Managerial Economics

M. A. Beg
Professor and Director (Management Studies)
Institute of Technology and Science
Former Senior Reader, Zakir Husain College;
University of Delhi

&

Manoj Kumar Dash
Assistant Professor
Institute of Technology and Science
Mohan Nagar (Ghaziabad)

GLOBAL
professional
publishing

Published by Global Professional Publishing Limited 2010

ISBN: 978-1-906403-39-3

Global Professional Publishing
Random Acres
Slip Mill Lane
Hawkhurst
Cranbrook
Kent TN18 5AD
United Kingdom

www.gppbooks.com

Preface

Over the past decade, Business School curriculum committees have taken several steps to strengthen the analytical and critical thinking skills of their students. Employers of business school graduates are demanding better thinkers. Many of us who teach Economics believe that training in economics not only helps students to understand and predict the economic forces shaping real-world business decisions, but also serves to develop and strengthen the overall analytical skills of students in all their major managerial decision. Managerial Economics brings together topics in microeconomics that can be applied to business decision making to create a valuable way of thinking about markets and business decisions. The objective of this book is to help business students become architects of business strategy rather than simply middle managers plodding along the beaten path of others.

Managerial economics, meaning the application of economic methods in the managerial decision-making process, is a fundamental part of any business or management course. This textbook covers all the main aspects of managerial economics: the theory of the firm; demand theory and estimation; production and cost theory and estimation; market structure and pricing; game theory; investment analysis and government policy. It includes numerous and extensive case studies, as well as review questions and problem-solving sections at the end of each chapter. This book will be invaluable to business and economics students, at both undergraduate and postgraduate levels, that have a basic training in calculus and quantitative methods.

The primary goal of this book has always been, and continues to be, to teach students the economic way of thinking about business decisions. Managerial Economics develops critical thinking skills and provides students with a logical way of analyzing business decisions. Managerial Economics is a self-contained book that requires no previous training in microeconomics. While maintaining a rigorous style, this book is designed to be one of the easiest ones in managerial economics from which to teach and learn. Managerial Economics carefully develops and applies the most useful concepts for business decision making. Starting with basic algebra and graph-reading skills, all other analytical tools employed in this book are developed within the text itself. While calculus is not a part of any chapter, instructors wishing to teach a calculus-based course can do so by using the Mathematical Appendixes at the end of most chapters. They employ calculus to analyze some of the key topics covered in the chapter.

One of the primary objectives in writing this book is to provide you, the student, with a book that enhances your learning experience in managerial economics. However, the degree of success you achieve in your managerial economics course will depend, in large measure, on the effectiveness of your study. I would like to offer you this one tip on studying. Emphasize active study rather than passive study. Passive study activities are those that do not require you to think for yourself. Reading the text, reviewing class notes and listening to lectures are 'passive' in nature because the authors of your textbook or your instructor are providing the analytical guidance for you. You are simply following someone else's analytical thought process, working only hard enough to agree with the authors or instructor.

In contrast, 'active' study techniques require you to think and reason for yourself. For example, when you close your book and put aside your lecture notes and try to explain a concept to yourself—perhaps sketching on a pad the graph or mathematical demonstration of a result—only then are you creating the path of logical analysis for yourself. The better you can explain the 'how' and 'why' of key concepts, the more thorough will be your understanding. Of course, some passive study is necessary to become familiar with the material, but genuine understanding and ability to use the decision-making skills of managerial economics require emphasis on active, rather than passive, study techniques.

M. A. Beg
Manoj Kumar Dash

Acknowledgements

At the outset, we wish to record our profound feeling of gratitude to the guiding angels of this humble work, Kausar Beg and Susmita Dash, to whom we owe the conception and compilation of the present work. Their words of encouragement every now and then, their friendly suggestions and their critical viewpoints, despite their own overwhelming scholastic pursuits and preoccupations, kept our spirits from flagging.

We owe sincere thanks to Prof. Shekhar Ghose, Director General, Institute of Technology and Science; Mohan Nagar, for his continuing encouragement and moral support. This work would never have been completed without his guidance.

Prof. Beg is grateful to the members of his family Kausar Beg (wife); Anam Beg (daughter) and Ashar Beg (son) for their encouragement and help to ensure that work was not interrupted. My parents' blessings have always showered strength and courage for the growth of my career.

M. A. Beg
Manoj Kumar Dash

Contents

PART - I

Part - I

- The Economic Nature of Decision Making
- The Goals of the Firm
- The Analysis of Value and Risk
- Maximization and Optimization
- Modelling the Decision Context
- Consumer Behaviour and Demand
- Elasticity and Demand Specification
- Production in the Short Run
- Production in the Long Run
- Costs in the Short Run
- Costs in the Long Run
- The Competitive Environment
- Pure Monopoly
- Monopolistic Competition
- Oligopolistic Competition
- Extending the Models
- Challenges to the Theory of the Firm
- Ethical Dimensions of Managerial Decisions
- The Role of the Government
- The Firm in Society
- Reallocation of Resources by Government
- International Commerce
- The Multinationalization of Enterprise
- Opportunities in Developing Economies

Chapter 1

The Economic Nature of Decision Making

Topics covered in this chapter

• The focus of managerial economics. • The significance of scarcity. • Bases for productive opportunities. • The benefits of specialization and division of labour. • The essential nature of the firm. • The popularity of the corporate forms of organization. • The potential for divisionalization. • The internal structure of the enterprise. • The internationalization of commerce. • The characteristics of multinationalization. • The entrepreneurial nature of strategic management. • Dimensions of the decision problem. • The nature of risk. • The nature of marginal change. • Expected values of multiple possible outcomes. • The consequence of uncertainty about outcomes.

Managerial economics is about the criteria for rational decision making by managers of business enterprises. The criteria elaborated here for business enterprises can also be applied to non-commercial decision settings, including government agencies, eleemosynary institutions, the home, and one's personal life. Before we proceed to an examination of these decision criteria, we shall review the essential economic nature of decision making in order to establish the fundamental principles upon which decision criteria may be based.

As noted in all first Principles of Economics courses, the world is characterized by scarcity rather than abundance. Human beings need certain things for survival, and they want to possess or consume a much larger variety of amenities. If all of these things were abundantly available, each person could simply gather as much as he or she wished, and still leave enough for everyone else to do likewise. Managerial decision making would require little more than determining the time sequence of acquisition.

In regard to most of the things that humans consume, scarcity is the rule and abundance is the exception. A scarcity of something means that the total of requirement or need for it exceeds the quantity available for human consumption. As a result, one person simply cannot take all that he or she might want without consequences for other persons. Something may be said to be scarce when its price exceeds zero (P greater than 0). The price may be expressed and paid in non-pecuniary terms as well as in money. There are a few things that have essentially zero prices, for example, air and the water available from a fountain.[1]

Some other things are available in greater quantities than people wish to consume. The quantities of such items so exceed simple abundance that their effective prices are negative (P less than 0). People will not pay positive prices to acquire more of such things, but they might be willing to pay others to get rid of them. Such superabundance may be regarded as nuisance goods (an obvious contradiction in terms), or 'bads.' Examples include garbage, sewage and any of the other environmental pollutants that have become troublesome.

It is because of scarcity that humans have to make choices. The 'economic problem' is the juxtaposition of productive resource scarcity against human want insatiability. In attempting to resolve the economic problem, humans must make choices of how to use the available scarce resources as efficiently as possible. Making choices is the essence of decision making, and making decisions is the central function of management. The management of any human activity is ultimately an exercise in economizing. Managerial economics focuses upon the criteria for making rational economic decisions regarding the use of scarce resources.

THE NATURE OF THE FIRM

Economic opportunities lie in the possibilities for supplying other humans with goods and services made with scarce resources. Opportunities may also be found in the removal or disposal of nuisance goods (bads). Productive opportunities are enhanced by specialization and division of labour. People have found that they can consume larger quantities of scarce goods and services when they specialize in the functions that they perform best, trading the fruits of their efforts with others in exchange for the things that they can produce most effectively.

The organization of individual capabilities into firms or enterprises can further enhance productive ability relative to that which individuals alone can achieve. The business firm accomplishes such enhanced productivity by serving as a vehicle for organizing the specialization and division of labour. R. H. Coase has noted (*The Nature of the Firm, Economica*, New Series, Vol. IV (1937), p. 393) that firms governed by hierarchical, authoritarian control usually can accomplish resource reallocations more efficiently (that is, at lower cost) than can be achieved by

---

1. We must make qualifications in regard to each of these examples. If someone wishes to breathe air of any particular quality or purity, he or she will have to go to some lengths to acquire it, and such pure air then is not a so-called 'free good'. The water that any one of us can 'freely' drink from a water fountain does in fact cost the larger society of which the drinker is a member something to acquire it, to transport it to the site, and to cool it to a desirable temperature.

human interaction through market mechanisms on a purely personal level. Coase notes that commercial enterprises may also function as 'players' on their own account in market interactions.

The management of such commercial enterprises involves the exercise of authority, usually from a top level of responsibility downwards through progressively lower levels of responsibility and function. The decisions made by the manager of the enterprise encompass both the acquisition of scarce resources from outside the enterprise, and the efficient allocation of those resources within the enterprise. Thus, the management of a commercial enterprise ultimately is an exercise in economizing. The motives, behaviour, legitimacy of authority, criteria for successful decision making and consequences of operations constitute the heart of the study of managerial economics.

THE VARIETY OF MANAGERIAL SETTINGS IN A MODERN FIRM

Managerial decision-making necessarily occurs within any of the organizational forms that modern business enterprises may take. Three principal forms of business enterprise are proprietorship, partnership and corporation. Our purpose in this section is to survey the ranges of decision settings in the larger, more complex commercial enterprises. In most cases, this means the corporation since both size and organizational complexity are severely limited in proprietorships and partnerships. Even so, some of the following remarks may be applicable to aspects of decision-making in the simpler organizational forms.

The modern corporation is characterized by a pyramidal, hierarchical organization. A manager may be situated in any setting ranging from that of a shop floor foreman, through lower and middle management echelons, to vice presidential and CEO (chief executive officer) positions. A manager may serve in all of these positions at one time or the other with progression through the managerial career.

The manager may also be placed in staff rather than line positions. A line position is so called because the manager is in a direct line of authority between the top level decision maker and those employees who carry out the essential business of the firm. A staff position, although it is not in the direct line of authority, provides supplemental services or analyses that enable managers to exercise authority more efficiently. Such staff positions include those in accounting, data processing, communications, statistical analysis, marketing, financial analysis and services, personnel and transportation, among others. Even though a staff officer is not in the direct line of authority over the essential business of the firm, he or she must still manage the resources under his or her control.

Every business firm has at least one office or plant, and many firms establish multiple places of business, each of which must be directed by an office or plant manager. Such multiple sites may be organized by function or by geographical region. Depending upon the mission of the office or plant, multiple tiers of managerial responsibility and authority may be established at each site. Managers at every site and at every tier are responsible for the efficient allocation of the resources assigned to them. Corporate operations sometimes become so extensive and complex that a single management team (or bureaucracy) cannot effectively oversee all the operations of the business. One possible remedy to this problem has been the divisionalization of the firm's operations. Divisionalization allows the establishment of separate management teams to direct the operations of the multiple divisions. The chief operating officer of the division may have a title such as division director, vice president of the division, or even president of the division. Whatever the title, the division manager reports ultimately to the CEO of the corporation.

There may emerge multiple tiers of managerial organization within the divisions of a corporation. The divisions may be organized along staff function lines, or by geographic regions if operations are widely dispersed geographically (including internationally). A division may also have multiple offices or plants assigned to it.

Corporate divisions are occasionally 'spun off' from the main corporation and constituted as separate corporations that are wholly or partially owned by the parent firm as subsidiaries. A subsidiary relationship may also come into existence when one firm acquires a controlling ownership interest in another firm, but chooses to preserve the acquired firm's corporate identity. Because of the ownership relationship, the management of the acquiring firm can dictate policy to the management of the acquired firm. If the acquiring firm has never conducted business operations or for some reason ceases physical operations but continues to direct the operations of one or more subsidiary operating companies, it may be referred to as a holding company.

The internal structures of enterprises, and their divisions and subsidiary relationships, may be organized horizontally, vertically or in conglomeration. As is common in the automobile and other American industries, numerous divisions of the same enterprise may perform parallel or identical functions, and may even be directed to compete with one another. This constitutes a horizontal structure. In other cases, the multiple plants or divisions of a firm may perform different functions in a vertical sequence ranging from the extraction of raw materials through the refinement of ores and the production of basic shapes, the fabrication of parts, various stages of assembly and distribution through jobber, wholesale and retail outlets. The multiple plants, divisions and subsidiaries of a corporation may be conglomerated in the sense that the functions performed or items produced are unrelated to one another, but are linked in the corporate family for financial or distributional reasons.

Whatever the structure of a firm and its affiliated entities, any line or staff officer of the firm, or any plant, division, or subsidiary manager, must make economic choices in the use of the scarce resources that are assigned to his or her control. It is in this sense that managerial decision-making in any of its settings is ultimately an exercise in economizing.

STRATEGIC AND TACTICAL DECISION-MAKING

Strategic management is concerned with the fundamental direction of the organization's activity, that is, the businesses that the organization intends to pursue and desired levels of achievement in them. Such decisions, by their very nature, must be made at the highest policy making level of the organization. The timeframe is from the present to as far into the future as the organization's time horizon. The organization's time horizon is limited to that of its least visionary policy maker who constrains the enthusiasm of its would-be innovators.

By virtue of the fact that such directional decision-making covers the long run and is laden with risk, it should be understood to be entrepreneurial rather than managerial in nature. Although the language of the business administration literature stresses strategic management, it should be more properly understood to be strategic entrepreneurship. In the late twentieth century, the term 'entrepreneurship' has come to be associated with new, small 'start-up' business ventures that are highly risky. Entrepreneurship is often not perceived to occur in established or 'going' concerns, especially if they have attained a large size in terms of assets, employment, market share or volume of sales.

Strategic entrepreneurship may occur at any level in any organization, whether a new local venture or a well-established multinational enterprise. In a new venture, entrepreneurship is exercised by the founder of the firm. To the extent that fundamental change is initiated at the boardroom level of an established enterprise, the function of the governing board is almost purely entrepreneurial since the board must assume the risks of its innovative decisions. If proposals for change are devised at lower levels in the administrative organization and only submitted to the governing board for approval, it is the site of the innovative proposal that is the true locus of entrepreneurship. However, in its approval, the governing board assumes a substantial portion of the risk of the proposed innovation, and in effect shares risk with the proposer of the strategic change.

There is some confusion over the meanings of the terms 'goals' and 'objectives.' We shall take 'goal' to refer to an ultimate end that the organization at its highest policy-making level determines to try to achieve. The term 'objective' is taken to refer to desirable intermediate situations or levels of performance to be achieved in pursuit of the ultimate goals of the organization. By their nature then, goals are long-term and strategic in orientation, whereas objectives are more short-term, immediate and partial in nature.

In military parlance, the term 'tactic' is usually juxtaposed with 'strategy' in referring to an action that is taken 'in the field' by a specific unit to accomplish a limited objective in pursuit of a strategic goal. The term 'tactic' and its various derivative forms are rarely used in discussions of strategic management. However, decisions taken at various levels in the administrative organization to implement an approved strategic change are oriented towards specific objectives (such as a target volume of sales or share of the market) rather than ultimate goals (such as a required return on investment in a particular line of business), and are thus essentially tactical in nature. In a new venture, goals and objectives may coincide, and strategic and tactical decision-making may converge in the mind of the founding entrepreneur.

In the established enterprise, tactical decision making at various administrative levels must confront choices that involve risks. A modicum of entrepreneurship may therefore be exercised by the mid-level manager in the tactical decisions that must be made. However, tactical decisions that involve simply deciding upon increases or decreases in activities already in progress belong to the realm of managerial decision-making. It is possible that nearly all of the decisions that must be made in a new business venture are strategic and entrepreneurial rather than tactical and managerial.

A prime example of strategic decision-making is found in the international business arena. It is not uncommon for corporations to engage in international transactions or operations, but proprietorships and partnerships may do so as well. By its very nature, much of the business decision-making concerning the international realm is entrepreneurial because of the inherent risks attendant upon extending operations into other countries. But once international operations have become established, tactical managerial decision making is required to adjust levels and rates of operations.

THE NATURE OF THE DECISION PROBLEM

Managers may make a myriad of decisions every day. Some of the decisions are trivial in the sense that the consequences of them do not matter very much. The consequences of other decisions, for example, which employee health insurance plan to adopt or whether to add or drop a product line from the company's product mix may be monumental.

We shall assume as an operating premise that human beings are basically interested in their own welfare. Rational human behaviour consists of trying to maximize the value of some positive quantity, or to minimize the value of something perceived as having negative connotations.

Although human nature is culturally influenced, we shall also presume that human beings are more-or-less materialistic, that is, more is better than less, and hedonistic, that is, that pain and displeasure are to be avoided or minimized. We consider in the succeeding chapters whether these behaviour premises are truly viable foundations upon which to erect models of managerial decision-making.

Human approaches to decisions may be categorized as capriciousness, conditioned response and deliberate, reasoned choice. The more trivial the consequences of the decision, the less time and effort are devoted to the decision process. Sometimes people seem to act without engaging in any apparent decision-making process.

The choices underlying such actions may have been nearly automatic, based upon an implicit summing-up of the current circumstance compared with the decision maker's accumulated stock of past experiences under similar circumstances. Occasionally, however, human beings indulge in a capricious action (an act without deliberate choice), even when the consequences may be non-trivial. If a capricious action constitutes a 'bad' decision, the actor must suffer the consequences.

DIMENSIONS OF THE DECISION PROBLEM

Multiple Goals

The decision-maker may be confronted with a multiplicity of goals. Since it is technically not possible to try to simultaneously maximize the values of multiple conflicting goals, the decision-maker has to choose one of the goals for primary pursuit. The other goals, expressed as minimum or maximum acceptable values, can then be regarded as constraints on the pursuit of the primary goal. The object of the decision is to maximize the value of the primary goal, subject to realization of satisfactory levels of subordinate goals. The mathematical modelling problems and possibilities with respect to multiple goals are elaborated in detail in the following chapters.

Multiple Strategies

With respect to any single goal, a decision involves multiple possible courses of action, or strategies. If there were no alternatives, no decision would be required other than selecting the goal for pursuit. The deliberate approach to decision making involves the identification of all possible courses of action and the benefits and costs likely to result from each of the alternatives. The rational choice is the alternative that yields the greatest relative positives or the largest sum of net benefits (positives less negatives), given the decision-maker's set of preferences.

Marginal Changes

In many cases, the choices are not mutually-exclusive alternative courses of action; rather they involve more or less the same course of action. The range of possible alternatives includes larger or smaller quantities to be selected. Typically, the decision problem is to select some quantity that is an alternative to the present one. Assuming that the alternative quantities are arrayed from smallest to largest, or vice-versa, choosing to shift from one to another involves additions to or subtractions from benefits or costs. Economists speak of such additions and subtractions as incremental changes, or marginal changes if they are the smallest possible changes that can be made. The rational choice in such cases is to make a quantitative change that will yield the greatest marginal benefit relative to marginal cost.

Multiple Outcomes

Often the possible alternative courses of action can be identified, but each decision alternative may have several outcome possibilities. If the decision maker can in some meaningful sense assess the probability, p, of the occurrence of each possible outcome and V for each of the alternative courses of action, he may then compute the expected value of each alternative. The expected value is a probability-weighted average of the possible outcomes for each decision alternative,

$$(1)\ EV = p_1V_1\ p_2V_2 + \ldots + p_kV_k,$$

or

$$(2)\ EV = S_{j=1,k}\,(p_jV_j),$$

where EV is the expected value of the alternative, p is the probability of the outcome V for each of the k possible outcomes of the alternative. The presumption here is that the sum of the probabilities of the possible outcomes is 1.0. Each outcome may itself be a net difference between benefit (b) and cost (c), or V = b–c. Other things remaining the same, the rational decision then is the choice of the alternative that promises the largest expected value of possible outcomes.

An extension of the expected value concept may be employed in decision situations that unfold in stages with subsequent stages depending upon what happens in the previous stages. In such cases, the probability of occurrence of an ultimate outcome is a conditional probability, that is, the product of the probabilities of the final outcome and all prior stages. Such a situation can best be visualized with a 'decision tree,' an example of which is illustrated in Figure 1.1. In this hypothetical situation, the decision-maker has to decide whether to develop a major shopping centre anchored by two department stores, or a small strip shopping centre with no department stores. In Figure 1.1, the decision point is represented by the box on the left side of the tree. The circles in the diagram indicate non-decision outcome branches. There is a 60 per cent chance that if a major centre is built, the county will construct a four-lane approach road to the centre, but a 40 per cent chance that the existing two-lane road will have to do. But if a small strip is constructed, there is only 20 per cent chance of construction of a four-lane road. Beyond the estimated completion of the project, there is a 20 per cent chance that the economy will boom, a 50 per cent chance of normal economic conditions, and a 30 per cent chance of recession.

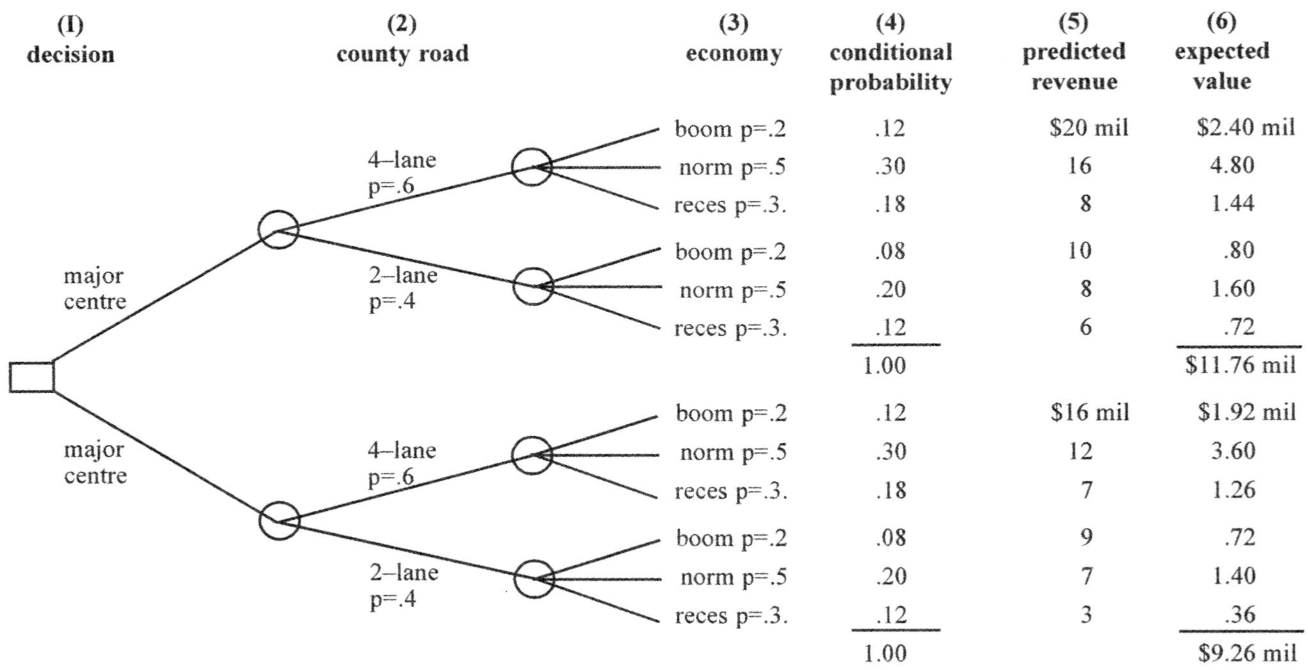

Figure 1.1. Conditional probabilities in a decision tree.

Table 1.1: Probable Outcomes of Two Possible Decision Alternatives

	Possible Outcomes $	*Prob of Occurrence* Per Cent
Alternative A	500	10
	650	20
	900	40
	1150	20
	1300	10
Alternative B	0	5
	450	20
	900	50
	1350	20
	1800	5

The expected values of the decision branches may be computed from the information in columns (4) through (6) of Figure 1.1. Column (4) shows the conditional probabilities computed as the products of the probabilities of conditions along the branches to the respective stems of the tree; the sum of the probabilities for each decision branch is 100 per cent. Column (5) contains the best available estimates of the first-year revenue flows that will occur under the different conditions. Column (6) reveals the expected values of the first-year revenue flows. The sum of the expected values of the revenue flows for each branch reveals the expected value (a conditional probability-weighted average of the outcomes) of each of the respective decision branches. Real-world decision settings may be far more complicated than illustrated in this example, and may involve multiple decision points as well as numerous states of nature. Other things remaining the same, the decision branch with the largest expected value is the decision choice.

Risk

Other things may not be the same, however, if the range of outcome variability differs from one alternative to another. It is typical for decision alternatives to have different expected values, but even if two decision alternatives have approximately the same expected values, one may have a wider range of possible outcome variability than the other. Risk is inherent in the dispersion of possible outcomes about the mean of all such outcomes. To illustrate, suppose that decision alternatives A and B may each result in any of five possible outcomes with probabilities of occurrence as indicated in Table 1.1. It is readily apparent that the possible outcomes for alternative A span a narrower range than do those of alternative B even though each has an expected value of $ 900. Figure 1.2 employs bar-charts in panel (a) to illustrate the probability distributions of the outcomes of the two alternatives. A common measure of risk associated with a decision alternative is the standard deviation (sigma) of the alternative's possible outcomes,

$$\sigma = [S_{j=1,k} (V_j - EV)^2 p_j]^{1/2}.$$

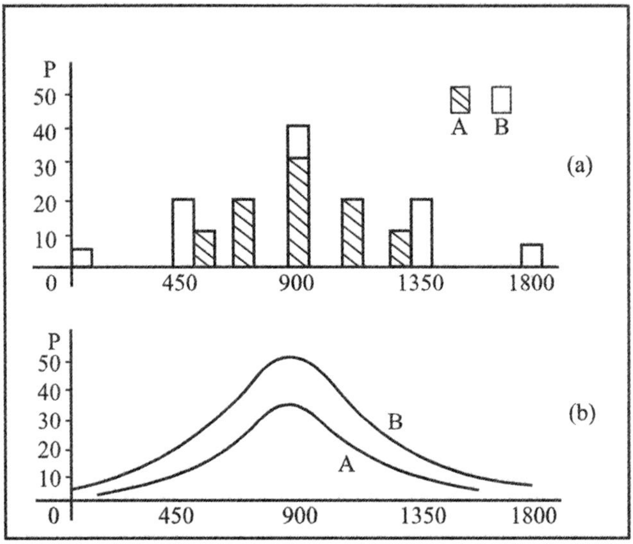

Figure 1.2. Probability distributions of two decision alternatives.

The justification for using the standard deviation as a measure of risk is the assumption that outcome probability distributions tend to be normally distributed about their means as illustrated by the smooth probability distribution curves drawn in the panel (b) of Figure 1.2. If this assumption is valid, then the mean of the distribution plus and minus (one/two/three) standard deviations contains (68.26/95.44/99.74) per cent of the outcomes in the distribution. The decision alternative with the wider range of outcome variability, that is, greater standard deviation, is said to be the riskier of the two. If the expected values are equal, the lower-risk decision alternative would be preferred by most people. Since s_A is only 238.7 while s_B is 402.5, alternative A is the lower-risk alternative.

However, when the expected values of two decision alternatives differ substantially, so also will their standard deviations be of different magnitudes, and will therefore not serve as a reliable basis for comparing risks. In such cases, the decision maker may compute a coefficient of variation, v, for each decision alternative, where v is the ratio of the standard deviation to its respective expected value,

$$v = \sigma / EV.$$

The decision alternative with the smaller coefficient of variation is the less-risky alternative.

It is not uncommon for a decision alternative with a higher expected value of outcomes to also be riskier in the sense of having a wider range of outcome possibilities. In addition to assessing the risk of the decision alternatives, the decision maker must also be able to rationally make comparisons of the expected values of outcomes (or returns) in light of their comparative risks.

Since a decision maker might be willing to trade off risk for return (that is, expected value), he must be able to decide whether the higher expected value of a decision alternative is adequate compensation for the additional risk that must be assumed. Theoretically, a preference function relating satisfaction (or utility) to any pair of desirable goods (or phenomena) may be constructed for a decision maker. Practically, the specification of such a preference function is difficult if not impossible to achieve. A functional notation representation of such a preference function might appear as

$$U = f(V,(1\text{-}\sigma) / \ldots),$$

where U is the amount of utility realized by the decision maker, V is the value of the return from a decision alternative, and sigma indicates the risk associated with the opportunity. The argument (1-sigma) is the complement of the amount of risk incurred, or the degree of certainty that a particular outcome within the range of all such possible outcomes will occur. Graphically, such a preference function for a normal decision maker might appear as depicted in Figure 1.3. Risk (degree of uncertainty) and return occupy the floor axes of the three-dimensional graph; utility is measured in the vertical dimension. The right-hand side of the utility surface can be identified because the degree of certainty reaches a maximum, that is, the degree of risk approaches zero. But the left-hand end of the risk-certainty axis cannot be specified since risk may increase without bounds. The utility surface may be 'sliced' parallel to the floor and at any altitude of utility. Four such slices are illustrated in Figure 1.3, and their vertical projections down into the floor of the surface have been drawn. These projections constitute so-called 'indifference curves' for the two phenomena represented on the floor axes, that is, return and degree of certainty. Any number of such indifference curves may be constructed by slicing the utility surface at any chosen utility altitudes.

Figure 1.4 depicts a map of selected indifference curves generated from the utility surface illustrated in Figure 1.3. In effect, the map depicted in Figure 1.4 is the sliced surface of Figure 1.3 viewed 'from above.' In Figure 1.4, a movement from left to right along the horizontal axis represents an increase of certainty about which outcome within the range of all possible outcomes will occur

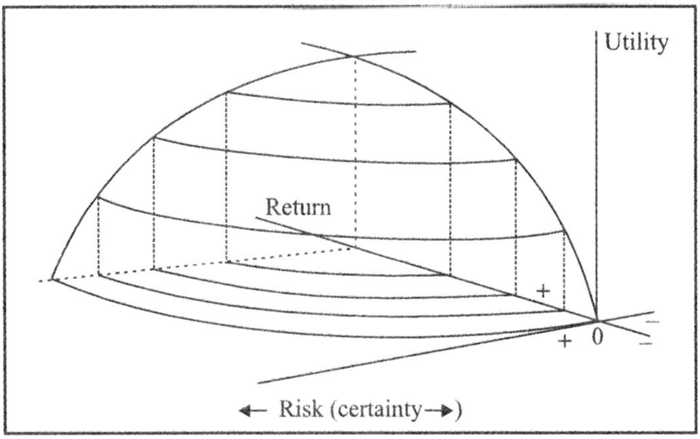

Figure 1.3. A utility surface for certainty and return.

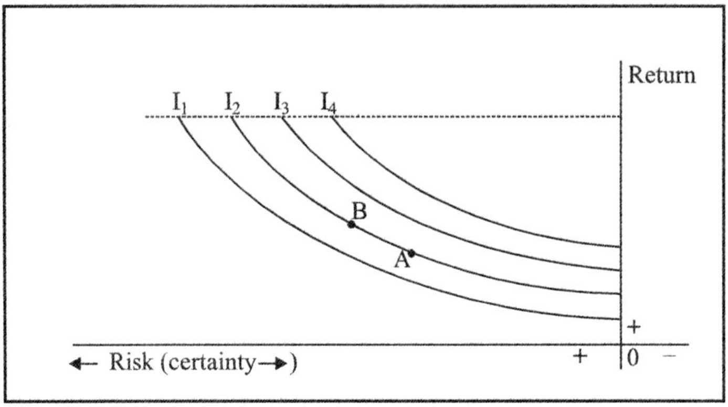

Figure 1.4. A risk-return indifference map

(and implicitly a narrowing of the range of possible outcomes). At the right end of the horizontal axis, the decision maker may be certain that there is only one possible outcome, and thus that risk is minimal (or zero). Risk therefore increases from right to left along the horizontal axis, but the left end of the axis may not be specified in the sense that risk may increase without bounds. Any point in the coordinate space of the map represents some combination of risk and return, and each point lies on some indifference curve, such as I_2, for a certain level of utility. Any movement along I_2 would leave the decision maker in a state of indifference. For example, the movement from point A to point B would result in an increase of risk (a 'decrease of certainty'), for which the decision maker would have to be compensated by an increase of return in order to remain at the same level of utility. Or, at the higher return associated with point B, the decision maker would tolerate more risk (less certainty). The indifference curves for a more risk-averse decision maker would be more steeply upward sloped (right to left) because such a decision maker would require even greater return for each level of risk.

Imperfect Knowledge

Only rarely does a decision maker have perfect knowledge of a decision environment, the possible alternative courses of action that may be taken, or the range of outcomes that may result from each choice. Where multiple outcomes are possible, a *risky* situation is said to exist if the decision maker can both identify all of the possible outcomes and meaningfully assess the probabilities of occurrence of each of the possible outcomes. An *uncertain* situation occurs if the decision maker either cannot identify some of the outcomes, or cannot meaningfully estimate the probabilities of their occurrence. The decision maker may attempt to deal with uncertainty by seeking additional information about outcomes or their probabilities of occurrence. But after all available information is acquired and there is a persisting aura of uncertainty, the decision still has to be made.

Decision theorists have suggested a number of decision rules for situations involving uncertainty, that is, where outcomes cannot be identified or their probabilities of occurrence cannot be meaningfully assessed. The two that seem to be most useful are the *maximin* and the *minimax regret* decision rules. In the former, the objective is to identify the worst-case outcomes of all of the decision strategies under consideration, and then choose the one that yields the least-negative effects, that is, the best of the worst-case scenarios. This is an extremely conservative approach that is most appropriate to the need to avoid ultimate failure of the enterprise. Its prime deficiency is that it considers only failure states, and does not take into account the possibilities of success.

The minimax regret rule requires that the decision maker perceives the best possible outcome of the decision strategies, and then computes the regret associated with all other strategies as the difference between each and the best of the alternate strategies. The strategy of choice then is the one that minimizes the regret that follows from failure to select the best outcome.

The Time Dimension

Economists refer to a time frame during which some matters can be changed (for example, the number of workers employed), but others cannot (for example, the size of plant or the number of assembly lines) as the short run. Short-run decisions usually affect the current situation or the immediate future. The long run is a period long enough so that any and everything can be changed. Long-run decisions usually have their impacts only after the passage of some time, and do not affect current operations in any significant sense. Most short-run decisions within the business enterprise are to increase or decrease something already being done and thus require marginal comparisons of benefits and costs. Long-run decisions usually affect the scale of the enterprise's operations, and often involve starting something new or stopping some operation currently under way. Given the sharpest possible contrast, short-run decisions are 'more-or-less,' whereas long-run decisions are 'go-no go' decisions.

Entrepreneurial Decisions

Finally, we may distinguish between managerial and entrepreneurial decisions. The managerial context involves making relatively low-risk, routine decisions in regard to processes that change in smooth, continuous fashion, about which much can be known or discovered, and to which marginal analysis is applicable. In contrast, the entrepreneurial decision is risk-laden because it involves innovative discontinuities in operations, about which little can be known in advance, and to which marginal analysis is less likely to be applicable. As a general rule, short-run decisions are often managerial in nature, whereas long-run decisions tend to be entrepreneurial. Managerial decisions are matters of doing more or less of something already in process, whereas entrepreneurial decisions involve starting or stopping activities or significantly altering the structure, scope, or pace of extant processes.

WHAT'S AHEAD

This brief survey of the range of settings for managerial decision making and the dimensions of the decision problem should convey something of the magnitude of the task before us in identifying the criteria for rational decision making in a variety of contexts. The study of managerial economics is, in effect, applied microeconomic analysis. But it is much more than an application of economic principles. Managerial economics brings together economic theory, the methodology of modelling relationships, the statistical process of function specification, and the application of algebra, geometry and calculus to the decision process. In addition, we shall have occasion to touch upon the subject matters of marketing, finance, accounting, organizational behaviour and international trade. The next chapter is devoted to an examination of the motives of decision makers and the patterns of decision making that follow.

Summary of Important Points

1. Managerial economics is about the criteria for rational decision making in business enterprises and non-commercial decision settings.
2. The world in which we live is characterized by scarcity rather than abundance.
3. Economic opportunities can be found in supplying economic goods or removing nuisance goods.
4. Specialization and division of labour enhance productive opportunities.
5. The firm may achieve internal resource allocation more efficiently with hierarchical, authoritative control than with market transactions.
6. The management of a commercial enterprise is an exercise in economizing.
7. Problems of coordination and control within the complex corporate organization may be remedied by divisionalization.
8. The internal structure of an enterprise may be horizontal, vertical, or conglomerated.
9. Strategic decision making, that involves the fundamental direction of the firm's activities, is essentially entrepreneurial in nature.
10. The enterprise may engage in international activities in a variety of forms.
11. Multinationalization of enterprise is achieved when managerial personnel are recruited world-wide without national prejudice.
12. Human beings are essentially materialistic and hedonistic; rational human behaviour consists of attempting to maximize the value of some positive quantity or to minimize the value of some negative quantity.
13. Human approaches to decision making may be characterized as capriciousness, conditioned response, or deliberate and rational choice.
14. The decision maker, confronted by a multiplicity of possible goals, must select one for primary pursuit and subordinate others to it; subordinate goals may serve as constraints upon the pursuit of the primary goal.
15. Any decision involves multiple possible courses of action among which the decision maker must choose.
16. Often the alternative courses of action are greater or lesser quantities of the same action; the choice of an alternative quantity involves an incremental or marginal change.

Contd.....

17. Any course of action may result in multiple possible outcomes; each possible outcome may span a range of variability; the wider the range of variability, the greater the degree of risk associated with the outcome.
18. The identities of some of the possible outcomes or their ranges of variability may not be known with certainty by the decision maker; the decision maker may attempt to reduce the uncertainty by seeking additional information about the outcomes.

Significant Terms

managerial economics
business enterprises
decision criteria
scarcity
economic, free, nuisance goods
want insatiability
choices
economic opportunities
specialization
division of labour
exchange
hierarchical, authoritarian control
line, staff positions
management team
divisionalization
subsidiary
holding company
internal structure, horizontal, vertical,
conglomerate
strategic decision making
goals, objectives
tactics, strategies
entrepreneurial, managerial
international transactions
multinationalization
materialistic, hedonistic
capriciousness
conditioned response
deliberate choice
decision problem
decision strategies
benefits, costs, net benefits
constraints
multiple goals; primary, subordinate
incremental, marginal change
outcomes; outcome variability
expected value
decision tree
conditional probability
risk
standard deviation
coefficient of variation
preference function
utility surface
indifference curves, map
imperfect knowledge
uncertainty
decision rules
short-, long-run
entrepreneurial, managerial decisions

—oo(O)oo—

Chapter 2

The Goals of the Firm

Topics covered in this chapter

- The role of modelling in economic analysis. • Eras of managerial behaviour patterns. • Choosing a behavioural premise. • Profit in the short and long runs. • An object of pursuit or an indicator of success.

THE ROLE OF MODELLING IN ECONOMIC ANALYSIS

Models in all of their possible formats (tabular, functional notation, graphic, equation, computer statement) constitute the primary instructional vehicles employed in economics texts (including this one) to convey to students understandings of the functioning of economic mechanisms. Modelling is the chief analytical vehicle employed by those economists who are pushing the frontiers of economic knowledge. Models, ranging from the highly simplified to the extremely complex, are designed in both the private and the public sectors to forecast the future courses of economic phenomena.

Perhaps the most productive use of modelling for managerial decision making is to structure a model of the manager's decision making context (the firm as a whole, or parts of it such as demand functions, production functions, and cost functions). If the structured model is a good enough depiction of the real mechanism, it may allow the manager the luxury of trying-out policies before having to implement real decisions that affect stock-holders, employees, suppliers, or customers. What are the consequences of making a bad decision in a **policy simulation** model? The benefit may be the realization of the likely detrimental effects of the decision so that it can be corrected before its 'real-time' implementation.

The approach of this managerial economics text is that of **model methodology**. The economic criteria for rational managerial decision making are elaborated with models; managerial behaviour patterns and consequences are depicted with models; and the procedures for policy simulation and economic forecasting modelling are presented. Appendix 2.1 to this chapter outlines the procedures that economists typically employ in attempting to model some economic phenomenon.

One of the first steps that the economic analyst must take in modelling an economic phenomenon is to select an appropriate **behavioural premise** to serve as a foundation upon which the model may be built. Economists usually presume that rational decision makers attempt to maximize some positive quantity or minimize something that has negative connotations for the decision maker. In modelling the commercial enterprise referred to as the business firm, economists have traditionally assumed that managers attempt to **maximize profits**. It is because this behavioural premise has been called into question that we devote this chapter to a critical consideration of it before proceeding to an elaboration of the mathematical analysis of model construction.

ERAS OF MANAGERIAL BEHAVIOUR PATTERNS

Survival is perhaps the single behavioural goal that has dominated individual productive effort across the span of human existence. It was the organization of human effort into enterprises enabling collective and cooperative effort that necessitated the exercise of management as it is known today. Until such time, however, we may perceive the survival behaviour pattern as the effort to minimize hunger and privation, or, if the producer had risen above the biological necessity threshold, to try to maximize the possession of creature comforts. With the emergence of the concept of 'income' in money using societies, we can perceive of the individual craftsman, trader, or agriculturalist as simple income maximizers.

By the late nineteenth century, economists such as Alfred Marshall theorized about proprietors and partnerships as autonomous owner-entrepreneurs who could attempt to **maximize profit**, the net difference between their incomes and their costs. Such entrepreneurs were simultaneously owners and managers of their productive enterprises. Little impinged upon their firms from outside to constrain them except for the pressures of competition from other, similar owner-managed enterprises. Their activities and scales of operation had yet to attract social concern, and government was hardly a force to impose curbs on their operations.

Even before Marshall and his contemporaries were contriving descriptions of such competitive conditions, the **corporate** form of commercial organization was becoming popular as a means of marshalling greater capital resources and enabling specialization and division of labour in management. As the scale of the corporations grew, it was inevitable that the owners would hire managers to run their enterprises for them. As long as owners of enterprises remained relatively close to their operations, they could impose their wills upon their managerial employees. While the managers may have had interests that diverged from those of their owner-employers, their decisions were still constrained by the wills of the owners imposed upon them, and they could still be perceived to be effective profit maximizers.

With the progressive **growth of scale** of operations, the ownership interests became ever more remote from the managers, whose personal interests could become at least as important as the profit interests of the owners. Such **personal interests** include, in the words of William Baldwin, "personal financial rewards, security, power and prestige within the organization, desire to be liked, human sympathy, the urge to create, and perhaps occasionally the desire for an easy life." ('The Motives of Managers, Environmental Restraints, and the Theory of Managerial Enterprise,' in *The Quarterly Journal of Economics*, May 1974, p. 249). While some of these interests may be compatible with the interests of owners, others are likely to be in conflict with them. The problem for the owners was to keep the emerging interests of their managers subsidiary to their own interests.

Two additional twentieth-century developments have affected the goals of managers and the patterns of their decision making: the **dispersion of ownership** of corporate shares, and a rising tide of social concern about the operations of the business community, together with managerial recognition of its social responsibilities. The first of these two phenomena emerged during the first half of the twentieth century. Its impact is aptly described by Kanji Haitani:

> As corporations raise large sums of funds by selling shares of stock, their ownership becomes widely dispersed. Very large corporations may have hundreds of thousands of shareholders. Thus, even though some large blocks of shares may be held by some individuals and institutions, these blocks are not likely to constitute more than a small fraction of the total shares of outstanding stock. One effect of the wide dispersion of voting shares is to give effective control of the corporation to its management team. The managers solicit proxy votes from shareholders and cast them in annual meetings ostensibly for the absentee shareholders. The management almost always has enough proxies to override any proposals presented to the meetings by outside groups. This ability to control the outcomes of shareholders' meetings gives the management the right to appoint directors of its choice. (*Comparative Economic Systems*, Prentice Hall, 1986, pp. 228-229).

The consequence of the control conferred by dispersion of stock ownership is that the personal interests of managers may ascend to dominance over the interests of owners. The essential conclusion is that profit-maximization may not be the behaviour assumption that is relevant to modelling the modern commercial enterprise; rather, it could be the maximization of any of the personal interests of managers.

The rising tide of social concern about the operations of the commercial enterprise is largely a product of the latter half of the twentieth century. Business-related social concerns have ranged from the level of concentration in industry to environmental pollution and the distribution of income between profits and wages. Whatever the impetus to such social concerns, the important point is that business managers have widely acknowledged a level of **social responsibility** unprecedented in human experience. William Baldwin indicates the emerging managerial attitude as follows:

> Management, it is claimed, is becoming a profession; and professional managers tend to regard themselves as trustees of corporate property, exercising their powers for the benefit of virtually all those who come into contact with the corporation and adjudicating conflicting claims of such beneficiaries as stockholders, employees, customers, suppliers, communities, and the general public. ('The Motives of Managers, Environmental Restraints, and the Theory of Managerial Enterprise,' in *The Quarterly Journal of Economics*, May 1964, p. 241.)

In those firms for which this is the prevailing perspective, the interests of the owners is but one among a wide variety of competing interests among which the managers must mediate. Although their decisions are certainly constrained by a variety of both internal and external factors, such managers cannot be perceived to be attempting to maximize or minimize any single identifiable quantity.

Thus, it is apparent that four historical developments have unfolded to lead us to question whether indeed managerial decision makers attempt to maximize profits: the advent and growing popularity of the corporate form of business organization; the increasing scale of operations resulting in the employment of managers who have little or no ownership interests; the progressive dispersion of ownership of the corporation leading to ever greater managerial control; and the emergence of social concerns acknowledged by the managers of large corporations. As these developments have unfolded, the goal of profit has moved from centre stage to become but one of the background characters in the drama. And constraints upon managerial decision making, at one time limited only to competitive pressures, seem to have attained the level of obsession with managers of at least some large enterprises.

ALTERNATIVE PREMISES

The stage is now set for an examination of a variety of alternative theses about the goals pursued by managerial decision makers and the behavioural patterns exhibited by them in pursuit of those goals. We could identify a large number of plausible behavioural premises and still not exhaust the possibilities. We shall specify five, and invite the reader to explore yet others.

1. The original, classic behavioural premise for the manager of a commercial enterprise is that of simple, absolute, unconstrained **profit maximization**. A mathematical model of the enterprise erected upon this premise can be developed in straightforward fashion by an application of the derivative calculus as elaborated. It is this behavioural premise that has served for a century as foundation for the so-called 'theory of the firm' in the following chapters.

While profit is usually taken to be the goal of the manager of the enterprise, recognition of other possible managerial goals requires us to admit that any of those enumerated by William Baldwin in the quotation cited above may be pursued instead of profit. We should then stipulate that the mathematical modelling procedures are the same irrespective of the identity of the dependent variable, that is, the presumed goal being pursued by the manager.

More than one of Baldwin's enumerated managerial goals may be handled in a model in which it is presumed that the objective of the manager is to maximize personal utility. Such a multi-argument **utility function** might be represented as

$$\text{Utility} = f(x_1, x_2, \ldots, x_n),$$

where x_1 to x_n are the various factors of importance to the manager. While this may be an intellectually satisfying approach to dealing with a multiplicity of possible goals that the manager may pursue, we must note the general impracticality of specification of utility functions. Also, even if a manager's utility function could be adequately specified, this approach provides no single managerial decision criterion upon which the manager can key decisions.

2. The manager of the enterprise may attempt to **optimize** the profits of the enterprise, that is, to maximize profits subject to one or more constraints. The constraints may be limitations on the operations of the enterprise imposed from exogenous sources that are not under the control of the management. Such forces may include physical conditions such as climate, weather, geography, and demography. Social, cultural, religious, and political realities may also constrain the operations of the enterprise.

Kenneth Boulding ('The Ethics of Rational Decision,' *Management Science*, February, 1966) has suggested that the multiple goals pursued by managers must be regarded in a hierarchy so that the manager can choose one of them for primary pursuit. The problem for the manager in regard to the other, or subordinate, goals is to keep them subordinated to the primary goal that the manager pursues. This is a problem because exigencies of the moment often lead to the 'insubordination of subordinate goals.' The **subordinate goals** can also be incorporated into the decision-making model by treating them as **constraints** upon the maximization of the primary goal. This treatment then is also a form of optimization.

3. As noted in (1) above, profit may not be the primary goal of the enterprise's management. William Baumol (in *Business Behavior, Value and Growth*, New York, U.S.A.: Harcourt Brace Javanovich, 1967) has theorized on the basis of extensive consulting experience that the primary goal of many enterprise managers is some **growth**-related variable such as unit sales, sales revenue, or share of market. Particularly, Baumol suggests that the goal of many enterprise managers is to maximize unit sales subject to a constraint in the form of a minimum acceptable amount of profit or rate of profit. If the goal is a so-called 'target rate of return' (TROR) on invested capital, the necessary amount of profit can be computed if the investment in capital is known. For example, if a million dollars has been invested in plant and equipment, and an 8 per cent return on investment is desired, then the manager must operate the enterprise to yield $ 80,000 per annum. Once this target has been met, the manager may be free to pursue another objective, for example, the volume of sales. An elaboration of a model of the firm incorporating the Baumol thesis is presented later.

4. Herbert Simon ('Theories of Decision Making in Economics and Behavioral Science,' *American Economic Review*, June, 1959, pp. 253-280) approaches the behaviour of the enterprise manager from the perspective of behavioural psychology:

> ... In most psychological theories the motive to act stems from drives, and action terminates when the drive is satisfied. Moreover, the conditions for satisfying a drive are not necessarily fixed, but may be specified by an aspiration level that itself adjusts upward or downward on the basis of experience.

From this starting point, Simon deduces that firm managers often attempt to achieve a satisfactory rate of profit rather than the maximum amount possible. Simon in effect created a new verb, 'to satisfice,' to describe the behaviour pattern. Business managers often indicate in surveys and interviews that they work towards meeting a target rate of return on invested capital. Such responses are taken by Simon to support his **satisficing thesis**.

Intuitive support for the satisficing thesis may also be found in the fictional story recounted by March & Simon about the tailor who had dropped the last of several needles on his shop floor that was covered with straw (in earlier centuries it was not uncommon for animals to be brought into the shop or dwelling at night, hence the straw on the floor). Before he could continue his work, the tailor had to find one of the needles, so he swept the straw up into the proverbial haystack. We may now pose the crucial question: what is it rational for the tailor to do? Find the sharpest needle in the haystack (which, incidentally, will require him to find all of them), or to find only one that is sharp enough to get the job done. We must admit that the latter is the more economic approach, and that also supports the satisficing thesis.

Simon also prefers the satisficing approach to managerial decision behaviour because of its adaptability:

> Models of satisficing behaviour are richer than models of maximizing behaviour, because they treat not only of equilibrium but of the method of reaching it as well. ...
>
> (a) When performance falls short of the level of aspiration, search behaviour (particularly search for new alternatives of action) is induced.
>
> (b) At the same time, the level of aspiration begins to adjust itself downwards until goals reach levels that are practically attainable.
>
> (c) If the two mechanisms just listed operate too slowly to adapt aspirations to performance, emotional behaviour—apathy or aggression, for example—will replace rational adaptive behaviour.

We may agree with Simon that satisficing models have great appeal because of their ability to handle adaptive behaviour. But while the adjustment principles could be easily expressed above in verbal terms, we must also acknowledge the extreme difficulty of structuring and specifying a decision model in mathematical terms that accommodates both satisficing and adaptive behaviour.

5. Enterprise managers who perceive themselves to be responsible to a variety of **constituencies** can probably not be construed as attempting to maximize or minimize any quantity. In fact, their behaviour may be in response only to constraints, with no clearly definable objective of pursuit other than 'survival.' The response pattern has been described as that of mediation among the competing constituencies, an essentially political process.

Adolph Berle has suggested that enterprise managers who give lip service to 'social responsibility' are in effect attempting to achieve an aura of legitimacy for the power that they wield. William Baldwin further hypothesizes that if successive generations of corporate executives repeat often enough their company's litany of social responsibility, they may come to actually believe it and begin to live by it.

The problem for modelling the behaviour of the enterprise is that economists have not ventured far enough into the wilderness of political processes to allow us to offer a clearly defined model of **constituent mediation** for the reader's consideration. We may envision the possibility that some of the management's constituencies may at any time become the primary object of the manager's concern, given the exigencies of the moment. In either case, optimization models may be appropriate for analysis of situations wherein one of the constituencies has, at least temporarily, become the focus of the manager's attention.

However, the manager may attempt only to minimize the value of some negative connotation associated with the constituency, subject to constraints imposed by the perceived need for deference to the other constituencies. Here the manager may be in the avoid-avoid dilemma illustrated by Kenneth Boulding in his example of the donkey between two skunks (this is in contrast to the donkey's approach-approach dilemma when it finds itself between two bales of hay). If optimization modelling can indeed be applied to the situation of constituent mediation, the manager must anticipate that the identities of the behavioural goal and its constraints will be exchanged from time to time as the concerns of one and then another constituency rise to the surface (the squeaky wheel gets the grease).

CHOOSING A BEHAVIOURAL PREMISE

In the previous section we outlined five possible behavioural premises and variations upon them that might be taken to serve as foundations upon which might be erected a theory of managerial decision making. Other behavioural premises could be considered, and perhaps in the future yet other possibilities will surface to prominence in the literature. We now come to the task of making a selection from among them to serve us through the remainder of this text.

By virtue of the fact that there is great diversity among the nearly twenty million identifiable business firms in the American economy, it might be defensible to argue that all five of the possible premises outlined above ought to be retained in view of the fact that there are without doubt numerous firms whose managers exhibit the behavioural characteristics of each premise. This would require the development of at least five different models of managerial behaviour, and such may indeed be appropriate. In order to economize on our effort (and the volume of matter that the reader must absorb), we shall pursue a strategy of adopting one premise for primary elaboration, but make reference to variations and alternatives where appropriate.

William Baldwin suggests the tack that virtually all writers in the field of managerial economics have followed during the past two decades:

> ...if we want a theory of managerial enterprise that assumes a single organizational objective subject to maximization or minimization, profit does appear to be more realistic than any of the alternatives offered. .... The findings reviewed in this paper strongly suggest...that profit maximization is a fairly close approximation to actual motives of the typical large corporation and that any losses suffered by abstracting from the complexity of interplay among real-world motives will be relatively minor.

Baldwin, concerned primarily with the 'typical large corporation,' concludes the **profit maximization** premise to be satisfactory; yet the corporate form of business organization accounts for only about 17 per cent of all business firms in the American economy. The simple, unconstrained profit maximization premise should be acceptable with even less question for the 74 per cent of the American firms organized as proprietorships. It may even serve adequately for the remaining nine per cent organized as partnerships in those firms within which the partners have reached some consensus of direction for the firm.

Milton Friedman ('The Methodology of Positive Economics' in *Essays in Positive Economics*, University of Chicago Press, Chicago, U.S.A., 1953) argues that the **realism of the assumptions** (a behavioural premise is an assumption) underlying a theory are less important than the **ability of the theory to explain or predict**. In Friedman's parlance, what is important is that people behave as if the assumptions about their behaviour are true, whether or not the assumptions are factually descriptive. Applying this concept to the present issue, we may argue that a model based upon the premise of profit maximization may be useful if managers behave as if they are attempting to maximize profits, irrespective of what they actually are attempting to do. So, it does not matter whether it is profit or some other behavioural objective, or whether the decision maker is attempting to maximize, satisfice, or only mediate; the relevant consideration is whether a model erected upon a profit maximization assumption can explain or predict well enough. Baldwin concluded in the quote cited above that the opportunity loss resulting from adopting the profit maximizing assumption would be small.

There may even be reason to believe that the simple profit maximization assumption will be adequate to the modelling of satisficing behaviour. Herbert Simon, the inventor of the satisficing idea, even though he judges satisficing models to be richer than maximizing models, acknowledges that "the psychological evidence on individual behaviour shows that aspirations tend to adjust to the attainable. Hence in the long run...the level of aspiration and the attainable maximum will be very close together." If this can be taken as a justification for employing a maximizing assumption where a satisficing assumption might be preferable, it is due to the richness of the satisficing approach that accommodates adaptation, rather than the adaptability of the maximization model.

Whatever it is that business decision makers are pursuing, and whatever their behavioural pattern with respect to the objective, our conclusion is that profit maximization can serve as a satisfactory proxy in developing the theory of managerial decision making. In consequent chapters we shall elaborate the mathematical modelling approach to both maximization and optimization (that is, maximization subject to one or more constraints), and in employ the maximization or optimization behavioural premises as appears appropriate, but we shall be prepared to refer to alternative objectives or other behavioural patterns as needed.

PROFIT IN THE SHORT AND LONG RUNS

The student of managerial economics should recognize from the outset that the unbridled pursuit of profit in any short-run setting could be detrimental to the earning of profit in any subsequent period (each future setting is of course its own short run), or even to the survival of the enterprise in the long run. A wise manager, one whose **time horizon** stretches beyond the immediate circumstances, upon occasion will see the need to **sub-maximize** with respect to a profit objective in the short run in the interest of both survival into the long run and the possibility of maximizing profits in future short runs. We thus acknowledge the rationality of deliberate non-maximizing behaviour during any particular short-term time frame if justified by long run considerations.

One approach to analyzing profit in the long-run time frame is that adopted by Brigham, Pappas & Hirschey in the various editions of their managerial economics texts (*Managerial Economics* and *Fundamentals of Managerial Economics*, Dryden Press, Chicago, U.S.A.). The essential notion in this approach is that the manager of the firm attempts to maximize the **value of the firm** in the long run. This idea then can accommodate both profit maximization and deliberate non-maximization behaviour in the sequence of short-runs that constitute the long-run. This decision perspective can be represented by the present value model:

$$PV = R_1/(1 + i) + R_2/(1 + i)^2 + \ldots + R_n/(1+i)^n.$$

The return, R, in each of the n short runs is the profit of the period that the manager may have attempted to maximize, but may have deliberately chosen not to maximize in the interest of outcomes in other short runs and the long run. The i in each of the denominator terms is the **discount rate** that reflects the remoteness of outcomes expected in the future time settings. The number, n, of future short runs that comprise the long run depends on the length of the manager's time horizon. The essential long run behavioural premise is that the manager attempts to maximize the **present value** of the enterprise, PV, even if non-maximizing behaviour is indulged in with respect to any of the short-run profits indicated by the R symbols.

AN OBJECT OF PURSUIT OR AN INDICATOR OF SUCCESS

A word of caution in regard to profit may be in order for the prospective business manager. Profit, after the fact, an easily measurable quantity, may be much like the more nebulous and hard-to-measure state of happiness. Personal happiness is a condition that virtually all human beings (exceptions being masochists) aspire to attain. But it often appears that if happiness *per se* is taken to be the object of personal pursuit, the harder one tries to achieve happiness, the more elusive it becomes. Particularly, members of a materialistic society often appear to pursue happiness by acquiring things such as bigger and nicer homes, cars, boats, condos at the beach or chalets in the mountains, etc., only to discover that once the object of desire has finally been acquired, they are in fact no happier than they were before. We philosophize to suggest that the more effective way to attain happiness is to pursue and achieve some other personally satisfying or socially beneficial end. Happiness thus would be the by-product rather than the object of pursuit, and may be achievable in greater abundance by not pursuing it than by pursuing it.

The application of this consideration to the context of managerial decision making is the possibility that if profit is the object of pursuit, it may turn out to be highly elusive. On the other hand, if the enterprise management takes some other more socially redeeming goal, for example, to provide well-designed, functional, high-quality merchandise at the lowest possible price, a larger volume of profit may result as a by-product and a reward for successful entrepreneurship than could have been achieved had profit been the primary object of pursuit. Here, the role of profit is to serve as an **indicator of success** in pursuing some other goal, rather than as the object of pursuit itself. Indeed, some writers have suggested that if profit is the only object of pursuit, profit will be the main product, with poor-quality and high-priced merchandise the by-product. We can only conjecture that the seeming obsession of American corporate enterprise (and the academia that attempts to explain its behaviour) with short-run profit is one of the factors in the declining competitiveness of American products on world markets.

Kanji Haitani offers the following indictment of an obsession with profit maximization:

> What is wrong, one may ask, with trying to maximize returns on corporate assets? Is it not, after all, what the corporate business is all about—maximizing the returns on

stockholders' equity? The answers to these questions hinge on the nature of control over assets. According to the 'new management principles,' corporate assets are viewed not as machines but rather as financial assets—that is, as dollars and cents. This preoccupation with tight financial controls inevitably leads to a neglect of engineering and production—the factory floor and the assembly line. Emphasis tends to shift away from research and development, innovations in products and production processes, and development of better working relations among people, to short-term cost savings. Sacrificed in this process is the long-term competitive health and vigour of the enterprise (p. 240).

Summary of Important Points

1. Autonomous owner entrepreneurs, with few external constraints, may attempt to maximize profits in an absolute sense; but for other contexts, the profit maximization behavioural premise has been called into question.
2. With growing scale of operations and separation of ownership and management, hired managers could pursue personal interests that diverge from those of owners.
3. The ensuing dispersion of ownership of corporate shares has led to the exercise of absolute authority by corporate managers, followed by a rising concern for corporate social responsibility.
4. Professional managers have begun to perceive their roles as mediating among a wide variety of interests, of which the ownership interest is but one.
5. Five prominent managerial behaviour premises are that managers attempt
   - (a) to maximize profits;
   - (b) to optimize profits subject to various constraints;
   - (c) to optimize some growth phenomenon subject to a profit requirement as a constraint;
   - (d) to satisfice with respect to profit; and
   - (e) to mediate among competing constituencies.

   Each of these premises may find relevance in some firms.
6. What is important to the development of a theory of managerial behaviour is that managers behave as if they maximize profits, irrespective of what they actually are attempting to achieve.
7. Managers may in the short run find rationales for sub-maximizing profits; in the long run they may rationally attempt to maximize the value of the enterprise.
8. Profit may be more readily achievable as a by-product of other pursuits than as an object of direct pursuit.
9. The seeming obsession of American corporate managers with short-run profits may underlie a declining competitiveness of American products on world markets.

Significant Terms

profit maximization
survival
hired managers
divergence of interests
dispersion of ownership
social responsibility
constraints
managerial utility
function
optimization
subordinate goals
growth-related variables
TROR
behavioural drives
satisficing
constituent mediation

Questions for Discussion

1. Explain why the original behavioural premise underlying the theory of the business firm has been called into question.
2. Discuss the effects of 'separation of ownership and management' upon the theory of the businesss firm.
3. How has the dispersion of ownership of corporate shares affected the decision making in the modern business firm?
4. Explain how rising interest in social concerns has affected the operations of business firms and the theory that purports to explain their behaviour.
5. Discuss the emergence of constraints upon managerial decision making, and how this has affected the theory of the business firm.
6. Identify alternative behaviour premises for the theory of the firm, and explain the rationale for each.
7. Describe the behavioural pattern of optimization and explain how it may be incorporated into the theory of the firm.
8. Explain how the multiple goals confronting a business decision maker may be incorporated into the theory of the business firm.
9. Explain how the profit of a business enterprise may serve as a constraint upon the pursuit of other goals by the management of the business firm.
10. Explain how a 'target rate of return on invested capital' may be incorporated into the theory of the business firm.
11. Discuss the phenomenon of 'satisficing,' and explain how it can be incorporated into the theory of the business firm.

12. Why does Herbert Simon assert that "models of satisficing behaviour are richer than models of maximizing behaviour?"

13. Explain how the behavioural pattern of 'constituent mediation' can be reconciled with the economist's optimization model.

14. Explain why William Baumol concludes that the profit maximization premise is satisfactory for a theory of the behaviour of the typical large corporation.

15. How does the 'as if' proposition advanced by Milton Friedman bear upon the theory of the business firm?

16. How does Herbert Simon reconcile maximizing and satisficing behavioural patterns in the theory of the business firm?

17. If business firm managers do not actually attempt to maximize profits (but rather pursue some alternate goal), what should be done with the theory of the business firm that is based upon the profit maximizing premise?

18. Discuss possible circumstances under which business firm managers might deliberately sub-maximize with respect to their profits.

19. Explain how long-run value maximization by business firm managers may be reconciled with short-run non-profit-maximizing behaviours.

20. Explain how the achievement of profit in the business firm may be a by-product of other activities rather than an object of direct pursuit. What are the managerial implications?

21. Discuss Kanji Haitani's indictment of the seeming obsession of American corporate managers with short-run profit maximization.

Appendix 2.1

ECONOMIC METHOD AND MODELLING

UNDERSTANDING ECONOMIC BEHAVIOUR

Over the past couple of centuries, economists have developed an effective approach to understanding 'the way the world works.' This approach, known as theoretical, deductive, or *a priori* method, may also be described as **model methodology**. The objective of economic modelling is to produce an abstract representation of a real economic context. Such a representation can be used to explain how the context works, to instruct about it, to forecast its behaviour, and to simulate policy in regard to its function.

Economists regard modelling as a form of scientific method. When the term 'scientific method' is mentioned, people often think of **experimentation** within a laboratory setting. Such experimentation generates data which can serve as the basis for an inference about the validity of a scientific theory or hypothesis. Economists have only upon occasion undertaken experiments as a means of discerning the economic nature of the world.

Several good reasons have been offered for the paucity of experimentation in economic inquiries. Social systems, economic mechanisms in particular, usually are regarded as too large and complex to be fitted into the confines of a laboratory. Indeed, young economists often are told that the world itself is their laboratory. More importantly, in any social system it is usually too difficult (which for the economist means too costly) to exercise **laboratory control** over all of the matters which are extraneous or peripheral to the social system. Also, there typically are **moral implications** to efforts by social scientists at experimenting on human subjects. The moral implications follow from the likelihood that any social experiment will leave the subjects of the experiment either better or worse off than before the experiment.

The most significant practical objection which can be raised with respect to experimentation on human subjects is the **Hawthorne Effect**, that is, that intelligent human beings, once they perceive that they are the subjects of experimentation, tend to engage in affected behaviour. This affected behaviour may be to try to present themselves in the best light in the eyes of the experimenter or those who will analyze the experimental data. Such behaviour has the effect of contaminating the experimental results so that they cannot be taken as indicative of normal behaviour. The only way to avoid the possibility of such affected behaviour is for the experimenter to try to keep the subjects from perceiving that they are subjects of experimentation, but there may be moral implications to this approach as well. For any of the reasons expressed above, economists have tended to avoid an experimental approach.

MODEL METHOD

The approach favoured by economists was pioneered by David Ricardo, who in his 1817 book, *Principles of Political Economy and Taxation*, described a hypothetical opportunity of England to exchange cloth with Portugal for wine. The purpose of this example was to elaborate the virtues of international specialization according to comparative advantage. The example was an abstraction because it was both imaginary and highly simplified. Although Ricardo's tabular information was not given graphic or equation format by him, it can still be considered an early model in the modern vein.

From Ricardo's time until about the middle of the twentieth century, economists employed roughly the same approach. They further developed the method to employ mathematics in order to give their models both graphic and equation representations. Their models enabled them to **deduce conclusions** (hence the name, 'deductive method'), but they rarely attempted to subject their deduced conclusions to empirical verification. Indeed, those holding more extreme views in this regard declared that there was no need for empirical testing. Such tests would be a waste of time since the deduced conclusions were true in an *a priori* sense (hence the name, '*a priori* method').

The basis for such an extreme position was their belief that since they started from accurate observations, made appropriate assumptions, and obeyed the laws of logic (both inductive and deductive), the conclusions which they derived had to be true (in the *a priori* sense). But, perhaps a more practical reason for a general reluctance to attempt verification of the *a priori* deductions was the extreme difficulty of computation in an era which lacked both mechanical and electronic calculators and computers.

The deductive or *a priori* approach started to 'come apart' early in the twentieth century as economists began to realize that some of their most fervently held conclusions about the economic nature of the world could not explain current happenings and conditions. In particular, the 'classical economists' (as John Maynard Keynes called them) presumed that their understanding of markets at the microeconomic level (deduced using good *a priori* procedures) would be applicable to the whole macro-economy. Accordingly, their theories failed either to predict or explain the 'Great Depression' of the decade of the 1930s. Nor could they recommend adequate policy prescriptions for dealing with the great contraction. Nonetheless, the early twentieth century economists were no more ready to give up their time-honoured method of analysis than they were to give up the theories derived from it.

Although the procedures and tools of modern statistical analysis were well developed by the 1920s, the tremendous computational effort required for statistical testing with empirical data continued to prevent many economists from undertaking the effort. It took a technological and information revolution after the middle of the twentieth century to bring about a significant change in the economist's model method. With the advent first of the calculator and subsequently the computer, economists began to modify their methodology. They would still employ a theoretical approach for developing a model; they would continue to employ deductive logic to derive model conclusions; but the deduced conclusions would no longer be regarded as *a priori* truths. Rather, the deduced conclusions would be treated only as **tentative hypotheses** to be subjected to efforts at **empirical verification**.

Although few of the 'principles of economics' elaborated in the economic texts of the 1940s had been verified with empirical data, today virtually all of them have been tested many times over. That they had not earlier been verified does not mean that they were untrue, only that their validities had not been determined. Upon occasion, empirical testing has led to the rejection of some long and firmly held economic beliefs, but in most cases the efforts at empirical testing have served to validate the conclusions deduced earlier by *a priori* methods.

MODERN MODELLING PROCEDURES

Although economists have not agreed upon a formalized list of procedures for modelling an economic phenomenon, we shall offer the following outline as a guide to the prospective economic model builder. We shall also note parallels and differences between the modelling approach and an experimental approach.

1. Any scientist, whether natural or social, is first attracted to a new topic by **observation** of some phenomenon. The observation may be perfectly casual, as when walking down the street one notices a peculiar pattern of leaves on a bush, or the behaviour of a child selecting an ice cream cone from a vendor. Alternately, the observation may be made in conjunction with some other formal inquiry, as, for example, when a chemist, in experimenting with a reaction between certain elements,

notices another element (present as a contaminant) also entering into the reaction. Or an economist, intent upon analyzing the real growth of a region, coincidentally notices a pattern in the price data which have been removed from the regional product data by process of deflation. In any of these cases, the first observation serves as a platform from which to depart into further analysis.

2. Given knowledge and experiences in the discipline, the scientist then **hypothesizes** a relationship between the object of interest (treated as dependent variable) and some number of determinants (treated as independent variables). The economist selects a fundamental **behavioural premise** to serve as a principle which governs behaviour. A behavioural premise is usually an assumption that someone is trying to minimize or maximize some quantity. The hypothesized relationship can be expressed in mathematical, functional notation as

$$y = f(x)$$

where y, the object of analysis, is the **dependent variable**, and x is an **independent variable**, that is, a determinant of the behaviour of y. More than one independent variable may be included in the model. The selected behavioural premise is implicit in the presumed functional relationship, f.

3. The economist as well as the natural scientist must now find some means of **simplifying** or abstracting from the complexity of the phenomenon under examination. Here the natural scientist often has an advantage over the economist in being able to accomplish the abstraction by means of laboratory control. The slash in the functional notation statement above separates the independent variables to be included explicitly in the analysis (those to the left of the slash) from those to be isolated from the analysis (those to the right of the slash represented by the ellipsis symbols). The natural scientist then designs an experiment so that the facilities of laboratory control may **hold constant** (or eliminate) the extraneous variables. The experiment is in effect isolated from the surrounding environment by means of the laboratory control. But, as we have noted above, economists find it to be extremely costly or physically impossible to effect laboratory control over the extraneous variables in an economic system. Their alternative approach, admittedly a second best to actually being able to **hold** the environment constant, is to **assume** all of the extraneous influences as given or constant for purposes of the analysis. The economist's method of abstracting from complexity of the phenomenon under study is *assumption of constancies*.

4. While the natural scientist proceeds to conduct an experiment in order to generate data, the economist employs **inductive logic** (that is,

reasoning from first observation and behavioural premise to a generalization about them) to structure a model. The model, including only those independent variables to the left of the functional notation slash, may be represented in the form of verbal assertions of relationships, mathematical equations, or graphs of the equations. Once the structure of the model is in place, the economist may employ **deductive logic** (that is, reasoning from a generalization to a particular conclusion) to derive conclusions about the model.

5. An economist who is a strict *a priorist* will be inclined to regard a deduced conclusion as an *a priori* truth to be accepted without further consideration. But the more usual present day approach is to treat the deduced conclusion as a **tentative hypothesis** to be subjected to empirical verification.

6. Assuming that the deduced conclusion is an hypothesis to be tested, the economist is confronted with the need for appropriate **empirical data**. In contrast, the natural scientist is provided with data generated in conducting the experiment (a stochastic process). The experiment is probably conducted numerous times, generating enough data for a statistical inference about the validity of the hypothesis. But what data should the economist use? Since experimentally generated data cannot be relied upon, the economist must turn to the world itself as a **stochastic process**. The on-going processes of the phenomenon which the economist has determined to study produce continuing experience which can yield data as soon as they are observed and recorded. The world itself is surely the most prolific of all stochastic processes. The analyst must simply watch what is going on and record observations about it. The economist's job is to find appropriate data already captured and published by others, or to engage in original **field research** to record the needed data from observations of natural processes. Once adequate data are in hand, the economist may employ the tools of statistical analysis to test the hypothesis, thereby accepting or rejecting it on grounds of statistical inference. The statistical procedures are usually conducted by computerized statistical software.

The economist still has a problem to resolve. The model was structured only after appropriate simplifying assumptions were made, but the data available for testing the model conclusions reflect natural processes for which nothing was or could be held constant. The economist must recognize the **dynamic** (changing over time) nature of the real world; it holds no aspect of itself constant for the convenience of the analyst. The dynamic natural process data are unlikely to match very closely the conclusions which were deduced from a model structured under various constancy assumptions.

One approach to dealing with this problem is to **add to the model** more of the determinants which were assumed constant in structuring the model, but this approach may ultimately defeat the purpose of modelling the phenomenon. An alternate approach is to **adjust the data** for the dependent variable to get rid of the influence of the determinants which were assumed constant. Once the influences of the extraneous determinants have been purged from the dependent variable data, the independent variable data are more likely to validate the model conclusions.

7. A final step in model method is one which often has been omitted, and occasionally by some very prominent economists. This final step is to relate the model conclusions (which were deduced under a variety of constancy assumptions) back to the real world phenomenon which the economist is investigating. The means for accomplishing this step is an intellectual exercise to **reconsider the deduced conclusions** in light of the assumed constancies, modifying them to take into account those factors which, though assumed constant, in fact do change.

John Maynard Keynes, widely regarded as the intellectual father of modern macroeconomic analysis, was guilty of a failure to take the last step in the modelling process. In constructing his concept of a consumption function, Keynes assumed many factors to be constant, among them the stocks of liquid assets (for example. the quantity of money) and real wealth. Keynes proceeded to structure his model of the macro-economy, deduce conclusions about how it worked, and recommend policy prescriptions to deal with the ensuing 'Great Depression.' But he failed to return to his model conclusions to reconsider the impacts of changes in liquid assets and real wealth. In so doing, Keynes himself set the stage for a resurgence of classical economics in the guise of Monetarism.

REVIEW

A brief review of these modelling procedures is in order. The economic analyst observes some phenomenon which attracts attention for further examination. The analyst hypothesizes a relationship and selects an appropriate behavioural premise upon which the model may be structured. The next step is to simplify from the complexity of the phenomenon under investigation by assuming constant all extraneous matters. The analyst then employs inductive logic to structure a model relating the dependent variable to the independent variables which have been chosen for treatment in the model, and deductive logic to derive conclusions about the functioning of the model. In the modern approach, the deduced conclusions are regarded as tentative hypotheses to be validated by statistical tests on data taken from real-world circumstances. Finally, if the model conclusions are supported by the data, they should be reconsidered in light of changes in factors which were assumed constant in structuring the model.

Appendix 2.2

MANAGING FOR QUALITY RATHER THAN PROFITABILITY

The view of profit as a by-product of pursuing other goals is congruent with the evolution of Total Quality Management (TQM) programmes during the late 1980s. The objectives of a TQM programme are:

1. To sensitize employees to the pursuit of quality in the delivery of their products or services;
2. To serve as a vehicle for changing an organizational culture of complacency;
3. To formalize a process for pursuing continuing quality improvement; and
4. To provide a means of involving others (than the decision makers) in the improvement process.

A great many companies in the private sector have adopted TQM programmes, among them IBM, Xerox, Ford, Yellow Freight, Texas Instruments, Florida Power and Light, GTE, and Southern Pacific Transportation. The principal motivation seems to be to improve the company's chances of survival in an increasingly competitive international environment.

Some companies report great success with the approach; others admit failure to achieve desired results. Success or failure seems to depend heavily upon two factors: the extent to which top-level executive management has committed to the process in its company, and the extent to which lower-level administrative personnel and line and staff employees have been infused with enthusiasm for the programme.

Many colleges and universities have also jumped onto the TQM bandwagon, not only to teach about it but also to attempt to implement the process in both their business affairs and academic areas. The principal motivation for public sector institutions is survival in the face of budget cuts by state legislatures. For private colleges it may be loss of funding or simply survival when faced with subsidized pricing by public institutions.

Some have regarded TQM as a trivial process, or as simply the latest bit of managerial alphabet soup—PERT (Programme Evaluation and Review Technique), SWOT (Strengths, Weaknesses, Opportunities, Threats), or MBO (Management by Objectives). It is easy for the management of an established organization to be complacent or to take an arrogant or elitist position that it is already a quality organization which does not need a quality-management programme like TQM.

'Quality management' means only the maintenance of existing levels of performance; TQM should really be understood to target continuing quality improvement (CQI) throughout the organization. The operating premise is that no matter how good an organization has become, there is always room for further improvement.

The first order of business in implementing a CQI process should be to review the organization's vision (long-run, strategic) and mission (short-run, tactical) statements. Then, since TQM is touted as a 'customer driven' process, the organization should identify its customers and their expectations of the organization's products. Gaps between current performance and customer's expectations should be identified, along with potential means for closing the gaps.

Procedures should involve establishing performance-expectation gap (PEG) teams to focus upon means of monitoring and achieving quality improvement in production processes as measured against vision and mission statements. Each PEG team is in effect an *ad hoc* committee established to focus upon a particular problem. Each employee may be assigned to several such PEG teams, depending upon his or her responsibilities, interests, or expertise.

TQM programmes are oriented towards inputs rather than outputs. A significant feature of TQM is 'midstream recursion' that is, continuing review of a process with running adjustments. This differs from statistical quality control, that is, statistical assessment of outputs to accept or reject the final product.

PEG teams should meet periodically to review progress towards elimination of gaps between current performance and customer expectations, and devise procedures for addressing remaining problems. A PEG team may be decommissioned (with celebration) once its performance–expectations gap has been eliminated.

The adoption of a TQM process is evidence that an organization is pursuing a goal of quality in the delivery of its products rather than profit, *per se*. If the organization is successful in its TQM programme implementation, its profitability may improve, not because it has resolved to become more profitable, but rather because it has diminished the gaps between its performance and its customers' expectations. Profitability then comes as a by-product of quality.

—oo(O)oo—

Chapter 3

The Analysis of Value and Risk

Topics covered in this chapter

• The nature of riskiness. • Distinctions between long- and short-run changes. • The effects of remoteness of future benefits and costs. • Decision criteria for the long run. • Human attitudes towards risk.• Means of allowing for risk in making long-run decisions. • Means of adjusting for anticipated inflation in long-run decisions.

Much of the substance of managerial economics is about marginal decision making affecting operations in the short-run time frame. Most of the rest of this text elaborates the marginal criteria for short-run decision making. This chapter is devoted to **long-run** decision considerations and the analysis of **risk**.

THE REMOTENESS OF THE LONG RUN

In addition to the differences noted in Chapter 1 between long and short runs, a major distinction remains to set the long-run decision problem apart from short-run decision making. Since the effects of the long-run decision can be expected to impact the enterprise in the future, some recognition must be made of the **remoteness** of those effects. The sense of the problem is that the expectation of a benefit to be realized in the future is **worthless** to the decision maker than an equivalent benefit received immediately. Specialists in finance often refer to this phenomenon as the 'time value of money,' but the phenomenon would exist even in a barter economy (one which does not use money). The phenomenon is described by the ancient adage that 'a bird in the hand is worth two in the bush.' The problem pertains to costs as well as to benefits. In addition, costs which must be paid at some future time are also less meaningful to the decision maker than those which must be paid today, although the wise decision maker should plan and make careful arrangements to cover expected future costs.

Since future possibilities are worth less than present realities, economists have acknowledged this phenomenon by **discounting** the expected future values at an appropriate rate. This rate is usually taken to be the **best market rate of interest** for which the enterprise can qualify. The interest rate is used as a discount rate on the premise that the equivalent of the expected future value, less the cost of interest, can be had at present by borrowing the future sum. This relationship should be true whether the borrowed principal and the interest to be repaid are expressed in barter or monetary terms. If we let the symbol i stand for the interest rate which will serve as discount rate, the present value of the expected future outcome can be expressed as

$$(1)\quad PV = \frac{V_1}{(1+i)} + \frac{V_2}{(1+i)^2} + \ldots + \frac{V_n}{(1+i)^n}$$

where V is a predicted future net benefit (or return) in each of n future periods (it is 'expected' if it is a probability-weighted average of all possible outcomes which may occur). The value of V is taken to be the net of the difference between the future benefit, b, and the cost of realizing it, c, or $V = (b - c)$. PV is less than the sum of the Vs because each V is divided by a number greater than 1, that is, 1 plus the discount rate i.

If there are no risk considerations to be taken into account, the appropriate decision procedure is to first compute, using formula (1), the present values of the expected future net benefits for each of the k outcome possibilities for each of the decision alternatives. Then the expected values of possible outcomes of each decision alternative can be computed as their probability-weighted averages using formula (1) of Chapter 2 into which the computed present values, PV, are substituted for the outcomes, V. The proper decision criterion is to choose the alternative with the **largest present expected value** of the possible outcomes.

A MARGINAL DECISION CRITERION FOR THE LONG RUN

In the present value formula (1), values for V and i are known or estimated, and the value of PV is computed. An alternative version of the present value formula permits computing the so-called internal rate of return,

$$(2)\quad K = \frac{V_1}{(1+r)} + \frac{V_2}{(1+r)^2} + \ldots + \frac{V_n}{(1+r)^n}$$

In formula (2), K is the **capital outlay** required to acquire and install an investment opportunity (since it is known today, it is the opportunity's 'present value'), and r is the **internal rate of return** on the investment opportunity. In this approach, the value of K and the values for V are known (or can be estimated), but the value of r is to be computed. Actually, equation

(2) cannot be easily solved for value r, but r may be estimated by successive approximation from annuity tables.

If we may abstract from the possibility of a scrap value of the capital at the end of its useful life, n, the conceptual sense of r is the **discount rate** which would be just sufficient to make the sum of the returns, V1...Vn, just equal to the capital outlay, K. The discount rate, r, is interpreted as a rate of return because if all of the net amounts represented by V were invested at an interest rate equal to r, they and their interest earnings would add up to the capital outlay, K. The investment criterion which justifies undertaking the investment opportunity is that its **rate of return**, r, is at least as great as the **best market interest rate**, i, for which the enterprise can qualify, or r >= i.

If we may assume that the predicted net returns, V1...Vn, can be estimated, the internal rates of return can be computed for each prospective investment opportunity currently under consideration by the enterprise's management. For example, suppose that the management of an enterprise is considering five prospective investment opportunities, designated A to E, which require the capital outlays and promise the internal rates of return reported in Table 3.1. These opportunities have already been arrayed in descending order of internal rates of return. When the capital outlays are 'stacked' from left to right on a set of coordinate axes with capital expenditures on the horizontal axis and internal rates of return on the vertical axis as in Figure 3.1, the plotted points A to E constitute a downward sloping path which John Maynard Keynes called the 'marginal efficiency of capital' (*The General Theory of Employment, Interest, and Money*, Harcourt, Brace & World, Inc., 1964, p. 135). Suppose that the enterprise can borrow funds from the capital markets at an interest rate i=8 per cent, represented by the horizontal dashed line. The marginal investment criterion then is to undertake additional investment opportunities in descending order of rates of

Table 3.1: Hypothetical Investment Opportunities and Rates of Return

Opportunity	*r* %	*Outlay* $	*Cumulative* $
A	16	140,000	140,000
B	14	218,000	358,000
C	10	250,000	608,000
D	6	98,000	706,000
E	4	124,000	830,000

return as long as the rates of return are at least as high as the interest rate, i, or r >= i. In the illustrated example, investment opportunities A, B, and C ought to be undertaken; opportunities D and E ought to be rejected because their rates of return would not be sufficient to pay the interest on borrowing to finance them.

We should note that this long-run investment decision criterion is appropriate even if the enterprise can finance its capital outlays from **internal sources**. The rationale is that funds accumulated internally by **depreciation allowances** and **retaining earnings** have been (or could

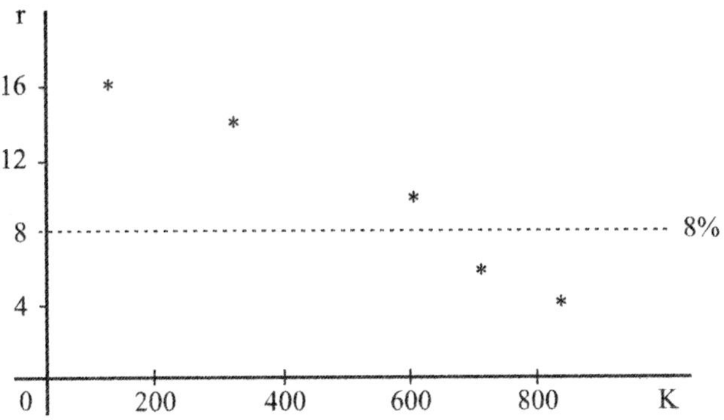

Figure 3.1. The marginal efficiency of capital.

have been) 'invested' on financial capital markets earning interest rate, i, which must now be forgone if the funds are used to finance the prospective investment opportunities instead.

ATTITUDES TOWARDS RISK

Decision makers' **attitudes towards risk** may vary widely. People who have strong preferences for risk assumption may turn out to be chronic gamblers. Such people get their 'kicks' from accepting adverse-odds bets (long shots) with negative expected values. Even though the odds are against them, it is more intellectually satisfying to them to win 'big' on rare occasions than to gain small sums more frequently on favourable-odds bets. **Risk preferrers** are likely to lose (on net balance) over the long run. Luckily for society (and themselves), they are in the minority. It is theoretically possible for a decision maker to be essentially **risk-neutral**, having neither preference for nor aversion towards risk. However, this is such a 'razor's edge' state that few people find themselves there.

The vast majority of all people who regard themselves as rational thinkers are **risk-averse**, and the more extreme of them are **risk avoiders** (they expect bad things to happen to them each morning as soon as they get out of bed). A normally risk-averse decision maker likely would not accept an even-odds bet on a two-possibility event (50 per cent chance each way) because the loss of the sum at risk would mean more to them (negatively) than would the gain of an identical sum would mean to them (positively). It is likely that most business decision makers, who tend to be a conservative lot, are risk averse. This does not mean that they seek to avoid risk altogether (if so they would not behave as entrepreneurs); rather, they attempt to **manage risk** by seeking more information in order to diminish it, by attempting to take offsetting positions, or by attempting to insure against the risk.

If it were practical to specify **personal utility functions** for decision makers, it would be possible to include the decision maker's attitude towards risk as an argument (that is, one of the independent variables) in the function. We might find the risk preferrer to 'consume' risky items under conditions of increasing marginal utility, the risk-indifferent decision maker to exhibit a linear

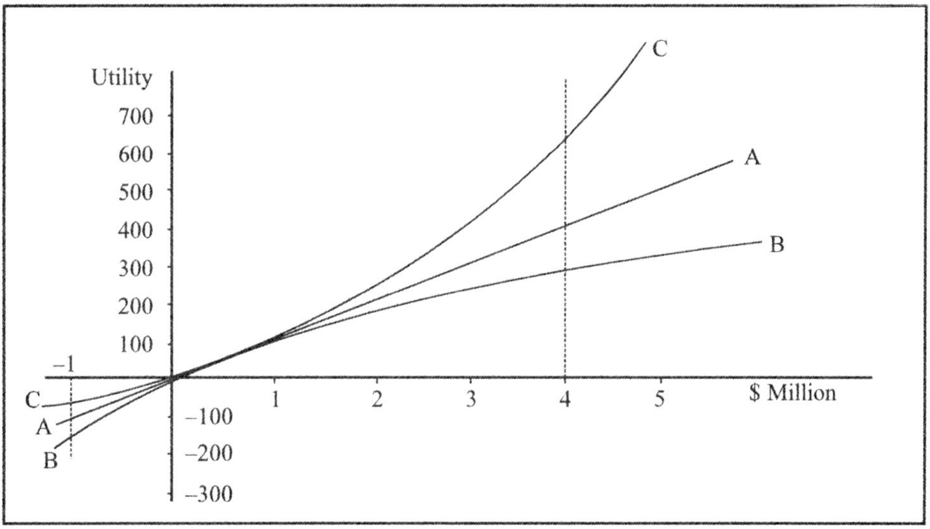

Figure 3.2. Possible shapes of total utility functions.

risk utility function, and one who is averse to risk experiencing diminishing marginal utility with respect to risk.

MARGINAL UTILITY AND RISK

The conditions under which a decision maker realizes satisfaction (that is, utility) with respect to income (whether monetary or 'in kind') are thought to influence his attitude towards risk. Three possible shapes of total utility functions are illustrated in Figure 3.2. For decision maker A, utility increases at a constant rate as income increases. Decision maker B's utility increases at a decreasing rate (the utility function, though positively sloped, is concave downward). This illustrates the so-called principle of **diminishing marginal utility**, and is thought to be descriptive of typical human behaviour with respect to the receipt of income. Decision maker C realizes additional utility at an increasing rate as income increases (that is, the curve is concave upwards). Although this utility pattern is thought to be atypical of human behaviour except in the very early stages of consumption, it would illustrate a phenomenon of **increasing marginal utility**. In all three cases, the utility function is extended into graphic quadrant III (negative values for both income and utility) for purpose of illustration. Although utility is hardly measurable, and certainly not comparable from one decision maker to another, we shall indulge in the heroic assumption of the same numeric scale on the vertical axis of all three graphs.

Suppose that these three decision makers are all presented with an investment opportunity that requires a capital outlay of $ 1 million, and which can be expected to result in only two possible outcomes, success yielding a $ 5 million return, or failure yielding a zero return. Although the three decision makers might estimate widely divergent probabilities of success and failure, for purposes of argument let us for the moment suppose that all three accept a conventional wisdom that 80 per cent of such ventures are doomed to failure, but 20 per cent succeed. The **expected value** of such an investment opportunity may be computed as follows:

$$EV = (\$ 5 \text{ mil} - \$ 1 \text{ mil}) \times .2 + (\$ 0 \text{ mil} - \$ 1 \text{ mil}) \times .8$$

$$EV = \$ 4 \text{ million} \times .2 - \$ 1 \text{ million} \times .8$$

$$EV = \$ 800 \text{ thousand} - \$ 800 \text{ thousand} = \$ 0.$$

The expected value of the decision alternative not to invest (which will require no capital outlay and yield no return) is also $ 0. On the basis of expected value of the returns, it would appear that all three decision makers should be indifferent between the decision to invest and not to invest (indeed, since the expected value of the opportunity is $ 0, why bother?).

However, an examination of their **expected utilities** (a probability weighted average of the utilities which they would realize) reveals a different story. The expected utility for decision maker A may be computed as

$$EU_A = 400 \times .2 - 100 \times .8 = 0 \text{ units of utility,}$$

which is the same utility realized from not investing. In this case, the conclusion is identical to that reached by examining the expected value of the opportunity.

Decision maker B realizes additional utility under conditions of diminishing marginal utility. The expected utility may be computed as

$$EU_B = 270 \times .2 - 150 \times .8 = -66 \text{ units of utility.}$$

Decision maker B would suffer an absolute loss of utility if the investment were undertaken, and would therefore prefer to realize a utility of zero from not investing.

The expected utility for decision maker C, who realizes additional income under conditions of increasing marginal utility, may be computed as

$$EU_C = 650 \times .2 - 70 \times .8 = 74 \text{ units of utility.}$$

Decision maker C would enjoy a net of 74 units of utility from undertaking the investment compared with zero units from not investing, and therefore can be expected to proceed with this 'long shot.'

Although there is no direct linkage here between marginal utility and risk, there is a rather strong presumption that decision maker B's **diminishing** marginal utility implies that he is risk **averse**, while decision maker C's **increasing** marginal utility leads to a **preference** for risk. Decision maker A's **constant** marginal utility function results in **indifference** with respect to risk.

Several important managerial implications follow from this analysis. One is that the **expected value** of a decision alternative is a good selection criterion only in the case of a decision maker who realizes increased satisfaction at an approximately constant rate. Alternately, if the marginal utility for a decision maker is approximately **constant** in the neighbourhood of the EVs of the available decision alternatives, the EVs may serve as adequate selection criteria. For other decision makers who realize increased satisfaction at **decreasing or increasing rates**, it is necessary to consider the **expected utilities** of the decision alternatives.

Even slightly different assessed probabilities may change the decision picture significantly. Suppose that the probability of success decreases to 15 per cent, while the probability of failure rises to 85 per cent. The recomputed expected value and expected utilities are as follows:

$$EV = \$\ 4 \text{ mil} \times .15 - \$\ 1 \text{ mil} \times .85 = -\$\ .250 \text{ mil}$$

$$EU_A = 400 \times .15 - 100 \times .85 = -25 \text{ units of utility}$$

$$EU_B = 270 \times .15 - 150 \times .85 = -87 \text{ units of utility}$$

$$EU_C = 650 \times .15 - 70 \times .85 = 38 \text{ units of utility}$$

In this case, the expected value is negative and decision makers A and B would rationally choose not to invest. But decision maker C would realize positive utility from the investment, even though the expected value of the venture is negative! Such a decision maker who experiences increasing marginal utility of income strongly enough to induce him to accept an **adverse-odds** venture with a negative expected value is surely a **gambler**. If the probability of success rises to 25 per cent while the probability of failure of the venture falls to 75 per cent, the computed expected values become:

$$EV = \$\ 4 \text{ mil} \times .25 - \$\ 1 \text{ mil} \times .75 = \$\ .250 \text{ mil}$$

$$EU_A = 400 \times .25 - 100 \times .75 = 25 \text{ units of utility}$$

$$EU_B = 270 \times .25 - 150 \times .75 = -65 \text{ units of utility}$$

$$EU_C = 650 \times .25 - 70 \times .75 = 110 \text{ units of utility}$$

Under these probability circumstances, the expected value of the venture is positive, but decision maker B is still so risk averse due to diminishing marginal utility as to be unwilling to undertake it. This is because the prospect of losing \$ 1 million in case of failure means so much more than the prospect of gaining \$ 4 million in case of success of the venture. Decision maker B would hate losing \$ 1 million more than the enjoyment of gaining \$ 4 million. The reader should confirm that in order for risk-averse decision maker B to realize a positive expected utility from the venture, the probability of success would have to rise to 36 per cent.

In the real world, three decision makers would likely experience not only different utility conditions, but may also come up with different **assessments of the probabilities** of success and failure of the decision alternatives before them. This means that two or more decision makers examining exactly the same decision opportunities may reach widely divergent conclusions about them. For example, suppose risk averse decision maker B assesses the probability of success of the venture at 36 per cent, which would yield a positive expected utility, while risk preferring decision maker C assesses the probability of success at only 9 per cent, which would yield a negative expected utility. Under these circumstances we might witness the irony of the risk averse decision maker undertaking the venture while the risk preferrer rejects it.

MEANS OF DEALING WITH RISK

A first approach to dealing with risk is to seek **more information** about the decision alternative. Additional information often reveals that the range of outcome variability is narrower than at first thought, and that the decision alternative is thus less risky than earlier imagined. But information itself is a **scarce resource** which is costly to acquire. The determination to acquire additional information is a managerial decision which is based on a comparison of the benefits of the additional information relative to the cost of acquiring it. At some point, the benefits of acquiring additional information must be judged as not outweighing the costs and the decision must be made under conditions of uncertainty or risk. The decision maker must then find some way to deal with (that is, manage) the remaining risk, possibly by insuring against it, offsetting it (possibly by hedging), or by simply accepting it. One of the essential functions of an entrepreneur is to assume risk in undertaking new ventures or in changing the operation of the enterprise.

Since it has not been found practical to specify utility functions, we shall take a more intuitive approach to how decision makers might deal with risk. A potentially useful concept for short-run decision analysis is that of the **certainty equivalent**. In this approach, the decision maker must ask himself what certain sum he would be willing to accept in lieu of the risky outcome at issue. The **risk-averse** decision maker can be expected to indicate a **lesser certain sum** than the risky possibility ('a bird in the hand is worth two in the bush'), whereas the **risk preferrer** would have to have a larger certain sum as a compensation for the insult of removing the gamble from his consideration. The certainty equivalent, CE, of the risky outcome, EV, is then substituted in the numerators of the ratios in the expected value (1) and present value (2) formulas:

$$(1') \quad PV = \frac{CE_1}{(1+i)} + \frac{CE_2}{(1+i)^2} + \ldots + \frac{CE_n}{(1+i)^n}$$

$$(2') \quad K = \frac{CE_1}{(1+r)} + \frac{CE_2}{(1+r)^2} + \ldots + \frac{CE_n}{(1+r)^n}$$

For a risk averse decision maker, CE < V; where the decision maker is risk indifferent, CE = V; and in the case of a risk preferrer, CE > V.

Although it may not be practical to specify preference functions, the certainty equivalent approach may be illustrated by the hypothetical risk-return indifference map first introduced in Figure 2.3. The map is reproduced in Figure 1.3. The preference function illustrated in this map is for a normally risk-averse decision maker. Suppose that a decision opportunity promises a return of \$ 6,000, but entails a risk of v_1. This particular combination of risk and return lies at point C on indifference curve I_3. If we now follow indifference curve I_3 downward to the right until the vertical axis is reached, we find that it intersects the vertical axis (where risk is zero) at \$ 3,000.

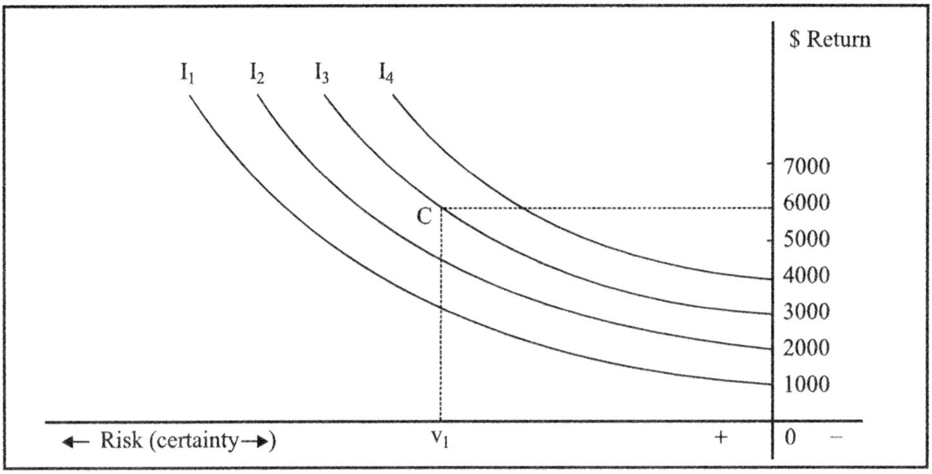

Figure 3.3. Risk-return indifference map.

The sum of $ 3,000 is thus the certainty equivalent of the $ 6,000 return which entails risk v_1. The certainty equivalent of any other risky sum may be found in similar fashion. The reader may imagine the appearance of an indifference curve map for a decision maker who prefers risk.

Another approach is possible in the analysis of risk in the long run. In the present value formula (2), a subjectively determined **risk premium**, a, is added to the interest rate discount in the denominator,

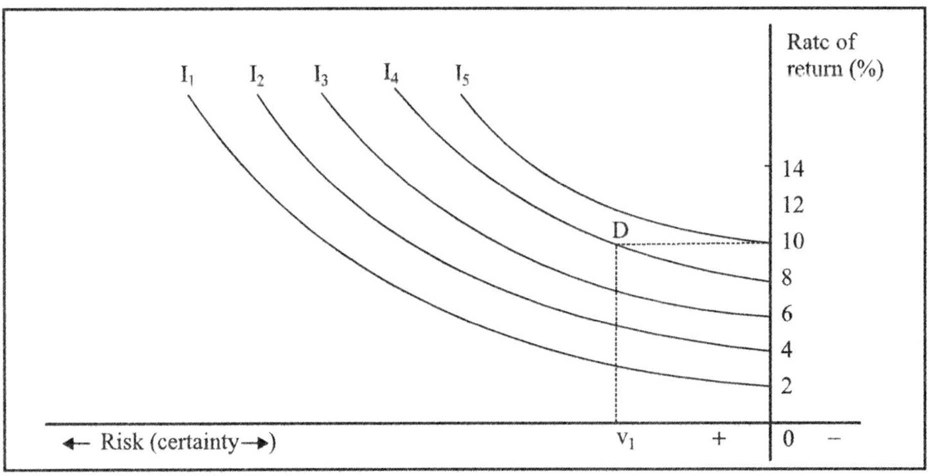

Figure 3.4. A risk-rate of return indifference map.

$$(3)\ PV = \frac{V_1}{(1+i+a)} + \frac{V_2}{(1+i+a)^2} + ... + \frac{V_2}{(1+i+a)^n}$$

The premium a constitutes a risk adjustment to the discount rate, i. The **risk-adjusted present value** will be smaller than before risk adjustment in reflection of the larger denominator. The risk-adjustment factors will differ from one decision opportunity to another, but their present values, adjusted for risk, will be more realistic selection criteria.

The determination of a risk adjustment factor may be illustrated by an indifference map which is a variation upon that illustrated in Figure 3.3. Figure 3.4 depicts a decision maker's indifference map with risk on the horizontal axis as illustrated above, but with percentage rates of return (rather than dollar amounts of returns) on the vertical axis. In this case, the procedure is first to find on the right-hand vertical axis the current risk-less return on something like a government bond, say 8 per cent. This identifies the relevant indifference curve, I_4, which may be followed. Then, when the risk factor, v_1, for the decision opportunity is computed, a vertical may be erected at v_1 on the horizontal axis to intersect indifference curve I_4 at point D. At point D the decision maker is indifferent between the low return on the risk-less government bond and the higher return on the risky decision opportunity. A horizontal may be drawn from D to the right-hand vertical axis to find the higher return, 10 per cent as illustrated. In the denominator of the present value formula, the value of i is taken to be 8 per cent, and the risk premium a is 2 per cent (that is, 10 per cent minus 8 per cent). If the market interest rate on government bonds changes, then some other indifference curve would become relevant and a new risk premium found in similar fashion.

The illustrated procedure for determining the risk adjustment factor is operational only if the decision maker's preference function can be specified (heroic at best), but this model does illustrate the thought process which must be used by a rational decision maker in selecting a risk adjustment factor. There is no scientific way to specify a schedule of either certainty-equivalent or discount rate adjustment factors. These are such **highly subjective** matters that they must be left to the personal judgement of each decision maker. This is one reason that different decision makers, confronted with the same scenarios and information, can reach such different investment conclusions. The naive or inexperienced decision maker may have no ability at all to determine either certainty equivalents or discount adjustment factors. The ability to determine either will come only with time and the accumulation of a **stock of experience** in considering risky alternatives.

ALLOWING FOR ANTICIPATED INFLATION

Finally, we should note that neither discounting to allow for the time value of money nor risk-adjustment of the discount rate constitutes an allowance for the risk of inflation. If over the n-period life of a decision opportunity inflation is expected to ensue, a **deflation factor** (that is, an inflation risk adjustment factor), d, may be included in the denominators of the terms of the present value equation,

$$(4)\ PV = \frac{V_1}{(1+i+a+d)} + \frac{V_2}{(1+i+a+d)^2} + ... + \frac{V_n}{(1+i+a+d)^n}$$

Table 3.2: Regret Matrix for Investment Decision

Strategy	*Outcomes*		*Regrets*	
	Success	*Failure*	*Success*	*Failure*
	(1)	(2)	(3)	(4)
Invest ($ million)	4	–1	0	1
Not invest ($)	0	0	4	0

Each deflation factor is a decimal equivalent, for example, .04, of an anticipated rate of inflation, for example, 4 per cent. The deflation factors may differ from term to term if inflation is thought likely to accelerate or decelerate over the life of the decision opportunity.

DECISION MAKING UNDER UNCERTAINTY

In the previous section we considered the utility implications of different probability assessments, but suppose that a decision maker simply cannot in any meaningful way assess the probabilities of the possible outcomes. How can the decision maker decide whether or not to invest in the venture described in the above example? Under the **maximin** decision rule, the decision maker would examine the worst-case scenarios, $ 0 for not investing and –$ 1 million if the investment is undertaken and fails; the choice under this rule would be not to invest because it yields the **least of the worst** scenarios.

The **minimax regret** rule, however, yields a different conclusion. A so-called 'payoff matrix' may help to illustrate the computations. In Table 3.2, columns (1) and (2) show the outcomes of the invest and do-not-invest alternatives if successful or failure. Columns (3) and (4) show the 'regrets' associated with each outcome if selected relative to the best possible outcomes of success and failure. The regrets in column (3) are computed by subtracting each entry in column (1) from the highest-valued entry in column (1). Likewise, the regrets in column (4) are computed as the differences between each entry in column (2) and the highest-valued entry in column (2). The zeros in columns (3) and (4) result from subtracting the highest-valued entries from themselves. According to the minimax regret rule, the alternative with the **least regret** of not selecting the best outcome should be chosen. In the example above, a much larger regret ($ 4 million) would be suffered from not investing if the investment turns out to be successful than would be realized ($ 1 million) from investing which is not successful. Therefore, under this rule, the decision maker should choose to invest.

WHAT'S AHEAD

The decision problem is a complex phenomenon with many dimensions. The next two chapters are devoted to an examination of the mathematical facilities for analyzing patterns of behaviour and the statistical procedures for modelling behavioural relationships.

Summary of Important Points

1. The consequences of a decision will emerge over a range of time; the more remote the benefits or costs of a decision, the less meaningful are they to the decision maker; the present value of a future event is less than it will be worth when it occurs; present values may be computed by discounting future values at an appropriate rate.
2. The internal rate of return on an investment alternative is the discount rate which would make its stream of future net returns just equal to the required capital outlay.
3. It is rational to undertake any investment alternative which promises an internal rate of return in excess of the market rate of interest, irrespective of whether the investment alternative is financed from internal or external sources.
4. One means of allowing for risk in the internal rate of return is to substitute the certainty equivalents of risky returns into the numerators of internal rate of return formula; another means is to adjust the denominators by including risk premiums.
5. Allowance for inflation may be made by including a deflation factor in the denominators of the internal rate of return formula.

Significant Terms

Remoteness of Benefits Costs
Time Value of Money
Discounting; Discount Rate
Present Value
Capital Outlay
Internal Rate of Return
Marginal Efficiency of Capital
External, Internal Sources of Funds
Personal Utility Function
Risk Preference, Neutrality,
Aversion, Avoidance
Risk Attitudes
Marginal Utility
Expected Utility
Gambler
Certainty Equivalent
Risk Premium; Risk Adjustment Factor
Inflation

Questions for Discussion

1. Distinguish the short run from the long run, and discuss how decision making differs in the two time frames.

2. Discuss the implications of 'remoteness' of future possibilities for decision analysis.
3. Identify the known and unknowns in present value and internal rate of return formulas. How can the unknowns be estimated?
4. Explain how the internal rate of return can serve as a managerial decision criterion.
5. Explain how attitudes towards risk may affect managerial decision making.
6. Survey the range of possible managerial responses to the perception of risk in decision alternatives.
7. Discuss two approaches to analyzing risk in a managerial decision setting.
8. Explain how the risk-adjusted present value of an investment opportunity may serve as a decision criterion.
9. Explain the relevance of the market rate of interest to an investment decision if the capital outlay can be financed internally.

—oo(O)oo—

Chapter 4

Maximization and Optimization

Topics covered in this chapter

• The applicability of marginal analysis. • The experience required for implementation of marginal analysis. • The treatment of extraneous variables. • How the marginal can serve as a decision criterion. • How the derivative can serve as a measure of a marginal value. • How derivatives can be used to find maximum or minimum values • The usefulness of the second derivative. • The applicability of partial differentiation • The process of optimization of a function. • The specification of a Lagrange function. • The applicability of mathematical programming.

A REVOLUTION IN THOUGHT

A veritable revolution in economic thought ensued in the 1870s. This revolution brought into economic analysis the use of **calculus**, the branch of mathematics that analyzes small changes in mathematical functions. The tools of the calculus were first developed by Isaac Newton and Gottfried Leibniz (working independently of each other) in the latter half of the 17th century. Although there were numerous forerunners of the use of calculus in economics, one name stands out in the development of the analysis of marginal change in economics:

William Stanley Jevons (1835-1882). Jevons, an English economist of the **classical school**, first described a 'final degree of utility' in a paper read in 1862. But it was not until the publication of his *Theory of Political Economy* in 1871 that the world at large was made privy to his description of the effects of consuming successive units of food. Jevons referred to the analysis of such effects as 'a Calculus of Pleasure and Pain.' Indeed, it was this introduction of the principles of derivative calculus into economic analysis that fomented the **marginalism revolution** and initiated the **neoclassical era** of economic thought.

The ensuing development of the analysis of change at the margin in the theories of consumer behaviour, production, and costs has yielded a powerful analytical tool to theoretical economists. Its impact in applied economics lies in the provision of decision criteria for marketing, production, and financial decision makers.

THE APPLICABILITY OF MARGINAL ANALYSIS

As we noted earlier, the types of managerial decisions range from selecting one among several alternative courses of action to deciding to accelerate or retard some activity already under way. If the choice involves a **discrete change** or discontinuity of operations, as for example in most entrepreneurial decisions, then marginal analysis may not be applicable.

Examples of decision contexts that are not particularly amenable to marginal analysis are the initiation or termination of business, the selection of items to produce or carry in inventory, the construction of a new plant or the disposition of an old one, and executive hires or fires. Such discrete changes in operations are usually associated with the **long run**, a period of time that is long enough to allow changes in all matters within the decision maker's realm of responsibility.

Marginal analysis comes into its own when a process under way changes in a relatively smooth, continuous fashion. Such changes occur within a **short-run** time frame when at least some matters are not amenable to alteration by the decision maker, for example, the size or capacity of the productive facility.

Where a process may **change smoothly** and continuously, the decision maker needs a criterion for deciding to do more or less of what is already being done. An example might be to produce a larger or smaller quantity of an item in the enterprise's product line.

Even if the process does change in a smooth and continuous fashion, marginal analysis is 'information hungry' in the sense that it presumes that the decision maker already possesses a substantial amount of information about the likely consequences of advancing or retarding the rate at which the process is occurring.

Such prior information can only be based upon an accumulation of **historical experience**, either the decision maker's own or someone else's. Marginal analysis cannot provide a useful decision criterion for how much of a newly invented item to produce in the first production run.

There is a broad range of decision contexts to which marginal analysis may be applied, even when the restrictions noted above are recognized. These include whether to increase or decrease the rate of production (or to keep on doing so), whether to use more or less of a particular productive input, and whether to raise or lower the price of an item. Marginal analysis has been extended to bridge the distinction between the short and long runs by providing criteria for adding or deleting items from the product line and increasing or decreasing the enterprise's capital investment.

THE MARGINAL IN MANAGERIAL DECISION MAKING

We shall assume that the decision maker is responsible for some process that changes in a relatively smooth and continuous fashion, and that the decision maker has access to a stock of accumulated experience with the behaviour of the process. The decision maker's concern then is whether to expand or contract the process, and in either case to keep on doing so.

As an analytical convenience, we shall suppose that the process can be represented in mathematical functional notation,

$$(1)\ y = f(x_1,\ x_2,\ \ldots,\ x_n)$$

where y, the dependent variable, is the object of the decision maker's control. The independent variables, x_1, x_2, ..., x_n, are the potential means by which **control** is exerted. Many of these independent variables are simply environmental constraints or conditions that affect the dependent variable but are not amenable to control by the decision maker. As a simplification, we shall assume that the decision maker has direct control over only x_1, and that all other independent variables, x_2, ..., x_n, are environmental matters not amenable to control by the decision maker, at least in the short-run decision framework. These other independent variables then may be **assumed to be constant** (or given, or accounted for). This assumption allows us to focus attention upon the relationship between y and x_1. The slash inserted in functional notation statement (2) indicates that all variables listed to the right of it are assumed constant:

$$(2)\ y = f(x_1/x_2,\ \ldots,\ x_n)$$

To illustrate the benefit of knowing marginal relationships, let us first suppose that in the process under decision making control, currently a y-value of 7 occurs when the value of the decision variable x_1 is 13. This may be graphed as point A, located at (x, y) coordinates (13, 7) in Figure 2.1. We may also suppose that it is the objective of the decision maker to increase the value of y (although there are circumstances in managerial control where a smaller value of y might be deemed desirable). On the basis of this so-called 'total' information (that is, the total amount of y when x_1 is 13), should the decision maker increase x_1 to 14 (or some higher value), or decrease it to 12 (or some lower value)? The simple fact is that there is no way to tell from the information considered thus far.

Suppose that the decision maker can estimate from his accumulation of past experience that point B at coordinates (14,8) in Figure 2.2 will likely be achieved when x_1 is increased by one unit (by assumption the smallest amount by which x_1 can be changed). In this simple example, the ratio of the $\Delta y/\Delta x_1$ when $x_1 = 1$ is referred to by economists as the marginal y, or the marginal to the y function. The value of the marginal in this example is a positive number. (In a subsequent discussion we will note circumstances in which the magnitude as well as the sign of the marginal is significant). The decision maker can now use this information as a decision criterion. He may be confident that when the marginal value of y is positive, an increase of decision variable x_1 will increase the value of y, the object of his control. We note in passing that the ratio $\Delta y/\Delta x_1$ measures the slope of a line passing through points A and B, and that the line slopes upward.

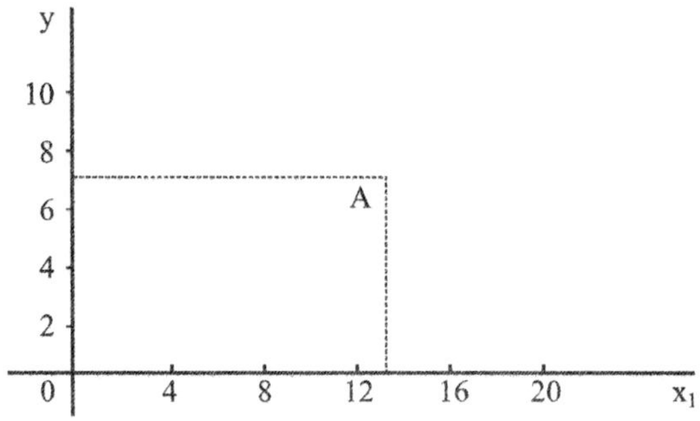

Figure 4.1. Initial values of dependent and independent variables.

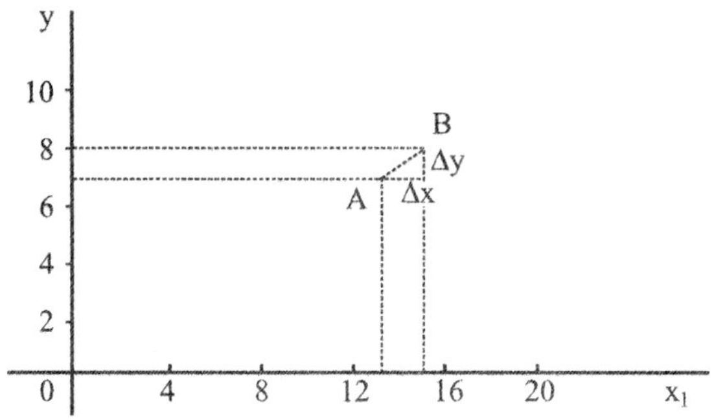

Figure 4.2. A second estimated point.

But suppose, as illustrated in Figure 4.3, that when x_1 is increased from 13 to 14, the value of y decreases to 6, reaching point C at coordinates (14, 6). In this case the positive one-unit change of y. Thus, the value of the marginal y, $\Delta y/\Delta x_1$, is now a negative number and the line passing through points A and C slopes downward. The negative marginal y can serve as a decision criterion. When the marginal y is negative, the decision maker should expect an increase of his decision variable x_1 to result in a decrease in y, the object of his decision making. If his objective is to increase the value of y, he should then decrease x_1 when the marginal y is negative. (The reader is encouraged to consider how information about positive or negative marginal y values should serve as decision criteria when the objective is to decrease the value of y, as for example when production costs are the concern of managerial decision making.)

The examples considered thus far have been ideal in the sense that Δx_1 was one unit (assumed to be the smallest amount by which x_1 can be changed) in both cases. This enables us to refer to the ratio of $\Delta y/\Delta x_1$ as the marginal y. However, the real world rarely allows a one-unit change of x_1. We should therefore note that when Δx_1 is not a one-unit change, the ratio Dy/Dx_1 does not accurately measure the **marginal** y, although it may be an approximation to the marginal y with some error depending upon how large the change is of x_1. In a subsequent discussion, we shall refer to the ratio $\Delta y/\Delta x_1$ where Δx_1 is larger than one unit as the **incremental** y, or the incremental

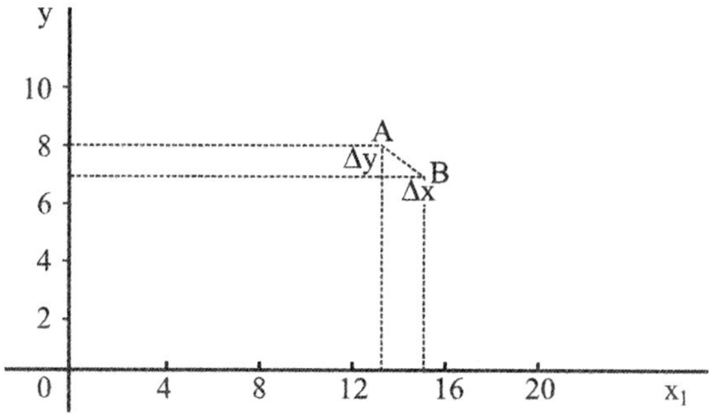

Figure 4.3. A decrease in the dependent variable.

to the y function. The significance of the incremental y is that while the marginal y is the appropriate decision criterion, it is rarely observable; the incremental y, though commonly observable, is **only an approximation** to the marginal y, and thus may serve only imperfectly as a decision criterion. The wise managerial decision maker should be cautious in employing an observable incremental y as a decision criterion. The incremental y will almost certainly be of a different magnitude than that of the marginal y, and it may be of different sign as well if the Δx is relatively large.

CALCULUS AND THE MARGINAL

In order to illustrate how the calculus can be brought to bear upon marginal analysis, let us suppose that the relationship given in functional notation statement (2) can be specified (or estimated employing appropriate statistical procedures) by an equation of some order, say 2. The highest power of a term in such an equation is the squared term. The format of a second order (or quadratic) equation is

$$(3)\quad y = a + bx_1 + cx_1^2.$$

The terms a, b, and c are constants that specify the way in which the dependent variable y relates to (or is affected by) the independent variable x_1. We note that independent variables $x_2,\ldots,x_n$ do not appear in equation (3) because they were assumed constant in functional notation (2). Suppose that in a particular specification of the equation, the constants a, b, and c take on the values 288, 64, and –2 (the estimation of these values is discussed in Chapter 3), respectively,

$$(4)\quad y = 288 + 64x_1 - 2x_1^2.$$

This equation, which plots as a parabola oriented about a vertical axis and opening downward (that is, vertex pointing upwards) as depicted in Fig 4.4, might well represent a total revenue function for a business firm.

The marginal y can be computed for any one-unit change of x_1, say from $x_1 = 4$ to $x_1 = 5$ as the slope of a chord connecting points A and B in Figure 4.4. The value of y increases from 512 to

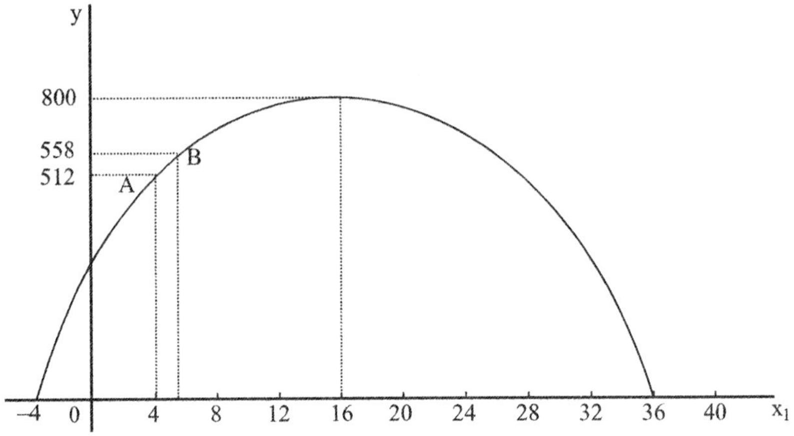

Figure 4.4. The graphic plot of a second-order equation.

558 (found by solving equation (4) for x_1 values of 4 and 5) an increase of 46 units. Hence, the marginal y over the 4 to 5 range of x_1 is 46. Thus when $\Delta x_1 = +1$, $\Delta y = +46$, and the ratio of $\Delta y/\Delta x_1 = 46/1 = 46$.

In the calculus, the derivative of a function that measures the rate of change of the function is conventionally represented as dy/dx, read 'the derivative of y with respect to x.' The value of the derivative may be computed by the formula

$$(5)\ y' = dy/dx = \lim \Delta y/\Delta x \text{ as } \Delta x \text{ approaches } 0.$$

This limit measures the **slope** of the function at a point on the function. The slope can be represented graphically as a **tangent** to the function at the point. This concept differs from the economist's concept of the marginal only in that in the denominator of the marginal ratio, Δx, takes on the value 1, which is assumed to be the smallest possible change of x, whereas the denominator of the derivative is presumed to approach, but not reach, zero. Thus, for all intents and purposes the mathematician's concept of the derivative approximates the economist's concept of the marginal. The practical value of this coincidence is that if the economist knows the equation of a function, he may compute the derivative of a function at a particular value of x to serve as a measure of the marginal y value. Employing conventional differentiation formulas, the derivative of equation 4.4 is

$$(6)\ y' = dy/dx_1 = 64 - 4x_1.$$

Thus, when x_1 is 4, the value of the derivative is 64 - 4(4) = 48. When x_1 is 5, the value of the derivative is 64 - 4(5) = 44. These two values lie on either side of the value previously computed using the marginal ratio over the range of x_1 from 4 to 5.

The important consideration then is that the process of differentiation estimates the slope of the function at a point on it (that is, when $x_1 = 4$ or when $x_1 = 5$), but the marginal is computed over the range between two points that are separated by only one unit of x_1 (in this case between 4 and 5). The differential of the function y estimates the slope of the function at either end of the range; the marginal computes the slope over the one-unit range. The differential is thus a close approximation to the marginal (and vice versa). It is for this reason that economists feel confident in employing differential calculus to estimate the values of marginal.

THE MARGINAL AS DECISION CRITERION

We have now established the usefulness of the marginal of the y function as a decision criterion in deciding whether to increase or decrease the value of x_1, and that the computed derivative of the function is a close approximation to the marginal. Remembering that the value of the derivative of the function at a particular value of x_1 measures the slope of the function, we may observe that the slope of the function illustrated in Figure 4.4 becomes ever shallower as the peak of the parabola is approached. At the peak itself, the slope of a tangent to the function would be zero, that is, the tangent would be horizontal. The graph of the original function is repeated in panel (a) of Figure 4.5. Panel (b) illustrates the graph of the so-called **first derivative** of the original function. Economists refer to this graph as the **marginal y function** where y might be revenue, cost, or product. It is the behaviour of the first derivative or marginal that permits us to employ an application of differential calculus to compute the value of the independent variable x_1 that yields a maximum value of the dependent variable y. Since the slope of a function is known to be zero at its peak (or its trough), the method is simply to set the derivative from equation (5) equal to zero and solve for the value of x_1:

$$64 - 4x_1 = 0$$
$$4x_1 = 64$$
$$x_1 - 16$$

The conclusion of this operation is that the function reaches a maximum y value when $x_1 = 16$. The maximum may be computed by entering 16 for x_1 in the original equation (4),

$$y = 288 + 64(16) - 2(16)2$$
$$= 288 + 1024 - 512$$
$$= 800$$

Thus, when $x_1 = 16$, y attains its maximum value of 800. The reader is invited to confirm this conclusion by trying x_1 values on either side of 16, for example, $x_1 = 15$ and $x_1 = 17$, to confirm that y is less than 800 in both cases.

The same methodology may be employed in the case of a function that reaches a trough rather than a peak, but without actually plotting points on a function it may not be obvious that a particular equation reaches a peak or a trough. Here the mathematician's concept of the **second derivative** may help to discern which, peak or trough, has been reached. The second derivative is the derivative of the first derivative; it measures the **rate of change of the rate of change** of the

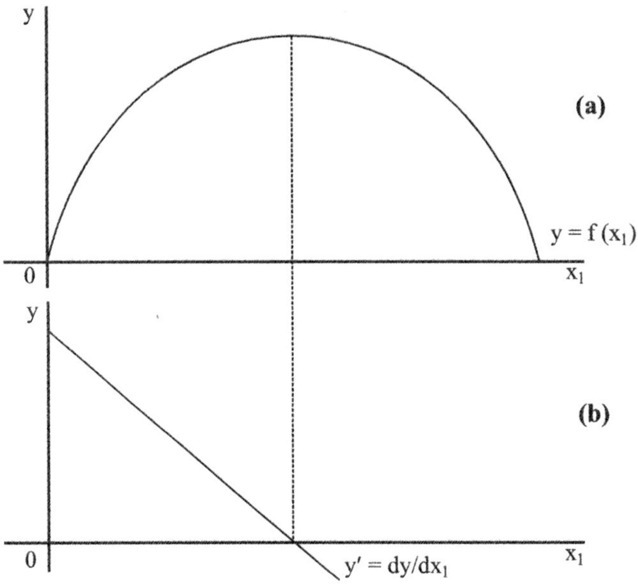

Figure 4.5. The graph of a first derivative to a second-order function.

original function, that is, the rate of acceleration of the original function. Economists regard the second derivative function as the marginal to marginal function, or the rate at which the marginal function changes.

Figure 4.6 illustrates in its panel (a) the graphic plot of an idealized third order (cubic) function of form

$$(7)\ y = a + bx_1 + cx_1^2 + dx_1^3.$$

The cubic function has two directions of curvature separated by an inflection point at A. Panel (b) illustrates the associated first derivative or marginal function, of form

$$(8)\ y' = b + 2cx_1 + 3dx_1^2.$$

The first derivative function is of one order lower than the original function, and has one fewer direction of curvature than does the original function. We note that the peak of the first derivative function occurs at the same x_1 quantity at which the inflection point of the y function occurs. The second derivative function also attains zero y values at the levels of x_1 at which the original y function reached both minimum and maximum.

Panel (c) illustrates the associated second derivative function of form

$$(9)\ y'' = 2c + 6dx_1.$$

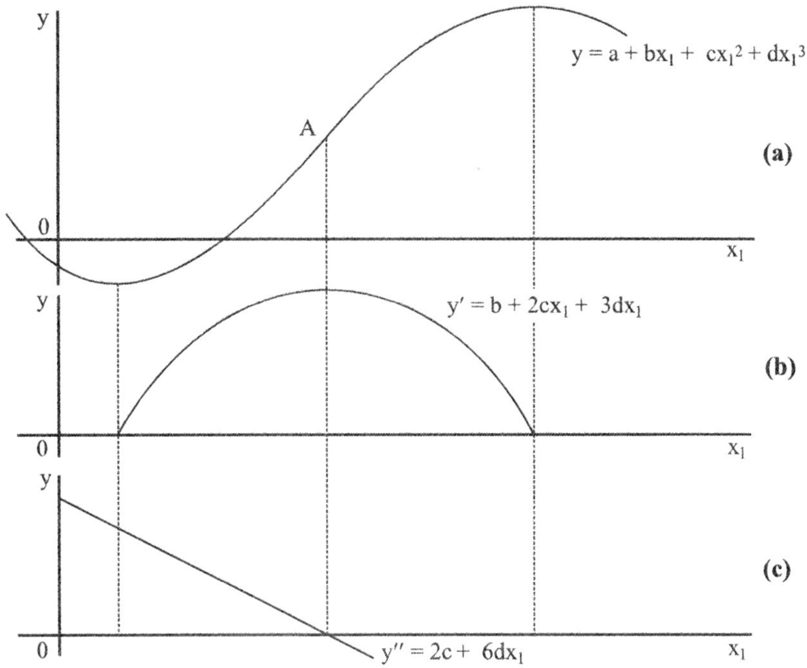

Figure 4.6. Graphs of an original third-order function and its first and second derivatives.

The second derivative function is one order lower than the first derivative function, and two orders lower than the original function. It has one fewer direction of curvature, in this case being linear, than does the first derivative function.

It is important to note that since the first derivative function reaches a value of zero when the original function is at either minimum or maximum, it is not possible without plotting the graphs of the functions to know from computing the first derivative alone whether the original function has reached a maximum or a minimum.

However, the **second derivative** provides a solution to this problem. Since, in Figure 4.6, the first derivative cuts the horizontal from below and is thus positively sloped at the x_1 value for which the original function is at a minimum, the value of the second derivative function is positive at this level of x_1. It is also true that the first derivative cuts its horizontal from above, and is thus negatively sloped at the x_1 level at which the original function is at maximum. Hence, the second derivative exhibits a negative value when the original function is at a maximum.

It is knowledge of these relationships that allows us to reverse the process and identify whether the original function has reached a maximum or a minimum without plotting its graph. The procedure is to:

(a) Compute the first derivative of the function.

(b) Set the first derivative equal to zero and solve for the value(s) of x_1. At these values of x_1, the function reaches either a maximum or a minimum value of y, a fact that cannot yet be discerned.

(c) Compute the second derivative of the function and evaluate the second derivative at the x_1 values for which the first derivative is zero. The criterion is that if the value of the second derivative is **positive**, an original function **minimum** has been identified; and if the value of the second derivative is **negative**, an original-function **maximum** has been found.

This application of the calculus has served economists and managerial decision makers well in the cases of a number of economic situations, including those of both production functions and revenue functions. However, there is an important class of economic functions for which these procedures will fail, and we should thus note that they are not applicable to these functions. Specifically, total cost functions, whose estimated equations typically plot as illustrated in Figure 4.7, never reach either maximum or minimum values for y.

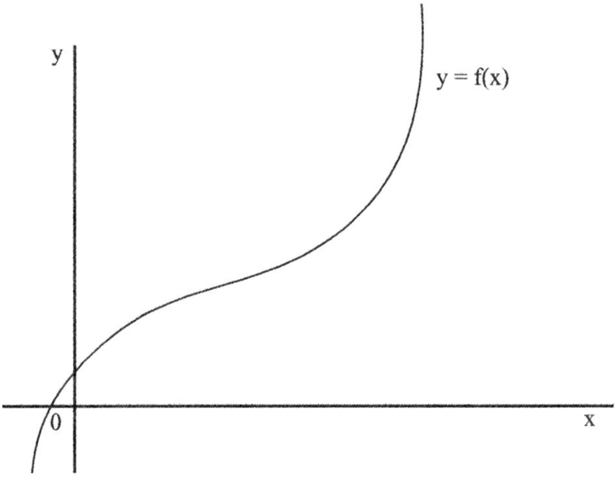

Figure 4.7. A total cost function that does not reach maximum or minimum.

While the marginal to a cost function can be computed by derivative calculus, when the derivative is set equal to zero, the y value solved for will be infinite. There is thus no point in asking where total costs reach minimum or maximum values (they never do); economists, however, do analyze the average or per-unit functions that can be derived from the total function (for example, average total cost), and find that the average function can be expected to attain a minimum value. Thus, the derivative calculus can be used to discover the value of x_1 for which the average function reaches minimum even though the total cost function reaches neither minimum nor maximum. Functions of this type are examined later.

MULTIPLE INDEPENDENT VARIABLES

Up to this point we have assumed that all independent variables but one are constant. An extension of the derivative calculus enables treatment of two or more independent variables. Functional notation statement (4-2) may be rewritten to accommodate two explicit independent variables, all others are assumed to be constant:

$$(10)\quad y = f(x_1, x_2/x_3, \ldots, x_n).$$

An example of an equation containing two independent variables is

$$(11)\quad y = ax_1 + bx_1^2 + cx_1x_2 + dx_2\ \varepsilon x2^2.$$

This particular equation is of second order in both x_1 and x_2, but an equation could be specified to any order in as many independent variables as the analyst wishes to include.

When two or more independent variables are present, the calculus enables the differentiation of the function with respect to each independent variable. In computing each derivative, all other independent variables are treated as if they are constants, and the derivatives, called partial derivatives, are signified by the lower case of the Greek letter, δ. In computing the partial derivative of y with respect to x_1, the variable x_2 is taken to be a constant (the derivative of which is zero):

$$(12)\quad \delta y/\delta x_1 = a + 2bx_1 + cx_2.$$

In computing the partial of y with respect to x_2, the variable x_1 is taken to be a constant:

$$(13)\quad \delta y/\delta x_2 = d + cx_1 + 2\varepsilon x_2.$$

Each of these partial derivatives then represents the rate of change of the y function when one variable changes but the other does not change. The graph of a function like (10) and equation (11) would be three dimensional with a parabolic appearance such as that in Figure 4.8. Here u and v are the x_1 and x_2 coordinates of the point directly below the peak of the surface. Supposing for the moment that u and v are known coordinates, if we were to move a point such as r along the path from v towards t, we could observe that the slope of the surface, as measured by a tangent to the surface at r, becomes ever shallower until it is zero at the peak. Likewise, if a point such as s is moved along the path from u towards t, the slope of the surface as measured by a tangent at s would also become ever shallower, and also reach zero at the peak. It is knowledge of this behaviour that allows us to find the values of u and v when they are unknown.

The unknown values of u and v may be found by setting the partial derivatives (12) and (13) equal to zero,

$$(14)\quad a + 2bx_1 + cx_2 = 0,$$

$$(15)\quad d + cx_1 + 2\varepsilon x_2 = 0,$$

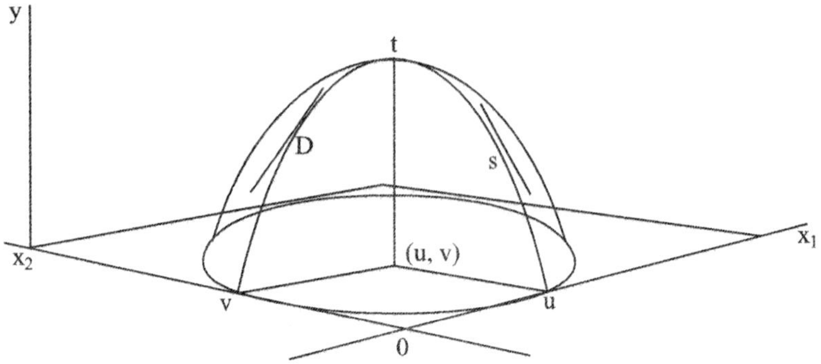

Figure 4.8. The graph of a second-order function with two independent variables.

and solving the pair of equations simultaneously for x_1 and x_2 to find that $x_1 = u$ and $x_2 = v$. Once these values are known, they may be substituted for x_1 and x_2 in the original function equation (11) to find that

$$y = au + bu^2 + cuv + dv + ev^2 = t$$

Thus the maximum value of y is t, which occurs when $x_1 = u$ and $x_2 = v$.

An example of this application of partial differentiation occurs in the case of a production relationship where the amount of output, y, is determined by two inputs, x_1 and x_2. Such a function graphs as a three dimensional surface similar to that depicted in Figure 4.7. Suppose that the productive process may be simulated by the equation

$$(16) \quad y = 30x_1 - 3x_1^2 + 3x_1x_2 + 5x_2 - 2x_2^2.$$

The objective is to find the maximum value of y that it is possible to produce when there are no limits on the availability of the x_1 and x_2 inputs. The first step is to compute the partial derivatives of output with respect to each of the inputs:

$$\delta y/\delta x_1 = -6x_1 + 3x_2 + 30,$$

$$\delta y/\delta x_2 = 3x_1 - 4x_2 + 5.$$

Next, these partial derivatives are each set equal to zero to form differential equations that may be taken together as a system of simultaneous equations to be solved for the values of x_1 and x_2:

$$-6x_1 + 3x_2 + 30 = 0$$

$$-4x_2 + 5 = 0$$

The second equation may be multiplied through by 2,

$$6x_1 - 8x_2 + 10 = 0,$$

and added to the first equation in order to eliminate the x_1 variable and solve for the value of the x_2 variable,

$$-5x_2 + 40 = 0,$$

$$x_2 = 8.$$

Then, 8 may be substituted for x_2 in one of the differential equations in order to solve for x_1,

$$3x_1 - 4(8) + 5 = 0,$$

$$3x_1 - 32 + 5 = 0,$$

$$x_1 = 9.$$

We note that the second derivatives, that is, the derivatives of the first derivatives, are both negative,

$$\delta^2 y/\delta x_1^2 = -6,$$

$$\delta^2 y/\delta x_2^2 - -4.$$

This confirms that the output reaches a maximum value when $x_1 = 9$ and $x_2 = 8$. We may find the maximized value of output by substituting these numbers in the original equation,

$$y = 30(9) - 3(9)^2 + 3(9)(8) + 5(8) \quad 2(8)^2,$$

$$= 270 - 243 + 216 + 40 = 128 = 155.$$

The conclusion is that 155 units of output is the most that can be produced from this production process.

While the examples illustrated here include only two independent variables in the equation of the function, more than two may be dealt with by computing the partial derivatives of the function with respect to each of the independent variables in their turn. If there are n independent variables in the equation, then n partial derivatives may be computed.

Each may be set equal to zero, and the resulting set of equations solved simultaneously to find the values of the independent variables that maximize (or minimize) the value of the dependent variable. It is not possible to render a graphic representation of a function with more than two independent variables.

MULTIPLE GOALS AND OPTIMIZATION

As noted in discussing the dimensions of the decision problem, it is possible (and probably not uncommon) for a decision maker to be confronted with multiple goals for simultaneous pursuit. The decision maker is lucky if two or more of the goals are compatible with a common strategy. An analogy from ballistics is where two or more targets can be lined up and hit by the same projectile. Otherwise the decision-maker may be torn among several conflicting objects of pursuit. A principle drawn from the algebraic theory of simultaneous equations (n unknowns require n equations for their solution) and that is often applied in macro policy is that as many policy tools (or weapons) are required as there are incompatible problems to be dealt with (or targets to be hit simultaneously).

If the decision maker cannot bring to bear as many means as there are conflicting goals to pursue, it will be necessary to select one goal for primary pursuit, and then regard all other goals as subordinate to the selected primary goal. Kenneth Boulding has noted the manager's difficulty in keeping these goals subordinated to the one selected for primary pursuit ('The Ethics of Rational Decision,' *Management Science*, February, 1966). Although the manager may simply give up pursuit of the subordinate goals in favour of the primary goal, in some circumstances it may be possible to incorporate them into the decision making process so as to regard them as constraints upon the pursuit of the primary goal. The term applied to this process is 'optimization', which we shall take to mean maximization (or minimization) subject to constraint(s). We shall examine two mathematical tools for optimization.

OPTIMIZATION USING THE CALCULUS

The procedure of partial differentiation serves as a tool of analysis in a decision setting best dealt with by attempting to optimize the value of the selected decision goal subject to various constraints that are in fact alternate, but subordinate goals. Suppose that all of the goals may be expressed in functional notational forms:

$$y_1 = f(x_1, x_2, x_3, \ldots, x_n),$$

$$y_2 = g(x_1, x_2, x_3, \ldots, x_n),$$

$$y_n = k(x_1, x_2, x_3, \ldots, x_n).$$

We should note that while some of the goal functions may share independent variables in their argument listings, not all independent variables will appear in each argument listing. Also, some argument listings may be mutually exclusive with other argument listings. To be amenable to treatment by differential calculus, three conditions must be met:

1. The multiple goal functions must share at least some of their arguments;
2. It must be possible to select one of the goals, say y_1, for primary pursuit (that is, to be maximized or minimized); and
3. It must be possible to specify the subordinate goals, $y_2, \ldots, y_n$, as equality constraints such

that the value of each y is a constant that must be met precisely. If the constraint goals are inequalities (that is, greater or lesser than some value), then the differential calculus cannot be applied.

Although we shall illustrate the calculus procedure for dealing with multiple goals with only two goal functions, we stress that the procedure can encompass any number. We assume that the goal functions have been specified as behavioural equations. The steps in the procedure are to:

1. Select the single goal for primary pursuit;
2. Express the subordinate goal(s) as constraint(s) by moving all terms to the left side of the equality, with only 0 on the right side;
3. Specify a new function, called the Lagrange (after the mathematician who first proposed the procedure) function, which is a combination of the primary and subordinate goals in the sense that it has the constraints built into the primary function; the constraint terms introduce new, artificial independent variables signified by the Greek letter lambda, $\lambda_1, \lambda_2, ..., \lambda_n$, one such artificial variable for each of the constraints;
4. Compute the partial differentials of the Lagrange function with respect to each of the independent variables;
5. Set each of the partial differentials equal to zero and regard the differential equations as a set of simultaneous equations; and
6. Solve the set of simultaneous equations for the values of the independent variables, including the artificial ones.

The resulting values of the original independent variables are those that maximize (or minimize) the value of the primary goal function subject to the constraint(s) imposed by the subordinate goal function(s). The value of the artificial variable may be interpreted as the marginal contribution to the value of the primary goal when the respective constraint is relieved by one unit.

To illustrate these procedures, let us suppose that the goal is still to maximize the output function (16). However, there are now only 15 productive units that can be set up as either x_1 or x_2 inputs. A second goal, then, is to keep the sum of the inputs within a maximum of 15 units. The two goal equations may be given as

$$y = 30x_1 - 3x_1^2 + 3x_1x_2 + 5x_2 - 2x_2^2,$$

and

$$15 = x_1 + x_2.$$

In the second goal equation, the value of the dependent variable is taken to be a constant, that is, an absolute goal that must be fulfilled. The independent variables x_1 and x_2 are common to both goal equations. The procedural steps are as follows:

1. The first equation is taken to be the primary goal such that the value of y is to be maximized subject to the constraint that the sum of the two independent variables must be equal to 15.

2. The subordinate goal is expressed in constraint format as

$$15 - x_1 - x_2 = 0$$

3. The Lagrange function is formed as

$$\lambda_y = 30x_1 - 3x_1^2 + 3x_1x_2 + 5x_2 - 2x_2^2$$
$$+ \lambda_1(15 - x_1 - x_2).$$

Note: Had there been other constraints, they would have been designated λ_2 through λ_n; then each of the constraints would have been added to the Lagrange function.

4. The partial differentials are computed as

$$\delta\lambda_y/\delta x_1 = -6x_1 + 3x_2 + 30 - \lambda_1$$
$$\delta\lambda_y/\delta x_2 = 3x_1 - 4x_2 + 5 - \lambda_1$$
$$\delta\lambda_y/\delta\lambda_1 = 15 - x_1 - x_2$$

5. The partials are set equal to zero and regarded as a set of simultaneous equations:

$$-6x_1 + 3x_2 + 30 - \lambda_1 = 0$$
$$3x_1 - 4x_2 + 5 - \lambda_1 = 0$$
$$-x_1 - x_2 + 15 = 0$$

6. The equations may be solved simultaneously by:

(a) Subtracting the second equation from the first:

$$-9x_1 + 7x_2 + 25 = 0$$

(b) Solving the third equation for x_1 and substituting:

$$x_1 = 15 - x_2$$
$$-9(15 - x_2) + 7x_2 + 25 = 0$$
$$-135 + 9x_2 + 7x_2 + 25 = 0$$
$$16x_2 = 110$$
$$x_2 = 6.875$$

(c) solving for x_1

$$-x_1 - (6.875) + 15 = 0$$

$$x_1 = 8.125$$

(d) and solving for l_1

$$3(8.125) - 4(6.875) + 5 - \lambda_1 = 0$$

$$\lambda_1 = 1.875$$

Thus, the maximum value of y occurs when $x_1 = 8.125$ units and $x_2 = 6.875$ units. Since x_1 and x_2 are indivisible units, we round them to $x_1 = 8$ units and $x_2 = 7$ units. When the 15 available inputs are set up as 8 x_1 and 7 x_2 units, the maximum output that may be produced is computed from the original production function equation,

$$y = 30(8) - 3(8)2 + 3(8)(7) + 5(7) - 2(7)2$$

$$= 240 - 192 + 168 + 35 - 98 = 153.$$

Thus, when only 15 input units are available and they are set up as 8 x_1 and 7 x_2 units, maximum output is 153 units. If the constraint can be relieved by one unit, output can increase by about two units ($\lambda_1 = 1.875$).

OPTIMIZATION BY LINEAR PROGRAMMING

The differential calculus as a means of optimizing a set of goals is a powerful but limited procedure. Its power lies in its ability to treat nonlinear functions and constraints. Its limitation is the fact that the constraints can be only equalities that must be met precisely. If any of the subordinate goals must be taken as inequalities (that is, greater or lesser than stipulated quantities), then the differential calculus may be applied to the decision problem only with qualification. In a case of maximization subject to inequality constraints, the calculus can be used to find only the outer bounds of the inequality constraints as if they were equalities; but the optimal input values may be less than the outer bounds. Unfortunately, in the vast majority of real-world decision problems that require an optimization approach, at least some of the constraints are inequalities.

A possible solution to the inequality constraint problem is to employ the procedures of mathematical programming, the most widely used variant of which is linear programming. Linear programming is an optimization technique that can accommodate inequality constraints. However, it suffers the limitation that the equations of the primary goal function and all of the constraint functions must be linear, that is, first order equations. This too is a serious problem for real-world decision analysis because many relationships in the real world simply are not linear. This objection can be relieved only by shifting to versions of mathematical programming that are so complex as to require substantial mathematical expertise and computational power to implement them. Such nonlinear mathematical programming techniques are generally inaccessible to most business decision makers, and thus are beyond the scope of this text.

However, a compromise is in order. We recognize that the nonlinear relationships found in the real world can often be approximated by linear functions for small changes in the near neighbourhoods of current values of the independent variables. It is for this reason that linear programming has found extensive use in various military, commercial, and industrial applications. The danger in the use of linear programming is in attempting to push it too far, that is, beyond the neighbourhoods of current values where the nonlinearities of real-world relationships become significant. But changes of such magnitude require us to depart from the realm of marginal decision analysis.

Because linear programming belongs more to the realm of operations management than economics, we choose not to elaborate it in the text of this chapter. However, Appendix 4.1 describes linear programming principles and the use of a linear programming computer programme for those who are interested in pursuing it.

WHAT'S AHEAD

The next chapter elaborates the means by which statistical analyses may be employed to model decision contexts. While the modelling procedures may in some cases yield linear relationships, we shall expect many real-world relationships to be non-linear.

Summary of Important Points

1. Marginal analysis is not useful when choices involve discrete change or discontinuity of operations; marginal analysis is applicable when a process can change in a smooth, continuous fashion.
2. The exercise of marginal analysis presumes extensive knowledge of the process that can only be derived from historical experience; marginal analysis cannot be applied to newly-initiated processes.
3. The extraneous (independent) variables in a behavioural function are assumed constant; the dependent variable changes with variation in the decision (independent) variables.
4. The marginal of the dependent variable represents its rate of change when there is a one-unit change of the decision variable; if there is a greater than one-unit change of the decision variable, the result is an incremental change of the dependent variable.
5. The marginal of the dependent variable is an appropriate decision criterion, but it is rarely observable; the incremental of the decision variable, though commonly observable, is only an approximation to the marginal, and thus is an imperfect decision criterion.

Contd....

6. The calculus concept of the derivative may be used as a measure of the economic concept of the marginal.
7. The maximum or minimum value of a function corresponds to the independent variable value for which the derivative of the function is zero.
8. The sign of the second derivative of a function can confirm the identification of a maximum or minimum value of the function.
9. Some functions that are of economic significance do not reach maxima or minima.
10. Partial differentiation allows analysis of functions with multiple independent variables.
11. As many decision variables are required as the number of incompatible goals to be pursued.
12. In a case of multiple independent goals that cannot be addressed with the same decision variables, the decision maker must choose one goal for primary pursuit, and treat other subordinate goals as constraints.
13. The Lagrange function builds equality constraints (subordinate goals) into the function to be maximized or minimized.
14. Where constraints are inequalities, calculus may not be used to find maximum or minimum values of a function; mathematical programming may be useful in such cases.

Significant Terms

Calculus	Differentiation Formulas
Change at the Margin	First, Second Derivatives
Marginal Analysis	Minimum, Maximum Values of a Function
Smooth, Continuous Change	Partial Derivatives
Historical Experience	Three Dimensional Surface
Functional Notation	Simultaneous Equations
Dependent, Independent Variables	Subordinate Goals
Environmental Constraints	Optimization
Constancy Assumption	Equality, Inequality Constraints
Total, Marginal Information	Lagrange Function
Incremental Change	Linear Programming
Derivative Function	

Questions for Discussion

1. Discuss the circumstances under which managerial analysis is applicable to decision making.
2. Identify the decision contexts within which marginal analysis is not useful.
3. Discuss the applicability of marginal analysis to the decision to add or delete items in the business firm's product line; ...to increase or decrease the production of items in its product line.
4. Distinguish marginal from incremental changes and discuss the managerial significance of the distinction.
5. Explain the relationship between the calculus concept of the derivative and the economic concept of the marginal.
6. Discuss the usefulness of differential calculus to the managerial problem of determining the firm's output level that maximizes its revenue.
7. Explain the usefulness of the second derivative to managerial decision analysis.
8. Identify the types of economic functions for which the procedures of differential calculus will fail to find minimum or maximum values.
9. Explain how the tools of differential calculus can be applied to functions including two or more independent variables.
10. Describe the process by which a decision maker may employ the calculus to deal with multiple goals that must be pursued simultaneously.
11. Under what decision circumstances can the calculus not be used to treat a multiplicity of goals?
12. Explain how the calculus can be used to analyze the process of optimization.
13. Explain the use of the Lagrange function to incorporate a multiplicity of constraints into a function to be maximized.
14. Compare and contrast the Lagrange function and linear programming for optimizing an economic function.

Problems

1. The manager of the Bullington Corporation has found that the company's single-product monthly demand function can be expressed as:

$$Q = 670 - (1/6)P.$$

(a) Explain how the manager might have discovered this relationship.

(b) Derive the associated total and marginal revenue functions.

(c) Identify the level of output at which total revenue would be maximized and indicate how you found this level.

(d) Specify the price ranges over which demand is elastic and inelastic and indicate how you identified these ranges.

(e) If Bullington is presently charging a price of $ 2,700 per unit, devise a strategy for increasing sales revenue; what are the implications if competition can be ignored? ...if Bullington operates in a so-called oligopolistic market?

2. Bullington has also discovered that its present plant can be analyzed by a monthly cost function with the following characteristics:

$TC = 150000 + 2400\ Q - 10\ Q^2 + 0.018\ Q^3.$

(a) What is the likely source of this information?

(b) Derive the associated TFC, TVC, ATC, AVC, and AFC functions.

(c) At what levels of output will ATC and AVC be minimized? How did you find these levels? Of what significance are they?

(d) What is the lowest price that Bullington should be willing to charge for its product and continue operating? Why this price?

3. Suppose that Bullington's management follows a classical profit-oriented operating strategy.

(a) Derive its total profit function and find the level of output that the company should produce. How did you find this level?

(b) What price per unit should be charged? Why this price?

(c) What is the elasticity of demand at this price? Why is this important?

(d) What are values of MC and MR at this output level and price? Why are these values significant?

4. Bullington's Board of Directors recently hired a Mr. Baumol to serve as a management consultant. He convinced the Board that a sales-maximization (subject to realizing a satisfactory return on invested capital) strategy is in the best long-run interest of the company. The Board decided that an annual return of 10 per cent on the company's $ 1,000,000 of invested capital was essential.

(a) Assess the feasibility of this strategy.

(b) Identify and specify the equation for the firm's new supply curve.

(c) Given the new strategy, what output should be produced? At what price should it be sold? How were these conclusions reached?

(d) What is the elasticity of demand at this price? Why is it significant?

(e) What profit will be realized at this price and output?

(f) What are MR and MC at this price and output? Why are these values significant?

Appendix 4.1

LINEAR PROGRAMMING

The Simplex Method

In most general terms, the 'Simplex Method' of solving a linear programming problem involves:

1. The specification of the primary objective function and all relevant constraints as linear equations or inequalities;
2. The solution of the set of such simultaneous equations to find the coordinates of points of intersection of pairs of constraints if the functions were plotted in coordinate space; and
3. The determination of the intercepts of the primary objective function equations which pass through the intersection points.

The intersection coordinate set which yields the highest value (if maximization is the object of decision making) or lowest value (if minimization is the object) of the dependent variable computed from the objective function equation which passes through the intersection point is taken to be the solution to the decision problem.

Variables, Equations, and Inequalities

The total number of variables, including all independent variables (x_1, x_2, etc.) and the dependent variable (y, the maximum or minimum value of which is to be found) may not exceed the number of equations and inequalities in the system, including the objective function and the constraints. In a simultaneous equations context, if there are more variables than equations and inequalities, the system is 'underdetermined' because values may not be found for all of the unknowns (that is, variables) in the system. A problem involving too few equations and inequalities (or too many variables) is not amenable to linear programming treatment.

It is possible for a problem to involve fewer variables than equations and inequalities. Indeed, it may be typical of situations which are amenable to linear programming solutions that there are more constraints than variables. In a simultaneous equations context, such a system would be 'overdetermined' because multiple solutions are possible. The linear programming problem then is to identify the one among the multiple solutions which yields the highest (in case of maximization) or lowest (in case of minimization) value of the dependent variable.

A LINEAR PROGRAMMING COMPUTER PROGRAMME

To illustrate the algebraic solution of a linear programming problem, a computer program has been included in the software set which accompanies this text. (The computational algorithm was taken from Lon Pool & Mary Borchers, *Some Common Basic Programs*, Adam Osborne & Associates, Inc., 1977; terminology, data entry, and display code have been modified to fit the requirements of this text.) In order to enter data into the computer program, each constraint equation or inequality must be arranged with variables (x_1, x_2, etc.) on the left of the equality or inequality sign, and the constant (k) on the right. The constraint equations and inequalities then must be arranged in the order of less-than inequalities first, equalities next, and greater-than inequalities last, illustrated as follows:

$$a_1x_1 + a_2x_2 + \dots + a_nx_n < kA$$

$$b_1x_1 + b_2x_2 + \dots + b_nx_n < kB.$$

$$g_1x_1 + g_2x_2 + \dots + g_nx_n = kG$$

$$h_1x_1 + h_2x_2 + \dots + h_nx_n = kH$$

::

$$r_1x_1 + r_2x_2 + \dots + r_nx_n > kR$$

$$s_1x_1 + s_2x_2 + \dots + s_nx_n > kS$$

The objective function must be arranged in the following order:

$$w_1x_1 + w_2x_2 + \dots + w_nx_n = y,$$

where y is the dependent variable, the value of which is to be maximized or minimized.

The programme user must indicate whether to perform a maximization or minimization linear programming solution, then enter the number of constraints and the number of variables so that the programme may prompt for entry of the coefficients of the equations of the constraints and the objective function.

Once all of the coefficients of the constraints and the objective function have been entered, the system is solved by the Simplex Method to find the coordinates of intersections of the constraint functions. Then the intercepts of the objective function equations which pass through the intersections are computed.

Finally, the values of the dependent variables are computed from the objective function equations at the intersection points. The solution to the problem is the highest (in the case of maximization) or least (in the case of minimization) value of the dependent variable, y, computed from an objective function equation which passes through a constraint intersection point.

Graphic Illustration

With more than two independent variables, it becomes impossible to illustrate a solution graphically because too many graphic dimensions are required. Simple linear programming problems with only two independent variables, say x_a and x_b, may be illustrated by drawing the paths of the constraint and objective functions in two-dimensional coordinate space.

Suppose that the problem is to maximize y in the objective function,

$$w_1x_1 + w_2x_2 = y,$$

subject to three explicit constraints,

$$a_1x_1 + a_2x_2 \leq kA,$$

$$b_1x_1 + b_2x_2 \leq kB, \text{ and}$$

$$c_1x_1 + c_2x_2 \leq kC,$$

and two implicit non-negativity constraints, that is, $x_1 >= 0$ and $x_2 >= 0$.

The non-negativity constraints impose a solution only in graphic quadrant I. It is possible that constraints might intersect in quadrants II (for negative values of x_2) or IV (for negative values of x_1). As we shall note below, if there are no constraint intersections in quadrant I, there will be no feasible solution to the linear programming problem.

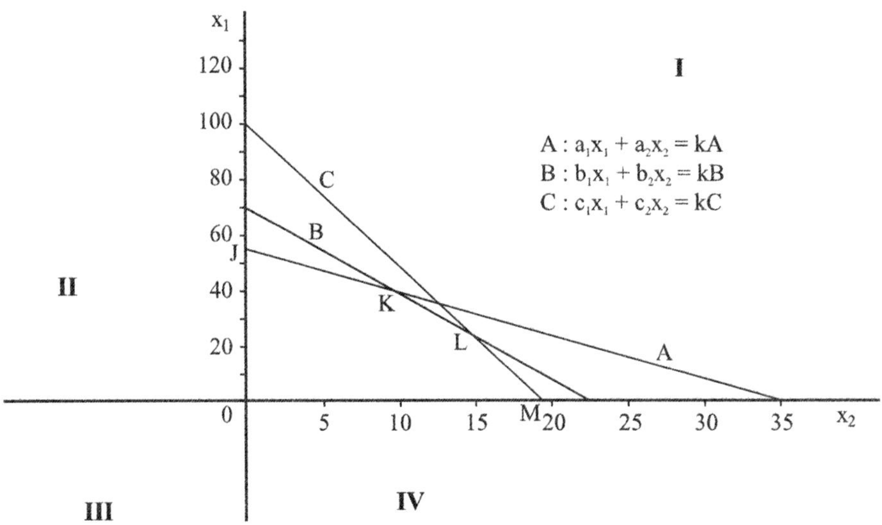

Figure A-IV(a). Three constraints for a maximization problem.

In a maximization problem, the constraints are usually equalities or less-than inequalities. The three constraints when taken as equalities can be plotted in x_1-x_2 coordinate space as illustrated in Figure A-IV(a). Since each constraint is a 'less-than or equal-to' relationship, the constraint path constitutes a boundary or frontier, points on or below which are possible solutions, but points above which are not. The region bounded by 0JKLM then is referred to as the 'feasible solution space.' Since this is a maximization problem, the solution will lie somewhere along the outer boundary JKLM.

The objective function may be solved for x_1,

$$x_1 = y/w_1 - x_2(w_2/w_1),$$

so that the slope of the objective function is w_2/w_1, and the x_1 axis intercept is y/w_1. In this formulation, the slope is known because both w_2 and w_1 are known, but the x_1 axis intercept is as yet unknown since the value of y (to be maximized) must be determined. There may be any number of objective function paths with slope w_2/w_1 plotted in Figure A-IV(a), depending upon the x_1 axis intercept. The linear programming problem is to find x_1 axis intercept of the one objective function which will yield the highest value of y. Except for a qualification to be noted below, this objective function will also pass through one of the points of intersection of a pair of constraints.

Figure A-IV(b) illustrates the graphic solution with the objective function path passing through point L at the intersection of constraints B and C. The x_1 axis intercept of the objective function is at point N. Since it is now known that $y/w_1 = N$, the value of y may be solved for as $y = N/w_1$, which is the maximum value of y which may be obtained from the objective function, given the constraints upon it.

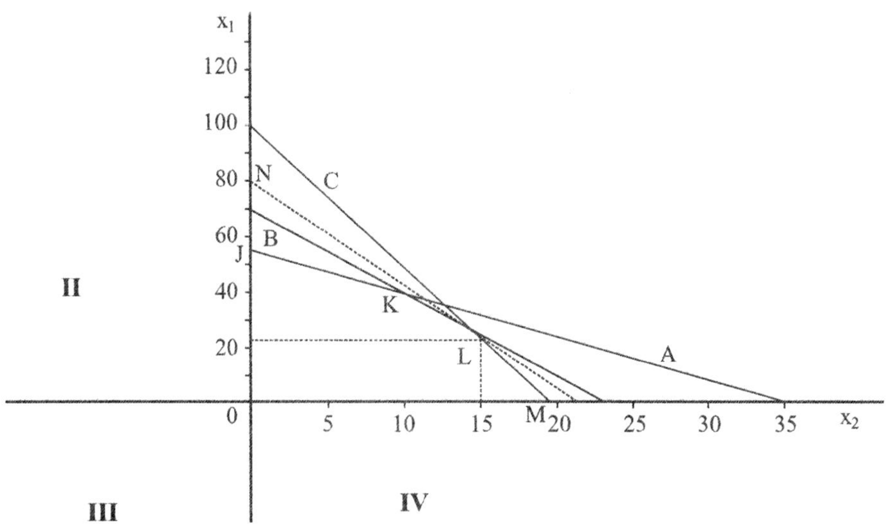

Figure A-IV(b). Graphic solution given the objective function.

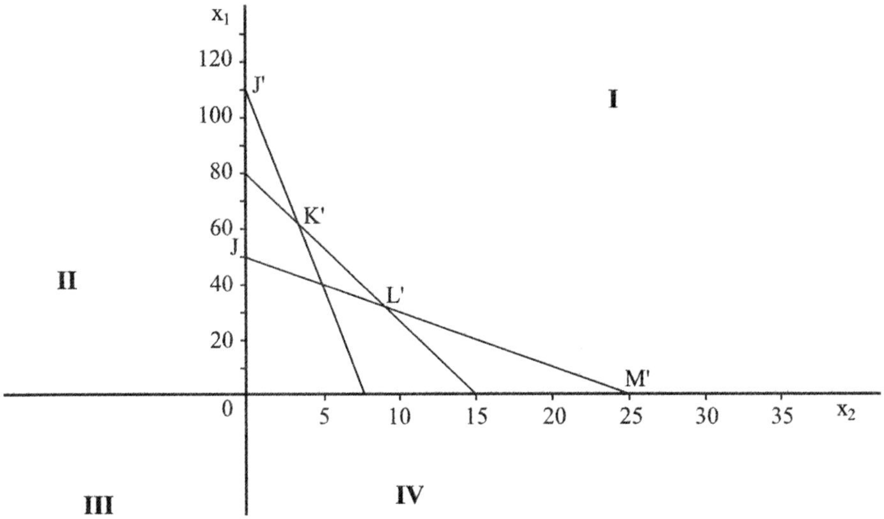

Figure A-IV(c). Three constraints for a minimization problem.

Had this been a minimization problem, the constraints would likely have all been either equalities or greater-than inequalities, which might be plotted as illustrated in Figure A-IV(c). Here the feasible solution space lies to the northeast of the constraint path J'K'L'M'. The graphic solution is similar to that of the maximization problem illustrated above, but with the objective function equation passing through the point of intersection of a pair of constraint paths which yields the minimum value of y.

QUALIFICATIONS

Three qualifications must be noted. If the slope of the objective function happens to coincide with the slope of one of the constraints, for example., constraint B in Figure A-IV(b), a unique maximum value of y does not exist. Rather, multiple solutions are possible since y can be maximized at any point along constraint B between points K and L.

If there happens to be another constraint, D, whose path lies wholly above the JKLM path as illustrated in Figure A-IV(d), it is redundant or non-binding. It may be said that only constraints A, B, and C are binding. In Figure A-IV(b), since the solution lies at the intersection of constraints B and C, but lies below constraint A, it may be said that constraint A is not binding as well.

Finally, it may also be possible that none of the constraints intersect each other and any path which the objective function may follow in quadrant I, that is, for positive values of all of the independent variables; in this case there is no feasible solution to the linear programming problem.

We should reiterate that these graphic illustrations are possible only for the simplest case of a problem involving only two independent variables. They serve only to illustrate the fundamental

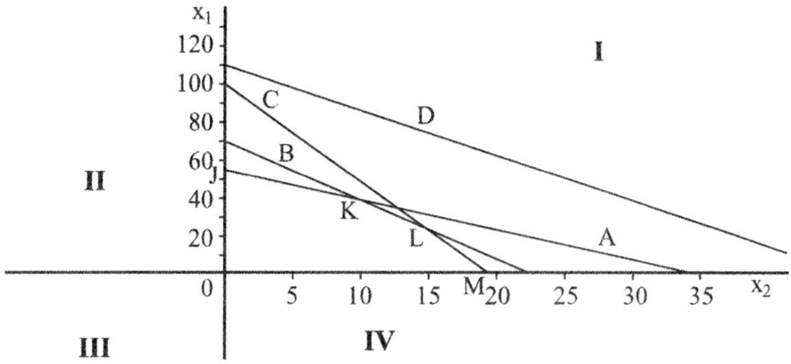

Figure A-IV(d). A non-binding constraint.

principles underlying linear programming analysis. Problems involving more than two independent variables are simply not amenable to graphic solution, and may be treated only algebraically.

THE DUAL LINEAR PROGRAMMING PROBLEM

A dual linear programming problem is implied by any so-called primal linear programming problem. If the primal linear programming problem is to find the maximum value of an objective function subject to constraints upon it, the dual problem is to find the minimum value of an associated dual objective function which may be derived from the primal objective function and its constraints.

The interpretation of the value of a dual independent variable is the opportunity cost of one unit of the capacity lost from a process, given its constraint. The opportunity cost of a process capacity unit forgone would be positive only if the constraint with respect to it is binding; the opportunity cost of a unit loss of capacity in a process for which the constraint is non-binding is zero.

The dual linear programming problem may be structured from the primal linear programming problem by employing as many artificial variables as there are constraints in the primal problem. Each artificial variable, v, represents the opportunity cost of the loss of capacity from the process for which the constraint was relevant. There will be as many constraints in the dual problem as there are variables in the primal problem.

Given the primal problem introduced earlier, that is, to maximize the function,

$$w_1x_1 + w_2x_2 = y,$$

subject to three explicit constraints,

$$a_1x_1 + a_2x_2 \leq kA,$$

$$b_1x_1 + b_2x_2 \leq kB, \text{ and}$$

$$c_1x_1 + c_2x_2 \leq kC,$$

and two implicit non-negativity constraints, that is, $x_1>=0$ and $x_2>=0$, the dual problem may be structured from the coefficients in the columns of the primal problem, that is, to minimize z in the dual objective function,

$$k_A v_A + k_B v_B + k_C v_C = z,$$

subject to the constraints,

$$a_1 v_A + b_1 v_B + c_1 v_C = w_1,$$

$$a_2 v_A + b_2 v_B + c_2 v_C = w_2,$$

and the non-negativity constraints that $v_A => 0$, $v_B => 0$.

We note that the coefficients of the variables in the dual objective function are the constants of the primal constraints. The coefficients in the first dual constraint are the coefficients from the column of x_1 primal constraint coefficients. The coefficients in the second dual constraint are the coefficients from the column of x_2 primal constraint coefficients.

Once the dual problem is structured, its solution follows the same procedures employed in solving the primal problem. However, the solution to the dual problem follows from the solution to the primal problem, and the solutions are usually found simultaneously.

AN EXAMPLE

The most critical aspect of a linear programming problem is to set it up properly for manual or automated solution. This involves properly interpreting the natures of the objective function and constraints so that their equations and inequalities may be properly structured and arranged. To illustrate this point, suppose that the problem is to maximize the profit, y, from two products, x_1 and x_2, which are produced by three processes, A, B, and C, each with limited capacities.

Experience indicates that the firm can expect \$ 21 of profit per unit of x_1, and \$ 85 per unit of x_2. The equation of the objective function is thus,

$$21x_1 + 85x_2 = y.$$

In process A, a unit of product x_1 requires 7 capacity units (for example, hours of processing time) while a unit of product x_2 requires 11 capacity units. But there are only 385 units of processing capacity available in the relevant time frame. The constraint for process A may therefore be expressed as,

$$\text{constraint A: } 7x_1 + 11x_2 <= 385.$$

By similar reasoning, the requirements of products x_1 and x_2 in processes B and C with their respective capacities result in the following constraints:

constraint B: $11x_1 + 35x_2 <= 770$,

constraint C: $19x_1 + 90x_2 <= 1710$.

When the linear programming computer programme is run, the user indicates that the primal problem is one of maximization, that there are two primal independent variables and three explicit primal constraints, and that all of the explicit primal constraints are less-than inequalities. Non-negativity constraints are implicitly assumed. The computer programme then prompts for entry of the coefficients and constants of each of the primal constraints, and the coefficients of the primal objective function. Once all of this information has been entered, the programme reports that 24.1379 units of x_1 and 14.4138 units of x_2 should be produced to yield a maximum profit of $ 1,732.07.

The structure of the dual problem is automatically derived from the primal problem, and the dual values are computed. The dual value of a capacity unit in process A is $ 1.5747, which is the amount of profit which must be forgone if a capacity unit in process A is lost. Since the dual values of capacity units in processes B and C are both zero, it may be inferred that the constraint of process A is binding, while those of processes B and C are not.

Appendix 4.2

DIFFERENTIATION RULES

There are numerous rules for differentiating functions of various types. We shall identify only six for use in the managerial economics context:

1. The simple derivative (d) of a function which is a constant is zero, that is,

   if $y = k$,

   then $dy/dx = 0$.

2. The simple derivative of a function in which the independent variable is raised to the power 1 is its constant coefficient, that is,

   if $y = kx$,

   then $dy/dx = k$.

   A variation upon this rule is that

   if $y = x$,

   then $dy/dx = 1$.

3. The simple derivative of a function in which an independent variable is raised to a power different than 1 is the power times the constant coefficient times the variable raised to the power less one, that is,

if $y = kx^a$,

then $dy/dx = akx^{a-1}$.

This differentiation rule works if a is less than 1 or if a is negative.

4. The simple derivative of a function containing multiple, additive terms is the sum of the derivatives of the separate terms, that is,

   if $y = kx^a + jx^b$,

   then $dy/dx = akx^{a-1} + bjx^{b-1}$.

5. If a function is a product of two functions, that is,

   if $y = u.v$

   where $u = f(x)$ and $v = g(x)$,

   then $dy/dx = v(du/dx) + u(dv/dx)$.

6. If a function contains two or more independent variables, then a partial derivative (p) may be computed with respect to each of the independent variables by treating the other independent variable(s) as if constant:

   if $y = kx^a + jz^b$,

   then $py/px = akx^{a-1} + 1$,

   and $py/pz = 1 + bjz^{b-1}$.

—oo(O)oo—

Chapter 5

Modelling the Decision Context

Topics covered in this chapter

• Model specification procedures. • Regression as a means of model specification. • Forms of regression models. • Means of fitting average relationship curves. • The stepwise regression procedure. • Polynomial regression modelling. • Multiplicative regression modelling. • Inferences about the regression model. • The existence and strength of relationship. • The significance of the independent variables. • Multiple regression problems.

Models constitute the primary vehicles for conducting economic analysis. Economic theorists, attempting to push the frontiers of economic knowledge, employ models to discern the economic nature of the world. Models constitute the nearly universally employed instructional vehicles of the economics classroom. Government as well as private-sector decision makers use models to forecast important environmental conditions. They also use specially tailored models for policy simulation purposes, that is, to examine 'what if' circumstances before actually having to make real-world decisions.

Models may be represented in any of several possible formats. The most rudimentary form is that of a verbal assertion of a relationship between a dependent and one or more independent variables. An example of such a verbal assertion is the law of demand, that is, that people will tend to buy items in larger quantities at lower prices, and *vice-versa*. Mathematical functional notations may be employed to represent the model, as, for example, $y = f(x_1, x_2, \ldots)$, where y is understood to be a dependent variable, the behaviour of which is determined in some sense by one or more independent variables, x_1, x_2, etc.

The specific structure of the model cannot be shown in functional notation format. The model can be made specific by putting it into an equation format, such as the so-called slope-intercept form of a linear relationship, $y = a + bx$. Here, a is the y-axis intercept, and b is the slope of the line representing the relationship between x and y. Other equation formats are also possible, as will be discussed below. And from the equation format, it is but a short step to the computer language statement to represent the model. Indeed, most economic models designed for forecasting and policy simulation purposes eventually find their ways into computerized implementations.

The process of specifying a model can be described in several identifiable steps. The first step is to model relationships between the dependent variable and one or more independent variables. The modelling process involves selection of independent variables thought most likely to affect the behaviour of the dependent variable, and guesses at the nature of the relationships (that is, whether direct or inverse, linear or curved, and if curved relationships, the direction of curvature). Such guesses lead to expectations of signs (+ or –) of the coefficients of the variables, positive for direct relationships, negative for inverse relationships. Prospective independent variables not expressly included in a model are treated as if they are constant (even if in actuality they are not).

The next step is to acquire data for all of the variables expressly included in the model. The data may be captured cross sectionally (that is, at a point in time but across a number of subjects) or as a time series (that is, for a single subject, but over a period of time). The process of data capture can be expected to be costly in terms of time, effort, and various explicit expenses.

The third step in the model specification process is to estimate the values of the parameters (or constants) of the hypothesized relationships. In the slope-intercept equation model format, the values of the constants a and b must be estimated. Although these values may be estimated by informal means (use of the imagination, 'eye-balling'), the remainder of this chapter will be devoted to elaboration of the formal statistical procedures that have been adopted nearly universally by economic analysts for the specification process. After the model has been specified, the final step in the process is to attempt to verify the model, or ascertain its adequacy to the end for which it was constructed. The tools of statistical inference are applied to this objective, but the ultimate test of a model is its ability to explain, predict, simulate, or instruct.

ESTIMATING A MODEL BY REGRESSION ANALYSIS

Regression analysis is the most widely used, formalized method of estimating the demand (or any other type of) functional relationship in economics and business administration settings. This chapter introduces the modelling capabilities of regression analysis, but a fuller elaboration of its capabilities and extensions into the realm economic forecasting will be provided in the following chapters..

SIMPLE REGRESSION MODELS

The simplest form of regression model relates two variables, of which one is described as dependent, and the other as independent. The format for this simplest regression model may be described in functional-notation form as

$$(1)\ Y = f(x)$$

where y is the dependent variable, and x is the independent variable. The linear form of the simple regression model could be expressed in slope-intercept form as

$$(2)\ Y = a + bx$$

where a is the intercept parameter, and b is the slope parameter. What statistical regression analysis will accomplish, given an adequate amount of data for x and y, is to compute values for the parameters a and b according to a certain mathematical principle. The data may have been gleaned from historical sources, or generated with experiments or sample survey techniques.

The simple linear regression analysis may be extended to multiple regression with the addition of terms for other independent variables, or to higher-order relationships with the addition of terms for values of the single independent variable raised (or transformed by self-multiplication) to successively higher powers. The general form of the linear multiple regression model is

$$(3)\ y = a + b_1x_1 + b_2x_2 + \ldots + b_nx_n.$$

Assuming for the moment a simple regression model as in equation (2), the data for variable y may be given graphic representation by plotting them in the vertical dimension relative to the data for the independent variable, x, in the horizontal dimension on a set of standard coordinate axes. Figure 5.1 illustrates a 'scatter diagram' of the data for two series.

This scatter diagram exhibits a great deal of variation about an upward-sloping path from left to right as the independent variable changes on the horizontal axis. It is possible to draw a smooth line, free-hand style, through the data plot. The smooth line may be straight or curvilinear.

Regression analysis functions to accomplish mathematically what the analyst may have drawn as a free-hand curve of average relationship using an 'eye-ball' fitting technique. Although there are several possible regression principles, the most commonly-used approach is to 'fit' the average relationship curve to the plotted points so as to minimize the squared deviations of the curve from the points.

Assuming this so-called 'least-squares' technique is properly applied, there is no other mathematical function that can be 'fitted' to the plotted points with any smaller average error relative to the location of the plotted points. The regression analysis produces estimates of the parameters (intercept, slope) of the best-fit average relationship curve.

Depending upon the amount of variation in the dependent variable, the resulting regression equation may be able to estimate, with some error, values of existing observations within the data set, and to predict values of hypothetical observations not included in the data set. This latter possibility constitutes the potential of regression analysis to serve as a modelling technique. Given a regression equation such as that developed from a 'least-squares' regression procedure on a set

VERTICAL AXIS VARIABLE 1

STANDARD DEVIATION	**9.8394**
MEAN	**247.7631**

HORIZONTAL AXIS VARIABLE 2

STANDARD DEVIATION	**11.9216**
MEAN	**235.4083**

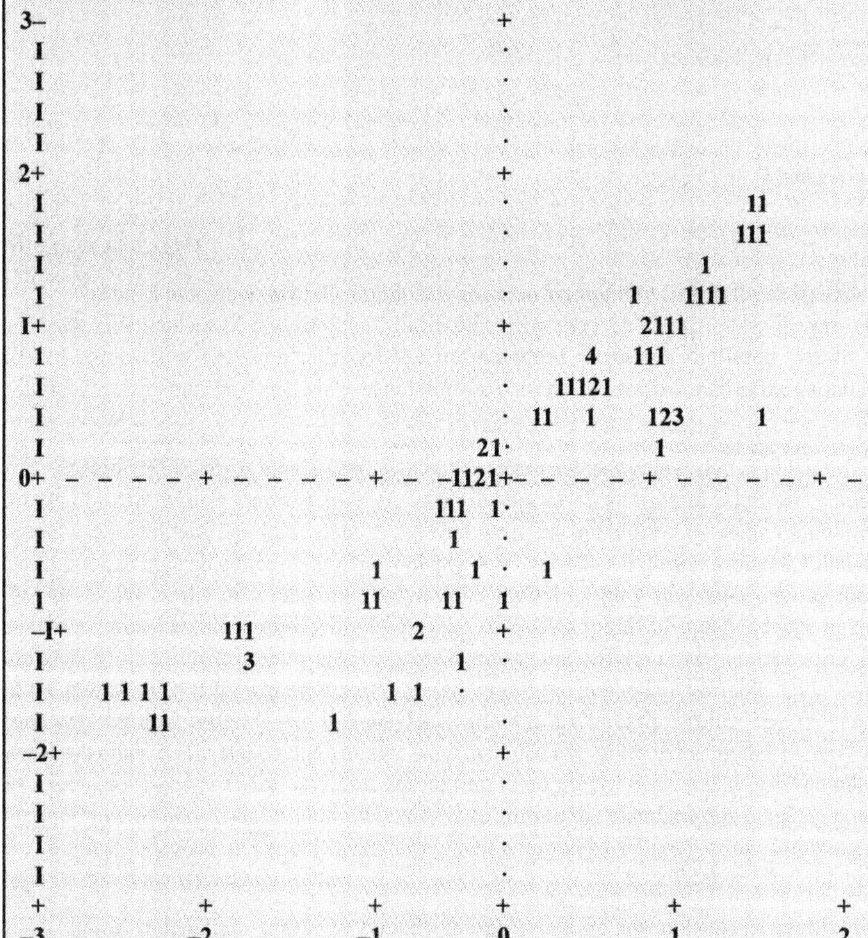

Note: Each of the plotted numbers above indicates the number of points plotted at that printspace.

Figure 5.1. Scatter diagram for variables y (vertical axis) and x (horizontal axis).

of data, unknown values of the dependent variable, y, may be estimated by inserting a known value of the independent variable, x, into the regression equation and solving for the dependent variable value. The error involved in estimating or predicting such values constitutes a potentially serious problem that will be discussed subsequently.

MULTIPLE REGRESSION MODELS

Some dependent variables can be adequately modelled with reference to a single independent variable, but other independent variables can be modelled only inadequately in this manner. There are two possibilities for these variables: either they are characterized so extensively by random noise that they cannot be modelled, or there are one or more other phenomena that govern or influence the behaviour of the variables. If comparable data for these other phenomena can be acquired, then conventional simple and multiple regression procedures may be invoked to model the relationships. The conventional formats for the simple and multiple regression models are given by equations (2) and (3) above.

Once a multiple regression model has been specified and the parameter values estimated, the analyst may discern the predictive ability of each of the included independent variables by examining the inference statistics for each of them as discussed later in this chapter. Any independent variable that in the judgement of the analyst does not make a satisfactory contribution to the explanation of the behaviour of the dependent variable data may then be deleted from the model when the model is re-specified. Many statistical software packages include options for stepwise deletion of inadequately contributing independent variables from the model according to some criterion specified by the programmer or the analyst. In the stepwise regression procedure, the full model including all variables selected by the analyst is first estimated, then the model is automatically re-specified in subsequent steps, omitting one variable in each step, until only one independent variable remains in the model. The analyst may then inspect the sequence of model specifications, looking for a significant drop in the overall level of explanation of the behaviour of the dependent variable. Once this loss is identified, the model specified prior to the deletion of the independent variable resulting in the significant loss is the optimal model.

NON-LINEAR REGRESSION MODELS

The multiple regression equation, linear in its equation (3) format, can be made to fit curvilinear data paths by converting it to a polynomial format. The polynomial equation includes one independent variable raised to successively higher powers. For example, a quadratic polynomial equation includes linear and second-order (or squared) terms in the format:

$$(4)\ y = a + b_1x + b_2x^2.$$

Data for the second independent-variable term are generated by performing a squared transformation on the data for the first independent variable. The general format for a k-th order polynomial model is

$$(5)\ y = a + b_1x + b_2x^2 + b_3x^3 + \ldots + b_kx^k,$$

Figure 5.2(a). A hypothetical scatter diagram illustrating a second-order relationship.

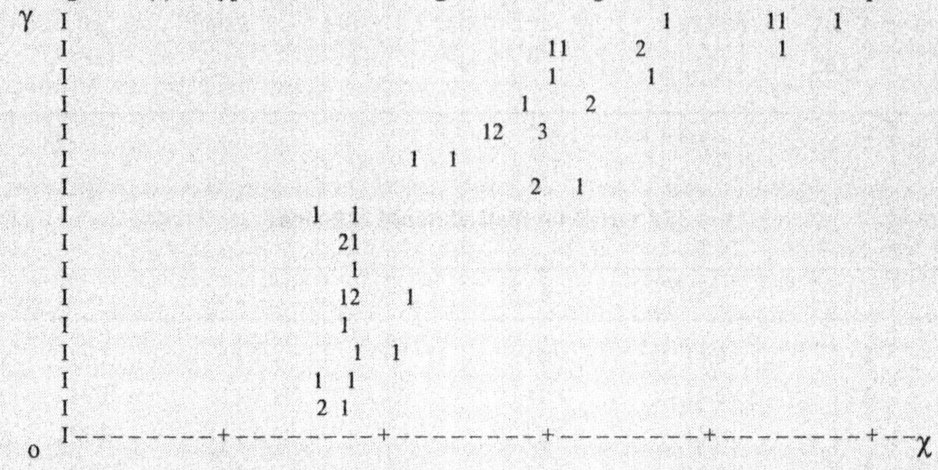

Figure 5.2(b). A hypothetical scatter diagram illustrating a third-order relationship.

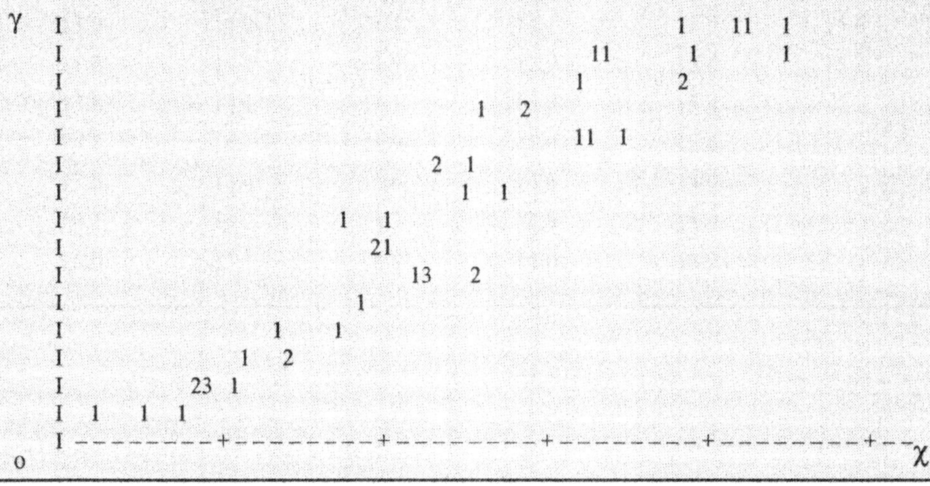

Figure 5.2. A hypothetical scatter diagram illustrating second and third order relationiships.

where data for all terms beyond the linear term are generated by subsequent transformations. Some software packages can automatically generate a specified k-th order polynomial regression model computationally (that is, without having to go through the data transformation phase). The analyst should consider a polynomial form of relationship when the scatter diagram exhibits a curved path that is not apparently amenable to linear modelling. As a general criterion, the analyst should specify a polynomial equation of order k that is equal to the number of directions of curvature apparent in the scatter diagram, plus 1. For example, if the scatter diagram exhibits one direction of curvature as illustrated in Figure 5.2, then a k=2, or second-order regression model should be specified. If the scatter diagram exhibits two directions of curvature, as illustrated in Figure 5.3, a k=3 or third-order (cubic) model of form

$$(6)\ y = a + b_1x + b_2x^2 + b_3x^3$$

should be specified. If the analyst is certain that the relationship is not linear but in doubt about the appropriate order of relationship, he could specify second-, third-, and perhaps fourth-order models, then choose the one with the smallest mean squared error (discussed below).

Finally, we should note that the multiple regression format can accommodate a mixture of all of the formats described to this point, and further incorporate moving averages as well as components of a decomposed time series For example, suppose the analyst finds that variable x_1 is a significant predictor of the behaviour of the object series, but that the explanation needs to be supplemented by the presence of two other independent variables, x_2 and x_3, the first linear and the other in a second-order relationship. Such a regression model might have the following appearance:

$$y = a + b_1x_1 + b_2x_2 + b_3x_3 + b_4x_3^2.$$

MULTIPLICATIVE MODELS

All of the models that we have illustrated to this point have been additive in the sense that the effects of all of the separate independent variables are simply added together to compose the total effect on the dependent variable. Each independent variable is assumed to have its impact on the dependent variable independently of any other independent variable. There may be reason to believe that two or more independent variables have joint or interactive impact on the dependent variable. An example might be found in utility analysis where the total utility realized from consumption of a particular good, for example, beer, can be expected to depend not only on the quantity of beer consumed, but also the quantity of pretzels available for consumption along with the beer. In cases like this, a multiplicative functional relationship such as that in equation (7) may be more appropriate:

$$(7)\ y = a\ x_1^b x_2^c.$$

Here, the total effect on y is the product of x_1 raised to the power b and x_2 raised to the power c, multiplied by a scale factor a. Equation (7) can be converted to a form that can be handled by (additive) multiple linear regression by taking the logarithms of all terms in the equation:

$$(8)\ \log y = \log a + b \log x_1 + c \log x_2.$$

Then, in order to estimate the function, it is necessary to convert the data for variables y, x_1, and x_2 to logarithmic format. Most computerized statistical systems can accomplish this by way of performing a logarithmic transformation on data for each variable. It should be noted, however, that such a regression equation will predict values for the log of variable y. The analyst must then take the anti-log (or exponential) of log y to find the predicted value of y.

INFERENCES ABOUT THE REGRESSION MODEL

Regression analysis purports to provide answers to a very specific question: 'What is the nature of the relationship between the dependent variable and an independent variable?' The question is answered by estimating values of the parameters in a best-fit equation. But regression analysis begs two other very important questions: 'Is there a significant relationship between the selected variables?' and, if so, 'How strong (or close, or reliable) is the relationship?' If there is no significant relationship, or even if the existing relationship is only trivial, a regression analysis will dumbly estimate the values of the parameters. It is therefore necessary to delve into the significance of the estimated relationships. The existence and significance of a hypothesized relationship should perhaps be brought into question even before the regression analysis is conducted. The statistical complement to regression analysis that attempts to address the questions begged by it is correlation analysis, a special application of the tools of statistical inference. Although the user of statistics is typically concerned with the results of both the correlation and the regression analyses, it is possible to conduct either analysis without making computations for the other.

THE EXISTENCE AND STRENGTH OF THE RELATIONSHIP

For our purposes, the evaluation criteria developed by the inference analysis will be divided into two groups. The first, usually described as 'analysis of variance,' yields four evaluation criteria that may serve as bases for inferences about the existence, strength, and validity of a regression model:

(a) The correlation coefficient, r or R, measures the degree of association or co-variation between the dependent variable and an independent variable in the regression model. One such simple correlation coefficient may be computed between the dependent variable and each independent variable in the model, and in a multivariate model between each pair of independent variables. Computerized statistical systems usually produce a matrix of such simple correlation coefficients so that the analyst may ascertain the correlations between the dependent and each of the independent variables, as well as among the independent variables (as illustrated on the following pages). If the model contains more than a single independent variable, a so-called multiple correlation coefficient, R, may also be computed to assess the overall association between the dependent variable and all of the included independent variables taken together. The domain of r is from -1 to $+1$, with positive values implying direct relationships, and negative values indicating inverse relationships. Values of r near the extremes of this range imply near perfect inverse or direct relationship between the two variables, depending upon sign. Values of r in the neighbourhood of zero (positive or negative), however, imply no statistically identifiable relationship between the variables.

(b) The coefficient of determination, r^2, is interpreted as the proportion of the variation in the dependent variable data that can be statistically explained by data for the independent variable for which the r^2 is computed. In a multivariate regression model, a coefficient of multiple determination, R^2, may be computed; if there is only one independent variable in the model, the computed R^2 will be equal to the only simple r^2. Since r^2 is computed as the squared value of the correlation coefficient, r^2 is unsigned, and falls within the range of zero to $+1$. Although computed values of r and r^2 contain essentially the same information (except for differences in sign), and each implies a value of the other, many analysts prefer to focus attention on r^2 because of its determination interpretation.

The interpretation of any computed r^2 statistic is subjective, and hence open to dispute. For example, how high (towards unity) does the r^2 have to be in order for the analyst to infer the existence and strength of a relationship? How low (towards zero) can an r^2 statistic be before the analyst may draw the inference that no statistically identifiable relationship exists between the dependent and an independent variable? Analysts in the natural sciences often expect r^2 values in excess of 0.9 (or even higher) to indicate the existence of a useable relationship.

Because of the degree of randomness, capriciousness, and ignorance that may characterize human decision making and behaviour in the aggregate, a social scientist may defensibly judge an r^2 that is in excess of 0.7 (or perhaps even somewhat lower) to be indicative of a statistically meaningful relationship. But most analysts are sceptical of the existence of a statistically meaningful relationship if the r^2 between the dependent and independent variables is below 0.3 (in statistical jargon, the null hypothesis, that is, that there is no relationship, is supported). For our purposes, the r^2 values of 0.3 and 0.7 will be taken as evaluation benchmarks: values of r^2 in excess of 0.7 are sufficient to reject the null hypothesis; values below 0.3 support the null hypothesis. But the reader should be aware that both of these values are rather arbitrarily selected and are subject to challenge.

Assuming that these values will serve satisfactorily as evaluation criteria, what of the r^2 range between 0.3 and 0.7? This constitutes a statistical 'no-man's land' wherein no strong inferences can be drawn about either the existence or the non-existence of a statistically meaningful relationship between two variables. The interpretation of r^2 values below 0.3 or in excess of 0.7 may be further refined with reference to the statistical significance of the regression model and particular variables within it.

(c) The computed F-statistic may be used as a basis for drawing an inference about the statistical significance of a regression model. Once the F-value is computed, the analyst must consult an F-distribution table (which may be found in any statistical source book or college-level statistics text). For the particular regression model under consideration, its computed F-value may be compared with F-distribution table values in the column for '1 degree of freedom in the numerator,' and on the row corresponding to the number of degrees of freedom (DF) of the regression model. The DF of a regression model is the number of observations less the number of variables (dependent and independent) in the model.

For a regression analysis including a dependent variable and two independent variables conducted with 60 observations, the DF is 57. If the regression model's computed F-value exceeds the F-distribution value read from the appropriate column and row in the table, the analyst may infer that the model is statistically significant at the level indicated in the heading of the table for the F-distribution (usually .05, that is, only five chances in 100 that the model is spurious).

Suppose that the computed F-value for a regression model is 4.73, with 60 degrees of freedom. An F-distribution table reveals that the F-value required for significance at the .05 level is 4.00; the F-value required for the .01 significance level is 7.08. These findings support the inference that the regression model is statistically significant at the .05 level, but not at the .01 level.

For many less-consequential forecasting purposes, most analysts probably would be willing to accept (though with hesitancy) a regression model with r^2 of 0.7 and statistical significance at the .05 level. If truly consequential decisions are to be based upon the regression model forecasts, the analyst may not be willing to use any model for which r^2 is less than some very high value (like 0.9 or 0.95), with statistical significance below some very low level (like 0.01 or 0.001).

(d) The standard error of the estimate (SEE) may be used to specify various confidence intervals for forecasts made with the regression model. Realistically speaking, the likelihood that the actual value at some forecast-target date will fall precisely on the value estimated in a regression model is nearly zero. In other words, the forecasted value is a 'point estimate' that the analyst hopes will be close to the actual value when it finally occurs. The computed SEE specifies a numeric range on either side of the point estimate within which there is an approximate 66 per cent chance that the actual value will fall. Two other confidence intervals are also conventionally prescribed. There is a 95 per cent probability that actual value will lie within a range of two standard errors of the forecasted point estimate, and a 99 per cent probability that the actual value will lie within three SEEs of the forecasted value. For example, suppose that a regression model forecasts a point estimate of 732 for the target date, with an SEE of 27. The 66 per cent confidence interval may thus be computed as the range from 705 to 759 (that is, 732 +/– 27); the 95 per cent confidence interval is from 678 to 786; and the 99 per cent confidence interval is from 651 to 813. It should be apparent that the higher the required confidence in the forecasts made with a regression model, the wider will be the range within which the actual value likely will fall. As a general rule, the SEE will be smaller the higher the r^2 and the lower the statistical significance of the regression model. Other things remaining the same, a regression model with a smaller SEE is preferable to one with a larger SEE. In any case, the analyst would be better off in reporting the results of a regression model forecast to specify confidence intervals rather than the single-valued point estimate that will almost certainly not happen.

THE SIGNIFICANCE OF THE COEFFICIENTS OF THE INDEPENDENT VARIABLES

Certain inference statistics are also computed for purposes of assessing the statistical significance of the regression coefficient (b, the estimated slope parameter) of each included independent variable.

(a) The standard error of the regression coefficient, SEC, is computed for each of the slope parameters estimated by the regression procedure. Unless the entire universe of values (all that have or can exist) are available for all variables included in a regression model, the regression analysis can do no more than construct an estimate of the true slope parameter value from the sample of data currently available. By its very nature, time series regression analysis could never encompass the entire span of time from the 'beginning' through all eternity. Data for various finite time spans will thus yield differing estimates of the true parameter of relationship between any two variables. The hope of the analyst, and one of the premises upon which regression analysis is erected, is that all such estimated parameter values will exhibit a central tendency to converge upon the true value of relationship, and that any single estimated regression coefficient will not be very far from the true value.

All such regression coefficient estimates are presumed to constitute a normally-distributed population for which a standard deviation (a measure of average dispersion about the mean) may be computed. This particular standard deviation is called the standard error of the regression coefficient. It may be used to specify the 66, 95, and 99 per cent confidence intervals within which the true coefficient value is likely to lie. As a general rule, the smaller the value of the SEC relative to its regression coefficient, the more reliable is the estimate of the regression coefficient.

(b) The t-value may be computed for each regression coefficient. In generalized inferential analysis, the 'student's t-test' may be used to test for the significance of the difference between two sample means. Applied to regression analysis, the t-value may be used to test for the significance of the difference between the estimated regression coefficient and the mean of all such regression coefficients that could be estimated. Since the latter is unknowable, the t-value is usually computed for the difference between the estimated regression coefficient and zero. As such, it can only be used to ascertain the likelihood that the estimated regression coefficient is non-zero. Once the t-value for a regression coefficient is computed, the analyst may consult a student's t-distribution table on the appropriate DF row to see where the computed t-value would lie. The t-table value just below the computed t-value identifies the column in the t-distribution table that specifies the significance level of the test. Suppose that the absolute value (unsigned) of the computed t-value for an estimated slope parameter is 1.73, with 60 degrees of freedom. A t-distribution table would show 1.73 lying between the values 1.671 and 2.000 on the 60 degree-of-freedom row. The column heading of the row containing the value 1.671 is the 0.1 significance level, implying that there is only one chance in ten that the estimated regression coefficient is not different from zero.

As a general rule, the lower the significance level of a regression coefficient, the more reliable are the forecasts that can be made using the model containing the independent variable for which the regression coefficient was estimated. For especially consequential decision making, the analyst may not be willing to retain any term in a regression forecasting model that is statistically significant above the 0.01 level. Since the t-value may be computed as the ratio of the estimated regression coefficient to its computed SEC, a rule of thumb may be prescribed that permits the analyst to avoid reference to a t-distribution table. If the absolute value of an estimated regression coefficient exceeds its computed SEC, the analyst may infer that the regression coefficient is statistically significant at the 0.33 level or lower. If the regression coefficient is more than twice the magnitude of its SEC, this implies a 0.05 significance level for the coefficient. Likewise, if b exceeds its SEC by a factor of 3, the implied significance level is below 0.01.

PROBLEMS WITH THE MULTIPLE REGRESSION CONTEXT

There are several possible problems that may emerge in the multiple regression model context. All are consequences of violation of one or another of the assumptions or premises that underlie the multiple regression environment. Adjustments may be made to the data or the analysis to deal with some of the problems, but in cases of others the analysis should simply be aware of the likely effects.

MULTICOLLINEARITY

The most fundamental of the multiple regression assumptions is that the independent variables are truly independent of one another. Multicollinearity may be identified by the presence of non-trivial correlation between pairs of the independent variables included within the model. Multicollinearity may be detected by examining the correlation matrix for all of the variables contained in the model.

Multicollinearity is almost certain to be present in any autoregressive or polynomial regression model of order higher than the first. Because the successive terms in a kth-order autoregressive model use essentially the same data as the first term, except shifted by some number of rows, the assumption of independence among the 'independent' variables is clearly violated. Likewise, because the successive terms in a kth-order polynomial model employ the same data as the first term, except as raised to successively higher powers, the assumption of independence again is clearly violated. Multicollinearity may also be present among the different independent variables included in the model, even if they are not autoregressive with the dependent variable, and even if they are each only the first order. If two independent variables are linearly similar, that is, very correlated with each other, it is as if the same variable were included two times in the model, thereby contributing its explanatory power twice, and thus amounting to so much 'deck stacking.' The usual effect of the presence of non-trivial multicollinearity is to inflate the standard errors of the coefficients of the collinear independent variables, rendering their computed t-values too low, implying excessively high levels of statistical significance (bad, since the lower the significance level the better).

Some statisticians prefer to remedy the presence of any non-trivial multicollinearity by removal of one or the other of the two collinear variables from the model. Others suggest that if there are good conceptual reasons for including both independent variables, they should both be retained in the model unless the multicollinearity is extreme (that is, the correlation between the collinear independent variables approaches 1.00 in absolute value), or unless the analyst is particularly concerned about the statistical significance of either of the collinear independent variables. In this latter case, if the independent variables are time series, the analyst might try differencing the collinear independent variables and re-specifying the model with the differenced series in place of the raw data series to see if significant information is contained in either of the collinear independent variables that is not also contained in the other.

AUTOCORRELATION

Another of the premises underlying multiple regression modelling is that the forecast errors constitute an independent random variable, that is, a random noise series. If there is a discernible pattern in the forecast error series, then autocorrelation is present in the dependent variable series. Autocorrelation may be detected by computing autocorrelation coefficients to some level of specified order of autocorrelation. Alternately, the analyst may construct a sequence plot of the forecast error series. The statistical software system may facilitate this procedure by allowing the user to have the forecast error series written to the next available empty column in the data matrix so that the sequence plot of that column may be constructed. If the forecast error series exhibits alternation of points above and below its mean, then the object series is negatively autocorrelated. Positive autocorrelation is present if the error series exhibits 'runs' of points above the mean alternating with runs of points below the mean in a cyclical (or seasonal) fashion. The expected number of runs if the series is truly random noise may be estimated for comparison with the actual (by count) number of runs exhibited by the series. If the actual number of runs is smaller than the expected number, then autocorrelation almost surely is present in the dependent variable series. The effect of the presence of autocorrelation within the dependent variable series is to render the r, F, and t statistics unreliable. In particular, the presence of autocorrelation will likely result in understated standard errors of the regression coefficients, thus causing overstatement of the t-values, implying better (that is, lower) significance levels for the estimated regression coefficients than warranted. Although the estimated regression coefficients themselves are unbiased (that is, not unduly specific to the particular data set), autocorrelation results in computed confidence intervals that are narrower than they should be.

Some degree of autocorrelation is likely to be present in every economic or business time series, and the analyst should probably ignore it unless it is extreme. As noted earlier in the chapter, one or more auto-regressive terms may constitute or be included in the regression model as the primary explanatory independent variables. If the analyst discovers the presence of non-trivial autocorrelation in a regression model that was specified without autoregressive terms, he might consider re-specifying it to include one or more such terms as the means of handling the autocorrelation. The approach in this case is to try to use the autocorrelated information rather than purge it from the model.

HETEROSKEDASTICITY

The problem of heteroskedasticity occurs if there is a systematic pattern between the forecast error series and any of the independent variable series. Homoskedasticity is the absence of such a pattern. Whether the model exhibits the property of heteroskedasticity may be discerned by having the forecast errors plotted against data for each of the independent variables in scatter diagrams. If the scatter of the plotted points exhibits any discernible path, then heteroskedasticity is present within the model.

If the regression model is non-trivially heteroskedastistic, the mean squared error and the standard error of the estimate will be specific to the particular data set; another data set may yield inference statistics that diverge widely from those computed from the first data set. Likewise, the inference statistics associated with the particular independent variables (SEC, t, and significance level) will also be specific to the data set. We shall leave the matter of heteroskedasticity with the warning to the analyst of the likely consequences for his model, that is, that its usefulness for modelling may be strictly limited to the range of data included in the object series.

AN APPLICATION

We conclude this chapter by applying the various models discussed here to data series presented in Tables 5.1 and 3.2. Figures 5.4, 5.5, and 5.6 display results of specifying simple linear, polynomial, and multiple regression models.

Table 5.1: Monthly Data for Series Y1

Month	*Year 1*	*Year 2*	*Year 3*	*Year 4*	*Year 5*	*Year 6*	*Year 7*
1.	233.4	249.4	234.1	240.7	245.6	252.1	253.3
2.	236.6	229.2	234.1	231.3	244.9	253.1	252.0
3.	239.8	229.5	229.7	245.3	248.3	254.3	256.2
4.	242.7	231.3	233.6	244.5	251.9	255.3	257.0
5.	245.2	233.7	234.1	249.1	253.9	256.4	259.3
6.	252.2	238.6	238.4	249.7	260.3	59.4	265.9
7.	252.3	239.7	237.0	248.1	255.1	257.5	259.9
8.	252.2	241.1	236.2	248.6	255.8	260.1	261.8
9.	251.1	238.0	237.1	249.1	255.8	257.3	264.6
10	251.1	240.8	235.5	247.4	255.5	256.8	264.4
11	252.2	240.2	236.0	248.2	255.1	253.6	262.7
12	251.7	242.3	232.8	246.6	254.3	257.2	263.9

Table 5.2: Monthly Data for Series Y2

Month	*Year 1*	*Year 2*	*Year 3*	*Year 4*	*Year 5*	*Year 6*
1	15.7	14.5	13.1	11.9	14.9	12.8
2.	14.3	13.7	14.6	11.8	15.6	18.6
3.	13.8	14.1	13.1	12.6	15.8	15.9
4.	13.6	14.8	13.6	13.3	14.9	14.1
5.	12.4	14.1	11.6	13.1	16.6	14.8
6.	13.9	14.2	11.1	14.1	15.9	15.6
7.	15.4	14.1	11.7	12.9	15.6	15.4
8.	13.8	14.1	11.1	13.5	15.4	
9.	14.1	14.1	11.9	15.0	15.6	
10.	13.5	13.4	11.6	14.6	14.9	
11.	14.1	14.2	11.3	13.9	15.9	
12.	15.0	13.1	12.8	14.0	14.2	

```
SIMPLE LINEAR REGRESSION: Y–A+ b(1)*X
DEPENDENT VARIABLE (Y) IS MATRIX COLUMN:                1  Y1          PERIOD
LAGGED: 2
INDEPENDENT VARIABLE (X) IS MATRIX COLUMN:              2  X1

COEF OF MULTIPLE CORRELATION (R)            .7825       CORRECTED R          .7825
COEF OF MULTIPLE DETERMINATION (RSQ)        .6223       CORRECTED RSQ        .6123
STANDARD ERROR OF THE ESTIMATE             6.1069       MSE                37.2938
ANALYSIS OF VARIANCE      SUMS OF SQUARES    DEGREES OF
                                               FREEDOM
TOTAL                          7696.2562         81
REMOVED BY REGRESSION          4712.7492          1
RESIDUAL                       2983.5070         80        F-VALUE     126.3680
INDEP VAR       SIMPLE R       COEF (b)     S.E. COEF   T-VALUE  SIGNIFICANCE
   2 X2           .7825         .6494         .0578      11.2414        .0000

INDEPENDENT VARIABLE NUMBER 1                                          253.4000
POINT ESTIMATE FORECAST OF DEPENDENT VARIABLE          260.0328
95 PER CENT CONFIDENCE INTERVAL                   247.8192 TO 272.2466
```

Figure 5.4. Simple linear regression analysis of dependent variable Y1 against independent variable Y2.

Summary of Important Points

1. The procedures employed in model specification follow the steps outlined earlier.
2. Regression analysis, widely used to specify economic models, accomplishes the fitting of an average relationship curve to data for the dependent and independent variables plotted in coordinate space.
3. Multiple regression models incorporate a multiplicity of independent variables that contribute to explanation of the behaviour of the dependent variable.
4. Stepwise regression deletes from the model variables that make inadequate contributions to the explanation of the dependent variable.
5. The multiple regression model can accommodate polynomial relationships.
6. Multiplicative models are used when independent variables are interrelated with one another.
7. Inference statistics reveal the existence and strength of relationship between the dependent and independent variables in a model.
8. The coefficient of correlation measures the degree of association or co variation between the dependent and an independent variable.
9. The coefficient of determination measures the proportion of the variation in the dependent variable data that can be statistically explained by data for the independent variable.

Contd.....

POLYNOMIAL REGRESSION
MODEL: Y(t) = (a) + (b)(1)*x + b(2)*X^2 + ··· + b(k)*X^k

DEPENDENT VARIABLE (Y) IS MATRIX COLUMN:	1 Y1	PERIODS LAGGED: 2
INDEPENDENT VARIABLE IS MATRIX COLUMN:	2 X1	
ORDER (k) OF EQUATION: 3		

COEF OF MULTIPLE CORRELATION (R)	.7924	CORRECTED R	.7265
COEF OF MULTIPLE DETERMINATION (RSQ)	.6279	CORRECTED RSQ	.6185
STANDARD ERROR OF THE ESTIMATE	6.0591	MSE	36.7123

ANALYSIS OF VARIANCE	SUMS OF SQUARES	DEGREES OF FREEDOM		
TOTAL	7696.2562	81		
REMOVED BY REGRESSION	4832.6945	3		
RESIDUAL	2863.0592	78	F-VALUE	46.8789

INDEP VAR	SIMPLE R	COEF (b)	S.E. COEF	T-VALUE	SIGNIFICANCE
X1 ^ 1	.7825	–91.3891	51.2027	1.7849	.0744
XI ^ 2	.7820	.3969	.3204	1.8010	.0719
XI ^ 3	.7807	–.0006	.0003	1.8037	.0715
CONSTANT (a)		7195.3124			

CORRELATIONS AMONG THE INDEPENDENT VARIABLES

1.0000		.9996	.9984
.9996	1.0000	.9996	
.9984	.9996	1.0000	

INDEPENDENT VARIABLE NUMBER 1	253.4000
INDEPENDENT VARIABLE NUMBER 2	253.4000
INDEPENDENT VARIABLE NUMBER 3	253.4000
POINT ESTIMATE FORECAST OF DEPENDENT VARIABLE	258.2437
95 PER CENT CONFIDENCE INTERVAL	246.1256 TO 270.3618

Figure 5.5. Simple linear regression analysis of dependent variable Y1 against independent variable Y2.

10. The F-statistic may be used as a basis for drawing an inference about the statistical significance of a regression model.
11. The standard error of the estimate may be used to specify various confidence intervals for forecasts made with the regression model.
12. The standard error of the regression coefficient may be used to specify various confidence intervals within which the true coefficient of relationship may lie.
13. The t-value for a regression coefficient may be used to test for the significance of the difference between the estimated regression coefficient and zero.
14. Multicollinearity is the regression problem of non-trivial correlation between pairs of independent variables.
15. Autocorrelation is the regression problem of a discernible pattern in the forecast error series.
16. Heteroskedasticity is the regression problem of a systematic pattern between the forecast error series and any of the independent variable series.

```
MULTIPLE LINEAR REGRESSION
MODEL:  Y(t) – a +   b(1)*X(2)  |  b(2) ^X(2)  + ···    * b(k)*X(k)
DEPENDENT VARIABLE  (Y) 18 MATRIX COLUMN:  1 Y1           PERIODS LAGGED: 2
NUMBER (k) OF INDEPENDENT VARIABLES: 3

COEF OF MULTIPLE CORRELATION (R):               .8506   CORRECTED R:            .0464
COEF OF MULTIPLE DETERMINATION (RSQ):           .7235   CORRECTED RSQ:          .7165
STANDARD ERROR OF THE ESTIMATE:                5.2236   MSE:                  27.2857

ANALYSIS OF VARIANCE:          SUM OF SQUARES         DEGREES OF FREEDOM
TOTAL:                              7696.2562                  81
REMOVED BY REGRESSION:              5567.9752                   3
RESIDUAL:                           2128.2810                  78    F-VALUE: 68.0208

INDEP VAR       SIMPLE R       COEF (b)       S.E. COEF  T-VALUE  SIGNIFICANCE
   X1             .7825          .8085           .0994     8.1325         .0000
   X2           – .1816         1.5023          1.5068      .9971         .6775
   X3           – .2613       – 1.7895          3.8825    – .4609         .6510
CONSTANT (a)                   48.3213

CORRELATIONS AMONG THE INDEPENDENT VARIABLES
          1.0000      –.5712      – .6460
         – .5711      1.0000        .9927
           .6463       .9927       1.0000

INDEPENDENT VARIABLE NUMBER 1:                               253.4000
INDEPENDENT VARIABLE NUMBER 2:                                10.5000
INDEPENDENT VARIABLE NUMBER 3:                                 4.0000
POINT ESTIMATE FORECAST OF DEPENDENT VARIABLE:               261.8035
95 PER CENT CONFIDENCE INTERVAL                 251.3564  TO 272.2507
```

Figure 5.6. Multiple linear regression analysis of dependent variable Y1 against Y2 and two other independent variables.

Significant Terms

equation	regression analysis
slope-intercept format	simple, multiple regression
dependent, independent variables	scatter diagram
expectation of sign	curve fitting
data capture	least squares
verification	estimated, predicted values
statistical inference	random noise

predictive ability
contribution to explanation
stepwise regression
polynomial equation
transformation
additive, multiplicative models
inference analysis
significance of relationship
correlation analysis
analysis of variance
coefficient of correlation
of determination
null hypothesis
F-statistic, F-distribution
standard error of the estimate
confidence intervals
point estimate
standard error of the regression coefficient
t-value
student's t-distribution
multicollinearity
autoregressive model
autocorrelation
number of runs
hetero-, homoskedasticity

Questions for Discussion

1. Explain how models can be used for policy simulation.
2. Describe the steps in the process of specifying an economic model.
3. Explain the significance of the expected signs of the coefficients of the variables in an economic model.
4. Compare and contrast informal and formal procedures for estimating the parameters of the variables in an economic model.
5. Explain the use of inference statistics in the model specification process.
6. Assess the usefulness of scatter diagrams to the model specification process.
7. Explain the meaning and significance of the concept 'fit' in the model specification process.
8. Explain the meaning and usefulness of the 'least squares' technique in the model specification process.
9. How can the predictive ability of an estimated regression model be determined?
10. How can an economic analyst determine which independent variables to retain or reject from a model being specified by regression analysis?

11. Describe the stepwise regression procedure and explain the sense in which it employs the opportunity cost principle.
12. Critically evaluate the stepwise regression procedure in connection with modelling methodology, and explain why some economists do not hold stepwise techniques in high esteem.
13. Explain how the multiple regression model may be converted to a polynomial format; where can analysts acquire data for the higher ordered (above first) variables?
14. Describe the process of data transformation and explain its usefulness in the model specification process.
15. How can an economic analyst tell whether a model of an economic process should be specified to first, second, or third order?
16. Explain how multiple independent variables that have joint or interactive effects upon the dependent variable may be treated in a multiple regression model.
17. Explain the meaning of the term 'statistical significance' and tell how the statistical significance of the coefficient of a variable in a regression model may be determined.
18. Explain why it is necessary to delve into the existence of an estimated relationship.
19. Explain how the 'analysis of variance' can help to assess the existence, strength, and validity of a regression model.
20. Explain the meaning of the coefficient of determination.
21. Explain how confidence intervals may be specified for predictions made with an estimated regression model.
22. Why is a standard error of a regression coefficient needed?
23. Explain how the statistical significance of a regression coefficient may be determined and discuss the usefulness of this information to the model specification process.
24. What is a specification error, and how can specification errors be alleviated?
25. Identify problems associated with multiple regression analysis and indicate remedies for each.
26. Explain why (multicollinearity/autocorrelation/ heteroskedasticity) is a serious problem in the specification of a regression model; how can the problem be relieved?

Chapter 6

Consumer Behaviour and Demand

Topics covered in this chapter

• Patterns of consumer behaviour. • Expected versus certain values of choice. • Comparison of actual outcomes to expected values. • The behaviour of the utility function. • Qualifications to the principle of diminishing marginal utility. • Managerial implications of utility relationships. • The meaning of the law of demand. • The utility basis of the demand curve. • Treatment of demand determinants in specifying demand relationships. • The distinction between change of demand and change of quantity demanded. • Demand shift as a demand surface phenomenon. • Managerial implications of the distinction between normal and inferior goods. • Managerial implications of substitutable and complementary goods. • The relationships among total average, and marginal revenues. • The significance of marginal revenue as a decision criterion.

Chapter 6 begins with the assertion that production is the central function of the organized business enterprise. **Production** is undertaken in the hope of relieving the economic problem of scarcity. But a rational decision to produce any particular good or service is predicated upon the existence of a social phenomenon: an **adequate demand** by other members of society for the fruits of the productive effort. This chapter focuses upon the managerial problem of identifying the characteristics of the demand that may be tapped by the productive enterprise, and the possibility of manipulating (creating, increasing, altering) that demand in the interest of the enterprise. We begin with a consideration of the principles of consumer behaviour.

CONSUMER BEHAVIOUR

We noted the possibility that people may act without engaging in any prior, deliberate decision making. Indeed, there is reason to believe that human beings often engage in such **conditioned responses**. Such responses often occur in circumstances where the decision maker has compiled a great deal of past experience with similar conditions, and where the consequences of choosing among alternative courses of action are essentially trivial. We must also admit the existence of **capricious** actions taken by people who give little or no consideration to the consequences, even when the alternative outcomes are likely to be non-trivial. Each of us probably engages in conditioned response behaviour much of the time, and everyone occasionally indulges in capricious action. While capricious behaviour can not be modelled, conditioned-response behaviour may be treated with a default forecasting model, that is, that tomorrow will be like today because today is like yesterday.

We now turn our attention to the phenomenon of deliberate, rational decision making on the part of the consumer. We must acknowledge two possibilities with respect to the information upon which the consumer must predicate the decision: the consumer either has perfect information about the possible alternatives to be purchased, or the consumer has some information but lacks knowledge of much that is relevant to the decision context. The task of analyzing consumer behaviour would be greatly facilitated if consumers always have all the needed information, but, unfortunately, the world is much different from this ideal situation. We must therefore employ the concept of the **expected value** of the possible outcomes from the consumer's choice. The expected value of a particular consumer choice is the probability-weighted average of all of the possible outcomes resulting from the choice. In the event that the probability of occurrence of one of the possible outcomes is 100 per cent, then the expected value becomes the certain value of the choice. Treating certain value as a special case of expected value, we shall make all subsequent references in this regard to expected value.

The time-honoured term that economists have used to refer to the expected value of the outcome of a consumer choice is 'utility.' **Utility**, or satisfaction, is an amalgam of a wide range of the consumer's attitudes with respect to the results of the choice. Its dimensions include the extent to which the choice is perceived to meet a particular need, and may extend to such nebulous concepts as the pleasure or enjoyment derived from the outcome of the choice. We must also acknowledge the possibility that the outcome of a consumer choice may be negative in the sense that the perceived need was not met by the choice, or that the choice resulted in displeasure or pain (emotional as well as physical).

In the cases of so-called 'big ticket' items that are typically purchased in discrete quantities of ones (for example, houses, cars, boats, cameras, stereo systems, mink coats, etc.), the consumer's choice usually is of the **all-or-nothing** variety, that is, whether or not to make the acquisition. Before the acquisition, the consumer can only estimate the expected value of the choice to acquire the item. Only after the fact of the acquisition (often, long after the fact) can a comparison of the actual outcome be made to the estimate of the expected value made before the acquisition. The rational decision criterion is whether the **expected value** of the choice to acquire is greater than the **cost of the acquisition**. The consumer's decision can be judged to be good or bad only in the retrospective comparison of the actual value of the outcome to the acquisition cost. Intelligent consumers will compile a stock of experience concerning pre-acquisition estimates of expected values compared to post-acquisition realized values. Sellers wishing to manipulate the prospective consumer's demands for their products may attempt to pursue strategies to get the consumers to over-estimate their expected values of the outcomes, or to ignore their accumulated experiences with ex-post realized values relative to ex-ante estimated values.

An even larger proportion of the consumer's choices is not all-or-nothing, but rather more-or-less choices. In these cases, the consumer, after deciding that some of the good or service is needed, must also decide how much to acquire. All of the principles described above apply to the fundamental decision to acquire any of the good or service. But the quantity question requires recognition of an additional decision criterion. Economists have deduced from a great deal of personal and collective experience that consumers, in acquiring successive additional units of most goods or services, tend to realize declining amounts of additional value (that is, utility or satisfaction). This phenomenon is referred to in the economics literature as the 'principle of **diminishing marginal utility**.'

Economists recognize that the consumer may experience an initial surge of realized value from consuming the first few units of the good or service, but they have also become convinced of the certainty of eventual diminishing marginal utility for most goods. The qualification is in regard to goods (alcohol, drugs) or activities (hobbies, sex) that may be addictive or compulsive. Although there is much that is yet unknown in regard to addictive behaviour, it may be hypothesized that the consumer realizes **increasing marginal utility** when consuming successive units of goods that are objects of addiction.

Figure 6.1 illustrates what economists think that a so-called total utility (TU) function and its derived marginal utility (MU) function might look like for a normal good, assuming all other factors are constant. The underlying functional relationship can be given by

$$(1)\ TU_x = f(Q_x / \ldots),$$

that is, the total utility realized in consuming good x is determined by the quantity of x consumed, given all other factors. The graph of the TU function can be perceived to be a two-dimensional section through a three-dimensional utility surface (illustrated in the Appendix to this Chapter). As it is illustrated in panel (a) of Figure 6.1, the TU curve is concave upward initially, over the range from the origin to Q_1. This is the initial consumption range over which the consumer may experience the surge of utility rising at an increasing rate. But beyond Q_1, and up to quantity Q_2, total utility **increases at a decreasing rate**. The key concept here is the decreasing rate of increase of total utility. It is apparent that the total amount of utility realized in the consumption of commodity x reaches a maximum at quantity Q_2. Successive units consumed beyond Q_2 actually yield negative satisfactions, so the total amount of utility decreases. The MU curve is derived from the TU curve according to the principles outlined earlier. We can observe that over the quantity range for which TU is increasing at an increasing rate, from the origin to Q_1, MU rises, reaching a peak at Q_1. Over the quantity range for which TU is increasing at a decreasing rate, MU falls, reaching a value of

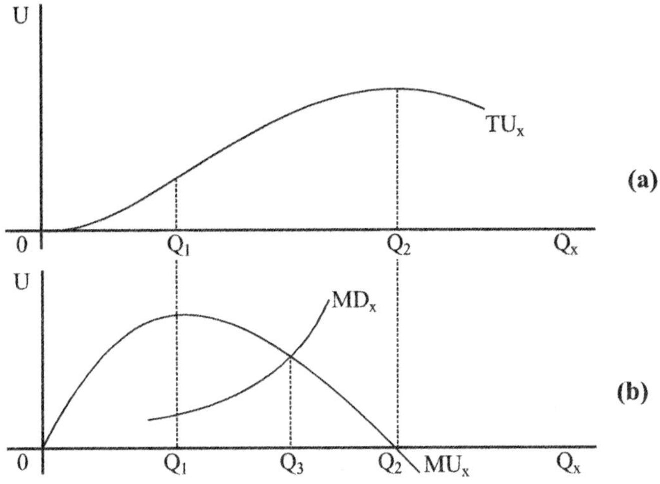

Figure 6.1. Relationship between UT, MU.

zero at Q_2 the quantity at which TU is maximum. The quantity range between Q_1 and Q_2 is described as the range of diminishing marginal utility. And it is this range that economists think represents the usual circumstances under which consumers make most of their choices. The reader is now invited to speculate on the likely appearances of the TU and MU curves for a commodity that is an object of addiction or compulsive consumption.

In the case of a non-addictive good or activity, the rational decision criterion is to continue to consume more of the good, even while realizing declining additional utility, until the marginal value realized in consumption is no longer greater than **the marginal cost of the acquisition**. In order to make such a comparison, the marginal cost of acquisition must be perceived in units comparable to those in which satisfactions are measured. One way to do this is to regard the acquisition cost in terms of dissatisfaction or disutility at having to part with purchasing power to make the acquisition. If the marginal utility does indeed decline, a point at which additional consumption should cease will be reached. In Figure 6.1, curve MD (marginal disutility) represents the marginal cost of acquiring additional units of the commodity (constant as illustrated). The consumer should push consumption to Q_3, beyond which the marginal utility falls below the marginal disutility realized in acquisition.

In the case of a good or activity that is an object of addiction, since the marginal utility always increases as successive units are consumed, no consumption-limiting criterion is ever reached unless the marginal disutility rises to exceed the increasing marginal utility. Even then, it cannot be assumed that the addictive subject can engage in rational choice. An enterprise wishing to promote the sale of its product or service may pursue a strategy designed to induce the consumer to **suffer the illusion** that marginal utility declines at a slower rate than it does in reality, or to believe that marginal utility only increases as with an addictive good or activity. In either case, the naive or unwary consumer may be induced to consume larger quantities than he might with more rational consideration. Intelligent consumers can be expected to add to their stocks of experience such comparisons between ex-ante estimates of expected values of satisfactions and ex-post realizations of actual satisfactions. The manager should be aware that intelligent, experienced, and mature consumers are likely to be more resistant to efforts at **manipulation of their preferences**. The obverse of this principle is that less-experienced consumers (especially children and adolescents) or less-capable adult consumers may be more amenable to preference manipulation. This possibility should raise ethical 'red flags' in the minds of conscientious managers.

Perhaps a less controversial approach to promoting sales of the product is for the enterprise to try to change one or more of the non-quantity **determinants of utility**, which to this point have remained unspecified and assumed constant. One of those surely is the consumer's **taste** for the good or service. An effective promotional strategy may improve the image of the good or service, thereby making it more desirable to the consumer. This will cause the TU curve, and with it the MU curve, to shift upwards and to the right. The reader is invited to envision a modification to Figure 6.1 to illustrate this phenomenon. The shifted MU curve should intersect the MD curve at a quantity larger than Q_3, thus achieving the seller's objective.

THE THEORY OF DEMAND

Demand is the desire for a good or service, together with the purchasing power to make the desire effective, both backed by the willingness of the consumer to part with the purchasing power. The **demand curve** is a graphic representation of the path along which the consumer would rationally choose to purchase quantities of the good or service at various prices. The so-called **Law of Demand** is the hypothesis that consumers will buy ever greater quantities of the good or service at progressively lower prices, that is, acquisition costs. The fundamental behavioural principle underlying the concept of the demand curve is the shape of the marginal utility curve over the range of **diminishing marginal utility**. The connection between demand and utility is that the seller must offer the consumer some inducement to purchase more of the good once his marginal utility has fallen to the level of the disutility realized in acquiring the last unit. The obvious inducement is a **lower price** or acquisition cost. Consumers can be expected to purchase more at lower prices. The inverse is also expected: consumers will purchase smaller quantities at higher prices.

In addition to the marginal utility principle, economists offer two other explanations for the law of demand, the income and substitution effects. The **substitution effect** occurs when an increase in its price leads consumers to shift their purchases away from the good or service and to its substitutes—hence the inverse relationship between the own-price of the good or service and its quantity demanded. A downward change in the price of an item leads to an increase in quantity demanded as consumers shift their purchases away from substitutes and towards the item.

The **income effect** of a price change results from recognition that the consumer is faced with a range of choices. For example, when the price of an item falls, the consumer can purchase more of the item itself, or more of other items that he consumes, or retain unspent purchasing power. The decrease in the price of the item then results in an **implicit** increase of his income. Conversely, an increase in the price of the item means that the consumer must purchase less of an item, less of other items that he normally purchases, or spend more than he has spent in the past. In either case, an inverse relationship between the price of the item and the quantity consumed of it is a consequence.

DEMAND CURVES AND DEMAND SURFACES

To this point we have spoken of demand in regard to the quantities of an item that might be purchased by a single consumer. But demand can also be regarded as a collective concept, that is, as the summation of the quantities of an item that would be purchased by a collection of consumers over the range of possible prices. The collection of consumers may include all who are 'in the market' for the particular item, but it may be more narrowly construed to those who are likely to purchase the item from a particular seller. In the former case we can speak of **market demand**, and in the latter case the demand faced by the particular seller, that is, the **firm's demand**. Whether that for an individual consumer or some collection of consumers, the functional notation representation of the demand relationship may be given by

$$(2)\ Q_X = f(\ P_X\ /\ \ldots\ ),$$

that is, the quantity demanded of a good or service is determined by the price of the good or service, given all other determinants. The functional relationship, f, is presumed to be **inverse** for the relationship between quantity and price. This inverse relationship, that is, the Law of Demand, can be illustrated by drawing a demand curve on a set of coordinate axes for price and quantity as in Figure 6.2. The downward (left to right) slope of the demand curve is a manifestation of the principle of diminishing marginal utility.

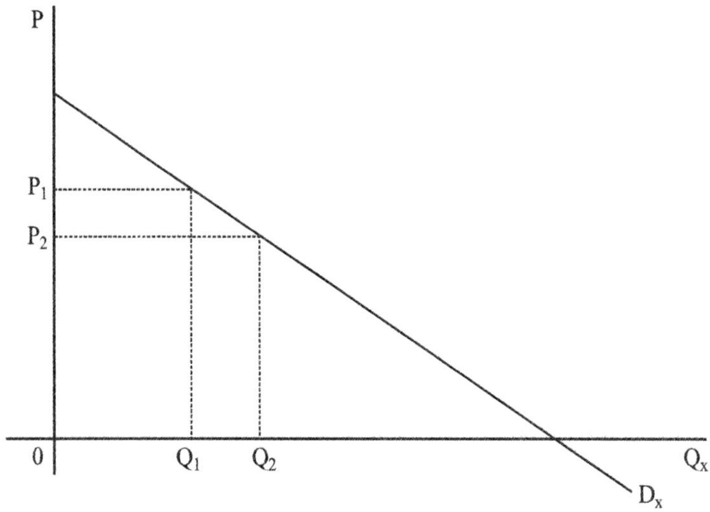

Figure 6.2. Demand curve.

We have drawn the demand curve in Figure 6.2 as a straight line with a negative slope. The equation for such a linear demand curve can be given in slope-intercept form as

$$(3)\ Q_X = c + d(P_X),$$

where c is the quantity-axis intercept, and d is the (assumed negative) slope of the demand curve. The linearity of this demand curve is assumed only for purposes of simplicity. In reality, a demand curve may exhibit any degree of curvature, and it may be concave upward or downward. Even if a straight line can approximate the price-quantity relationship, the linear demand curve may exhibit a range of slopes, from nearly horizontal at one extreme, to almost vertical at the other. And even these extremes are not effective limits on the possible slopes that demand curves may take. If the income effect of a price change of an inferior good were great enough to outweigh the substitution effect, the demand curve would slope upwards from left to right in apparent contradiction to the law of demand.

If the demand curve illustrated in Figure 6.2 can be presumed to be a realistic representation of a real demand relationship for good x, then a decrease of the price from P_1 to P_2 can be expected to lead to an increase in the consumer's purchases of x from Q_1 to Q_2. Economists refer to such a movement from one point to another along a fixed-locus demand curve as a 'change of quantity demanded.' Such a change of quantity demanded is attributable exclusively to a change in the price of the good, given all other determinants.

The demand for any good or service is actually determined by many factors in addition to the price of the good or service. In fact, for some items the price may be one of the lesser-significant determinants of its demand. A more general specification of a demand curve may be given by

$$(4)\ Q_X = f(\ P_X, I, T, B, \ldots, P_y, P_z, \ldots\ ),$$

where I is the income of the consumer, T stands for 'tastes and preferences' (the same tastes and preferences referred to above as determinants of utility), B is the consumer's current level of indebtedness, P_y is the price of a relevant substitute good, and P_z is the price of a related complement good. The ellipsis symbols (...) between B and P_y suggest that there are other non-price demand determinants that have not yet been specified (or even identified). Those following P_z allow for prices of yet other substitute and complement goods.

There is nothing particularly significant about the order in which the determinants of demand are listed on the right side of the equation. The order of the listing can be changed at will, and any one of them can be moved to the head of the queue as required. The price of the good itself (per cent, the good's 'own price') is typically listed in the first position because, historically, the attention of economists turned to this determinant first. Also, in the cases of most goods and services, the **own price** may indeed be the most important or significant (in a statistical sense) determinant of the quantity demanded. Yet any such hierarchy of determinants is something to be discovered by analysis, rather than assumed at the outset.

In order to draw the two-dimensional representation of the demand curve illustrated in Figure 6.2, it was necessary to treat all of the non-own price demand determinants as if they were constant, even if they in fact were not constant (more about this below). A revision of equation (3) to represent this specification is given by

$$(5)\ Q_x = f(\ P_x\ /\ I,\ T,\ D,\ \ldots\ ,\ P_y,\ P_z,\ \ldots\ ),$$

where the slash (/) is used to separate the single demand determinant that is presumed to be variable (P) from all the rest, that are assumed not to change. Indeed, if any of the other determinants are variable, it is technically not even possible to draw a discrete locus for the demand curve in the two-dimensional space of the P-Q coordinate axes.

Economists employ the term 'change of demand' to refer to the circumstance where some determinant of demand other than the item's 'own price' has changed. The effect of such a change is to shift the own-price demand curve from its former locus to some position, as illustrated in Figure 6.3. Here, D_1 is the original locus of the demand curve, and D_2 is the new locus after something other than the price of the good has changed. For example, improving tastes and preferences for the good or service, or a decrease in consumer indebtedness, could possibly explain the illustrated right-ward shift of the demand curve.

Another perspective on the demand-shift phenomenon is provided by a three-dimensional graphic representation of the demand relationship. In this representation, the slash of equation (5) is moved one item to the right,

$$(6)\ Q_x = f(\ P_x,\ I\ /\ T,\ B,\ \ldots\ ,\ P_y,\ P_z,\ \ldots\ ).$$

In this relationship, two demand determinants, P and I, are presumed variable, while all

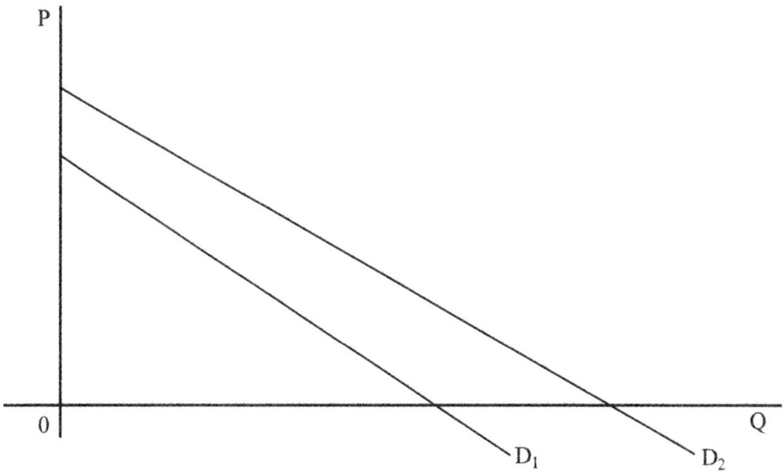

Figure 6.3. Shifing of demand curve.

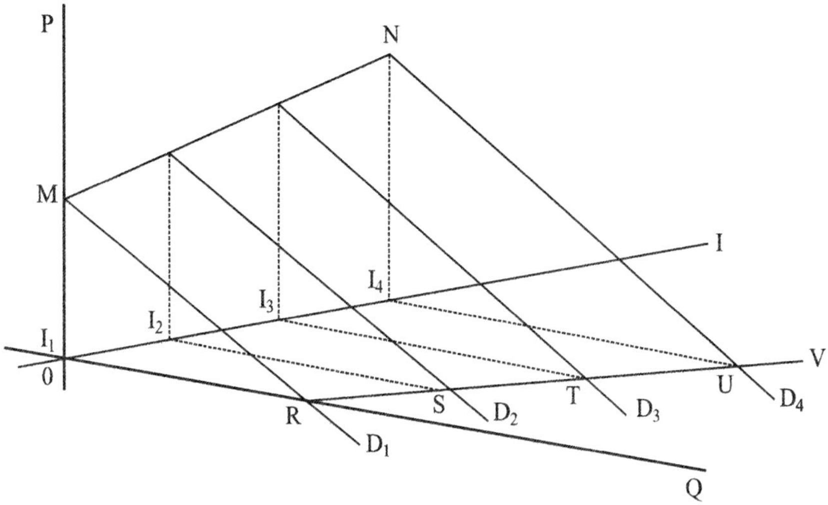

Figure 6.4. Relationship between demand curve.

other possible determinants are treated as if they were constant. A graphic representation of this relationship is given in Figure 6.4, where the third dimension (depth) is occupied by the income determinant. A number of 'slices' (or vertical sections) have been made through the three-dimensional demand surface at different income levels. If the three-dimensional surface were viewed from a perspective opposite the price-quantity plane, in effect collapsing the surface into two dimensions, the viewer would see something like that represented in Figure 6.5. Here, the several vertical slices through the three dimensional surface appear as a demand curve that shifts in two dimensions.

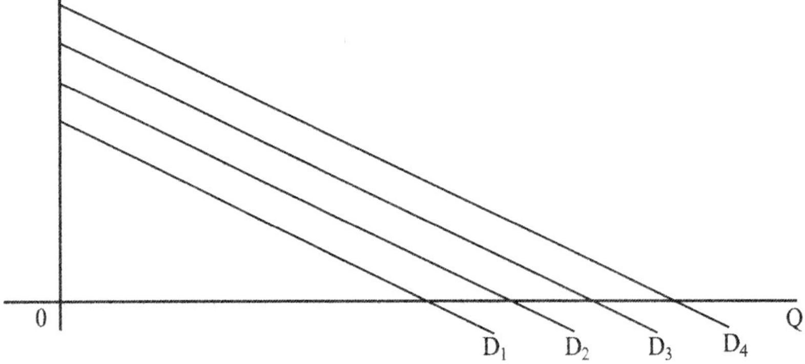

Figure 6.5. Shifing of demand curve.

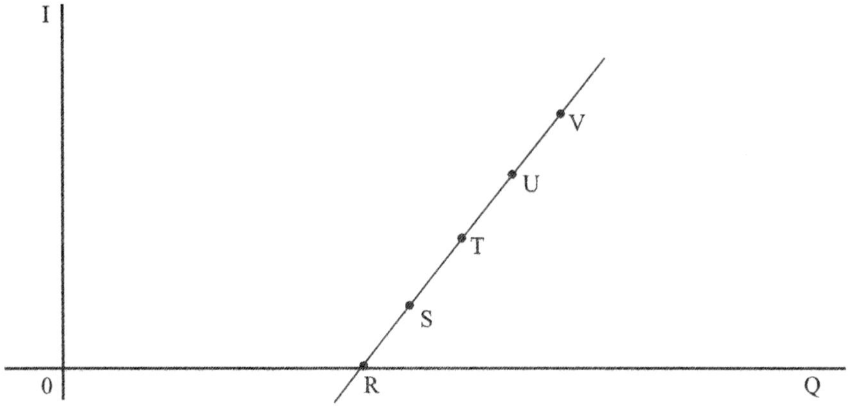

Figure 6.6. 3D Demand curve.

VRML 3-D VIEW

The three-dimensional perspective enables another important observation. In Figure 6.4, the intersection of the demand surface with the floor (the income-quantity plane) traces out path RSTUV, which when viewed from above yields the two dimensional graph illustrated in Figure 6.6. In this figure, income is measured on the vertical axis, and is thus taken to be the demand determinant relative to quantity demanded on the horizontal axis. The path, RSTUV, thus traces out an income-demand curve (or Engel Curve, as it is referred to in the literature), for which the functional notation relationship would be given as

$$(7)\ Q_x = f(\ I\ /\ P_x,\ T,\ D,\ \ldots\ ,\ P_y,\ P_z,\ \ldots\ ).$$

In equation (7), the only variable determinant of demand is presumed to be income, while all other demand determinants, including price, are taken to be constant. As we noted above, price may not be the most significant demand determinant, and it is legitimate to move any of the demand determinants to the head of the list of determinants so that it may be analyzed, assuming all other determinants as givens.

The three-dimensional surface represented in Figure 6.4 is for two demand determinants, own-price and income, relative to quantity demanded. It is unfortunate that we can have access to no more than three graphic dimensions, because this necessarily limits our analysis to no more than two demand determinants at one time as long as we wish to stay with the graphic analysis. (We can treat more than two determinants at one time only by exiting the graphics and entering the realm of multivariate algebra.) However, within the realm of three-dimensional graphics, we can move any two determinants to the head of the determinant queue in order to construct a three-dimensional surface showing the relationship between quantity demanded and the two selected determinants. And by judiciously slicing the three-dimensional surface, we can extract two-dimensional demand curves showing the relationship between quantity demanded and any single demand determinant.

Normal and Inferior Goods

The income-demand curve illustrated in Figures 6.4 and 6.5 happens to slope upwards from left to right (that is, to exhibit a direct relationship between quantity demanded and income), and is therefore illustrative of the phenomenon of a 'normal' good. A normal good is one for which quantity demanded increases when income rises, or decreases when income falls. An 'inferior' good is one for which quantity demanded decreases when income rises, and increases when income falls. The two-dimensional income-demand curve for an inferior good would slope downwards from left to right, with appearance similar to that of an own-price demand curve drawn on a set of price-quantity axes.

Most of the goods and services consumed by human beings are likely to be normal in the sense that people will consume more of them when their incomes rise. But there are also many examples of inferior goods to examine, although the items with respect to which they are inferior should be identified. For example, in the late twentieth century American culture, ground beef is probably inferior to most solid beef cuts; margarine is probably inferior to real butter, and Ford Escorts are probably inferior to Lincoln Town Cars. The word 'probably' is included in the foregoing sentence because of the highly personal nature of preferences.

We should also stress that the characteristics of normalcy and inferiority are time and culture bound. For example, potatoes were probably regarded as inferior substitutes for mutton by eighteenth century Irish peasants, whereas twentieth century Americans tend to regard potatoes as complement to both steaks and hamburgers. The inferiority of potatoes relative to meat has ceased to be an issue for Americans, although the issue may be reopened in a choice between potatoes and rice.

The normalcy or inferiority of a good may be revealed in the income effect consequent upon a price change, as well as with an explicit change of income. We earlier identified the income and substitution effects of a price change as further (in addition to the principle of diminishing marginal utility) explanations of the law of demand. In the case of a normal good, the income effect may be expected to reinforce the substitution effect: when the price of a normal good falls, people will tend to increase their purchases of it, not only because it is now less expensive relative to substitutes, but also because they have realized an implicit increase of income due to the price change. In the case of an inferior good, however, the income effect will offset the substitution effect: when the price of the good falls, people will tend to consume more of it than more expensive substitutes, but the realization of its inferiority retards the increased consumption. Although economists have found little evidence of its existence, it is hypothesized that the income effect in the case of an inferior good may be so great as to more than offset the substitution effect. If such a phenomenon should occur, the own-price demand curve would appear to slope upwards from left to right, and would thus be an apparent violation of the law of demand.

What are the managerial decision implications of inferiority and normalcy? In a growing economy, or during a period of cyclical expansion, the enterprise should attempt to produce normal goods or services since their demands will increase at the same or a faster rate than incomes are rising. The enterprise should avoid production of inferior goods since their demands will increase at a slower rate (or may even decrease) as incomes rise. However, during a period of cyclical decline, the enterprise would be better off in producing inferior goods because their demands will tend to decrease more slowly (or possibly even increase) as incomes fall. But, suppose that the main product lines of the enterprise are inferior goods that must continue in production through periods of expansion as well as contraction. In this case, the design strategy of the enterprise might be to alter the real nature of the product so that it becomes perceived to be a normal good relative to substitutes. Alternately, the enterprise's promotional strategy might be directed towards improving the clientele's tastes and preferences for the good, or altering the image of the good so that it is perceived to be normal rather than inferior.

Substitutes and Complements

Two other demand determinants that deserve the attention of the manager are the prices of substitutes (P_y) and complements (P_z). Each of these determinants may of course be moved to the head of the determinant queue for analysis while assuming all other determinants (including the own-price of the item) constant. The functional notation equation of a substitute good demand relationship would appear as

$$Q_x = f(\ P_y\ /\ P_x,\ I,\ T,\ D,\ \ldots\ ,\ P_z,\ \ldots\ )$$

for which a so-called cross-price demand curve can be constructed. In the case of a substitute good, the cross-price demand curve slopes upwards from left to right because when the price of the substitute P_y is raised, although its quantity demanded Qy will decrease, the quantity demanded of the good Q_x will increase. This increase can be illustrated as a movement upward along the cross-price demand curve, but would be a cause of a rightward shift of the own-price demand curve illustrated in Figure 6.3. We leave it to the reader to imagine the shape of the cross-price demand curve for a complement good, and the own-price demand shift implications of a change in the price of the complement.

The enterprise rarely has ability to directly influence the prices of goods that are substitutes or complements for those produced by the enterprise. But the management of the enterprise should be aware that competitors do produce substitutes for those produced by the enterprise, and that the pricing decisions of competitors can be expected to cause shifts of the own-price demand curves for the enterprise's products. Likewise, the management of the enterprise should be aware that its own pricing decisions will likely result in shifts of the competitor's own-price demand curves, and may induce strategic responses from them. These possibilities will be considered again in a later chapter.

Demand and Revenue

The price of the product can be understood to be its average revenue (AR), or the revenue per unit of the product sold by the enterprise. Thus, the total revenue (TR) that the enterprise will realize on the sale of Q units of its product can be computed by the formula

$$TR = P \times Q,$$

or if total revenue is known, the average revenue, or price, can be computed by solving equation (8) for P, or

$$AR = P = TR/Q.$$

Knowledge of these relationships enables us to derive an equation for a total revenue function from the equation for the demand function, or an equation for the demand function if that for the total revenue function is known. Either such equation can be specified employing the procedures discussed in the last section of this chapter. Suppose that demand equation (3) above has been specified with parameter values c = 20 and d = –4, resulting in equation (10),

$$(10)\ Q = 20 + (-4)P.$$

We have omitted the subscript 'd' in equation (3) for clarity of exposition. In order to derive the total revenue equation, we must first solve equation (10) for P,

$$(11)\ P = 5 - .25Q.$$

Since from equation (8) we know that $TR = P_xQ$, we may derive the total revenue equation (12) by multiplying equation (11) through by Q,

$$P \times Q = 5Q - .25Q^2,$$

$$(12)\ TR = 5Q - .25Q^2.$$

Alternately, had TR equation (12) been specified first, since AR = TR/Q, the AR equation could be derived by dividing the TR equation through by Q,

$$TR/Q = 5Q/Q - .25Q^2/Q,$$

$$(13)\ AR = 5 - .25Q,$$

which is the same as equation (11) when it is recognized that P is the same as AR.

The derivation of these equations by simple algebraic manipulation enables us to illustrate in two dimensions the graphic relationship between AR and TR. The TR curve is shown in panel (a)of Figure 6.7; its associated demand curve (AR) is shown in panel (b). Corresponding average and total revenue curves for a linear demand relationship. Because the demand curve is linear with a negative slope, its associated total revenue curve is a second-order (or quadratic) equation that graphs as a parabola that opens downward and spans the positive-price range of the demand curve on the quantity axis. In Figure 6.7 we have also drawn a box in panel (a) below the demand curve formed by a horizontal at price P_1 and a vertical at quantity Q_1, the quantity that will be sold at price P_1. We have also drawn a vertical in panel (b) below the TR curve a quantity Q_1. By the formula for the area of a rectangle (area = length × width), we can assert that the area of the box in panel (a) measures the total revenue resulting from selling quantity Q_1 at price P_1. This same area is also represented by the altitude of the vertical at Q_1 up to the TR curve in panel (b).

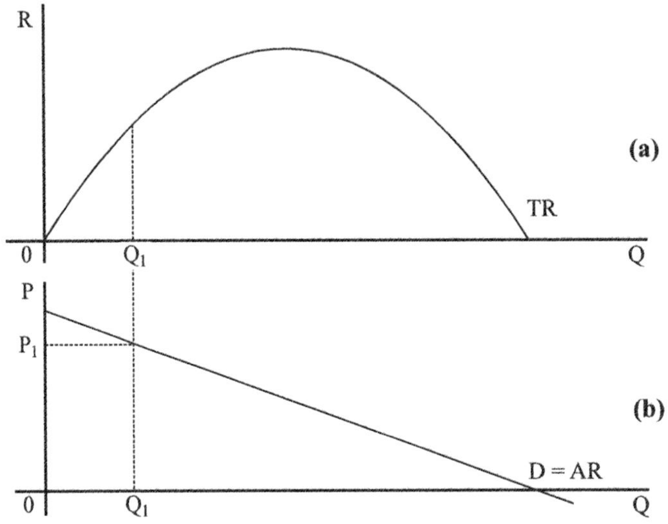

Figure 6.7. Relationship between TR, AR.

Figure 6.8 is a reproduction of Figure 6.7, but with several additional price-quantity boxes drawn below the AR curve, and corresponding verticals drawn below the TR curve. The reader should verify by inspection of the boxes that as price falls towards P_3 and quantity increases

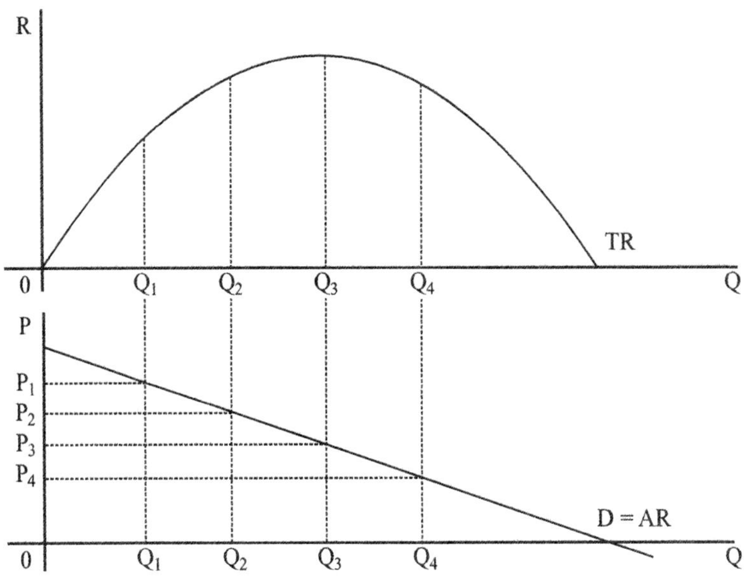

Figure 6.8. Relationship between TR, AR.

accordingly, the boxed areas increase to a maximum corresponding to the tallest vertical below the vertex of the TR parabola. If the demand curve is indeed linear, the maximum total revenue will occur at a quantity that is half the horizontal axis intercept of the demand curve. In Figure 6.8, prices successively lower than P_3 yield revenue rectangles of progressively smaller area. The graphic approach illustrated in Figure 6.8 provides one means of identifying the price-quantity combination that yields the maximum total revenue, but it is not a means that yields an effective decision criterion. However, an alternate approach that employs concepts from the calculus can provide a useful revenue-maximization decision criterion.

The value of Q for which TR is at its maximum value can be found by differentiating the TR function with respect to Q, setting the differential equal to zero, and solving the resulting differential equation for Q. Thus, for TR equation (10),

$$TR = 5Q - .25Q_2,$$

$$(14)\ dTR/dQ = 5 - .5Q.$$

Setting dTR/dQ = 0,

$$0 = 5 - .5Q,$$

and solving for Q,

$$Q = 10.$$

Thus, if the demand curve in panel (a) of Figure 6.8 is a graph of equation (3), the value of Q at Q_3 is 10 units. Further, by substituting 10 for Q in the TR function, the maximized total revenue is found to be

$$TR - 5(10) - .25(10)2 = 25.$$

The revenue maximizing price can be found by substituting Q=10 into the average revenue equation,

$$AR = 5 - .25(10) = 2.5.$$

Thus, if the price denomination is the U.S. dollar and the unit denomination is 1,000 each, a maximum total revenue of \$ 25,000 can be realized by selling 10,000 of the item at a price of \$ 2.50 each.

Economists refer to the differential of TR with respect to Q as the 'marginal revenue' (MR). Conceptually, marginal revenue is the addition to total revenue consequent upon selling one more unit of the item, or

$$MR = \Delta TR/\Delta Q,$$

where ΔQ is 1 unit of the item. This is the approximate equivalent of the definition of the derivative,

$$TR/dQ = \Delta TR/\Delta Q$$

as ΔQ approaches zero. MR can be reconciled to dTR/dQ if it is recognized that the closest that ΔQ can approach to zero is one unit of the item.

Equation (14), the differential of the TR function with respect to Q, can be rewritten as

$$(15)\ MR = 5 - .5Q.$$

A comparison of the MR equation (15) to the AR equation (13) leads to the inference that the two curves must share a common price-axis intercept (in this case 5), but that the slope of the MR function (.5) is twice that of the AR function (.25), and both are negative. This means that the MR curve must slope downwards more steeply than does the AR curve. Figure 6.9 is a reproduction of Figure 6.7 but with the MR curve drawn in. The most important observation to make in regard to Figure 6.9 is that the MR curve reaches zero at the quantity level for which the TR parabola attains its maximum value. This corresponds to the calculus procedure of setting the differential of TR equal to zero in order to find the Q for which TR is maximum.

The relationships described above provide a most useful managerial decision criterion. If the objective of the enterprise is to produce a quantity of an item and sell it at a price that yields the maximum possible revenue, it can do so by finding the quantity for which marginal revenue is zero.

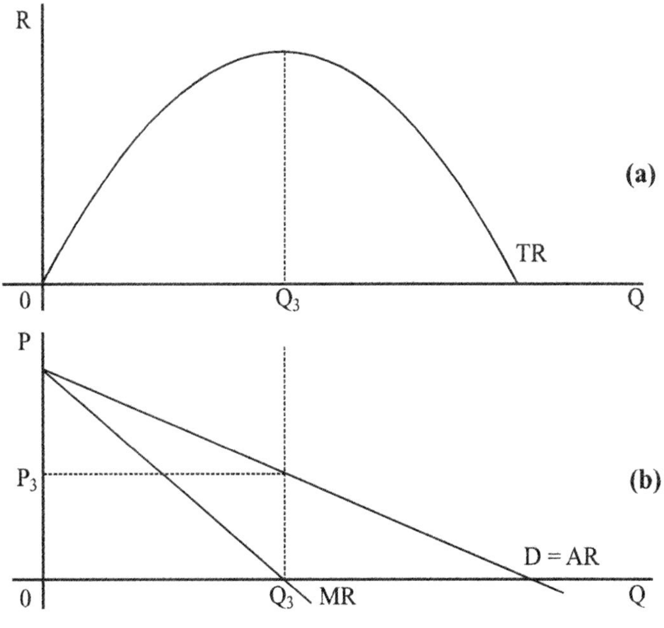

Figure 6.9. Relationship between TR, AR & MR.

We qualify this conclusion immediately by noting that simple revenue maximization may not be the behavioural objective of the management of the enterprise. Rather, the management may be oriented towards profit maximization (which, as we shall see in later chapters, is not likely to coincide with revenue maximization). Even so, we shall discover subsequently that marginal revenue is one of the two decision criteria that are relevant to profit maximization.

WHAT'S AHEAD

The following chapter extends the concepts developed in this chapter into the realm of the statistical estimation of the demand function. A decision criterion, elasticity of demand, is first elaborated, then the implications for elasticity of demand of various specification problems are considered.

Summary of Important Points

1. The theory of consumer behaviour underlies the theory of demand.
2. Because consumers typically lack perfect *ex ante* information about their decision contexts, they must base their acquisition decisions upon a comparison of *ex ante* expected values with acquisition costs.
3. With notable exceptions, the realization of satisfaction in consumption obeys the principle of diminishing marginal utility.
4. Objects of compulsive consumption or addiction may violate the principle of diminishing marginal utility.
5. Managerial strategies may include efforts to manipulate the preferences of consumers or to change the non-quantity determinants of utility.
6. The law of demand is based upon the principle of diminishing marginal utility as well as substitution and income effects.
7. The own-price demand curve, a visual representation of the relationship between quantity demanded and the item's own price, all other determinants assumed constant, may be perceived as a two-dimensional slice through a three-dimensional surface.
8. A change in the price of the item will result in a change of quantity demanded, represented as a movement from one point to another along the own-price demand curve.
9. The locus of an own-price demand curve depends upon the non-price determinants of demand; the own-price demand curve shifts (or a different slice is taken through the surface) if any of the non-price determinants of demand change.
10. An income demand curve depicts the relationship between quantity demanded and income, all other determinants assumed constant; the income demand curve exhibits a direct relationship for a normal good, and an inverse relationship for an inferior good.

Contd.....

11. Managers will be expected to prefer to produce normal goods in a growing economy and during economic expansion; it would be rational to choose to produce inferior goods in a declining economy or during an economic contraction.
12. A cross-price demand curve depicts the relationship between the quantity demanded of an item and the price of a substitute or a complement; changes of cross prices cause shifts of the own-price demand curve.
13. The total revenue resulting from sale of an item is the product of its price and quantity sold; the average revenue, identical with price, is total revenue per unit sold.
14. If the demand curve for an item is linear, the total revenue from its sale is maximum at the price-quantity combination represented by the midpoint of the demand curve.
15. The output required for revenue maximization may be found by differentiating the revenue function, setting the differential equal to zero, and solving for the output level; the marginal revenue is zero when total revenue is maximum.

Significant Terms

Behaviour
conditioned response
capriciousness
deliberate decision
expected value
certain value
utility; total, marginal
diminishing marginal utility
addictive, compulsive behaviour
demand, law of demand
income, substitution effects
demand curve
individual, market demand
inferior good
change of quantity demanded
determinants of demand
own price
change of demand
demand shift
demand surface
normal good
substitutes, complements
cross-price demand curve
revenue
average revenue

Questions for Discussion

1. Explain how conditioned response behaviour can be modelled and forecast.
2. How can a decision context be modelled if the decision maker has some information, but lacks knowledge of much that is relevant to the decision context.
3. What is the economic criterion for a consumer to use in deciding whether or not to acquire an item?
4. How can a consumer judge whether a choice to acquire an item was a good decision?
5. Critically evaluate a seller strategy to try to get consumers to over-estimate the expected value of the outcome of a consumer purchase.
6. Explain how an 'all-or-nothing' acquisition decision differs from a 'more-or-less' acquisition decision; how do the decision criteria differ?
7. Describe the phenomenon of 'diminishing marginal utility' and discuss its decision significance.
8. Explore possible exceptions or violations to the principle of diminishing marginal utility, and discuss the decision implications.
9. Explain how a marginal utility function can be derived from a total utility function, and describe the shape of the latter in relation to the shape of the former.
10. Why would a rational consumer continue to consume more of a good even while realizing declining additional utility?
11. Identify an appropriate criterion that might be used by a consumer in deciding whether to continue to consume additional units of a good.
12. Critically evaluate utility-related strategies that the management of a firm might attempt to use in getting its customers to purchase more of its product.
13. How does the law of demand relate to utility theory?
14. Explain why demand curves normally slope downwards from left to right.
15. Discuss possible exceptions to the law of demand and indicate the sources of the exceptions in utility theory.
16. Explain how variables other than the good's 'own price' are treated in the construction of a two-dimensional demand curve.
17. Distinguish a 'change of demand' from a 'change of quantity demanded' and indicate possible causes of each; what is the managerial significance of the distinction?
18. Explain a 'change of demand' with reference to a three-dimensional demand surface.

19. Describe the possible shapes of an income-demand curve and indicate the possible causes of the different slopes.

20. Distinguish inferior from normal goods and explain how these characteristics are revealed in own-price and income demand curves.

21. What are the managerial decision implications of inferiority and normalcy of goods in the firm's product line?

22. Distinguish substitutes and complements and explain the effects of changes in the prices of such goods upon the own-price demand curve.

23. Identify a so-called 'cross price' demand curve and discuss the significance of it to managerial decision making.

24. Explain how, once the equation of a demand curve has been estimated, the analyst can generate the equations of the total and marginal revenue functions.

25. Describe the relationships among total, average, and marginal revenue graphs, and discuss the managerial significance of the relationships.

26. Show how the marginal revenue can be derived from a total revenue function via differential calculus.

27. Discuss the managerial decision significance of marginal revenue.

Appendix 6.1

PREFERENCE AND INDIFFERENCE

In this appendix, we pursue the alternative approach for analyzing consumer behaviour. In the following discussions we shall not attempt an exhaustive exploration of the approach, but shall develop only those concepts necessary to requirements in subsequent chapters.

THE HORIZONTAL SLICE

Figure AVI(a) illustrates a consumer's three-dimensional utility surface with utility measured vertically against the quantities of two goods, X and Y, represented on the floor axes. The functional notation representation of the utility surface is

$$U = f(X, Y / \ldots),$$

or 'utility depends upon the quantities of goods X and Y consumed, given all else.' The total utility function may be perceived to be a vertical slice through the three-dimensional utility surface taken parallel to the X axis and at some (given) quantity of good Y. Any number of such vertical slices

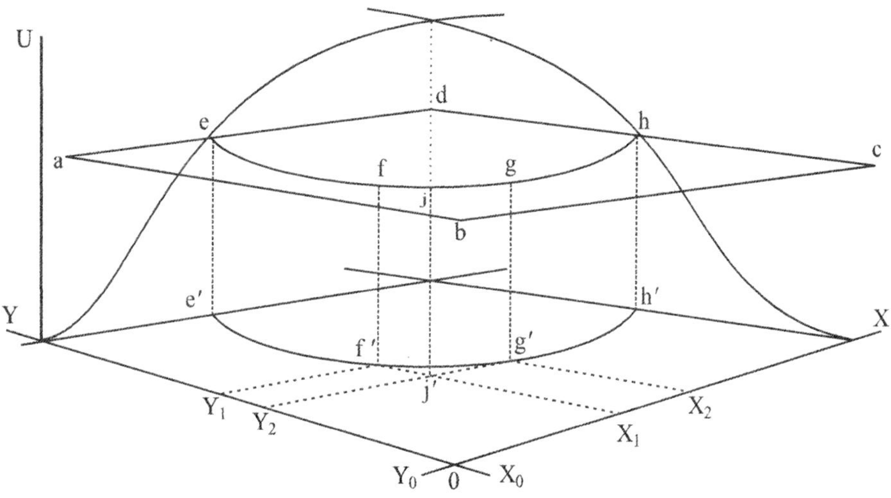

Figure A-VI(a). Three dimensional utility surface.

may be taken at various quantities of good Y, or vertical slices may be taken parallel to the Y axis for various quantities of good X.

As illustrated in Figure A-VI(a), the alternative analytical approach to consumer behaviour is to pass a plane, abcd, parallel to the floor of the utility surface at some utility level altitude, say I_4, tracing out the horizontal slice, efgh. The path, e'f'g'h', in the floor of the surface is the vertical projection of the slice through the surface. Slice efgh is only one of an infinite number of slices which could be taken through the surface at different utility altitudes.

THE INDIFFERENCE CURVE MAP

Figure A-VI(b) shows a two-dimensional view from a perspective above the surface illustrated in Figure A-VI(a). In effect, the three-dimensional surface appears to be collapsed into the floor when viewed from above, but the path e'f'g'h' represents the slice through the surface at utility altitude I_4. Economists refer to the e'f'g'h' path as an iso-utility curve (meaning same utility) because it represents a sequence of points, the (K,L) coordinates of which are the combinations of the two goods which can yield the I_4 level of utility. For example, utility I_4 can be realized with the X_1 quantity of good X combined with the Y_1 quantity of good Y. Utility I_4 can also be realized with Y_2 if a larger, X_2, is consumed. This suggests that good X and good Y are to some extent substitutable for one another in the consumer's preferences. Since path e'f'g'h' is drawn as a continuous curve, the implication is that there are an infinite number (or as many as there are points along the path) of combinations of X and Y which can yield the I_4 utility level.

Economists also refer to path e'f'g'h' as an 'indifference curve. The reason is that the consumer should be indifferent between the combinations of goods represented by different points

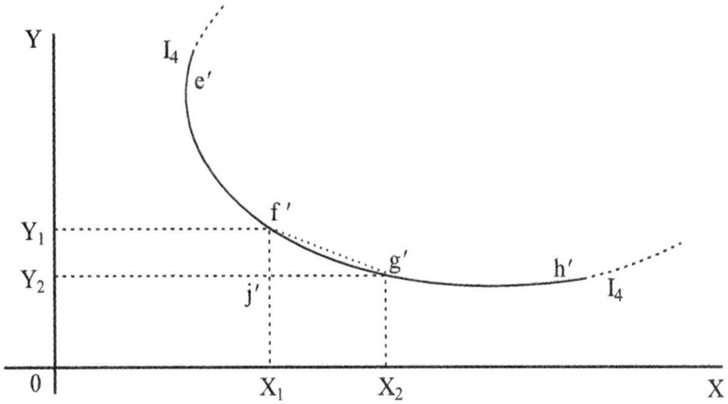

Figure A-VI(b). Two dimensional utility surface.

along the same iso-utility curve because they all yield the same level of utility. Combination (X_1, Y_1) at point f' yields the I_4 level of utility, but so also does combination (X_2, Y_2) at point g'. However, the consumer would prefer combinations of X and Y at utility level I_4 to any combination of X and Y which yields a lower level of utility. But the consumer would give preference to any combination of X and Y which yields a higher level of utility than I_4. We will refer to such curves as indifference curves rather than iso-utility curves in subsequent discussions.

Suppose that instead of selecting an (X,Y) combination represented by a point along the indifference curve, the consumer chooses the Y_2 quantity of good Y with the smaller X_2 quantity of good X, reaching point j on the utility surface in Figure A-VI(a), and j' in Figure A-VI(b). It should be apparent that the smaller quantity of good x combined with less of good y will yield some utility level lower than I_4.

Figure A-VI(c) is an elaboration of Figure A-VI(b) to show the paths of several other 'representative' indifference curves which could be generated by horizontally slicing the surface at altitudes other than I_4. It is now apparent that the X_1 quantity of good X along with the Y_2 amount of good Y can yield only the I_3 level of utility, which is less than I_4 level. Theoretically, any number of such indifference curves could be generated by slicing the utility surface at different altitudes so that the floor of the surface might appear 'dense' with concentric indifference curves. The collection of representative indifference curves may be referred to as an indifference curve map. The indifference curve map may be likened to the collection of isotemp or isobar lines on a weather map, or to the contour lines on a geological or military map.

Suppose that the horizontal slices taken through the surface to generate the indifference curve map illustrated in Figure A-VI(b) were taken at successively higher utility altitudes which are equal utility increments apart. In this case, (I_2- I_1) would be equal to (I_3- I_2), and so on. When viewed from above the surface in Figure A-VI(a), the indifference curve map illustrated in Figure A-VI(b) betrays the likely shape of the surface which cannot be seen explicitly in Figure A-VI(b). From indifference curve I_1 up to indifference curve I_4 the indifference curves appear to be getting

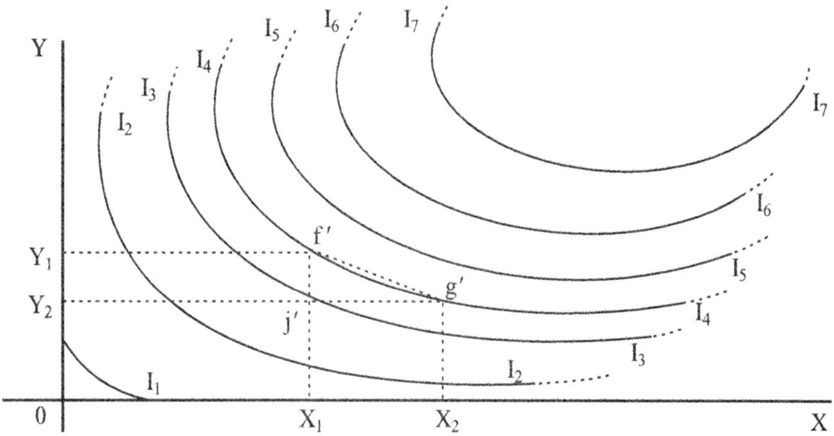

Figure A-VI(c). Several indifference curve.

closer together, implying that the surface is increasing at an increasing rate in the utility dimension. This corresponds to the range from the origin to Q_1 along the total utility curve illustrated in panel (a) of Figure 6.1. From indifference curve I_4 through indifference curve I_7 the indifference curves appear to become farther apart, suggesting that utility is increasing at a decreasing rate. This corresponds to the range from the origin to Q_1 along the total utility curve illustrated in panel (a) of Figure 6.1. The reader is invited to analyze the likely shapes of the indifference curve maps which could be generated from the surfaces linear and second-order (quadratic) shapes.

THE MARGINAL RATE OF SUBSTITUTION

The slope of an indifference curve at any point may be measured by the slope of a tangent drawn to the curve at the point, or it may be approximated by the slope of a chord connecting two points near to each other along the indifference. For example, the slope of the I_4 indifference curve over the f' to g' range in Figure A-VI(c) can be approximated by the slope of the chord from f' to g', or

$$(1)\Delta Y/\Delta X = (Y_2 - Y_1)/(X_2 - X_1) = f'j'/j'g'$$

The technical name for this slope is the Marginal Rate of Substitution (MRS). The MRS is interpreted as the rate at which the consumer can substitute good X for good Y while remaining at the same level of utility. Over the f'g' arc of the I_4 indifference curve, the consumer can maintain utility at the I_4 level as the good Y amount is reduced from Y_1 to Y_2 only by increasing the quantity of good X consumed from X_1 to X_2. It should be obvious that between f' and g' the MRS is negative since Y_2 is less than Y_1. The MRS will normally be negative over the economic range of consumption.

It will be instructive to examine the right triangle formed by the points f', g', and j'. As we have just noted, the ratio of the sides of this triangle, f'j'/j'g', measures the slope of the third side (or hypotenuse), which forms the f'g' chord. The diagonal movement from f' to g' may be regarded as two separate adjustments represented by the vertical and horizontal sides of the triangle. Specifically, the movement from f' to j' is a decrease in the consumption of the Y good ($-\Delta Y$) which, other things remaining the same, would decrease the consumer's utility from I_4 to I_3, or $-\Delta I_1$. The movement from j' to g' is an increase in the consumption of X (ΔX), which by itself would cause output to increase from I_3 to I_4, or ΔI_2. ΔI_2 is of the same magnitude, but opposite sign, as ΔI_1, so we shall use ΔI without sign or subscript to refer to both quantities. Identification of the utility changes allows us to specify the marginal utilities of good X and good Y as

$$(2)\ MU_Y = \Delta I/\Delta Y \text{ and } MU_X = \Delta I/\Delta X$$

Further, we may note that the ratio of the marginal utility of good X to the marginal utility of good Y also measures the MRS:

$$(3)\ MU_X/MU_Y = (D\Delta I/\Delta X) / (\Delta I/\Delta Y) = \Delta Y/\Delta X = MRS.$$

This point will prove of value in subsequent discussion.

THE CONSUMER'S BUDGET

The indifference curve map provides information about consumption possibilities, but by itself cannot provide the consumer with a criterion for selecting an optimal combination of two goods. Additional information is needed in the consumer's budget (or that portion which is reserved for the two goods) and the prices of the two goods, X and Y. Suppose that the prices of good X and good Y are P_X and P_Y, and the consumer has determined that the budgeted outlay must be limited to the dollar sum B. This information can be brought together in the following equation:

$$(4)\ X*P_X + Y*P_Y <= B.$$

The sense of this equation is that the product of the number of units of good X consumed (X) times its price (P_X) plus the number of units of good Y consumed (Y) times its price (P_Y) cannot exceed the budgeted outlay (B). The consumer could under-expend the budget, but suppose that the consumer typically commits the entire budget to the purchase of quantities of good X and good Y so that the inequality symbol may be ignored. What quantities of each good should the consumer purchase in order to maximize the consumer's utility?

Equation (4) can be usefully rearranged in the following format:

$$(5)\ Y = (B / P_Y) - (P_X / P_Y) * X.$$

Equation (5) is linear and in the so-called 'slope-intercept' format, $y = a + bx$, where the slope of the line which represents the equation is the ratio of the price of labour (P_X) to the price of capital (P_Y). It should be noted that this ratio is negative. The conceptual interpretation of this

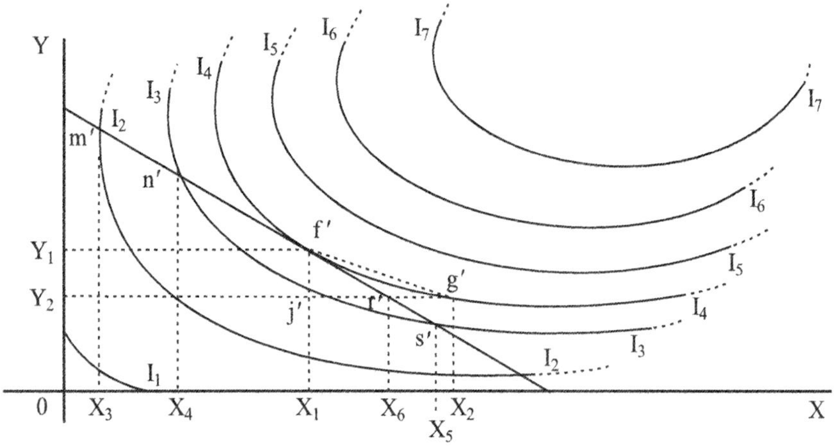

Figure A-VI(d). Equilibrium on indifference curve.

slope is the rate at which the consumer can substitute good X for good Y while remaining within the budget. The vertical axis intercept is the ratio of the budgeted outlay (B) to the price of good Y (P_Y), which determines the maximum amount of good Y which could be purchased by the consumer if he or she purchased none of good X. Equation (5), henceforth referred to as the budget line, can be plotted on the same set of coordinate axes containing the indifference curve map. We may suppose that the values of B, P_X, and P_Y are such that the budget line is plotted as in Figure A-VI(d).

THE OPTIMAL COMBINATION OF GOODS

At what point along the budget line should the consumer select a combination of good X and good Y? As the reader has likely already guessed, the relevant decision criterion is a comparison of the slopes of the indifference curve and the budget line, that is, whether

$$(6)\ \text{MRS} >=< (P_X / P_Y).$$

Point m' is one option involving a large amount of good Y with a small amount of good X. At point m' the slope of the indifference curve, though negative, is very steep, implying that if the consumer were to give up the (Y_3- Y_4) quantity of good Y, he or she could purchase the (X_4- X_3) quantity of good X while remaining within the budget. This additional quantity of good X is a great deal more than the consumer would have to have to remain at the I_2 level of utility. In fact, to exchange the (Y_3- Y_4) quantity of good Y for the (X_4- X_3) quantity of good X would enable the consumer to move to a higher level of utility on indifference curve I_3 at point n'. This is obviously a good move which the consumer should undertake. The reader is now invited to repeat this analysis using point n' as the departure point.

Suppose that the consumer maker had first determined to try the input combination represented by point s'. At this point the consumer purchases a relatively large quantity of good X along with substantially less of good Y. The MRS at point s' is negative, but quite small (that is, the slope of the indifference curve is shallow). The consumer is considering replacing the $(X_5 - X_6)$ quantity of good X with additional good Y. Only a small amount of additional good Y will be needed to allow the consumer to remain at the same level of utility, I_3. However, by giving up the $(X_5 - X_4)$ quantity of good X the consumer can still remain within the budget by purchasing the $(Y_6 - Y_5)$ quantity of good Y, which will enable the consumer to increase utility almost to the I_4 level. This is a good move which the consumer should undertake.

As may be readily deduced, the consumer will find a utility-increasing incentive to substitute good X and good Y by moving downwards along the budget line from points such as m' and n' until the incentive disappears. Likewise, a similar incentive will be found to move upwards along the budget line from points such as r' and s' until the incentive is eliminated.

When does the substitution incentive expire? This occurs when a point is reached along the budget line where the slope of the budget line is just equal to the slope of the indifference curve. At such a point, for example, f' in Figure A-VI(d), the conceptual interpretation is that the rate at which the consumer can substitute good X for good Y while remaining at the same level of utility (the MRS) is just equal to the rate at which the consumer can substitute good X for good Y while remaining within its outlay budget (P_X/P_Y). This is the point of tangency of the budget line with an indifference curve. It is also the highest-utility indifference curve which the budget line can reach. At this point the consumer will have found the utility-maximizing combination of good X and good Y, given the limitation of the budgeted outlay.

SUBSTITUTION AND INCOME EFFECTS

In Figure A-VI(e), budget line B1 represents the initial conditions under which the consumer can purchase quantities of X and Y, given their respective prices, while not exceeding the budget. The slope of the budget line is measured by the ratio, P_X/P_Y. The consumer thus can maximize utility at point J, the tangency of the budget line with indifference curve I_4, purchasing the quantities X_1 and Y_1.

Suppose that the price of one of the items, say X, falls. In order to illustrate the point with a graphic change which can be easily examined, we shall make the heroic assumption that the price falls by half, thus allowing the consumer to purchase twice as much X relative to each quantity of Y as before the price change. The new budget line is illustrated as B_2 in Figure A-VI(e). Now the consumer can realize a higher maximum utility at point K, the tangency of the B_2 budget line with indifference curve I_5, purchasing quantities X_2 and Y_2.

However, this increase of utility consequent upon the price change is composed of two effects, a substitution effect as the consumer shifts purchases away from other goods to X, and an income effect due to the fact that with a lower price of something in the consumer's budget, the consumer can now purchase more of all goods. These two effects may be illustrated by hypothetically removing enough from the consumer's budget at the new P_X/P_Y price ratio to return the consumer to the former level of utility, I_4. This would be represented by the budget line B3, which reaches

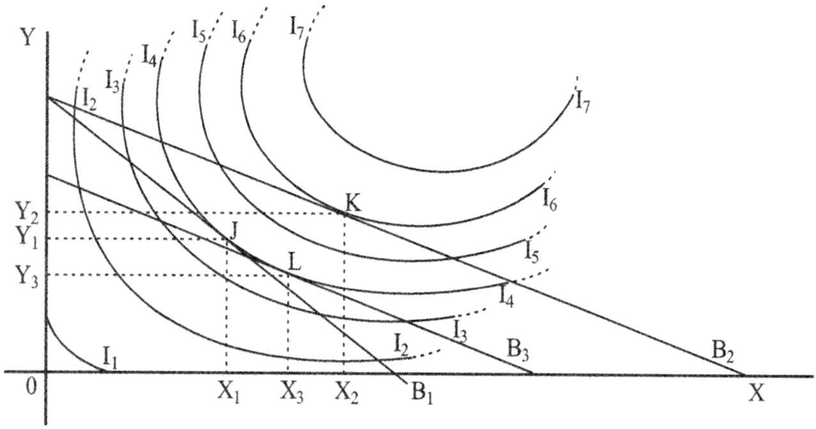

Figure A-VI(e). Equilibrium on indifference curve.

tangency with indifference curve I_4 at point L where the consumer would purchase quantities X_3 and Y_3.

The substitution effect now can be illustrated in Figure A-VI(e) as the movement along the original indifference curve, I_4, from point J to point L. In order to remain at the same level of utility as the price of X falls, the consumer would purchase a larger quantity, X_3, but a smaller quantity, Y_3. However, with the implicit increase in purchasing power of the consumer's income consequent upon the fall in the price of X, the budget line implicitly shifts from B_3 to B_2, allowing the consumer to purchase the larger quantities, X_2 and Y_2.

We may note that in the case of a normal good as illustrated, the income effect is in the same direction as the substitution effect, and thereby reinforces the substitution effect. With the fall in the price of X the consumer purchases more of X due to the substitution effect, and yet more of X due to the income effect. In the case of a normal good, the demand curve slopes downwards from left to right for two reasons; the substitution effect and the income effect. The reader is invited to construct a graphic analysis to illustrate the substitution and income effects consequent upon a price increase.

In the case of an inferior good, the income effect is in the opposite direction to that of the substitution effect, and therefore offsets (at least partially) the substitution effect. In such a case, with a fall in the price of X, more of good X is purchased due to the substitution effect, but not as much more as might have been purchased had there been no offsetting income effect.

In the case of an inferior good, the demand curve still slopes downward from left to right, but only because the substitution effect is strong enough to be only partially offset by the income effect, but not overwhelmed by it. The reader is invited to imagine the shape of the indifference curve map for two goods, X and Y, to illustrate the case of an inferior good consequent upon price changes in either direction.

Alfred Marshall, in his 1890 *Principles of Economics,* made anecdotal reference to a phenomenon reputed to have been observed by Sir Robert Giffen during the 19th century potato famine in Ireland. With the decrease in the availability of potatoes, a staple of the Irish peasants' diet, the price of potatoes increased substantially. Because the peasants' income were so meagre, they could not get enough calories by substituting more expensive sources, such as mutton, for the higher-priced potatoes. So according to Giffen they attempted to buy more potatoes at the higher prices to replace even the small amounts of mutton they had formerly consumed in their diets. Economists have subsequently looked far and wide for empirical evidence of the existence of so-called 'Giffen goods.' However, the search has to date been fruitless since no verifiable empirical evidence has yet been found to substantiate the actual existence of a Giffen good.

Giffen goods if they could be identified, would be inferior goods with such strong and offsetting income effects as to completely over-power their substitution effects when their prices change. In the case of a Giffen good, the demand curve would be sloped upwards. Again, the reader is invited to imagine the likely shapes of the indifference curves in an indifference curve map of a good which has such a strong offsetting income effect that it would be a Giffen good.

The managerial implications of income and substitution effects lie in determining the degree of price elasticity of the demand curve.

—oo(O)oo—

Chapter 7

Elasticity and Demand Specification

Topics covered in this chapter

• The slope of the demand curve as a decision criterion. • Own-price elasticity of demand as a decision criterion. • The ranges of own-price demand elasticity. • The revenue significance of demand elasticity. • The general applicability of the elasticity concept. • Use of calculus in computing demand elasticity. • The need for an average arc elasticity formula. • Income elasticity as an identifier of normal, inferior goods. • Cross elasticity as an identifier of substitute, complement goods. • Cross elasticity as an index of penetration, insulation. • The process of estimating a demand function. • Formal vs. informal estimating methods. • Assessment of the statistical significance of an estimated demand function. • Cross-sectional and time-series data approaches. • Causes of specification errors. • Causes of identification problems. • Remedies for specification errors and identification problems. • The relationship between the identification problem and the elasticity of demand.

In this chapter we extend the concepts developed in earlier chapters into the realm of statistical estimation of the demand function. First, we consider the concept of elasticity of demand as a decision criterion. Then, after we have discussed the procedures for the specification of a demand function, we consider the implications of various specification problems for the elasticity of demand.

REVENUE AND ELASTICITY

The **slope** of the own-price demand curve, $\Delta Q/\Delta P$, contains some information which may be useful to the management of the enterprise. It may be interpreted as the number of units by which quantity sold can be expected to change in response to a change in the price of the item, given all other determinants of demand. If the management is interested in nothing more than predicting the number of additional units which can be sold by changing price, the slope of the own-price demand curve is an entirely adequate decision criterion. However, if the management is concerned about profitability or one of its components, the revenue generated in selling the item, the simple slope of the own-price demand curve is an inadequate decision criterion. The reason for its inadequacy is that the slope of a linear own-price demand curve never changes over its entire positive-price range, but, as became apparent in the previous chapter, **total revenue** does differ from one point to another along the demand curve.

Even if the slope of the demand curve does change because it is not linear, the simple slope still fails to convey information about how the revenue of the firm changes consequent upon a price change. A more useful revenue-oriented decision criterion can be constructed by computing the ratio of the percentage change of quantity demanded to the percentage change in the price which resulted in the quantity change, or

$$\%\Delta Q \ / \ \%\Delta P.$$

Economists refer to this ratio as the **own-price elasticity of demand**, and they interpret it as a measure of the sensitivity (or responsiveness) of quantity demanded to a change in the item's own price. The revenue-related importance of the own-price elasticity can be illustrated by demand equation Qx = 80 - 4Px, which is graphed in Figure 7.1. The linear demand curve has been divided into ranges indicated by brackets. The upper portion of the demand curve, from price of $ 20 down to $ 10, is labelled the **elastic range**. It is characterized by positive marginal revenues and elasticity ratios (absolute values) greater than unity. The lower portion of the demand curve,

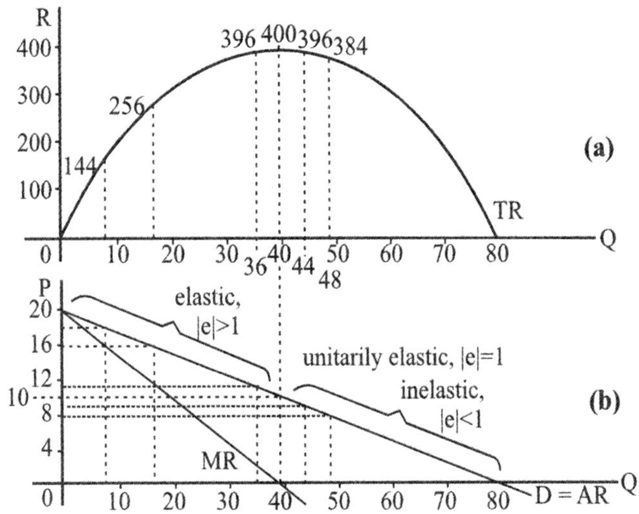

Figure 7.1. Demand, revenue, and elasticity for Q_x=80 - 4P_x.

from price $ 10 down to $ 0, is labelled the **inelastic range**. It is characterized by negative marginal revenues and fractional elasticity ratios (again, absolute values). The midpoint of the linear demand curve (at price $ 10) is labelled the **unitarily elastic** point because the absolute value of the demand elasticity ratio is precisely 1.0 at this point. Demand at the unitarily elastic point is also characterized by zero marginal revenue.

In the elastic range of the demand curve, any particular percentage decrease of price will result in a larger percentage increase of quantity demanded. Thus, what is lost to revenue by cutting price is more than made up for in increased quantity sold, so total revenue increases. For example, if price is lowered from $ 18 to $ 16, quantity demanded will increase from 8 units to 16 units, and total revenue will increase from $ 144 to $ 256. Price fell by 11 per cent, but this was more than made up for by a 100 per cent increase in quantity sold.

However, in the elastic range of the demand curve, any particular percentage increase of price will result in a larger-percentage decrease of quantity demanded, thus causing a decrease of total revenue. In this case, what is gained in raising the price is more than offset by the loss in quantity sold. Thus, if the manager can verify that the enterprise is presently selling the item at a point in the elastic range of the demand curve, the appropriate direction in which to change price in order to increase revenue is down.

The opposite conclusions emerge for the inelastic range of the demand curve. A price cut in the inelastic range will result in an increase of quantity demanded, albeit one of a smaller percentage magnitude, so that total revenue can be expected to decrease. If the objective is to increase revenue, price should be raised because a smaller-percentage decrease in quantity demanded will result. In the example illustrated in Figure 7.1, a price cut from $ 9 to $ 8 will result in an increase of quantity sold from 44 to 48 units, but a decrease of total revenue from $ 396 to $ 384.

Small percentage changes of price in the near neighbourhood of the unitarily elastic point of the demand curve will be offset by the same percentage changes of quantity demanded (but in the opposite direction), thereby leaving revenue unchanged. In our example, if price is raised from $ 9 to $ 11, quantity demanded will fall from 44 to 36 units, leaving total revenue unchanged at $ 396.

If the enterprise were to progressively lower price, moving down the demand curve from its intercept with the price axis towards its intercept with the quantity axis, total revenue would increase to a maximum (at the unitarily elastic point), and then decrease; concurrently, marginal revenue would decrease from positive values, through zero (at the unitarily elastic point), to negative values. And, elasticity would fall from (absolute) values greater than unity to (absolute) values less than unity.

The significance of own-price elasticity of demand is that it is indicative of what is likely to happen to the enterprise's revenues when it changes the price of an item which it sells. Enterprise managers may not explicitly compute elasticity ratios, and they may not use the term 'elasticity of demand'. However, we may infer that they must have employed an elasticity thought process in making a rational decision to change price if their enterprises have survived and are profitable.

To this point we have assumed that the demand curve is linear, but only for purposes of simplicity. Since only one point on a demand curve exists at any moment (all other points are only

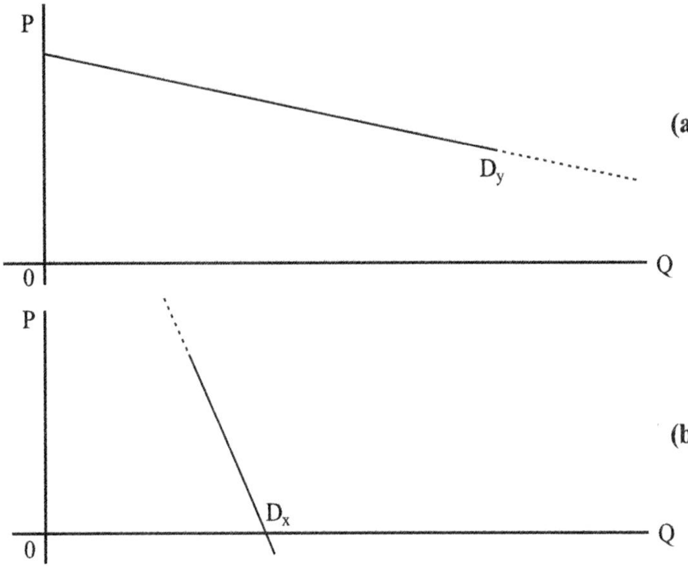

Figure 7.2. 'Elastic' and 'inelastic' demand curves.

hypothetical or virtual), it can be argued that the shape of the demand curve away from the extant point (whether curved, bent, kinked, etc.) is really a non-issue. But, even if the demand curve is curvilinear, all of the elasticity formulas introduced in this chapter can be applied to compute or estimate the elasticity of demand. Graphically, whether demand is elastic or inelastic at a particular point on a non-linear demand curve can be discerned by observing the characteristics of a tangent drawn to the curve at the point.

The demand curve for an item may take any slope, although a negative slope is expected according to the law of demand. Negatively-sloped demand curves which approach the vertical, as illustrated in panel (b) of Figure 7.2, are often said to be 'inelastic demand curves'. It would be more accurate to note that the relevant price range spans only the inelastic portion of the demand curve. There is an elastic range (off the vertical axis scale), but it is irrelevant under current pricing conventions. We should also note that the marginal revenues associated with points on the visible portion of this demand curve are all negative. This point is important because it is not possible for an enterprise to reach a profit maximizing equilibrium in the inelastic range of its demand curve since its marginal cost can never be negative..

A similar consideration should also be noted in regard to demand curves with very shallow slopes, approaching the horizontal, as illustrated in panel (a) of Figure 7.2. While such demand curves are often described as being 'highly elastic,' it would be more accurate to say that the relevant quantity range encompasses only the elastic range of the demand curve. There is an inelastic range, but only at quantities which are unattainable under current market and supply conditions. Marginal revenues associated with elastic points on such shallowly sloped demand curves will be positive, and thus can accommodate a profit-maximizing equilibrium solution for the enterprise.

ELASTICITY FORMULAS

Our discussion of elasticity to this point has focused on the own-price elasticity of demand, but elasticity is a more general concept not restricted exclusively to own-price. The demand elasticity ratio can be computed with respect to any relevant **demand determinant**, including own-price. Letting the symbol 'X' refer to an unspecified demand determinant, its elasticity can be computed by any of the following formulas, given the requisite information:

$$(1)\ \text{X elasticity} = \%\Delta Q/\%\Delta X = (\Delta Q/Q)/(\Delta X/X).$$

A simple algebraic rearrangement of this elasticity formula yields

$$(2)\ \text{X elasticity} = \Delta Q/Q \cdot X/\Delta X = \Delta Q/\Delta X \cdot X/Q.$$

If the limit concept of the calculus is applied,

$$(3)\ \text{X elasticity} = \Delta Q/\Delta X \cdot X/Q = dQ/dx \cdot X/Q,$$

at the limit as ΔX approaches 0.

The net of this formula development process is that X elasticity can be computed as the product of the **derivative** of the demand function with respect to X, and the ratio of the amount of X to the quantity Q. If there are other relevant demand determinants than X, the X elasticity ratio should be computed as a **partial** (rather than a simple) derivative, that is,

$$(4)\ \text{X elasticity} = \delta Q/\delta X \cdot X/Q.$$

This formula is referred to as the **point elasticity** formula because it can be computed from information about one point on the X demand curve if the equation of the demand curve is known.

Alas, this latter condition, that is, that the **equation** of the demand curve must be known, may constitute a serious barrier to the employment of the elasticity ratio as a decision criterion because the equation often is not known, or cannot be satisfactorily estimated. However, an approximation to point elasticity, known as **arc elasticity** can be computed if information about two points along the X demand curve are known, even if the equation of the X demand curve is not known. Formula (5) can be constructed from formula (2):

$$(5)\ \text{X elasticity} = \%\Delta Q/\%\Delta X = (\Delta Q/Q)/(\Delta X/X)$$
$$= ((Q_2 - Q_1)/Q_1)\ /\ ((X_2 - X_1)\ /\ X_1).$$

where the subscripts refer to the two points identified as points 1 and 2. The expression $(Q_2 - Q_1)$ constitutes 'ΔQ,' and the expression $(X_2 - X_1)$ is 'ΔX.' We note that point 1 is taken as the base or starting point for the computation. However, this particular formulation exhibits a deficiency in that different values for the computed X elasticity ratio emerge if the identities of points 1 and 2 are reversed. This deficiency can be relieved by estimating the **average elasticity** over the arc of the demand curve between points 1 and 2 using formula

$$(6)\ X\ \text{elasticity} = [(Q_2-Q_1)/((Q_2+Q_1)/2)]/[(X_2-X_1)/((X_2+X_1)/2)]$$

where $(Q_2+Q_1)/2)$ constitutes the average of Q_2 and Q_1, and $((X_2 + X_1)/2)$ is the average of X_2 and X_1. Finally, formula (6) can be simplified because the 2s in the denominators of the ratio cancel each other, resulting in

$$(7)\ X\ \text{elasticity} = [(Q_2-Q_1)/(Q_2+Q_1)]/[(X_2-X_1)/(X_2+X_1)].$$

This final formulation, the so-called 'average arc elasticity' formula, can be computed if only two points on the X demand curve are known, but it must be recognized as only an approximation to the true elasticity at either known point, or any point on the arc between the known points. Depending upon the shape (that is, concavity) of the X demand curve, the average arc elasticity ratio may be an over- or under-statement of true point elasticity. The reader is invited to explore the conditions resulting in over- or under-statement.

ELASTICITY AND OTHER DEMAND DETERMINANTS

We now explore the conceptual sense of several specific X-demand elasticity ratios. The so-called **income elasticity of demand** may be computed if information about the clientele's income is known and other demand determinants remain unchanged. Any of the elasticity formulas elaborated in the previous section may be employed simply by substituting income for X in the selected formula, for example,

$$(8)\ \text{income elasticity} = [\%\Delta Q]/[\%\Delta I].$$

The computed income elasticity of demand for a **normal good** is expected to be positive, while that for an **inferior good** is expected to be negative. But conclusions should never be assumed before conducting empirical research. From this perspective, a computed positive income elasticity of demand ratio may be taken as the basis for an inference that the item is a normal good; likewise, a computed negative income elasticity ratio implies that the item is an inferior good. But even if the item is deemed normal, the value of the elasticity ratio may contain useful information. Positive income elasticities less than unity imply that the demand for the item is **relatively inelastic** (that is, unresponsive) with respect to income changes. Income elasticities greater than unity suggest that the demand for the item is **relatively elastic** with respect to income changes. The reader is invited to review the earlier section of this chapter which suggested reasons for managerial preferences to produce normal and inferior goods.

The management of the firm may have chosen to take an aggressive approach to the demand for its item by mounting a promotional effort. The relevant question in this regard is whether the demand for the item is elastic with respect to the promotional expenditure (for example, the advertising budget for a particular medium). The relevant elasticity formula can be expressed as

$$(9)\ \text{advertising elasticity} = \%\Delta Q/\%\Delta \text{ Advertising Budget}.$$

The management might be pleased to find a positive advertising elasticity ratio greater than unity. The reader is left to imagine the management's reactions to advertising elasticity ratios less than unity (or, heaven forbid, negative!).

Finally, we consider the sense of the so-called **cross** (or cross-price) elasticity of demand ratio. This term may be understood in comparison with the term 'own-price' elasticity of demand. A **cross-price demand curve** shows the graphic relationship between the quantity demanded of one item, say x, relative to the price of another item, y or z. As noted earlier, y and z may refer to substitutes and complements, respectively, for x. The cross-elasticity of demand for the substitute good y can be expressed as

$$(10)\ \text{substitute cross elasticity} = \%\Delta Q_x/\%\Delta P_y,$$

and that for complement good z as

$$(11)\ \text{complement cross elasticity} = \%\Delta Q_x/\%\Delta P_z.$$

The sign of the **substitute** cross elasticity ratio is expected to be **positive**: when the price of y rises, less of y will be demanded, but more of its substitute x will be demanded. And the sign of the **complement** cross elasticity ratio is expected to be **negative**. Again, neither substitutability nor complementarity should be assumed; empirical evidence should be compiled to reveal whether two goods appear to be substitutes or complements, and the magnitudes of the computed ratios (in absolute value, greater or lesser than unity) should indicate how good or strong is the relationship. The substitute cross elasticity ratio has been proposed as an index of the ability of a competitor to **penetrate the market** of the enterprise by cutting price (or the ability of the enterprise to insulate itself from competitor's price changes).

We have now considered the managerial implications of own-price, cross-price, income, and advertising elasticity of demand. The principles underlying these concepts are applicable to demand elasticities of yet other determinants which have not been specified. Each item can be expected to have a set of demand determinants which are specific to it, and which may not be pertinent to many or any other items.

While demand elasticity can be computed for any demand determinant for which sufficient information is available, we do not mean to suggest that successful managers must make explicit demand elasticity computations before each and every demand decision. Rather, the concept of demand elasticity is the economist's explanation of a thought process through which the successful manager must have passed in making the decisions which resulted in the success of the enterprise. Whether or not any demand elasticity ratio has been computed, the manager has to have asked the question of whether a contemplated demand determinant change is likely to result in a larger or smaller percentage change in the quantity demanded of the item. We shall subsequently discover that the elasticity concept can be extended into the realm of supply, production, and cost.

THE EMPIRICAL ESTIMATION OF DEMAND

Ideally, the enterprise manager should predicate pricing decisions upon an accurately-formulated **demand function** for each item that the enterprise sells. This ideal is feasible only for enterprises which sell one or only a small number of items. The task of estimating a demand function is sufficiently arduous and costly that few firm managers are willing to devote the necessary resources to the task when demands for more than a few items must be estimated. In extreme cases, for example the grocery retailer or hardware wholesaler who stocks literally thousands of items, the task of estimating demand for all items becomes a physical and economic impossibility.

For the moment we shall focus upon the procedures for estimating the demand for a single item, for example dozens of grade A large eggs, or half-gallons of 2 % butter-fat milk. The first step in specifying a demand function is to **model the relationship** between quantity demanded as dependent variable, and all demand determinants which the analyst thinks might affect quantity demanded as independent variables. The modelling process should follow the procedures outlined to select the possible independent variables and the likely form of relationship of each (linear, polynomial) to the dependent variable and to other independent variables (additive, multiplicative). The modelling process should also hypothesize the expected sign of the coefficient of each independent variable, for example, negative for own-price, cross-price of a complement, and income in the case of an inferior good; positive for cross-price of a substitute and income in the case of a normal good.

Once the function has been modelled, the manager can **estimate the parameters** of the function in a manner similar to Fritz Machlup's educated guess based upon a summing up of the situation compared to experience with similar situations in the past ('Marginal Analysis and Empirical Research,' in *Essays in Economic Semantics*, W. W. Norton & Company, 1967, p. 167). Or, he can engage in the more-formal process which we shall elaborate in the remainder of this section. The Machlup-like seat-of-the-pants method is likely what managers do most of the time and in regard to most of the items which they sell, especially when their enterprises sell large numbers of items. Although no explicit equation results from this process, an implicit demand equation does underlie each educated guess of the number of units saleable, given various values of the relevant demand determinants. This informal approach may be the only one possible in the case of a new item for which no current information or historical data can be obtained.

The following discussion of the formal estimating procedure is important both because the manager may indeed wish to estimate the demand function for some of the items sold by the enterprise, and because knowledge of the formal procedure can be beneficial to the informal summing-up process even if the demand function is not explicitly specified.

The formal estimating procedure culminates in an **explicit equation** which can be used to compute (that is, predict, estimate) the unit sales of the item under various demand-determinant conditions. The equation may be linear or polynomial, additive or multiplicative, and may include as many independent variables as the analyst deems significant to the explanation of unit sales. The typical form of such a linear, additive demand equation is

$$(12)\ Q_d = a + b_1X_1 + b_2X_2 + \ldots + b_nX_n,$$

where X_1 through X_n are such demand determinants as own-price, cross-prices, incomes of prospective clients, advertising expenditures, etc.

If there is only one demand determinant, say own-price, the equation will be of the slope-intercept format similar to that of equation (1) of Chapter 6. However, if there are more determinants than one in the equation, the constant a cannot be interpreted as an intercept parameter for any one of the demand determinants.

A typical second-order (or quadratic) demand equation including only one independent variable would take the following form,

$$(13)\ Q_d = a + b_1X_1 + b_2X_1^2.$$

Higher-ordered terms for X_1 can be present, and terms for other variables (X_2, X_3, ...) can be included to any order (squared, cubed) as deemed important.

Once the demand function has been modelled, and assuming that the item is already being sold so that pertinent data can be obtained, the usual procedure for estimating the parameters of the demand model is **regression analysis**. The associated **inference statistics** provide means for assessing the statistical significances of the estimated coefficients of the included variables. The analyst should attempt to include in the model as independent variables as many demand determinants as are likely to make significant contributions to explanation of the behaviour of the quantity demanded. Then, any variables for which estimated coefficients are judged not to be statistically significant can be deleted from the model before it is re-specified.

Occasionally the analyst will find data appropriate to the demand specification process published in industry or trade sources, or compiled by government or private agencies. More often than not, however, demand data for individual items in specific locales do not exist, and must be captured as a matter of original **field research**. The first field research decision which the analyst must make is whether to capture the data **cross sectionally** (that is, across a number of subjects at a point in time), or as a **time series** (that is, for the same subject over a period of time). A cross-sectional approach is preferred if it is thought that demand determinants not explicitly included in the model might change over time. However, a cross-sectional approach might require access to competitors' demand information, which they are likely to be reluctant to provide voluntarily.

If the analysis must be restricted to a time-series approach, the analyst should take care to include within the model all demand determinants which are likely to change over time. The analyst may also include so-called 'dummy variables' (values of 0 and 1) as a means of quantifying such qualitative conditions as type of outlet (for example, convenience store versus full-line grocery store) or whether or not a special promotion is in effect.

A student's demand specification research paper is included as Appendix to this chapter to illustrate the procedures and some of the problems that were encountered in estimating a demand function.

Table 7.1: Data for Specification of a Demand Function

	Quantity (1)	*Price* (2)	*Income* (3)	*Index*$_I$ (4)	*Adjusted Q* (5)	
A.	23.0	5	150	1.50	15.33	K.
B.	27.0	8	210	2.10	12.86	J.
C.	22.0	10	176	1.76	12.50	I.
D.	24.5	3	140	1.40	17.50	H.
E.	20.0	6	150	1.50	13.33	G.
F	20.0	2	100	1.00	20.00	F.

SPECIFICATION ERRORS AND THE IDENTIFICATION PROBLEM

A so-called **specification error** is often indicated by a coefficient of multiple determination (R^2) which is substantially below unity. The specification error occurs either because one or more important determinants of demand were **omitted from the model**, or because an included variable was raised to the wrong power (for example, linear instead of quadratic or cubic).

Another type of specification error, an **identification problem**, may not be indicated by any inference statistic. The best indicator that an identification problem may have occurred is a sign on an estimated regression coefficient which is different than expected, for example, a positive sign on the own-price regression coefficient. The cause of an identification error is a simultaneous relationship between the dependent variable (quantity demanded) and some determinant (for example, consumer income) which was omitted from the model.

As an illustration of the problem, let us suppose that a cross-sectional data capture process yielded the quantity and price data in columns (1) and (2) of Table 7.1. The row-wise pairs of observations in the quantity and price columns serve as coordinates for plotting points A, B, C, D,

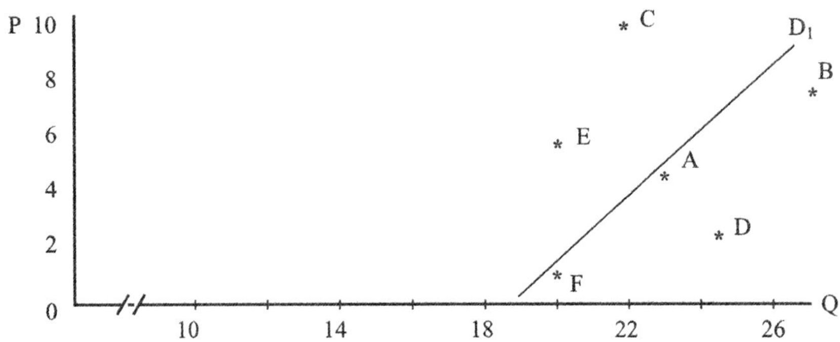

Figure 7.3. Price and quantity data plotted on coordinate axes.

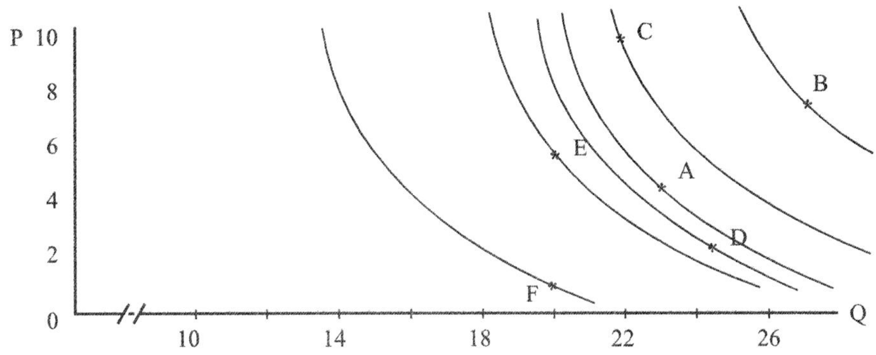

Figure 7.4. The identification problem revealed.

E and F in Figure 7.3. Because these points scatter around an upward-sloping curve, D_1, the coefficient of determination is quite low, 0.07, so a specification error may be indicated. Also, the slope of the curve D_1 is positive, thus suggesting a violation of the law of demand. The problem is that points A, B, C, D, E, and F do not lie along a common own-price demand curve. Each point lies on a separate own-price demand curve which differs from the others because another determinant which has not been included in the model, income, has varied from observation to observation. These separate own-price demand curves are illustrated in Figure 7.4.

Additional data, shown in column (3) of Table 7.1, were subsequently obtained for the average incomes of the clients at stores where the original price and quantity data were collected. Column (4) of Table 7.1 contains an index of the income data; a convenient income observation was selected to serve as the index base. The column (4) index numbers were then used to adjust the column (1) quantity data (the adjustment is analogous to the process of deflating a money-value series by a price index) to remove the effects of the income variations. The adjusted quantity data

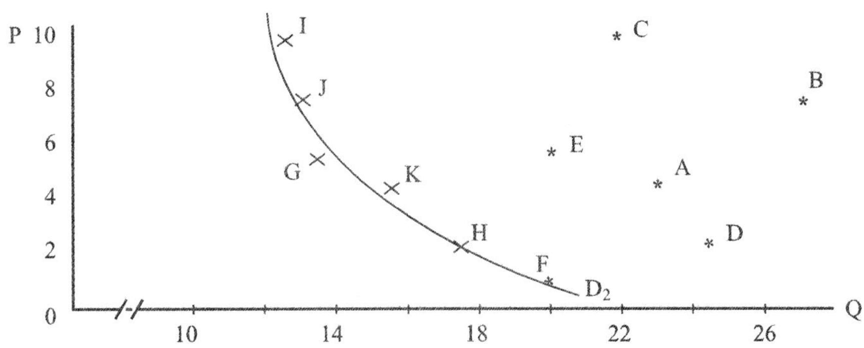

Figure 7.5. An -income-constant demand curve.

are recorded in column (5) of Table 7.1. Now, when the adjusted quantity data are plotted against the price data from column (2), points F, G, H, I, J, and K emerge in Figure 7.3. A curve D_2 has been fitted through these points which yields a coefficient of determination of 0.86. Also, the slope of D_2 is negative as expected from the law of demand.

The curve D_2 in Figure 7.3 can be interpreted as an income-constant demand curve. Curve D_1 exhibits an identification problem because, since the points lie on different demand curves due to the income variation, the true locus of the own-price demand curve could not be identified. The identification problem occurred because of the simultaneous change between own-price (included in the model) and income (not included in the model).

THE IDENTIFICATION PROBLEM AND DEMAND ELASTICITY

Suppose that an analyst estimates a demand function like curve D_1 in Figure 7.1, but fails to recognize the presence of an identification problem. If the own-price elasticity of demand is computed at any point along D_1, it will have a positive sign, which indicates a perverse own-price demand elasticity. However, if the identification problem is eliminated using a procedure similar to that described in the previous section so that own-price elasticity can be computed for curve D_2 in Figure 7.3, the expected negative own-price elasticity ratio will result.

In many cases, however, an **unexpected sign** of a computed elasticity ratio or the **wrong slope** of the estimated demand curve may not occur as a clue to the presence of an identification problem. Figure 7.4 illustrates a downward-sloping path of plotted demand data points, but the simultaneous occurrence of change of income causes a shift of the true income-constant demand curve from locus D_3 to D_4 and then to D_5.

The path traced out by points K, L, and M constitute not a true demand curve, but rather a demand **expansion path**. If a demand equation is estimated from data for points K, L, and M, it will have the expected negative slope, but the slope will be shallower than that of the true demand curve at any of its loci. Also, if average arc elasticity is computed from information about points K

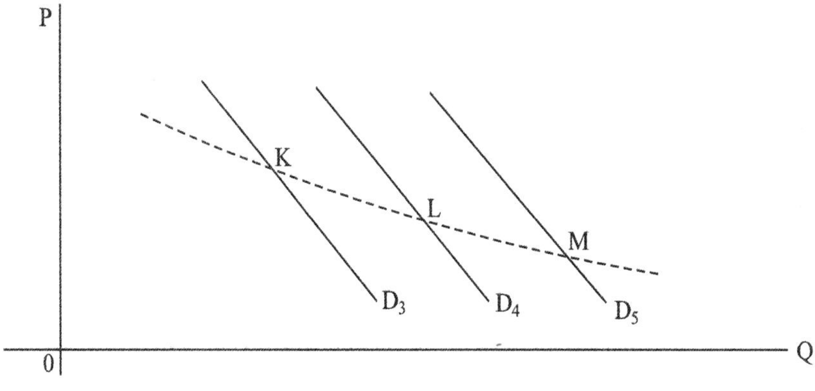

Figure 7.6. An elastic demand expansion path.

and L, the elasticity ratio will be negative as expected, but will imply that demand is far more elastic than it truly is along any locus of the true income-constant own-price demand curve. In fact, the implication may be that own-price demand is elastic when it truly is inelastic. A price decision maker who bases a price change decision on such an erroneously computed elasticity ratio will likely lower price when it should be raised.

The moral of the story is that the analyst should take great care to be sure that the demand function is being estimated from points along a **common, fixed-locus, own-price** demand curve (that is, one which exhibits no identification problem). Great care should be taken to ascertain that the two points from which the average arc elasticity ratio is computed do lie along the same demand curve.

CONCLUSION

The concept of the demand function provides the economist with a formalized vehicle for analyzing the demand for an item. Enterprise managers usually function to 'size-up' and estimate the quantity demanded of an item without formally estimating a demand function. But more sophisticated managers who require more accuracy in their demand estimates may be willing to devote the necessary time and effort to the formal estimation procedures which we have outlined in this chapter. Later, we shall see how demand and cost analyses can be brought together to assist the rational manager in his effort to maximize the profits of the enterprise.

Summary of Important Points

1. The slope of the demand curve is an adequate criterion for predicting a change of unit sales consequent upon a price change.
2. The own-price elasticity of demand is a more appropriate criterion for assessing the revenue implications of a price change.
3. In the elastic range of the demand curve, price must be reduced in order to increase revenue; in the inelastic range of the demand curve, price must be raised in order to increase revenue.
4. Maximum revenue is achieved at the output level for which marginal revenue is zero and own-price elasticity of demand is unitary.
5. Demand elasticity ratios can be computed with respect to any relevant demand determinant.
6. The 'point elasticity' of demand may be computed using the calculus if the equation of the demand curve is known or can be estimated; otherwise, the 'arc elasticity' formula may be used to estimate average elasticity across the arc between two known points on the demand curve.
7. The sign of the income elasticity of demand ratio may be used to identify whether a good is normal or inferior.

Contd.....

8. The sign of the cross-price elasticity of demand ratio may be used to identify whether the good is a substitute or complement for another good.
9. If the firm has survived and been profitable, its managerial decision makers must have employed a demand elasticity thought process (whether they actually computed elasticity ratios or not) when contemplating demand determinant changes.
10. Demand functions may be estimated employing either informal summing-up or formal modelling procedures.
11. Statistical regression analysis is the most commonly-used formal procedure for estimating the values of model parameters.
12. Data for regression analysis may be captured in time series or cross sectionally.
13. A coefficient of multiple determination which is substantially below unity may be indicative of a specification error, that is, omitting some variable(s) which should be included in the model.
14. A possible consequence of a specification error is an identification problem, that is, estimating the equation of a curve relating two variables using data for points on different curves; this is attributable to variation in some variable(s) assumed constant and thus omitted from the model.
15. A demand identification problem will likely result in an over- or under-statement of the true demand elasticity relationship.

Significant Terms

Own-price demand curve
Slope
Elasticity of demand
Elastic, inelastic ranges
Revenue
Unitarily elastic demand
Extant, virtual points
X-elasticity of demand
Point-elasticity formula
Arc-elasticity formula
Income elasticity of demand
Cross elasticity of demand
Substitute, complement
Penetration, insulation index
Empirical estimation
Expected sign
Inference statistics
Contribution to explanation
Data capture
Field research
Time-series, cross-sectional data
Dummy variables
Coefficient of multiple determination
Specification error
Identification error
Demand expansion path

Questions for Discussion

1. Compare and contrast the decision significance of the slope of an own-price demand curve with the own-price elasticity of demand.
2. Describe the elasticity ranges of the linear own-price demand curve and discuss the decision significance of this information.
3. Explain the relationship between marginal revenue and elasticity of demand; why is this relevant to managerial decision making?
4. If management's objective is to maximize revenue, devise a price-change strategy if demand is thought to be {elastic/inelastic} at the present price.
5. Discuss the managerial implications of {raising/lowering} price in the {inelastic/elastic} range of the demand curve.
6. How can the elasticity of demand at a point on a non-linear demand curve be determined?
7. Why is there no such thing as a completely {elastic/inelastic} demand curve?
8. Show how differential calculus can be used to compute the elasticity of demand at a point on the demand curve.
9. Under what circumstances can the average arc elasticity formula be used to estimate elasticity of demand when the point elasticity technique cannot be used.
10. Explain why the average arc elasticity formula may over- or under-estimate the true elasticity of demand.
11. How can the computed income elasticity of demand reveal whether a good is normal or inferior?
12. What are the managerial implications of the income elasticity of demand?
13. How can the computed cross elasticity of demand reveal whether another good is a substitute or complement for the good in question?
14. What are the managerial implications of {substitute/complementary} relationships between goods?
15. What is the possible relevance of demand elasticity concepts if real-world decision makers do not actually compute demand elasticity ratios?
16. Compare and contrast formal and informal means of estimating demand relationships.
17. Identify possible sources of data which may be used in the estimation of a demand function.
18. Discuss the positives and negatives of using cross-sectional and time-series approaches to capturing data to be used for estimation of a demand function.

19. What is a demand specification error? How can such an error be detected? What are possible remedies for such errors?

20. What is a demand identification problem? How can such a problem be detected? What are the possible causes of such a problem?

21. What can be done to eliminate or relieve a demand identification problem?

22. How are computed elasticity of demand ratios related to identification problems?

23. What are the managerial decision implications of the incidence of a demand identification problem?

Appendix 7.1

THE ECONOMIC TASKS OF MARKETING

Marketing is one of the four functional areas of business administration (management, finance, accounting, marketing), and as such is a variant of applied economic policy in the microeconomic arena. Marketing is concerned with the cost side of microeconomic decision criteria only in providing the demand enabling conditions for spreading overhead costs in the short run and exploiting scale economies in the long run. From an economic theory perspective, there are three tasks for marketing to accomplish in regard to demand:

1. Upon introduction of a new product or entry into a new market, to establish the initial locus of the demand curve;
2. Subsequently, to shift the product demand curve to the right, or prevent it from shifting leftward; and
3. To improve the attitude of the demand curve or prevent its attitude from deteriorating.

1. When a new product is introduced, whether in a home or foreign market, virtually nothing is known *ex ante* the introduction about the locus of the product's demand curve in that market. This may be illustrated graphically in Figure A-VII(a) by a demand curve which is coincident with the vertical (price) axis. The immediate marketing problem is to conduct research to gain information adequate to determining where the demand curve might lie in price-quantity coordinate space at the start-up of sales of the product in the new market.

For an absolutely new product never before marketed, the information resulting from market research may be little more than speculation. For products which have been sold before in markets with characteristics similar to the target market, the procedure may simply be an extrapolation of what is known about the established markets to the new target market, with appropriate adjustments to account for environmental and cultural differences between the established markets and the new target market. The problem is compounded for foreign target markets since environmental

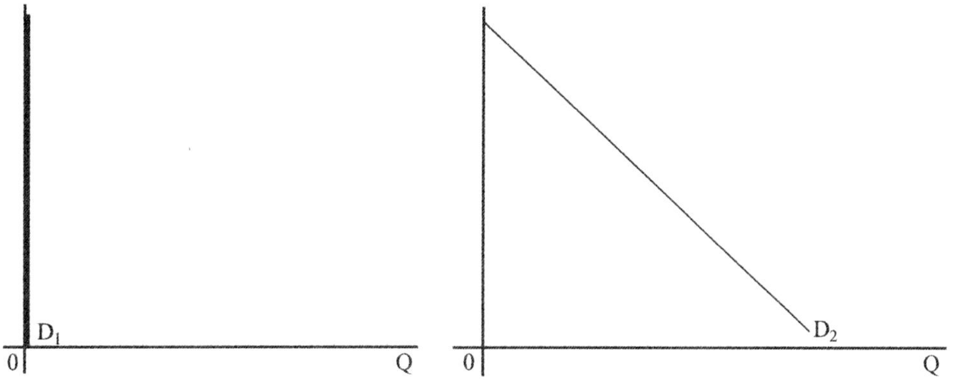

Figure A-VII(a) (i). Hypothetical location of a demand curve for a new product.

and cultural settings may be sufficiently different from those of established markets that simple adaptive tranference of information is not effective.

In such circumstances the product may have to be actually marketed or test marketed at the new site in order to generate the first information upon which reliable demand analysis may be based. Figure A-VII(a).(i),(ii) shows a hypothetical location of a demand curve for a new product upon its initial offering in a new market.

Once a 'fix' can be got upon the properties of the product demand curve in the new market, it should be possible to assess price elasticity of demand over some range of product prices. Price elasticity of demand may be measured as a percentage change in quantity demanded divided by the percentage change in price, assuming no other causative factor has changed. Price elasticity of demand information can serve as criteria for determining an appropriate price relative to the firm's behavioural objectives (for example, profit maximization or satisficing, growth measured by volume of sales, sales revenue, performance relative to recent history, or share of market, or yet other behavioural objectives). If demand is elastic, the firm can increase its revenues only by lowering price; if demand is inelastic, revenues are increased by raising price.

Demand elasticity is accurately measured over an arc (that is, between two points) on a single demand curve which has not shifted. A matter which may cause assessment difficulties with measures of price elasticity of demand is that causative factors other than the product's price may have caused the demand curve to shift simultaneous with a change of product price. This problem is referred to by economists as an 'identification problem' since with points on two different demand curve locations a single demand curve is not uniquely identified. Depending upon whether

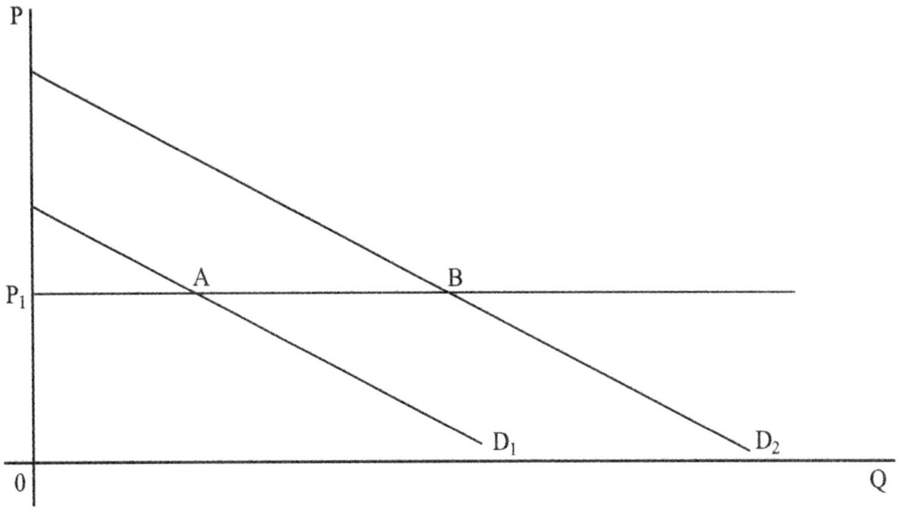

Figure A-VII (a) (ii). Hypothetical location of a demand curve for a new product.

the demand shifted right or left when price is decreased, measured elasticity will tend to be over- or understated.

2. The second task of marketing is manipulation of the locus of the demand curve. With the passage of time, changing non-price determinants of demand can be expected to shift the demand curve, with consequent changes in price elasticity of demand. On-going monitoring of price elasticity of demand should enable rational price change decisions. For example, as illustrated in Figure A-VII.(a),(ii) increases of demand (illustrated as rightward shifts of demand curves) tend to render demand less price elastic at any established price level. Decreases of demand (leftward shifts) cause demand to become more elastic at the going price. In Figure (ii), point A on curve D_1 is in its elastic range. To increase revenue the firm would have to lower price. As demand shifts rightwards towards D_2, elasticity progressively decreases. From point B on D_2 in its inelastic range, the firm can increase revenue by raising price.

The firm may choose to respond passively to favourable shifts of demand, for example, rightward shifts attributable to population growth and rising incomes. Firms which are oriented towards growth rather than profitability will be inclined towards aggressive marketing efforts designed to shift their product demand curves to the right. Rightward demand shifts lower elasticities of demand and facilitate price increases. Adverse shifts of product demand may occur in response to economic contractions or intensifying competition. Should the demand for one of the firm's products shift adversely due to changing conditions, demand tends to become ever more elastic at the established price level, and militates in favour of cutting prices. The marketing task is to mount an appropriate campaign to reverse or slow the pace of the adverse shift.

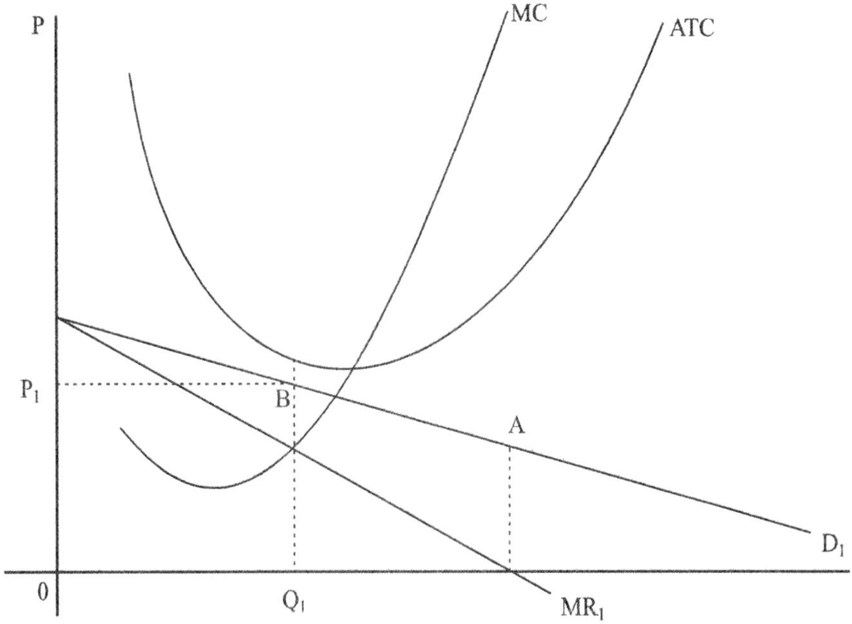

Figure A-VII(b). Hypothetical situation when demand is below average total cost (ACT).

3. The 'attitude' of a demand curve is its slope. A demand curve with a fairly shallow slope has a relatively poor attitude from the perspective of managerial decision making because demand is highly elastic over the relevant output range. This means that management has little pricing discretion. It also means that the firm must be prepared to cut price in order to increase revenues. From a managerial decision perspective, the attitude of the demand curve may be improved by doing something to cause it to become more steeply downward sloping. Even if the demand for a product is not increasing (or cannot easily be increased by marketing promotion), it may be possible to design a marketing programme to enhance perceptions of the image of the product in the public mind to the end of rendering the demand curve more steeply downward sloping. As a demand curve rotates to become more steeply downward sloping (left to right), elasticity at any given price level will decrease toward inelasticity.

This may be an especially important matter under certain circumstances, for example, when demand is fairly shallowly sloped and below average total cost (ATC) as illustrated by D_1 in Figure A-VII(b). Point A lies at the mid-point of the linear demand curve, below which marginal revenue (MR_1) is zero.

Demand is of unit elasticity (absolute value equal to 1) at the midpoint. Demand above and to the left of point A is in the elastic range (absolute value greater than 1).

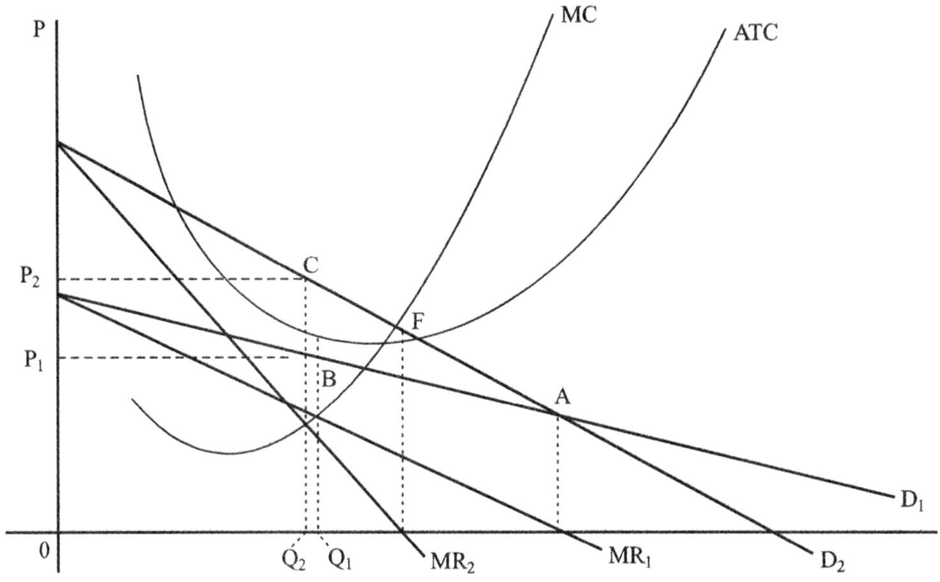

Figure A-VII(c). Hypothetical situation when demand marketing effort succeeds in rotating the demand curve.

Given this locus of demand curve D_1, the firm is obviously operating at a loss, but can minimize the loss by finding Q_1 where marginal revenue is equal to marginal cost. Of course, if price falls below the firm's average variable cost (not shown), it should shut down operations and suffer only the fixed (overhead) costs.

In order to achieve profitable operation the firm needs to be able to raise price relative to average total cost. However, a price increase will decrease revenue; only a price cut will increase revenue, but it will not solve the firm's problem in this case.

But suppose that the firm can mount a marketing effort to enhance the perception of the product in the public's eye sufficient to improve the attitude of the demand curve. So that it cannot be construed as a demand shift, let us suppose that in Figure A-VII(c) the marketing effort succeeds in rotating the demand curve around its former midpoint at A to the new locus designated D_2 with corresponding marginal revenue curve MR_2. The new profit maximizing output is now Q_2, only slightly lower than Q_1. However, demand curve D_2 now rises above the ATC curve to enable profitable operation, and the profit maximizing price is P_2 which is substantially higher than P_1. Point F is the midpoint of D_2 where demand is unit elastic. At point C, the profit maximizing point on the demand curve, demand is still elastic, but less so relative to midpoint F than was point B on demand curve D_1 relative to its midpoint at A. The marketing effort has succeeded, not in shifting

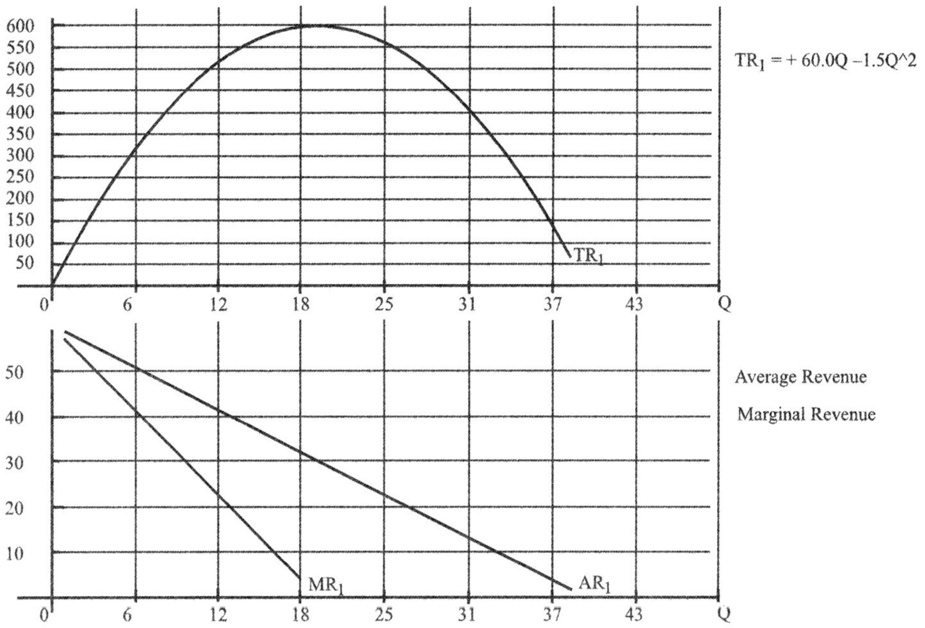

Figure A-VII(d). The initial loci of the total, average, and marginal revenue functions.

the demand curve, but rather in improving its slope attitude to enable increasing price enough to achieve profitable operation.

Appendix 7.2

In Appendices to earlier chapters we introduced the SIMMOD Java applet computer programme as a model simulation system. Our purpose in this appendix is to elaborate its potential usefulness in the analysis of demand and revenue relationships. Suppose that an initial revenue function is given by the equation,

$$R = +\ 60Q + -1.5Q^2.$$

We note that there is no constant in the equation. More properly, the implicit value of the missing constant is zero. The SIMMOD display of this function is illustrated in Figure A-VII(d).

SIMMOD allows the user to change any of the parameters of the revenue model. Suppose

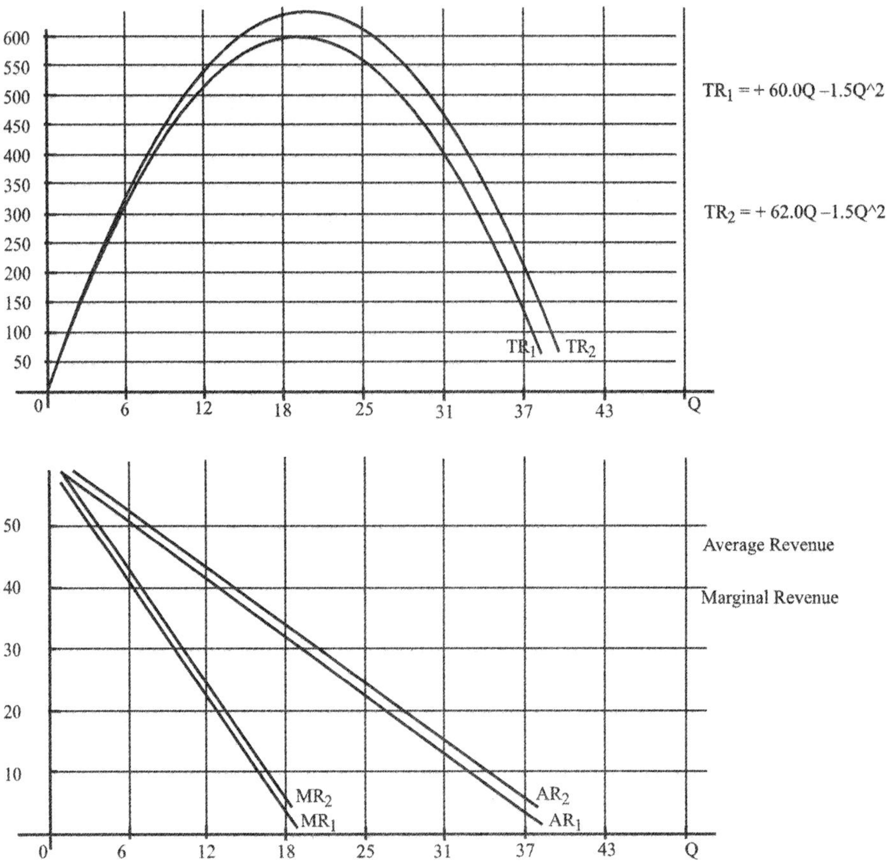

Figure A-VII(e). The initial (1) and subsequent (2) loci of the total, average, and marginal revenue functions.

that the coefficient of the linear term (Q) is changed from 60 to 62. The revised equation becomes

$$R = +\ 62Q + -1.5Q^2.$$

The Q coefficient change has the effect of shifting the TR, AR, and MR functions to new locations as illustrated in Figure C2B-2.

What are the circumstances under which such information about the implications of a parameter change might be useful? The business firm's product demands are normally subject to the buffeting of market forces which cause the demand curve to shift left or right, and the total revenue function to shift accordingly. If the firm can achieve any degree of monopoly power, it can exert some control over its price. It may also be able by engaging in appropriate strategies to shift its demand curve to the right to capture a larger market share. Or, it may be able to prevent the leftward shift of its demand curve in the face of aggressive marketing drives by its competitors.

Assuming that by market research to gather data and regression analysis to estimate parameters the management of the firm has a good idea of the equations of its demand and revenue functions, it can model them with SIMMOD. When market forces cause the demand to shift, the management can then make corresponding changes to the revenue function in SIMMOD to approximate the market shifts, and thereby analyze the likely effects. Or, with adequate monopoly power, the management of the firm may devise possible offensive strategies to shift demand and revenue functions to the right, or defensive strategies to prevent their leftward shifts. In either case, prospective shifts of functions may be simulated in SIMMOD to allow examining the likely implications of the strategies.

—oo(O)oo—

Chapter **8**

Production in the Short Run

Topics covered in this chapter

• Production as the central function of the enterprise. • The significance of specialization and division of labour. • How efficiency is achieved. • The raison d'etre of the business enterprise. • Essential entrepreneurial functions. • Crucial managerial questions. • The nature of the production function. • The distinction between the short and long runs. • The distinction between returns to a variable input and returns to scale. • The governing principle of production relationships. • The behaviours of marginal and average products. • Marginal and incremental products as decision criteria. • The symmetry of the stages of production. • Means of increasing the marginal productivity of an input.

PRODUCTION IS THE CENTRAL FUNCTION OF THE ENTERPRISE

In fact, the possibility of engaging in production activity is the reason that enterprises are organized. The occasion for production activity follows directly from the existence of the **economic problem**: scarcity and the hope of relieving it by concerted, organized effort.

VARIETIES OF PRODUCTION ACTIVITY

In the broadest possible sense, production activity encompasses nearly all of human effort. Even if life were characterized by abundance, the things desired for consumption would still have to be gathered and transferred or transported to the point of consumption, and then possibly held until the propitious moment. The gathering, transporting, and holding activities certainly are forms of production activity.

The act of production is the transformation of raw substances (including human labour itself) into other forms that are distinguished by their more desirable functional, locational, or temporal characteristics. Production of tangible goods encompasses gathering, extracting, refining, combining, assembling, packaging, transporting, and distributing activities. Production of services includes performance activities as well.

ORGANIZING PRODUCTION

Any single person can produce a variety of goods and services that are more desirable than the natural substances from which they were produced. Why go to the trouble to interact with other human beings to cooperate in a production process? Such effort is warranted because of the potential inherent in specialization and division of labour to improve the efficiency of the production process. Boiled down to its essentials, the economic problem is to use the scarce resources as efficiently as possible in the effort to alleviate the insatiability of demand.

Efficiency is the name of the economizing game. Efficiency is served in either of two ways: by producing a larger volume of output from a given amount of inputs, or by employing smaller amounts of the inputs in the production of a target output. Experience has demonstrated that in both cases organized human effort is typically more efficient than is isolated effort.

MANAGERIAL PROBLEMS IN THE PRODUCTION PROCESS

Suppose that all production resulted as a matter of individual effort. In an economic system organized around markets, the market itself provides the mechanism for distributing the results of the productive effort. Since the market can perform this function, what justifies the appearance of such authoritarian organizations as **business firms** to undertake the production process? Experience has demonstrated that organized productive effort under hierarchical control (that is, managed from the top down) often is more efficient than are individual efforts. The business enterprise, in several of its organizational guises (proprietorship, partnership, corporation), has provided the vehicle for the organization and control of production in modern society. As R. H. Coase has noted, commercial enterprises are established and thrive where it is less costly (that is, more efficient) to organize production in centralized, authoritarian power structures than via interaction among individuals participating in market transactions. [R. H. Coase, 'The Nature of the Firm.' *Economica*, New Series, Vol. IV (1937), p. 393.]

The essential **entrepreneurial** functions are the perception of an unfilled market demand and the assumption of risk in organizing a productive process to exploit the market potential. The three crucial **managerial** problems are

1. to select an appropriate technology for implementation of production,
2. to discern the right volume of output to meet the market demand, and
3. to choose the optimal combination of inputs to produce the target level of output.

Associated with these three broad problem areas are a myriad of detailed functions ranging from choosing the site for the production facility, procuring inputs and scheduling production, and packaging and distributing the final product.

Real-world production processes may be quite detailed and complex. Our task in this chapter shall be to discern general production decision criteria that can be transferred to specific production situations. What we are about is learning how to think about production problems rather than what to do in specific situations.

PRODUCTION PRINCIPLES

THE RELEVANT QUESTIONS

Every production decision maker must confront four basic questions:

1. What is an appropriate technology for producing the desired output?
2. What size plant should be constructed to implement the selected technology?
3. At what volume of output (or rate of production) should the constructed plant be operated?
4. What are the appropriate quantities of input to combine to produce the target output.

The first two are entrepreneurial decisions; the last two are managerial in nature.

These fundamental production questions will not always be addressed in the same sequence. Some of them must be confronted simultaneously. The perceived market demand ultimately constrains the answer to the volume-of-output question and suggests a response to the size-of-plant question. The target production volume may then limit the eligible range of technologies. Assuming that the target volume is known, we shall address the technology question later in this chapter. Our immediate task is to confront question (4), the appropriate quantities of inputs to be combined to produce output.

THE PRODUCTION FUNCTION

The analysis of production requires an examination of how inputs are combined to produce output. The analysis may also be directed to the effects upon the volume of output of changing any of the employed inputs. Economists have adopted the functional notation conventions of mathematics to describe production relationships. Let broad categories of physical inputs be represented by the symbols,

L = labour

R = resources

K = capital

then a generalized **production function** can be represented as,

$$(1)\ Q = f(L, R, K, \ldots)$$

where Q is the volume of output.

But equation (1) is an incomplete specification of the production function. There are two possible ways to complete it. One is to further specify additional aspects of production that are represented as implicit inputs:

$$(2)\ Q = f(L, R, K; T, E, M).$$

Here the symbols T, E, and M stand for technology, entrepreneurship, and managerial capacity. They are grouped together and separated from the list of physical inputs by the semicolon because they are not *per se* physical inputs. Rather, they both enable and constrain the combination of the physical inputs in the production of outputs.

In recognition that T, E, and M are not physical inputs, some analysts prefer the following representation of the production function:

$$(3)\ Q = f(L, R, K)$$

$$(4)\ f = g(T, E, M).$$

This representation clearly indicates the relationship between physical inputs and output in equation (3), but signifies with equation (4) that the production function itself is a function of other conditions, that is, technology, entrepreneurship, and managerial capacity.

While these are abstract production function representations, a production function that is specific to a particular production process might include in its input listing various types of labour, materials, and capital. An example of a production function to which almost anyone can relate is any kitchen recipe for the preparation of an edible dish. Boiled down to essentials, a production function is nothing more than a list of ingredients together with instructions for combining them in the preparation of a desired output.

THE PRODUCTION SURFACE

In order to examine production input-output relationships, it will be convenient to envision three-dimensional surfaces that represent output (Q) on the vertical axis, and two inputs, such as labour (L) and capital (K), on the horizontal (or floor) axes. The functional notation for such a surface may be given as

$$(5)\ Q = f(L, K / \ldots)$$

where the slash is the conventional indication that all items in the input list appearing to the right of it (in this case, 'all other variables') are assumed constant.

Four hypothesized shapes for the three-dimensional production surfaces are illustrated in

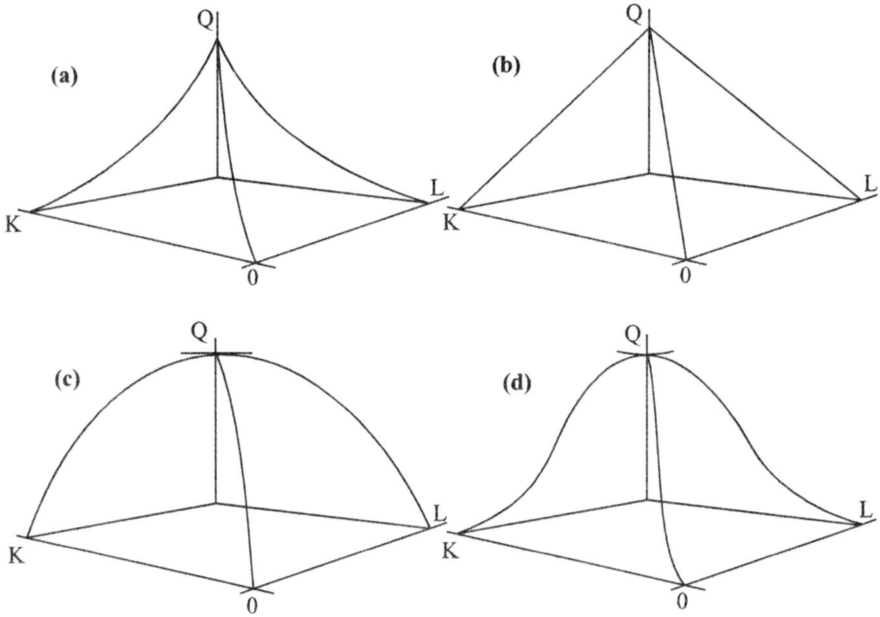

Figure 8.1. Hypothesized shapes of production surfaces.

Figure 8.1. The four panels show, respectively, the following output patterns as the quantities of the inputs are increased:

(a) output increases at an increasing rate;

(b) output increases at a constant rate;

(c) output increases at a decreasing rate; and

(d) output increases at varying rates in the sequence of increasing, constant, and decreasing rates of increase.

There are of course other possible patterns that might be imagined, including an absolute decrease of output consequent upon employing more of the inputs. The output-decrease possibility is a logical extension of patterns (c) and (d) for excessively large increments to the inputs.

Not all of these hypothesized shapes are plausible representations of real-world production relationships. Panels (a) and (b) illustrate two patterns that are thought to be inconsistent with observed production phenomena over any but the shortest ranges of the inputs. It is thought that most real-world production processes exhibit the behaviours represented by panel (c), or possibly the generalized shape of panel (d) which incorporates over limited input ranges all three of the other hypothesized shapes.

THE LONG AND SHORT-RUN TIME FRAMES

The three-dimensional surfaces illustrated in Figure 8.1 imply that production decision makers might enjoy a great deal of freedom in varying the two inputs, or in choosing any eligible combination of inputs represented by the coordinates of points in the floors of the diagrams. In reality, such freedom of choice is constrained by the time-frame setting of the decision context.

In the analysis of how input variation affects output, given a selected technology, economists distinguish three situations:

(a) a single input is changed vis-à-vis fixed quantities of all other inputs;

(b) all inputs are changed (positively or negatively) by the same proportion (greater or lesser than 100 per cent); or

(c) inputs are changed in varying proportions vis-à-vis each other.

The first case describes the analysis of **returns to a variable input**; the second describes **returns to scale**; the third describes the general situation, **variable proportions**, inferences about which may be drawn from an analysis of the first two situations. We shall defer consideration of returns to scale and variable proportions to a later section of this chapter.

The realm of returns to a variable input permits us to distinguish the short run from the long run. In the **long run**, all inputs are presumed to be variable. The analysis of returns to scale thus belongs to the long-run. A change of a single input, given fixed quantities of other inputs, is then clearly an analysis of the short run. The **short run** can be described as the period of time during which at least one of the inputs cannot be changed. The duration of the short run is until the yet-unchanged input can be changed. In the real world, production decision makers may plan for the long-run changes that they intend to make, but all decisions are made in short-run settings, even the decisions to make long-run changes. In this sense, then, the freedom of the decision maker to vary inputs is constrained by the temporal setting.

It is tempting to identify capital as the input class that typically is fixed in the short run, but we must recognize that this concept is not descriptive of all real-world situations. An example of this caveat consists in the family-owned business (a farm or a commercial establishment) where the labour force is the fixed input (mom, pop, children, cousins, etc.). The relevant input question in the short run is how much land or capital equipment to use (rent, buy), not how much labour to employ.

THE VERTICAL SLICE APPROACH

[This is one of two possible approaches, the other being a 'horizontal-slice' approach. The author has chosen to elaborate the vertical-slice approach in the body of this chapter because he believes it to be less abstract and to lead to more operational decision criteria than does the horizontal slice approach. Instructors who prefer an isoquant-isocost approach may find an elaboration of it in the appendix to this chapter.]

We now have in place all of the conceptual tools so that we can begin the analysis of production in the short run. Our objective is to identify the relevant criteria that may be used to

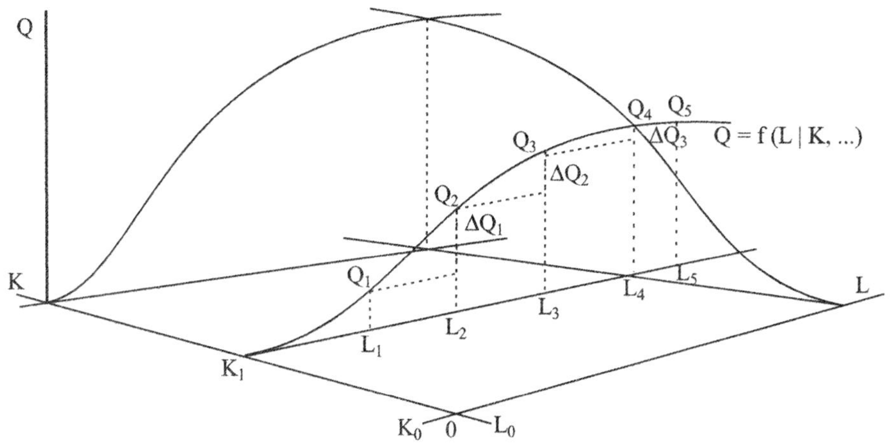

Figure 8.2. A labour-variable section through a production surface.

guide production decision making by rational and perceptive production decision makers. Because of its behavioural inclusiveness, we shall adopt the generalized shape of the production surface illustrated in Figure 8.1, panel (d). It is reproduced in an enlarged format in Figure 8.2. We should note two essential caveats before proceeding with the analysis. First, many real-world production processes may satisfactorily be modelled with the simpler linear or second-order shapes illustrated in panels (b) and (c) of Figure 8.1. Second, the smooth, continuous surface illustrated in Figure 8.2 is only an heroic representation of what certainly are discontinuous real-world relationships. In fact, no more than a few points on or near such a surface may be observable for any real-world production process.

THE VERTICAL SLICE

A short-run production perspective may be analyzed in Figure 8.2 by taking a vertical slice through the surface, parallel to either floor axis. Let us assume that some quantity of capital, K_1, is available from an already-constructed plant, so that the vertical slice is cut parallel to the labour axis, and emanating from the point K_1 on the capital axis. We shall repeat this analysis shortly, but with a vertical slice taken parallel to the capital axis.

The problem for the production decision maker is to choose an appropriate amount of labour to employ with capital input K_1. The analysis may be conducted by assuming alternate labour-employment decisions that follow the path across the floor of the diagram from L_1 through L_2 and L_3. Theoretically, any other quantities of labour along this path might have been chosen; these are simply a few representative quantities. But, the real-world production process might be characterized by a few, discrete labour-quantity choices, such as L_1 or L_3.

As the labour employed with capital K_1 is increased from L_1 toward L_4, output increases along the path on the surface from Q_1 to Q_2, Q_3, and Q_4. Given the adopted shape of this production surface, it is apparent that over the labour input range from L_1 to L_2, output increases at an increasing rate (the surface is concave upward) from Q_1 to Q_2. Point Q_2 in the surface path is near what mathematicians would call the inflection point, that is, where a curve changes concavity, in this case from being concave upwards to being concave downwards. As the labour input is further increased from L_2 to L_3, output continues to increase to Q_3, but at a decreasing rate of increase. Further increases of the labour input from L_3 to L_4 yield additional output, also at a decreasing rate over the Q_3 to Q_4 range. It should be clear that the DQ_3 output increment is smaller than the DQ_2 output increment. This phenomenon of output increasing at a decreasing rate continues beyond Q_4, and until the output path peaks around Q_5 and turns downwards.

The labour input range from K_1 to L_2 is described by economists as the increasing returns range. It is thought to be an early or temporary phenomenon in the production process, and may not be observable in most real-world production situations. This range is missing entirely in the surface illustrated in panel (c) of Figure 8.1.

THE GOVERNING PRINCIPLE

The labour input range from L_2 to L_5 is described by economists as the range of **diminishing returns**. Its essential characteristic is that output increases at a decreasing rate as the labour input increases. Its graphic illustration is the downward concavity of the production surface, and the output path formed by the vertical slice through the surface. Note that the range of diminishing returns to the variable input ends at the peak of the output path. Beyond L_5 and its associated Q_5 in Figure 8.2, output can be expected to decrease in absolute terms as the then-excessive quantities of labour greater than L_5 are employed.

The principle of diminishing returns is thought to govern all real-world production processes. Diminishing returns may not be evident in the very early stages of production characterized by low levels of labour employment, but it becomes obvious as progressively more labour is employed. It is simply implausible to believe and unreasonable to expect that output can continue to increase at increasing or even constant rates forever as the labour input is progressively increased vis-à-vis a given plant size. This physical relationship was recognized earliest in agricultural settings and subsequently in engineering situations. It has been adopted by economists as the fundamental behavioural premise in the explanation of input-output relationships. Although diminishing returns are rarely subject to direct examination or empirical testing, the essential truth of the principle may be verified by the logical process of reduction to absurdity.

As an example, consider a typical peasant farm in South Asia, perhaps 15 acres in size, equipped with a fixed amount of capital equipment including a yoke of oxen and a wooden plough with metal tip, and perhaps two or three other digging or cultivating implements. The peasant farmer by himself can exact some volume of agricultural production from the 15 acres. It is likely that the farmer and his son, working together, can produce more than twice what the farmer alone could produce (the range of increasing returns). As successive additional workers (usually family members) are employed on the farm, output can be expected to continue to increase, but eventually at a decreasing rate, and ultimately to actually decrease if too much labour is employed. In case the reader is sceptical of this conclusion, we invite him to think about the possibilities of employing five workers on the 15 acres, then 10 workers, 15, 20, 50, 100, 1000, 1 million workers on 15 acres. Is there any doubt that the principle of diminishing returns has to be true and applicable (at least, eventually) to every real-world production process?

TOTAL, AVERAGE AND MARGINAL PRODUCTS

Theoretically, any number of different vertical sections, parallel to the labour axis, could be cut through the production surface of Figure 8.2. Each one would differ from the others by the amount of capital (that is, the size of plant) in use. Practically, the number of discrete plant sizes that can be built is likely to be rather small. For the time being we shall continue to analyze the representative section illustrated in Figure 8.2 by extracting it from the surface and laying it out on a set of two-dimensional coordinate axes in panel (a) of Figure 8.3. Here the production function section traces out a path that economists refer to as a total product (TP) curve. This TP curve is specific to a given technology, entrepreneurial ability, managerial capacity, and plant size; variation along it is accounted for solely by variation in the labour input.

Employing analytical techniques noted earlier, we can now trace out in panel (b) of Figure 8.3 the average product (AP) and marginal product (MP) curves that correspond to the TP curve in panel (a). The **average product of labour** may be defined and computed as the amount of output, Q, divided by the quantity of labour, L, employed in its production, given all other inputs, that is,

$$(6)\ AP_i = Q_i / L_i,$$

for the ith amount of labour employed. For example, the average product of the L_2 volume of labour employed is Q_2/L_2. With this concept in mind, we should be able to discern the behaviour of the labour AP curve by observing the slopes of rays drawn from the origin to successive points on

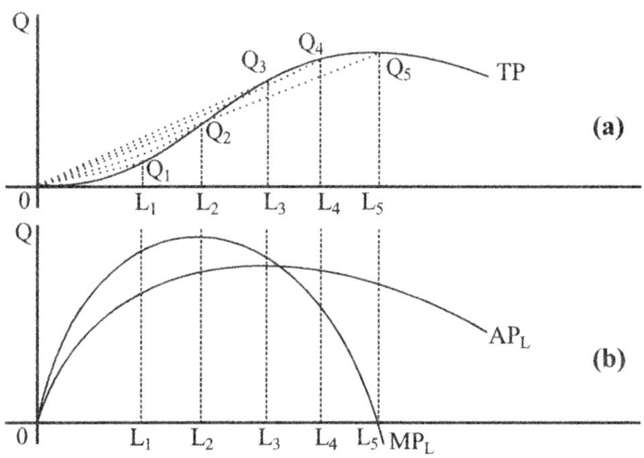

Figure 8.3. Total, average, and marginal product curves.

the TP curve. This is so because the slope of the ray drawn to a point on the TP curve is the hypotenuse of a right triangle formed by the horizontal axis and a vertical erected from the labour quantity point on the axis to the TP curve. Then, the trigonometric tangent of the angle so formed is the ratio of the opposite to the adjacent sides of the triangle, for example, Q_2/L_2, which we have already defined as the average product of the L_2 quantity of labour. In panel (a) of Figure 8.3, rays to the successive points along the TP curve have progressively steeper slopes until Q_3 is reached, beyond which the rays become shallower of slope. Thus we can draw the AP curve in panel (b) as rising from the origin to a peak at the L_3 quantity of labour, beyond which it falls back towards the horizontal axis. The vertical axis units in panel (b) have been expanded relative to those in panel (a) so that the behaviour of AP can be made quite obvious. The relationships among the computed average products for the points along the TP curve illustrated in Figure 8.3 are:

$$(7)\ Q_1/L_1 < Q_2/L_2 < Q_3/L_3 > Q_4/L_4 > Q_5/L_5.$$

The average product of the variable input is relatively easy to measure; the only information required is the amount of output and the corresponding quantity of the input required to produce the output. Because it is easy to measure, the AP of the variable input is a tempting criterion for production decision making. However, economists usually reject it in favour of the MP of the variable input. The average product of labour does find usefulness in aggregate production settings where it is commonly referred to as the output per capita of the labour force. The downward-sloping range of the aggregate AP of labour curve has been compared to the hypothesized subsistence level of income in neo-Malthusian studies.

The **marginal product of labour** (MP_L) may be defined as the ratio of an increment of output (ΔQ) divided by the smallest possible increment of labour (ΔL), that is,

$$(8)\ MP_L = \text{limit}\ (\Delta Q/\Delta L\ ),$$

as ΔL approaches zero.

This definition should be suggestive of an application of the calculus: the first derivative of the TP function with respect to the labour input, that is, dQ/dL, may be used as a measure of MP_L. If there are other inputs present, a partial derivative must be computed. The MP_L measures the rate of change of TP, and can be illustrated graphically as the slope of a tangent to the TP curve at a selected point.

This concept provides the means for discerning the behaviour of the MP_L. Tangents have been drawn to each of the representative points on the TP curve illustrated in panel (a) of Figure 8.3. As the labour input is increased, and output consequently increased, the slopes of the tangents become progressively steeper. The maximum steepness is reached at point Q_2, beyond which they become shallower until a zero slope is reached at Q_5. Beyond Q_5 the slopes of tangents to points on the TP curve are negative. Thus, we draw the MP of labour curve as rising from the origin to a peak at the L_2 level of labour input, then falling until it is zero at the L_5 level of labour input, beyond which it is below the horizontal axis.

Since the AP_L and the MP_L curves are superimposed in panel (b) of Figure 8.3, we may note the corresponding behaviours of the two curves. Over the initial range of labour input, MP_L rises much faster than does AP_L. For example, at Q_1 the slope of the tangent is steeper than the slope of the ray to Q_1. MP_L remains greater than AP_L even after the peak of the MP_L curve is reached. MP_L decreases and passes through the peak of the AP_L curve at the labour input level L_3. Here, the tangent to the TP curve at Q_3 is coincidental with a ray from the origin to Q_3. For all labour input levels greater than L_3, MP_L is both decreasing and less than AP_L. The slope of the tangent at Q_4 is shallower than the slope of the ray drawn to Q_4.

For reasons that shall become apparent in subsequent discussion, economists advocate the use of MP as a production decision criterion. However, the MP is a more abstract concept than is the AP, and the true marginal product of a variable input is substantially more difficult to measure and compute than is the average product. In order to compute the marginal product, the equation of the TP function must be known or estimated before the derivative can be computed. The equation of a function can be guessed at, 'eyeball' fashion, but the generally accepted means of equation estimation is statistical regression analysis of historical data for the Q and L variables. The data for the regression analysis may have been generated by experimental procedures or captured by observing natural production processes in operation. These procedures are troublesome, time-consuming, and costly. It is no wonder that real-world production decision makers have an aversion to using the MP as a production decision criterion.

Economists make a distinction between the marginal product and the **incremental product** (IP) of a variable input. While the true MP may be measured as the limit of the ratio $\Delta Q/DL$ as ΔL approaches zero, the incremental product may be measured as the ratio, $\Delta Q/\Delta L$, for any measurable ΔL. With reference to Figure 8.3, panel (a), the incremental product of labour over the L_2 to L_3 input range can be computed as

$$(9)\ IP_L = (Q_3 - Q_2) / (L_3 - L_2).$$

In this sense, the incremental product may be measured as the slope of a chord connecting any two points on the TP curve. This is so because the chord forms the hypotenuse of a right triangle drawn to the two points.

Although the true marginal product of a variable input is troublesome to compute, the incremental product is relatively easy to compute. The only data needed are the quantities of output and labour input for the two points on the TP curve. It is important to note two caveats in this regard. First, two observed production points may not be on the same TP curve if one or more of the other (than L) determinants of output have changed (that is, there may be an identification problem). If the two points happen to be on different TP curves, the computed IP ratio will over- or under-state the IP that might have been computed for points on the same TP curve. Second, even if the two observed points are on the same TP curve, the computed IP will over- or under-state the true MP computed by differentiation for a point at either end of the chord connecting the two points.

Where does this leave us? MP is the ideal production decision criterion (we shall substantiate this point shortly), but it is troublesome to compute. IP is in practical terms both measurable and

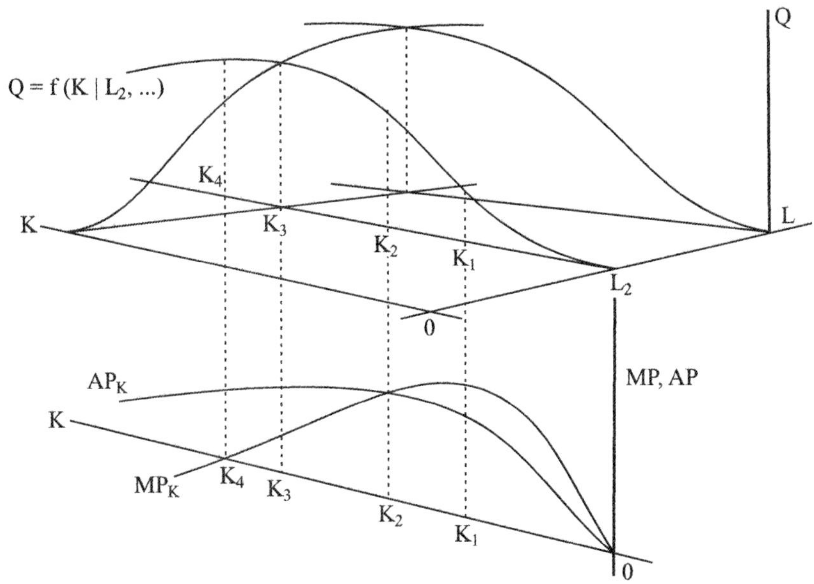

Figure 8.4. A capital-variable (labour-constant) section of the surface.

computable with relative ease, but it is likely to over- or under-state the true MP. The production decision maker is urged to go to the trouble to compute MP if it is not too costly to do so; otherwise, the IP may be computed and used as a decision criterion, subject to the recognition that it is only an approximation to the true MP of the variable input.

THE PRODUCTIVITIES OF OTHER INPUTS

Thus far we have illustrated a vertical slice through the production surface, parallel to the labour axis, on the premises that capital is the fixed input and labour is the variable input in the short run. But we have also noted the possibility of the opposite identities of the fixed and variable inputs in a short-run setting. Any number of vertical slices may be taken through the production surface, parallel to the capital axis, thus simulating fixed quantities of labour, with variable quantities of capital. We could also repeat all of the discussion on the last several pages, but in reference to capital as the variable input. We shall decline to reproduce this discussion, but we invite the reader to study Figure 8.4, which depicts a labour-constant, capital-variable slice through the production surface, in order to confirm the applicability of the analysis to the alternate situation.

THE STAGES OF PRODUCTION

Now that we have demonstrated the applicability of the production principles to either labour or capital as the variable input, the stage is set to identify the so-called relevant range of

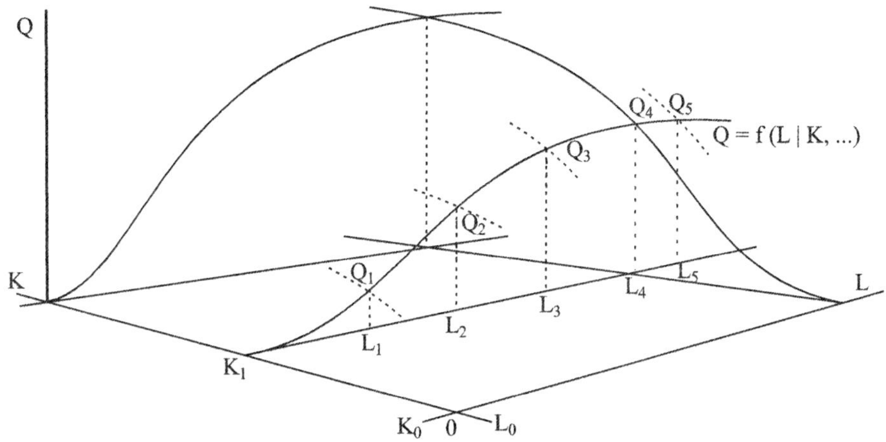

Figure 8.5. Each point on a total product curve for labour is also on a total product curve for capital.

production. To this end we reproduce in Figure 8.5 the surface and vertical slice through it illustrated in Figure 8.2, but with obvious alterations. We retain the assumption that capital is the fixed input with plant K_1 in place; the slice parallel to the labour axis implies that labour is the variable input in the short run.

Any point like Q_2 on the production surface lies on both a TP curve for labour as variable input and a TP curve for capital as variable input. Thus we have drawn line segments cross-wise to the path of the slice at each of the selected points along the labour-variable TP curve. These cross-wise line segments represent tangents to the surface, the slopes of which measure the marginal products of capital. Even though the quantity of capital does not change, we should be able to compute for every different amount of labour employed both the MP of labour and the MP of capital.

How do the marginal products of labour and capital vary with respect to each other? Figure 8.6 illustrates a TP curve for labour as a variable input, assuming one unit of installed capital. In this illustration, the TP curve is carried to the point where so much labour has been employed that output has fallen to zero. For purpose of illustration, we assume that the horizontal axis between the origin and the point at which TP returns to zero can be divided into 10 equal labour units.

In panel (b) of Figure 8.6 we represent the explicit labour-variable MP and AP curves that correspond to the TP curve, and further plot selected points along implicit MP and AP curves for capital as if it were the variable input. Along the horizontal scale we note that even though the labour input increases explicitly from zero to ten units, the capital input remains constant at one unit.

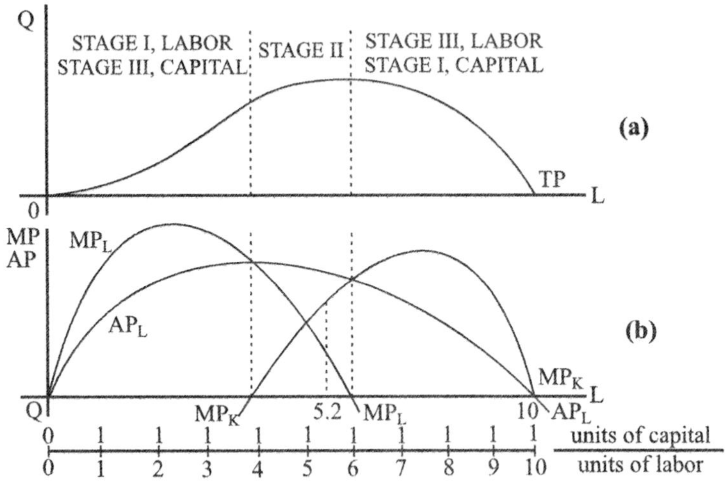

Figure 8.6. Marginal productivities in the stages of production.

In Figure 8.6 we may examine the results of explicitly decreasing the labour input from 10 towards zero units. When this happens, the quantity of capital employed per unit of labour implicitly increases from 1/10 of a unit to 1/9 of a unit, then to 1/8, 1/7, and so on. Conversely, when the quantity of labour is explicitly increased from one unit to two units, the quantity of capital per unit of labour is implicitly decreased from 1/1 unit to 1/2 unit. Recognition that the relative quantity of each fixed input does implicitly change consequent upon an explicit change of a variable input is essential to an understanding of how the marginal products change vis-à-vis each other.

As may be seen in panel (b) of Figure 8.6, over the initial range of labour input, the MP of labour increases to a peak, then begins to decrease; but the MP of capital is negative. Economists identify this range as the Stage I of production for labour, but the Stage III of production for capital. Likewise, moving from right-to-left as the quantity of capital is implicitly increased, the MP of capital rises to a peak and begins to decrease; but the MP of labour is negative. Economists identify this range as the Stage I of production for capital, but the Stage III of production for labour. A rational and perceptive production decision maker would not choose to operate in either Stage I or Stage III. In labour's Stage I (capital's Stage III), labour is underutilized while capital is over-utilized (implied by the negative marginal productivity of capital). In labour's Stage III (capital's Stage I), labour is over-utilized (implied by the negative marginal productivity of capital) while capital is underutilized.

We may thus identify Stage II (common to both inputs) as the relevant range of production. Within Stage II the marginal products of both inputs are positive, although they vary in opposite directions. The boundaries for Stage II for each input are found at the point of zero MP for the other input, which coincidentally correspond to the intersections of the MP and AP curves for each of the inputs.

Some very important behavioural relationships may now be noted. Within production Stage II, as either input is increased in quantity, its MP decreases, but the MP of the other input (which explicitly does not vary) increases. Conversely, if the quantity of either input is decreased, its MP will increase, but the MP of its complement(s) may be expected to decrease. Knowledge of this relationship enables us to answer a very important question for the production manager: how can the (marginal) productivity of labour be increased? Two answers are possible: either by decreasing the labour input, or by providing labour with more capital equipment. The former response is typically regarded as a short-run adjustment, the latter as a long-run change.

THE EQUAMARGINAL PRINCIPLE

But where within Stage II should the production manager choose to operate? It is tempting to pick the intersection of the two MP curves, but this would be the appropriate point only in a very special circumstance. To answer the question, we need two additional pieces of information, the prices per unit of the two inputs. Then, whatever happens to be the ratio of the unit prices of the two inputs, it follows logically that a corresponding ratio between their marginal products would be warranted, that is,

$$(10)\ MP_L/MP_K = P_L/P_K.$$

An alternate version of this relationship may be expressed as:

$$(11)\ MP_L/P_L = MP_K/P_K.$$

This very important relationship is known as the Equamarginal Principle. Stated as an operational decision criterion, the optimal combination of labour and capital is the one for which the marginal product per dollar's worth of labour is equal to the marginal product per dollar's worth of capital. But this is really not a decision criterion; rather, it is an equilibrium condition. The practical decision criterion might better be stated:

$$(12)\ MP_L/P_L >=< MP_K/P_K.$$

Following this decision criterion, if the MP per dollar's worth of capital is greater than the MP per dollar's worth of labour, the production decision maker should employ more capital and/or less labour. By so doing, the MP of capital will fall and the MP of labour will rise, thereby tending to bring about an equality of the marginal product per dollar's worth of the two inputs. We leave it to the reader to explore alternate possibilities. In Figure 8.6, if the price of a unit of capital is twice the price of a unit of labour, then approximately 5.2 units of labour should be employed to operate the one unit of capital since at 5.2 units of labour the MP of capital is approximately twice the MP of labour.

COST MINIMIZATION VS. PROFIT MAXIMIZATION

The Equamarginal Principle as elaborated in the previous section can serve only as a decision criterion for finding the least-cost combination of the factor inputs. It cannot however find the resource input combination that maximizes profits because it encompasses only the physical productivities of the resources and their prices or, from the perspective of the firm, their costs. It fails completely to account for the firm's revenue possibilities. As we shall confirm, cost minimization and profit maximization are unlikely to occur at either the same level of output or with the same resource input combination.

A variant of the Equamarginal Principle can be specified to enable discovery of the input combination that maximizes profits. To do so, we must define a new concept, **marginal revenue product** (MRP). The MRP of a resource is the addition to the firm's total revenue due to selling the additional output resulting from using one more unit of the resource. In a purely competitive context, MRP can be computed as the marginal product of the resource multiplied by (evaluated at) the price per unit of the product (that is, $MRP_R = MP_R \times P$). In an imperfectly competitive situation, because the firm's product demand curve slopes downward from left to right, the MRP is computed as the marginal product of the resource multiplied by the marginal revenue resulting from selling the additional product, or

$$(13)\ MRP_R = MP_R \times MR.$$

We note that MR=P in the purely competitive context, so specification (13) is good for both the purely competitive and imperfectly competitive contexts. The schedule of MRP values for different quantities of the resource used by a firm constitutes its demand curve for the resource, $D_R = MRP_R$, as illustrated in Figure 8.7.

If the firm purchases the resource in a competitive market, the resource price, P_R, is the firm's **marginal factor** cost (MFC); the firm's MFC_R curve would be horizontal and coincident with its resource supply curve at the level of P_R. But if the resource is bought in an imperfectly

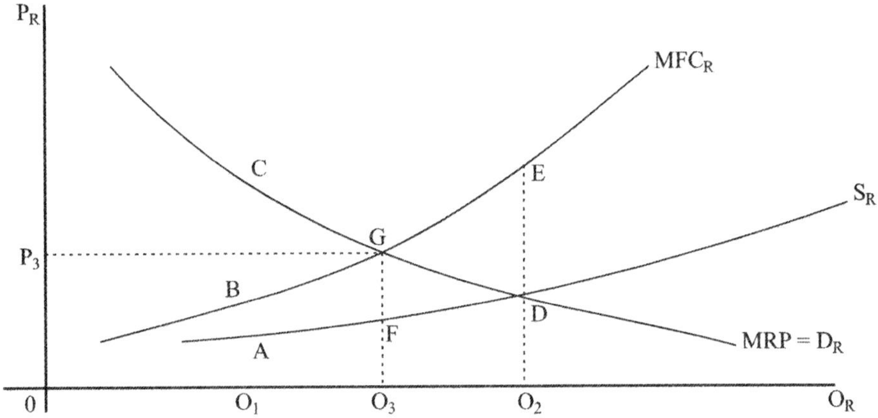

Figure 8.7. Resource demand and supply in an imperfectly competitive market.

competitive market, the MFC of employing an additional unit of the resource is greater than its price. This is so because the firm has to offer successively higher prices to purchase larger quantities of the resource, and the higher prices normally apply to all units of the resource purchased, not just the additional units. In an imperfectly competitive resource market the resource supply curve slopes upward. The marginal factor cost schedule also slopes upward and lies above the resource supply curve as illustrated in Figure 8.7.

These resource market relationships enable specification of the criterion for finding the resource utilization level for any single resource that maximizes the firm's profits, given all other resources:

$$(14)\ MRP_R >=< MFC_R.$$

At any resource utilization level for which $MRP_R > MFC_R$, for example, Q_1, the firm can by using one more unit of the resource add more to its total revenue when the additional output is sold than will be added to its total costs by employing the resource unit. Or, if $MFC_R > MRP_R$, for example, at Q_2, the firm should reduce its utilization of that resource. This will decrease its total revenues and total costs, but total costs will fall by more than total revenue will decrease. The firm should stop making adjustments to its level of utilization of the resource as soon as there is nothing more to be gained, for example, at Q_3, where

$$(15)\ MRP_R = MFC_R.$$

When this equality is attained, profit is maximized. This relationship can be rearranged as

$$(16)\ MRP_R/MFC_R = 1.$$

While this criterion is appropriate to a single resource input, given all others, it can be extended to multiple variable inputs as

$$(17)\ MRP_L/MFC_L = MRP_K/MFC_K = \ldots = MRP_X/MFC_X = 1.$$

If any inequality emerges anywhere in this string of relationships, an adjustment to the resource input combination needs to be made. Such an inequality may emerge as technologies, product prices, or resource supply conditions vary. For example, suppose that one of the resources, L, becomes more abundant and its price to the firm falls. This will decrease MFC_L, the denominator of the first ratio, thereby causing the value of the ratio to increase. In this scenario the firm should adjust its input combination to use more of the resource L, or less of other resources. Using more of L will have the dual effect of decreasing its marginal productivity and bidding its market price up. Both effects will cause the ratio MRP_L/MFC_L to fall until the string of equalities is re-established.

Two points need reiteration. First, the resource input combination resulting in the equalities of MRP/MFC across all of the inputs and equal to unity (1) will be the profit maximizing resource input combination. Second, the profit maximizing input combination found by equating the MRP/MFC ratios will not necessarily (in fact, not likely) coincide with the cost minimizing combination of resource inputs that is found by equating the MP/P ratios across all inputs.

WHAT'S AHEAD

In this chapter we have examined the implications of changing one input while all other inputs remain constant. This has been essentially short-run analysis. In the long run, all inputs are variable.

Summary of Important Points

1. Production is the central function of the enterprise; the act of production is the transformation of raw substances into other forms that are distinguished by their more desirable functional, locational, or temporal characteristics.
2. Productive effort is warranted because of the potential inherent in specialization and division of labour to improve the efficiency of the production process.
3. Efficiency is served by producing a larger volume of output from a given amount of inputs, or by employing smaller amounts of the inputs in the production of a target output.
4. Experience has demonstrated that organized productive effort under hierarchical control often is more efficient than are individual efforts; the business enterprise has provided the vehicle for the organization and control of production in modern society.
5. The essential entrepreneurial functions are the perception of an unfilled market demand and the assumption of risk in organizing a productive process to exploit the market potential.
6. Three crucial managerial problems are to select an appropriate technology for implementation of production, to discern the right volume of output to meet the market demand, and to choose the optimal combination of inputs to produce the target level of output.
7. The analysis of production requires an examination of how inputs are combined to produce outputs, a relationship that economists analyze with a production function.
8. A graphic representation of a production function may exhibit any of several possible shapes.
9. The analysis of returns to scale belongs to the long run; a change of a single input, given fixed quantities of other inputs, is an analysis of the short run.
10. Production decision makers may plan for the long run, but all decisions are made in short-run settings.
11. Vertical slices through a production surface enable analysis of production relationships.

Contd....

12. An essential characteristic of a production relationship is that as an input increases vis-à-vis other fixed inputs, (eventually) output increases at a decreasing rate; this exhibits the principle of diminishing returns, which is thought to govern all real-world production relationships.
13. The average product of labour (AP_L) may be computed as the slope of a ray from the origin to a point on the total product (TP) curve corresponding to the labour input.
14. The marginal product of labour (MP_L) may be computed as the slope of any tangent to a point on the TP curve.
15. The facts that the AP_L and MP_L curves reach peaks beyond which they slope downward are indicative of the principle of diminishing returns.
16. The incremental product of labour (IP_L) may be computed as the slope of any chord drawn between two points on the TP curve; the IP_L, though easily computed from available data, is only an approximation to the MP_L.
17. Marginal and average products may also be computed for other inputs even though they do not explicitly vary; every point on the TP curve for labour as the variable input also lies on a TP curve for capital as the variable input.
18. The 'Stages of Production' for labour and capital are symmetrical; labour is underutilized in its stage I (capital's stage III) and over-utilized in its stage III (capital's stage I); within stage II (which is common to both inputs), labour's marginal productivity diminishes as capital's marginal productivity increases (and vice versa).
19. The two ways to increase the marginal productivity of any input are to use less of it or more of the complementary inputs.
20. The appropriate combination of two inputs may be found within stage II where the marginal product per dollar's worth of each input is just equal to the marginal product per dollar's worth of the other input.
21. The rational input decision criterion for cost minimization is to use more of any input for which its marginal product per dollar's worth is greater than the marginal products per dollar's worth of other inputs.
22. Profit maximization may be achieved when the ratio of the marginal revenue product to the marginal factor cost for each input is just equal to the same ratio for every other input, and all such ratios are just equal to unity (1).

Significant Terms

production

specialization, division of labour

economic problem

demand insatiability

efficiency

distribution mechanism

hierarchical control

appropriate technology

production function
physical inputs
production enabling conditions
production surface
returns to a variable input, to scale
variable proportions
short, long run
vertical, horizontal slice approaches
diminishing returns
total, average, marginal product curves
derivative
incremental product
fixed, variable inputs
stages of production
explicit, implicit input changes
stage boundaries
complementary inputs
equamarginal principle
marginal product per dollar's worth
marginal revenue product
imperfectly competitive product markets
marginal factor costs
resource demand, supply

Questions for Discussion

1. There is no reason for any enterprise to exist except to engage in some form of production. Discuss.
2. Eleemosynary institutions (like churches, charitable organizations, and colleges) are *de facto* productive enterprises. Discuss.
3. Discuss the role of efficiency in managerial decision making.
4. Why is organized human effort likely to be more efficient than individual human effort?
5. What is the justification for the existence of hierarchical, authoritarian business firms in competitive markets?
6. Discuss the role of the entrepreneur in the productive process for some selected good. ...for some selected service.
7. Identify the four basic production questions and indicate how each is addressed in a market economy.
8. Distinguish physical inputs from enabling conditions in the productive process and indicate how each affects the production of output in a selected product market.
9. Explain the sense in which a recipe for your favourite food is actually a production function.
10. Explain how more than two independent variables can be analyzed in the production function for a specific item that you have selected.

11. Explain why not all of the hypothesized shapes of three-dimensional production functions are plausible representations of real-world production relationships.

12. Explain why a production function that is linear in all independent variables might serve satisfactorily as an analytical device; what are the limits on its use?

13. Explain why the manager's freedom of choice in selecting input combinations in a productive process is usually constrained by the time-frame of the decision context.

14. Distinguish 'returns to a variable input' from 'returns to scale' and 'variable returns,' and identify the time frames associated with these terms.

15. Describe a real-world productive process with which you are familiar in which capital is not the input that is fixed in the short run.

16. Contrast the productive relationships of 'diminishing returns' and 'increasing returns' to a variable input and assess the viability of each to real-world production processes with which you are familiar.

17. Explain the sense of a 'vertical slice' through a production function and indicate what variables are assumed to be fixed and changeable.

18. Explain the managerial significance of the 'inflection point' along a vertical slice through a production surface.

19. Explain why the principle of 'diminishing returns' may be taken as the governing principle of most real-world production processes.

20. Why is it "implausible to believe and unreasonable to expect that output can continue to increase at increasing or even constant rates forever as the labour input is progressively increased vis-à-vis a given plant size"?

21. Discuss the implications of progressively increasing the amount of labour employed on a 100-acre farm until the entire unemployed population of the country is being used.

22. Explain how average and marginal product functions may be derived graphically from a total product function; what assumptions must be made in the derivation?

23. What are the managerial implications of the behaviour of the average product of labour?

24. Distinguish the 'marginal product of labour' from the 'incremental product of labour' in a production function, and contrast their respective usefulness.

25. Explain why economists usually advocate the use of the marginal product rather than the average product as a production decision criterion; under what circumstances might the average product of a variable input be judged an adequate decision criterion?

26. Explain why the incremental product of labour is likely to be inferior to the marginal product of labour as a decision criterion. Why would a production decision maker choose to rely on information about the incremental product?

27. Describe the analytical process for deriving information about the marginal product of capital from a three dimensional production surface; what assumptions must be made in this process?

28. Explain why both the marginal products of labour and capital may be analyzed for any combination of labour and capital possible in a production process; what are the managerial implications of this possibility?

29. Explain how one may infer the marginal products of the 'fixed input' in a production process when the 'variable input' is explicitly changed.

30. Identify the boundaries for the stages of production and indicate their managerial significances.

31. Explain why most rational and knowledgeable production decision makers would choose not to operate in production stages I or III.

32. Explain why economists identify production stage II as the relevant range of production; how does the production decision manager ensure operation in stage II?

33. Explain the role of the prices of the inputs in a productive process in determining their optimal combination.

34. How can information about marginal products of inputs and their market prices serve as a criterion for production decision making?

35. Distinguish 'marginal revenue product' from 'marginal physical product' and indicate why a production decision maker might choose to pay attention to the former rather than the latter.

36. Contrast the relevant production decision criteria for the objectives of cost minimization and profit maximization; why might they not coincide for the same input combination?

Appendix 8.1

THE HORIZONTAL-SLICE APPROACH

In this appendix we pursue the alternative approach to that elaborated earlier for developing the Equamarginal Principle. In the following discussions we shall not attempt an exhaustive exploration of the approach, but shall develop only those concepts necessary to reaching the objective.

THE HORIZONTAL SLICE

We could choose to analyze any of the production surface shapes illustrated in Figure 8.1. Following the convention established we shall focus on the generalized surface shape illustrated in panel (d) of Figure 8.1. Figure A-VIII(b) illustrates such a production surface where a plane, abcd, parallel to the floor at quantity altitude Q_4, has been passed through the production surface tracing

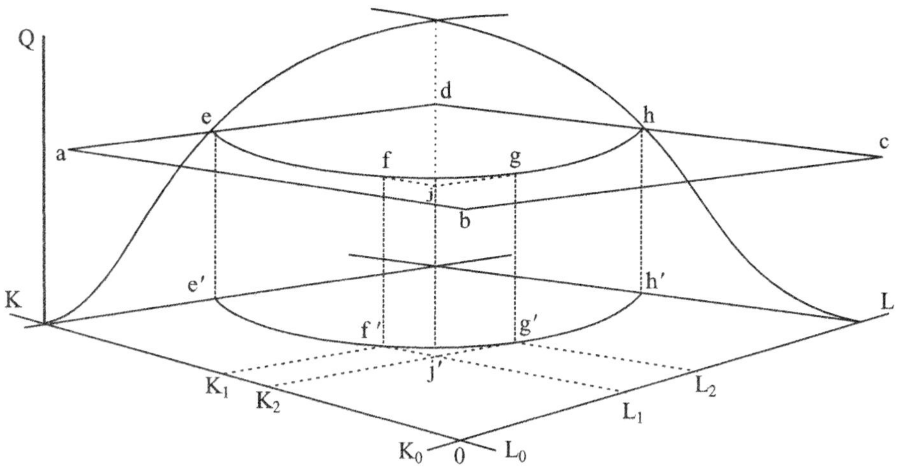

Figure A-VIII(a). A horizontal slice through a production surface.

out the horizontal slice, efgh. The path, e'f'g'h', in the floor of the surface is the vertical projection of the slice through the surface. Slice efgh is only one of an infinite number of slices that could be taken through the surface at different quantity altitudes.

THE ISOQUANT MAP

Figure A-VIII(b) shows a two-dimensional view from a perspective above the surface

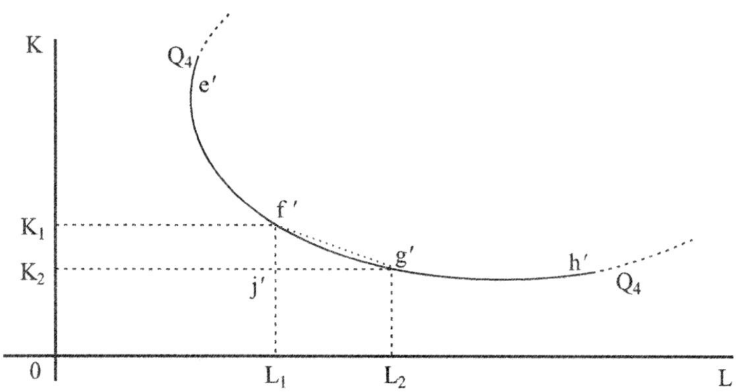

Figure A-VIII(b). An isoquant.

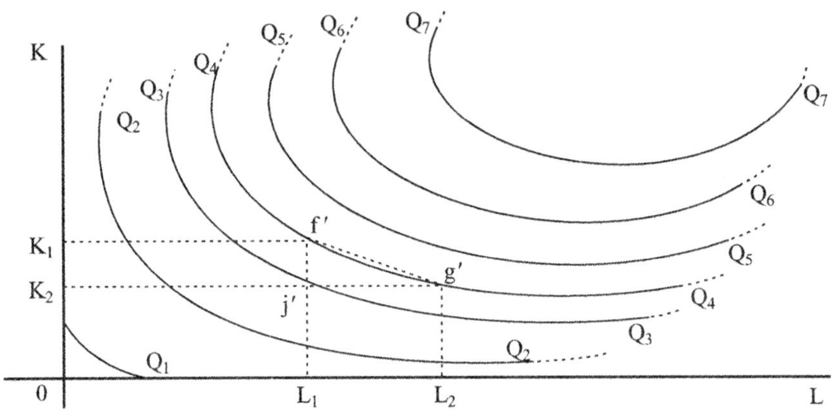

Figure A-VIII(c). An isoquant map.

illustrated in Figure A-VIII(a). In effect, the three-dimensional surface appears to be collapsed into the floor when viewed from above, but the path e'f'g'h' represents the slice through the surface at quantity altitude Q_4. Economists refer to the e'f'g'h' path as an isoquant (meaning same quantity) because it represents a sequence of points, the (K,L) coordinates of which are the input combinations that can produce the Q_4 level of output. For example, output Q_4 can be produced with the L_1 quantity of labour employed with the K_1 quantity of capital. Output Q_4 can also be produced with less capital, K_2, if a larger labour quantity, L_2, is utilized. This suggests that labour and capital are to some extent substitutable for one another. Since path e'f'g'h' is drawn as a continuous curve, the implication is that there are an infinite number (or as many as there are points along the path) of combinations of K and L that can produce the Q_4 output. In reality, technological considerations may limit the effective number of such combinations to a relatively small number.

Suppose that instead of selecting a (K,L) combination represented by a point along the isoquant the production decision maker chooses to use the K_2 quantity of capital with the smaller L_2 quantity of labour, reaching point j on the production surface in Figure A-VIII(a), and j' in Figure A-VIII(b). It should be apparent that the smaller quantity of labour working with less capital will produce some output smaller than Q_4.

Figure A-VIII(c) is an elaboration of Figure A-VIII(b) to show the paths of several other 'representative' isoquants that could be generated by horizontally slicing the surface at altitudes other than Q_4. It is now apparent that the L_1 quantity of labour using the K_2 capital input can produce only the Q_3 output, which is less than Q_4. Theoretically, any number of such isoquants could be generated by slicing the surface at different altitudes so that the floor of the surface might appear 'dense' with concentric isoquants. The collection of representative isoquants may be referred to as an isoquant map. The isoquant map may be likened to the collection of isotemp or isobar lines on a weather map, or to the contour lines on a geological or military map.

Suppose that the horizontal slices taken through the surface to generate the isoquant map illustrated in Figure A-VIII(b) were taken at successively higher quantity altitudes that are equal quantity increments apart. In this case, (Q_2- Q_1) would be equal to (Q_3- Q_2), and so on. When viewed from above the surface in Figure A-VIII(a), the isoquant map illustrated in Figure A-VIII(b) betrays the likely shape of the surface that cannot be seen explicitly in Figure A-VIII(b). From isoquant Q_1 up to isoquant Q_4 the isoquants appear to be getting closer together, implying that the surface is increasing at an increasing rate in the quantity dimension. From isoquant Q_4 through isoquant Q7 the isoquants appear to become farther apart, suggesting that output is increasing at a decreasing rate. The reader is invited to analyze the likely shapes of the isoquant maps that could be generated from the surfaces illustrated in panels (a), (b), and (c) in Figure A-VIII(c).

THE MARGINAL RATE OF TECHNICAL SUBSTITUTION

The slope of an isoquant at any point may be measured by the slope of a tangent drawn to the point, or it may be approximated by the slope of a chord connecting two points near to each other along the isoquant. For example, the slope of the Q_4 isoquant over the f' to g' range in Figure A-VIII(c) can be approximated by the slope of the chord from f' to g', or

$$(1)\ \Delta K/\Delta L = (K_2 - K_1)/(L_2 - L_1) = f'j'/j'g'$$

The technical name for this slope is the Marginal Rate of Technical Substitution (MRTS). The MRTS is interpreted as the rate at which the firm can substitute labour for capital (that is, use more labour and less capital) while remaining at the same level of output. Over the f'g' arc of the Q_4 isoquant, the firm can maintain output at the Q_4 level as the capital input is reduced from K_1 to K_2 only by increasing the quantity of labour used from L_1 to L_2. It should be obvious that between f' and g' the MRTS is negative since K_2 is less than K_1.

The MRTS will normally be negative over the economic range of production (we shall identify production Stage II towards the end of this appendix). It will be instructive to examine the right triangle formed by the points f', g', and j'. As we have just noted, the ratio of the sides of this triangle, f'j'/j'g', measures the slope of the third side (or hypotenuse), which forms the f'g' chord. The diagonal movement from f' to g' may be regarded as two separate adjustments represented by the vertical and horizontal sides of the triangle.

Specifically, the movement from f' to j' is a decrease in the use of capital (–DK) which, other things remaining the same, would decrease output from Q_4 to Q_3, or $-\Delta Q_1$. The movement from j' to g' is an increase in the use of labour (ΔL), which by itself would cause output to increase from Q_3 to Q_4, or ΔQ_2. ΔQ_2 is of the same magnitude, but opposite sign, as ΔQ_1, so we shall use ΔQ without sign or subscript to refer to both quantities. Identification of the output changes allows us to specify the marginal products of capital and labour as

$$(2)\ MP_K = \Delta Q/\Delta K \text{ and } MP_L = \Delta Q/\Delta L.$$

Further, we may note that the ratio of the marginal product of labour to the marginal product of capital also measures the MRTS:

$$(3)\ MP_L/MP_K = \Delta Q/\Delta L/\Delta Q/\Delta K = \Delta K/\Delta L = MRTS.$$

This point will prove of value in subsequent discussion.

THE CAPITAL OUTLAY BUDGET

The isoquant map provides information about production possibilities, but by itself cannot provide the production decision maker with a criterion for selecting an optimal input combination. Additional information is needed in the firm's production budget and the prices of the two inputs, K and L. Suppose that the prices of Labour and Capital are P_L and P_K, and the firm's management has determined that the production cost outlay must be limited to the dollar sum C. This information can be brought together in the following equation:

$$(4)\ L^*P_L + K^*P_K <= C.$$

The sense of this equation is that the product of the number of units of labour utilized (L) times its price (P_L) plus the number of units of capital consumed (K) times its price (P_K) cannot exceed the budgeted outlay (C). The firm could under-expend its budget, but suppose that the management has decided to commit the entire budget to the purchase of quantities of labour and capital so that the inequality symbol may be ignored. What quantities of each input should the firm employ?

Equation (4) can be usefully rearranged in the following format:

$$(5)\ K = C/P_K - P_L/P_K \cdot L.$$

Equation (5) is linear and in the so-called 'slope-intercept' format, y = a + bx, where the slope of the line that represents the equation is the ratio of the price of labour (P_L) to the price of capital (P_K). It should be noted that this ratio is negative. The conceptual interpretation of this slope is the rate at which the firm can substitute labour for capital *while remaining within the budget*. The vertical axis intercept is the ratio of the budgeted outlay (C) to the price of capital (P_K), which determines the maximum amount of capital that could be purchased by the firm if it purchased no labour at all. Equation (5), henceforth referred to as the budget line, can be plotted on the same set of coordinate axes containing the isoquant map. We may suppose that the values of C, P_L, and P_K are such that the budget line is plotted as in Figure A-VIII(d).

THE OPTIMAL RESOURCE ALLOCATION CRITERION

At what point along the budget line should the firm choose to employ a combination of labour and capital? As the reader has likely already guessed, the relevant decision criterion is a comparison of the slopes of the isoquant and the budget line, that is, whether

$$6)\ MRTS >/< P_L/P_K.$$

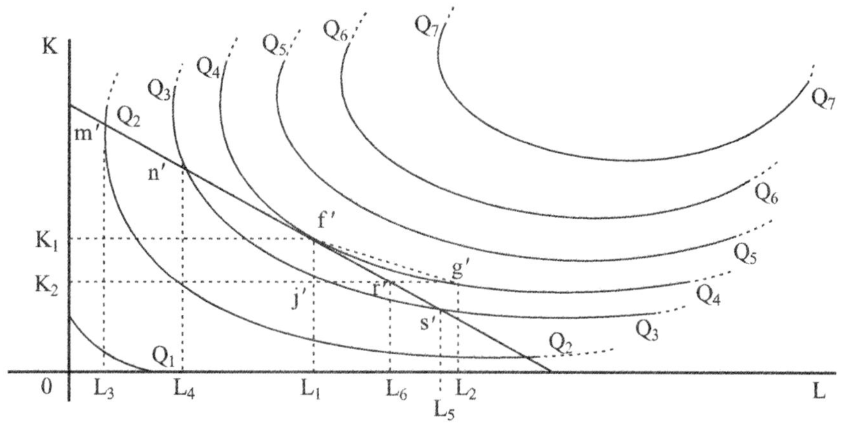

Figure A-VIII(d). An isoquant map and a budget line.

Point m' is one option involving a large capital input used with a small amount of labour. At point m' the slope of the isoquant, though negative, is very steep, implying that if the firm were to give up the (K_3- K_4) quantity of capital, it could purchase the (L_4– L_3) quantity of labour while remaining within its budget. This additional quantity of labour is a great deal more than the firm would have to have to remain at the Q_2 level of output. In fact, to exchange the (K_3- K_4) quantity of capital for the (L_4- L_3) quantity of labour would enable the firm to move to a higher level of output on isoquant Q_3 at point n'. This is obviously a good move which the firm should undertake. The reader is now invited to repeat this analysis using point n' as the departure point.

Suppose that the production decision maker had first determined to try the input combination represented by point s'. At this point the firm employs a relatively large quantity of labour with substantially less capital. The MRTS at point s' is negative, but quite small (that is, the slope of the isoquant is shallow). The production decision maker is considering replacing the (L_5- L6) quantity of labour with additional capital. Only a small amount of additional capital will be needed to allow the firm to remain at the same level of output, Q_3. However, by giving up the (L_5– L_4) quantity of labour the firm can still remain within its budget by purchasing the (K6- K5) quantity of capital, which will enable it to increase output almost to the Q_4 level. This is a good move that the firm should undertake.

As may be readily deduced, the production manager will find an output-increasing incentive to reallocate labour and capital by moving downwards along the budget line from points such as m' and n' until the incentive disappears. Likewise, a similar incentive will be found to move upwards along the budget line from points such as r' and s' until the incentive is eliminated.

When does the input-reallocation incentive expire? This occurs when a point is reached along the budget line where the slope of the budget line is just equal to the slope of the isoquant. At such a point, for example, f' in Figure A-VIII(e), the conceptual interpretation is that the rate at which the firm can substitute labour for capital while remaining at the same level of output (the

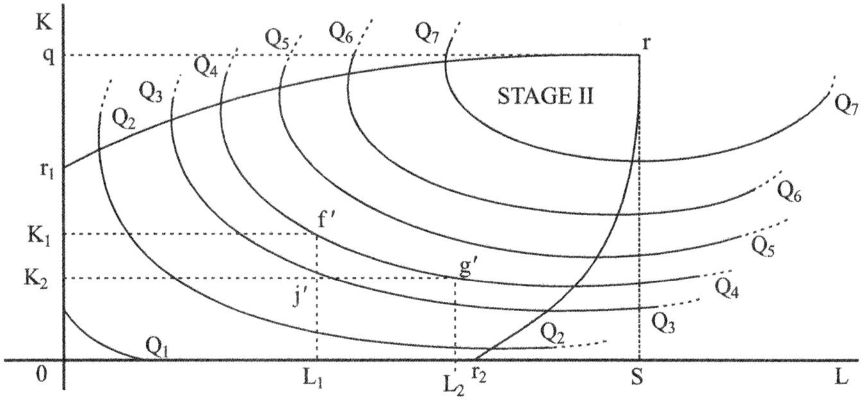

Figure A-VIII(e). The stages of production in isoquant analysis.

MRTS) is just equal to the rate at which the firm can substitute labour for capital while remaining within its capital outlay budget (P_K/P_L). This is the point of tangency of the budget line with an isoquant. It is also the highest output-level isoquant that the budget line can reach. At this point the production manager will have found the output-maximizing combination of labour and capital, given the limitation of the budgeted capital outlay. It is then also the cost-per-unit minimizing combination of labour and capital that can be accommodated by the capital-outlay budget.

THE EQUAMARGINAL PRINCIPLE

Cost minimization occurs at the point representing the input combination that meets the criterion,

$$(7)\ MRTS = P_L/P_K.$$

And since we have already shown in equation (3) that MRTS also measures the ratio of MP_L to MP_K, equation (7) can also be expressed as

$$(8)\ MP_L/MP_K = P_L/P_K.$$

which by algebraic rearrangement can be expressed as

$$(9)\ MP_L/P_L = MP_K/P_K.$$

Thus we have arrived at the same Equamarginal Principle that was recognized as the optimal resource allocation criterion via the approach of horizontal slices through the production surface.

STAGES OF PRODUCTION IN ISOQUANT ANALYSIS

Before we leave the horizontal slice approach, we should also note that the stages of production can be identified on an isoquant map by specifying two ridge lines. One ridge line follows a path formed by the points on the isoquants where they are vertical, the path r_1r in Figure A-VIII(e). At any point below r_1r an increase of the capital input will increase output because a higher isoquant will be reached. This implies that the MP_K is positive. However, at any point above r_1r an increase in the capital input will decrease output (lower quantity altitude horizontal slices will be reached), implying a negative MP_K. We may infer then that the region above r_1r is Stage III for capital, while that below r_1r is capital's Stage II.

We leave it to the reader to examine the logic leading to the inference that at any point to the left of r_2r the MP_L is positive, while at any point to the right of r_2r the MP_L is negative. This recognition then identifies Stages II and III for labour. The final step is to recall from discussion in Chapter 8 the coincidences of capital's Stage III with labour's Stage I, as well as that for labour's Stage III and capital's Stage I, and the isoquant stage analysis is complete. The MRTS at any point along an isoquant in Stage II will be negative, and the marginal productivities of both inputs in Stage II will be positive. Outside of Stage II, the MRTS will be a positive slope, and the marginal productivity of one or the other of the inputs will be negative.

—oo(O)oo—

Chapter 9

Production in the Long Run

Topics covered in this chapter

• Analysis of returns to scale. • Impacts of technology, entrepreneurship, and management changes on production relationships. • Appropriate technology for a production process. • The specification of a production function equation. • The empirical estimation of a production function. • Identification problems in estimating production functions. • Production functions as simulation models.

THE LONG- AND SHORT-RUN TIME FRAMES

As we noted earlier, the three-dimensional surfaces imply that production decision makers enjoy a great deal of freedom in varying the two inputs, or in choosing any eligible combination of inputs represented by the coordinates of points in the floors of the diagrams. In reality, such freedom of choice is constrained by the time-frame setting of the decision context.

In the analysis of how input variation affects output, given a selected technology, economists distinguish three situations: a single input is changed vis-à-vis fixed quantities of all other inputs; or all inputs are changed (positively or negatively) by the same proportion (greater or lesser than 100 per cent); or inputs are changed in varying proportions vis-à-vis each other. The first case describes the analysis of **returns to a variable input**; the second describes **returns to scale**; the third describes the general situation, or **variable proportions**, inferences about which may be drawn from an analysis of the first two situations. It is to the second and third cases that we now turn in the present chapter.

The realm of returns to a variable input permits us to distinguish the short run from the long run. In the short run, some (at least one) inputs may not be changed. In the long run, all inputs are presumed to be variable. The analysis of returns to scale thus belongs to the long-run. In the real world, production decision makers may plan for the long-run changes which they intend to make, but all decisions are made in short-run settings, even the decisions to make long-run changes. In this sense, then, the freedom of the decision maker to vary inputs is constrained by the temporal setting.

To this point we have taken the short-run view that some quantity of one or another of the inputs is fixed while quantities of other inputs are variable. Over the long run, quantities of all of the inputs into the production process can vary. While some can be varied almost continuously (for example, labour), others can be adjusted only in discrete increments (for example, sections of land, additions to warehouses, new assembly lines).

VARIABLE PROPORTIONS AND RETURNS TO SCALE

We shall describe the more general case where the quantities of the inputs change in different proportions vis-à-vis each other as the case of variable returns or **variable proportions**. Variable proportions encompasses the possibility that quantities of some inputs decrease as others increase. While this is certainly the typical case in the real world, let us first consider the special case wherein all of the physical inputs are assumed to change in the same direction and by the same proportion, that is, to the same scale. This is the phenomenon of **returns to scale**.

Returns to scale can be analyzed with graphs of production surfaces similar to those illustrated in Figure A-VIII(a). As we did in Figure A-VIII(b), we shall focus on the generalized production surface in panel (d) of Figure A-VIII(a). Again we shall cut a vertical slice through the surface, but along a linear path emanating from the origin at some angle (any, it does not matter) with the labour and capital axis. The angle with respect to either axis is the 90-degree complement of the angle with respect to the other axis. In Figure 9.1 the path to be followed on the floor of the surface (a ray from the origin) is 0ABCD. The corresponding path traced out on the surface is $0Q_1Q_2Q_3Q_4$.

A CONSTANT CAPITAL-LABOUR RATIO

The angle chosen for the ray from the origin implies a certain capital-labour ratio which remains fixed as long as the line input path is followed, that is,

$$K_1/L_1 = K_2/L_2 = K_3/L_3 = K_4/L_4.$$

If the firm has been producing Q_1 by employing the L_1 quantity of labour in a K_1 size plant, the firm can increase its scale of operations by increasing both inputs (and all others not explicitly included in the three dimensional diagram) by the same factor or proportion. For example, it might double both the plant size and the employed labour force to reach point B where it will employ the L_2 labour force in the K_2 plant which will enable it to produce the Q_2 output. To reach output Q_3 while maintaining a fixed capital-output ratio, the firm would have to increase both of its capital and labour inputs by another 50 per cent (the same absolute increments as previously) to reach point C. To produce the Q_4 output would require another one-third increase (again, the same absolute increment as in the earlier examples) of both inputs to arrive at point D.

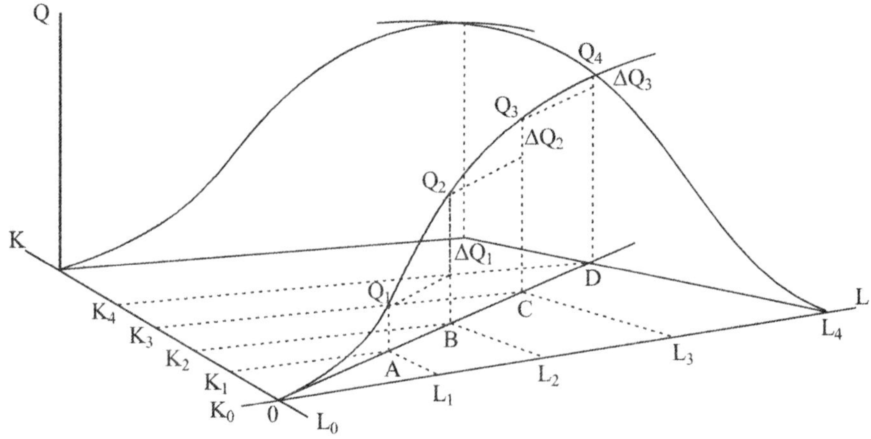

Figure 9.1. Return to scale.

RETURNS TO SCALE

As the scale of operations has increased while the capital-labour ratio has been preserved, what has happened to output? Consequent upon the shift from point A to point B in the floor of the diagram (a 100 per cent increase in both inputs), output has increased by (Q_2-Q_1), which appears to be a nearly 400 per cent increase. We may describe the A to B input change as an output range of increasing returns to scale. The B to C input shift (an increase of 50 per cent for both inputs) resulted in an output increase, (Q_3– Q_2), of about the same proportion, 50 per cent. We can describe the B to C input change as an output range of approximately constant returns to scale. We leave it to the reader to classify the nature of the returns to scale associated with the C to D input change.

We are now in a position to specify some general principles with respect to returns to scale. For any particular change of all inputs in a production process by the same proportion, if the output change is in the same direction and

(a) of smaller proportion than the input change, this is a case of **decreasing** returns to scale;

(b) of the same proportion as the input change, this is a case of **constant** returns to scale;

(c) of larger proportion than the input change, this is a case of **increasing** returns to scale.

A particular production process may exhibit only decreasing, constant or increasing returns to scale over the available range of input and output data as do those illustrated in panels (a), (b), and (c) of Figure A-VIII(a). But it is also possible that a single production process might also exhibit ranges of all three types as illustrated in panel (d) of Figure A-VIII(a).

It may be quite difficult for production decision makers to perceive the effects of returns to scale. In Figures A-VIII(b) and A-VIII(d) we sliced the production function parallel to one of the input axes in order to describe the phenomenon of diminishing returns to a variable input, given some quantity of a fixed input. In Figure A-VIII(a) we sliced the production function diagonally along a ray from the origin in order to discuss the effects of returns to scale. But a real-world production process will likely involve a meandering path across the floor of the production surface, or possibly a path with a stair-step appearance implying a sequence of short-run adjustments situated within a longer-run time frame. The consequence is that it may not be possible to separate those output changes which are a result of diminishing returns from those which are attributable to changes of scale.

SCALE AND THE PRODUCTION FUNCTION

The mathematical properties of a production function may now be easily specified. Returning to the production function specification (1) introduced in the previous chapter, suppose that all of the inputs are multiplied by the same factor, v (a positive or negative real number which may be larger or smaller than 1), and output changes in the same direction by proportion u,

$$uQ = f(vL, vR, vK/\ldots).$$

The production function exhibits

(a) decreasing returns to scale if u is less than v;

(b) constant returns to scale if u is equal to v; or

(c) increasing returns to scale if u is greater than v.

A production function may contain input terms (L, K, R, etc.) which are linear (that is, the highest power to which a term is raised is 1), second order (squared terms are the highest order present), third order (cubics), or even higher. However, orders higher than third are rarely estimated and it would be very difficult to give them economic interpretations. Examples of the equation forms of linear, second-, and third-order production functions are given in equations (1), (2), and (3), respectively:

$$(1)\ Q = a + bK + cL.$$

$$(2)\ Q = a + bK + cK^2 + dL + eL^2.$$

$$(3)\ Q = a + bK + cK^2 + dK^3 + eL + fL^2 + gL^3.$$

However, a single production function may have mixed orders for the various inputs, for example linear in K but second order in L:

$$Q = a + bK + cL + dL^2.$$

Because different inputs may be present in the production function to different orders, it may be difficult to say whether to expect constant, increasing, or decreasing returns to scale from any particular function. We may indulge in a few broad generalizations. If the equation is linear in all included inputs, we may be confident that it will exhibit constant returns to scale over all ranges of the included inputs. It will then have a pyramidal or conical appearance when graphed in three dimensions. If the highest ordered term for all included terms is second, the equation will exhibit increasing or decreasing returns (but not both), depending on the signs (positive or negative) of the included terms. Such a second-order equation might plot as illustrated in panel (a) of Figure A-VIII(a), but it is more likely to have the decreasing-returns appearance of that in panel (c). Finally, if the highest-ordered terms for all inputs included in the equation are cubic (third order), the production function can be expected to exhibit increasing, constant, and decreasing ranges of returns to scale as illustrated in panel (d) of Figure A-VIII(a) (we note that the opposite sequences of ranges is possible but highly unlikely in real production circumstances). In a production function with mixed orders of the included terms, the nature of returns to scale will depend upon the angle of the ray from the origin which determines the capital/labour ratio.

Equations (1), (2), and (3) are additive in the sense that the effect on Q of all of the inputs is simply the sum of the independent effects with no mathematical interaction among the inputs. If interaction among the included terms is likely, then a multiplicative equation form may be more appropriate. A commonly-used equation format of this type is the so-called Cobb-Douglas production function:

$$(4)\ Q = aK^bL^c.$$

This function can be modelled by ordinary least squares regression in the transformed format

$$(5)\ \log Q = \log a + b \log K + c \log L,$$

where the parameters a, b, and c can be estimated by the regression procedures. In this multiplicative power-equation form of the production function, the returns to scale depend entirely upon the values of the powers b and c.

The Cobb-Douglas production function exhibits

(a) decreasing returns to scale if $(b + c)$ is less than 1;

(b) constant returns to scale if $(b + c)$ is equal to 1; or

(c) increasing returns to scale if $(b + c)$ is greater than 1.

A decreasing returns Cobb-Douglas production function has the appearance of the surface illustrated in panel (c) of Figure A-VIII(a). Since it never quite reaches a peak (rather, it approaches some output level asymptotically), it has no production Stage I or III. All input combinations for a Cobb-Douglas production function lie in Stage II.

CHANGES IN TECHNOLOGY, ENTREPRENEURSHIP, MANAGERIAL CAPACITY

All of the production functions illustrated thus far have been specified assuming some particular technology, given amounts of managerial capacity and entrepreneurial ability. This point is incorporated in the functional notations (2), (3), and (4) of the previous chapter. If there is any significant change in any of these enabling conditions, the production function must be re-specified, and the geometric surface representing it redrawn. Failure to do so may lead to an identification problem in the production context, with the consequence that production decisions may be based upon erroneous criteria.

Some technological, entrepreneurial, or managerial changes will have the effect of **shifting the production surface** upwards (in the output dimension) or downwards while preserving its essential shape. A technological change which shifts the production surface upward is an advance which improves productive efficiency in the sense that a larger volume of output can be produced with any combination of the inputs. A downward shift, perhaps because the firm has lost managerial capacity or deliberately chosen to retrench to some simpler or more primitive technology, constitutes a decrease in productive efficiency.

Some technological changes may have the effect of twisting or warping the production surface instead of simply shifting it. Such changes may have the effect of using more intensively one factor of production (and hence, less intensively the other factors). The firm's management may deliberately choose such a surface-twisting technological change if, for example, factor supply conditions change in such a way as to make one factor significantly more costly or another less costly. An example of the former might be the union organization of the firm's labour force which results in rising wage rates, thereby inducing management to install labour-saving technologies when the occasion arises for capital replacement. An example of the latter might be found in a technological advance which renders a previously uneconomic resource now commercially exploitable, for example, new technologies enabling the extraction of shale oil or the gasification of coal.

This leads to a consideration of the criterion for selecting an appropriate technology in any commercial setting. Given market conditions, the best technology is not necessarily the most recently developed, the most 'advanced,' the most complex, or the one used most commonly by other firms or in other countries. Rather, the appropriate technology for implementing any productive process is the one which employs extensively the most abundant (cheapest) factors of production, and conserves most on the scarcest (dearest) factors of production. Failure to recognize or abide by this criterion has on too many occasions led enterprises in developing countries (which often are labour-abundant and capital scarce) to adopt the most advanced, capital-intensive technologies available in the West.

Technological changes are almost always implemented via capital investment. Capital replacements are almost always current-technology instead of the earlier vintage being replaced. Likewise, capital expansions typically opt for a later technology than that already in place. Care should be taken by management when any capital replacement or expansion is underway to question whether some technological change is also being effected. If so, the firm's production functions should be re-specified in order to avoid erroneous production decisions which may result from an unrecognized identification problem.

In earlier discussion of returns to scale, we described the phenomenon but failed to indicate why it occurs. We are now in a position to suggest that even if all of the physical inputs (labour, capital, and materials) are variable in the same or varying proportions, there still must be some ultimate enabling or limiting conditions which govern the scale phenomenon. We may speculate that these enabling and limiting conditions are the entrepreneurial ability, managerial capacity, and technologies which can be understood and implemented by the firm. The firm may possess or acquire abilities far beyond those which it presently is using, so that all of the physical inputs can be utilized more effectively at a larger scale. But eventually the scale of operations can exceed the ability of the management's abilities for coordination and control, with the result of decreasing returns to scale.

THE EMPIRICAL ESTIMATION OF PRODUCTION FUNCTIONS

As in the estimation of demand functions, it should be possible to apply regression analysis to empirical data for output and inputs in order to estimate the parameters of a best-fit equation. For many reasons, the job of estimating a production function may be even more difficult at the microeconomic level of the firm than at the macroeconomic level of the aggregate economy or even an industry.

An immediate problem is that most firms produce a variety or range of products and some are joint products resulting from a common production process. If the firm produces several products in independent productive processes, a separate production function may be needed for each of the processes. Where joint products result from a common production process, it may be necessary to identify output as a product mix which is measured in value rather than quantity terms.

Another problem is that the production function by its nature assumes quantities of resources used and output produced such that measures of flows of inputs and outputs are needed for modelling purposes. Examples of flows are labour hours employed and capital consumed (that is, used up) in the production process. But flows are much more difficult to measure than are stocks, such as the number of labourers employed or the number of machines or value of capital invested. Where data for flows are unavailable or too costly to generate, the analyst may attempt to use available data for associated stocks as proxies for the missing flows data.

The management of the firm may need a short-run production function, that is, for the particular plant which can be assumed to be in place and unchangeable. In this case the hypothesized relationship can be given as

$$(5)\ Q_{gross} = f(\ L,\ R,\ X_1,\ldots,X_n\ /\ K;\ E,\ M,\ T\ ),$$

so that the only data needed for the regression analysis are for the output flow, the volume of labour (L) utilized and materials (R) consumed, and various other inputs ($X_1,\ldots,X_n$) such as energy which vary with the level of output. The subscript indicates 'gross' output in the sense of total number of units or total value of output produced. If the management can accept a value-added-by-manufacture (or processing) as the measure of net output, then the materials and other variable inputs can be assumed to be given (or at least to be enabling), so that the functional-notation representation of the production function becomes:

$$(6)\ Q_{net} = f(\ L\ /\ R,\ X_1,\ldots,X_n,K;\ E,\ M,\ T\ ).$$

In this case, only data for value-added (as the measure of Q_{net}) and labour used are needed in order to estimate the production function via regression analysis.

If the management needs a long-run production function (that is, for plant-size and all other physical inputs variable), then K must be moved to the left of the slash,

$$(7)\ Q_{gross} = f(L, R, X_1, \ldots, X_n, K/E, M, T)$$

or

$$(8)\ Q_{net} = f(L, K/R, X_1, \ldots, X_n; E, M, T).$$

Data for capital consumed in the production process are also needed.

Yet another potentially serious problem consists in the quantity of data required by the regression analysis for estimation of a statistically significant production function model. Cross-sectional data can be used only if data are available for other, similar production processes, that is, production by other firms which are likely to be competitors.

As a practical matter, competitors are usually quite reluctant to share such sensitive internal information as production volume and input requirements data, except possibly under the auspices of a trade or manufacturer's association. Even if data from other firms or other plants within the same organization are available, they are likely for different plant sizes (not a problem if a long-run production function is to be estimated), or different technologies, managerial capacities, or entrepreneurial abilities.

If any of these differences are present in the cross-sectional data, then an identification problem is likely to emerge because the data will be for points on different production functions rather than a common production function.

The potential for an identification problem can be minimized by using data only for the firm itself, but this requires the use of time-series data instead of cross-sectional data. The use of time-series data opens other problems. If monetary values (instead of quantity units) are to be used, they should first be adjusted for changes in price levels (that is, deflated or inflated), and this begs the question of the appropriate price index to use as deflator, if indeed an appropriate index even exists. When this problem is surmounted, there remains yet another problem.

If a short-run production function is to be estimated the time series must be short enough that the size of the plant has not changed. Or if a long-run production function (encompassing plant size changes) is to be constructed, in order to avoid an identification problem the analyst must still restrict the range of the time series so that no significant changes in technology, managerial capacity, or entrepreneurial ability have occurred. The effect of restricting the length of the time series may be that too little data are available to estimate a statistically significant production function model.

The thrust of the foregoing discussion may suggest the heroic nature of an effort to estimate a production function from empirical data. It is a difficult, but not an impossible, task. Our purpose is to alert the analyst to the requisites and potential pitfalls so that they may be accounted for or avoided as required.

MANAGING PRODUCTION

Suppose that the firm's management has been successful in estimating production functions for as many of its production processes as are needed. How can these production functions assist the management in its production decision making? The answer of course is to use the production function equations as models to simulate changes in the resource inputs. Since the cost-minimizing or profit-maximizing combinations of inputs are rarely self-evident, management may use the models to try a 'what-if' approach to understanding the likely effects of alternatives to the present input combinations.

The firm's management should be sensitive to the effects upon its production processes of changing input supply conditions, technological advances, and the gains or losses of managerial or entrepreneurial capacities. In addition to responding passively to such changes which impinge upon the firm, the management may aggressively determine to try to alter its productive processes by acquiring different technologies or managerial or entrepreneurial abilities.

On a closing note, we should assert that even if the management never undertakes or succeeds in adequately modelling any of its productive processes, an acquaintance with the concepts which we have examined in this chapter should provide the basis for more effective production-related decision making.

Summary of Important Points

1. The analysis of returns to scale belongs to the long run; a change of a single input, given fixed quantities of other inputs, is an analysis of the short run.
2. Production decision makers may plan for the long run, but all decisions are made in short-run settings.
3. Returns to scale may be analyzed when all inputs change in the same proportion.
4. A case of constant (increasing/decreasing) returns to scale occurs if output changes in the same (a greater/a smaller) proportion than the change of all inputs in the production process.
5. Production function equations may be specified as additive or multiplicative, and to any required order.
6. If there is any significant change in technology, entrepreneurship, or managerial capacity, the production function surface will shift and the production function equation must be re-specified.
7. The appropriate technology for implementing any productive process is the one which employs extensively the most abundant (cheapest) factors of production and conserves most on the scarcest (dearest) factors of production.
8. Technological changes are almost always implemented via capital investment; when any capital replacement or expansion is under way, the firm's production functions should be re-specified to account for possible technology changes.

Contd.....

9. A production function may be estimated by applying regression analyses to empirical data for output and inputs.
10. A separate production function should be estimated for each of the products (or product mixes) produced by the firm.
11. An identification problem may emerge in the estimation of a production function if changes occurred in any inputs which were assumed constant.
12. Production function equations may be used to simulate the effects of changes in inputs and output.
13. Even if the management never undertakes or succeeds in adequately modelling any of its productive processes, an acquaintance with the production function concepts should provide the basis for more effective production-related decision making.

Significant Terms

Returns to a Variable Input, to Scale

Variable Proportions

Short, Long Run

Vertical, Horizontal Slice Approaches

Variable Returns

Capital-Labour Ratio

Returns to Scale

Constant, Decreasing, Increasing

Multiplicative Relationship

Identification Problem

Appropriate Technology

Empirical Estimation of Production Function

Joint Products

Flows, Stocks of Inputs

Short, Long Run Production Functions

Simulation Model

Questions for Discussion

1. Explain how production decision making differs in long- and short-run time frames.
2. Distinguish the production context of variable proportions from that of returns to scale; which is most likely to be encountered in the real world; why?
3. Explain the analytical significance to production of a constant labour-capital ratio; what is assumed about other inputs?

4. Explain how returns to scale can be indicated in a production function; what is the managerial significance of returns to scale?
5. Why is it likely to be difficult for production decision makers to perceive the effects of returns to scale?
6. Why might a multiplicative form of production function be preferred over an additive form? How can a multiplicative form be analyzed with common regression analysis?
7. Explain how a Cobb-Douglas form of production function exhibits returns to scale; what are the managerial significances of different return-to-scale scenarios?
8. Identify the likely impact upon a production function of changes in technology. ...of changes in entrepreneurship. ...of changes in managerial capacity.
9. Why might a technological change have the effect of twisting or warping the surface of a production function? What is the managerial significance of this phenomenon?
10. What is the economic criterion for selecting an 'appropriate technology' for a particular production process?
11. What are the implications for a firm if its management chooses a technology for a production process which is inappropriate to the extant conditions?
12. Describe the procedures typically employed in the estimation of a production function; what information is required in order to do this; how can the analyst tell if the estimation process has been successful?
13. Explain the difference between stocks and flows in a production function; indicate which is preferable for purposes of estimating a function, and discuss the implications of using the other in the estimation process.
14. Distinguish between a short-run and a long-run production process and indicate the differences in the data requirements for estimating each.
15. Distinguish cross-sectional from time-series production data and indicate how each should be employed in estimating short- and long-run production functions.
16. Explain how an identification problem might arise in the estimation of a production function; what are the consequences of such a problem; how might such a problem be averted?
17. Explain how estimated production functions may be used in managerial decision making.

—oo(O)oo—

Chapter 10

Costs in the Short Run

Topics covered in this chapter

• Costs are a consequence of production. • The nature of implicit costs. • The distinction between relevant and irrelevant costs. • The nature of opportunity costs. • The distinction between disbursement and no disbursement costs. • The nature of depreciation. • Correspondence between depreciation allowance and capital consumption. • The distinction between direct and overhead costs. • The distinction between the short run and the long run. • Why costs must be matched to relevant time frames. • The relevance of spill-over costs. • The distinction between accounting profit and economic profit. • The derivation of cost functions from production functions. • The computation of average, marginal, and incremental costs. • The relationship between marginal cost and marginal product. • The decision relevance of overhead costs. • Cost functions as simulation models.

THE INEVITABILITY OF COSTS

Costs, the age-old plague of the production manager, are a necessary evil—something you cannot live with, but you cannot do without. 'You've got to spend money to make money.'

The manager of any production process, whether formally organized as an enterprise or informally conducted as in household cookery, must come to terms with the cost phenomenon. What should be the manager's attitude with respect to costs? Any production process where scarce resources are employed must incur costs. But the incurred costs offset the realized benefits (including revenues if the product is sold in a money-using economy). That is, the costs diminish the net benefits (including profits in the money-using economy) and may render them negative. Why not just get rid of the costs or avoid them? We can't...the necessary evil! If output is to be produced by combining scarce resource inputs, costs are going to be incurred. So, the inevitable must be accepted...incur more costs to get more output. But this suggests a direct and causative relationship: costs vary with output, and increasing output results in greater costs. It also begs the question of whether the additional benefits (revenues) will be as great as the incurred costs.

We show in this chapter that while there is a tendency for costs to rise as output increases, the relationship between output and costs is not a one-for-one correspondence. And costs are a consequence of production, not a cause of it. The manager would do better to regard costs as something to control rather than something to manipulate as a causative factor in producing output.

What is the fundamental nature of costs? Why do they exist? Why can't we get rid of them? The existence of costs of production is attributable directly to the existence of **scarcity**. We may recall from introductory economics courses that scarcity exists if there is less of something (a consumable good or a productive resource) than people have or want. A price greater than zero is a certain indicator of the existence of scarcity. And since anyone's price is someone else's cost, the scarcity of the resources used in productive processes means that costs will plague the productive enterprise.

A short digression about an admittedly unrealistic condition may prove helpful. Suppose that the world were characterized not by scarcity, but rather by its opposite, abundance. There is enough of everything (consumable goods and productive resources) to 'go around' so that no one has to pay anyone else for anything. Everyone can have as much as he or she needs of anything simply for the taking, and enough will be left for everyone else's use. The prices of all things in this unrealistic world are at highest zero (we admit the possibility that they may be negative). Suppose that all things have precisely zero prices. Again, since everybody's price is someone else's cost, all costs in this world of abundance will also be zero. Not only would the economic problem be solved: so also would that of the production manager. In fact, in a world of abundance we would need neither economists nor managers.

Unfortunately for society (although fortunately for the employment needs of economists and managers) the world is not so characterized by abundance. Because they are scarce, the prices of most things are positive, and non-trivial costs are incurred by productive processes. However, there are a few things (or substances) in nature which are, for all intents and purposes, abundant relative to wants, and which are also absolutely essential to production. The prime example is the air (containing oxygen) which is a necessary input in any internal combustion engine. There are no (we should stipulate 'explicit') costs of using common air. However, should commonly-available air begin to contain too little oxygen or too much of certain impurities, even this text-book example will cease to be useful.

RELEVANT COST

We shall proceed upon the operating premise that any aspect of a production process that has negative implications for the production decision maker is a cost of production that is relevant to the production decision. We may also identify the corollary premise that any aspect of production with a positive implication for the decision maker is a relevant benefit (or revenue if the benefit is denominated in money terms). We should note that this premise could be germane to a barter economy (where no money is used to effect transactions) as well as to the monetized economies with which we are familiar. This means that even in a monetized economy where we are accustomed to denominating costs in money terms, some costs of production are essentially personal, or emotional, or psychic, and hence are not (easily) quantifiable and expressible in pecuniary equivalents.

Implicit Costs

We shall refer to non-pecuniary costs as implicit costs, and those which are regularly incurred in money terms as explicit costs. A hypothetical example of an implicit cost might be the negative sense which a production manager feels when he purchases an input from a party whom he personally dislikes (perhaps because he is an alumnus of the state university which is the arch-rival of the production manager's alma mater), even though the money price per unit is lowest from that supplier. Such negative feelings, or **psychic costs**, could be so substantial as to induce a production decision maker to indulge in the apparently irrational decision to procure inputs from a well-liked supplier at higher prices.

Aside from such psychic implicit costs, economists identify **opportunity costs** as another category of implicit costs. An opportunity cost is incurred when a decision maker either knowingly (for non-economic reasons) or unwittingly opts for a lower-valued opportunity than the highest-valued alternative available. The classic text-book example is that of a single proprietor who chooses to continue to run his own business while realizing an accounting profit (to be defined shortly) which is less than the salary which he could realize in managing one of his chain-store competitor's outlets. We admit that the negative feeling experienced by a production decision maker which induces him to forgo the lower-priced inputs in favour of those from a fellow alumnus is in effect also an opportunity cost.

Explicit Costs

Another term commonly used for explicit cost is accounting cost by virtue of the fact that such money-denominated costs are visible, readily monitored, and hence easily included by accountants when they design accounting systems. Accountants should be congratulated upon their meticulous efforts to account for all of the 'hard' (that is, money-denominated) costs incurred by a productive enterprise. By the same token they may be chastised for their reluctance to address those non-pecuniary psychic or opportunity costs and benefits which are no less relevant to the production decision. Because such non-pecuniary or psychic costs are excluded from formal cost accounting systems, it is up to the production decision maker to recognize them and account for them in the decision-making process.[1]

---

1. One reason that accounting systems are designed to account only for the explicit costs is that this is the requirement of the tax authority that the accounting profit (that is, explicit revenues minus explicit costs) can be identified and taxed.

Accounting costs may be subdivided into two categories: disbursement and non-disbursement costs. **Disbursement costs** are those which result in money out-payments from the enterprise to parties who provide services or resources to the enterprise. Examples are the salaries, payments for energy used, and disbursements to vendors of the raw and partially processed materials, components, and sub-assemblies brought together in the production process.

There is one type of **no disbursement** accounting cost: **depreciation** (the macroeconomic equivalent is 'capital consumption'). Depreciation is an allowance for the decline in the value of the capital stock which is attributable to the using-up of part of the enterprise's capital equipment during the production (usually the accounting) period. Such using-up or consumption of capital may occur as wear on the equipment or by weathering (exposure to the elements), whether the capital is used or not. These processes gradually diminish the production capabilities of the capital equipment. The phenomenon of **obsolescence** due to technical advance should not, however, be treated as a depreciation or capital consumption phenomenon. Obsolescence may reduce the market value of a piece of capital equipment, but it does not *per se* diminish the physical productive capacities. Nor should a **disaster** (for example, fire, flood, and earthquake) be regarded as a capital consumption phenomenon even though it may suddenly and catastrophically diminish both the market value and productive capability of the equipment.

An allowance for depreciation is not paid out (disbursed) to any party outside the enterprise; rather it is in a sense paid to the enterprise itself for the use of the capital equipment owned by the enterprise. Because it is not paid-out, but still is allowed as an expense against money revenue in computing the taxable profits, the enterprise's tax liability is thereby reduced. For this reason, depreciation may be regarded as a means of **outlay recovery**, supplying funds internally to the enterprise to finance subsequent reinvestment in its capital stock. But we should be careful to note that capital consumption is a real phenomenon which occurs whether or not a tax authority exists, and regardless of the tax authority's rules for computing the depreciation allowance.

Because it is impossible to know in advance what will be the actual life of any piece of capital equipment, and because the tax authority may change the depreciation-allowance rules for macroeconomic reasons (that is, in an effort to stimulate or retard the growth of the economy), it is highly likely that any tax allowance scheme designed by the accountant or permitted under the tax authority's current rules will diverge from the real phenomenon of capital consumption. The depreciation allowance could either exceed or be less than the real wearing out of capital. In the former case, the capital equipment will cease to function before the full amount of the capital outlay has been recovered ('written off'). In the latter case, the capital equipment continues to function productively even after it is fully depreciated. The important point to be recognized by the production manager is that the accounting allowance may not closely match the real weathering and wearing process. Since it is the real process which contributes the relevant cost, the production manager must be prepared to make decision allowances (positive or negative) beyond those designed by accountants or allowed under the tax authority's rules.

We have made more than one reference to the concept of **relevant cost**. We have already noted that any negative-implications phenomenon which is consequent upon the production process is a relevant cost, whether it is denominated in money terms or not. We should also note that there may be negative-implications phenomena that are not relevant to a particular decision context, but that may be mistaken as being relevant to it. For example, cost factors which do not change in response to any particular managerial decision are not relevant to that decision.

VARIABLE AND FIXED COSTS

One example lies in the distinction between direct costs and overhead costs, or to use the economist's preferred terms, between **variable costs** and **fixed costs**. Variable or direct costs are those which vary with the level (or rate) of productive output. Variable costs are always relevant to the rate-of-production decision. Fixed or overhead costs are associated with the existence of the manager, the plant, and the equipment. Examples are contractual salaries and insurance premiums. They continue at the same levels or rates irrespective of the rate of production, even if it is zero. Once the plant has been put in place, these fixed or overhead costs are, so to speak, 'sunk' costs, and sunk costs are not relevant to any rate-of-production decisions.

THE SHORT AND THE LONG RUN

The distinction between variable and fixed costs also permits us to distinguish between the time frames of the short and long runs. The **short run** is the period of time within which some contractual obligations associated with management, plant, and equipment are not alterable by changing the firm's managerial capacity or its scale of operations. The duration of the short run of course varies from enterprise to enterprise and situation to situation, and thus cannot be specified in discrete terms.

In the **long run** all aspects of the enterprise's operations can be adjusted. All costs are variable in the long run. Any long run consists of a sequence of short runs. All decisions affecting both the enterprise's scale and rate of operation are made in short-run settings, even those decisions affecting the long runs. The distinction between the short and long runs may be more pertinent to academic analysis than to operational decision making. But once we have distinguished the concepts of the short and the long runs, we can assert that the costs that are relevant to short-run decisions (that is, the rate of production) include no overhead or fixed costs, that is, **sunk costs** are 'gone costs,' and hence irrelevant to short-run decision making. Fixed costs, though irrelevant to rate-of-production decisions in the short run, become relevant to the scale-of-operations decisions of the long run.

TEMPORAL MISMATCHING OF PRODUCTION AND COSTS

Another example of explicit costs which may be irrelevant to decision making **in a particular time frame** are those which are incurred within the time frame but which affect operations in other time frames. Prime examples are maintenance and repair expenses. Preventive maintenance services are performed in one period to ensure the continuing functionality of the equipment in subsequent periods. Repair service expenses are incurred in one period due to operations in previous periods. If the enterprise is pushing hard to meet a production target or delivery schedule during one period, both preventive maintenance and some repair services may be delayed, and the resulting costs thereby deferred to a subsequent slack period. Such costs then, when they are incurred, are irrelevant to decisions of the period within which they were incurred, but are relevant to some earlier or later period. The moral of this story is that the astute decision maker may have to go to some lengths to match the relevant costs with the appropriate temporal settings, and not rely blindly upon the available cost accounting data.

SPILL-OVER COSTS

A final example of costs which are irrelevant to current decision making consists in what economists define as social or spill-over costs. The reader may recall that our operating premise is that a relevant cost is any aspect of a production process which has negative implications **for the production decision maker**. But what about negative aspects of production which descend upon members of society other than the production decision maker? For example, air, water, and noise pollution are the unfortunate by-products of production processes which affect parties outside the enterprise. These **spill-over costs**, however, are irrelevant to the production decision context unless or until either the production decision maker experiences a twinge of conscience, or the authorities require the firm to abate, prevent, clean-up, or compensate those who have been harmed. We may say, then, that while such spill-over costs currently are irrelevant to the production decision context, they always have the **potential for becoming relevant costs** and should not be ignored entirely by the production decision maker.

ECONOMIC PROFIT

Once we have identified relevant costs (as well as relevant revenues), we are in a position to specify the distinction between accounting profit and economic profit. **Accounting profit** is the explicit, money-denominated revenues realized by the enterprise during an accounting period, less the explicit, money-denominated costs which are incurred in that same period. Accounting profit does not include any implicit (psychic or opportunity) costs, recognizes no divergence between depreciation allowance and the real phenomenon of capital consumption, and often makes no allowances for the temporal mismatching of production and costs. To the extent that these aspects are omitted from consideration, the computation of an enterprise's accounting profit may over- or under-state its true (economic) profit and thereby lead to erroneous decisions.

The concept of **economic profit** is the result of the economist's effort to recognize all benefits (implicit as well as money revenues) and costs (psychic and opportunity costs as well as accounting costs) accruing to the enterprise. **Economic costs** are all of the costs which are relevant to decision making, whether or not money disbursements were made and whether or not they are recognized in formal accounting systems. The critical significance of economic costs is that they must be paid (or at least given adequate recognition or compensation) in order to retain the services of all factors of production supplied to the firm.

The magnitude of the economic cost of any productive factor is its opportunity cost, that is, at least as large a return as it can realize in its most favourable alternative use. The consequence of failure of an enterprise to pay all of the relevant or economic costs of its factors of production will be their departure to their best alternative employments. We admit that ignorance or irrationality on the part of the owner of the resource may result in the resource remaining in its present employment in spite of economic realities. A critical distinction between a 'good management' and 'poor management' may lie in the ability of the decision maker to recognize the implicit costs and benefits of managerial decisions.

THE COST-PRODUCTION NEXUS

It should be clear from the foregoing discussions that the phenomena of costs and production are inextricably intertwined. The analysis of the behaviour of costs and the specifications of cost-related decision criteria follow directly from the production principles outlined in an earlier chapter. Costs behave as they do because of the underlying production relationships. In fact, the principle of diminishing returns serves as a common governing principle in the behaviours of both production and cost relationships.

In an earlier chapter we developed the analysis of production behaviour via the **production function**, both algebraically and graphically implemented. We may now pursue the analysis of costs via a cost function which may be developed directly from the production function. We shall begin with the graphic exposition and move to the algebraic specification.

THE TRANSITION FROM THE PRODUCTION FUNCTION TO THE COST FUNCTION

In order to begin our graphic analysis of costs we make three **simplifying assumptions**, which we can subsequently drop. First, we assume that the enterprise already has an installed capital base which determines its plant scale and a particular output range. Second, we assume that there is only one explicitly variable input; for convenience we choose labour, but we could choose any other. There may be other inputs such as materials and energy which must also change with the rate of output, but we can assume that supplies of them are adequate to permit them to be handled with the labour. Third, we assume that labour is hired in a purely competitive labour market such that any quantity of labour can be hired at the going wage rate.

With these three assumptions in place we have the classic short-run decision question confronting the manager: how much output to produce, or at what output rate should the given plant be operated? Although we must wait until further chapters to discover the possible answers to this question, we are ready to analyze the cost implications in the remainder of this chapter.

We may begin our analysis of the behaviour of costs in the short-run by departing from the total, average, and marginal **product curves** illustrated in Figure 8.1 and reproduced with only minor modification in Figure 10.1. The first step in the transition from production to cost analysis is to rotate the axes so that L is on the vertical axis and Q is on the horizontal axis. This permits us to focus on Q rather than L as the deterministic variable. As illustrated in two panels of Figure 10.2, this has the effect of reversing the concavities of the TP curve, but there are as yet no other significant changes.

The second step in the transition from production to cost analysis is to evaluate the labour units now on the vertical axis at their unit cost, the wage rate (which, it is assumed, does not change as more labour is employed because labour is hired in a purely competitive market). The vertical axis label may now be changed to $W \times L$ in recognition of this evaluation. We note that if W is constant, the shape of the curve is not altered when we change the vertical axis units from physical units of labour to value (or cost) of labour employed. The product of $W \times L$ can also be regarded as the total labour variable cost, TLVC, or, since labour is the only variable input, simply

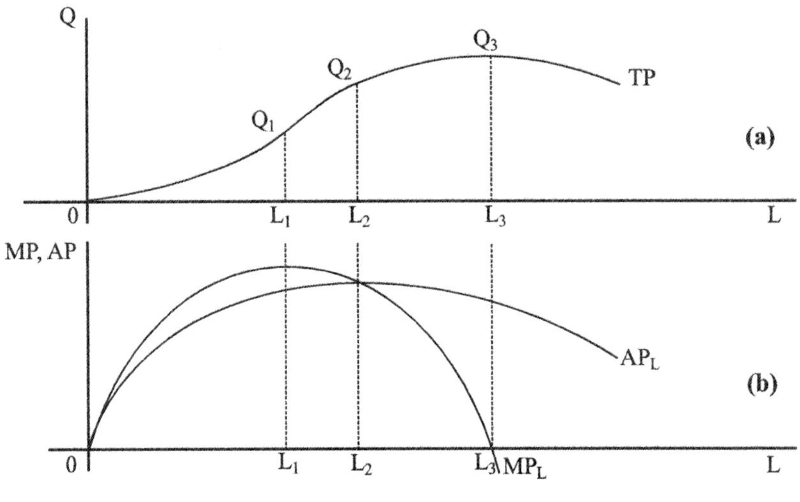

Figure 10.1. Total, average, and marginal product curves.

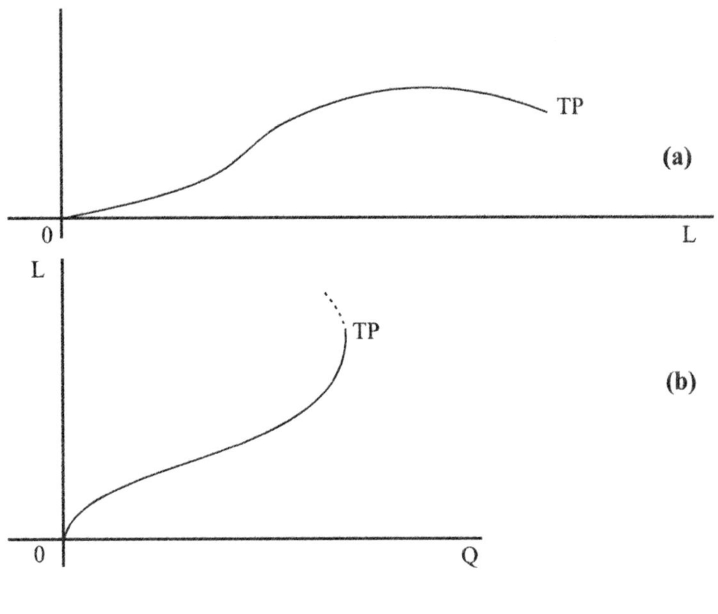

Figure 10.2. Rotating the axes of a total product curve.

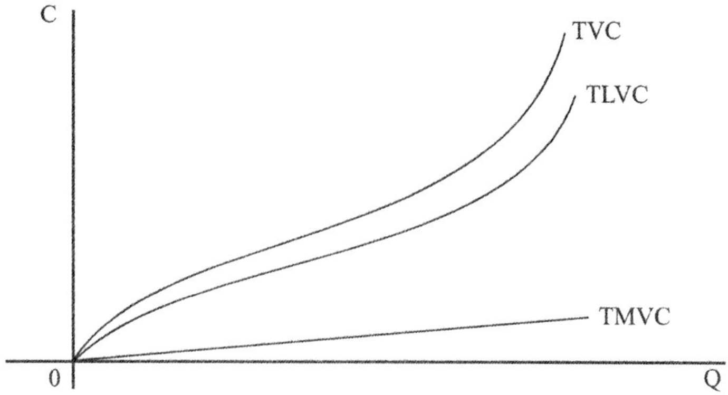

Figure 10.3. TVC as the sum of TLVC and TMVC.

as the **total variable cost**, TVC. Although we had to make several simplifying assumptions to do so, we have now accomplished the transition from the analysis of production to the analysis of costs.

DROPPING THE ASSUMPTIONS

We assumed that labour was the only variable input, but now let us suppose that the materials input is also variable, but it varies with output independently of the labour input. For purpose of illustration, we suppose the total materials cost, TMVC, to be linear as illustrated in Figure 10.3, so that the total variable cost, TVC, is the (vertical) sum of the TLVC and TMVC. As is apparent in Figure 10.3, the TVC curve lies above the TLVC curve by the amount of the materials cost of each output level, but the shape of the TVC is essentially the same as that of the TLVC curve, which we recall was derived from the TP curve. In similar fashion, as many variable cost curves as are relevant can be brought into the analysis and summed to compose the TVC curve.

These other-input variable cost curves may have a variety of shapes, but economists believe it to be unlikely that their shapes will be so perverse relative to that of the TLVC curve as to render the shape of the TVC curve fundamentally different from that of the TLVC curve. If this is true, then the principle of **diminishing returns**, which underlies the shape of the TP curve, also dominates the shape of the TVC curve, even if there are other variable inputs in addition to labour.

We also assumed that labour was hired from a purely competitive labour market so that W could be treated as a constant. But if labour is employed from an **imperfectly competitive** labour market, ever higher wages must be offered to attract successively larger quantities of labour. This phenomenon will change the locus of the TLVC curve by rotating it upwards, perhaps introducing a stair-step pattern if the wage increments occur in discrete stages. But in this case as well, economists are generally of the belief that the imperfections of the labour market are unlikely to fundamentally alter the shape of the TVC curve from that dictated by the principle of diminishing returns.

THE LAW OF INCREASING COSTS

In the previous section we went to some lengths to convey the notion that the principle of diminishing returns dominates the shape of the TVC curve. But we also noted that in the transition from the analysis of production to the analysis of costs, the concavity of the curve is reversed. In the production context, as the labour input is increased, output may initially increase at an increasing rate; but corresponding to this Stage I phenomenon, variable costs tend to increase at a decreasing rate. In the production context we noted that beyond some point, further increases of the variable input resulted in output increasing at a decreasing rate, that is, the phenomenon of diminishing returns. And corresponding to this Stage II phenomenon, costs will increase at an increasing rate. Economists refer to this phenomenon as a revelation of the **law of increasing cost**. The law of increasing cost is the cost analysis variant of the production principle of diminishing returns.

AVERAGE VARIABLE COST

Diminishing returns and increasing costs can also be illustrated with marginal and average functions derived from the TVC function. The average variable cost (AVC) curve, illustrated in panel (b) of Figure 10.4, may be derived from the TVC curve in the same fashion that the AP curve was derived from the TP curve. Specifically, AVC at any level of output, Q_1, may be measured as

$$AVC = TVC/Q$$

The ratio of TVC/Q may be measured graphically as the slope of a ray from the origin to the TVC curve at the selected Q. For successively larger outputs, it can be seen in panel (a) of Figure 10.4 that the rays from the origin at first decrease in slope, reach a minimum at Q_3, and then increase in slope as output increases beyond Q_2. Correspondingly, the AVC curve illustrated in panel (b) of Figure 10.4 decreases to a minimum at Q_3, and then increases beyond Q_3. The increase of AVC beyond Q_3 is attributable to the principle of diminishing returns, and is illustrative of the law of increasing costs.

MARGINAL COST

Likewise, the **marginal cost curve**, MC, illustrated in panel (b) of Figure 10.4, may be derived from the TVC curve in the same fashion that the MP curve was derived from the TP curve. Marginal cost may be computed as

$$MC = \Delta TVC/DQ$$

in the limit as ΔQ approaches zero (realistically the smallest possible ΔQ is 1 unit). Following the convention established, **incremental cost**, IC, an approximation to MC, can be computed as

$$IC = \Delta TVC/\Delta Q$$

for a ΔQ of any magnitude.

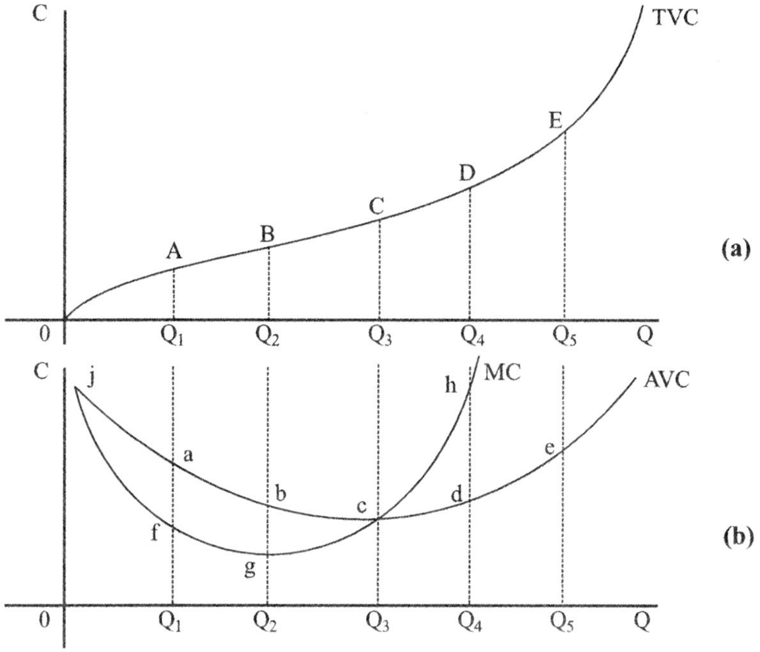

Figure 10.4. AVC and MC curves derived from the TVC curve.

Graphically, IC may be measured as the slope of a chord connecting any two (near-neighbourhood) points along the TVC curve such as the chord AB in panel (a) of Figure 10.4. MC may be measured as the slope of a tangent to the TVC curve (the tangent to the curve is the limiting position of a chord as either end-point of the chord approaches the other end-point). The shape of the MC curve then may be inferred by observing the slopes of tangents to successive points along the TVC curve as Q increases. It is apparent in panel (a) of Figure 10.4 that the slopes of the tangents to points up to B decrease (mathematicians refer to a point like B as the 'inflection point' where the curve changes concavity). For ever-larger quantities beyond point B, the slopes of tangents to points like C, D, and E become progressively steeper. Correspondingly, the MC curve illustrated in panel (b) of Figure 10.4 falls to a minimum at Q_2, then rises as output increases beyond Q_2. The increase in the MC beyond Q_2 is attributable to the principle of diminishing returns, and is illustrative of the law of increasing costs. We may assert that the phenomenon of increasing costs starts at the output level for which MC is minimum (Q_2 in Figure 10.4).

What are the managerial significances of AVC, IC, and MC? The average variable cost is easiest to compute (only two pieces of information are needed, the current total variable cost and the quantity being produced), and for this reason it is tempting to try to base output decisions upon it. Indeed it can be used as an output **decision criterion** if the goal of the enterprise is to minimize per-unit variable costs

If the goal of the enterprise's management is **profit maximization**, then AVC is an inadequate criterion; the appropriate cost-related decision criterion for profit maximization is **marginal cost**. But here is a problem, because MC is rarely observable (that is, for a one-unit change of output). It can be computed mathematically (differentiation) if one has an equation which adequately represents the cost function. However, to develop such an equation by statistical means requires information about an adequate number of cost and quantity combinations (usually 20 or more).

In lieu of such extensive information, the IC can be computed from four pieces of information: quantities produced at two points in time (preferably very close to each other in time and involving as small a quantity change as possible), and the corresponding totals of the direct production costs. Even for a very small ΔQ, the IC will be at best only an approximation to MC because it will over- or under-state MC, and may thereby lead to erroneous output-change conclusions.

Where does this leave us? MC is the ideal cost-related decision criterion, but is hardly observable and may be very costly to compute. Even IC, its approximation, though cheaper to compute, may lead to erroneous conclusions. AVC, though not acceptable as a cost-related decision criterion when the goal is profit maximization, is easily computed from a minimal amount of readily-observable information. There is a circumstance, however, under which AVC may serve satisfactorily as a profit-maximizing decision criterion: if TVC is linear (or approximately so), then AVC decreases and approaches MC, which is constant. As it turns out, empirical data for many industries suggest that TVC may in fact be approximately linear across a wide range of output in the vicinity of the commonly-produced output level.

RELATIONSHIPS AMONG TOTAL, AVERAGE AND MARGINAL COST

We may now observe the unique relationships among the curves illustrated in Figure 10.4.

(a) Over the output range for which TVC is increasing at a decreasing rate, both AVC and MC decreases, but MC is less than AVC.

(b) MC reaches its minimum point at the Q for which TVC reaches its inflection point; at its minimum, MC is less than AVC.

(c) AVC reaches its minimum point at the Q for which a ray from the origin to the TVC is of minimum slope (point C in panel (a) of Figure 10.4). Coincidental, the ray from the origin to this point is a tangent to the TVC, so MC and AVC are equal at this output level (Q_3 in Figure 10.4). MC is less than AVC up to this point.

(d) For all output levels beyond the minimum of the AVC, both AVC and MC increase, with MC rising at a faster rate (that is, MC lies above AVC).

(e) Neither TVC nor AVC nor MC is ever negative.

Although the reader may not at this point see the significance of the relationships outlined in this section, the astute production manager will find a knowledge of these relationships to be invaluable as criteria for production decisions.

RELATIONSHIPS BETWEEN COST FUNCTIONS AND PRODUCT FUNCTIONS

In subsequent chapters we shall be addressing the question, 'What is the appropriate **level of output** for the enterprise to produce in order to meet its goals?' Once the answer to this question is determined, a subsidiary question must be addressed: 'What are the appropriate **amounts of inputs** to use in producing the target level of output?' Since these two questions are so closely related, it is now appropriate to review certain relationships between cost and production functions. The reader may confirm the following relationships by comparing Figures 8.1 and 10.4.

1. The output range over which TVC is increasing at a decreasing rate (and MC is falling) corresponds to the variable input range over which TP is increasing at an increasing rate (and MP is rising).
2. The output levels at which AVC and MC are at minima correspond, respectively, to the variable input levels at which AP and MP are at maxima.
3. The output range over which TVC is increasing at an increasing rate (and MC is rising) corresponds to the variable input range over which TP is increasing at a decreasing rate (and MP is falling).

The reason that these relationships between the cost function and the production function are so significant is that our understanding (or theory) of the **behaviour of costs** is based so exclusively upon the principle of **diminishing returns**. If the principle of diminishing returns is not true, or not descriptive of the way the world really is, then our understanding of the behaviour of costs is also defective and will lead to erroneous production decisions. The other side of this coin is that if we do have an adequate grasp of a principle which truly is descriptive of the way the world works, then production managers need to know how their costs are related to the principle.

OVERHEAD COSTS IN THE SHORT-RUN

We shall take up the nature of overhead or fixed costs in this section, but we run the risk of conveying a misimpression to the reader about the significance of fixed costs to short-run decision making. So, at the outset of this discussion we repeat our assertion from an earlier section of this chapter that overhead costs are 'sunk and gone,' and are thus costs which are **not relevant** to short-run production decision making. We shall be examining the nature of fixed costs in the short-run context purely **for information**, and not as prospective decision criteria.

Overhead costs, usually fixed by contractual obligation at the same level as long as the existing plant, equipment, and management are intact, can be illustrated in panel (a) of Figure 10.5 as a horizontal line TFC, at the altitude of the total of the fixed costs. Then, to the fixed costs can be added the total variable cost at each level of output to measure the total cost, represented by curve TC in panel (a) of Figure 10.5. It should be apparent that the TC curve lies above the TVC curve by a constant vertical distance (the magnitude of TFC), and that the two curves are parallel to each other along verticals. This means that along any vertical which crosses both curves, a tangent to either curve will be parallel to a tangent to the other curve. The significance of this relationship lies in the fact that a common MC curve, already illustrated in panel (b) of Figure 10.4 and reproduced in panel (b) in Figure 10.5, serves both the TC and TVC curves.

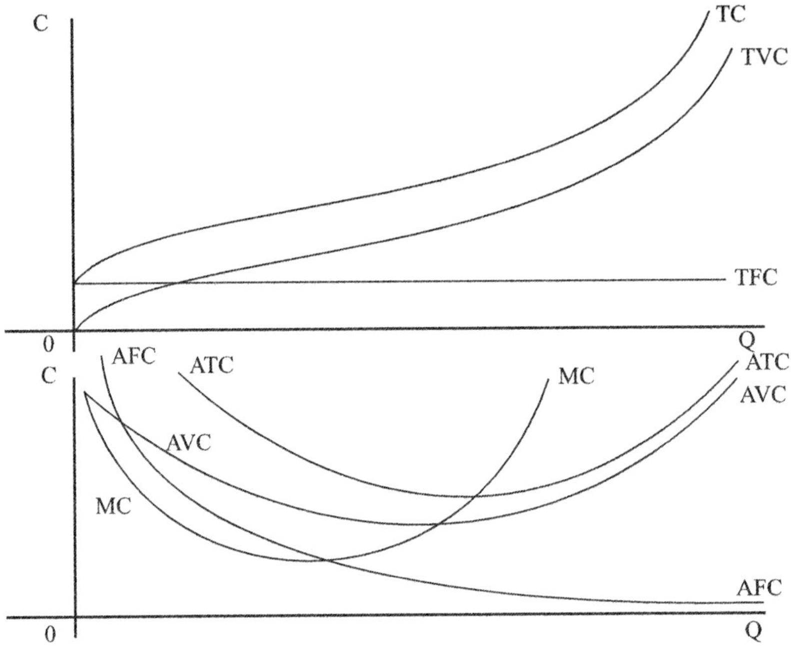

Figure 10.5. The TC and ATC curves.

The same methodology, that is, drawing rays from the origin to points along the total curve, can be used to ascertain the behaviour of the average fixed cost, AFC, which can be computed as

$$AFC = TFC/Q.$$

It should be apparent that the slopes of rays from the origin to points F, G, H, I, and J in panel (a) of Figure 10.5 diminish as output, Q, is increased. Correspondingly, the AFC curve is drawn in panel (b) of Figure 10.5 as a downward-sloping, upward-concavity curve which approaches the horizontal axis asymptotically.[2] The fact that the AFC curve always decreases as output increases is illustrative of the so-called **spreading of the overhead** costs to a larger number of units as output is increased.

In similar fashion to finding the position of the TC curve by adding TVC to TFC, the locus of the average total cost curve, ATC, can be determined in panel (b) by vertically summing the AVC and AFC curves. The reader should confirm that any level of output the ATC curve lies above the AVC curve by the amount of the average fixed cost at that output level, which is also the altitude of the AFC curve. It may also be noted in passing that the MC curve passes through the minimum

2. It may also appear to approach the vertical axis asymptotically, but in reality it begins at a finite point where Q=1 and at altitude = TFC.

point of the ATC as well as the minimum point of the AVC curve, but that the minimum of the ATC lies somewhat to the right of the minimum of the AVC. This latter relationship is true because in panel (a) of Figure 10.5 the tangency of the ray from the origin to the TC curve occurs to the right of the tangency of the ray from the origin to the TVC curve.

In panel (a) of Figure 10.5, the TC and TVC curves appear to converge toward the upper end. However, they do so only in the horizontal dimension; the vertical distance between them is maintained constant. But as illustrated in panel (b), the ATC and AVC curves do tend to converge in both the horizontal and vertical dimensions because of the spreading of the overhead as Q increases.

To return to the caution issued at the beginning of this section, what are the short-run significances of the TFC, the TC, the AFC, and the ATC curves constructed upon recognition of the overhead costs? Before the making of short-run output and pricing decisions, they should be ignored as irrelevant costs; after the point of decision, they may be regarded purely as information to be considered in any forthcoming long-run decision set. Particularly, the decision maker should not attempt to set price to cover overhead costs or total costs (including overhead); the output decision should not be oriented specifically toward the spreading of the overhead.

WHAT'S AHEAD

The criteria for appropriate pricing and output decisions are developed in the next chapter. After the fact of selecting the price and output upon appropriate criteria, the manager **may in retrospect observe** whether or not total costs were covered, and by how much the overhead was spread across the number of units produced. If the total costs were not covered, or the overhead costs were not met, then a long-run change may be warranted. It is to costs in the long run that we turn in the next chapter.

Summary of Important Points

1. Any production process where scarce resources are employed must incur costs which offset the realized benefits; costs are a consequence of production, not a cause of it.
2. Although most productive costs are money denominated, some costs of production are essentially personal, emotional, or psychic, and hence not easily quantifiable in pecuniary terms.
3. Both explicit and implicit costs are relevant to decision making.
4. An opportunity cost is incurred when a decision maker either knowingly or unwittingly opts for a lower-valued opportunity than the highest-valued alternative available.
5. Another term for explicit cost is 'accounting cost' because such money-denominated costs are visible, readily monitored, and hence easily included by accountants when they design accounting systems.

Contd....

6. Accounting costs may be subdivided into two categories, disbursement and non-disbursement costs; an example of the latter is depreciation, an allowance for the decline in the value of the capital stock which is attributable to the using-up of part of the capital equipment during the production period.
7. Obsolescence may reduce the market value of capital equipment, but does not *per se* diminish its physical productive capacities.
8. An allowance for depreciation is not disbursed, but rather is 'paid' to the enterprise itself for the use of the capital equipment owned by the enterprise, thereby supplying funds to finance subsequent reinvestment in its capital stock.
9. The accounting allowance for depreciation as permitted by tax authority rules may not closely match the real weathering and wearing process.
10. Any negative-implication phenomenon which is consequent upon the production process is a relevant cost, whether it is denominated in money terms or not.
11. Direct or variable costs vary with the level of output; overhead or fixed costs continue at the same levels or rates irrespective of the rate of production.
12. The short run is the period within which some contractual obligations associated with management, plant, and equipment are not alterable by changing the firm's managerial capacity or scale of operations.
13. In the long run all aspects of the enterprise's operations can be adjusted, so all costs are variable in the long run.
14. No overhead or fixed costs are relevant to decision making in the short run.
15. Explicit costs which are irrelevant to decision making in a particular time frame are those which are incurred within the time frame but which affect operations in other time frames, for example, repair and maintenance expenses.
16. Spill-over costs have negative implications for members of society other than the production decision maker and are thus irrelevant to the immediate decision context; however, they may have potential for becoming relevant in the future.
17. Accounting profits are the difference between money-denominated revenues and explicit costs; they do not include any implicit costs, recognize no divergence between depreciation allowances and real capital consumption, and may make no allowances for temporal mismatching of production and costs.
18. Economic costs include all costs which are relevant to the decision context; they must be paid (or recognized) in order to retain the services of all factors of production supplied to the firm; they are at least as large as the resource's opportunity cost.
19. The analysis of the behaviour of costs and the specifications of cost-related decision criteria follow directly from the production principles.
20. A total labour variable cost (TLVC) curve can be derived directly from a total product curve.

Contd.....

21. Variable cost curves for inputs other than labour may have a variety of shapes, but economists believe it to be unlikely that their shapes will be so perverse relative to that of the TLVC curve so as to render the shape of the total variable cost (TVC) curve different from that of the TLVC curve.
22. Economists believe that imperfections in the labour market are unlikely to fundamentally alter the shape of the TVC curve from that dictated by the principle of diminishing returns.
23. The law of increasing cost is the cost analysis variant of the production principle of diminishing returns.
24. The average variable cost (AVC) at any level of output can be measured as the slope of a ray from the origin to the corresponding point on the TVC curve; the increase of AVC beyond its minimum point is attributable to the principle of diminishing returns.
25. Marginal cost (MC) can be measured as the slope of any tangent to the TVC curve; the increase of MC beyond its minimum point is also attributable to the principle of diminishing returns.
26. Incremental cost (IC) can be measured as the slope of any chord connecting two points on the TVC curve; IC is an approximation to MC which may over- or under-state MC at either end of the chord.
27. MC is rarely observable and may be difficult to compute because of a lack of required data; IC may be easily computed from readily available data, but is only an approximation to MC.
28. Output ranges exhibiting variations of MC correspond to input ranges for variations of marginal product (MP).
29. Overhead costs are 'sunk' and are not relevant to short-run production decision making; the decision maker should not attempt to set price to cover overhead costs or total costs (including overhead); in retrospect, the manager may observe whether or not total costs were covered.

Significant Terms

costs

benefits

price

scarcity, abundance

relevant cost

non-pecuniary costs

implicit, explicit costs

psychic, opportunity costs

accounting costs

disbursement,
non-disbursement costs

depreciation, capital consumption

wear, weathering, obsolescence

irrelevant costs

direct, variable costs
overhead, fixed costs
sunk costs
short, long run
preventive maintenance
repair services
social costs
spill-over costs
economic costs
economic profit
diminishing returns
production function
variable, total costs
law of increasing costs
marginal, average costs
incremental cost
average fixed cost

Questions for Discussion

1. Explain why costs are not a cause of output.
2. Why are costs not avoidable in the production process?
3. Explain how costs relate to the fundamental economic problem.
4. Distinguish the types of costs which are not relevant from those which are relevant to the process of production.
5. Distinguish implicit from explicit costs and indicate which are relevant to managerial decision making.
6. Distinguish accounting from economic costs and indicate which are relevant to managerial decision making.
7. Give examples of psychic and opportunity costs and assess their relevance to the managerial decision context.
8. Why are non-disbursement accounting costs relevant to managerial decision making? How are they taken into account?
9. Why are accounting systems typically designed to account only for explicit costs of operation; what is the role of the manager in regard to implicit costs?
10. Explain how the rules of the tax authority with respect to depreciation might tend to distort managerial decision making if not taken into account.
11. Explain how the decision making time frame bears upon the distinction between relevant and irrelevant costs.
12. How should maintenance and repair expenses be accounted for in managerial decision making?

13. Explain the meaning of the term 'spill-over cost' and assess the relevance of such costs to managerial decision making.

14. Distinguish economic from accounting profits and assess the managerial decision significance of each.

15. Explain how cost functions can be derived graphically from production functions; what assumptions have to be made to do this; what are the consequences of dropping the assumptions?

16. How are cost relationships related to the principle of diminishing returns? What if the principle of diminishing returns is not descriptive of a particular production process?

17. Explain how an average variable cost function can be derived graphically from a total variable cost function; how is the principle of diminishing returns revealed in the shape of the average variable cost curve?

18. Distinguish marginal cost from incremental cost and indicate which is the preferable managerial decision criterion; under what circumstances might the other be used as a decision criterion?

19. What are the managerial significances of AVC, IC, and MC?

20. Why is AVC an inadequate decision criterion if the goal of the enterprise's management is profit maximization?

21. Explain the behavioural relationships among TVC, AVC, and MC, and assess the managerial significance of each.

22. Explain how the principle of diminishing returns is revealed in the behaviour of the marginal cost function. Why is this significant?

23. Why is it significant that neither TVC or AVC nor MC is ever negative?

24. Discuss the decision significance of overhead costs in the short-run decision time frame.

25. Explain why the TC and TVC curves seem to converge towards their upper ends.

26. Explain what happens to overhead costs as the output of the production process is progressively increased without limit.

27. Discuss the managerial decision significance of total costs.

—oo(O)oo—

Chapter 11

Costs in the Long Run

Topics covered in this chapter

• The distinction between short run and long run. • Why costs must be matched to relevant time frames. • The decision relevance of overhead costs. • Means of specification and estimation of cost functions. • Problems associated with cost function estimation. • The social implications of cost conditions.

In Chapter 10 we made a distinction between relevant and irrelevant costs. Any negative-implications phenomenon which is consequent upon the production process is a relevant cost, whether it is denominated in money terms or not. We also noted that there are some negative-implications phenomena which are not relevant to a particular decision context, but often are mistaken as being relevant to it.

One example lies in the distinction between direct costs and overhead costs, or to use the economist's preferred terms, between variable and fixed costs. Variable- or direct-costs are those which vary with the level (or rate) of productive output. Variable costs are always relevant to the rate-of-production decision. Fixed or overhead costs are associated with the existence of the manager, the plant, and the equipment.

Examples are contractual salaries and insurance premiums. They continue at the same levels or rates irrespective of the rate of production, even if it is zero. Once the plant has been put in place, these fixed or overhead costs are, so to speak, 'sunk' costs, and sunk costs are not relevant to any rate-of-production decisions.

THE SHORT AND THE LONG RUN

The distinction between variable and fixed costs permitted us to distinguish between the time frames of the short and long runs. In regard to costs, the short run is the period of time within which some contractual obligations associated with management, plant, and equipment are not alterable by changing the firm's managerial capacity or its scale of operations. The duration of the short run of course varies from enterprise to enterprise and situation to situation, and thus cannot be specified in discrete terms.

In the long run all aspects of the enterprise's operations can be adjusted, so all costs are variable in the long run. Yet, as we noted, any long run consists of a sequence of short runs. All decisions affecting both the enterprise's scale and rate of operation are made in short-run settings, even those decisions affecting the long runs. The distinction between the short and long runs may be more pertinent to academic analysis than to operational decision making. But once we have distinguished the concepts of the short and the long runs, we can assert that the costs which are relevant to short-run decisions (that is, the rate of production) include no overhead or fixed costs (that is, sunk costs are 'gone' costs and hence irrelevant to short-run decision making). Fixed costs, though irrelevant to rate-of-production decisions in the short run, become relevant to the scale-of-operations decisions of the long run.

OVERHEAD COSTS

Before the making of short-run output and pricing decisions, overhead costs should be ignored as irrelevant costs; after the point of decision, they may be regarded purely as information to be considered in any forthcoming long-run decision set. Particularly, the decision maker should not attempt to set price to cover overhead costs or total costs (including overhead); the output decision should not be oriented specifically towards the 'spreading of the overhead.' After the fact of selecting the price and output upon appropriate criteria, the manager may observe in retrospect whether or not total costs were covered, and by how much the overhead was spread across the number of units produced. If the total costs were not covered, or the overhead costs were not met, then a long-run change may be warranted.

COSTS IN THE LONG RUN

In the long run, all aspects of the enterprise's circumstances are changeable; all costs are variable. The impetus for long-run change may come from a variety of sources:

(a) recognition from short-run decision contexts that total and overhead costs are not being adequately covered;

(b) increasing or decreasing demand which requires changes in the scale of operations;

(c) the departure or acquisition of managerial ability and entrepreneurial capacity;

(d) technological advances which alter production functions or result in new products;

Possibilities (c) and (d) above will cause shifts and perhaps twists or warps in the production surface as described in an earlier chapter, with consequent alterations in the short-run cost curves which may be generated from any total product curve sliced through the production surface. How any such change in technology, management, or entrepreneurship may likely affect costs must be analyzed on the merits of each change.

We can reach some general conclusions on how costs are affected when the long-run change is to adjust the scale of the enterprise's operation by constructing a larger or smaller plant. A larger plant than the one represented by the K_1 quantity of capital in Figure 8.2 results in another slice through production function surface at, say K_2, as illustrated in Figure 11.1.

The total product curve drawn from K_2 likely rises higher into the output dimension, and may reach its peak at a larger volume of labour utilization than does the K_1 total product curve. Any number of successively larger plants could be represented by cutting total product slices through the production surface at quantities of capital greater than K_2.

The total cost curves associated with the K_2 plant likely lie farther to the right than those associated with plant K_1, as illustrated by TC_2 relative to TC_1 in panel (a) of Figure 11.2.

Correspondingly, the average total cost curve for plant K_2, illustrated by ATC_2, in panel (b) of Figure 11.2, likely lie slightly to the right of the position of ATC_1 for plan K_1, and ATC_2 may reach minimum at a lower per-unit cost level than does ATC_1.

Figure 11.3 illustrates an idealized representative set of such ATC curves which might result from building a sequence of ever larger plants, given the same technology and managerial capacity. This is an admittedly heroic representation since most firms would have the occasion to build only

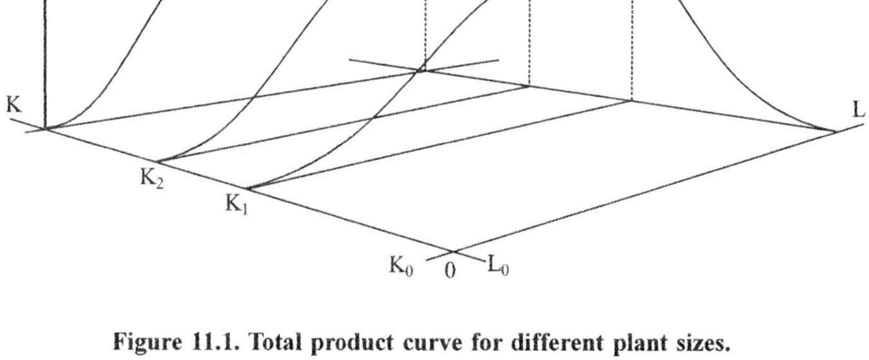

Figure 11.1. Total product curve for different plant sizes.

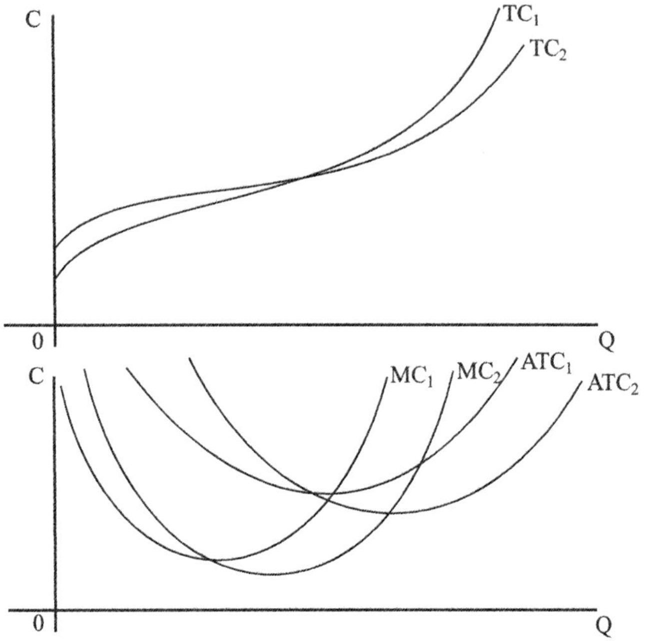

Figure 11.2. Total cost curves for different plant sizes.

one plant for any particular technology. However, if we may indulge in the presumption that the management might at least contemplate the construction of any of a range of possible plant sizes, we may note that the successively larger plants initially achieve ever higher and wider output ranges accompanied by falling per-unit costs.

This occurs up to point A in Figure 11.3. Economists describe this phenomenon as the range of economies of scale and note that the decreasing costs correspond to the phenomenon of increasing returns to scale. Increasing returns to scale, with the consequent scale economies, are attributable to greater division and specialization in the use of labour, or (and perhaps to say the same thing in other terms) more efficient use of plant and equipment.

Beyond point A in Figure 11.3 the ATC curves, though they reach higher output ranges, incur ever increasing per-unit costs. Economists describe this as the range of diseconomies of scale which are associated with the phenomenon of decreasing returns to scale.

Scale diseconomies are most often attributed to limitations on the abilities of management to coordinate and control the ever more complex productive relationships involved in the larger-scale operations.

THE LONG RUN AVERAGE COST CURVE

The curve in Figure 11.3 which is tangent to the sequence of ATC curves is a long run

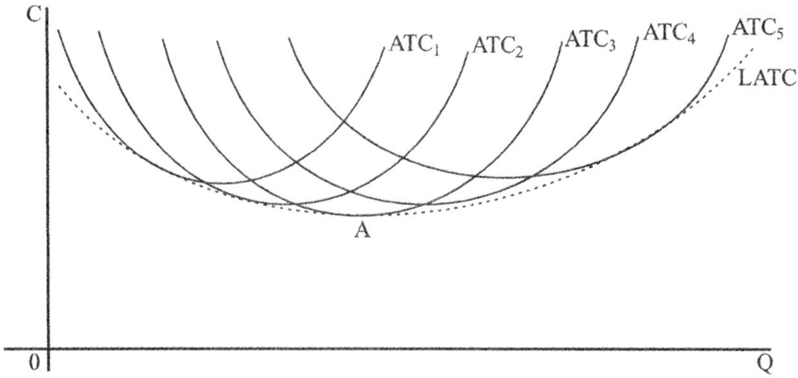

Figure 11.3. Average total costs in the long run.

average total cost curve, LATC. It is also referred to as an 'envelope' curve because it envelopes the sequence of ATC curves.[3]

Each of the ATC curves represents the cost conditions for a plant of particular capacity which the enterprise may construct. The LATC curve, however, represents no single such entity, but rather is a sequence of points each on a different ATC curve. As we shall, each of these points represents the single optimal plant size, rate of production, and cost level to meet a particular level of demand. The LATC curve may therefore be regarded as a long-run 'planning horizon' concept which may assist the production manager in selecting the appropriate plant size, given the existing or anticipated level of demand for the product. We shall return to this concept to examine the criteria for such a long-run decision in further chapters.

The LATC curve of Figure 11.3 is an idealized representation of production conditions in the long run because, given its U-shape, it contains ranges representing both scale economies (the down-sloping portion) and scale diseconomies (the up-sloping portion). Other shapes for the LATC curve are possible, and empirical data for a variety of industries suggests that some of the other shapes may be more common than the theoretical U-shape. Figure 11.4 illustrates three possible alternate shapes.

That shown in panel (a) suggests possible early (small-plant) scale economies, but after a rather small least-cost plant size has been reached, diseconomies of scale if the company attempts to build larger-scale plants. These long-run cost conditions are conducive to the development of a market populated by a rather larger number of smaller firms (or firms with a multiplicity of

3. Jacob Viner, the inventor of the LATC concept, first drew it as passing through the minimum points of the successive ATC curves, but in a subsequent note acknowledged that it should envelop the ATC curves. The original article and supplementary note are both reprinted in *Readings in Price Theory* (Homewood, Ill., U.S.A.: Richard D. Irwin, 1952, pp. 198-232).

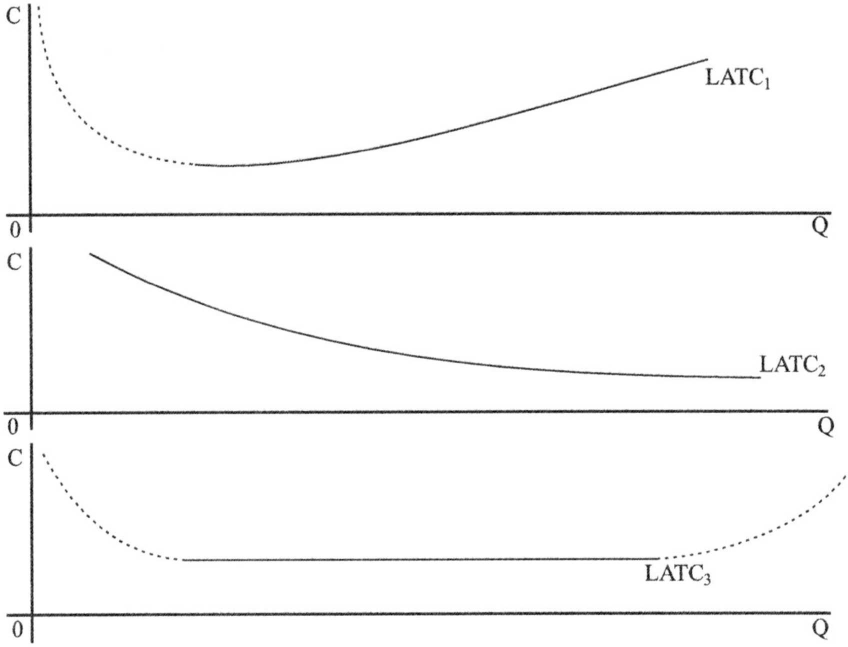

Figure 11.4. Possible shapes of the long run average total cost curve.

small-capacity plants). Alternately, a market populated by a large number of small firms will likely be characterized by a long-run cost curves similar to that depicted in panel (a).

Panel (b) of Figure 11.4 depicts long-run cost conditions characterized by the progressive, though gradual, exploitation of economies of scale which never seem to reach exhaustion. A market characterized by these long-run cost conditions will tend to be populated by a rather smaller number of larger-sized firms, and perhaps ever fewer firms as time passes and competition ensues. Economists classify such a market as oligopolistic. The ultimate end of competitive evolution in such a market might be a single, very large surviving firm, a so-called 'natural monopoly.' Real-world industries with a small number of large firms are likely to have reached such a state by exploiting scale economies while realizing no significant diseconomies of more growth.

The LATC curve illustrated in panel (c) of 11.4 may have involved a few minor scale economies as firms grew from very small size at start-up, and could eventually reach a range of diseconomies of large scale if existing firms grow much larger. But the salient characteristic of the panel (c) LATC curve is that it is flat-bottomed, that is, there are no significant scale economies to be exploited or diseconomies to be suffered over a very wide range of plant sizes. Another way to say this is that there appears to be no purely cost-related incentives or penalties to further growth.

The significant implication of a flat-bottomed LATC curve is that small-sized firms (or firms with small plants) may coexist with and thrive alongside of much larger firms (or firms with very large plants). It is not possible to predict with confidence whether such a market will be populated by many or few firms with large or small plants, but many economists believe that the growth pressures felt by managerial personnel in such industries likely militate in favour of an evolution towards a smaller number of larger firms. These long-run cost conditions may be even more favourable to the oligopolistic evolution than are those depicted in panel (b). Empirical data for a variety of industries suggest that many are in fact characterized by flat-bottomed LATC curves.

We shall draw our discussion of costs in the long run to a close with a reconsideration of the implications of technological, managerial, and entrepreneurial change. These changes in any of these factors likely shifts the entire production surface upward or downward from its previous position, and may have the effect of twisting or warping it with respect to the input axes. These may be exogenously sourced changes to which the management must adjust; for example, a key member of the management staff may leave the enterprise or die, or some natural disaster may destroy the plant or equipment.

Other such changes may be sought and initiated by the management of the firm in response to changing market realities or scientific developments. An example of the former might consist in the falling market price of one input or the rising market price of another input which induces management to seek to replace existing technologies with those using the lower-priced inputs more intensively, possibly even displacing the higher-priced inputs to the extent that they are substitutable. Technological advances not only produce new products for which new production processes are developed and production functions must be formulated; they may also render some inputs so much more productive than they were formally that managers will find incentive to replace the old technologies with the new as occasion arises.

MATHEMATICAL SPECIFICATION AND EMPIRICAL ESTIMATION OF COST FUNCTIONS

Fundamentally there are two ways for a managerial decision maker to regard the information about costs presented thus far in this chapter: grasp the essential theoretical relationships and employ the understanding of them to make 'seat-of-the-pants' (but informed) decisions (as suggested by Fritz Machlup, 'Marginal Analysis and Empirical Research.' *Essays in Economics and Semantics,* W. W. Norton & Company, 1967); or, take the information provided thus far as a platform for departure into the realm of attempting to model the enterprise's cost functions by mathematical specification and statistical estimation.

It is likely that the vast majority of all who study the behaviour of costs take the former route, so we give the reader an opportunity at this point to skip to the last section of this chapter.

One who chooses to attempt to model the cost function may use an intuitive rather than a statistical approach to the specification process. This involves making an informed judgement about the likely shape of the cost function (for example, linear, quadratic, cubic).

The function is then tailored to the specific situation by guessing at the magnitudes and signs of the constant coefficients of the variables in the equation of the function which will make it simulate the actual behaviour of costs.

Since no statistical curve-fitting procedures are employed, the validation process involves trying the model equation as data become available, and then making adjustments to the magnitudes and signs of the coefficients until the function behaves like the actual cost phenomenon. The analyst may go through several iterations of adjustment before getting the function to behave closely enough to the real situation. If one is attempting to model the cost relationships for a new product or a new production technology for which no historic data exist or can be generated, the intuitive approach may be the only reasonable way to proceed.

The statistical estimation of a cost function is an arduous task at best, and one which has a high risk of yielding an unsatisfactory result. Why should one go to the effort? If one can adequately model the enterprise's cost conditions, the cost model can be used to simulate (or 'what-if') the effects upon his costs of output and other changes. And if appropriate data are at hand, the statistical procedures may be able to do a better job in tailoring the equation to the specific situation than can the intuitive approach.

The functional-notation representation of a cost function can be given as

$$(1)\ C = f(X_1, X_2, \dots, X_n),$$

where C is cost, Q is output, and X_1 through X_n are possible independent variables which the analyst feels may be significant to the explanation of the behaviour of costs. One obvious candidate for inclusion as an independent variable in time series data is t, a time period counter to indicate trend if the productive capacity of the capital equipment is thought to diminish due to weathering or obsolescence. Other independent variables to be included may be dummy variables (values of 0 or 1) to indicate the presence or absence of some condition, for example, whether or not the work force in each plant is unionized.

The analyst may attempt to model short- or long-run cost conditions. If the objective is analysis of the short-run, then the analyst may choose to model a total variable cost, an average variable cost, or a marginal cost. It really does not matter which form is chosen to model since it is possible by algebraic manipulation to derive the other two forms. For short-run analysis, if the enterprise produces only one product, the analyst could just as well model the TC relationship as the TVC relationship since TC and TVC have the same shapes (that is., they are parallel along verticals) and share a common MC.

However, if (as is usually the case) the enterprise produces a multiplicity of products, some of which may be jointly produced, there is a problem of how to allocate the overhead costs to the various products. This problem can be avoided by choosing to analyze only direct costs, that is, the TVC relationship, and this is entirely appropriate since overhead costs are not relevant to short-run decision making anyway. If the object is to model the long-run cost relationship, then the appropriate focus of attention should be upon TC (that is, including both direct and overhead costs) since in the long run all costs are variable and there is no difference between TC and TVC.

The usual statistical-estimation procedure is to subject the available data to regression analysis assuming a higher-order relationship than is expected. Then, if the highest-ordered terms are not statistically significant, the next lower-ordered regression equation may be tested. The highest-ordered total cost equation tested usually is cubic (the conceptual sense of an equation of higher-order than three is obscure) of form

$$TVC = b_0 + b_1Q + b_2Q^2 + b_3Q^3,$$

from which may be derived

$$MC = dTC/dQ = b_1 + 2\ b_2Q + 3\ b_3Q^2$$

and

$$AVC = TVC/Q = b_0/Q + b_1 + b_2Q + b_3Q^2.$$

If b_3 turns out not to be statistically significant but both b_1 and b_2 are significant, the model may be re-specified as a quadratic of form

$$TVC = b_0 + b_1Q + b_2Q^2,$$

from which may be derived

$$MC = dTVC/dQ = b_1 + 2\ b_2Q$$

and

$$AVC = TVC/Q - b_0/Q + b_1 + b_2Q.$$

And if upon regression analysis of the quadratic form the coefficient b_2 appears not to be statistically significant, the equation may be re-specified as a linear form,

$$TVC = b_0 + b_1Q,$$

from which may be derived

$$MC = dTVC/dQ = b_1,$$

and

$$AVC = TVC/Q = b_0/Q + b_1.$$

If none of the coefficients, b_1, or b_2, or b_3 is statistically significant, then the effort to model the cost relationship by statistical means has failed.

Figure 11.4 illustrated the theoretically expected shapes of the TVC, AVC, and MC functions for a cubic (3rd order) relationship. Figures 11.5 and 11.6 illustrate the expected shapes of the quadratic (second order) and linear (first order) cost functions, respectively. Since so many real total cost functions turn out to be approximately linear over the range of data that are available, we

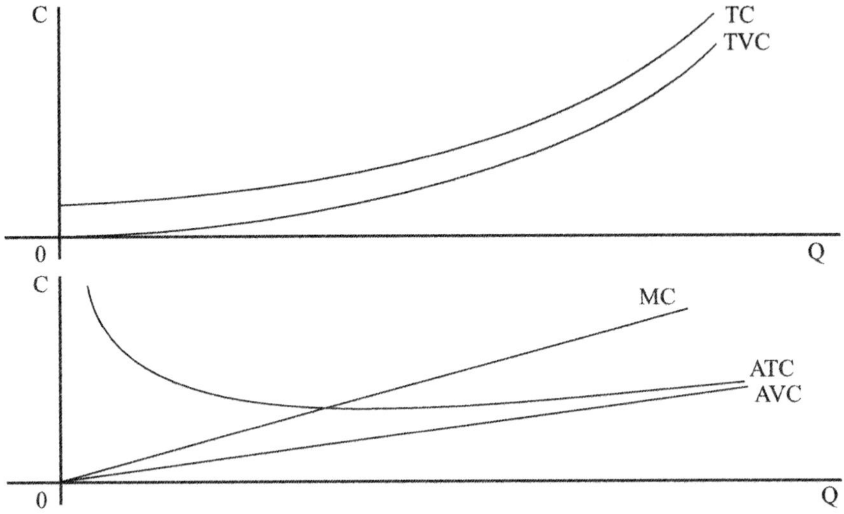

Figure 11.5. Marginal and average costs for a quadratic total cost curve.

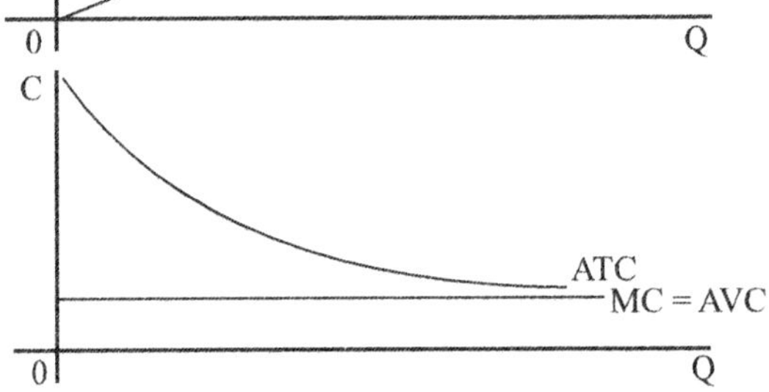

Figure 11.6. Marginal and average costs for a linear total cost curve.

should point out the fact that if TVC is linear, MC is constant (a horizontal line), and AVC falls to converge upon MC. The significance of this fact is that it may be possible to base output decisions upon the readily available average cost data (rather than the difficult-to-compute marginal costs) since average and marginal costs are approximately equal beyond some level of output.

DATA REQUIREMENTS

The methods for specifying and statistically estimating a cost function are clear enough; the real difficulty is in getting enough useable data to permit specification of a reliable cost function. The problems fall into three categories: ensuring that the cost data include all relevant costs and only relevant costs; identification of output where joint-products are produced; and selecting the time period for data collection.

RELEVANT COSTS

Most of the data for cost analysis will have been compiled by formal accounting systems which may have been designed for tax-reporting rather managerial decision-making purposes. One can of course employ the straight accounting data as reported to estimate what we shall call an 'accounting cost' function, but the cost decision maker is urged to recognize and remember when using it for simulation purposes that it overstates some costs and understates other costs. Also, any cost function estimated from historic data will be valid for simulation of future circumstances only if historic patterns persist into the future.

The analyst will have to make adjustments to the accounting cost data to estimate a relevant-cost function. No hard data exist at all about opportunity costs (what the firm is not presently doing but could be doing); only the managerial decision maker can estimate the opportunity costs based upon awareness and perceptions of the foregone alternatives. Needless to say, different managers will have different perceptions and assessments of the available opportunities, and some managers will be more successful than others because of their successful recognition of the pertinent opportunities. The well-designed cost accounting system should recognize temporal cost-output mismatching, but if it does not then some effort must be exerted to allocate certain costs (for example, repair and maintenance expenses) to the proper time periods.

If the objective is to estimate a short-run cost function, care must be taken to exclude all overhead costs. This may be especially difficult if the cost-accounting system obscures the distinction between some direct and some overhead costs. For example, maintenance and repair expenses often are lumped together (they are typically performed by the same in-house crews or outside contractors), but regular maintenance expenses (presumably at approximately the same expense levels period after period) should be treated as fixed costs. However, repair expenses, to the extent that they are not regular occurrences, should be treated as variable costs. Then there is the problem of matching the repair expense to the appropriate time period since the circumstances culminating in the need for the repair may have spanned several production periods.

Depreciation is an especially knotty problem for the determination of relevant costs. Should it be treated as a variable cost to be included in the estimation of a short-run cost relationship? We have already made reference to the likely divergence between the accounting allowance for decrease in the value of the capital stock and the real phenomenon of capital consumption. Real capital consumption surely does vary with the rate of production, which may be quite uneven from period to period. But since it is not possible to know with certainty in advance what will be the actual physical life of the plant or equipment, it may not be possible to meaningfully impute a cost value to the amount of capital consumption to be allocated as a direct cost to a particular production period.

The accountant handles this problem by selecting a depreciable life (on the basis of past experience, as permitted by the tax authority's rules, or simply arbitrarily), and designing an allowance schedule which may be straight-line, accelerated, or retarded (again, as permitted by the tax authority's rules). If a straight-line allocation method (the same proportion of the capital value charged as cost during each period) is used, then a case can be made for excluding depreciation from the list of costs relevant to the short run, because even though it represents a direct cost it does not vary with output. But even if an accelerated or retarded depreciation schedule is used, the proportions of the capital value to be allowed as costs change smoothly, predictably, and monotonically (a mathematical term meaning in one-direction only and hence are unlikely to correspond to real variations in output and the capital consumed in producing it. Given these problems, then, a case can be made for excluding depreciation from the estimation of a short-run cost function, but including repair expenses (properly matched to time periods) as mirroring the real consumption of capital, that is, the expenditure necessary to restore the real decrease in productive capacity caused by use of the capital.

Another short-run cost estimation problem occurs in time series data if there has been non-trivial variation in the prices of the variable inputs. Short-run costs certainly vary with the prices of inputs, so the analyst must make a methodological choice: either choose to 'deflate' each of the TVC components (that is, TLVC, TMVC, etc.) by a price index appropriate to that cost, or choose to include as other independent variables (that is, the $X_1, X_2, ..., X_n$ in equation 11.1) the prices of the inputs which are thought to be varying significantly. The regression analysis will reveal which in fact are statistically significant determinants of TVC.

Identification of Output

Theoretically, the physical units produced (or some multiple) should be used for Q in the regression model. A problem arises if the firm produces a multiplicity of products, some of which are jointly produced. In this case, Q may have to be the 'product mix' normally resulting from the production process. If the market values of the jointly-produced products differ significantly, it may be necessary to use a composite index of the jointly-produced outputs where the weights are the current market prices of the products. Finally, if the objective is to estimate a firm-wide cost curve where the firm is producing multiple products, it may be desirable to use data for value of output evaluated at current market prices. If time series data are employed, both the output and input value data should be deflated by appropriate price indexes.

Selection of an Appropriate Time Period

The alternative heading for this section might be 'Getting Enough Useable Data.' In sourcing his data, the analyst is first confronted with a choice between time-series and cross-sectional data. A short-run cost function assumes given technology, managerial capacity, and entrepreneurial abilities. Much recommends the cross-sectional choice for short-run cost estimation since the data are taken across firms or plants, but at a point in time. There is thus no problem of dealing with changes of plant size or of technology, managerial capacity, or entrepreneurial ability. It is perhaps easier to identify the use of the same technology than to find comparable amounts of managerial capacity and entrepreneurial ability in different firms. In this regard, the analyst will simply have to exercise judgment. Alas, there remains a critical problem with cross-sectional data for short-run cost estimation that is difficult to surmount for most firms: data are required from different firms or plants, but competitors often are reluctant to share such sensitive information.

The use of time series data for the firm's own plant(s) obviates the need to solicit data from competitors. Here the analyst must take care to choose a time span which is not so long that there have occurred changes in technology, management, or entrepreneurship, else data will be for points on different cost functions. This may be a period covering several years, but may be as short as a few months. Then the analyst must divide the period into an adequate number of data collection intervals to yield enough observations for estimation of a statistically-significant cost function. Usually 20 to 30 observations are adequate for this purpose. The duration of the data-collection period may then dictate daily, weekly, or monthly observation intervals. A new short-run cost function must be estimated every time that technology, management, or entrepreneurial ability changes.

In the estimation of a long-run cost function, all costs should be included. It may not be feasible, however, to use a time-series approach since the intervals should be long enough to permit variation in plant size (but still no changes in management or entrepreneurship). In order to get enough long-interval observations, the duration of data collection may have to span several years. Alterations in management or entrepreneurship during the data-collection period will result in points on different long-run cost functions. These conditions may be heroic at best. The use of cross-sectional data, if they can be obtained from other firms and plants, may accommodate requisite variations in plant size, but care must be taken in selection of subjects to avoid different technologies, managerial capacities, or entrepreneurial abilities. Again, these may be heroic conditions.

Whether the analyst is attempting to estimate short- or long-run cost functions, the necessary premise is that each plant is being operated efficiently, with no significant waste of any resources, that is, at an appropriate point on its cost curve. If at any time or in any plant included in the sample there are wasteful conditions, the observed data will be for a point above the locus of the firm's true cost curve. If this circumstance occurs in more than a few instances, the estimated cost function will lie above its theoretically true (efficient) location, and will yield erroneous conclusions in simulation exercises.

THE MANAGEMENT OF COSTS

Whether the management of the firm develops a cost-function simulation model or not, the cost-related job involves many facets:

1. In the long run, selecting the most efficient technology for producing the enterprise's selected products;
2. With that technology, selecting the scale of plant with an output range which is most compatible with current and expected future levels of demand for the products;
3. Given the right scale of plant, selecting the appropriate output level to meet the enterprise's goals (profit maximization, cost minimization, optimization, etc.);

4. For the target level of output, selecting the appropriate internal allocation of the enterprise's resources, that is, the most efficient combination of inputs, given the available input prices;
5. Operating efficiently and without waste, that is, to operate at points on the enterprise's production function surface (not below it) and on its respective cost curve (not above it).

Furthermore, economists can argue that if the goal of the enterprise is to maximize profits, and if it does so operate to maximize profits without monopolizing its markets or exploiting its resources, it will also meet a desirable social objective of efficiency in the allocation of resources among industries, among firms within the industries, and between products. Assuming that monopolization and exploitation are averted (admittedly a serious problem), this happy circumstance can be expected to emerge even if social well being and social economic efficiency are not explicitly managerial goals of the enterprise.

Summary of Important Points

1. The long-run average total cost (LATC) curve is a planning-horizon concept which envelops the firm's ATC curves associated with different plant sizes.
2. The shape of the LATC curve helps to determine whether a market will be populated by a larger number of smaller firms, a smaller number of larger firms, or firms of varying sizes.
3. The majority of business decision makers use their accumulated knowledge of cost relations, but rarely attempt to model cost functions by mathematical specification and statistical estimation.
4. Any negative-implication phenomenon which is consequent upon the production process is a relevant cost, whether it is denominated in money terms or not.
5. Direct or variable costs vary with the level of output; overhead or fixed costs continue at the same levels or rates irrespective of the rate of production.
6. The short run is the period within which some contractual obligations associated with management, plant, and equipment are not alterable by changing the firm's managerial capacity or scale of operations.
7. In the long run all aspects of the enterprise's operations can be adjusted, so all costs are variable in the long run.
8. No overhead or fixed costs are relevant to decision making in the short run.
9. Overhead costs are 'sunk' and are not relevant to short-run production decision making; the decision maker should not attempt to set price to cover overhead costs or total costs (including overhead); in retrospect, the manager may observe whether or not total costs were covered.
10. The usual statistical estimation procedure is to subject the available cost data to regression analysis to determine the statistical significance of terms in the specified equation.

Contd.....

11. In collecting data for cost analysis, care must be taken to include data for all relevant costs, but exclude data for irrelevant costs.
12. If the firm succeeds in maximizing profits without monopolizing its markets or exploiting its resources, it will also meet a desirable social objective of efficiency in the allocation of resources among industries, among firms within the industries, and among products.

Significant Terms

scale of operations; scale economies, diseconomies

managerial ability

entrepreneurial capacity

technological advance

specialization, division of labour in management

long run average total cost

envelope curve

planning horizon

natural monopoly

natural disasters

overhead, fixed costs

sunk costs

short, long run

mathematical specification

empirical estimation

order of cost functions

deflation

jointly-produced products

product mix

short-run, long-run cost functions

efficient technology

social objectives

economic efficiency

Questions for Discussion

1. Distinguish the long from the short run and explain the relevance of the distinction to cost analysis.
2. Identify various impetuses to long-run change and explain the impact of each on the shapes or loci of the firm's cost functions.
3. Explain how the firm's cost analysis should be changed consequent upon constructing a new larger plant implementing the same technology as the extant plant. ...implementing a new technology.
4. Distinguish economies from diseconomies of scale, and suggest possible causes of each.
5. How is the firm's short-run average total cost curve (and all others associated with it) affected by the construction of a larger plant which exploits scale economies?

6. Explain the construction and conceptual sense of the long-run average total cost curve. Why does its shape matter?
7. Explain how the shape of the long-run average total cost curve helps to determine the size composition of the population of firms in a market.
8. Discuss the implications for the growth of an industry in which long-run average total cost curves seem to be 'flat-bottomed'.
9. What is the significance to the management of a firm in an industry which is characterized by long-run costs which seem ever to decrease with the construction of larger and larger plants?
10. Explain how variation in the market prices of productive inputs might provide impetus for the management of a firm to shift to a different (for example, resource saving or using) technology.
11. Describe the intuitive approach to modelling cost relationships and the means of validating the functions so determined.
12. Describe the statistical-estimation approach to modelling cost relationships and the means of validating the functions so estimated.
13. Distinguish short- from long-run cost functions and indicate how the data requirements for estimation of each might differ.
14. Discuss the role of overhead cost data in the estimation of a short-run average variable cost function.
15. Contrast the expected shapes of the average total cost functions which may be derived from linear, quadratic, and cubic total cost functions; what are the managerial significances of these different shapes?
16. Discuss the pitfalls associated with using data compiled by the typical cost-accounting system in statistically estimating a cost function.
17. Explain why depreciation is an especially knotty problem in the determination of relevant costs.
18. Explain why the identification of output is a potential problem in the estimation of a firm's cost functions.
19. Explain why the selection of an appropriate time frame is critical to the successful estimation of a cost function.
20. Contrast the possibilities of employing cross-sectional and time-series data for the estimation of cost functions.
21. Identify the short- and long-run managerial decisions which must be made in regard to the firm's costs.
22. What are the managerial implications of the estimation of a cost function from cross-sectional data for firms, some of which are operating inefficiently?

—oo(O)oo—

Chapter 12

The Competitive Environment

Topics covered in this chapter

• Decision options are constrained by the nature of competition. • The nature of pure competition. • The distinction between pure and perfect competition. • Profits in pure competition. • Pricing and output discretion in pure competition. • Criteria for profit maximization. • Operate and shut-down criteria. • The effects of entry and exit on competition. • Social valuations of price and costs in pure competition. • Decision incentives in the long run.

Now that the theoretical foundations for the analyses of both revenue and costs are in place, we can proceed to bring the two together and begin an examination of goal-oriented decision criteria. To begin this analysis we assume that the decision maker is deliberately trying to maximize the economic profit of the firm. Along the way we shall give consideration to alternative behavioural objectives (costs, production scheduling, inventory control, employment, social responsibility, etc.) and behaviour patterns (minimization, optimization, satisficing, etc.).

The decision options of the enterprise manager are constrained by the types and intensities of competition confronting the enterprise in the market for its products. We shall describe a range of competitive types along a continuum between two extremes. In broad terms, the two extremes represent a maximum intensity of competition and no effective competition at all. We readily admit at the start that very few industries and markets in the real world can be characterized by conditions at either extreme. Our objective in this chapter and the next is to identify and describe the limits of the competitive spectrum.

THE MAXIMUM-COMPETITION EXTREME

We can imagine the descriptive characteristics of a market at the highly competitive extreme of the continuum:

1. There is a large number of very small firms which operate within the same product market.
2. The single product which they produce and market is essentially homogeneous across the member firms.
3. The member firms have virtually identical managerial capacities; they use essentially the same technologies; no one of them has or can acquire any special expertise which is not available to all of the others.
4. All participants in the market have access to the same information about changing market conditions.

Economists describe a market with these characteristics as 'purely competitive.' They also identify a more stringent (and even more unrealistic) extreme as 'perfect competition' which, in addition to all of the characteristics enumerated above, includes perfect market knowledge and instantaneous and costless adjustment. While the 'perfection' of competition is an even more rarefied concept than that of pure competition, it does serve at the extreme to point up departures from competitive perfection, for example, less market knowledge, less widely-shared information, and various frictions or impediments to adjustment which absorb time and incur costs. We shall examine the effects of the imperfections of competition later in this chapter.

Given these descriptive characteristics, we can deduce likely consequences and behavioural patterns for firms in the purely competitive market:

(a) Entry into the market is easy; entry may be accomplished quickly (though not instantaneously) because of the ready availability of common technology, and with very little capital investment.

(b) Exit from the market is likewise easy, that is, the firm can dispose of its capital assets quickly and with very little loss of value.

(c) Once a decision has been made to enter the competitive market there is likely to be very little incentive or effort to exercise further entrepreneurship, except the decision to exit the market.

(d) The atomistic size and limited financial resources of the competitive firm militate against its acquisition of any special managerial or technical expertise; firms are unable successfully to differentiate their products, and no firm can attain any position of market dominance.

(e) Because of the common knowledge of changing market conditions, all participants in the market become aware of such changes simultaneously, and all adjust at approximately the same rates.

(f) Because of the large number and atomistic size of sellers, competition is essentially anonymous; no seller is aware of or concerned about the identities of other sellers.

(g) A common price likely emerges in the market, and no market participant finds incentive to try to charge any price higher or lower than the market price.

(h) Due to the absence of successful product differentiation, there is little or no point in advertising the firm's product characteristics or its price.

(i) Supernormal and subnormal profits in the competitive market, although they may occur, are fleeting; profits tend towards the economically normal level of opportunity cost (what the firm can realize in the next best alternative application of its resources).

Various of these behavioural patterns or consequences deserve further elaboration, which we shall provide in conjunction with the ensuing graphic analyses.

SHORT-RUN ADJUSTMENT IN THE COMPETITIVE INDUSTRY

In Figure 12.1 we illustrate in panel (a) the market conditions for a purely-competitive market. Market prices will adjust towards an equilibrium at price P_1 and quantity Q_1. Because all firms in the market are similar to one another and significant differences are unlikely to emerge, we can analyze the behaviour of a 'representative firm' in panels (b) and (c). No single firm in the competitive market will find incentive to charge any price but the market price, P_1; at any higher price no one will buy from the firm; the firm can sell all that it can produce at the market price. Therefore, the firm is what we call a 'price taker;' it exercises no discretion concerning price except to get into line with the market price when it changes. For this reason, the representative firm's demand curve is drawn as a horizontal line at price P_1. We can deduce from principles described earlier that when demand is linear and horizontal, total revenue, TR, is a straight line emanating from the origin of its axes, and the marginal revenue curve, MR, is coincident with the demand curve.

We are now in a position to analyze the effects upon the firm of decisions to produce at selected output levels. Output quantities q_1 and q_2 are variable-cost **break-even** levels. At outputs smaller than q_1 or larger than q_2, total variable cost is greater than total revenue; likewise average variable cost exceeds average revenue. At any output between q_1 and q_2 the firm covers **all operating costs** and makes some contribution to covering overhead costs and profit.[1] Output q_3 is one of the output levels between q_1 and q_2 for which revenue exceeds variable costs, TR > TVC, and makes a **contribution to overhead** costs and profit. At q_3, a small increase of output will increase total revenue by more than it will increase total cost. We can discern this relationship graphically in panel (c) because the slope of the TC curve is shallower than is the slope of the TC

1. We do not at this point show the locus of the total cost curve in panel (c) or the average total cost curve in panel (b) of Figure 12.1 because fixed costs are not relevant to short-run decision making. All that the manager should attempt to discern in the short run is whether, after the fact of the decision, the operating costs are covered. An appropriate long-run consideration is whether revenues also cover the overhead costs and make a contribution to profit, hence the concept of a 'contribution margin.'

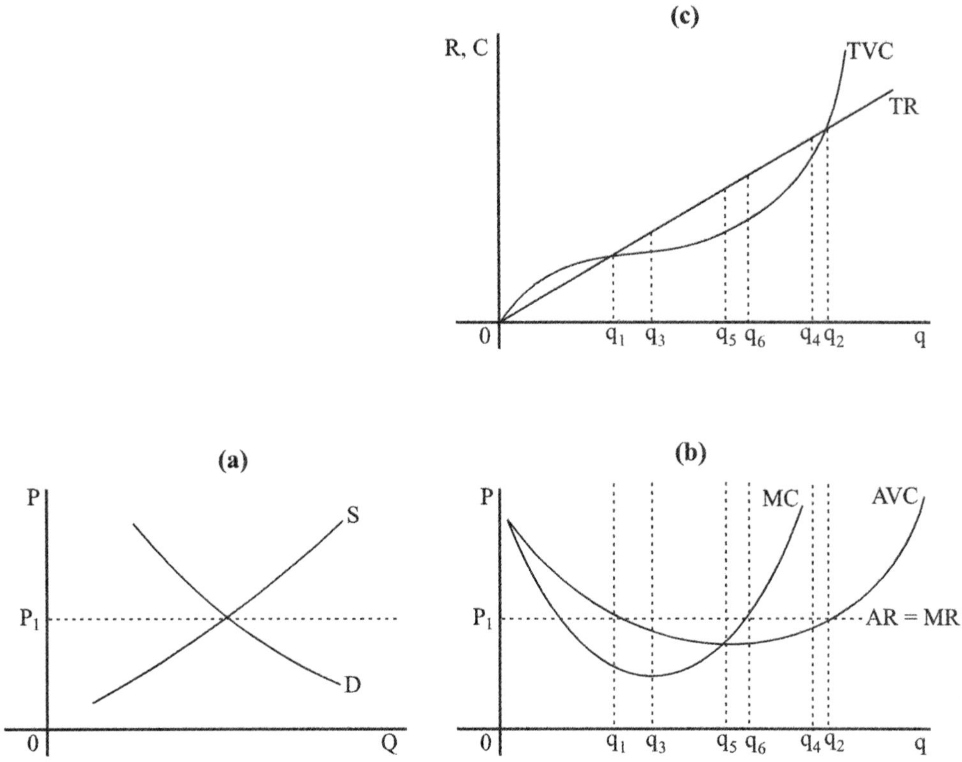

Figure 12.1. A firm in a purely competitive industry.

curve at output q_3. This relationship can be verified in panel (b) of Figure 12.1 where at q_3 the marginal revenue curve (coincident with the demand curve) lies above the marginal cost curve. If the decision maker's goal is **profit maximization**, it is clear that an increase of output from q_3 will add more to total revenue than to total cost, and thereby either increase profit or diminish loss. The appropriate decision criterion is a comparison of **marginal revenue** and **marginal cost**. If marginal revenue is greater than marginal cost, MR > MC, then output should be **increased**. Output q_4 is also in the range of q_1 to q_3, but at q_4 marginal cost is greater than marginal revenue. An increase of output from q_4 will have the effect of adding more to total cost than to total revenue, thereby diminishing profit or increasing loss. A decrease of output will decrease both total revenue and total cost, but total cost will decrease by more than total cost decreases, thereby decreasing loss or increasing profit. Again, if the goal of the manager is to maximize profit, the firm should **decrease** output when marginal cost is greater than marginal revenue, that is, MR < MC.

We could examine other output levels between q_3 and q_6 to draw inferences similar to those drawn for q_3. Likewise, we could examine other output quantities between q_4 and q_6 in order to draw inferences similar to those drawn for q_4. The general principle which should govern output decision making when the goal is to maximize profit is to **increase output** if marginal revenue is greater than marginal cost, MR > MC, but to **decrease output** if marginal cost is greater than marginal revenue, MR < MC. Marginal revenue is easy to identify in the purely competitive market because it is equal to price, and the MR curve is coincident with the demand curve.

However, we recall from Chapter 11 that marginal cost is not directly observable. It can be computed for any output level if the equation of the TC or MC curve is known, but knowing either of these equations probably required the exercise of a costly data collection and model specification and estimation process. Incremental cost can be computed more cheaply from data for two different output levels, but it is only an approximation to true marginal cost.

It is tempting then to look at **average revenue** and **average cost** as possible decision criteria because it is so easy to compute both at any level of output. Average revenue at any output level such as q_2 can be computed as TR_2/q_2, but in the purely competitive market, average revenue is also equal to the price of the product. Average variable cost is easily computed as TVC_2/q_2 at output level, q_2. These magnitudes, AR_2 and AVC_2 are so easy and cheap to compute, what would be the problem in using them as the output decision criteria? It should be apparent in panel (b) of Figure 12.1 that the profit-maximizing output level cannot be found simply by comparing AR and AVC unless all possible outputs between q_1 and q_2 are examined.

Another way to say this is that the comparison of AR and AVC can reveal whether or not the firm is covering its operating costs, but can yield no guidance about whether to **increase or decrease** output. The comparison between AR and AVC can serve as a useful decision criterion, however, if the goal of the management of the firm is to **minimize per-unit costs** (this occurs at output level q_5 in Figure 12.1), or if the goal is simply to operate at any output level for which revenues cover operating costs.

The moral of this story is that MR and MC are the appropriate decision criteria if the goal of the firm is to maximize profit. A qualification to this principle should be noted. In the event that the total cost curve is also linear as described in Chapter 11, Figure 11.6, the marginal cost curve will be linear and horizontal, paralleling the linear and horizontal marginal revenue curve. In this case neither averages nor marginals can provide any guidance in regard to profit maximization or cost minimization. If TR lies above TC (MR also will be above MC and be parallel to it), the firm can always increase its contribution to overhead and profit by increasing output. But it is unlikely that TC will be linear for ever as output increases; eventually the principle of diminishing returns will have its way with the firm's costs, but the firm may have grown beyond the confines of pure competition.

THE OPERATE VS. SHUT-DOWN CRITERION IN THE SHORT RUN

Zero is also a possible level of output which may be chosen in the **short-run**, and it may be rational to shut-down operations if the revenue generated by selling the output cannot cover even the **operating costs** (or variable costs) of producing the output. Assuming cubic production and cost functions, the **shut-down** criterion can be illustrated in panel (b) of Figure 12.1 at any output for which AR < AVC, or in panel (c) at any output for which TR < TVC.[2] Graphically, TR would lie completely below TVC, and P=AR=MR would be below MC at all output levels. In these circumstances, the firm should not operate because the revenue resulting from operation would not cover all of the operating costs, and could make no contribution at all to the overhead costs.[3] In shutdown mode, the firm minimizes its losses by incurring only the fixed costs. The fixed costs, which continue in the short run whether the firm operates or not, can be saved (or avoided) only by exiting the industry, a long-run decision.

There are many exogenous phenomena which may impinge upon the firm in the short run but are not under the discretionary control of the firm's management. For example, as we noted in Chapter 10, the variables $X_1,..., X_n$ in the cost function may include the prices of the inputs (labour, materials, energy, etc.). A change in the price of an input will have the effect of **shifting** the firm's short-run cost curves upwards or downwards and may thereby create a shutdown or restart situation. Such a short-run change may create the need or basis for a long-run decision to exit the industry if the problem cannot be satisfactorily remedied by short-run adjustment. In the long run, revenues must cover all costs of production because there are no fixed costs in the long run. The long-run **exit** criterion applies to any output in panel (b) of Figure 12.2 for which AR < ATC, which also corresponds in panel (c) to any output for which TR < TC.

SHORT-RUN INDUSTRY ADJUSTMENT OF THE COMPETITIVE INDUSTRY

Figure 12.2 is an extension of Figure 12.1 to include the TC curve in panel (c) and the ATC curve in panel (b). We may recall from Chapter 9 that TC is greater than TVC by the amount of the total fixed costs, and ATC is greater than AVC by the average fixed cost at each level of output. Under the circumstances illustrated by P_1 and TR_1, firms presently operating in the market can cover all of their variable and fixed costs and enjoy a profit at the current market price. When these profits are perceived by outsiders, and if these profits are greater than can be earned in other markets, the outsiders may exercise their entrepreneurship to enter the market and try to share in the supernormal profits. This entry into the market will have the effect of increasing market supply, shifting it to the right to some position like S_2 in panel (a) of Figure 12.2. As a result, market price will fall towards P_2, which will become the new locus of the demand and marginal revenue curves as well. Correspondingly, the TR curve will rotate downwards to its new position, TR_2. As a consequence, the firm's profit-maximizing output level will change to q_7, and the profit earned by the firm will be smaller.

---

2. As depicted in Figure 11.6, a linear TVC function has a linear and horizontal AVC curve. In this unlikely case, the shut-down criterion obtains when the slope of TR becomes less than the slope of TVC, such that the horizontal AR curve lies below the horizontal AVC curve. As depicted in Figure 11.5, a second order (quadratic) TVC function has a linear and upsloping AVC curve that never reaches a minimum. In this more likely case, the shut-down vs. operate criterion fails because AR can never (in Quadrant I) become less than AVC.
3. It is tempting to think that the shutdown criterion should be the failure of revenues to cover overhead costs, but as we have stipulated earlier, overhead costs are not relevant to short-run decision making. The identification of the proper shutdown criterion is another reason that we have declined to draw the TC and ATC curves into Figure 12.1.

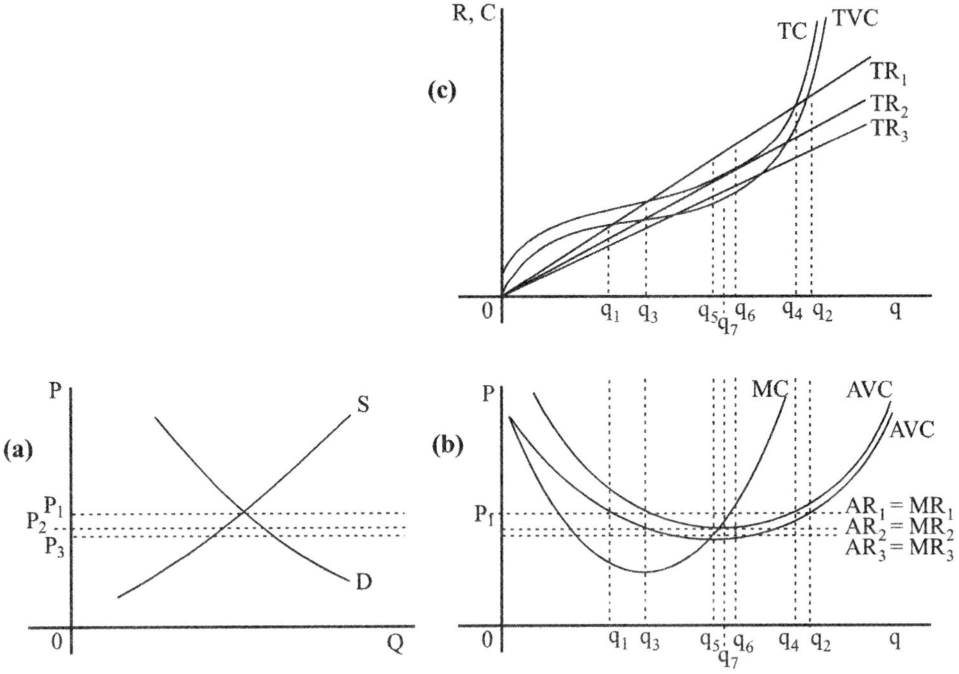

Figure 12.2. Purely competitive adjustment in the long run.

Theoretically, this adjustment process, driven by continuing entry into the market, could continue until the price falls to P_2 and the total revenue curve rotates to position TR_2; here, supernormal profits are eliminated and the market price just covers the firm's variable and fixed costs, allowing only a normal return to the firm's ownership interest. The important point is that with no effective way for firms to prevent entry into the market, all supernormal profits will be competed away. But no firm in the market will be suffering because each will be paying or earning normal returns for all of the resources under its employ. Capital and entrepreneurship, having entered the market, will continue in their present occupation until the prospect of supernormal profits appears elsewhere.

Perfect market knowledge is never a fact in the purely competitive market. Suppose that there is a time lag in the dissemination of information so that potential entrants into the market fail to realize that enough new firms have already entered the market to cause price to fall to the level of ATC. Continued entry by new producers who are yet unaware that supernormal profits are no longer possible in the market will cause price to fall to below the minimum point of ATC, and the total revenue curve to rotate downward to TR_3 which lies below TC. Now firms in the market are realizing insufficient revenue to cover all of their costs. At price P_2, all of the direct or variable costs are covered, and a contribution is being made towards the overhead or fixed costs, so the firm should keep on operating in the short run. However, if due to excessive entry into the market price should happen to fall below the minimum point of AVC, the firm should then shut down and suffer only the fixed costs.

If the situation persists, the management of the firm should give thought to making the long-run decision to exit the market. The managements of some firms will decide to do just this; their exit from the market will decrease market supply, causing market price to rise towards the level where all costs, direct and overhead, can again be covered, and the firms remaining in the market can once again earn normal profits. The competitive market is in equilibrium when all firms still in the market are realizing normal profits, and there are no supernormal profits to tempt entry or subnormal profits to induce exit.

LONG-RUN ADJUSTMENTS IN THE COMPETITIVE INDUSTRY

In the short run the firm's management is limited to making output-related adjustments. Output is adjusted by changing the amounts or rates of utilization of inputs. We can bring together the functional-notation relationships of Chapters 8 and 10 as follows:

$$TC = f(\, Q, X_1, \ldots , X_n \,/\, \ldots),$$

$$Q = g(\, L, M \,/\, K \,)$$

$$g = h(\, E, M, T \,).$$

Costs are a function of output; output is a function of the variable inputs (labour, materials, etc.), given the existing plant and the productive environment. The productive environment is a function of the available entrepreneurial capacity, managerial ability, and the technology in use. The latter three plus plant size constitute the long-run parameters which the firm's management may alter.

The decision options of the long-run extend to

(a) entering or exiting a market;

(b) adding to the firm's plant or equipment, disposing of capital assets, or letting them depreciate to non-functionality without replacement;

(c) building a larger or smaller plant of the same technology;

(d) choosing a different technology, and consequently an appropriate plant size to implement that technology; technologies new to the firm may be acquired externally by licensing, purchasing new equipment, or hiring new personnel, or they may be developed internally through research and development (R&D) efforts;

(e) gaining of managerial capacity internally by experience and training or externally by employment of new personnel; or losing managerial capacity through retirement, death, or movement of personnel to other firms; or

(f) gaining or losing entrepreneurial ability.

An alteration of any of the environmental parameters (technology, management, or entrepreneurship) means that the firm's production and cost functions, short- and long-run, have shifted and should be redefined by intuitive or empirical estimation means. How the functions shift, and whether they exhibit warps or twists relative to previous attitudes, depend entirely upon the particular change.

A change of plant size within the same technology is amenable to analysis using the long-run average total cost curve introduced in Chapter 10. Such a plant-size change may have scale economy or diseconomy implications if the LATC curve is U-shaped. If the management can discover enough about the shape of its LATC curve, it may devise a long-run (capital investment) strategy to change plant size in anticipation of exploiting scale economies or avoiding scale diseconomies. Also, as market demand changes, the managements which know enough about their costs in the long run may seek to construct plants of more optimal capacity to meet market demands.

These points can be illustrated with the ATC and LATC curves depicted in Figure 12.3. Suppose, for whatever historical reason, the firm has constructed the plant represented by ATC_1 and MC_1. At price P_1 it maximizes profits by producing the q_1 output. But we note that there is a more optimal plant for producing the q_1 output. This plant is ATC_2, the one for which average total cost curve is tangent to the LATC curve at q_1. The profit-maximizing output for plant ATC_2 is not q_1, but rather q_2 where MC_2 crosses the MR curve. However, there is an even lower-cost plant which could be constructed to produce the q_2 output level, ATC_3, but the profit maximizing output level for ATC_3 is q_3. Points a, b, and c are on the respective marginal cost curves and lie directly below the points of tangency of the respective ATC curves with the LATC curve. These points trace out a path which can be construed as a long-run marginal cost curve, LMC.

Unless the firm's managers have perfect knowledge of the firm's long-run cost conditions (that is, they know the loci of all of the possible short-run cost curves), it will be through a process of discovery that the firm will eventually be led to build the ATC_m plant and operate it at the q_m level of output where the firm will maximize profits. Given market price P_1, plant ATC_m i the plant

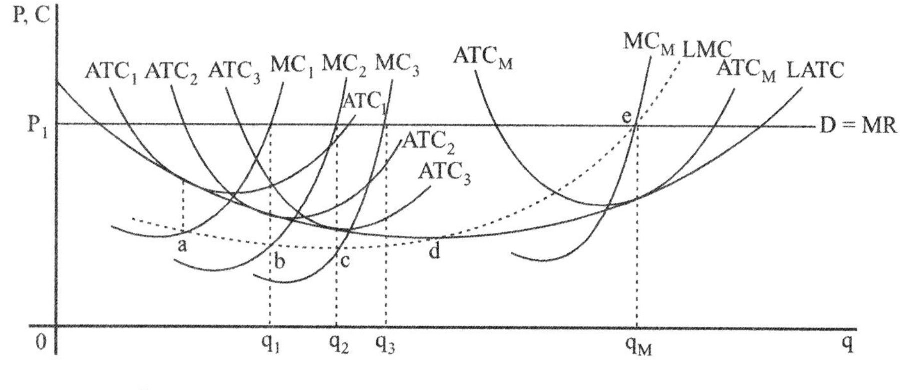

Figure 12.3. Long-run costs for a purely competitive firm.

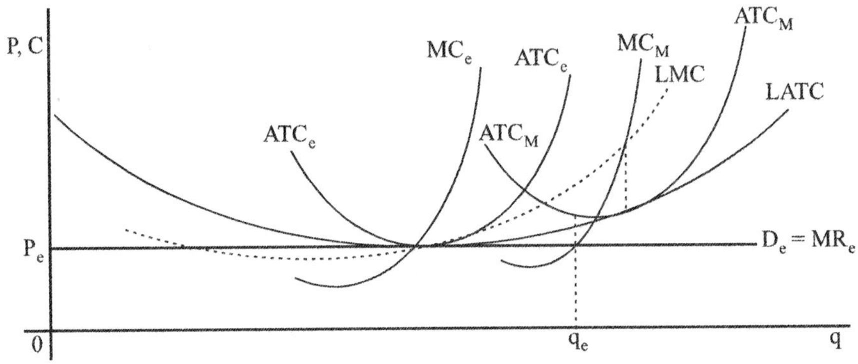

Figure 12.4. A competitive firm in long-run industry equilibrium.

which will yield the largest mass of profit for the firm. At output level q_m, the short-run ATC_m curve is tangent to the LATC curve; there is no other plant which is more appropriate for producing the q_m output. Theoretically, this plant can be found at the intersection of the LMC curve with the MR curve. The appropriate plant then is the one whose MC curve crosses MR at the intersection of the LMC curve with the MR curve.

Let us suppose for a moment that the manager of the competitive firm does have perfect knowledge of its production and cost functions, but completely lacks foresight of likely future market changes. Given price P_1 and assuming that it will persist for ever, he makes the long-run decision to build plant ATC_m, intending to operate it at q_m level of output. Managers of many other competitive firms do likewise. This phenomenon, plus the effect of entry of new firms into the market to try to capture a share of the supernormal profits can be expected to bid the market price down towards P_e in Figure 12.4, for which demand curve D_e and marginal revenue curve MR_e happen to be tangent to the minimum point of the LATC curve. When prices reach P_e, the appropriate plant size is described by ATC_e, which is tangent to the LATC curve at its minimum point. And the manager who opted for plant ATC_m when price was P_1 can now be seen to have been both naive and short-sighted because plant ATC_m incurs unit costs (even at its minimum point) which are greater than market price P_e.

Managers who committed to plants like ATC_m or ATC_1 may find their firms realizing losses relative to firms whose managers more astutely chose to build a least-cost plant. They are stuck with plants which are too small or too large for the duration of the lives of the plant and equipment. Their short-run options are to continue to operate while suffering losses if P_e happens to exceed their average variable cost, or to shut down if P_e is less than their average variable cost. If price remains as low as P_e, the firms which are realizing losses have the option of exiting the market. Exit from the market will likely involve capital losses if the plant and equipment cannot be economically converted to other applications, or if they must be sold at prices below their depreciated book values.

In reality, managers of competitive firms have neither perfect foresight of market conditions nor perfect knowledge of their production and cost functions. Collectively they will be led through processes of discovery to the construction of optimal plants (ATC_e in Figure 12.4) as market price falls toward P_e. Some will build suboptimal plants and others will build super-optimal plants. It is these who will prematurely exit the market. The ones who survive and remain in the market are those who through exceptional knowledge of their own long-run cost possibilities, astute understandings of future market dynamics, or sheer good luck, are induced to build the right-sized plants and operate them at the right levels of output. Competition smiles upon those who learn enough about their costs and are knowledgeable of market dynamics. Competition ruthlessly dismisses those who are ignorant of their costs or naive of market realities.

Our purpose is to examine decision-making criteria from the perspective of the manager, but in passing we shall note that from the perspective of society as a whole, plant ATC_e operated at output level q_e when price is p_e is also a socially-optimum condition. Competitive firms are induced to build least-cost plants and operate them at least-cost output levels while covering all economic costs but realizing no supernormal profits. The market price of a good can be interpreted as society's valuation of the good; the marginal cost of producing a good can be interpreted as the cost to society of using the resources to produce the good rather than other goods. Because in competitive equilibrium the firm's marginal cost of producing the output is just equal to market price, it may be said that the social cost of using resources to produce the output is just equal to the social valuation of the output produced. From this may be drawn the inference that the resources used in the production of the output are efficiently allocated. Enough, but not too much, of the output is being produced.

Finally, it may be noted that the functioning of the competitive market has brought about a coincidence of social welfare and private profitability.

THE MANAGERIAL IMPLICATIONS OF PURE COMPETITION

It may be possible to capture supernormal profits in a highly competitive market that can be easily entered with small amounts of capital and commonly available technologies. Entrepreneurs who perceive such possibilities should be aware that those supernormal profits will be fleeting at best. Good advice would be to 'gather ye rosebuds while ye may' and 'make hay while the sun shines.' Only normal returns (no greater than the returns which can be realized in other opportunities) can be earned in the competitive market in the long run.

The competitive firm manager would be well advised to take pains to identify and build the least-cost plant for the long run, even if there appears to be a more appropriate plant size to build under current conditions. It is better to take smaller profits from a plant which can be operated through its physical life than to take maximum profits this month from a plant which may have to be shut down next month and disposed of next year.

Since no manager can know in advance and with precision what is absolutely the correct rate of output at which to operate its existing plant in the short run, the manager should expect to proceed iteratively, that is, to try one rate of production and then another higher or lower rate, using as decision criterion whether marginal cost (or an approximation to it) is greater or lesser than marginal revenue (price in a competitive market.

We entered this chapter with a disclaimer: the extremes of the competitive spectrum are hardly representative of real-world situations. Are there no examples of pure competition in the real world? A search for good examples of pure competition is likely to be fruitless, but this may only mean that we have asked the wrong question. A better question, given a market in which we are already operating or considering entering, is whether the decision-making characteristics of the market can best be analyzed with the purely-competitive model or some other model that will be introduced in subsequent pages. Is the DVD movie rental business a good example of a purely competitive market? We can't say. Is the purely competitive model an appropriate vehicle for analyzing the DVD movie rental business? Possibly.

At the beginning of this section we specified the descriptive characteristics of the purely competitive market. We then noted the consequences and behavioural patterns that follow from the characteristics. These consequences and patterns rather severely limit the range of entrepreneurial discretion to the choices to enter or exit the market. It limits the range of managerial discretion to choosing the right plant size in the long run, and the right rate of output in the short run.

If there ever were a purely competitive market, it would likely cease to be such rather quickly because of the inherent differences of entrepreneurial capacity and managerial abilities from firm to firm. Entrepreneurs of exceptional ability will discover new markets to enter, new product lines to produce, and new, more efficient technologies to employ; they will discover how to make their products more appealing to consumers by differentiating them from other products. And in so doing they will gain competitive advantage over other firms in the market. This of course means that the market can no longer be characterized as purely competitive. What are the managerial implications? As one wag has put it, the way to get ahead in life is to be a goat while everyone else is being a sheep. A goat in the middle of a flock of sheep is a natural leader. Being a goat amidst a flock of sheep is what entrepreneurship is all about.

Summary of Important Points

1. The decision options of the enterprise manager are constrained by the types and intensities of competition confronting the enterprise in the market for its products; at the extremes are pure competition and pure monopoly.
2. Pure competition may be described as a very large number of very small firms with no special managerial capacity, producing a homogeneous product, the market for which is easily entered or exited.
3. No seller in the purely competitive market is aware of or concerned about the identities or actions of competitors.
4. Super- and subnormal profits in pure competition will be fleeting.
5. Firms in a purely competitive market can exert virtually no pricing discretion.
6. In the short run, the profit maximizing (or loss minimizing) level of output occurs where marginal revenue equals marginal cost.
7. Marginal revenue and price (average revenue) are identical in a purely competitive market.

Contd....

8. The firm should continue to operate (even while suffering losses) as long as price is greater than average variable cost.
9. Entry and exit will dissipate super- or sub-normal profits in pure competition.
10. In the long run the pure competitor will find incentive to build the least-cost plant possible and operate it at the least-cost level of output while realizing no supernormal profits.
11. The market price of a good can be interpreted as society's valuation of the good; the marginal cost of producing a good can be interpreted as the cost to society of using the resources to produce the good rather than other goods.
12. Because in competitive equilibrium the firm's marginal cost of producing the output is just equal to market price, it may be said that the social cost of using resources to produce the output is just equal to the social valuation of the output produced.

Significant Terms

behavioural premise
pure, perfect competition
product homogeneity; differentiation
imperfections of competition
entry, exit
entrepreneurship
anonymity
super-, subnormal profits
equilibrium
break-even
contribution to overhead, profit
marginal revenue
shut-down
variable, direct costs
short-run adjustment
research and development
depreciation
environmental parameters
long run average total cost
scale economies, diseconomies
long run marginal cost
social valuation, cost
efficient allocation
least-cost plant

Questions for Discussion

1. Why do there appear to be so few good examples of cases at the extremes of the competitive continuum?
2. Identify the descriptive characteristics of firms in a purely competitive market.

3. Distinguish perfect from pure competition and discuss the decision implications of the distinction.
4. Identify the behavioural characteristics of firms in a purely competitive market; which seem to require greatest stretches of the imagination to accept them?
5. Why is it feasible to analyze conditions in a competitive market with reference to a 'representative firm'?
6. Why would the manager of a purely competitive firm be reluctant to produce an output below the lower revenue-cost break-even point? ...above the upper break-even point?
7. Explain how the manager of a purely competitive firm should attempt to find the best level of output to produce between the revenue-cost break-even points.
8. Why is the locus of the total cost curve not relevant to short-run decision making in the purely competitive firm?
9. Explain how the marginal revenue curve may be identified for a firm in a purely competitive market.
10. Why are MR and MC more appropriate as managerial decision criteria than are AR and AC in a purely competitive firm?
11. Describe a plausible scenario for the transition of a purely competitive market into an imperfectly competitive market.
12. Discuss the managerial decision implications of a linear total cost function for a purely competitive firm.
13. Describe the criteria which the manager of a purely competitive firm should use in a consideration of whether to not to cease operating (that is, shut down).
14. Explain the appropriate role of average fixed cost in a purely competitive firm manager's decision to continue operating.
15. Describe the market forces which lead firms in a purely competitive market to build the 'right' size plants and operate them at the 'right' levels of output.
16. What are the possible incentives for entrepreneurs to enter a purely competitive market? What are the likely consequences for firms already in the market?
17. Explain the sense in which entry into and exit from a market are both entrepreneurial decisions.
18. Describe the long-run parameters which a purely competitive firm's management may alter; what follows from each?
19. Describe the long-run decision options available to the managers of firms in purely competitive markets; how are these decision options different from their short-run decision options?
20. Describe the effects of exploitation of scale economies by purely competitive firms in the long run.

21. Discuss the consequences of incurring scale diseconomies by purely competitive firms in the long run.
22. Why might the management of a firm in a purely competitive market build a non-optimal sized plant? What are the likely consequences in such a situation?
23. Explain the relationship between the welfare of society and the profitability of firms in a purely competitive market.
24. How is it possible for firms in a purely competitive market to capture supernormal profits? Describe the likely market response to such a circumstance.
25. What are the managerial implications of operating in a purely competitive market?
26. Without perfect market knowledge, how is it possible for managers of firms in purely competitive markets to find appropriate output levels.
27. Why would a purely competitive market likely have a rather short life?

Appendix 12.1

PRICE CHANGES IN COMPETITIVE MARKETS

In an abstract representation of a competitive market mechanism such as the panel (a) of Figure 12.1 in Chapter 12, economists assert that when price is too high for equilibrium, market forces will cause it to fall until quantity demanded is just equal to quantity supplied and inventories are no longer accumulating. Or, when price is too low for equilibrium, market forces will cause price to rise until quantity demanded is just equal to quantity supplied, and inventories are no longer depleting. The resulting equilibrium is then a 'state of rest' with no further change until the mechanism is disturbed by a change in one or more of the determinants of demand or supply which have been assumed constant.

What are the market forces which actually cause market price to fall or to rise? Demand must be understood to be a schedule of the collective *intentions* of all of those who hope to acquire quantities of the good from the market at different possible prices. Likewise, supply is a schedule of the collective *intentions* of those who wish to offer quantities of the good on the market at different possible prices. At any price other than the equilibrium price, the intentions of only one set of market participants (either demanders or suppliers) can be met. The intentions of the other set of market participants are not met. Only in equilibrium can the intentions of both sets of market participants be met. It is in this sense that it is sometimes said that equilibrium describes a sort of 'bliss state' in a market.

When price is too high for equilibrium, only the intentions of demanders can be fully met because they can purchase all of the good that they want to purchase at the too-high price. The intentions of suppliers, wishing to offer a larger quantity of the good on the market than demanders wish to purchase, are at least partially frustrated. Either all suppliers will sell some of what they offered, or some suppliers will sell as much as they want to sell while others sell little or none. In any case, it is the quantity demanded which will actually be transacted on the market. Suppliers collectively are pushed or forced off their schedule of intentions. It is thus suppliers who are unhappy at the outcome, and it is suppliers who can be expected to become the activists in the market to do something about their discomfort. The immediate response to the problem of increasing inventories is to cut price. Another way of saying this is that it is the suppliers who feel an itch (increasing inventories) which they feel compelled to scratch (by cutting price).

When price is too low for equilibrium, only the intentions of suppliers can be fully met because they can sell all of the good that they want to sell at the too-low price. In this case, it is the intentions of demanders, wishing to acquire a larger quantity of the good from the market, which are at least partially frustrated. Some demanders (perhaps the first to arrive at the market) may be able to purchase all of the good that they want at the too-low price, but others (the later arrivals) will have to leave the market empty-handed or with less than they would like to have purchased. The quantity supplied is the quantity which is transacted on the market. It is demanders whose intentions cannot be fully met, and who will sense an itch (to acquire more of the good at the too-low price) which requires a scratch (to offer a higher price in hopes of capturing a larger quantity of the good).

Demanders may or may not be able to scratch their itch when the price is too low for equilibrium. In bazaar trading situations where there is interactive bidding and offering (dickering, haggling) between buyers and sellers, demanders can scratch their itches to acquire more of the good by bidding the market price upward, and price will continue to be bid upwards by demanders until their intentions can be met. Bazaar trading is a common mode of commerce in many of the so-called 'third-world' countries. Examples of this possibility in the 'first' world include auctions, flea markets, yard sales, and new and used real estate and automobile markets.

People in Western nations are perhaps more accustomed to purchasing their needs in fixed-price retail shops where the prices of items are specified on stickers on the items themselves or on labels on the racks or shelves holding the items. There is no opportunity to dicker over the price in such a shop (unless some flaw or damage can be identified). The customer's only options are to purchase an item at the specified price or leave it in order to search for a better price at another shop. In fixed-price retail shops, it is up to the seller to lower price when price is too high for equilibrium, and to perceive the opportunity to raise the price when it is too low for equilibrium.

The forces of market adjustment are the unmet intentions of market participants. These forces of adjustment are inherent in the market mechanism, although they may lay dormant as long as a market is in equilibrium. The forces are called into action when the intentions of one set or the other of the market participants cannot be met at the going price. But once price has adjusted to a new level at which all intentions of market participants can be met, the forces of adjustment go dormant again.

This functioning of the market mechanism gives rise to a description of a market as an 'automatic, self-correcting mechanism,' much in the same sense that a thermostat-controlled heating and air conditioning (HVAC) system works automatically. When the ambient temperature departs from the set criterion temperature, the thermostat calls the heating or cooling mechanism into operation. The unmet intentions of market participants function as the adjustment triggering mechanism in a market.

Both markets and HVAC systems may also be described as 'adjustment self-limiting mechanisms' in the sense that adjustment continues until the respective criterion is met, but then adjustment ceases. The HVAC system continues to heat or cool until the ambient temperature reaches the criterion temperature, and then the thermostat shuts down the HVAC system and it remains in an idle state until something again disturbs the ambient temperature to cause it to diverge from the criterion temperature. Likewise, price adjustment continues to occur in a market until the intentions of demanders and suppliers can be met by matching the quantity demanded with the quantity supplied in the market. Then, price adjustment ceases and price remains at the equilibrium level until changes occur in the determinants of demand or supply.

In a dynamic world, equilibrium may not ever be an observable state because the determinants of demand and supply are ever changing. This does not mean that equilibrium is an irrelevant mental construct which exists only in the minds of economists. It is a real phenomenon which functions as an ever-moving target towards which the market mechanism continually attempts to adjust. Its usefulness to the economic analyst is an attempt to predict the direction in which price (or quantity) will move towards a new equilibrium once changes in demand or supply are identified.

Appendix 12.2

SIMULATION MODELLING OF A FIRM IN A COMPETITIVE MARKET

In an earlier Appendix we introduced a graphic model simulation system. We have discussed its applicability to revenue and demand analysis, and its usefulness to the analysis of costs. Our purpose in this appendix is to bring together the revenue and cost functions for a firm in a competitive market and examine the applicability of the graphic simulation model to the analysis of the marginal criteria for selection of the competitive firm's profit-maximizing price and output in the short run. We assume that the competitive firm has no pricing discretion so that it simply accepts the market price as a 'given,' that is, it is a 'price taker.' This implies that its demand (average revenue) and marginal revenue curves are horizontal and coincident.

The initial total revenue function was given by the linear equation,

$$TR_1 = 20Q,$$

from which may be derived the demand equation,

$$AR_1 = P = 20,$$

and the marginal revenue equation which is identical to the demand equation,

$$MR_1 = 20.$$

The total cost function is given by the third-order equation,

$$TC_1 = 120 + 30Q + -1.7Q^2 + .04Q^3,$$

from which may be derived the average cost equation,

$$AC_1 = 120/Q + 30 - 1.7Q + .04Q^2,$$

and the marginal cost equation,

$$MC_1 = 30 - 3.4Q + .12Q^2.$$

The graphs of these functions and the average and marginal functions derived from them are illustrated in Figure A-XII(a).

Figure A-XII(a) illustrates the graphic display for a simultaneous solution of the two marginal equations. The profit-maximizing value for Q is between 24.9 and 25.0 units. The quantity 25.0 entered into the demand and marginal revenue equations yields average revenue (price) of $ 20.0 and marginal revenue of $ 20.0. The average total cost of $ 17.3 may be determined by entering the value of Q into the average total cost equation; marginal cost for this value of Q is $ 20.0. The difference between the price and average cost at quantity 25.0 units is the per-unit profit contribution of $ 2.7.

Suppose that the coefficient of Q in the total revenue equation is decreased from 20 to 15. The new total revenue function equation is

$$TR_1 = 15Q,$$

from which may be derived the new average revenue equation,

$$AR_1 = P = 15,$$

and new marginal revenue equation (identical to the average revenue equation),

$$MR_1 = 15.$$

The cost functions remain unchanged.

Figure A-XII(b) shows the results of decreasing the coefficient of Q in the total revenue equation from 20 to 15. A comparison of the two graphic displays reveals that the total revenue function rotated downwards consequent upon the decrease in the coefficient of Q; the average and marginal revenue curves (coincident) are also shifted downwards. The marginals now intersect

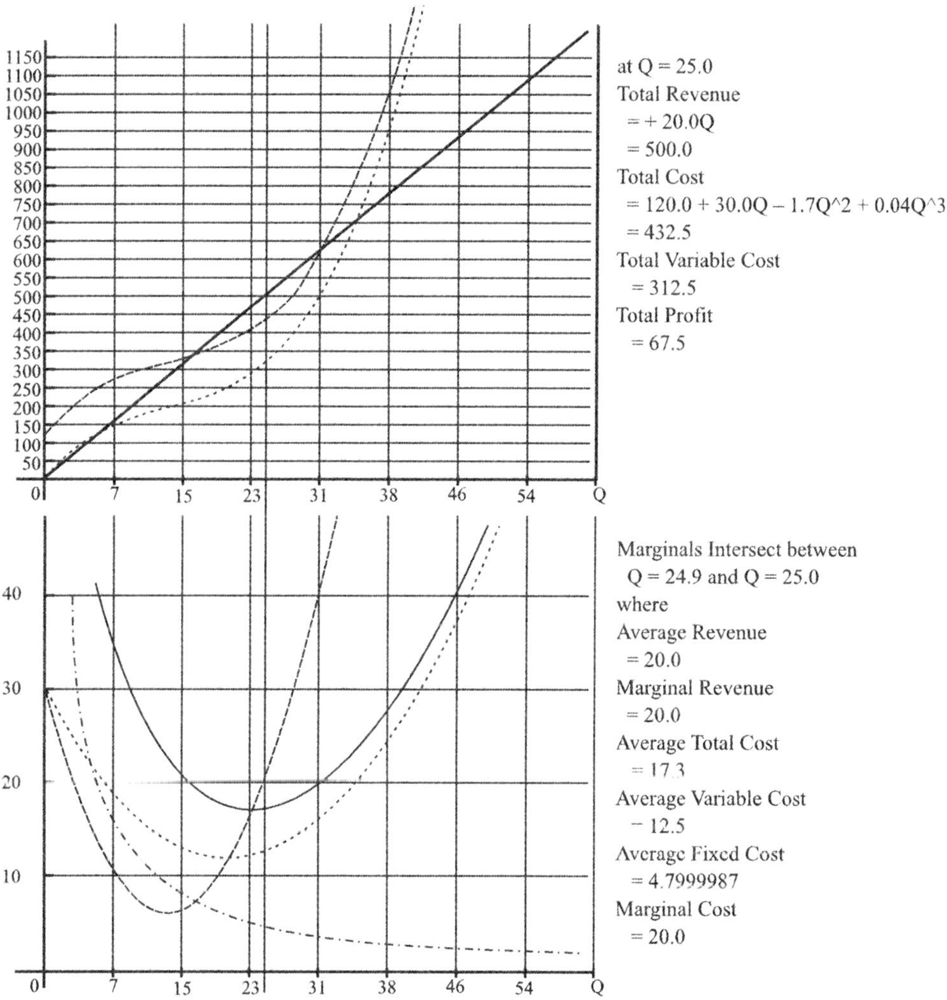

Figure A-XII(a). Derivation of marginal revenue curve.

between 22.8 and 22.9 units of output. Using the value of 22.9 for Q in the AR, MR, ATC, AVC, and MC equations, we find that the profit-maximizing price is now \$ 15.00 and marginal revenue is also \$ 15.00; average total cost is \$ 17.29 and marginal cost is \$ 15.07. At a quantity of 22.9 units, the difference between price and average cost is now a per-unit loss of \$ 2.29. Since price of \$ 15.00 is still greater than average variable cost of \$ 12.05, the firm should keep operating, covering all of its operating costs (that is, average variable cost) and making a contribution of \$ 2.95 per unit of product sold to covering overhead (fixed) costs.

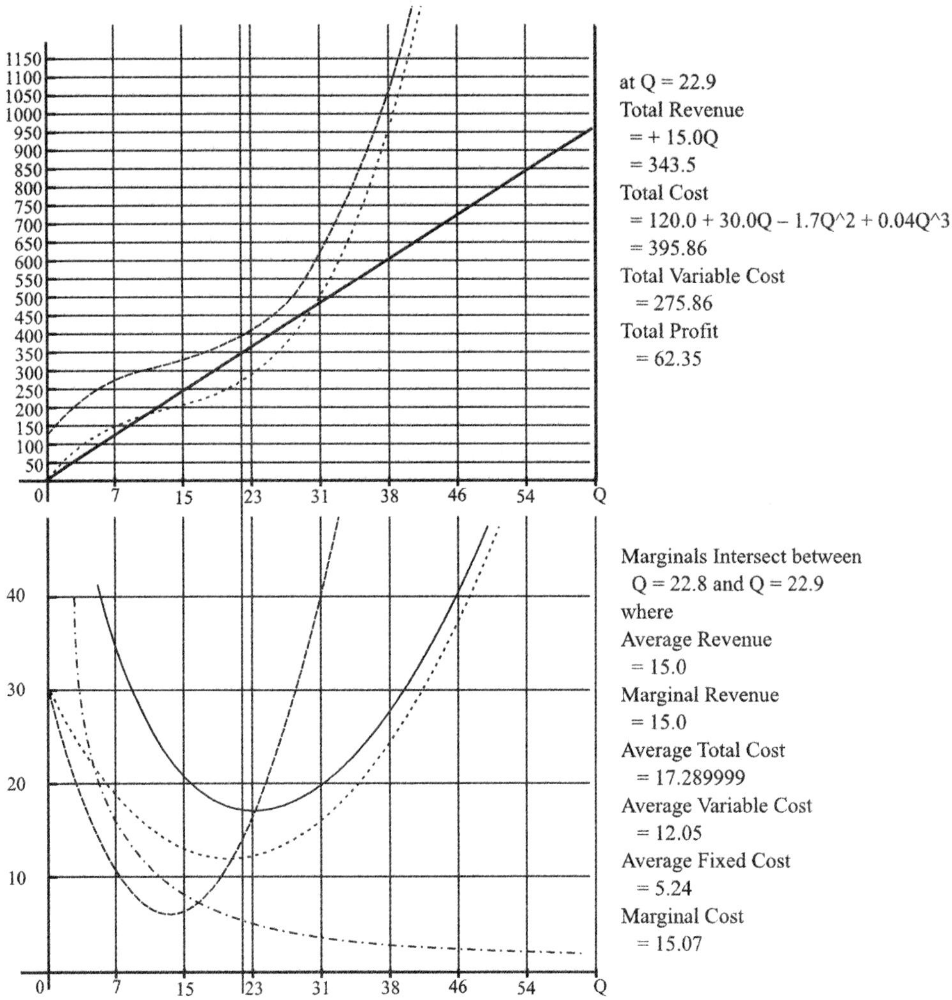

Figure A-XII(b). Relationship between TR & MR.

In this example we have illustrated the ability, using a graphic simulation model, to analyze the effects upon the profitability of a firm in a competitive market of a change in one (or more) of the parameters of its revenue and cost functions. The reader may similarly analyze the likely effects of changes in the revenue and cost functions for any firm or product line if the functions can be known or estimated from historical data via regression analysis.

—oo(O)oo—

Chapter 13

Monopoly

Topics covered in this chapter

• The nature of pure monopoly. • The distinction between monopoly and pure competition. • The bases for pure monopoly. • The nature of entry into a monopolized market. • Pricing and output discretion in pure monopoly. • Output and pricing criteria in pure monopoly. • Alternative behavioural patterns of pure monopolists. • Scale economies in pure monopoly. • Managerial preferences for monopoly.

At the other extreme of the competitive continuum from pure competition is the market structure which economists designate as pure monopoly. Its descriptive characteristics are as follows:

1. The 'market' is supplied by a single firm.
2. There are no close substitutes for the product(s) sold by the firm, that is, the product is significantly differentiated from all others.
3. There are several possible bases for the monopoly position, including
   (a) the exploitation of scale economies;
   (b) a technological uniquity which may have been developed (internally, by research and development) or acquired (externally, from the inventor);
   (c) the grant of an exclusive position by government, for example, by franchise, patent, trademark, or copyright;
   (d) a resource-control uniquity; and

(e) predatory or acquisitive behaviour leading to the demise or absorption of former competitors.

The maintenance of a monopoly position may involve a combination of these bases.

These descriptive characteristics of a pure monopoly lead to a number of consequences or behavioural patterns:

1. Entry into the monopolist's market is very difficult or costly, and may be blocked entirely by some combination of circumstances. For example, the firm's research and development operation may have developed the technology for a new product or process, which is then protected by an exclusive government grant in the form of a patent. Another example is that of a utility (publicly or privately owned), the operations of which would be uneconomic if competitors existed. In recognition of this problem, governments usually grant an exclusive franchise to the utility which is regarded as a 'natural monopoly.' Yet another example may be a firm which has attained monopoly position by exploiting scale economies, and has become so large that the capital requirements for entry by a prospective competitor are so great that none can mount an effort to start up at a large enough scale to match the monopolist's low per-unit costs.

2. Exit from the market may be equally difficult; if the monopolist has attained large enough scale, exit may be possible only by failure and dissolution.

3. The monopolist has exclusive control over the market price of the product. However, this does not mean that the firm can charge 'any price it wishes,' or can send prices 'out the ceiling' as may be a common misconception. The monopolist is still subject to the discipline of market demand; there is some revenue-maximizing price, some profit-maximizing price (probably different from the revenue-maximizing price), and some price which is high enough that the public will not (or cannot) buy any of his products, even if it is the only source of it.

4. Supernormal profits and control over its situation are the two prominent benefits which monopoly position confers upon a firm. Supernormal profits are not a certainty, even for a monopolist, but if they are achieved, it may be possible to sustain them indefinitely if effective competition can be forestalled and entry into the market blocked. But even if supernormal profits cannot be achieved (as appears to be common for some utilities), the control over the market, the comforts of entrenchment, and the absence of a need to compete may be sufficient rewards for the monopolist.

SHORT-RUN ADJUSTMENTS BY THE MONOPOLIST

Figure 13.1 illustrates the short-run revenue and cost curves for a pure monopolist. The reader is invited to compare these with those in Figure 13.1 for a representative firm in pure competition. There are two obvious differences. First, the market demand and supply curves illustrated in panel (a) of Figure 13.1 are apparently missing from Figure 13.1. They are in fact present in Figure 13.1, but a separate set of coordinate axes is not needed to house them. This is so because the monopolist's demand curve is the market demand curve when there is only one seller in the market. And the market supply curve consists of one of the monopolist's short-run cost curves, depending upon the monopolist's behavioural objective.

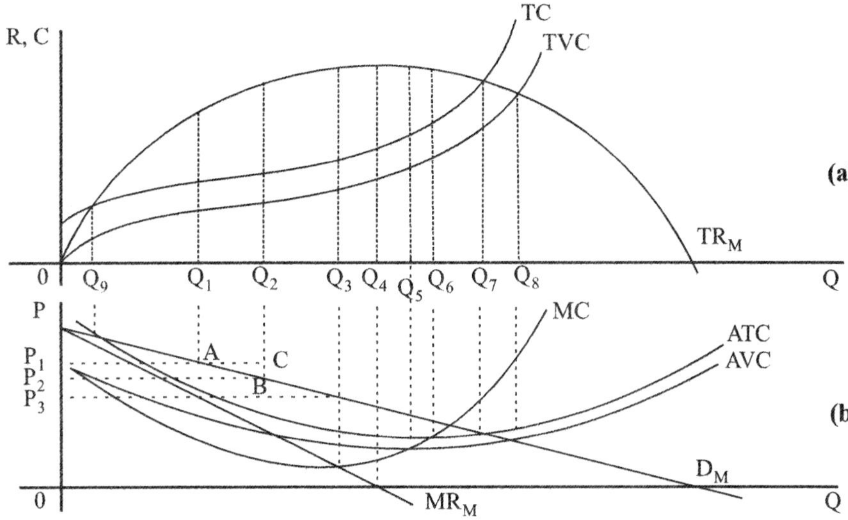

Figure 13.1. Cost and revenue curves for a pure monopolist.

The second obvious difference between Figures 12.1 and 13.1 is that the monopolist's total revenue curve, TRm, is drawn as a parabola opening downwards (rather than a straight line), and its demand curve (which is also its average revenue curve), D_m, slopes downwards from left to right. The marginal revenue curve, MRm diverges from the demand curve and lies below it when the total revenue curve is a parabola.

The practical reason that D slopes downwards is that the monopolist, in order to increase sales, finds it necessary to lower the product price (or do something to cause the demand curve to shift to the right). The conceptual reason that marginal revenue is always less than average revenue (that is, MR lies below D) is that the lowered price applies to all units which are sold, not just to the additional unit sales resulting from the price decrease. Since marginal revenue is the addition to total revenue consequent upon selling more units, marginal revenue decreases because total revenue increases at a decreasing rate. This can also be stated in the opposite direction: when TR increases at a decreasing rate, MR decreases. Because marginal revenue eventually reaches zero and negative values, total revenue correspondingly reaches a peak and becomes negatively sloped beyond the peak.

The cost curves illustrated for the pure monopolist in Figure 13.1 have essentially the same appearances as those illustrated for the pure competitor in Figure 13.1. Short-run cost relationships are not the real differences between the pure competitor and the pure monopolist. In a local market, or in the case of a newly-invented product, the pure monopolist could be physically as small a firm as we assume a pure competitor to be, in which case the cost curves could be identical. We usually imagine the monopolist to be a gigantic firm, having gotten so by growth and exploiting economies of scale. In this case, the quantity units scale on the horizontal axis may cover a much larger range than would be expected of the small-firm pure competitor, but we can still expect the short-run cost curves to be of similar shape, only to spread horizontally across the larger range.

The thought process which the pure monopolist must use in selecting the right output level is virtually identical to that of the pure competitor. The same decision criteria are pertinent to both pure competition and pure monopoly. Output should be increased if marginal revenue exceeds marginal cost because more will be added to total revenue than to total cost, thereby increasing profit (or diminishing loss if the firm is operating unprofitably). Such is the case at output level Q_1 in Figure 13.1. If marginal cost is greater than marginal revenue, as at output level Q_2, output should be decreased; the resulting decrease in total cost will be less than the decrease in total revenue, so that profit will be increased (or loss diminished).

The major difference between the pure monopolist and the pure competitor lies in the fact that the pure monopolist has at least two realms of decision discretion whereas the pure competitor has only one. The pure competitor is a price taker; it has no alternative but to accept market price as a given. The pure monopolist not only can alter market price if it wishes; it must change market price if it wishes to change the quantity which it sells. For example, suppose that it has been selling the Q_1 quantity at price P_1 (point A in Figure 13.1). The manager realizes that since marginal revenue is greater than marginal cost output should be increased to Q_2. If the manager now does not also lower price to P_2, a larger quantity will be produced than can be sold at the unchanged price, resulting in an inventory accumulation of $Q_2–Q_1$, or the line segment AC in Figure 13.1. It would certainly be nice to be able to sell the larger quantity, Q_2, at the unchanged price, P_1, but point C does not happen to be on the firm's demand curve. In fact, to increase output without correspondingly decreasing price will result in increased total costs but no increase in total revenue. The impact on profit would be precisely the opposite of the desired effect.

To accomplish the desired objective of increasing profits, the monopolist must move along the demand curve to some point like B. Such a movement is a 'change of quantity demanded,' which any student who has had a course in principles of economics knows to be caused by a change of price. In order to get to a point like C, the monopolist would have to effect a 'change of demand,' that is, to shift the demand curve to the right. This may indeed be possible by mounting an effective promotional effort. Even if the monopolist does not have perfect knowledge of the shapes and loci of his revenue and cost curves (management almost never will), an iterative process (trial and error) employing as decision criteria the comparison between marginal revenue and marginal cost (or their proxies) can lead the monopolist towards the profit maximizing price and output levels, P_3 and Q_3 in Figure 13.1. Output level Q_3 is that for which marginal revenue is equal to marginal cost. Given the locus of the demand curve at D_m, there is no other quantity sold at any alternative price which can yield any more profit than can the Q_3 output sold at the P_3 price. In addition to Q_3, there are other output levels which are also notable:

Q_4, the output which maximizes total revenue;
Q_5, the output which minimizes average variable cost;
Q_6, the output which minimizes average total cost
Q_7, the upper break-even output level
Q_8, the maximum output at which all variable costs are covered; and
Q_9, the lower break-even output level.

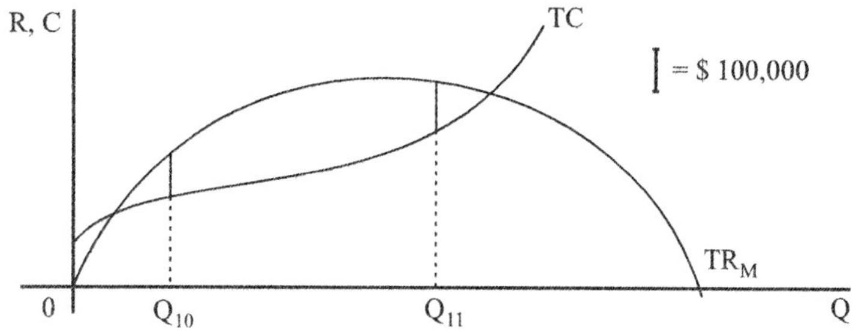

Figure 13.2. A monopolist's profit-satisficing level of output.

Each of these is notable because it could be a decision objective of the firm in lieu of profit maximization. For example, suppose that the objective of the firm is growth rather than profit. Output Q_7 is the largest quantity that can be produced and sold without incurring loss. Output Q_8 is the largest output that can be produced and sold while covering all variable costs, but sustaining a maximum loss equal to the average fixed costs. Output Q_9, the lower breakeven output, could be an objective if the firm is attempting to present a low profile to the antitrust authorities: it is the smallest output which can be produced and sold without incurring a loss.

Earlier, we noted that the manager of the firm might pursue a satisficing behavioural strategy with respect to profits. One form of satisficing is to select a target rate of return (TROR) on invested capital. For example, if the firm has \$ 1 million invested in plant and equipment and the management wishes to earn 10 per cent on this investment, it must realize a profit of \$ 100,000. This sum can be represented as a vertical line segment of an appropriate length relative to the vertical axis scale. This vertical line segment can then be moved into Figure 13.2 until it just 'fits' between the TR and TC curves, thus 'finding' the minimum output level, Q_{10}, which will just satisfy the TROR requirement. Alternately, it may be fitted to the right side of the lens-shaped area formed by the TR and TC curves to find Q_{11}, the maximum output which is compatible with the TROR requirement. In either case the management would further have to estimate the market price at which each output could be sold, but there are no marginal decision criteria which can help him in this respect. However, if the management has enough information about cost and revenue relationships to permit estimation of cost and revenue functions, it could solve the difference between the two functions (TR-TC) for the Q which just meets the TROR requirement.

Before we leave the realm of short-run decision making for the monopolist, we should note that it has even more decision-making discretion than just price and output. There is a wide variety of non-price determinants of demand which the marketing decision maker can manipulate in the effort to shift the demand curve, that is, to effect a 'change of demand.' In regard to Figure 13.1 we noted that the effort to get to point C will be unproductive if the demand curve lies at position D_m. But by creative advertising or other promotional effort, the marketing staff may succeed in shifting the demand curve to the right until it does pass through point C. Then the firm could produce the larger output Q_3 and sell it at the unchanged price P_1. The additional revenue will be offset by the increased promotional expense. Both the revenue and the cost curves will be shifted by such an effort, thus establishing a new profit-maximizing price-output combination. At any time that such changes occur, the cost and revenue functions should be re-specified either intuitively or by empirical estimation. The problem is that when such a change is effected, no historical data for the altered situation exist to permit the empirical estimation. The manager is then in the position of making 'best-guess' intuitive modifications to the parameters of the cost and revenue functions until enough new data can be compiled to enable empirical re-estimation of the functions.

LONG-RUN ADJUSTMENT BY THE MONOPOLIST

The monopolist's long-run average total cost curve is more likely to be flat-bottomed or to slope downwards from left to right rather than to have the classic U-shape. The monopolist's demand and marginal revenue curves are downward-sloping as depicted by curves D_1 and MR_1 in Figure 13.3. If market demand, D_1, is still small relative to scale economy possibilities, the monopolist should select plant size ATC_1, for which its marginal cost curve crosses the long-run marginal cost curve at the latter's intersection with MR_1.

Although it may be heroic for the monopolist to know so much about its revenue and cost possibilities as to be able to find such an intersection, there is no more efficient plant for meeting the D_1 demand than the ATC_1 plant. However, selection of plant size ATC_1 could be short-sighted if there are prospects for market demand to shift to the right from position D_1. It might do so if the economy is growing and the income elasticity of demand for the product is positive. The monopolist may also promote its rightward shift by engaging in effective marketing activity. If either of these prospects is significant, the monopolist might be wise to build a plant to meet the demand forecast for some number of years into the future, even though it may yield suboptimal profits or even losses at present demand levels. The rightward shift of demand through time may enable the monopolist to exploit potential scale economies if LATC slopes downwards. By the time that demand has shifted to position D_2, plant ATC_2 can be constructed and operated profitably. It will yield lower unit costs and extend to a larger output range than can be attained by plant ATC_1. The

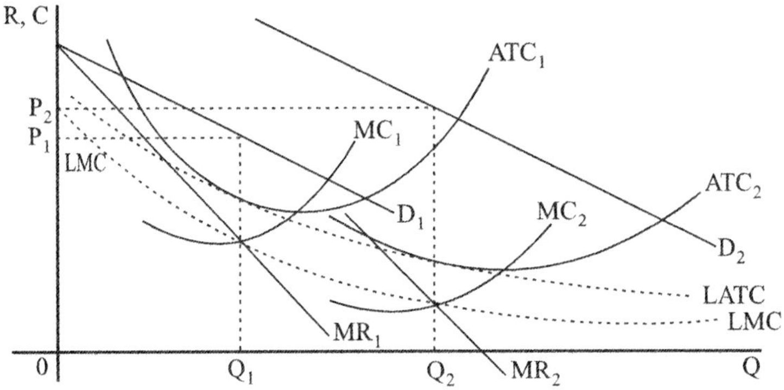

Figure 13.3. Long-run adjustment by the monopolist.

exploitation of scale economies as demand increases can contribute to the profitability of the monopolist.

Some industries grow, but others contract with technological advances or the dynamics of comparative advantage. Sometimes a monopolist is faced with contracting demand conditions. In these circumstances, a firm which has built a plant like ATC_2 in Figure 13.3 may find demand to have collapsed to some level like D_1. Given demand D_1, there is no level of output at which plant ATC_2 can be operated profitably. The monopolist's options are to continue to operate plant ATC_2 as long as output can be sold at a price above average variable cost, or to shut down when price falls below AVC. The manager can then give consideration to exiting the market or building a smaller plant, such as ATC_1.

THE MANAGERIAL IMPLICATIONS OF PURE MONOPOLY

From the perspective of the manager of the commercial business firm, monopoly would seem to be the most desirable position to be in. Except for governmental interference, the monopolist can exert greater control over his own destiny than can managers of firms in any more competitive environments. This position is not without cost, however. It must be maintained, defended, and protected on a continuing basis. The monopolist must be ever vigilant, not only for attempts at entry, but also for changes in demand and technology which can provide opportunity for growth or threaten the firm with failure. Although the monopoly position can be comfortable, its operations seem inevitably to attract the attention of the public or the authorities. Once the monopolist comes under the scrutiny of an antitrust authority which decides either that its existence or its behaviour is not in the public interest, the monopolist's position may cease to be so comfortable.

COMPETITION VS. MONOPOLY

The market structure of choice for the manager of the business firm would surely be pure monopoly, but it can be argued that the interests of society are best served by pure competition. As we noted at the beginning of this chapter, industries in the real world are rarely at either extreme of the competitive continuum. We have devoted earlier chapters to an examination of the extremes so as to describe the limits within which real-world market structures lie. We now proceed to further chapters for elaboration of two more realistic market structures, monopolistic competition and oligopoly.

Summary of Important Points

1. Pure monopoly lies at the opposite extreme of the competitive continuum from pure competition.
2. Pure monopoly may be described as a single seller of a product for which there are no close substitutes.
3. Bases for pure monopoly include economies of scale, technological or resource-control uniquity, governmental grant of exclusive position, and predatory or acquisitive behaviour.

Contd....

4. Entry into the monopolist's market is very difficult or costly, and may be blocked entirely by some combination of circumstances.
5. While the monopolist may exercise perfect pricing discretion, it is still subject to the constraint of market demand.
6. Persisting supernormal profits and control over its situation are the two prominent benefits which monopoly position confers upon a firm.
7. The firm's demand is coincident with the market demand in pure monopoly.
8. If the monopolist is oriented towards profit maximization, a comparison of marginal revenue and marginal cost can serve as decision criteria for output level and price.
9. Even the monopolist is unable to control price and quantity independently of each other.
10. The monopolist may pursue goals other than profit maximization.
11. An increasing demand will enable the monopolist to exploit economies of scale.
12. From the perspective of the manager of the commercial business firm, monopoly would seem to be the most desirable position to be in.

Significant Terms

pure monopoly

technological, resource-control uniquities

predatory behaviour

exclusive grants, franchises, patents,trademarks

failure, dissolution

supernormal profits

blocked entry

market supply curve

decision discretion

change of quantity demanded

decision objective

satisfying

target rate of return

change of demand

Questions for Discussion

1. Identify the descriptive characteristics of a pure monopolist. What behavioural consequences follow?
2. Explain how entry into the market may be blocked in the case of a monopoly market.

3. Explain how the decision discretion of a pure monopolist differs from that of the manager of a firm in a purely competitive market.
4. What enables a firm in a pure monopoly market to capture supernormal profits?
5. Describe the differences between the revenue and cost curves for firms in purely competitive and pure monopoly markets.
6. Explain why the monopolist's total revenue curve is parabolic, and what this means for its average and marginal revenue curves.
7. Describe the thought process which the manager of a pure monopolist firm must use in selecting the right level of output.
8. In the absence of perfect market knowledge, how can a monopolist find the profit-maximizing price and output levels?
9. Describe possible decision objectives for the monopolist which might be plausible alternatives to profit maximization; what decision criteria would the monopolist use in each case?
10. Why might the manager of a pure monopolist firm choose to implement a satisficing strategy? What decision criteria could be examined in pursuit of such a strategy?
11. What strategy might a monopolist pursue in attempting to sell at a price-output combination to the right of its demand curve?
12. Describe the likely shape(s) of long-run average total cost curves for pure monopoly firms; what are the managerial decision implications of such cost curves?
13. Why might a monopolist be faced with contracting demand conditions? How can the monopolist adjust to such conditions?
14. Explain why monopoly is a desirable state for the management of a firm to aspire to achieve, but a less-than-desirable state from the perspective of the society in which the firm operates. How can these two perspectives be reconciled in democratic society?

—oo(O)oo—

Chapter 14

Monopolistic Competition

Topics covered in this chapter

• The need for other theories of market organization. • The nature of monopolistic competition. • The distinction between monopolistic competition and pure competition. • The similarity between monopolistic competition and pure monopoly. • Profits in monopolistic competition. • Pricing and output discretion in monopolistic competition. • The social consequences of product differentiation.

In Chapters 12 and 13 we considered what life would be like for the manager of a firm operating at either extreme of the competitive continuum. We noted that both extremes were unrealistic relative to what is typical of commercial relationships in late-twentieth century Western societies. But perhaps we should not so hastily dismiss the extremes, because at some earlier time both may have been more realistic than they seem to be today.

Prior to the middle of the nineteenth century when the corporate form of business organization became more popular, most business enterprises were organized as proprietorships or partnerships, and were generally of quite small scale. Under these circumstances the hypothetical construct which economists have labelled 'pure competition' may have been more than adequate to the task of analyzing circumstances and providing criteria for managerial decision making.

With the popularization of the corporate form of business organization during the latter half of the nineteenth century, the scale of the enterprise could grow very rapidly. And business entities competed fiercely during the late nineteenth century, driving some of their competitors out of business and combining with others to effect what economists came to understand as 'pure monopoly.' Indeed, Alfred Marshall's first edition of *Principles of Economics* in 1890 contained essentially complete expositions of both pure competition and pure monopoly, but mentioned nothing in between. Very little has been added to our understanding of pure competition and pure monopoly since 1890. But perhaps these two model types were entirely adequate for describing and analyzing most real-world commercial and industrial contexts of the day.

As business organization, management, competition, and particularly governmental involvement in the commercial and industrial sectors evolved in the twentieth century, economists became ever more acutely aware that their theories of competition and monopoly represented polar extremes. These theories served progressively less satisfactorily to describe and analyze the emerging competitive situations between the extremes. By the 1930s, economists were attempting to devise theories to fill the void between the extremes, and the adjective 'pure' became the common descriptor of the theories at the ends of the competitive continuum.

By the late 1940s the emerging intermediate theories became classified into two broad categories to be known as 'monopolistic competition' and 'oligopoly,' the latter term implying a small number of sellers in the market. We should pause at this point to distinguish American usage from British terminology. An American economist, Edward Chamberlin, and an English economist, Joan Robinson, almost simultaneously, but independently, proposed virtually identical explanations of competition with monopolistic elements. Chamberlin described his theory as that of 'monopolistic competition,' but Robinson called hers 'imperfect competition.' American economists and textbook writers naturally adopted the term 'monopolistic competition' while British economists became accustomed to talking about 'imperfect competition,' although when American and British economists got together they became aware that they were talking about the same phenomenon going by different labels.

American practice found a use for the term 'imperfect competition' which was likely not intended by Robinson or her English associates. In American economic parlance, the term 'imperfect competition' came to refer to everything between the extremes of pure competition and pure monopoly, including both monopolistic competition and oligopoly. But when she described imperfect competition, Robinson had in mind a very specific set of characteristics which did not encompass what we today know as oligopoly. The title of this chapter follows the American practice.

DECISION MAKING UNDER MONOPOLISTIC COMPETITION

The descriptive characteristics of monopolistic competition in its modern incarnation are as follows:

1. As in pure competition, there is a large number of very small firms which operate within the same product market (hence the 'competitive' part of the term).
2. Unlike pure competition, the firms produce similar but not identical products, although they are enough alike to be regarded by the public as very close substitutes in use. The products may be differentiated in fact by colour, texture, structure, function, etc., or only in the imagination of the consuming public. In

a sense, monopolistic competition may be said to be like pure monopoly in that each seller is a monopolist of his own product design and brand name (hence the 'monopolistic' part of the term).

3. Like pure competition, firms in the market have comparable managerial capacities and use approximately the same technologies, but unlike pure competition, individual firms may develop or acquire managerial distinctives which are sufficient to enable the pursuit of market strategies. They may also develop or acquire technological variations which are sufficient to differentiate each firm's product.

With these descriptive characteristics in mind we can deduce the likely consequences and behavioural characteristics of monopolistic competition. Since monopolistic competition is so much more like pure competition than pure monopoly, we shall be focusing on the consequential differences between monopolistic competition and pure competition.

(a) As in pure competition, entry into the monopolistically-competitive market is easy because of the small capital requirements and commonly-available technology.

(b) Exit from the monopolistically competitive market is also easy, as it is in pure competition.

(c) Because of the possibility of developing managerial distinctives and market strategies, there may be significant incentive for managements of monopolistically-competitive firms to exercise entrepreneurship in order to distance themselves and their products from other competitors and their products.

(d) In spite of the small size and limited financial resources of the monopolistically-competitive firm, it may seek to gain special managerial abilities and technological variants in order to try to achieve some measure of market dominance.

(e) Even with ready access to commonly available knowledge of market conditions, and because of the possibility of managerial distinctives, monopolistically competitive firms may react differently from their competitors.

(f) But like pure competition, monopolistic competition is essentially anonymous; each monopolistic competitor perceives changes only in 'the market,' and thus reacts only to 'the market' rather than to the particular actions of any specific competitor whose identity can be known (we stress this point now because this is be one of the significant differences between monopolistic competition and oligopoly).

(g) Because of the ease of entry into the monopolistically-competitive market, there is a tendency towards convergence upon a common price. Because of the great number of competitors supplying very close substitute products, the monopolistic competitor's demand curve is highly elastic (though not perfectly elastic as in pure competition). The downward slope of the monopolistic competitor's demand curve, however slight, provides the manager of the firm some small measure of pricing discretion, and from time to time he may be tempted to experiment with price. Most of the time, however, he will perceive himself to be adjusting to a changing market price rather than initiating a new price.

(h) Because of the possibility of differentiating the product, either physically or only in the perceptions of prospective clients, the manager of the monopolistically competitive firm will be prone to advertise or otherwise promote his product extensively in the hope of attracting the attention of the consuming public. Any promotional effort incurs an expense which is like an overhead cost because once a commitment has been made to the promotional programme, its cost is in effect 'sunk.' It will be the same level of outlay whether successful or not, that is, whether the firm produces and sells a larger or smaller volume of output.

(i) As in pure competition, super- or sub-normal profits will be fleeting due to the ease of entry and exit. Profits will tend towards the economically normal level of opportunity cost.

SHORT-RUN ADJUSTMENTS IN THE MONOPOLISTICALLY-COMPETITIVE MARKET

In the discussion of pure competition in Chapter 11 we spoke of a 'representative firm in the market.' This terminology may not be appropriate to monopolistic competition because products are not homogeneous, and because monopolistic competitors may develop managerial distinctives. The differentiated products, however, are enough alike to be construed as being within the same market group. We shall analyze the operation of a typical firm in the monopolistically-competitive market group.

Figure 14.1 represents the revenue and cost curves for such a typical monopolistic competitor. The cost and revenue curves for the typical monopolistic competitor illustrated in Figure 14.1 differ from those for a representative purely competitive firm in that the market is not separately represented, the demand curve slopes downwards from left to right (even if only slightly), the MR curve diverges from the AR curve, and the TR curve has some downward concavity. The Figure 14.1 curves are actually quite similar to those for the pure monopolist with the exception of the relative shallowness of the slope of the AR and MR curves, and the fact that the TR curve is of such slight concavity that its peak and downward-sloping range lie well beyond the total cost curves.

We shall not impose upon the reader a 'replay' of the Chapter 11 discussion of the process which the manager of the firm might go through in finding the output Q_1 and the corresponding price P_1 for which the monopolistically-competitive firm maximizes profits. Suffice it to say that the comparison of marginal revenue with marginal cost serves just as well for the manager of the monopolistically competitive firm as it does for the pure competitor or pure monopolist in discovering whether to increase or decrease output.

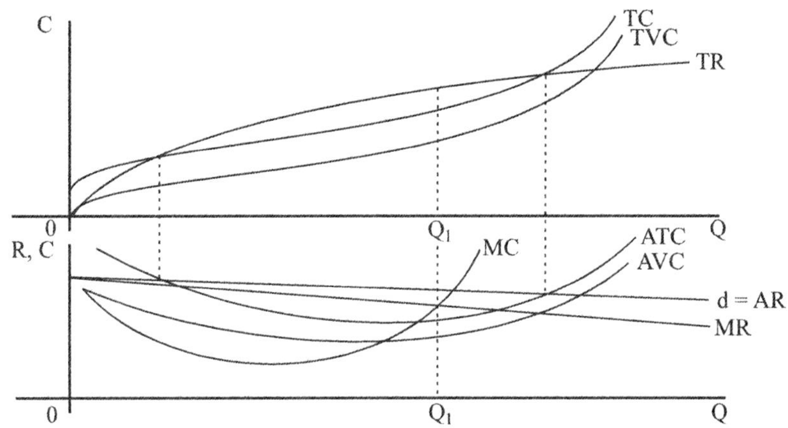

Figure 14.1. Revenue and cost curves for a monopolistically competitive firm.

If the monopolistically-competitive firm depicted in Figure 14.1 is typical of all such firms in the market group, the large amount of supernormal profit realized at the profit-maximizing price and output level will not go unnoticed by entrepreneurs presently outside the market. There will likely ensue a rush to enter the market in order to likewise reap such handsome above-normal returns, but they will surely be competed away just as in pure competition. How this happens requires further elaboration.

Chamberlin employed two demand curves, similar to those depicted in Figure 14.2, to explain the market adjustment process. The demand curve of Figure 14.1 is reproduced in Figure 14.2, and was intentionally labelled with a lower-case letter 'd' so that Chamberlin's other demand curve could be introduced and labelled with the capital 'D' in Figure 14.2. Chamberlin referred to demand curve d as the firm's 'species' demand curve because it is specific to the particular firm; it is the one with respect to which the manager must plan most of its short-run strategies. But the

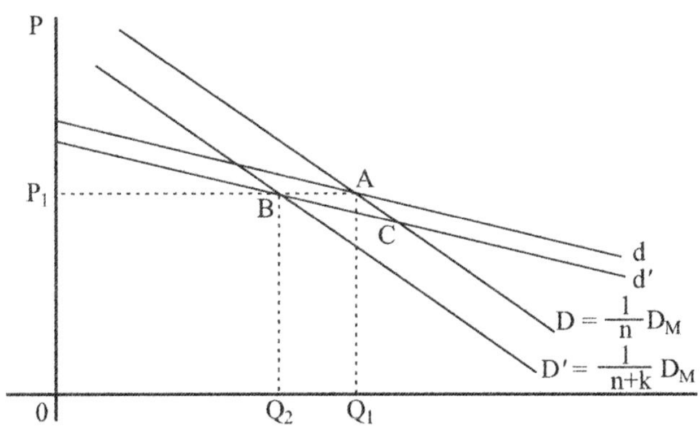

Figure 14.2. Genus and species demand curves in monopolistic competition.

manager cannot avoid giving consideration to the other demand curve, D, which Chamberlin referred to as the 'genus' demand curve because it is generic to the market group.

Suppose that the entire market demand, D_m, for all of the close-substitute products which comprise the market group can be identified, and that there are n such typical firms in the market group. Unless any of them can distinguish itself and its product to capture a larger share of the market demand, each can expect to exploit a 1/nth share of the market demand, or $D = 1/n\ D_m$. When, in response to the perception of the supernormal profits being realized in the market, k additional firms enter the market, each firm in the market (new as well as old) now can count on only a 1/(n+k) share of market demand, or $D' = 1/(n+k)\ D_m$.

Thus, the firm's generic demand curve shifts to the left consequent upon the entry into the market, and according to Chamberlin carries with it the firm's species demand curve as we have illustrated it in Figure 14.2. The leftward shift of each firm's set of demand curves consequent upon a diminishing share of the market induces each firm's management to accept a progressively lower price consistent with the goal of maximizing profits. The effect of the decreasing market share and falling price is to decrease the profits of each of the typical firms. Theoretically, enough additional firms, j, will enter the market until all supernormal profits have been competed away, and each of the typical firms is left in a state similar to that depicted in Figure 14.3. This state may be described as market (–group) equilibrium.

This result is similar to the market equilibrium in pure competition in that the typical firm in the market is covering all of its economic costs, including normal returns to the entrepreneur and management, but is not realizing supernormal profit. It is different from the purely competitive conclusion because the typical firm operates at an output rate, Q_m, which is below that at which the pure competitor would produce, Q_c, and sells at a price which is slightly higher than that of the representative pure competitor in market equilibrium.

Carried into the long run, which we will leave to the reader to analyze with reference to Figure 14.3, the manager of the monopolistically-competitive firm will be led to build a (slightly) too-small plant, operate it at a (slightly) too-low rate of output, and charge a (slightly) too-high price, all while realizing no more profit than would have been realized by the representative pure competitor.

With the small amount of pricing discretion implicit in the shallowly-sloped species demand curve, the manager of the monopolistically-competitive firm may be tempted to experiment with price. In the interest of increasing the market share, a price cut is much more likely to be attempted than a price increase. The highly elastic species demand (the one which appears to govern his market) leads to the belief that a small price cut can vastly increase sales, thereby to increase both revenues and profits. And this strategy would work, too, if none of his competitors noticed the price cut.

Alas, some of the competitors at first will become aware that price has fallen somewhere in the market (but because there are so many sellers, they will be oblivious to the identity of the perpetrator) and cut their prices as a defensive measure. More and more firms will meet what is rapidly becoming the reality of a new market price. As this phenomenon ensues, each firm will find itself sliding down its genus demand curve rather than travelling down the species demand curve

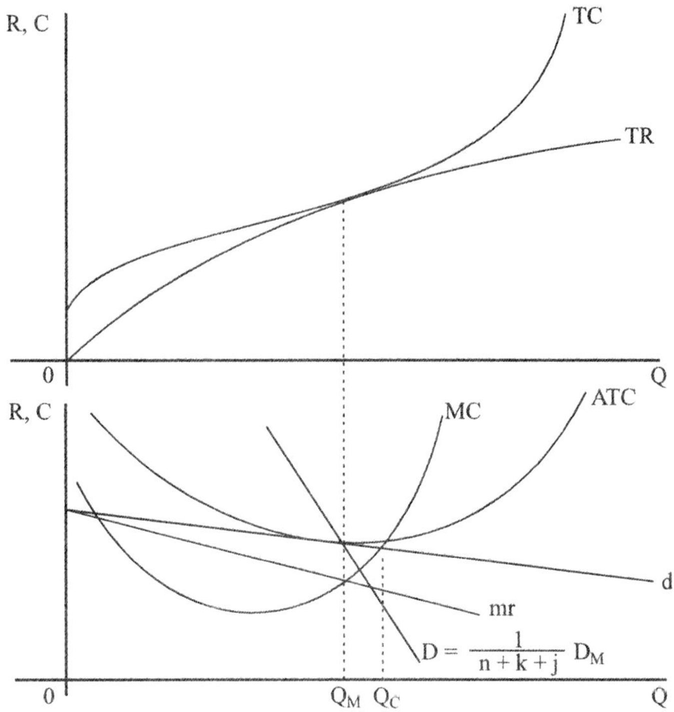

Figure 14.3. A monopolistically-competitive firm in industry equilibrium.

as was the intention of the manager of the first firm to have cut price. They will all sell a few more units of the product (people do tend to buy more at lower prices), but if the movement along the genus demand curve is into the inelastic range, each firm's revenues will actually decrease and profit will fall. The perpetrator of the price cut, so full of hope that cutting price will get him a larger market share and more profit, will have gotten burned by playing with the matches of price experimentation. It is experiences like this which make managers of monopolistically-competitive firms much more amenable to non-price forms of competition and promotion.

Detractors of the monopolistically-competitive (or any imperfectly competitive) market structure speak of the 'wastes of monopolistic competition,' call attention to the redundancy involved in 'pointless' heterogeneity, note the excess capacity implicit in operating at a rate of output below the least-cost output rate. They deduce that resources are at one-and-the-same time both over-allocated (the excess capacity) and under-allocated (too little is produced at the too-high price) to goods produced for such a market.

Those more tolerant of the monopolistically-competitive market structure note that the slightly-higher price, the slightly-lower output, and the smaller-than-optimal plants are small prices to pay for product variety in a society that values freedom of choice (after all, a range of alternatives must be available in order to be able to exercise the privilege of choosing). Also, the excesses of monopolistic competition may seem mild in comparison with the alternatives of oligopoly and monopoly. Other things remaining the same, if society could make no-cost choices of the market structures for producing its outputs, pure competition would win hands down. But even those who think they have found an example of monopolistic competition in the real world (have they been asking the wrong question?) are hard-pressed to come up with a workable public policy for transforming the monopolistic market into a purely competitive one.

MANAGERIAL IMPLICATIONS OF MONOPOLISTIC COMPETITION

The entrepreneur who decides to enter a monopolistically-competitive market should do so with eyes wide open to the likelihood that those supernormal profits will disappear very quickly. The manager's only serious hope for sustaining the supernormal profits is to make the product and its support system (location, convenience, delivery, service, etc.) as distinctive in a positive way as possible, and thereby to prevent the leftward shift of the demand curve. To this end the manager of the monopolistically-competitive firm may engage in efforts to promote and differentiate the product, but not without cost.

The relevant question here is whether the increased demand for the product will generate enough additional revenues to cover the costs of differentiation and promotion. Figure 14.4 illustrates a successful effort at promotion which adds to overhead costs but shifts the demand curve far enough to the right, for example, to position D_2 to yield enough additional sales revenue to both cover the promotional cost and pad the profits. But there are entrepreneurial risks in monopolistic competition, and this happy result is not guaranteed. If the manager of one typical monopolistic firm can devise an innovative marketing scheme, so too can the managers of other similarly typical firms, and their efforts may simply cancel each other out. In this case they might end up spending more and enjoying less profit, for example, if demand remains at D_1 in Figure 14.4.

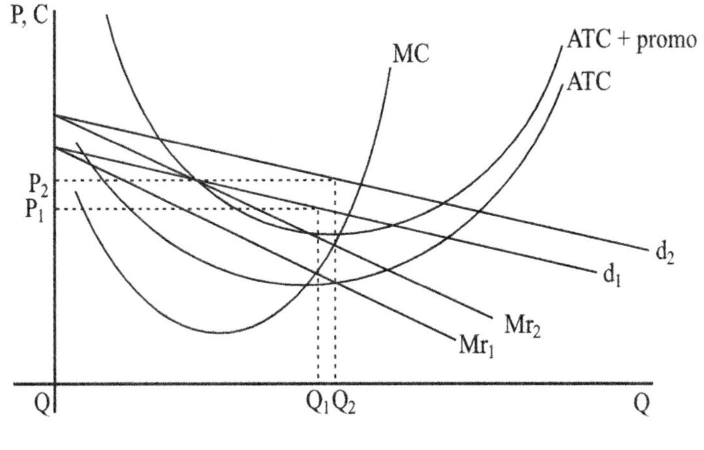

Figure 14.4. A successful promotional effort by a monopolistic competitor.

To the extent that a monopolistically competitive firm is successful in differentiating and promoting its product to gain a larger-than-typical market share, it and a few other successful firms may be on their way into the realm of oligopoly, and it is to this market structure that we soon turn our attention.

Are there many (or any) good examples of monopolistically-competitive markets? We should remember from our discussion that this may be the wrong question to ask. For a particular market under examination, is the model of monopolistic competition an appropriate vehicle of analysis? This is the better question. It may be answered in the affirmative if certain criteria are met. If there is a relatively large number of fairly small sellers in a market which is easy to enter, then either pure competition or monopolistic competition is indicated. If the managements of the firms can be observed to be trying to differentiate their products, then either monopolistic competition or possibly oligopoly is indicated. But there are two acid-test criteria: if competitors are essentially oblivious of each other's identities, and if profits tend to be dissipated due to entry of new firms into the market, then monopolistic competition is almost certainly the appropriate model to apply.

On the other hand, if the competitors are conscious of each other's identities to the point of devising market strategies oriented towards specific competitors, this is a sure sign of oligopolistic competition. Profits may be dissipated in oligopoly as well as in monopolistic competition, but due to price competition rather than entry. The detection of price leadership/followership behaviour might be taken as an identification of oligopoly rather than monopolistic competition, but if competitors 'follow the market' without specific knowledge or concern about the identity of the perpetrator of a price change, monopolistic competition is the appropriate model. The number of competitors was not stressed above as a critical distinction between monopolistic competition and oligopoly. This is due to the importance of an identification of the relevant geographic market. For example, in any Standard Metropolitan Statistical Area (SMSA) there are literally hundreds of retail petrol stations which are differentiated from each other by brand name and locality. Does this sound like monopolistic competition? If the owner or manager of each station sets prices vis-à-vis the prices of those other stations within sight up and down the street, the relevant geographic market likely consists of a half-dozen or fewer stations in the near neighbourhood. This renders retail petrol distribution essentially oligopolistic.

WHAT'S AHEAD

The critical criterion for distinguishing oligopolistic from monopolistic competition is not number of sellers, but rather consciousness of identities of competitors. Experience indicates that the majority of real-world competitive contexts are more appropriately analyzed with oligopolistic models than with monopolistically-competitive models. Chapter 15 elaborates theories of the oligopolistically competitive environment.

Summary of Important Points

1. The extremes of the competitive continuum may have been satisfactory to explain business organization during the 19th century, but have served progressively less satisfactorily during the 20th century to explain business structure and behaviour.
2. Two intermediate theories emerged during the 1930s and 1940s to describe competitive structures between the extremes: monopolistic competition and oligopoly.
3. Monopolistic competition can be described as a large number of small firms with similar managerial capacities, selling differentiated products in a market which is easily entered and exited, and within which there is little concern about the identities of particular competitors.
4. Supernormal profits will dissipate in a monopolistically competitive market due to entry.
5. The monopolistic competitor has a small amount of pricing discretion.
6. In the long run, monopolistic competitors tend to build plants which are slightly too small, operate them at a slightly too-low rate of output, and charge slightly higher than purely competitive prices, but realize no supernormal returns; these matters may simply be the costs of product variety.
7. Because geographic markets often are rather limited in scope and sellers do pay attention to particular competitors, the monopolistically competitive model may be of limited usefulness in analyzing real-world competitive markets.

Significant Terms

competitive continuum
pure competition, monopoly
proprietorship, partnership, corporate forms of organization
monopolistic, imperfect competition
product differentiation
managerial distinctive
entry, exit
market strategies
anonymity
price convergence
pricing discretion
opportunity cost
typical firm
market group
species, genus demand curves
demand elasticity
price experimentation
wastes of competition
resource misallocation
freedom of choice
supernormal returns
costs of differentiation, promotion
identities of competitors

Questions for Discussion

1. Speculate on why Alfred Marshall made no reference to market structures between competition and monopoly.
2. Distinguish monopolistic competition from imperfect competition.
3. Identify the descriptive characteristics of monopolistic competition and discuss the behavioural implications.
4. Explain how monopolistic competition is like pure monopoly in some respects, but like pure monopoly in others.
5. Explain how monopolistic competition differs from pure competition. ...from pure monopoly.
6. Discuss the role of entrepreneurship in the monopolistically competitive firm as contrasted to the purely competitive firm.
7. What are the enabling conditions to the exercise of entrepreneurship in the monopolistically competitive firm?
8. How may monopolistic competition be distinguished from oligopoly? What are the managerial implications of the distinction?
9. Explain how the managers of firms in monopolistic competition react differently from the managers of firms in oligopoly in regard to 'the competition.'
10. Contrast the pricing discretion which may be exercised by the managers of firms in monopolistic competition and pure competition.
11. Contrast the potential for product promotion in purely competitive and monopolistically competitive firms.
12. Explain the sense in which promotional expenses are like overhead costs.
13. Explain why the concept of a 'representative firm in the market' is not appropriate to monopolistic competition; explain how firm behaviour in monopolistically competitive markets may be analyzed.
14. Explain how the manager of a firm in a monopolistically competitive market may find the 'right' output level and the price at which to sell it.
15. How can supernormal profits occur in a monopolistically competitive market? Describe the market adjustment process which ensues when supernormal profits appear; what are the managerial implications?
16. Distinguish between 'genus' and 'species' demand curves in a monopolistically competitive market, and discuss the managerial implications of the distinction.

17. Why might entry occur in a monopolistically competitive market? In what sense does this represent an exercise of entrepreneurship? What happens to market share when entry occurs? What are the managerial implications?

18. Contrast the characteristics of short- and long-run equilibrium in monopolistically competitive and purely competitive markets.

19. Describe the likely attitudes of managers of monopolistically competitive firms with respect to price and non-price forms of competition.

20. Why are 'wastes' reputed to occur in monopolistically competitive markets?

21. Given the apparent theoretical superiority of pure competition relative to monopolistic competition, are there any redeeming features of monopolistic competition?

22. Discuss the managerial implications of a monopolistically competitive market.

23. Describe a scenario for the transition of a monopolistically competitive market into the characteristics of an oligopolistically competitive market.

24. Identify possible examples of monopolistically competitive markets with which you may be familiar; what is your basis for judging them to be examples of monopolistic competition?

25. How can you tell whether the appropriate model for analyzing a particular market is monopolistic competition or some form of oligopoly?

—oo(O)oo—

Chapter 15

Oligopolistic Competition

Topics covered in this chapter

• The nature of oligopoly. • The distinction between oligopoly and monopolistic competition. • The nature of entry in oligopoly. • The significance of identities of competitors. • Possible oligopoly behaviour patterns. • The impetus to price warfare. • The impetus to price rigidity. • The effects of antitrust law and its enforcement. • Bases of price leadership. • Motives for price followership. • Competition as a means of social control of industry.

Chapter 14 ended with a question of whether there are any good examples of monopolistically competitive markets. It was noted that this may be the wrong question to ask. The better question for any particular market under examination is whether the model of monopolistic competition is an appropriate vehicle of analysis. If there is a relatively large number of fairly small sellers in a market which is easy to enter, then either pure competition or monopolistic competition is indicated. If the managements of the firms can be observed to be trying to differentiate their products, then either monopolistic competition or oligopoly is appropriate.

As we noted in Chapter 14, there are two acid-test criteria for distinguishing the applicability of monopolistic and oligopolistic competition models. If competitors are essentially oblivious of each other's identities, and if profits tend to be dissipated due to entry of new firms into the market, then monopolistic competition is almost certainly the appropriate model to apply. On the other hand, if the competitors are conscious of each other's identities to the point of devising market strategies oriented towards specific competitors, this is a sure sign of oligopolistic competition.

The **number of competitors** was not stressed in Chapter 14 as a critical distinction between monopolistic competition and oligopoly due to the importance of the relevant geographic market. We noted that in any Standard Metropolitan Statistical Area (SMSA) there are literally hundreds of retail petrol stations that are differentiated from each other by brand name and locale. If the owner or manager of each station sets prices vis-à-vis the prices of those other stations within sight up and down the street, the relevant geographic market likely consists of a half-dozen or fewer stations in the near neighbourhood. This makes retail petrol distribution essentially oligopolistic. The critical criterion is not number of sellers, but rather **consciousness of identities** of competitors. Experience indicates that the majority of real-world competitive contexts are more appropriately analyzed with oligopolistic models than with monopolistically-competitive models.

DECISION MAKING IN OLIGOPOLY

More-or-less standard specifications may be described for pure competition, monopolistic competition, and pure monopoly. Oligopolistic competition, perhaps the most common form of Western industrial and commercial market structure, is the one for which the least standard analytical specification exists. In laying out its descriptive characteristics, we shall focus upon the differences and similarities with both monopolistic competition and pure monopoly.

1. The oligopolistic market consists of a relatively **small number** of firms, but as we noted in the previous section, the number of firms in the market is not the most critical criterion for distinguishing oligopoly from monopolistic competition. The lower limit of oligopoly is duopoly which is a market populated by only two firms.
2. The products (goods or services) sold by the firms in the oligopolistic market may be **homogeneous** (examples might be asphalt once laid, concrete once poured, a grade of petrol once in the tank) or **differentiated** (locale, billing practices, and levels of service distinguish even pavers, ready-mix concrete suppliers, and retail petrol stations). But if differentiated, the products must be close-enough substitutes in use or function that prospective consumers give serious consideration to the alternative products before purchasing.
3. Unlike monopolistic competition, in oligopoly there may occur significant differences in **managerial abilities** and organizational structures. Also, widely divergent **technologies** may be employed by different oligopolistic competitors to produce identical or close substitute products.
4. Unlike monopolistic competition, firms in an oligopolistic market have differing levels of access to **information**, some of which may have been acquired by deliberate research. Some information is specific to each firm, particularly its own prices, production plans, and marketing strategies. This information is likely to be kept secret and protected so that it is not readily available to other firms. There are likely to be few enough firms competing in the market that the manager of each one can know the particular identities of each of the other competitors in the same market.

These descriptive characteristics lead to the following behavioural characteristics of oligopolistic competition:

(a) As with pure monopoly, scale of operation, technological complexity, or governmental grant of exclusive position (by certification, franchise, patent, or trademark) may constitute effective **barriers to entry** of new competitors into the market. It may even be possible for existing competitors, by some form of concerted action, to erect entry barriers. However, the incentive for a single oligopolist to unilaterally erect entry barriers is likely to be slight because competitors can be **free riders** in enjoying the benefit of another firm's efforts.

(b) As in monopoly, exit from the market is always possible by failure and dissolution, but oligopolists wishing to exit a market may have another option not available to the monopolist, that is, to **combine** with or dispose of assets to a competitor.

(c) Unlike monopolistic competition and pure competition, oligopolistic competition is hardly anonymous. Because there are few enough sellers for each to know the identities of the others, virtually every market-oriented and productive decision needs to take into account the range of possible **reactions** by competitors as well as the most likely reaction. And even if no deliberate decisions are under consideration by the management of the oligopolistically competitive firm, its manager needs to monitor the activities of the competition and be prepared to react accordingly.

(d) Oligopolists, like monopolists, have a great deal more **pricing discretion** than do monopolistic competitors, but the pricing discretion may be severely constrained by the pricing practices of competitors and their likely pricing reactions.

(e) Because of the inherent or contrived barriers to entry into an oligopolistic market, **supernormal profits** may persist. Yet, price competition among oligopolists, as among monopolistic competitors, may tend to dissipate any supernormal profits even if no new entry occurs. Managers of oligopolistic firms may even deliberately initiate a price war which is intended to take profits to subnormal levels long enough to induce competitors to exit the market.

(f) As in both pure and monopolistic competition, there may tend to be a market-wide convergence upon a **common price**, but for different reasons in the oligopolistically competitive market. These may range from an effort to limit price to a **profit submaximizing level** to forestall entry into the market, through various forms of **price leadership**/followership behaviour, to **overt collusion** among the oligopolistically competitive firms in the market. The oligopolist's demand curve likely will be of somewhat steeper downward slope than that of the monopolistic competitor, and it may account for some fraction of the total market demand that is greater or less than $1/n$ if there are n firms in the market. The steeper downward slope of the oligopolist's demand curve suggests greater pricing discretion, but this may be rather illusory for all of the firms in the market except the price leader.

(g) Difficulties with pricing strategies and price leadership/followership relationships in the oligopolistically competitive market may lead the managers to prefer **non-price forms of competition** which are similar to the efforts to differentiate and promote the product in monopolistic competition. But practically everything that can be said about price leadership/followership in oligopoly can be repeated for non-price competition leadership/followership. That is, there may occur design, service, or promotion competition, and a market leader may emerge in any of these areas. The leader then initiates aggressive decisions while the followers make defensive decisions of the 'catch-up' or 'me-too' variety.

The object of competition in oligopoly often becomes **market share** rather than profit or any other behavioural goal. A common problem for oligopolists engaging in non-price competition is to incur design, service, or promotion costs (fixed costs) which simply cancel out each other's efforts, leaving their market shares unchanged (the 'smoking-more, enjoying-it-less' syndrome). To the extent that non-price competition has **self-cancelling effects**, profits are diminished. The market leader may have the best hope of gaining market share, and that may be only temporary.

For each of the other market structure types (that is, pure competition, pure monopoly, and monopolistic competition), we were able to describe one fairly standard model generally accepted by economists. Unfortunately, this is not possible for oligopolistic competition because the circumstances and the potential for competitor reaction render each oligopolistic situation unique. Since no two oligopolistically competitive situations are alike, it is necessary to model each one to fit the specifics. There is no single oligopoly model as there is a single monopoly model. **Oligopoly Models are legion**.

We can, however, identify a limited number of oligopolistic behavioural patterns into which nearly any oligopolistic situation can be classified. A general type of model can be specified for some of the patterns. We shall describe seven broad behavioural patterns:

1. Oligopolistic competitors may choose to **ignore** each other in a 'live-and-let-live' attitude, each pursuing their own goals. This may in fact be the reality for most of the trivial and day-to-day decisions made by the manager of a firm in oligopolistic competition. However, as we shall show in our discussion of price leadership/followership, choosing to ignore the competition's market-related decisions can have serious market-share or growth consequences.
2. Managers of oligopolistically competitive firms may engage in open price- (or design-, service-, promotion-) **warfare** or other predatory or even criminal behaviour to the end of eliminating competitors so that monopoly (or more-limited oligopoly) position can be achieved.
3. Oligopolistic managers may be so fearful of the possible deleterious effects of a ruinous price (or other kind of) war that they enter into extreme **decision rigidity** (for example, price rigidity) in a 'don't-rock-the-boat' or 'don't-make-waves' attitude.
4. Oligopolistic managers, to avoid both price rigidity and price warfare, may engage in overt (open, public) collusion. Collusion may be only occasional consultation, or it may be conducted on a continuing basis. Such **overt collusion**, if formalized by contract or treaty, constitutes a cartel. The monopoly

model described in Chapter 12 is adequate to the analysis of the behaviour and identification of decision criteria for an effective cartel. However, collusive relationships and cartel arrangements are inherently unstable because of the difficulty of maintaining discipline among the members as to agreed-upon decisions or policies. They are prone to cheating by members who engage in 'under-the-table' transactions. It has been said that if a near-universal cartel exists, the best position to be in is outside the cartel in order to be able to subvert the cartel's prices, promotions, etc.

5. If overt collusion among separate firms is frowned upon by the authorities, the same end may be accomplished by **combination** (acquisition, merger, forming 'trusts') among the competitors to achieve monopoly position.

6. If combination to achieve monopoly is frowned upon as well by the authorities, then competitors may try to engage in implicit or **covert collusion** with no apparent agreement or even contact among themselves. Such so-called 'conscious parallelism of action' may be effected through the use of common rate schedules, transportation basing points, catalogues or price books, or trade-association reporting schemes. No one talks to anyone else, but everyone knows that each of the others is following a common policy. In the latter case, although the information reported is historic, there may emerge a consensus about how near-future prices may be predicated upon recent past prices.

7. And finally, even if none of the above occurs, some type of price **leadership/followership** is likely to emerge. This author is of the opinion that the existence and effective administration of antitrust law inevitably causes price leadership/followership relations to become the most common patterns of oligopolistically-competitive interaction in Western industrialized nations. This is not to imply that price leadership/followership is the pattern of choice among oligopolistic competitors. Left to their own devices (that is, without constraint or interference from governmental authority), oligopolistic competitors would choose not to compete, but rather would collude, cartelize, or combine. If these avenues to monopolistic position are foreclosed by effective antitrust administration, price leadership/followership will emerge by default. Then there remains the residual question for government authority of whether leadership/followership relationships are deleterious to the public interest, and if so, what is to be done about them. This and other questions should be of extreme interest for managers of oligopolistically competitive firms.

MODELS OF OLIGOPOLISTIC ADJUSTMENT

Patterns (4), (5), and (6) may be satisfactorily analyzed with the **pure monopoly** model described in Chapter 12. If *de facto* monopoly is achieved through any of these avenues, then the remaining problems are those of maintaining discipline and dividing the spoils (that is, the monopoly profits). These are essentially political problems which we shall not attempt to model with economic theory. The models which we shall describe for patterns (2), (3), and (7) can all be adequately

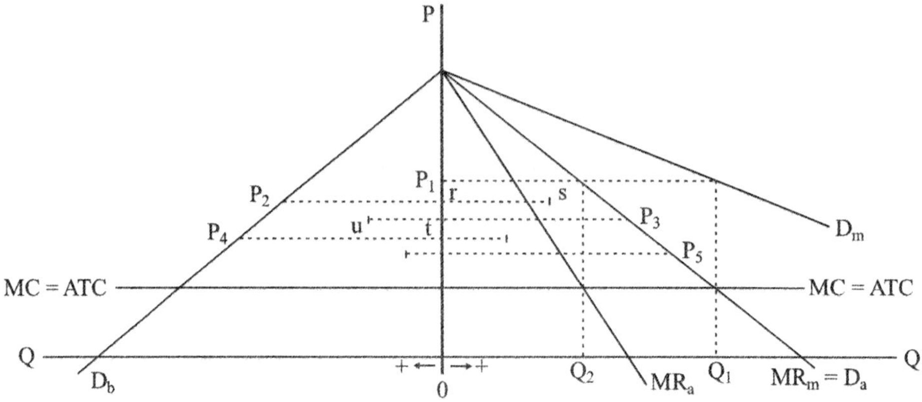

Figure 15.1. A duopoly model of price warfare.

elaborated assuming a two-firm market, duopoly. Each model could be extended to more than two firms with added degrees of graphic complexity.

Price Warfare

The earliest of what might be considered oligopoly models were described by Augustin Cournot, Joseph Bertrand, and F. Y. Edgeworth during the nineteenth century. The Edgeworth variant described a simple duopoly whose managers are incredibly naive, but the model can serve to illustrate the effects of price warfare. A model similar to Edgeworth's is illustrated in Figure 15.1. The manager of Firm A, the first to set up shop, naturally assumes himself to be a monopolist who can exploit the entire market demand. He builds a plant which by assumption has constant variable costs represented by MC=ATC, and with plant capacity Q_1, the output at which monopoly profits would be maximized when sold at price P_1.

The second seller, Firm B, enters the market. Its manager realizes that Firm A is already in operation, and naively assumes that Firm A will continue to sell at price P_1. Firm B builds a plant also with capacity Q_1; the manager takes as its demand curve D_1, which is half of the total market demand. The D_b demand curve is represented in Figure 15.1 as a Janus curve facing left (that is, output increases from right to left) which backs on the D_m demand curve at its vertical axis. The manager of Firm B, however, realizes that if he will undercut price P_1 by a small margin, say at price P_2, he can sell his whole output, invading the market of Firm A by line segment rs.

Meanwhile, the manager of Firm A has become aware of the presence of Firm B, accepts it as a fellow duopolist, and now takes Firm A's demand curve to be D_a, which also is half of the market demand. The manager of Firm A, who now makes the naive assumption that Firm B will continue to sell at price P_2, cuts price to P_3 and dumps Firm A's entire capacity output on the market, invading Firm B's market by amount tu.

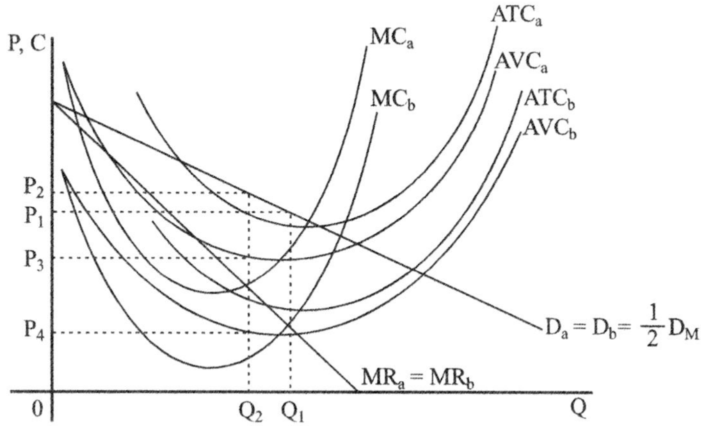

Figure 15.2. Exploiting of a cost advantage by an oligopolist.

It is easy to see that as long as each manager naively makes the assumption that the other firm will continue to sell at its current price, the competitive price cutting will continue through several more iterations until the price charged by one of the firms, B in Figure 15.1, reaches the level of its average total cost. The manager of Firm A notices (with sudden and unexplained astuteness) that Firm B has done its worst; it is dumping its entire capacity output on the market at a price just equal to ATC. It dare not go to a lower price, else it will suffer losses. So the manager of Firm A reasons that there is nothing to lose by returning to its profit-maximizing price, P_1, and to produce and sell Q_2. And the whole price war starts all over from P_1 back down to P_6.

The moral of this story is that if the managers of oligopolistically competitive firms are so naive as to assume that competitors will continue to charge the same price for ever, and if they are incapable of learning from experience, they will get into price wars where price oscillates between the preferred profit maximizing price and the level of ATC.

Real-world business firm managers are neither so naive nor incapable of learning from experience. As intelligent and perceptive decision makers, they are unlikely to lapse into such mindless competition. However, as noted earlier in this chapter, if the manager of one oligopolistically competitive firm has a cost advantage or a greater financial capacity relative to competitors, a price war may be initiated with the intention of driving price down below the AVC of the competitors, thereby to induce them to shut down in the short run, and to exit the market if the low price continues long enough.

In Figure 15.2, suppose that two duopolists equally share the market demand so that their demand curves are coincident and each equal to 1/2 of market demand, D_m. Firm B, however, has lower costs, represented by ATC_b, AVC_b, and MC_b. Firm A's costs are higher at ATC_a, AVC_a, and MC_a. Firm A would like to maximize profit at P_2, while Firm B prefers the lower price, P_1, for maximization of its profits. But if the manager of Firm B knows enough about both the firm's own costs and those of Firm A, he or she will realize that price can be taken as low as P_4 before incurring a loss greater than average fixed costs. Price P_3 is at the minimum point of Firm A's AVC curve. Firm A's options now are either to meet price P_4 and go out of business in the long run (because P_4 is less than its AVC), or to stay at Price P_2 and lose market share as its demand curve shifts leftwards far enough for it to go out of business because of declining market demand for its product. Thus, by pursuing a deliberate profit-non-maximizing strategy in the short run, Firm B may be able to achieve monopoly position which will allow it to maximize profits in the long run. But this sort of behaviour is likely to be regarded as predatory by the antitrust authority.

Extreme Price Rigidity

During the late 1930s, the prices in certain oligopolistic industries, notably tobacco products, were observed to be constant for years at a time. During the late 1930s, economist Paul Sweezy proposed an oligopolistic model to explain extreme price rigidity among competitors ('Demand under Conditions of Oligopoly,' *Journal of Political Economy*, vol. XLVII (1939), pp. 568-573). Sweezy reasoned that competitors are likely to react asymmetrically with respect to price increases and price decreases initiated by one of the firms in the market. Sweezy implicitly assumed recession economic conditions (the effects of assuming an expanding economy are explored in the appendix to this chapter). Given these conditions, competitors are far less likely to follow a price increase than a price decrease. Sweezy then reasoned that demand would be relatively more elastic above the current price, but relatively more inelastic below the current price. This implied that the oligopolistic competitor's demand curve is bent or kinked at the price as illustrated in Figure 15.3.

If the demand curve for the oligopolist's product really is kinked at point A in Figure 15.3, then a price increase to P_2 will result in a larger percentage decrease of quantity demanded (to Q_2) than the percentage increase (to Q3) which will result if price is cut to P_3. Assuming that demand is elastic above the kink, but inelastic below the kink, this alone will provide a revenue disincentive for the manager to change price from P_1. It may be recalled that a price increase when demand is elastic will reduce total revenue; and a price cut when demand is inelastic will also reduce total revenue. The manager is in a lose–lose situation. There is no price above or below P_1 at which the firm can increase its revenue. Hence, price remains rigidly at P_1. A second possible explanation of

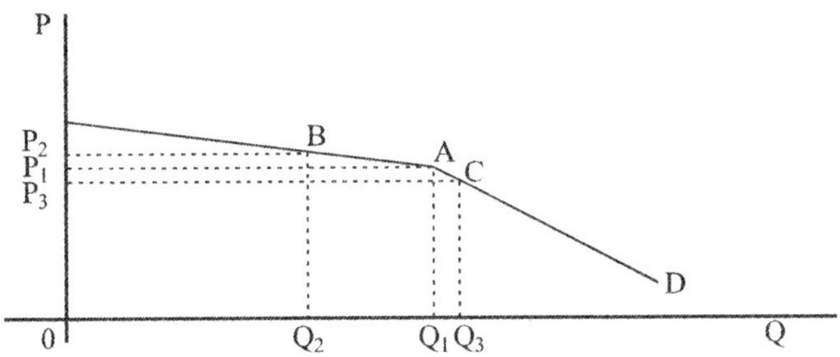

Figure 15.3. Sweezy's Kinked demand curve.

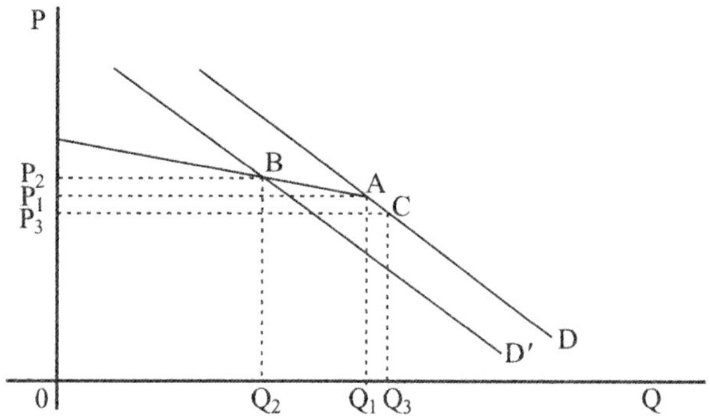

Figure 15.4. Asymmetrical price leadership for price increases and decreases.

extreme price rigidity lies in what is reputed to be a gap or vertical segment in the marginal revenue curve below the kink. This hypothesis is also examined in the appendix to this chapter.

There are several problems with the so-called kinked-demand hypothesis. One is that it provides no explanation of how any actual price, like P_1, is established in the first place. Second, when price is increased but competitors do not follow, customers can be expected to defect from the firm's product to those of its competitors. This is an example of an unsuccessful effort at price leadership, and it constitutes a change of one of the determinants of demand, that is, the cohort of the consumers purchasing the firm's product. The consequence of a change of such a non-price determinant of demand is a demand curve shift (in this example, to the left). The movement from point A to point B is really not along the same demand curve; rather, the firm's genus demand curve (a concept borrowed from Chamberlin's monopolistic competition model) shifts to the left as illustrated in Figure 15.4. Point B is on a relocated genus demand curve, D'.

The path from A to B is in this example a contraction path. The demand curve is not kinked; rather, it has simply shifted to create an identification problem (as described in Chapter 7). Point C is on the original demand curve, D, and is reached when the firm cuts its price to P_3, and all of its competitors follow suit (in this case, the firm is a successful price leader). All of the firms in the market sell some more of the product at the lower price, but there is no realignment of customers with sellers, so the demand curves do not shift.

Leland Yeager has suggested that there is only one actual point, like A, on any demand curve ['Methodenstreit over Demand Curves,' *Journal of Political Economy*, vol. LXVIII (February, 1960), pp. 53-64)]; all others are 'virtual' in the sense that they may be revealed under other circumstances (different prices). So it is not possible to be confident that a demand curve has any particular shape, whether straight, curved, or kinked, away from the single existing point.

Even if a demand curve is not truly kinked as reputed in the Sweezy model, asymmetrical responses of competitors to a firm's increases and decreases of price could result in the theorized rigidity. If the firm cuts price when demand is inelastic and other firms follow the price cut, revenues will decrease because of the demand inelasticity. If the firm raises price and other firms do not follow, the firm's revenues will decrease because its demand curve shifts left (but not because its demand is elastic). Although economists have looked very hard for empirical evidence of kinks in demand curves, virtually none has been reported in the professional literature over the past half century. This implies either that the kinked demand curve is a relatively rare circumstance, or that economists have been looking for the wrong thing (kinks rather than shifts).

Price-Leadership/Followership

We have made a case that oligopolistic competition is the most prevalent form of commercial organization in Western society; and we have asserted the most common pattern of oligopolistic interaction where antitrust laws are vigorously enforced to be price leadership/-followership. But we recognize that each price leadership circumstance is unique and demands its own model for analysis. All that we can do in this section is to select a few of the more prevalent types of price leadership to model as guides for the reader to use in encounters with price leadership circumstances.

Economists have identified four broad categories of price leadership:

1. **Asymmetrical price leadership** occurs if the firm is successful in one direction of price change, but not in the other; the kinked demand model is reputed to be an example.
2. **Barometric price leadership** is where the manager of one of the oligopolistic firms establishes a reputation for perceptiveness and sensitivity to changing market conditions, and a record of making timely and successful adjustments to those perceived changes. Managements of other firms then watch the price leader's activities and attempt to emulate his decisions.
3. **Dominant firm price leadership** is where the market consists of a dominant firm surrounded by a competitive fringe of smaller firms. The dominant firm behaves as a benevolent monopolist, tolerating the existence of the smaller firms and allowing them to sell any amount of the product which they wish at the price that the dominant firm prefers. The dominant firm then takes its demand as the residual of the market demand not met by the competitive fringe firms, and proceeds to behave as a pure monopolist in maximizing profits. There is no doubt that dominant-firm price leadership examples (in the automotive and computer industries, to name but two) can be found, but we venture the guess that they come into being only as a consequence of vigorous antitrust enforcement which constrains the predatory tendencies of the dominant firm. In Figure 15.5, the market demand is D_m. The competitive supply, S_c, is the sum of the marginal cost curves of the competitive fringe firms. The locus of the dominant firm's demand curve, D_d, is found by subtracting the competitive supply from D_m at each possible price. The dominant firm then sets price at P_1 to maximize its profits by selling output Q_1, while the competitive firms behave as purely competitive price takers to sell quantity $(Q_2\text{-}Q_1)$. This form of oligopolistic market organization is quite workable, and can persist as long as antitrust law is vigorously enforced and the dominant firm behaves

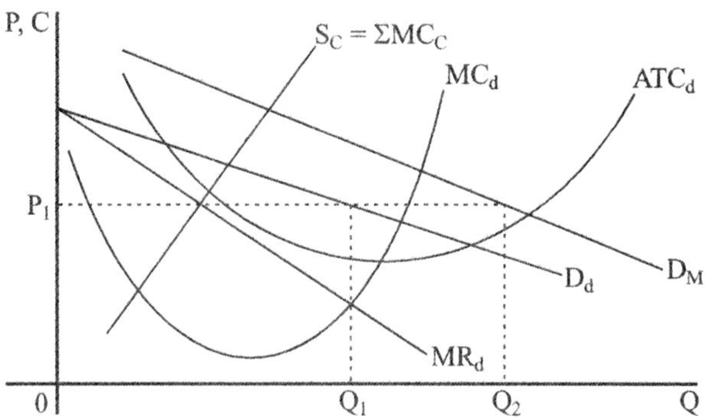

Figure 15.5. A model of dominant-firm price leadership.

itself. The dominance of the dominant firm may break down when one or more of the competitive firms begins price experimentation or product differentiation/promotion in the effort to capture a larger share of the market.

4. **Differential characteristics price leadership** may be based on three aspects of the constituent firms' characteristics:

   (a) differences in per-unit costs;

   (b) differences in sizes of plant; or

   (c) differences in market shares.

Combinations of these differences may also be bases for price leadership.

Suppose, in Figure 15.6, that there are two firms in a market, and that, as illustrated in panel (a), they initially share the market demand equally, that is, the demand curves are coincident at D_f, each of which is one-half of market demand. Firm B has a **cost advantage** (it hires labour or buys material inputs, components, or energy in lower-cost resource markets) than does Firm A. In order to maximize its profits, Firm B would prefer the lower price, P_B, at which it sells quantity Q_B, than that preferred by Firm A, P_A, at which it sells the smaller quantity Q_A in order to maximize its profits. Which firm has the potential for exercising price leadership?

If Firm A chooses to charge its preferred price, P_A, ignoring Firm B's preferred lower price, P_B, some of Firm A's customers will defect to purchase from Firm B. This constitutes a change of a non-price determinant of demand for both firms, that is, the population of consumers purchasing from each firm. Firm A's demand curve will shift to the left towards position D_A as illustrated in panel (b), carrying with it its marginal revenue curve towards position MR_A, with the consequence that Firm A will prefer an ever-lower price. Firm B's demand curve will shift to the right towards position D_B in panel (b), carrying with it its marginal revenue curve toward position MR_B, with the consequence that it will prefer an ever-higher price. Theoretically, these shifts will continue until

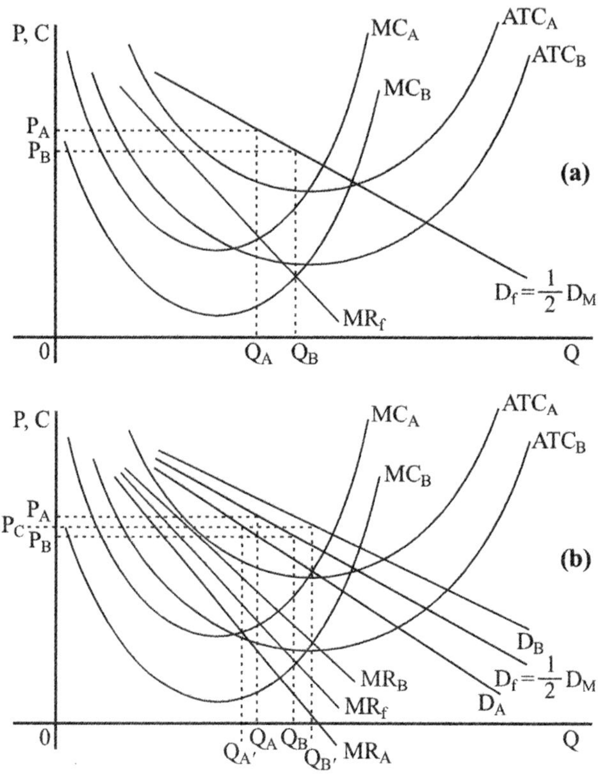

Figure 15.6. Price leadership based on cost differences.

the preferred prices converge to a common price, P_C, but with a significant difference: the two firms now have divergent market shares, Firm B now with a larger share than Firm A. Firm A will sell an even smaller quantity, Q_A', and Firm B will sell an even larger quantity, Q_B'.

Alternately, had the manager of Firm A been willing to meet Firm B's preferred lower price (a deliberate profit sub-maximizing strategy in the short run), it could have preserved its share of the market. Thus, the firm naturally preferring the lower price (in this case, Firm B) has the potential to be the price leader when demand or cost circumstances change. The other firm(s) may choose to follow or not; they can either go ahead and meet the leader's preferred lower price (and thereby preserve market share), or they can lose market share and end up preferring the same price as the leader.

The same phenomenon can be seen where there is no cost or demand difference between firms, but there is a difference in **plant sizes**. In Figure 15.7, the two firms again have equal initial market shares. They also use the same technology and have access to the same labour and materials

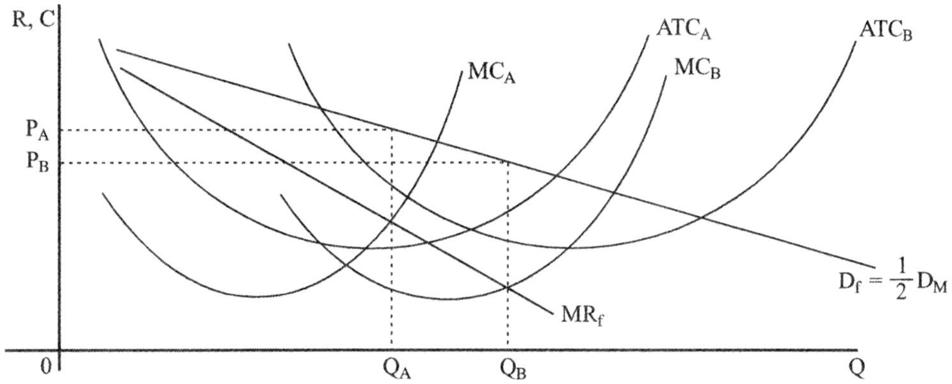

Figure 15.7. Price leadership based on plant size differences.

markets, or different markets with the same market prices. The evidence of this is that their ATC curves have the same shapes and reach bottom at the same per-unit cost levels. Firm B, however, has a slightly larger plant evidenced by the overlap of its ATC curve to the right of Firm A's ATC curve. Again, Firm B has the potential for price leadership because it naturally prefers a lower price in order to maximize profits. But in this case, the basis for price leadership lies in Firm B's larger plant.

Finally, we suppose in Figure 15.8 that the two firms have identical plants and hire labour and purchase materials from the same resource markets. These conditions are evidenced by the fact that their ATC curves are coincident. Firm B, however, initially has a slightly **larger market share** than does Firm A. In this case, Firm A prefers the lower price in order to maximize its

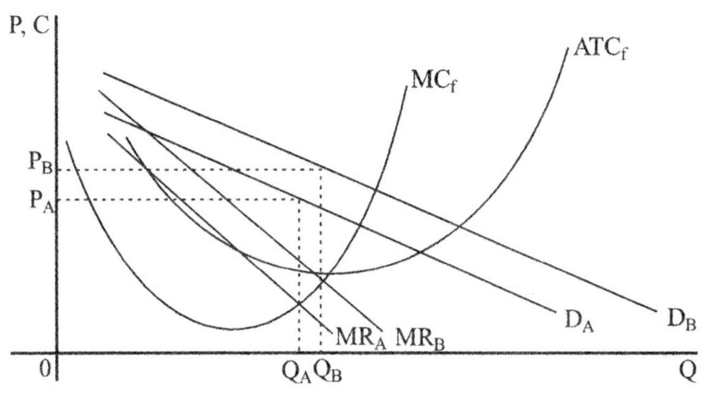

Figure 15.8. Price leadership based on unequal market shares.

profits, and thereby has the potential for price leadership. In this example, the basis for price leadership lies in the smaller initial market share (we can only imagine that Firm A's sales force is pushed to be more aggressive, "We're Number 2, we try harder!"). If Firm B now does not meet the lower price preferred by Firm A, it (Firm B) will lose market share to Firm A. This process theoretically could continue until they have the same market shares and thus prefer the same market price.

While the potential for price leadership can readily be discerned in each of these models, it does not follow that the actual price leader will coincide with the potential price leader. The theoretical follower could 'take the bull by the horns' and undercut the price preferred by the theoretical leader in each example. But by doing so he risks the initiation of a price war as described earlier.

THE MANAGERIAL IMPLICATIONS OF OLIGOPOLISTIC COMPETITION

We have reached the end of our survey of possible behaviour patterns in oligopolistically-competitive markets, but we have by no means exhausted the range of possibilities. What should the manager of the oligopolistic firm pay attention to? It all depends upon the circumstances of the specific situation. The oligopolistic market can range from a fairly comfortable 'live-and-let-live' mentality to an intensely competitive situation characterized by predatory behaviour on the part of some of the managements. Some managers thrive in such an environment while others would rather get out. Business failure will get some of the faint-hearted out of the market, while others will try to escape the intensity of oligopolistic competition by efforts to achieve monopoly. In Western societies where antitrust law exists and is effectively administered, the oligopolistic competition can count upon government scrutiny of its practices and policies.

THE SOCIETAL IMPLICATIONS OF OLIGOPOLISTIC BEHAVIOUR AND INDUSTRY STRUCTURE

Oligopolistic industries are populated by firms which range in size from the corner petrol station to the mega-buck corporation. Oligopolistic competition among petrol retailers probably militates in the consumer's interest by ensuring the lowest possible prices and the narrowest possible profit margins consistent with the continued provision of retail petrol distribution services. Unless collusion among competitors accomplishes a measure of monopoly control and the realization of supernormal profits, oligopolistic competition at the larger-firm end of the spectrum contributes to technological advance in productive efficiency, better product designs, and better service of the product.

Competition, if not subverted by collusion, predatory behaviour, the erection of barriers to entry, or the grant of exclusive position by government, can serve as a mechanism for the social control of industry and commerce. Competition does not have to be pure in order to exert its controlling function. Even the competition present in the oligopolistically-competitive market in the form of price leadership/followership can be an effective vehicle of social control because the threat of market share loss will induce competitors to meet the lowest price preferred by any firm in the market. Society's job in formulating public policy with respect to oligopoly then is to suppress collusive behaviour which exploits consumers, prevents predatory behaviour which destroys existing competitors, and disallows the creation of entry barriers which diverts potential competition.

Summary of Important Points

1. An oligopolistic market may be described as a small-enough number of sellers of a homogeneous or differentiated product that each knows the identities and pays careful attention to the actions of competitors in the market.
2. Natural, legal, or artificial barriers to entry are characteristic of oligopoly.
3. Because oligopolistic sellers know the identities of their competitors and have some pricing discretion, decision strategy is important in oligopoly.
4. Possible oligopoly behaviour patterns include ignoring competition, price warfare, price rigidity, combination, cartelization, collusion, and price leadership/followership.
5. Price warfare may occur due to the naiveté of competitors, or may be initiated deliberately to drive competitors out of business.
6. Expected asymmetrical competitor response to possible price changes may lead to extreme price rigidity in oligopoly
7. Where antitrust laws are vigorously enforced, price leadership/followership will likely emerge as the most common form of oligopoly behaviour.
8. Price leadership may be based on differences in per-unit costs, differences in plant size, differences in market share, or the will of one of the competitors in the market.
9. The oligopolistic firm which naturally prefers the lowest price in order to maximize profits will tend to be the price leader in the market.
10. The potential price leader may not be the actual price leader in an oligopolistic market.
11. Competition, if not subverted by collusion, predatory behaviour, the erection of barriers to entry, or the grant of exclusive position by government, can serve as a mechanism for the social control of industry and commerce.

Significant Terms

identities of competitors	access to market information
oligopoly	barriers to entry
number of firms	price warfare
homogeneous, differentiated products	price (etc.) leadership/followership

market share
self-cancelling effects of competition
decision rigidity
overt, covert collusion
cartel
combination conscious
parallelism of action
antitrust law
naive behavioural assumptions
deliberate profit non-maximizing strategy
extreme price rigidity
asymmetrical price leadership
kinked demand hypothesis
non-price determinants of demand
identification problem
actual, virtual points
barometric price leader
dominant firm price leader
social control
marginal revenue gap

Questions for Discussion

1. How may oligopolistic competition be distinguished from monopolistic competition?
2. Why is the number of competitors in the market not a sufficient basis for identification of oligopolistic competition?
3. Identify the descriptive characteristics of oligopolistic competition.
4. Discuss the role of product differentiation in an oligopolistically competitive market.
5. Discuss the role of entrepreneurship in an oligopolistically competitive market.
6. Explain the significance of the availability of information to firms in an oligopolistically competitive market.
7. How do the behavioural characteristics of an oligopolistic market differ from those of a monopolistically competitive market? ...from those of a pure monopoly?
8. Explain the significance of non-price competition to oligopolistic competitors.
9. Explain how supernormal profits may occur in an oligopolistically competitive market. How does the market tend to react to the appearance of such profits?
10. Explain why the manager of a firm in an oligopolistically competitive market might deliberately initiate a price war. ...a non-price competitive war.
11. Why might there be a tendency for an oligopolistically competitive market to converge upon a common price? Why might price differentials among the products sold by oligopolistically competitive firms persist?

12. Discuss the role of price leadership/followership behaviour in an oligopolistically competitive market. What are the managerial implications of successful (unsuccessful) efforts at price leadership by one of the competitors?

13. Why might share-of-market become a more significant goal than profit maximization for some firms in an oligopolistically competitive market? What are the managerial implications?

14. Why is it not possible to devise a single model to analyze all oligopolistically competitive circumstances?

15. Identify typical oligopolistically competitive behaviour patterns and discuss the managerial implications of each.

16. Why might oligopolistic competitors try to avoid engaging in price warfare with competitors?

17. Why might oligopolistic competitors find incentive to engage in collusion with competitors?

18. Distinguish between overt and covert forms of collusive behaviour in an oligopolistically competitive market, and indicate why competitors may resort to the latter rather than the former.

19. Why might oligopolistic competitors attempt to combine with or acquire competitors? What might prevent this from occurring?

20. Explain the meaning of the term 'conscious parallelism of action.' Explain why this type of behaviour might emerge, and discuss the managerial implications if it does.

21. Why is price leadership/followership behaviour likely to emerge in oligopolistic markets in democratic societies? What are the managerial implications of price leadership?

22. Discuss the desirability of the various forms of competitive and anticompetitive behaviour which might emerge in oligopolistic markets and survey the remedies available to governmental authorities. What are the managerial implications of governmental responses?

23. Why do cartels tend to be inherently unstable? What are the managerial implications for members of the cartel? ...for non-members of the cartel?

24. Discuss the implications of naiveté on the part of managers with respect to competitors' pricing strategies in an oligopolistically competitive market.

25. Explain how behavioural asymmetry in an oligopolistically competitive market may result in price rigidity for long periods of time. What are the managerial implications?

26. Critically evaluate the Sweezy kinked-demand thesis; what are the managerial implications if the thesis is not valid?

27. Explain why the demand curve in the Sweezy model is really not 'kinked.' What are the managerial implications?

28. Identify possible bases upon which price leadership/followership might emerge in an oligopolistically competitive market.

29. Explain how a firm might come to dominate competition in an oligopolistic market. What are the managerial implications for the dominant firm? ...for the other firms in the market?

30. Explain how differences in per-unit costs (sizes of plant, market shares) among firms in an oligopolistically competitive market might lead to price leadership/followership behaviour. What are the managerial implications for the leader (followers) in each case?

31. Explain why the management of a firm in an oligopolistically competitive market might resort to following the pricing leadership of another firm in the same market.

32. Discuss the significance of non-profit goals to firms in oligopolistically-competitive markets.

33. Explain why the managements of firms in an oligopolistically competitive market might resort to predatory behaviour with respect to competitors. ...with respect to customers. What are the managerial implications of the likely responses of governmental authorities to such predatory behaviour?

34. Explain the sense in which competition among firms in an oligopolistically competitive market may serve as a vehicle of social control. Under what circumstances might such social control break down?

Appendix 15.1

In Chapter 15 we showed how the asymmetrical responses of competitors to price increases and decreases by one of the firms in an oligopolistically-competitive market could make it appear that the firm's demand curve was kinked. We dispelled this notion, however, by calling attention to the fact that the firm's genus demand curve actually shifts leftwards when it raises price but its competitors do not follow suit, thereby tracing out a more-shallowly sloped contraction path which has the appearance of a species demand curve. A rightward shift of the genus demand curve, however, does not follow upon a price cut by the firm which is followed by competitors. The resulting asymmetry of response by competitors theoretically renders price rigid at the current level.

Proponents of the kinked-demand model further extend it to a consideration of the marginal revenue conditions associated with the kink. As illustrated by Figure A-XV(a), the marginal revenue curve is reputed to have a gap or vertical segment immediately below the kink. This discontinuity is attributed to the mismatching of the two ends of the marginal revenue curve which are derived from the portions of the demand curve above and below the kink. The gap or vertical segment is reputed to allow the firm's marginal cost curve to freely shift upwards or downwards within the gap without bringing about conditions which would be the basis for a price change. This phenomenon thus constitutes a second explanation of the rigidity of prices in an oligopolistically-competitive market.

However, when the phenomenon is recognized to be an asymmetrical demand shift phenomenon rather than a kinked-demand phenomenon, it must also be concluded that the marginal

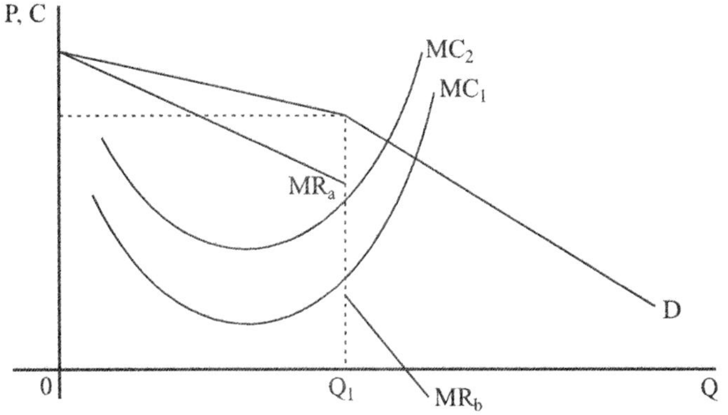

Figure A-XIV(a). The gapped marginal revenue curve.

revenue curve also shifts in an asymmetrical fashion: it does not shift rightwards when price is cut and competitors follow the price cut, but it does shift leftwards along with the demand curve when price is raised and competitors do not follow suit. This phenomenon is illustrated in Figure A-XV(b). The marginal revenue curve is not gapped or vertical below the 'kink;' it shifts in one direction but not in the other with price changes. Since there is no gap or vertical segment in the marginal revenue curve, this does not constitute a second explanation of price rigidity.

The original Sweezy kinked-demand thesis implicitly assumed recessed economic conditions. To further demonstrate the implausibility of the kinked-demand, gapped-marginal revenue thesis,

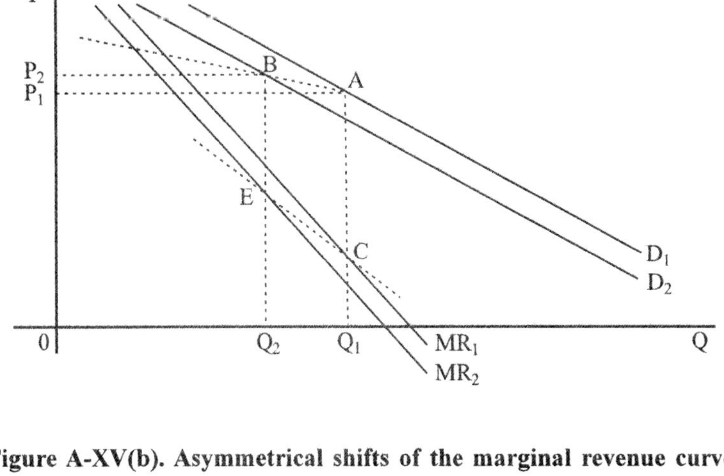

Figure A-XV(b). Asymmetrical shifts of the marginal revenue curve.

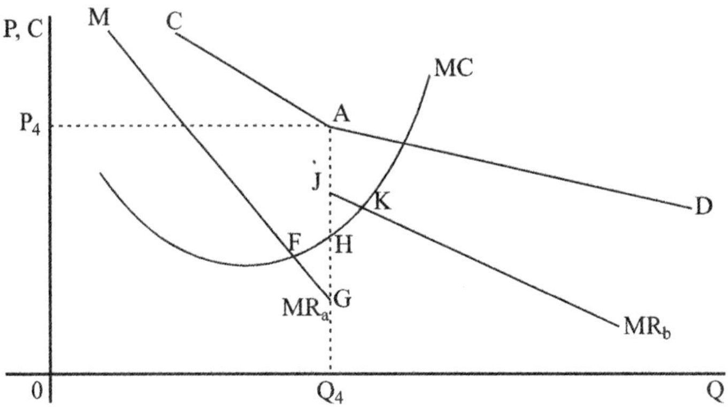

Figure A-XV(c). Kinked demand under inflationary conditions.

let us assume a buoyant economy accompanied by some inflation. In this case, competitors are more likely to be looking for an excuse to raise price than to lower it since their costs of production are probably also increasing. Under these circumstances the demand curve would have to be kinked in the opposite direction, with a zigzag marginal revenue curve as illustrated in Figure A-XV(c). Here, any price other than P_4 would be better than P_4. Because demand appears more inelastic above the kink, a higher price will increase revenues; and because demand appears more elastic below the kink, a lower price will increase revenues. Therefore, price P_4 is an unstable price. The relevant question would be whether to raise or lower price from P_4.

One suggested solution is to observe where the marginal cost curve cuts the various portions of the marginal revenue curve; there are of course three such intersections. According to this suggested solution, if the leftward triangular portion is of larger area than the rightward triangular portion, the firm should raise price; it should lower price with the opposite triangular areas. Needless to say, the comparison of areas of triangles can hardly serve as a practical decision criterion. We leave it to the reader to discern the asymmetrical demand-shift implications of price changes in inflationary circumstances.

—oo(O)oo—

Chapter 16

Extending the Models

SIMPLE MODELS AND COMPLEX REALITIES

The models which we examined in Chapters 11 to 15 assumed the simplest possible context for a commercial enterprise: a business with a single plant, employing a single variable input, producing a single product, which is sold in a single market, and which is run by a single manager. The organization of the market varied in structure and complexity, ranging from pure competition through monopolistic and oligopolistic competition to pure monopoly. But there are very few real-world businesses which are so simple.

Business enterprises typically produce a multiplicity of goods and services which often can be organized into lines of complementary and sometimes competing items. Occasionally the goods produced by the business are conglomerated in the sense that there are no apparent relationships among them. Often the multiple goods are joint products resulting from a common production process. And commercial enterprises often sell their products in a multiplicity of separable market areas.

They employ a great many variable inputs bought or hired from different resource markets. It is not unusual for a business to have several production facilities or plants, and each plant may be subdivided into several assembly lines, each of which can function as a more-or-less autonomous production unit. And the management of the business may include many decision makers, each with limited areas of expertise, decision-making authority, and responsibility. They may be organized into multiple, hierarchical tiers of authority. The facets of intricacy and complexity of the modern business enterprise are almost innumerable.

How can the simple-minded models be relevant to any real-world business organizations other than those which match the models in simplicity? The great virtue of such simple contexts is that they allow us to peer through the haze of complexity in order to come to understanding the principles governing the behaviours of revenues, costs, profit, production, and competition itself without the encumbrances of a plethora of detail. They may serve their academic purposes well, but from a practical perspective, the applicability of such simple models is still not apparent.

There are three planes upon which the models which we have been examining may be beneficial to practical decision contexts. First, the general principles discovered and learned by examining the models in an academic setting can be used as guides to what we shall call 'seat-of-the-pants' decision making (see Fritz Machlup, 'Marginal Analysis and Empirical Research,' in *Essays in Economic Semantics*, W. W. Norton & Company, 1967, pp. 154-155).

Here the decision maker proceeds from an accumulation of experience in similar circumstances to an assessment of the present situation. A rational decision is made by comparing the best available information about the situation to the decision criteria discerned in the academic study of the principles. While this decision-making procedure may sound a bit loose and uncertain, we believe that the vast majority of all business decision makers who have engaged in any formal study of economic principles are likely to proceed in just this fashion.

The second plane upon which simplistic models can be used is to simulate small parts of the complex business decision context. For example, if a business has one plant in each of several completely separate markets, and each plant produces several mutually-exclusive products for sale in the market where that plant is located, it should be possible to specify a revenue and a cost function for each of the products in each of the markets in order to establish the relevant marginal decision criteria.

This approach becomes cumbersome and costly in the case of a wholesale distributor which regularly carries 30,000 different items (in the case of screws, each combination of thread pattern, head design, finish, diameter, and length constitutes a separate item) in its warehouse. The approach breaks down entirely if some of the items are jointly-produced, or if they are produced in a single plant for sale in several markets, or if they are produced in multiple plants but sold in a single market.

On the third plane the simplistic models must be elaborated to handle the intricacies of the situation. The model builder attempts to make the assumptions underlying the model ever more realistic, the structure of the model ever more accurately descriptive of the real context which is being modelled, and the parameters of the model ever more closely tailored to the particular circumstances of the required decision. The progressive elaboration of a model inevitably increases its complexity and detail. The number of equations in the model increases, and particular equations may have to have more and higher-ordered terms in them.

ON REALISM, ACCURACY, AND SPECIFICITY IN MODELS

Economists have traditionally valued simplicity in models, for after all is said and done a model is intended to be a simplified representation of a more complex reality. But economists have also debated the importance of the realism of assumptions and the descriptive accuracy of the structure of their models. Most inevitably have come to the conclusion that it may not be possible to construct a simulation model which is perfectly realistic in its assumptions and accurately descriptive in its structure without making it as complex as the real situation from which it is supposed to be an abstraction. This of course would defeat the purpose of attempting to structure a simplified representation of the more complex reality.

A respected economist, Milton Friedman, has argued that the realism of assumptions and the accuracy of the structure of a model are of lesser importance than is the predictive ability of the model ('The Methodology of Positive Economics' in *Essays in Positive Economics*, University of Chicago Press, 1953).

The acid test for a model is how it performs in doing what it was designed to do. According to Friedman, a simplistic model based on unrealistic assumptions may perform satisfactorily; what is important is whether people behave as if the assumptions of the model are realistic, even if the assumptions bear little or no resemblance to the reality.

An 'economic' perspective on the process of elaborating a model to make it more specific to the context being modelled would examine the benefits and the costs of the elaboration process. A more complex model based on more realistic assumptions may indeed yield better decision criteria, but the process of specifying any model is costly in terms of time and effort, and in money terms if the expertise has to be hired from outside the organization.

The cost of specifying an ever more complex model probably obeys the principle of diminishing returns (or its variant, the law of increasing costs) no less so than does any other real production phenomenon. Model-building costs rise at an increasing rate the farther the model builder attempts to go in detailing the model. The relevant economic question then is whether the value of the additional effectiveness of the model is worth the extra cost of improving the fit.

Our advice is to apply Occam's Razor to the model-building context. Under this principle, one should (use the Razor to) 'cut off' the unnecessary complexity of a model: let suffice the simplest model which will perform satisfactorily. When several needles are lost in a haystack, rational behaviour on the part of the tailor is to search until he finds one which is sharp enough to do the sewing job, not until he has found the absolutely sharpest one. But, this is not a recommendation to make no enhancements to the model. Some models are 'simply too simple' to fit the realities under analysis.

Our purpose in the next section of this chapter is to point the reader in the directions of some potentially productive model elaborations. But we do caution the fledgling model builder to take an economic approach by comparing the possible benefits with the likely costs.

EXTENSIONS OF THE MODEL OF THE FIRM

Non-Price Determinants of Demand

Economists focus almost obsessively upon price as the primary determinant of demand. In an earlier chapter we postulated a more general demand function with several quantity determinants, any one of which could be moved to the head of the queue to serve as the primary determinant. Once any one of them has been designated the primary determinant, others are assumed constant. This procedure enables the construction of a two- or (at most) three-dimensional graphic model to illustrate and analyze the demand relationship. A change of any of the assumed-constant determinants (that is, the ones not represented explicitly on any of the coordinate axes) results in a shift of the curve (in two dimensions) or the surface (in three dimensions). If such a change occurs without being recognized by the analyst, an 'identification problem] arises. The decision-significance of the occurrence of an identification problem is that the decision criteria will tend to be over- or under-stated, and could thereby lead to erroneous decisions.

Economists, in structuring the kinds of models we have examined in earlier chapters, usually assume price to be the primary determinant of quantity demanded, but it is also a convenience to have a deterministic variable which is directly comparable to average and marginal costs. Business decision makers attempting to employ the economic models should pay attention to the non-price demand determinants because autonomous changes in any of them can shift the company's demand curves in unexpected ways.

While these are phenomena to be aware of and prepared to adjust to, it may also be possible to make the non-price determinants of demand into components of the firm's promotional strategy. For example, a successful advertising campaign (promotional effort is one such non-price determinant of demand) should have the effect of increasing the company's demand (that is, shifting the demand curve to the right), or at least preventing it from decreasing (shifting left) in the face of a competitor's promotional effort.

NON-QUANTITY DETERMINANTS OF COSTS

Economists also focus almost exclusively upon quantity produced as the primary determinant of cost. But we also noted that non-quantity determinants of costs may be incorporated into the cost function. Possible candidates are the market prices of the labour and materials inputs which the firm purchases.

It is a convenience to take costs primarily to be functions of quantity produced because this allows direct comparison of per-unit costs (average and marginal) with price and marginal revenue. A change in any of the non-quantity determinants of costs can be expected to shift the per-unit cost curves upward or downward.

As in the case of the non-price determinants of demand, it may be possible to incorporate the non-quantity determinants of costs into the company's production and marketing strategies. For example, one way to gain a 'leg-up' on the competition would be to develop a more productive (that is, lower cost) technology, or to find or negotiate lower-priced sources of supply of the materials or labour inputs than competitors can employ. This would certainly increase the company's profits (or reduce its losses) by shifting its per-unit cost curves downwards. If the company's average variable cost curve shifts far enough downwards, the manager may be encouraged to initiate a price war.

MULTIPLE MARKETS

The markets in which a firm sells can be classified on at least four bases: product, geographic, demographic, and temporal. We shall defer consideration of multiple products to a subsequent section. The geographic market for a particular product is the locale within which the company sells, and where there is effective competition by other companies selling closely competitive products. For most products, the geographic market is almost certainly not the world or even the whole geographic area of a country. Most companies sell in multiple geographic markets which are separated by distance and the cost of transport so that clienteles are effectively compartmentalized. Furthermore, the company may face varying intensities of competition in its different geographic markets: it may be a monopolistic competitor in some markets, an oligopolist in some, and a nearly-pure monopolist in a few. It may need to pursue different marketing strategies according to the nature and intensity of the competition faced.

Varying demand conditions make price differentials among the markets feasible. The charging of different prices for the same item where there are no differences in the costs of serving the different customers constitutes price discrimination which is prohibited under law in most Western societies. By the same token, the charging of the same price where there are different costs of serving different customers is also price discrimination, but this form of price discrimination usually escapes detection or prosecution under the law.

For example, many companies deliver products in their own trucks instead of using third-party shippers. Often the costs of own-truck delivery are not charged explicitly, but rather absorbed in the product prices. To the extent that this occurs, the delivered price is the same to the nearby customer as to the distant customer.

Price discrimination results as a consequence of charging the same price to the different customers. The antitrust authorities would likely never finish if ever they decided to start prosecuting this form of price discrimination. Although the law usually prohibits the practice of overt price discrimination where there is no cost justification for the price discrimination, price discrimination between markets should be expected to emerge as a normal concomitant of different demand elasticities in the different markets.

The company may also sell to separate temporal and demographic markets within the same geographic market. The bases for demographic market separation may include age, race, ethnicity, religion, place of birth, citizenship, etc. Price (and any other kind of) discrimination based on race or ethnicity are usually prohibited by law. The most common demographic forms of price discrimination are by age and citizenship. Theatres typically offer lower-priced children's tickets, even though the seat is as fully occupied by the child as by an adult, and even though the adult really did not want to see the children's feature.

Restaurants as well as theatres may price differently through the day (the 'luncheon menu' versus the 'dinner menu,' the 'afternoon matinee' versus the 'evening feature'). State universities often price-discriminate against citizens of other states who apply for admission, and denominational colleges occasionally price-discriminate in favour of their own members or the offspring of their ministers and missionaries. Airlines and hotels conventionally price discriminate by days of the week and from one season to the next.

Commercial classification may constitute yet another basis for price discrimination. Wholesalers usually identify 'legitimate' retail vendors who then are eligible to buy 'at wholesale' whereas members of the general public can qualify only for the higher retail price. Some wholesalers as well as some manufacturers maintain several customer classifications, each of which is eligible for a certain price level or discount from the company's standard price (wholesalers often express

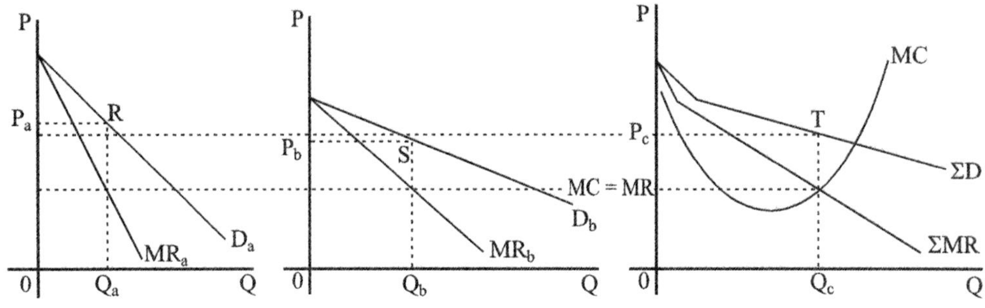

Figure 16.1. A model of price discrimination.

their price schedules as various levels of discount from manufacturer's suggested retail price). Such classification schemes break down when a buyer classed in one group has access to someone classed in another group. Most of us know 'a guy who's got a brother-in-law who can get it for us at wholesale.' Also, the recent advent of 'wholesale buying clubs' has served to obscure the distinction between retail and wholesale.

Any of these forms of price discrimination is enabled only because demand elasticity varies among groups or from time to time, and it is not feasible for a prospective client to jump from one group or time frame to another. If clients can jump market segments, the basis for price discrimination is destroyed. It can be shown mathematically that if two conditions can be met, the company can increase its profit by price discriminating across its markets: (a) demands are of different elasticities in the different markets; and (b) there is some means of segmenting markets and keeping customers in the different market segments from jumping segments or from buying for one another.

Figure 16.1 illustrates the possibility of price discrimination across two separable markets, A and B. Demand in Market A is somewhat more inelastic than is demand in Market B. When the demands are summed (horizontally), D_c (the combined demand) has the appearance of a bend where D_b is joined to D_a, so that the marginal revenue curve, MR_c is as drawn in panel (c). The firm has a single plant for which its marginal cost curve is MC.

The intersection of MC with SMR identifies the quantity Q_c and price P_c which would maximize profits without price discrimination. The total revenue will be the area $0P_cTQ_c$. Suppose now that the manager of the company identifies the quantities and prices in the two markets separately for which MR in each is equal to MC, the common marginal cost. On this criterion, Q_1 can be sold at P_a in market A, and Q_b can be sold at P_b in market B. P_a is higher and P_b is lower than P_c. A careful examination of total revenue rectangles OP_aRQ_a and OP_bSQ_b should reveal that the sum of their areas is greater than that of total revenue rectangle $0P_cTQ_c$.

Thus, whatever the firm's costs happen to be, its revenues with price discrimination will be greater than its revenues without price discrimination, so price discrimination will yield more profit than can be realized without price discrimination. An appendix earlier elaborates a mathematical model of price discrimination which supports this contention.

The managerial implications are clear. The manager of an imperfectly competitive company may by price discrimination increase the company's revenues, but only by incurring the costs of establishing and enforcing market separation, and often by risking antitrust prosecution. It may be very troublesome (and trouble translates into costs) to seal off the markets from one another. The costs of enforcing market separation may be greater than the additional revenue realized from discrimination.

What does it take to certify that a person really is under 13 years of age in order to qualify for the child's price, or over 55 years of age to qualify for the senior citizen's discount? How much does it cost to verify each prospective customer's claimed authorization to buy at wholesale? What is the probability of incurring antitrust prosecution, and what is the likely fine if the verdict is 'guilty?' As with any other managerial decision, the rational approach is to compare the expected benefits with the likely costs before deciding to proceed.

MODELLING FOR PRICE DISCRIMINATION

Suppose that the manager of a company which has a single plant thinks that it might be more profitable to divide the market into two segments in order to price discriminate. In order to ascertain the appropriate quantities to ship into each sub-market and the prices at which to sell them, the company must estimate its demand functions in the form of $P = f(Q/...)$ and then find the total revenue function by multiplying the demand function through by Q, or $TR = P \times Q$ (alternately, the company might first estimate its total revenue function, then derive the average and marginal functions mathematically):

$$TR_1 = P_1 \times Q_1 = Q_1 \times f(Q_1),$$

and

$$TR_2 = P_2 \times Q_2 = Q_2 \times f(Q_2).$$

It must also estimate its cost function, $TC = f(Q)$, where

$$Q = Q_1 + Q_2.$$

It must then compose its total profit function as $TN = TR_1 + TR_2 - TC$, so that the two marginal profit expressions can be computed by partial differentiation,

$$MN_1 = \delta TN/\delta Q_1$$

and

$$MN_2 = \delta TN/\delta Q_2.$$

These marginal profit expressions may then be set equal to zero (because the slope of the profit function is zero at its peak),

$$\delta TN/\delta Q_1 = 0$$

and

$$\delta TN/\delta Q_2 = 0,$$

allowing for solution of values for Q_1 and Q_2. Then, using these values in the estimated demand functions, values for P_1, P_2, TR_1, and TR_2 may be found. And finally, the maximized profit, TN, may be computed. An example of this process has been elaborated earlier.

MULTIPLE PRODUCTS

As we have already noted, if the company produces multiple products for sale in as many product markets, its production and marketing operations in each product market can be modelled separately. For short-run decision making purposes, this analysis can be handled without reference to the overhead costs since they are irrelevant to the price and output decisions (in the last section of this chapter we will consider a model for pricing to cover fully-allocated costs).

In the long run the allocation of the overhead costs in a multi-product plant becomes critical to the question of whether to delete any particular items from the product line, or to add new items if excess capacity exists. In order for any item currently in the product line to continue to be produced, its price must make an adequate contribution to its overhead costs as well as cover all of the direct costs of its production.

This is not an argument for price to be set to cover overhead as well as direct costs; rather, once price has been determined with appropriate economic criteria (MR, MC), the question is whether or not it covers all relevant costs. Since there appears to be no objective criterion for allocating overhead costs among multiple products, this assessment must be based upon the judgement of the decision maker who, in any case of deleting or adding products, is engaging in an entrepreneurial decision.

If the company has excess productive capacity and is considering whether to add items to its product line, the decision maker must make a prior judgement (again, in an entrepreneurial capacity) as to whether the new item can be sold at a price which is high enough to cover all of its direct production costs and make some contribution to covering the overhead costs as well. It can be argued that since the excess capacity already exists, the overhead costs are in effect 'sunk costs' and thus not pertinent to the question of adding the item to the product line.

Yet, even if an item is added on the basis that its price will be sufficient to cover all direct costs plus some contribution to overhead costs, for the item to be retained in the product line in the long run it will have to be judged to be making an adequate contribution to overhead costs and profit. If the company is considering adding an item when it has no excess capacity, then the appropriate criterion is that the item should not be added unless it is possible to sell the item at a price which will cover both its direct costs and the overhead costs resulting from the added capacity. In any case, the rational entrepreneur should add items to the product line in descending order of perceived profitability.

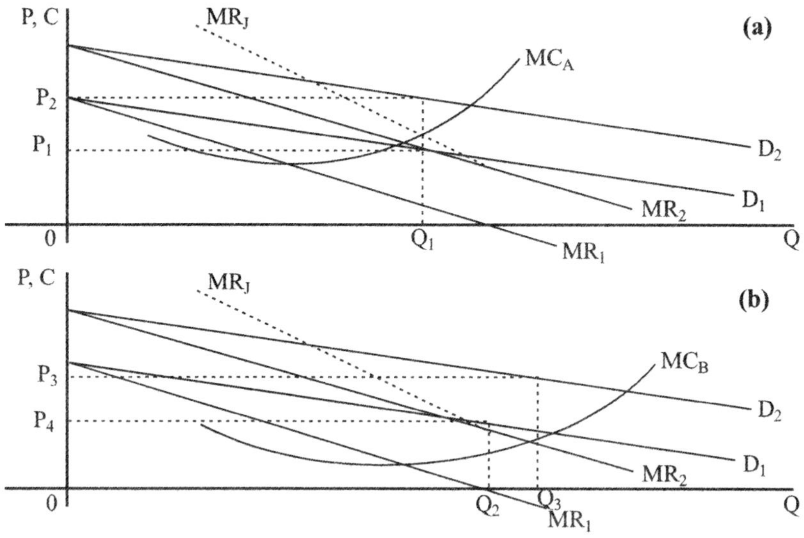

Figure 16.2. Jointly-produced products produced in fixed proportions.

JOINTLY-PRODUCED PRODUCTS

The specification of decision criteria for jointly-produced products poses another difficult problem. Jointly-produced products are those which result from a common production process. Classic examples are beef and hides, petrol and fuel oil, mutton and wool. Even where the objective is to produce one primary product, for example, metal stampings for auto body parts, there are likely to be marketable by-products such as the metal scrap. In any short-run situation, such joint products are produced in fixed proportions. The relevant questions are what quantity of the output mix is to be produced and at what prices are the individual items in the mix to be sold. In the long run, the management often can vary the output proportions, so that the relevant question for the long run is the profit-maximizing output combination.

The short-run decision problem can be analyzed with a variant on the multi-market price discrimination model. In Figure 16.2, the marginal revenue curves for the jointly produced products are summed vertically (they were summed horizontally in the price discrimination model) to construct the joint marginal revenue curve, MR_J. We note that for all outputs larger than Q_2, MR_1 is negative so that the MR_j curve is coincident with the path of MR_2. The relevant short-run decision criterion is the comparison of marginal cost with joint marginal revenue. The manager should increase output as long as joint marginal revenue exceeds marginal cost, or decrease output if joint marginal revenue is less than marginal cost . In panel (a) of Figure 16.2, if marginal cost is given by MC_A, the product 1 profit-maximizing price is P_1 at which output Q_1 of product 1 should be sold. Price P_2 should be charged for product 2, and all units of both products should be sold.

If marginal cost should fall to MC_B in panel (b) of Figure 16.2, it intersects the joint marginal revenue curve to the right of where MR_1 has become negative. Since it would be irrational to sell so large a quantity of any product as to reduce total revenue (that is, where MR is negative), output Q_3 of both products is produced, but only Q_2 of product 1 should be sold at price P_4. The rest of product 1 (Q_3-Q_2) should be withheld from the market and possibly destroyed or 'dumped' in another market (dumping is then a special case of price discrimination). All of product 2 produced, Q_3, should be sold at price P_3. Plant managers typically have little discretion in varying the product mix in the short run. To alter the output mix usually requires a long-run adjustment to plant, equipment, and technology to be effected through capital investment. Without perfect prior knowledge of the costs and revenues of alternative product-mix combinations, the company's manager, acting in an entrepreneurial capacity, can only proceed iteratively to try an alternative combination when the next occasion for capital reinvestment arises. If the new product mix increases profitability (a successful entrepreneurial decision), the manager can assume that an adjustment in the proper direction has been made.

The long-run decision to vary the proportions in which joint products are produced can be illustrated with an isorevenue map superimposed over an isocost map, similar to the isoquant-isocost analysis of production elaborated in the appendix to Chapter 8. We choose not to elaborate the theoretical isocost-isorevenue model in the text of this chapter because the ability to estimate the equations of surfaces from which isocost curves can be extracted requires near-perfect prior knowledge of the company's multiple-product production possibilities. This is typically far more information than can be mustered in most real decision settings.

INCREASING SIZE AND COMPLEXITY

To this point we have assumed the convenient fiction that the management of the company consists of the single person, the 'manager,' who makes decisions in pursuit of the profit objective. The owner-entrepreneur of a small-scale single proprietorship fits this description nicely, and there are throughout the world tens of thousands of such one-person companies in existence, many of them well-managed, successful enterprises.

But as other companies, organized as partnerships and corporations, have become much larger than could ever have been accommodated under the proprietorship form of organization, a wide variety of approaches have emerged for dealing with the resulting problems of coordination and control. As noted in Chapter 10, these problems usually show up as decreasing returns to scale in the production function, and as diseconomies of scale in the long-run cost function. Virtually all of the attempted remedies have been means of specializing and dividing the labour of decision making among a multiplicity of managers. They include:

(a) distinguishing line from staff functions;

(b) the functional specialization of line managers to ever narrower realms of discretion and responsibility;

(c) the establishment of multiple tiers of managerial responsibility organized along hierarchical lines of authority; and

(d) divisionalization of the company's operations.

We shall leave the further elaboration of the first three of these approaches to texts in organizational theory. The purpose of divisionalization is to create several smaller decision units to replace (or in lieu of) a single, large, unwieldy administrative unit. Divisionalization may be along horizontal or vertical lines. The **horizontal divisionalization** of the company may be organized along geographic or product lines. Each such horizontal division may be construed as a near-autonomous entity over which the appointed management staff is given the responsibility to be profitable (or to meet some other specified company goals), and the decision-making discretion and authority to pursue this end (hence they may be designated 'profit centres'). The horizontal divisions may have been created by dividing a previously unified organization. More likely, a horizontal divisional structure is the outcome of one or more acquisitions or mergers where complete integration of the combined companies has not been achieved, and may not even be intended by the acquiring owners. In many cases, the fellow divisions are expected to compete with each other as well as with other companies. In any case, they must vie with each other for access to the parent company's financial resources.

Since there is often no particular economic reason for the horizontal divisions to be parts of the same company (unless the objective is merger to avoid competition), the justification for their common ownership lies in the 'deeper financial pockets' of the larger company. We leave further examination of this angle to the auspices of corporate finance. In most cases of horizontal divisionalization, the models which we have already elaborated should be adequate to the analysis of both short- and long-run decision criteria.

TRANSFER PRICING

To this point we have assumed each company to be perfectly **vertically integrated**, that is, to perform all operations in proper sequence to convert a batch of raw materials into a final product. This fiction (or reality in a few, rare cases) allowed us to discuss the construction of a single production function, implicitly encompassing all sequential operations without reference to any particular operations. It also permitted us the luxury of imagining the specification of a single cost function encompassing all of those separate operations. Without making it explicit, we have assumed that the intermediate product was simply 'work in process' to be passed from one processing stage to the next without having to be 'costed' or 'priced.' Any profit (normal or supernormal) which resulted would accrue to the company as a whole without any necessity of distributing or attributing it to the various productive operations.

The alternative to vertical integration is **vertical segmentation** (or disintegration) where each identifiable productive operation is performed by a separate company. Each company in performing its operation adds value to the intermediate product. The partially-processed product is then sold to another company which adds more value by performing the next operation in sequence, and so on until the state of 'final product' is attained.

If a production process were perfectly vertically segmented, each of the companies in the vertical sequence would maximize profits by finding the price and quantity for which marginal revenue is equal to marginal cost. The price which each company would charge would be equal to its marginal revenue if market conditions were purely competitive, but price would exceed marginal revenue in imperfectly competitive markets. In a vertically-segmented production process, each company's price would become part of the next company's per-unit costs.

From a social perspective, the application of **marginal decision criteria** in a competitive market would lead to an efficient allocation of resources among the successive operations and profits among the separate companies. From the company perspective, efficiency (and hence, profitability) is served by applying the marginal decision criteria among its vertically related divisions. Virtually all manufacturing companies are to some extent vertically integrated in that they perform more than one identifiable operation in the sequence necessary for the production of the final product. No additional modelling or analysis is required if the vertically integrated company is organized as a single unit for which one production function and one cost function may be estimated.

However, the vertically integrated company may be organized into separate, **semiautonomous divisions** within which managers are given discretion for determining output and responsibility for controlling costs and earning profits. It then becomes necessary to determine the prices of the intermediate goods as they are transferred from each division to the division which will undertake the next stage of processing. Realistic **transfer prices** are as important to the allocation of resources between divisions within the vertically integrated company as realistic intermediate goods prices are to the allocation of resources between companies in a vertically segmented production process. A too-low transfer price will result in a sub-normal profitability of the division (profit centre), and resources will tend to be under-allocated to the division as division output is decreased. Since the too-low transfer price becomes a too-low per-unit cost to the next division, profits there will be supernormal, and resources will tend to be over-allocated to that division.

Transfer pricing among divisions is an especially critical matter if executive or employee compensation across the divisions is based upon the profitability of the divisions. Profitability differentials among the divisions which are due to errors or deliberate distortions in transfer pricing will inevitably lead to a deterioration of executive or employee morale.

Parent companies with subsidiaries in other countries may devise a transfer pricing strategy to **shift cash** from one country to another. For example, if the parent company sets prices well above costs on inventory shipped to a foreign subsidiary, cash is shifted to the parent company. Vice-versa, if inventory shipped from the subsidiary to the parent is overpriced relative to costs, cash is shifted from the parent to the subsidiary.

The matter of realistic transfer pricing is even more critical if the division manager is also allowed the discretion to sell some of the output to buyers outside of the company as an alternative to transferring all of the intermediate good to the next processing division within the company. If the in-house transfer price is set too low, the company may find it more profitable to sell to outsiders at market prices than to transfer intermediate product to the next in-house division, in which case vertical disintegration will occur as the company becomes less vertically integrated. The company may instruct one division to price-discriminate in favour of a fellow division and against an outside buyer, but this may lead to interdivisional differentials of profitability, and it is likely to attract the attention of the antitrust authorities. For example, consider the implications if the Saginaw Division of General Motors were to sell power steering units to the Buick Motor Division of General Motors at a more favourable price than to Chrysler for installation in Jeep vehicles.

Suppose that a division manager is given the authority to source intermediate goods requirements from outside the company even though a fellow division produces the intermediate

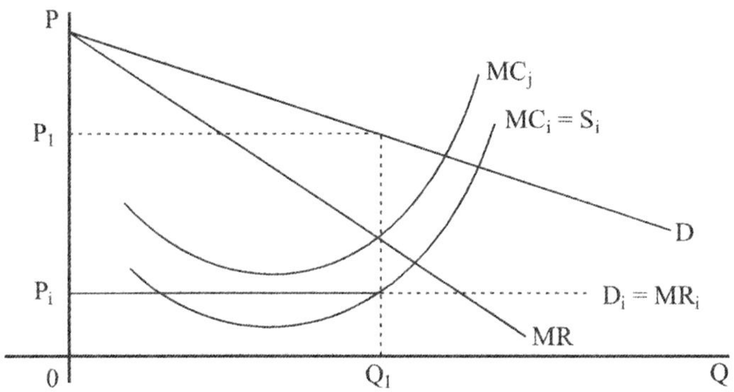

Figure 16.3. Transfer pricing with no external market for the output.

good. A too-high transfer price for the intermediate good will lead to vertical disintegration as the division manager shifts to the externally-sourced supply of the intermediate good at lower market prices.

Figure 16.3 can be used to illustrate the determination of the transfer price at any stage of production when the manager of the division is given no discretion to source the intermediate product from the market or sell product to the market after the division's processing of it. The product demand and marginal revenue curves are represented as D and MR. The product is assumed to go through j stages of processing where each stage is accomplished in a semi-autonomous division of the company. The marginal cost curve after the final, or jth, stage of processing is MC_j. The company will maximize profits at output level Q_1, the output level at which MR is equal to MC_j.

As processing ensues through the stages of production from the first to the jth, the marginal cost curves (as well as the average variable and average total cost curves) for the respective stages can be imagined to step upwards, approaching MC_j as the limiting and final-product position. The rationale for the upward stepping of the MC curves is that the transfer price set in any stage becomes the per-unit cost of the intermediate product at the next stage, to which the marginal costs at the next stage are added to find the next transfer price.

Thus the transfer price at each stage is higher than the transfer price at the previous stage of processing. On analogy, if the unit prices of the materials inputs in any production process were to increase, the whole set of per unit cost curves (average variable, average total, and marginal cost) would shift upward. In the divisionalized, vertically integrated company, the price of the intermediate product rises as more value is added to it at each stage of processing.

Given that the executive decision has been made to produce Q_1 units of output to be sold at the P_1 price, and assuming that the required cost functions can be specified and statistically estimated at each stage of production (that is, by each division), the transfer price for the ith division can be found at the intersection of the vertical from Q_1 with the division's marginal cost curve, MC_i. In a competitive industry, this marginal cost curve above its AVC minimum would constitute the ith division's intermediate product supply curve.

The demand by division i+1 for the output of division i is in effect perfectly elastic at the marginal cost of producing the value added by processing at the ith stage of production, but only up to output level Q_1. Beyond Q_1, division i+1 has no demand at all (nor does anyone else) for the output of the ith division.

Hence, since $MR_i=D_i$ when demand is perfectly elastic, MR_i is equal to MC_i at output Q_1, and the appropriate transfer price for the ith division is P_i, which is just equal to the marginal cost of the value added to the intermediate product by processing it in the ith division. Whether division i is functioning profitably at transfer price P_i then depends on the level of its average variable costs, the magnitude of the overhead costs, and how the overhead costs are allocated to the various divisions.

Suppose that division i+1 can purchase an equivalent intermediate product from a competitive external market at a market price below P_i. In this case, disintegration is likely to ensue since none of the output of the intermediate product should be purchased by division i+1 from division i. All of the required intermediate product should be purchased from the external market, and the company should dispose of division i.

We can imagine that the intermediate product after processing by division i-1 might be sold to another company to perform the ith stage of value-added processing, then be purchased by division i+1 for further processing, thereby completely skipping the ith stage of processing within the company. This phenomenon occurs in effect when a company contracts with another company to perform a certain stage of processing, then proceeds with further processing in-house. An executive decision might be made to mandate the purchase of the intermediate product by division i+1 from division i even at a transfer cost above the external market price.

In this case, other divisions of the company subsidize the higher-cost division. The likely consequence is distortion of both the allocation of resources within the company and the attribution of returns among the divisions.

Suppose that division i finds that it can sell the intermediate product after its processing on a competitive external market at a price above P_i, say P_t in Figure 16.4. The manager of division i should take the demand and marginal revenue curves to be D_t and MR_t, respectively, and will find incentive to push his division's output to Q_2. With this larger output being produced, Q_1 will be transferred to division i+1, while quantity (Q_2- Q_1) can be sold on the external market. However, since the marginal cost of producing the larger quantity is higher, the transfer price to division i+1 will be the higher price P_t rather than P_i.

This will have the effect of shifting upwards all of the marginal cost curves of the subsequent processing divisions, including that of the final product, MC_j. This will likely reduce the maximum profit output for the firm below Q_1. This can be imagined to set in motion a series of iterative readjustments by processing divisions all along the vertical sequence until a new equilibrium solution is found.

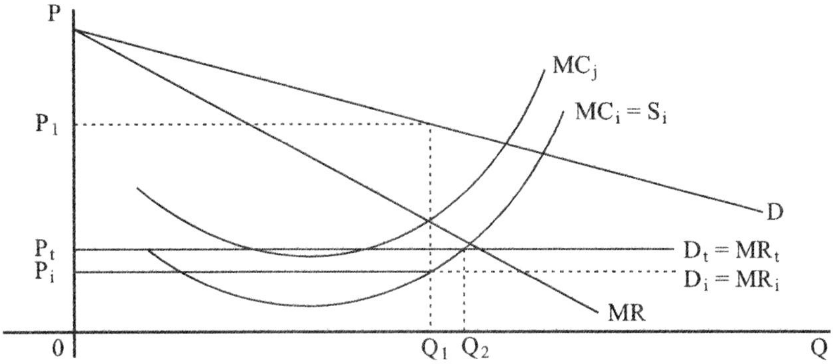

Figure 16.4. Transfer pricing with an external market for the output.

WHAT'S AHEAD

This chapter has explored a number of possibilities for adding realism to the simple models elaborated in Chapters 12–15. These possibilities are not intended to be exhaustive, but only suggestive of the directions in which model elaboration might be taken. We examine a number of challenges to the theory of the firm which is based on the assumption of single-minded orientation of the management towards profit maximization.

Summary of Important Points

1. Modern business enterprises may be organized into multiple, hierarchical tiers of authority; the facets of intricacy and complexity of the modern business enterprise are almost innumerable.
2. Models are simplified representations of complex realities; their great virtue is that they allow us to peer through the haze of complexity and come to understanding fundamental principles.
3. The general principles discovered by examining the models can be used as guides for 'seat-of-the-pants' decision making, a process probably followed by the vast majority of business decision makers.
4. Abstract models can be used to simulate small parts of more complex business decision contexts.
5. Model builders may attempt to elaborate their models to exhibit the intricacies of the real world.
6. A simplistic model based on unrealistic assumptions may be satisfactory if it behaves as if the assumptions are realistic.

Contd.....

7. An economic approach to model elaboration is to consider the benefits and the costs of further elaboration.
8. Economists focus in their demand analyses almost exclusively upon price as the primary determinant of demand; but models may be structured to relate demand to non-price determinants.
9. Economists focus their cost models almost exclusively upon price as the primary determinant of costs; but models may be structured to relate costs to non-quantity determinants.
10. The markets in which a firm sells can be classified on product, geographic, demographic, or temporal bases.
11. Varying demand conditions across markets make price differentials among the markets feasible.
12. Price discrimination across markets may be profitable if demands are of different elasticities in different markets and there is some means of segmenting the markets.
13. If the firm produces multiple products for sale in as many markets, its production and marketing operations in each market can be modelled separately.
14. While overhead costs are irrelevant to short-run decision making, in the long run the allocation of overhead costs among products is critical to the question of whether to retain or delete products from the product line.
15. Since there appears to be no objective criterion for allocating overhead costs among multiple products, this assessment must be based upon the judgement of the decision maker.
16. Jointly-produced products result from a common production process; the manager should increase output as long as joint marginal revenue exceeds marginal cost.
17. In a large and complex business enterprise, problems of coordination and control show up as decreasing returns to scale or diseconomies of scale in the long-run cost function.
18. Remedies for diseconomies of scale are means of specializing and dividing the labour of decision making among a multiplicity of managers.
19. The purpose of divisionalization is to create several smaller decision units to replace a single, large, unwieldy administrative unit.
20. In a vertically segmented production process, each productive operation is performed by a separate firm or a separate division within a vertically-integrated firm.
21. The determination of appropriate transfer prices within a vertically integrated firm is critical to efficient allocation of resources within the firm.
22. Inappropriate transfer pricing may lead to vertical disintegration of the firm.
23. The appropriate transfer price for the product of each division is the marginal cost of the value added to the intermediate product by processing in that division.

Significant Terms

intricacy, complexity
simulation model
reality, abstraction
predictive ability
modelling costs
diminishing returns
Occam's Razor
non-price determinants of demand
identification problem
non-quantity determinants of cost
geographic product market
price discrimination
temporal, demographic, commercial bases for market segments, separation
costs of enforcement
differential demand elasticities
direct, overhead costs
contribution to sunk costs
jointly-produced products
marketable by-products
output, product mix
coordination, control
returns to scale, economies of scale
specialization, division of decision making
line, staff functions
divisionalization
horizontal, vertical
vertical integration, segmentation
value added
intermediate, final

Questions for Discussion

1. Describe the facets of intricacy and complexity which characterize the typical modern business firm in a financially mature economy.
2. How can the simple-minded models elaborated in previous chapters be made relevant to the complex circumstances found in the real world?
3. Explain the role of theoretical models to the 'seat-of-the-pants' decision making engaged in by the vast majority of all business decision makers.
4. Explain how theoretical models can be used to simulate the operations of a real-world business enterprise. What are the limits of the manager to use models in this fashion?
5. Identify the problems involved in elaborating a model to reflect the details of the real mechanism which has been modelled.

6. Critically evaluate Milton Friedman's criterion for assessing the validity of a model.
7. Identify an economic criterion for continuing to elaborate a model to reflect the details of the circumstances being modelled.
8. How can an identification problem arise in the specification of a model to represent a real phenomenon?
9. What are the managerial implications of changes in non-price determinants of demand for a product sold by the firm?
10. Explain how it might be possible to make non-price determinants of demand into components of the firm's promotional strategy.
11. Explain how a change in a non-quantity determinant of costs likely affects the firm's cost relationships. What are the managerial implications?
12. Why is the fact that companies sell in multiple markets of managerial significance?
13. Explain how a firm may compartmentalize its market on various bases. What can the firm achieve by so doing?
14. What are the necessary conditions which enable the successful practice of price discrimination? What does price discrimination achieve for the firm?
15. Discuss the problems associated with effectively segmenting a market in order to effect price discrimination.
16. Discuss the problem of allocating overhead costs when the firm produces and sells multiple products.
17. Discuss the sense in which decisions concerning adding or deleting products from the firm's product line are essentially entrepreneurial in nature.
18. Distinguish the short- and long-run significances of overhead costs in the decision to add a product to the firm's product line.
19. Distinguish the short- and long-run managerial decision problem in regard to jointly-produced products.
20. Identify the relevant managerial decision criterion for increasing or decreasing the output of products which are jointly produced in fixed proportions.
21. Discuss the alternatives for disposing off a jointly produced product for which marginal revenue is negative at the profit-maximizing output level.
22. Identify the entrepreneurial decision criterion for capital reinvestment in a facility which produces multiple (jointly-produced) products.
23. Describe the approaches which have emerged for dealing with increasing size and complexity of modern business organizations.

24. Explain how divisionalization of the firm's operations might help to alleviate certain managerial problems.

25. Why might vertical segmentation of the production process constitute managerial decision problems for the firm?

26. Identify the relevant output/price decision criteria for companies in a perfectly vertically segmented production process to use in maximizing their profits.

27. Why are realistic transfer prices between the divisions of a company important to its profitability?

28. Explain the importance of transfer pricing to executive compensation across a company's divisions.

29. Explain how companies with multinational operations might use transfer pricing as a means or shifting cash internationally.

30. Discuss the implications of price discrimination in transfer pricing between divisions of the same company relative to other companies.

31. Discuss the likely consequences of setting one division's transfer price too low to the next division within the same company.

32. Discuss the likely consequences if the manager of one division of a company finds the transfer price of an intermediate product from another division of the same company to be higher than from an outside source.

33. Explain what happens to marginal cost curves through successive stages of processing in separate divisions of the same company when the intermediate good is transferred from each division to the next for further processing.

34. Identify the appropriate transfer pricing criterion which should be used in a divisionalized company in order to ensure proper internal allocation of company resources.

35. In a vertically integrated divisionalized company, explain the incentive to 'out-source' or 'out-process' at a certain level of processing.

36. Describe circumstances under which vertical disintegration of a firm might occur.

Appendix 16.1

A MATHEMATICAL MODEL OF PRICE DISCRIMINATION

In this appendix we show the mathematical steps necessary to compute the profit-maximizing prices and quantities for a company considering price discrimination in the sale of one item in two separable markets. Suppose that the company has, via regression analysis, estimated its demand functions for markets 1 and 2 as

$$Q_1 = 12 - 2\ P_1,$$

and

$$Q_2 = 15 - 3\ P_2,$$

where output is measured in lots of 100,000 each, and price is denominated in U.S. dollars. Solving each demand function for price,

$$P_1 = 6 - .5\ Q_1$$

and

$$P_2 = 5 - .3333\ Q_2,$$

permits specification of the total revenue function for each market as the product of price times quantity:

$$TR_1 = P_1Q_1 = 6\ Q_1 - .5\ Q_1^2,$$

and

$$TR_2 = P_2Q_2 = 5\ Q_2 - .3333\ Q_2^2.$$

The company has also estimated its total cost function,

$$TC = 20 - 4\ Q + .5\ Q^2,$$

or, when it is recognized that Q must be divided into Q_1 and Q_2,

$$TC = 20 - 4\ (Q_1 + Q_2) + .5\ (Q_1 + Q_2)^2$$
$$= 20 - 4\ Q_1 - 4\ Q_2 + .5\ Q_1^2 + Q_1Q_2 + .5\ Q_2^2.$$

Then, its total profit function can be specified as

$$TN = 6\ Q_1 - .5\ Q_1^2 + 5\ Q_2 - .3333\ Q_2^2 - 20 + 4\ Q_1 +$$
$$4\ Q_2 - .5\ Q_1^2 - Q_1Q_2 - .5\ Q_2^2$$
$$= 10\ Q_1 + 9\ Q_2 - Q_1^2 - 5/6\ Q_2^2 - Q_1Q_2 - 20.$$

In order to find the outputs in each market at which profit is maximized, the partial derivatives of profit with respect to each Q must be computed,

$$dTN/dQ_1 = 10 - 2\ Q_1 - Q_2$$
$$dTN/dQ_2 = 9 - 5/3\ Q_2 - Q_1$$

and set equal to zero, forming two equations which can be solved simultaneously:

$$10 - 2\ Q_1 - Q_2 = 0$$
$$9 - Q_1 - 5/3\ Q_2 = 0$$

Q_1 = 3 and 2/7 or 3.28571 units of 1 million
Q_2 = 3 and 3/7 or 3.42857 units of 1 million.

Thus, in order to maximize profit, the company should produce 6 and 5/7 million units of the product, sending 3 and 2/7 million units to markets 1 and 3 and 3/7 million units to market 2.

The prices to be charged in each market can be computed by inserting the solved values for Q_1 and Q_2 into the respective demand curve equations and solving for P_1 and P_2.

$$P_1 = 6 - .5\ Q_1 = \$4.36$$
$$P_2 = 5 - .3333\ Q_2 = \$3.86.$$

So, 3 and 2/7 million units should be sold in market 1 at a price of $ 4.36 each, and 3 and 3/7 million units should be sold in market 2 at a price of $ 3.86 each.

The total revenuc, total cost, and total profit may be computed from their respective functions:

$$TR = P_1Q_1 + P_2Q_2 = 14.316 + 13.224 = \$27.541$$
$$TC = 20 - 4\ Q + .5\ Q_2 = 20 - 26.857 + 22.541 = \$\ 15.684$$
$$TN = 10\ Q_1 + 9\ Q_2 - Q_12 - 5/6\ Q_2 - Q_1Q_2 \quad 20 - \$\ 11.857$$

in millions.

The elasticities may be computed for each price-quantity combination:

$$e_1 = dQ_1/dP_1 \times P_1/Q_1$$

and

$$e_2 = dQ_2/dP_2 \times P_2/Q_2.$$

Then,

$$e_1 = -2.652$$

and

$$e_2 = -3.375$$

which are clearly different. So, price discrimination between the two markets would be profitable if the clients can be kept separate. But, is price discrimination more profitable than charging the same price in both markets?

Without price discrimination, the total demand across the two markets can be computed as

$$Q = Q_1 + Q_2 = 12 - 2\ P_1 + 15 - 3\ P_2.$$

Since P_1 must be equal to P_2, the total demand function is

$$Q = 27 - 5\ P.$$

Solving for P,

$$P = 27/5 - Q/5,$$

the total revenue equation can be specified my multiplying through by Q, that is,

$$TR = P \times Q = 27/5\ Q - 1/5\ Q^2.$$

Given the estimated total cost function,

$$TC = 20 - 4Q + .5Q^2,$$

the total profit function can be specified as TR – TC, or

$$TN = 27/5\ Q - 1/5\ Q^2 - 20 + 4Q - .5Q^2,$$

$$= 47/5\ Q - 7/10\ Q_2 - 20,$$

and marginal profit can be computed as the derivative of the total profit function,

$$dTN/dQ = 47/5 - 14/10\ Q = 47/5 - 7/5\ Q.$$

Then, marginal profit may be set equal to zero,

$$47/5 - 7/5\ Q = 0,$$

in order to solve for the Q which will maximize TN,

$$7/5\ Q = 47/5$$

$$7\ Q = 47$$

$$Q = 6\ 5/7 \text{ units of } 100{,}000 \text{ each.}$$

The profit maximizing price may be found by inserting the solved value for Q into the combined demand function and solving for P:

$$P = 27/5 - (47/7)/5 = 27/5 - 47/35 = 189/35 - 47/35$$
$$= 142/35$$
$$= \$\,4.057.$$

Total profit may be computed from the profit function as

$$TN = 47/5\ Q - 7/10\ Q^2 - 20 = 63.114 - 31.557 - 20$$
$$= \$\,11.557 \text{ million (without price discrimination).}$$

It is clear that if the company price discriminates between markets 1 and 2, it can realize a profit of \$ 11.857 million, but only \$ 11.557 million without price discrimination, a difference of \$ 300, 000. If the cost of enforcing market separation is less than \$ 300, 000, it will be worthwhile for the company to price discriminate at the prices computed in the first part of this example.

Appendix 16.2

JOINT PRODUCTS PRODUCED IN VARIABLE PROPORTIONS

The problem of joint products produced in varying proportions can be illustrated with a graphic model. Assuming a three-dimensional cost function where the dependent variable, TC, is a function of two outputs, Q_a and Q_b, for products A and B, the cost surface has the appearance of

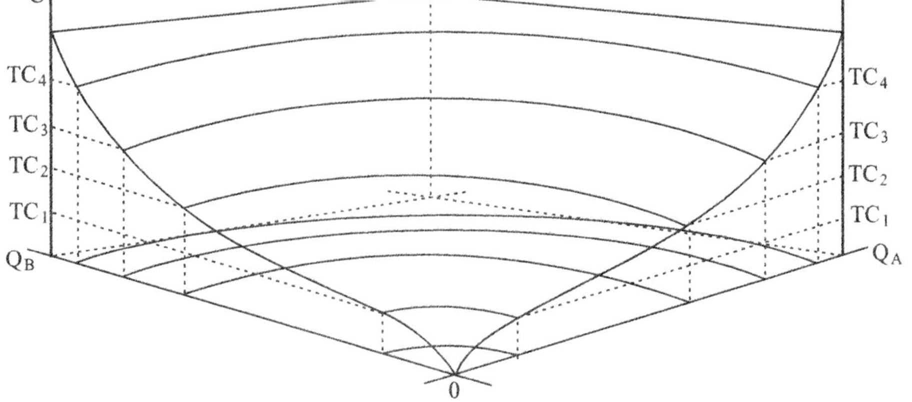

Figure A-XVI(a). A total cost surface for two products.

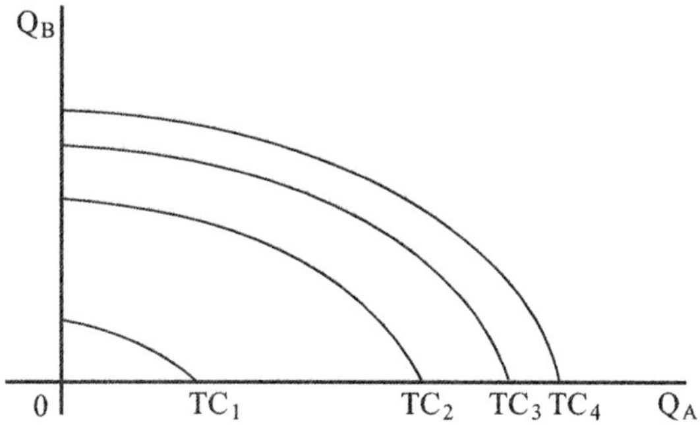

Figure A-XVI(b). An isocost map derived from the total cost surface.

that in Figure A-XVI(a). The equation for such a cost function might take the following form which is cubic in both independent variables:

$$TC = a + b\,Q_a^3 + c\,Q_a^2Q_b + d\,Q_aQ_b^2 + e\,Q_b^3.$$

Other equation forms are possible. A joint-products cost equation could be of different orders in the included variables, and there may be more than two jointly-produced products to be encompassed in the cost function equation. The analyst, in attempting to estimate such a function might try including higher-ordered terms than may be relevant, then inspecting the inference statistics for the statistical significance of the terms.

The TC surface could be sliced vertically, parallel to either floor axis for particular quantities of the item represented on the other floor axis, thereby generating the conventional two-dimensional TC curves which we have analyzed in Chapter 8. However, Figure A-XVI(a) illustrates horizontal slices taken at successively higher altitudes (that is, cost levels or amounts budgeted for expenditure on production of the two items). The projections of the slices through the cost surface into the floor generate a set of concentric isocost curves, which, when looked at from above, have the appearance of the isocost map illustrated in Figure A-XVI(b). Along any single isocost, for example, TC_3, are points the coordinates of which represent the combinations of quantities of A and B which can be produced at the same level of expenditure on production, TC_3. The isocost curves in Figure A-XVI(b) appear to get closer together to the northeast because the surface rises more steeply in this range.

A three-dimensional total revenue function where TR depends on the prices of A and B and the quantities of each sold,

$$TR = f(P_a, P_b, Q_a, Q_b),$$

or

$$TR = P_a \times Q_a + P_b \times Q_b,$$

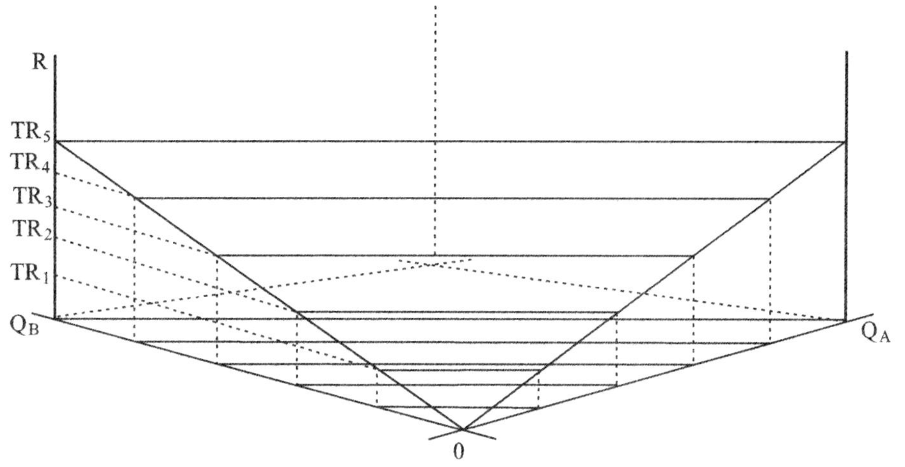

Figure A-XVI(c). A total revenue surface for two products.

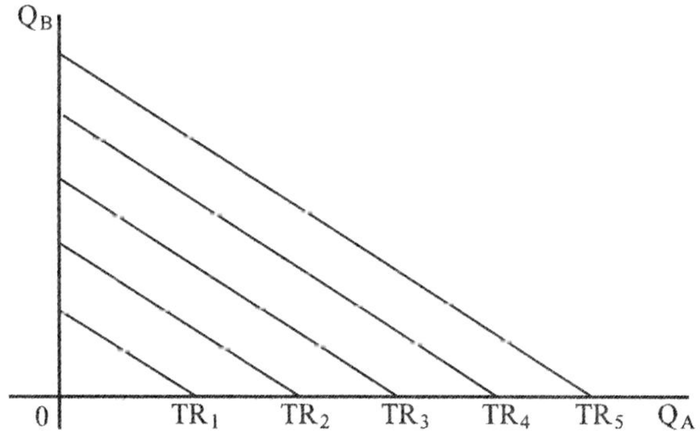

Figure A-XVI(d). An isorevenue map derived from the total revenue surface.

can be represented as in Figure A-XVI(c), assuming pure competition in both product markets (the reader might speculate on how the shape of the surface would be changed in any form of imperfect competition). When this TR surface is sliced at different altitudes (that is, levels of revenue), and the slices are projected down into the floor, this gives the appearance when viewed from above of the iso-revenue map illustrated in Figure A-XVI(d).

Given the equation of the total revenue function,

$$TR = P_a Q_a + P_b Q_b,$$

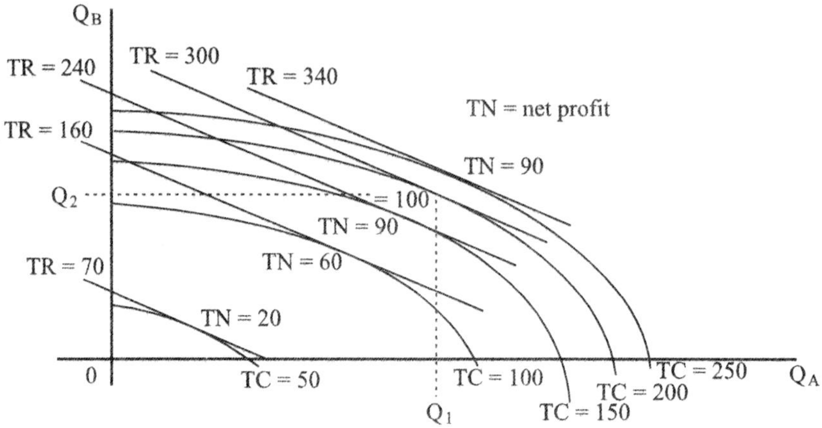

Figure A-(XVI(e). Superimposed isocost and isorevenue maps.

it may be solved for Q_a,

$$P_a Q_a = TR - P_b Q_b,$$

$$Q_a = TR/P_a - P_b/P_a \cdot Q_b,$$

which is in the slope-intercept form of a straight line with slope, $-P_b/P_a$. All of the isorevenue curves have the same slopes, determined by the prices of items A and B. The isorevenue map may be superimposed over the isocost map as depicted in Figure A-XVI(e) (or in three-dimensions the revenue surface may be shown cutting the cost surface). Because the isorevenue map is dense (that is, the revenue surface can be sliced at any and all altitudes), isorevenue curves of the same slope are drawn where needed tangent to the isocost curves. The profit can be computed at the tangency of each isocost curve with an isorevenue curve by subtracting the total cost from the total revenue. The largest profit, in this case profit = 100, occurs at the tangency of TC200 with TR300, and the coordinates of the point of tangency represent the quantities of A and B which will maximize the profits from the jointly-produced products. No point along an isocost that is not at a tangency with an isorevenue curve can yield as much profit as that realized at a tangency point.

What decision criteria can be extracted from the isorevenue-isocost analysis of jointly-produced goods? Suppose that the company is currently producing at point R, the coordinates of which represent the quantities of items A and B being produced. Although the company can reallocate its production in any direction from point R, let us suppose that it limits its changes to moving along either an isorevenue curve or an isocost curve.

If the company moves downwards along the isorevenue curve toward point T, its revenues will remain the same as it produces more of item A and less of item B, but its costs will fall (it reaches ever-lower isocost curves). If the company moves downwards along the isocost curve, its costs will remain the same while again it produces more of item A and less of item B, but its revenues will increase (it reaches higher isorevenue curves). In either case, profits will increase. We leave it to the reader to deduce what would happen to profits if the company should move upwards along either the isocost or the isorevenue curve from point R.

The slope of the isorevenue curve, P_b/P_a, measures the rate at which item A can be substituted for item B within the company's product mix while remaining at the same level of revenue. This rate will be referred to as the marginal rate of revenue substitution (MRRS) of A for B.

The slope of the isocost curve, $\text{delta}Q_b/\text{delta}Q_a$, measures the rate at which item A can be substituted for item B within the company's product mix while remaining at the same level of cost. This rate will be referred to as the marginal rate of cost substitution (MRCS) of A for B. The MRCS can further be understood by breaking the movement from R to S down into two component parts, the movement from R to U, and the movement from U to S. The movement from R to U results in a decrease of production cost, $-\text{delta}TC_b$, consequent upon a decreased output of B, $-\text{delta}Q_b$ the ratio of which measure the marginal cost of item B (assuming a smallest-possible $\text{delta}Q_b$):

$$-\text{delta}TC_b/-\text{delta}Q_b = \text{delta}TC_b/\text{delta}Q_b = MC_b$$

Likewise, the movement from U to S results in an increase in production costs, delta TC_a, as the production of item A is increased. And the ratio of the two measures the marginal cost of item A:

$$\text{delta}TC_a/\text{delta}Q_a = MC_a$$

The changes of total cost are of the same magnitude, but of opposite sign, so the subscripts on deltaTC can be ignored. Then, by algebraic manipulation it can be shown that the ratio of the two marginal costs,

$$MC_a/MC_b = (\text{delta}TC/\text{delta}Qa)/(\text{delta}TC/\text{delta}Qb) = \text{delta}Qb/\text{delta}Qa,$$

which we have already identified as the slope of the isocost, MRCS. To reiterate the significant point, the ratio of the marginal costs (MC_a/MC_b) measures the marginal rate of cost substitution.

Now a decision criterion can be specified. If the MRRS is greater than the MRCS, that is,

$$\text{MRRS} > \text{MRCS},$$

the company can increase its profits by producing more of item A and less of item B. Graphically, if the slope of the isorevenue curve (the MRRS) is steeper than the slope of the isocost curve (the MRCS), the company should produce more A and less B to increase profits (both the isocost and isorevenue curves have negative signs). The sense of this is that if the rate at which costs can be reduced while revenue remains constant (that is, by moving along the isorevenue curve) is greater than the rate at which revenue can be increased while costs remain constant (that is, by moving along the isocost curve), profits can be increased by producing more of item A and less of item B. The reader is encouraged to reread this paragraph, making appropriate alterations on the assumption of a reversal in the direction of the inequality, and starting from some point such as V in Figure A-XVI(e). These rates are not directly observable. But, with sufficient knowledge of the markets for items A and B (that is, the prices at which they can be sold) and the joint-production total cost function, all of the ingredients are available or can be computed to establish practically useable decision criteria. The marginal costs of items A and B can be found by computing the partial derivatives of the TC function, that is,

$$MC_a = dTC/dQ_a$$

and

$$MC_b = dTC/dQ_b,$$

and the ratio of the marginal costs, MC_a/MC_b, can be computed as the measure of MRCS. The MRRS can be computed as the ratio of the prices of items B and A, that is, P_a/P_a. Then, the practical decision criterion is

$$MRRS >/< MRCS$$

or

$$MC_a/MC_b >/< P_b/P_a.$$

We have shown graphically in Figure A-XVI(e) that the greatest profit is found at the tangency of an isorevenue curve with an isocost curve. This implies that when

$$MRRS = MRCS$$

a maximum-profit combination has been found, but it may be at any point along the expansion path CDEFG in Figure A-XVI(e). The manager of the company may still have to experiment with scales of operations to find the absolute maximum profit which can be realized.

—oo(O)oo—

Chapter 17

Challenges to the Theory of the Firm

Topics covered in this chapter

• Real-world use of marginal criteria. • Means of dealing with multiple goals. • Non-price decision criteria. • Implications of alternative pricing techniques.

All of the models surveyed and elaborated in previous chapters have been based upon the premise that the manager of the company will apply marginal decision criteria in the single-minded effort to maximize the company's profits. But personal experience, casual observation, and a mounting volume of empirical evidence suggest that real-world business managers often do not use marginal decision criteria. In response to survey questionnaires they typically indicate that profit is only one among several goals which command their attention. And even when profit is the dominant goal, they usually specify their objective as seeking a satisfactory return on invested capital rather than the maximum sum which it is possible to achieve. These considerations have led in some cases to doubt and scepticism about the conventional models, and in other cases to alternative approaches.

MULTIPLE GOALS

As we noted in Chapter 2, the multiple goals pursued by the managers of companies may include, in addition to profit, personal compensation, the enjoyment of perquisites ('perks'), professional and social recognition, the exertion of authority and control over human and physical resources, and the pursuit of commercial growth. The latter may be indicated by any of a wide range of quantities, including numbers of employees, invested capital, sales volume, and share of the market. A rational way to deal with multiple goals is to select one for primary pursuit, so that others can be regarded as subordinate goals. Kenneth Boulding has written about the extreme difficulty of the subordination of subordinate goals (*Management Science*, Volume 12, Number 6, February, 1966, pp. B-161–B-169). The subordinate goals can be construed as constraints upon the pursuit of the primary goal. This is the process of optimization, or constrained maximization, to which the calculus and the Lagrange multiplier may be applied.

William Baumol has developed a constrained sales maximization model which may be illustrated by the diagrams in Figure 17.1. The total profit function, TN, can be derived as the vertical difference between the total revenue, TR, and the total cost, TC, curves. Suppose that the manager treats profit as subordinate to the primary objective of maximizing sales volume. Here, a minimum satisfactory amount of profit specified by the manager can be represented by the altitude of the horizontal dashed line drawn across the total profit function. It is now possible to identify several pertinent output levels. Outputs Q_1 and Q_2 are the break-even levels; outputs below Q_1 and above Q_2 will incur losses, while any output level between these extremes will yield a positive profit. Output Q_3 is the profit-maximizing output level where the slope of the TC curve is just equal to the slope of the TR curve (that is, marginal cost is equal to marginal revenue), and the slope of the TN curve is zero. The intersection of the horizontal dashed line with the TN curve finds the output level, Q_4, which is the maximum output which can be produced and sold before profit falls below the minimum acceptable level. Using this criterion, the company can maximize sales volume subject to a minimum-profit constraint. But, suppose that the company is under the scrutiny of antitrust authority and needs to maintain a low profile. Output Q_5 is the lowest output level which is consistent with the minimum profit requirement.

Suppose that the manager is so obsessed with increasing sales volume that a loss may be tolerated, but that the maximum loss which is acceptable is represented by the depth of the dot-and-dashed horizontal line drawn below the horizontal axis. Now it is possible to recognize Q_6 as

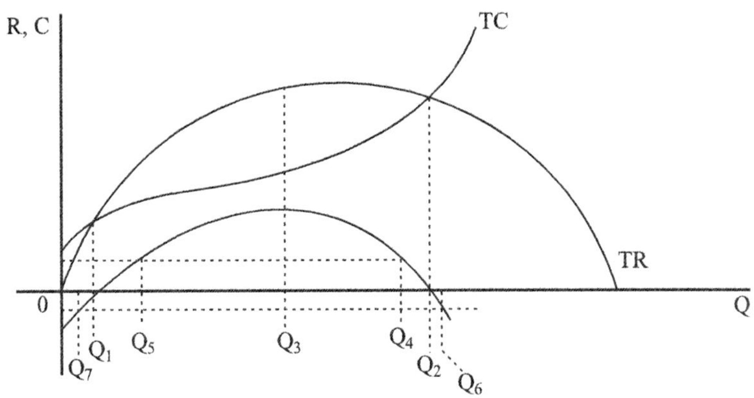

Figure 17.1. Baumol's constrained sales maximization model.

the maximum output which can be produced and sold before the incurred loss exceeds the maximum acceptable loss. And in case the low profile strategy is in effect, Q_7 is the least output which can be produced before the loss becomes unacceptably large.

The Baumol model can also be handled algebraically if the equation of the profit function is known or can be derived from known revenue and cost functions. In order to find Q_4 and Q_5 in Figure 17.1, the profit function is solved simultaneously with the minimum profit constraint expressed as an equation (alternatively, the minimum profit constraint can be substituted into the profit function to allow solving for Q). But while 'the answers' can be found using either a graphic or an algebraic approach, neither yields decision criteria which can be used to decide whether to increase or decrease output and raise or lower price (remember, if profit maximization is the objective, such a decision can be based on a comparison of marginal revenue and marginal cost). All that the manager can do is to proceed iteratively, that is, to try one output-price combination, then another, in search of the acceptable profit or loss level.

NON-MARGINAL DECISION CRITERIA

Real-world business managers rarely use the economist's ideal decision criteria, marginal revenue and marginal cost. Aside from the possibility that they may not be acquainted with the correct decision criteria, such criteria employ information which is not directly observable. Although marginal revenue and marginal cost may be inferred, estimated, or computed from observable information, the process of capturing an adequate amount of such information and generating the required decision criteria becomes progressively more difficult the more complex is the decision setting. For example, a wholesale distributor of hardware (tools, nails, screws, pipe fittings, hinges, locks, etc.) may carry 20,000 or more different items in the warehouse. It would be a heroic task to gather the required data for estimation of demand and cost functions for each and every one of the warehoused items so that marginal revenues and marginal costs could be computed.

Business managers usually respond in questionnaires that they employ an alternative pricing procedure to determine price, then sell as much of each item as they can at the set price. The alternative procedure is a rule-of-thumb approach variously known as cost-plus (variable cost plus an overhead cost/profit contribution), mark-up (from manufacturer's price), mark-down (from a 'suggested retail' price), add-on, or full-cost pricing. The usual procedure is to

(a) select a normal rate of production as some moderate proportion of plant capacity, usually between 70 and 80 per cent;

(b) estimate the per-unit direct (or variable) cost of producing the item at that production rate (for a distributor, it is the price from the manufacturer plus shipping expense); and

(c) add a standard mark-up-up as a 'profit contribution' which will cover overhead expense and allow for a net return.

This standard mark-up may have emerged as a matter of experience over an extended period of operation. It is likely to be in the neighbourhood of a conventional mark-up level used throughout the industry, but small differences may persist among competing firms. Indeed, the mode of competition in a highly-competitive industry may settle upon the percentage rate of mark-up rather than upon price *per se.* For example, in the wholesale hardware industry, it is conventional to add between 40 and 50 per cent to the manufacturer's price to get the wholesale price which is offered to retail vendors. The mark-up then must cover all of the other direct and overhead costs and allow a profit margin. But competition among wholesalers will tend to whittle the mark-ups down to the lowest level which can be sustained and allow them normal returns on their invested capital (the warehouse, handling equipment, delivery trucks, etc.). Retail vendors typically add something in the neighbourhood of 33 to 40 per cent to the wholesaler's price to get their retail prices. Small variations of retail prices among competing retail vendors who buy from the very same vendor can be accounted for by their differential mark-ups applied to the vendor's price.

A variant of this approach which is more appropriate to manufacturing than to wholesale or retail distribution is 'full-cost' pricing. The objective here is to fully allocate all overhead costs to the various items in production. This is no problem in the single-product firm: all overhead (that is, fixed) costs go to the single product, and are then 'spread' across all of the units produced. However, in a multi-product company, since there is no objective way to allocate overhead expenses among the company's product lines, the allocation process becomes highly arbitrary. A typical approach is to use as allocation shares the percentage of the company's gross revenues accounted for by each item.

To illustrate how full-cost pricing is accomplished, suppose that the direct production cost for a particular item is $ 4.17 per unit, and that the item's share of overhead expense (however arbitrarily allocated) divided by the number of units of the item produced (the method of 'spreading the overhead') is $ 6.37. The sum of the per-unit direct and overhead expenses is thus $ 10.54. Then, an additional mark-up to allow for profit, say 25 per cent or $ 2.63, is added to establish the final price of $ 13.17. The manager then may 'psychologically price' the item at $ 12.99 or $ 13.49.

An extension of this mark-up pricing approach may illustrate the satisficing hypothesis advanced by Herbert Simon ('Theories of Decision Making in Economics and Behavioral Science,' *American Economic Review*, volume 49, number 3, June 1959, pp. 253-280). According to Simon, many business managers do not attempt to maximize profit in any absolute sense. Rather, they try only to realize a satisfactory level of profit, usually expressed as a target rate of return (TROR) on invested capital. In the previous example, the 25 per cent mark-up to allow for profit was stipulated only arbitrarily. Suppose that the company has $ 1 million dollars invested in its plant and equipment for producing the item, and expects to produce 50,000 units of the item per year at 75 per cent of capacity. If the company targets a 10 per cent return on investment, then it must realize a profit of $ 100,000 per annum, which when divided by the 50,000 units means that the mark-up allowance for profit should be $ 2 per unit. The price which will then satisfice with respect to the TROR requirement is $ 12.54.

AN ASSESSMENT OF NON-MARGINAL PRICING PRACTICES

From the perspective of the economist, any sort of mark-up or full-cost pricing technique is inappropriate to the goal of profit maximization. The reason is that it is based exclusively upon costs. The demand side of the relationship is completely ignored. No elasticity conditions or

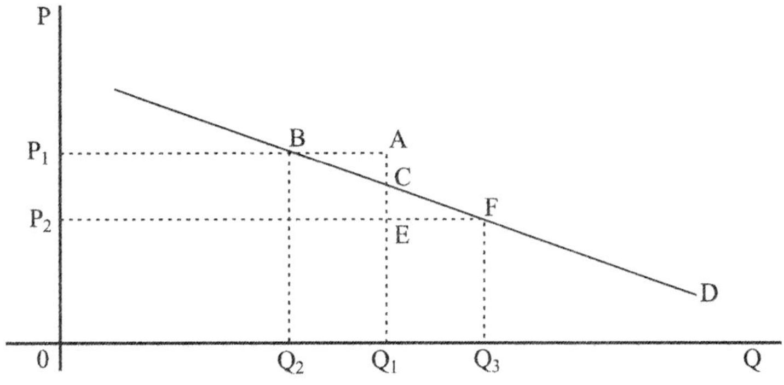

Figure 17.2. Pricing without regard to demand conditions.

competitive pressures are recognized by such procedures. The danger in employing such one-sided pricing techniques can be illustrated in Figure 17.2. Here the manager first selects a normal output, say Q_1, as the 75 per cent of plant capacity, then sums the per-unit direct and overhead costs, and finally adds a profit-contribution mark-up to arrive at a target price. Suppose that the full-cost price is P_1, such that the coordinates (Q_1, P_1) find point A. Since no consideration has been given to demand conditions, represented by the demand curve D, it would be purely coincidental for point A to lie on the demand curve.

As illustrated in Figure 17.2, point A lies above the demand curve. If the company insists on trying to sell the Q_1 output at full-cost price P_1, it will suffer an inventory accumulation of Q_1- Q_2. Alternately, if the full-cost price happens to be P_2, the coordinates (Q_1, P_2) find point E which lies below the demand curve. If the company insists on trying to sell output Q_1 at price P_2, an inventory depletion of Q_3– Q_1 will result if indeed the company has that much of the item in inventory. If not, then an opportunity-loss occurs due to the lost sales. In either case, the manager will have to abandon the full-cost price in order to relieve the ensuing inventory problem. Or, if the company is competing in an industry characterized by price followership, it may have to abandon the full-cost price if another company prefers a lower price.

Mark-up competition often emerges as the primary vehicle for recognizing competitive pressures. Sale prices and discounts become the means for recognizing price elasticity differentials among products or between geographic markets.

Phenomena such as these lead many economists to conclude that non-marginal pricing techniques eventually result in the same (or nearly the same) prices which would have been established had the marginal pricing criteria been employed. This conclusion is most pertinent to successful companies, that is, those which have survived over the 'long-haul.' The rule-of-thumb approaches, though clearly suboptimal in a theoretical sense, are lower-cost means of getting to the same conclusion which could have been reached only at the greater expense of modelling and statistical estimation.

Should we throw out the theoretical models based on marginal decision criteria in pursuit of profit maximization? Not if Professor Friedman is correct: what matters is that managers behave *as if* they utilize the marginal decision criteria.

Summary of Important Points

1. A rational way to deal with multiple goals is to select one for primary pursuit and regard subordinate goals as constraints.
2. Business managers rarely use marginal decision criteria in any explicit sense; evidence indicates that the process of capturing adequate information for computing marginal values is prohibitively costly.
3. Alternative pricing procedures may include cost-plus and full-cost pricing techniques; these procedures may approximate satisficing behaviour.
4. The principal objection to alternative pricing procedures is that they disregard the demand side of the market.
5. Mark-up competition among firms may lead to an approximation of marginal revenue-marginal cost pricing.

Significant Terms

marginal decision criteria

primary, subordinate goals

optimization

non-marginal decision criteria

mark-up pricing

full-cost pricing

profit contribution

overhead allocation

psychological pricing

satisficing

target return

mark-up competition

marginal rates of revenue, cost substitution

Questions for Discussion

1. Why have doubts and scepticism arisen about the conventional theoretical models of the firm?
2. How can a multiplicity of goals be rationally dealt with by the management of a business firm?

3. Discuss the role which profit plays in Baumol's constrained sales maximization model.
4. Identify conditions under which the management of a firm might deliberately choose not to try to maximize the firm's profit; in each case what is the relevant decision criterion?
5. Explain why marginal decision criteria may not be useable when the objective of the firm is to pursue some goal other than profit maximization.
6. Explain why real-world business decision makers rarely attempt to use marginal decision criteria in any explicit sense.
7. Describe the most commonly-used non-marginal decision criteria which business decision makers in the real world seem to employ.
8. How is a 'standard mark-up' usually determined by real-world business price makers?
9. How may small differences in retail prices of the same (or similar) items offered by different firms be explained?
10. Why would an economist likely recommend against a full-cost pricing technique to be used by a firm in pricing its products?
11. Describe the TROR pricing technique employed by some firms in determining the prices of the products which they sell; why would an economist judge this technique to be inappropriate?
12. Why do some economists conclude that non-marginal pricing techniques may result in approximately the same prices which would have emerged had marginal pricing criteria been employed?
13. If the use of non-marginal pricing techniques can achieve approximately the same prices as can marginal pricing techniques, what is the justification for continuing to use theoretical marginal pricing models?

—oo(O)oo—

Chapter 18

Ethical Dimensions of Managerial Decisions

ETHICS IN MANAGEMENT

Ethical dimensions of managerial decision making were not much discussed prior to the late twentieth century, perhaps because discussion of them might betray the existence of problems. There are now both management textbooks and management courses with titles containing the term 'ethics.' Of course, there really is no such thing as a particular variety of ethics peculiar to the managerial decision setting. The discussion should be not about ethics in the generic sense, but as applied to managerial decision settings.

Managerial decision making involves complex interactions between producers and consumers, employers and employees, managers and owners, business executives and members of the communities in which their firms operate. While these relationships are essentially economic in nature, they also have ethical dimensions. Some of these dimensions include the work environment, the effects of pollution and depletion of natural resources, and the safety of consumers.

Managerial decision making, whether in the profit, not-for-profit, or public sectors, must be based upon moral foundations if relationships are to be reliable and predictable. Nonetheless, we hear and read of a variety of practices in both public and private sectors which most people would judge to be unethical, among them bribery, embezzlement, breaking contracts, price fixing, collusion, deceptive advertising, falsification of expense accounts, underreporting of income or padding of expenses on tax reports, use of substandard materials, producing and selling products which fail to function as advertised, failing to divulge to consumers possible product dangers, and so on. Any of these behaviours may erode the moral foundation of commerce and make business activity both unreliable and unpredictable.

In the private sector, the pursuit of **profit** has traditionally been viewed as the chief motivation to engage in productive activity. The pursuit of profit cannot be regarded as a morally neutral activity because the receipt of profit income may lead to inequality in the distribution of income between those who are entrepreneurially successful and those who are not or who do not choose to behave in an entrepreneurial fashion.

A challenge to the legitimacy and authority of privately owned and managed business enterprise has emerged in the United States during the second half of the twentieth century. The challenge focuses upon the legitimacy of business, its right to exist, and the right of people to own and use business property to their own private benefit. Statistical evidence in support of this contention is implicit in numerous surveys and polls which indicate that many Americans believe that the ethical standards of business are lower than those of American society as a whole.

A FRAMEWORK FOR THINKING ABOUT ETHICS

In order to provide a framework for thinking about ethics in managerial decision contexts, it will be convenient to employ a classification scheme provided by W. Michael Hoffman and Jennifer Mills Moore in *Business Ethics: Readings and Cases in Corporate Morality* (McGraw-Hill, Inc., New York, U.S.A., 1990).

In simplest terms, **morality** may be defined as what is good or right for human beings. **Ethics** involves choices in regard to moral precepts. A choice may be ethical or unethical depending upon whether behavioural rules are obeyed, or whether the choice yields good or right outcomes for those who are parties to the decision, and perhaps also for 'innocent third parties.' Hoffman and Moore identify three ethical orientations which cover most of the positions which can be taken by business decision makers.

1. **Ethical relativism** is the position that there is no one universal standard or set of standards by which to judge the morality of an action. An ethical relativist may hold the same act to be morally right for one society, but morally wrong for another. A similar distinction may be applied to two individuals within the same society. An act which is taken to be moral in one set of circumstances may be regarded as immoral in another (situational ethics). A problem of ethical relativism is that each person's ethics are specific to the person; no comparative moral judgements are possible. An ethical relativist may base morality upon social customs and conventions. Students of international business often are urged to adopt a polycentric world view (tolerance and appreciation for cultures alien to one's own) incorporating ethical relativism. 'When in Rome, do as the Romans do,' even if it involves engaging in acts that would be unacceptable at home (like paying bribes).
2. At the opposite end of the ethical spectrum from ethical relativism is **ethical absolutism**. Ethical absolutists believe in the existence of universal standards of ethical behaviour. For Immanuel Kant (1724-1804), ethical criteria were 'categorical imperatives' in the sense that they are absolute and unconditional, irrespective of the consequences. Examples of Judeo-Christian scriptural dictums which may serve as categorical imperatives include those found in the Ten Commandments

(for example, prohibition against stealing and lying), scriptures relating to oppression (see the accompanying essay on 'Exploitation'), the Golden Rule ('Do unto others as you would have them do unto you'), and Jesus' command to love one's neighbour as oneself (Matthew 19:19, 22:39; Mark 12:31, 33; Luke 10:27). Religious fundamentalists of the late twentieth century, whether Moslem, Jew, or Christian, would perhaps be most comfortable with categorical imperatives in the form of scriptural dictums to guide their behaviour.

3. The intermediate range of the ethical spectrum is occupied by a variety of positions which focus upon the outcomes of behaviour. **Consequentialism** is the belief that the consequences of an action are the sole bases for judging whether an action is right or wrong. For a consequentialist there is no universal standard of ethical behaviour; any action which yields a desirable outcome can be rationalized as ethical. For a consequentialist the end justifies the means as ethical, or if it is an undesirable end, the end indicts the means as unethical.

CONSEQUENTIALIST POSITIONS

Consequentialism dichotomizes into ethical egoism and utilitarianism. **Ethical egoism** is the belief that every person ought always to act so as to promote the greatest possible balance of good over evil *for himself*. Therefore, an act contrary to one's self interest is an unethical act. Ethical egoists can argue that others' interests should be respected because treating others well also promotes their own self interest in the long run. The Golden Rule is not incompatible with ethical egoism.

In contrast to ethical egoism, **utilitarianism** holds that people ought to act so as to promote the greatest total balance of good over evil, or the greatest good for the greatest number. A **rule utilitarian** would obey those rules which experience has shown generally promote social welfare, even when doing so does not always lead to good consequences. An **act utilitarian** may hold that one ought to act so as to maximize total good even if doing so violates rules which usually promote social welfare.

Milton Friedman in *Essays in Positive Economics* (The University of Chicago Press, Chicago, U.S.A., 1953) raises an interesting question in regard to means and ends: If the end does not justify the means, then what does? He goes on to suggest that if a person is serious in raising this question, for him the means are actually a more important end than the end which had been contemplated. We may infer that such a person is less likely to be an act utilitarian than a rule utilitarian or a categorical imperativist.

We may infer that some variety of consequentialism must underlie the rationale of any dictator who assumes absolute political authority. A society which finds itself with a dictator can only hope him or her to be a benevolent act utilitarian rather than an autocrat who is an ethical egoist. Likewise, societies with democratic polities should attempt to elect act utilitarians rather than ethical egoists. Act utilitarianism is perhaps the ethical orientation most consistent with the pragmatism of late-twentieth century American social and political liberalism. Late twentieth-century Christians who are religious liberals might tend towards rule utilitarianism, whereas Christian fundamentalists are more likely to be categorical imperativists.

While numerous scriptural references imply care for other members of society, there do not appear to be any explicit scriptural dictums which are congruent with act utilitarianism. Although Cain's question in Genesis 4:9 ('Am I my brother's keeper?') went unanswered, an affirmative answer often is adduced to it. A liberal translation of 'brother' to refer to all of humanity would seem to suggest an act utilitarian orientation. In Luke 10:29, a lawyer asks Jesus, 'And who is my neighbour?" Jesus replies with the story of the Good Samaritan which concludes that the neighbour is the one who showed mercy to the injured man. Although never stated explicitly, the implication is that 'neighbour" refers to anyone encountered, and in the limit all of humanity. The latter interpretation implies an act utilitarian ethical orientation.

In 1776, Adam Smith (who trained as a moral philosopher) tied ethical egoism and utilitarianism together when he asserted (in *The Wealth of Nations*) that pursuit of self-interest by each member of society may contribute more to the common weal (welfare) than the individual either knows or intends.

THE ROLE OF JUSTICE IN ETHICS

The concept of justice plays an important role in ethical considerations in American society. **Procedural justice** is achieved when appropriate procedures are employed, as for example when universal rules are obeyed. However, the use of just procedures may not yield desirable results. The Golden Rule, 'Do unto others as you would have them do unto you,' is an example of a categorical imperative which would achieve procedural justice, but which may not result in desirable consequences if others choose not to reciprocate.

Distributive justice is achieved when benefits and burdens of economic activity are distributed fairly, but this begs a question of what constitutes **fairness**. The egalitarian notion of distributive justice is an equal (or as nearly equal as possible) distribution of benefit and burden. Non-egalitarians may hold that fairness is achieved when the benefits and burdens are distributed on the basis of some specific criterion, such as need, merit, effort, hard work, or contribution to society.

The principle of justice underlying American capitalism has tended to emphasize contribution to society recognized by market demand as the criterion for judging the fairness and hence the justice of distribution. Americans typically have not expected everyone to end up with an equal share of benefits and burdens; rather, those who receive more do so because of their greater contribution.

ETHICAL ORIENTATIONS OF MANAGERIAL DECISION MAKERS

It can be argued that managerial decision makers must behave relatively more ethically than less so in order to ensure continuance and reliability of commercial relationships. Are managerial decision makers, by training, social conditioning, or innate character (among those who select themselves into commercial occupations), inclined to be ethical relativists, ethical egoists, utilitarians, or categorical imperativists? We are likely to find some of each kind in any walk of life, including commerce. A pure speculation is that the for-profit sector has a natural attraction for ethical egoists. Those who are intimately engaged in international business operations probably become drawn to ethical relativism. Managers who are professing Christians are more likely to be rule utilitarians or categorical imperativists. Social liberals who are act utilitarians are likely to be drawn into public sector managerial settings or politics.

Although American business interests may be characterized by egoism as a predominant guiding principle of their ethics, Adam Smith's premise that there often is a convergence of private interest with the public weal goes a long way towards explaining why some may engage in actions which serve their own self interests while at the same time engaging in rhetoric to the effect that they are also contributing to the public welfare. Whether there is reality beyond the rhetoric is subject to scrutiny and debate. This issue is made more obscure because some in the non-business public take self-righteous positions in criticizing the apparently self-serving actions of American business decision makers.

SOCIAL RESPONSIBILITY

In the last couple of decades, the American business community has given the appearance of becoming more socially aware and responsible. This may be a manifestation of the quest for legitimacy in the face of the challenge to the power and authority wielded by business executives. Many businesses have created and displayed business ethics statements. Some have gone to great lengths to indoctrinate their employees to act upon the tenants of their company ethics statements. For others such statements may be little more than marketing ploys. To the extent that business executives take their corporate ethics statements seriously and back them up with civic generosity and ethical behaviour, this suggests that they are becoming less egoistic and more utilitarian in ethical orientation.

—oo(O)oo—

Chapter **19**

The Role of the Government

Topics covered in this chapter

• The significance of the type of economic system. • Legitimate roles for the state. • The mission of the not-for-profit organization. • The applicability of managerial decision criteria in the not-for-profit sector. • The implications of the budget constraint. • Managerial performance incentives and linkage in the not-for-profit sector. • Problems of bureaucracy. • Benefit-cost analysis and marginal decision criteria. • The problem of subjectivity in analysis. • Points of contact between the firm and the government. • Threats and opportunities in the involvement of government in the economy. • Rationales for governmental involvement in the economy. • Managerial implications of relationships with government.

We have made numerous allusions in previous chapters to the interrelations between the firm and the government. Our purpose in this chapter is to delve into these relationships, but our task is made all the more interesting and challenging by the recent events transpiring in Eastern Europe, the former Soviet Union, China, and other parts of the world where socialism has been the predominant form of economic organization for a half century or more.

FORMS OF ECONOMIC SYSTEMS

The nature of the relationship between the microeconomic productive unit (that is, the 'firm' in our previous discussions) and the state depends critically upon the form of economic system in place in society. Although it is possible to identify a wide range of economic system types (including communalism, tribalism, feudalism, and traditionalism), we shall limit consideration to the three which seem to be most pertinent to circumstances of the modern world: socialism, capitalism, and fascism.

In the extreme form of authoritarian socialism, the microeconomic productive unit may be little more than an appendage of the state. Indeed, there is little point in making distinctions among micromanagement (that is, the management of the productive unit), industrial organization and policy, and the macro-management (that is, the implementation of macro-policy) of the entire economy. They are all tied up together. For all intents and purposes, there is virtually no freedom of enterprise in authoritarian socialism.

Efforts at centralized and authoritarian direction of the economy seem to have revealed inefficiencies almost everywhere they have been tried. However, societies employing such forms of economic organization seem to be backing away from them in favour of capitalism. Capitalism is distinguished by private ownership of productive resources which are organized by markets. Rather than being highly centralized, decision making in capitalism is widely dispersed to the managements of a myriad of microeconomic productive units, that is, individuals and the firms or enterprises which compose the economy.

In most forms of capitalism there is a cleavage between the microeconomic productive units and the state which functions as government. In the purest form of capitalism, the state owns no productive resources and engages in no productive activity. Its role is closely circumscribed to providing a legal and social environment which is hospitable to the functioning of the private economy. By the same token, the privately-owned productive units have no significant governing responsibility or authority, but they enjoy a maximum of freedom of enterprise. It is these entities which have been the focus of managerial economic analysis thus far in this text.

Between the extremes of authoritarian socialism and pure capitalism is possible a wide range of governmental productive activity as well as the use of market mechanisms in conjunction with central planning. The terms 'mixed capitalism' and 'mixed socialism' are used to describe these intermediate forms of economic organization. The exercise of decision-making authority by the managers of enterprises depends critically upon the nature of the relationship between their organizations and the government.

Fascism is a curious combination of the characteristics of socialism and capitalism. Resources remain privately owned as in capitalism, but the state (often in the form of a dictatorship) exercises centralized authority to impose production quotas to be met by the privately-owned enterprises. In fascism, freedom of enterprise is severely restricted. Although fascism has an infamous twentieth-century history, the most prominent examples of it have been eliminated from the world scene. But there almost certainly are examples of functional fascism in today's 'third world.' And some Western societies are experimenting with a softer variant, statism, which involves increasing willingness to rely upon the powers of the state to treat social, political, and economic problems.

THE APPLICABILITY OF MANAGERIAL DECISION CRITERIA

The managerial economic principles and decision criteria elaborated in earlier chapters have been postulated for the context of privately-owned, profit-motivated business enterprises operating within market capitalism. It is not clear that these principles and criteria are also applicable to microeconomic production units in a centrally planned and directed economy. Nor is it clear that they can apply to governmental departments and their subdivisions and agencies, or to organizations in the not-for-profit sector of a market economy (churches, charitable organizations, educational institutions, health-care organizations, etc.). These are similar in that while each is oriented towards pursuit of some mission, that mission is not to realize the maximum possible amount of net income. It therefore appears that decision criteria which are postulated for profit-oriented firms may not be applicable to not-for-profit organizations.

One problem is that in both the government agency and the not-for-profit sector, the financial requirement is simply to remain within budget (that is, a budgetary non-negativity constraint), rather than to maximize profit (net revenue). A similar constraint usually is imposed upon a factory in a centrally-planned economy. However, this is not unlike satisficing, that is, the pursuit of a target return on invested capital, in the for-profit sector of a market economy as originally hypothesized by Herbert Simon. In the government agency and the not-for-profit organization, the target return is simply zero rather than some positive net amount. If for-profit business firm managers can target some (any) positive amount of net income (rather than try to realize the maximum possible), it should be feasible for the managers of not-for-profit organizations to employ the same decision criteria in pursuit of a zero or non-negative return. Zero should be as good a target as some positive amount.

In Chapter 4 we examined the thesis that managers of some for-profit business firms may attempt to optimize rather than maximize with respect to profit. Optimization (elaborated in Chapter 7) means maximization of a primary goal subject to one or more constraints which are imposed by the existence of subsidiary goals. William Baumol hypothesized that many managers, instead of attempting to achieve the maximum possible profit, actually pursue some non-profit goal, for example, sales volume or share of market, subject to a minimum acceptable profit constraint (for example, a target return on invested capital). The Baumol model is elaborated in Chapter 17

In the not-for-profit sector, the organization always has some mission to accomplish or some goal to pursue. Often the mission or goal can be expressed in some quantifiable but non-pecuniary form. For example, in a charitable organization such as the Salvation Army, the mission may be to provide the most welfare services (meals, shelter, etc.) to constituents while not over-expending the budget. The manager of a (former) Soviet factory may be required to meet an output quota imposed by the central plan while remaining within the factory's budget. These are fairly straightforward applications of the Baumol thesis taking the minimum acceptable amount of profit as zero (that is, no loss or negative profit).

Production units in centrally planned economies and not-for-profit organizations in market economies are notorious for inefficient operation in the sense that costs tend to be excessive and goal achievement seems to be deficient in comparison to comparable for-profit enterprises. A significant problem in these situations is that it is very difficult to provide the manager with performance incentives. It is also difficult to link the process of mission pursuit to any factor which constitutes a performance incentive for the manager. This linkage often is achieved in the for-profit sector of the market economy by letting the manager share in the net income of the enterprise (bonuses, stock options). But this is a problem of linkage, not a problem of the applicability of managerial decision criteria.

A final problem which we shall note is that of organizational bureaucracy. Typically there are several levels of management in any complex organization. The managerial decision criteria which we have described in earlier chapters are most appropriately employed at the highest level of managerial policy making where the managers can take a view which oversees the whole enterprise. These principles may be of lesser applicability at any intermediate level within the bureaucracy where the department or division-level manager (bureaucrat) can see and exercise control over only the few variables associated with the department. But bureaucracy is no less a problem for the corporation in the for-profit sector than for a charitable organization in the not-for-profit sector or the factory in a centrally planned economy.

The conclusion to which we have been moving is that the managerial decision criteria elaborated in earlier chapters should be applicable to decision making in not-for-profit organizations and government agencies, but there are other problems of performance-incentive linkage and bureaucracy which must be dealt with.

BENEFIT-COST ANALYSIS

If the principal objective of a not-for-profit organization is to maximize some aspect of its non-pecuniary mission, the marginal comparison criteria applied in the for-profit sector to revenues and costs should be equally applicable in the not-for-profit sector to the quantifiable characteristics of the mission being pursued. 'Benefit-cost' analysis may provide decision criteria for the organization manager in the government and not-for-profit sectors. The sum of all benefits (non-pecuniary as well as revenue) resulting from mission pursuit constitutes the numerator, B, of the benefit-cost ratio. Its denominator, C, consists of the sum of all costs (non-pecuniary as well as pecuniary) incurred in pursuing the mission. If the value of the ratio is a number greater than unity (that is, $B/C > 1$), then the activity under analysis is justifiable; any benefit-cost ratio less than unity (that is, $B/C < 1$) suggests that the activity is unwarranted.

Simple benefit-cost analysis has been extended to the concept of marginal benefit-cost analysis. This version is applicable to situations where the question is whether to do more or less of the activity which is already in progress. The numerator of the marginal benefit-cost ratio includes only the additional benefits which are expected to flow from some increment of the activity; the denominator sums only the increased costs incurred by the activity increment. The same decision criterion holds for the marginal as for the simple benefit-cost ratio: a value greater than unity warrants the activity increment while a value less than unity indicates that the activity increment should not be undertaken. While marginal benefit-cost analysis has been used most often as a decision criterion in the not-for-profit sector, it is apparent that the for-profit criteria of marginal revenue and marginal costs are special cases of marginal benefits and costs where the benefits and costs are pecuniary values (or equivalents).

Both simple and marginal benefit-cost analyses are subject to bias and fraught with the potential for abuse. The bias follows from the requirement to include all benefits (psychic and other non-pecuniary benefits as well as any revenues resulting from the activity) and all relevant costs (non-pecuniary psychic and opportunity costs as well as explicit money costs). The problem is that a decision maker who has a predisposition favouring a proposed activity tends to exhaustively identify all possible benefits and also tends to overestimate their money value equivalents. A decision maker with such a predisposition also tends to be more casual about identifying the relevant costs, and may also be inclined to underestimate their money value equivalents. By the same token, a decision maker with a predisposition against an activity tends to do the opposite, that is, to casually overlook some benefits and underestimate the values of those identified, while exhaustively finding all relevant costs and carefully estimating their full money-value equivalents. Because of the subjectivity involved, it is entirely possible for two decision makers, confronted by precisely the same prospects and with the same information, to estimate widely divergent benefit-cost ratios and reach opposite decisions about whether to proceed with the activity.

POINTS OF CONTACT BETWEEN THE FIRM AND THE GOVERNMENT

Because capitalism (or market economy) is the form of economic organization to which the world seems to be drawn, we shall presume its general characteristics in subsequent discussion of the role of government. Given this presumption, there are six principal points of contact between firms and the government.

1. Along with other entities in the economy, the government is a demander of goods and services from private-sector business firms; that is, firms function as suppliers to the government. Since the government is likely to be the single largest economic entity in any economy, the prospect of supplying the government should provide market opportunities for a great many firms in the economy. However, firms seeking to function as suppliers to government should beware of becoming too highly dependent upon government orders.
2. Firms pay taxes to the government. The taxes may be related to the firms' profits, their sales, their inventories or other assets, or the wages which they pay to their employees. Tax-related record keeping and reporting often become burdensome to business firms, and tax liabilities and rates are subject to change at the dictatorial or parliamentary whims of the state.
3. Depending upon the government's particular political, social, and military programmes, various firms in the economy may become objects of support by the government. Such support may take the forms of subsidies, approval of licences, preferential contracts, or other encouragements. The government may attempt to structure such activity as a coherent industrial policy for the promotion of international competitiveness of domestic companies.
4. In pursuit of its agenda, government's interests in firms may extend beyond support to efforts to control the activities of firms. Objects of governmental controls may include directions of research and development efforts, determination of product mixes and item specifications, selection of capital investment alternatives, eligibilities for import or export licences, and employment practices. These activities may become elements in a more comprehensive industrial policy.
5. The private sector may become an object of regulation by the government in the interest of employees, consumers, or other interests in the economy. Such regulation almost always imposes additional costs upon business firms, and consequently squeezes profits or results in higher market prices.

6. And finally, the private sector may become the object of efforts either to promote and encourage competition, or to stifle or prevent competition. In the former case, 'antitrust' or 'anti-monopolies' laws may be enacted and enforced; in the latter case the government may become the prime mover in the effort to 'rationalize' or cartelize industry (also a possible component of industrial policy).

In their extreme manifestations, points (1) and (4) above may devolve to the characteristics of fascism. We may also note that the government can effect a ready transformation to the characteristics of socialism simply by nationalizing private-sector firms so that they become government-owned and directed enterprises. Our purpose in making these observations and otherwise identifying the various points of contact between firms and the government is to note that the operation of government in a capitalistic economy may pose threats to private sector firms as well as provide opportunities which they may attempt to exploit.

RATIONALES FOR GOVERNMENTAL INVOLVEMENT IN THE MARKET ECONOMY

The most fundamental role for government to play in the market economy is the maintenance of an environment which is hospitable to the functioning of market economy and the exercise of entrepreneurship. At very minimum this means establishing the rules for holding, transferring, and arbitrating disputes over the possession of private property, determining weights and measures, providing a stable money supply, ensuring the sanctity of contracts, and otherwise maintaining law and order. John Stuart Mill during the nineteenth century referred to these minimal roles for government as the 'night-watchman' functions.

Beyond the night-watchman functions are four other significant rationales for governmental involvement in the market economy: to maintain competition, to reallocate resources, to redistribute incomes, and to stabilize the economy. Each of these rationales is founded upon some fault, shortcoming, or failure in the functioning of the market.

From this perspective it may be noted that any problem in the functioning of a market may invite some response from government to address the perceived problem. And if market mechanisms exhibit traumatic failure or become fundamentally distrusted by the political leadership of the society, these constitute the rationales for shifting to fascism by conferring product-mix decision making upon a central authority, or to socialism by nationalizing privately-owned productive resources and imposing central planning and direction. By the same token, failure of authoritarian socialism constitutes the rationale for shifting from authoritarian control to some form of market economy. It appears that this latter phenomenon is being widely experienced in Eastern Europe even as some economies of the West experiment with more statist orientations.

THE MAINTENANCE OF COMPETITIVE CONDITIONS

Viable competition among business firms in each market is the *sine qua non* of market capitalism. It is competition which ensures that firms efficiently produce only those goods and services demanded by the consumers of the society. But there is an inherent divergence of interest between the firms in an industry and their customers. Although customers surely benefit from adequate competition (lower prices, higher quality merchandise, greater product variety), firms might achieve greater profits in cooperation with each other or as sole monopolists of their respective markets.

Firm managements find incentive to attempt to achieve monopoly by internal growth, acquisition of competitors, or engaging in practices to destroy the abilities of competitors to effectively compete. If the achievement of monopoly is blocked by public policy (for example, antitrust law and its effective enforcement), they may attempt to cartelize the industry. If cartelization is prevented, firms may attempt to collude with competitors to set prices or allocate sources of materials or markets. If all of these avenues are blocked, the firms in an industry may engage in price leadership-followership behaviour. Each of these behaviour patterns is discussed in Chapter 11.

Governments of democratic societies then find rationale to undertake the promotion and preservation of competitive conditions in their economies. This is usually done by enacting legislation which declares the existence of monopoly to be unlawful (in the U.S.A. this is accomplished by Section 1 of the Sherman Antitrust Act) and the perpetrator of monopoly to be guilty of an unlawful act (Sherman, Section 2), or which enumerates specific acts or activities which diminish competition and which are thus unlawful (the Clayton, Robinson-Patman, and Wheeler-Lea acts). But the enactment of legislation alone is not enough. The government must further establish an enforcement authority (in the U.S.A., the Federal Trade Commission and the Antitrust Division of the Department of Justice) and resolve to make effective the enforcement of the relevant legislation. This resolve may differ significantly according to the political party in office and the particular agenda which it is attempting to implement.

The managerial implications of the determined enforcement of laws which are intended to preserve and maintain competition are that managers of business firms must make themselves knowledgeable of the pertinent laws, and they must make calculated judgements as to whether to risk violating such laws in any of their sourcing, producing, or marketing activities. It may also be worthwhile to note that in a society governed by law (as is the U.S.A.), innocence is presumed until guilt has been established. The significance of this is that no act undertaken by the management of a business firm is necessarily in violation of the law until it has been tested in the courts.

In a legal environment of presumed innocence, even though a law may declare a certain act unlawful and other firms engaging in the act have been indicted and successfully prosecuted, the act may be repeated by yet another firm. In order for the firm to be penalized under the law, the act must be detected, indicted by an appropriate legal authority, and successfully prosecuted in court. Because failure may occur at any of these stages, the management of a firm may behave rationally to assess the probability of detection, the probability of indictment if detected, the probability of successful prosecution if indicted, and the magnitude of the penalty if found guilty under the law. Then if the 'expected value' of the penalty (that is, the conditional probabilities multiplied by the likely penalty) is judged small enough, the management may deliberately assume the risks of detection and prosecution by engaging in the act. Indeed, it is not uncommon for business firms to maintain legal staffs or contingency funds to cover legal fees and any penalties which are actually assessed.

Two cautionary notes are appropriate at this point. First, even though the behaviour described in the paragraph above may be rational, the reader should not take this acknowledgement as an advocacy of the assumption of risk in knowingly breaking the law. And second, although the liability of corporate shareholders is limited to their investment in the firm, corporate managers should beware of the possibility of both criminal prosecution and civil liability suits when their firms have been found guilty of violation of the law.

RATIONALES FOR REALLOCATION, REDISTRIBUTION, AND STABILIZATION

We shall devote Chapter 15 to the governmental rationale for reallocating resources in the economy. Suffice it to say at this point that the rationale is based upon the conclusion that the particular allocation of resources resulting from the normal functioning of the market economy is not satisfactory and needs adjustment. This conclusion may emerge if there are so-called 'public goods' desired by society but not producible in response to market incentives, or if there are positive or negative externalities (or 'spillovers') resulting from the market production of goods or services. The managerial implication of this rationale is that declining profits or losses will likely emerge in industries from which resources are diverted, but profitable opportunities should be found in industries towards which resources are reallocated.

The income redistribution rationale follows from a social and political judgement that incomes are being inequitably distributed across the population of the society by the normal functioning of the market economy. There is little doubt that any market economy distributes incomes unequally because of the fundamental reward mechanism of capitalism: to each according to his or her contribution to the process of production of demanded goods and services. Since members of any population possess differential abilities and experience varying intensities of drive and motivation, there will occur different contributions to the production process, and as a consequence an unequal distribution of income.

Social action becomes warranted only when it is judged that the inequality of distribution is also inequitable. The governmental vehicles for redistribution include progressivity of income and profits taxation, the taxation of capital appreciation, and any of a wide range of possible transfer payments. One managerial implication of governmental redistribution is that business net incomes, assets, and wages paid are likely to be objects of taxation to raise revenue for redistribution to lower-income members of society. Another is that businesses catering to transfer recipient clienteles may benefit from the redistributions. However, there may be little hope for managements of business firms to exert significant control or influence upon the political process which determines how incomes are to be redistributed.

THE GOVERNMENT'S POTENTIAL FOR STABILIZING THE ECONOMY

The rationale for bringing the offices of government to bear upon the stability of the economy is based upon the view that market economies are naturally unstable, that the degree of instability is intolerable, and that some force must be applied to counteract the natural instability of the market economy. Of course, the only entity in the economy which can possibly bring enough force to bear upon the problem of instability is the government.

Summary of Important Points

1. The relationship between the firm and the government, which depends critically upon the form of economic system in place, is changing in various parts of the world.
2. In the extreme of authoritarian socialism, the microeconomic productive unit may be little more than an appendage of the state with virtually no freedom of enterprise.
3. Capitalism, in place through much of the Western world, is distinguished by private ownership of productive resources which are organized by markets.
4. In the purest form of capitalism, the role of the state is circumscribed to providing a legal and social environment which is hospitable to the functioning of the private economy.
5. Between the extremes of authoritarian socialism and pure capitalism is a wide range of governmental productive activity as well as the use of market mechanisms in conjunction with central planning.
6. In fascism, freedom of enterprise is severely restricted because although resources remain privately owned as in capitalism, the state exercises centralized authority to impose productive quotas.
7. In a centrally planned economy, a government agency in a market economy, or an organization in the not-for-profit sector of a market economy, activity is oriented towards the pursuit of some mission, but the mission is not to realize the maximum possible profit.
8. The requirement of such organizations to remain within budget is similar to the pursuit of a zero target rate of return on invested capital in the for-profit sector.
9. It should therefore be feasible for the managers of not-for-profit organizations and governmental organs to employ the same decision criteria as in the for-profit sector, but with a constraint of a zero or non-negative return.
10. In the not-for-profit sector, a variation on the Baumol thesis, that is, that the manager attempts to pursue some non-profit objective subject to a (zero- or non-negative) profit constraint, should be applicable.
11. A problem of the not-for-profit sector or a government organ is that it is very difficult to provide the manager with performance incentives or to link the process of mission pursuit to any factor which constitutes a performance incentive, but this is not a problem of the applicability of managerial decision criteria.
12. Bureaucracy is no less a problem in the not-for-profit sector and government organs than for business firms in the for-profit sector.
13. Benefit-cost analysis, a variation on the marginal decision criteria in the for-profit sector, has been developed to provide decision criteria for the organization manager in the government and the not-for-profit sectors.

Contd.....

14. The marginal decision criteria of the for-profit sector are special cases of the marginal benefit-cost criteria where the benefits and costs are pecuniary values.
15. Both simple and marginal benefit-cost analyses are subject to bias and fraught with the potential for abuse.
16. Because of the subjectivity involved, two decision makers might estimate widely divergent benefit-cost ratios and reach opposite decisions.
17. Points of contact between the firm and the government include: government demands output of firms; firms pay taxes; firms may become objects of governmental support; firms may become objects of governmental control; the activities of firms may become objects of regulation; and competition among firms may be promoted.
18. Government can effect a transformation to the characteristics of socialism by nationalizing private-sector firms.
19. Government in a market economy may pose threats to private sector firms as well as opportunities to exploit.
20. Rationales for governmental involvement in a market economy include: maintenance of an environment hospitable to enterprise; maintenance of competition; reallocation of resources; redistribution of incomes; and economic stabilization.
21. Viable competition among business firms in each market is the *sine qua non* of market capitalism, but firm managements find incentive to attempt to achieve monopoly.
22. The maintenance of competition requires the enactment of legislation and the vigorous enforcement of it.
23. The management of a firm may behave rationally to assess the probability of detection of a nominally illegal act, the probability of indictment if detected, the probability of prosecution if indicted, and the magnitude of penalty if found guilty, then proceed if the expected value of the penalty is judged small enough.
24. A governmental rationale for reallocating resources is based upon the conclusion that the extant allocation of resources is not satisfactory; declining profits (or losses) will likely emerge in industries from which resources are diverted, but profitable opportunities should be found in industries towards which resources are directed.
25. A governmental rationale for income redistribution follows from a social and political judgement that incomes are inequitably distributed by the market economy; business net incomes, assets, and wages paid are likely objects of taxation to raise revenue for redistribution.
26. A governmental rationale for stabilization is based upon the view that market economies are naturally unstable in intolerable degree.

Significant Terms

form of economic organization
economic system
authoritarian socialism
capitalism
fascism
micromanagement
industrial policy
macro-management
market mechanisms
dispersed decision making
legal and social environment
mixed capitalism, socialism
freedom of enterprise
for-profit, not-for-profit sectors
mission
marginal decision criteria
budgetary non-negativity constraint
optimization
constraint
performance incentives
linkage
organizational bureaucracy
benefit-cost analysis
simple, marginal
bias, potential for abuse
predisposition
demander, supplier
dependent
taxes
object of support
industrial policy
object of regulation
competition
antitrust
nationalization

Questions for Discussion

1. How have the transformations in the former Soviet Union, the former Soviet bloc countries, and China changed entrepreneurial and managerial incentives to peoples in those countries? ...to people in the outside world?
2. Discuss the role of the manager of a microeconomic productive unit in an authoritarian socialist state.
3. Distinguish micromanagement, industrial organization, and macro-management.
4. Discuss the managerial and entrepreneurial implications of constraints on freedom of enterprise in authoritarian socialism and fascism.

5. Discuss the appropriate role for government to play in an economy of pure capitalism; ...of mixed capitalism; ...of fascism; ...of authoritarian socialism.
6. Discuss the applicability of marginal decision criteria in microeconomic production units in a centrally planned and directed economy; ...in government agencies within market economies; ...in organizations in the not-for-profit sector of a market economy.
7. Discuss the applicability of marginal decision criteria when a behavioural goal or constraint is to remain within a prescribed budget.
8. Explain how the Baumol constrained sales maximization thesis can be applied to the not-for-profit sector.
9. Why are production units in centrally planned economies notorious for inefficient operation?
10. Discuss the problem of linkage in a not-for-profit organization.
11. Discuss the problem of the applicability of marginal decision criteria in a bureaucracy.
12. Explain the relationship between benefit-cost analysis and marginal decision criteria.
13. Explain how benefit-cost analysis can provide managerial decision criteria for organizations in the not-for-profit sector.
14. Why is benefit-cost analysis subject to bias and fraught with the potential for abuse?
15. Explain how an analyst's predisposition with respect to a proposed project may bear upon a benefit-cost analysis of the project.
16. Identify points of contact between business firms and the government of the economy within which they operate.
17. Explain how points of contact between business firms and the government may provide opportunities (pose threats) to the business firms.
18. Contrast the interests of business firms and the society of which they are a part in regard to competition.
19. Explain how governments may effect transformations of their economies from capitalism to fascism; ...to socialism. What are the managerial implications?
20. Discuss the problems which countries of Eastern Europe and the former Soviet Union seem to encounter in the effort to shift from central planning to market economy. What are the managerial implications?
21. Discuss the governmental rationale to maintain competition (to redistribute incomes; to reallocate resources; to stabilize the economy) in a market economy.
22. Describe the social transformations likely to ensue from traumatic failure of market capitalism; ...of authoritarian socialism. What are the managerial implications in each case?

23. Why do the managements of firms in market capitalism find incentive to try to achieve monopoly of their markets? What are the managerial implications of society's efforts to prevent them from doing so?

24. Discuss the managerial implications of a presumption of innocence until proven guilty.

25. Given a legal presumption of innocence until proven guilty, describe rational behaviour on the part of firm managements in regard to activities which may be unlawful.

26. Why does the incidence of externalities constitute a rationale for governmental response in market capitalism? What are the managerial implications?

27. Why does the identification of 'public goods' constitute a rationale for governmental response in market capitalism? What are the managerial implications?

28. Why are income distributions typically unequal in market capitalism? Why does this circumstance constitute a rationale for governmental response? What are the managerial implications?

29. Why do market economies exhibit characteristics of instability? Why does this constitute a rationale for governmental action? What are the managerial implications?

—oo(O)oo—

Chapter 20

The Firm in Society

Topics covered in this chapter

• The raison d'etre of business firms. • Distinctions between productive enterprises in authoritarian and market economies. • The contributions made by business firms to their host societies. • The potential for misbehaviour of business firms. • Opportunities and threats in the business firm's societal contacts. • Consequences of the aggressive exercise of producer sovereignty. • Rational approach to dealing with multiple constituencies. • The economics of public choice. • How the market economic ideally works. • Remedies when market mechanisms work imperfectly. • Opportunities and threats in the host society. • How governments may intervene in their economies. • The nature of an efficient allocation of resources. • How an efficient allocation of resources may be unsatisfactory to its society • The importance of honesty and integrity in business.

As noted in Chapter 9, the central function of the business enterprise, or 'firm' as we have called it, is production. We construe the term 'production' broadly to include all of the functions associated with extraction, processing, assembly, packaging, and distribution; it also encompasses the provision of services. The business firm is a creation of members of society to improve the efficiency of production by enabling specialization and division of labour and management. This statement presupposes that society has organized its economic arrangements as market capitalism and that the extant government at very minimum tolerates the existence and activities of such business firms.

However, even if the society in question has adopted some authoritarian form of economic organization (for example, fascism or socialism) rather than capitalism, efficiency in its productive relationships is still to be served by organizing production in units which enable specialization and division of labour and management. For example, in a Soviet-style planned economy, such production units exist and often are referred to as 'enterprises.' They are distinguished from firms in capitalism in that they are owned by the state while the latter are privately owned by members of society. Another distinction is that their managements are required to respond to dictates of the planning authority, whereas managements of firms in market capitalism are free to respond to market incentives.

Our further examination of the firm's situation in its societal relationships presupposes a setting of market capitalism, but the tone suggested in the first two paragraphs of this chapter belie alternatives which managers should keep in mind: society, or its government, may cease to be so tolerant of the existence or activities of privately owned and managed business firms. Alternatives include governmental efforts to modify or constrain the management and operations of the privately owned enterprise, or to take over the enterprise and run it as an organ of the state.

THE FIRM'S ROLES IN SOCIETY

Business firms in market capitalism make a great many contributions to the societies which host them. First and foremost is the provision of the goods and services demanded by society. It is indeed a high and noble activity to perceive human needs and function successfully to fulfil them. The private enterprises of Western market economies have demonstrated to the world their great capacities both to provide a flood of high quality goods and services, and to generate tremendous wealth in the process.

Second, in a social context where the principal avenue to consumption is by productive employment to earn spendable income, business firms are the chief providers of jobs. Western market economies have demonstrated abilities to provide productive employments to well over 90 per cent of their growing labour forces. The production of goods and services thereby serves to generate incomes which are distributed to both the owners and the employees of the firms. During the twentieth century in Western market economies, the proportion of the generated income which has been distributed as wages and salaries has gradually risen from around two-thirds towards four-fifths.

Third, business firms are tax payers, and thereby constitute important sources of revenue to governments at all levels. Business-related revenue sources have included property taxes on the firms' assets, floor taxes on their inventories, value-added taxes, sales and excise taxes, import tariffs, export licences, payroll taxes, business licences and associated fees, and corporate income taxes. It is not unusual for business-related taxes to account for 40 per cent or more of governments' revenues in Western market economies.

Finally, business firms themselves are citizens of their societies. Firms organized as corporations are also legal persons. Whether corporate persons or not, citizen firms have a presence in their communities. Their offices, plants, and warehouses have significant impacts upon the appearances of the communities within which they are situated. Their employees are active in the schools and churches of their communities. Many firms make valuable monetary and in-kind contributions to their communities.

This brief discussion has not exhausted the many contributions made by business firms to their communities. As firms contribute to their communities, they also incur responsibilities in their communities. While the roles mentioned above reveal the significance of business firms to society, each is also fraught with the potential for misbehaviour by firms. It is such misbehaviour which may lead society to become less tolerant of the continued unfettered operation of firms in the private sector.

THE FIRM'S SOCIETAL CONTACTS

Business firms in market economies come into contact with a great many different types of people as they conduct their productive activities. Their raison d'etre is to serve their customers by providing the goods and services demanded by them. Many business firms take only a passive role in attempting to discover demands which they may undertake to fill, but some firms aggressively attempt to create or manipulate such demands. The term 'consumer sovereignty' describes the former case, whereas a firm which succeeds in first determining what it will produce and then creating a demand for it has exercised producer sovereignty. The host society may tolerate a significant amount of such producer sovereignty, but if it is perceived to become troublesome the government of the society may exercise state sovereignty to nationalize the firm and operate it as a state enterprise. The managerial implications of this prospect should be clear although it is much less likely to occur in the democracies of North America and Europe than in some countries of Africa, Latin America, and Asia.

As we noted, managers of private sector business firms often feel that they must answer to a number of constituencies in addition to their customers. With the process of separation of ownership and management during the nineteenth and twentieth centuries, the owners became another significant constituency of the firms being managed. As long as the owners maintain effective control of their firms, the managers must meet the owners' expectations of returns or other goals, and this may be a matter of satisficing rather than maximizing. But as we also noted, the widespread dispersion of the ownership of corporate stock may enable the management of a corporation to so gain control over its own destiny that it can pursue its own private goals without fear of owner interference. The account of the takeover of RJR-Nabisco in the book *Barbarians at the Gate* by Bryan Burrough and John Helyar (Harper Collins Publishers, 1991) is illustrative of this point.

The firm's employees are another constituency which may constantly tug at the managers of the modern business firm. The principal employee concerns are wages, working conditions, amenities, and such benefits as health insurance and pension fund contributions. In a growing economy which experiences inflation, the interest of employees is in advancing wages at a rate fast enough to offset the effect of inflation which would decrease the purchasing power of their incomes, and to further capture as large a share of the fruits of growth as possible. The resulting tug-of-war is about the division of the growing 'income pie' between the interests of labour and capital.

In theoretical terms, each productive resource employed by the firm seeks to receive an income which is at least as large as its marginal revenue product; if it fails to do so, it becomes the subject of exploitation. A potential problem for management is that labour often can muster significant political influence over elected or appointed government officials to make them believe that labour is being exploited (whether it truly is or not), and that government should use its state sovereignty to curb the power of capital or redistribute income in the interest of labour. It is significant that in most Western democracies during the twentieth century, the proportion of national income going to wages and salaries has trended upwards from 60 towards 80 per cent.

The firm's suppliers may sometimes become a vocal constituency whose voices must be heard by the managers of the firm. In competitive resource markets, suppliers are always seeking to gain the attention of the firm's purchasing agents, and thereby to gain supply contracts at the expense of competitor suppliers. If suppliers gain monopolistic advantage in the control of unique resources, they may be able to exercise their monopoly powers to raise resource prices above competitive levels, and thereby capture a larger share of the 'income pie' at the expense of the firm. Such circumstances often encourage firms to extend their degrees of vertical integration by attempting to acquire their suppliers and thereby gain monopolistic position in regard to unique resources. If a firm can gain a monopsony position (monopoly as a buyer) in a resource market, it may be able to dictate price and delivery schedule conditions to its suppliers. But the attainment of monopoly or monopsony position may attract the attention of governmental authorities and invite unwanted responses.

As we have noted, in oligopolistic markets (which may in fact encompass most real-world commercial and industrial activity) the firm's competitors certainly constitute one of its most important constituencies. Because of the relatively small number of firms in each geographic and product market, each firm must be concerned not only with what each of its competitors may do, but also with how competitors may respond to any action taken by the firm. The potential for inducing undesirable competitive response may be so great that the firm's management finds itself in a mould of decision rigidity. But even if this extreme condition does not result, the firm's managers must assess the competitive response risks attendant upon any strategy which they are contemplating.

The process of dispersion of stock ownership also opens the door to responsiveness to yet other constituencies as managers begin to feel some sense of social responsibility to 'third parties,' that is, innocent bystanders to the actions and activities of the firm. Sometimes the externalities or so-called 'spill-over effects' are benefits which are conferred upon neighbours due to simple proximity to the business firm. Examples include better roads and street lighting. But there are also possibilities of negative externalities such as the various forms of environmental pollution and congestion associated with the firm's activities. Positive spill-overs may be rewarded with plaques given at meetings of civic organizations, but complaints about negative spill-overs often attract the attention of society at large and its elected or appointed government officials who tend to become ever less tolerant of the unconstrained operations of the firm.

These and other constituencies continually pull at the managements of modern business firms. As we suggested, it is unrealistic for the managers to try to pursue multiple goals simultaneously. Practically speaking, what usually happens is that the 'squeaky wheel gets the grease,' that is, the most vocal constituency at the moment captures the attention of the firm's management. That constituency's interest becomes the goal selected for primary pursuit, and all other constituencies' interests function as constraints upon the pursuit of the primary goal. Once the constituency's concerns have been adequately addressed, some other constituency's complaint will rise to the surface to dominate the attention of the firm's management. But if the management cannot or will not satisfactorily address the voiced concerns of its constituencies, it can expect intervention by some governmental authority.

THE WORKINGS OF ECONOMIC MECHANISMS

The economics of public choice is the study of how societies decide whether economic decisions are to be made in the private or the public sectors. A brief examination of the workings of the market economy will bring us to a fundamental principle of public choice decision making. In the market economy organized as pure capitalism (a hypothetical situation with no real-world examples), all productive assets are privately owned and all decisions concerning their use are made by their private owners. Resource owners are presumed to be motivated by prospects of personal gain or profit. Information about changing economic conditions is disseminated throughout the market economy by prices which change in response to shifts of market demands and supplies. Competition among participants in the market economy serves to enforce compliance with the dictates of the market changes, that is, the prospect of profit or loss invites appropriate adjustment, but competition ensures that appropriate adjustment ensues. Those who perceive the emerging opportunities and act upon their perceptions are rewarded with profits and survival; those who either do not perceive the opportunities or simply ignore them are penalized with losses and failure. The perceptive, responsive, and efficient survive and prosper. The imperceptive, unresponsive, and inefficient suffer losses and fail.

Societies which favour dispersed and participatory modes of social determination are generally pleased to leave economic decision making to the members of society unless there emerges widespread belief that private decision making yields results which are detrimental to the general welfare of the society. When such perception emerges, the government of the society has two fundamental alternatives: to try to make the private decision mechanism work to the satisfaction of society, or to substitute public decision making in place of private discretion. This is the fundamental issue of public choice. And it was consequent upon the emergence of this issue that the distinction between the private sector and the public sector was born.

The principal means for improving the functioning of private sector decision mechanisms are to reduce or eliminate market imperfections, and to curb the unbridled desires of decision makers to accumulate wealth or to gain exclusive control over their situations. These motives may lead private sector decision makers to indulge in unethical or even criminal behaviours. Market imperfections include restrictions upon the availability of information and the ability of market participants to adjust. They also encompass the achievement of monopolistic position in a product or geographic market. The relief of market imperfections may come via technological advances which improve information flows or reduce the costs and time requirements of resource mobility. But these same technological advances may also serve as bases for the achievement of monopoly position.

In Western democratic societies it often seems easier to replace the errant market mechanism with an authoritarian decision making structure than to devise means of making the market mechanism function more satisfactorily. More often than not, when a private sector decision mechanism is perceived to work unsatisfactorily, some substitute for private decision making is sought. The obvious substitute for private decision making is public or authoritarian decision making, perhaps in the form of a regulatory commission to determine such things as prices or distribution and quality of services.

An irony of this issue may be seen in societies which historically have opted for authoritarian decision mechanisms. For example, from 1918 onwards in the Soviet Union, socialism became the predominant form of economic organization. In the purest form of socialism (of which there are also no real-world examples), all of the society's productive assets are owned by the state, and all decisions in regard to their use are made by administrative fiat. When shortcomings are perceived in regard to the exercise of such governmental authority, some substitute for the authoritarian mechanism is sought. The obvious substitute for authoritarian decision making is individual discretion exercised by private decision makers in market mechanisms. The Soviets upon numerous occasions found themselves falling back upon market mechanisms when authoritarian decision making resulted in shortages or other problems.

There are no real-world examples of either pure capitalism or pure socialism. All economies are 'mixed' in the sense that they incorporate varying degrees of private discretion and authoritarian decision making. The U.S. economy is appropriately described as mixed capitalism to indicate that market mechanisms are the primary economic decision making vehicles, but that there is also a significant role for government to play in the economy. Before its demise, the Soviet Union could be described as mixed socialism in which authoritarian decision making in the form of central planning and direction was the primary decision vehicle. Economies of other nations may be described as varying mixtures of private and authoritarian decision making.

OPPORTUNITIES AND THREATS TO THE FIRM

The discussion to this point is intended to support the central thesis of this chapter, that is, that the firm's situation within its host society provides innumerable opportunities which it may exploit, but also poses a variety of threats to the manager's decision making discretion, and possibly to the very existence of the firm as an organization independent of the society's governing authority.

Societies through their governments may intervene in their economies in a variety of ways including:

(a) determining weights and measures;

(b) providing a stable money supply which can grow along with the economy;

(c) providing for law and order, that is, an environment conducive to enterprise;

(d) establishing the security of private property, the conditions under which title to it may be transferred, and the means to arbitrate disputes over the ownership of it;

(e) maintaining competitive conditions;

(f) stabilizing the macro-economy;

(g) redistributing income and wealth; and

(h) reallocating resources.

The opportunities and threats to private business firms lie in how extensively the government intervenes in the economy and how effectively it succeeds in achieving the goals of its interventions. For example, if the values of weights and measures are not certain, or if the purchasing power of the unit of money is volatile, there will be mostly threats to the success and survival of private-sector firms. If the private ownership of property is not adequately secured, firms will be threatened by declining investment in their assets. A redistribution of income will provide opportunities for firms servicing customers who receive additional income, but pose threats to firms whose clients suffer income losses. The enactment of antitrust legislation and its vigorous enforcement will constitute threats to firms bent upon achieving monopoly positions, but will enable opportunities for firms which are attempting to achieve entry into profitable markets. As noted in Chapter 18, governmental efforts to stabilize the macro-economy are also a mixed bag of opportunities and threats to private-sector firms, especially since it is not at all clear that deliberate efforts at stabilization accomplish their ends without further destabilizing the macro-economy.

The private sector of any economy will yield a certain allocation of resources which can be construed as efficient if there are few externalities and little exercise of monopoly power. It is efficient in the sense that under competitive conditions, output of each good will be adjusted until its marginal cost (society's valuation of the resources used to produce the good instead of some other goods) is just equal to its marginal revenue (or price, society's valuation of having one more unit of the good rather than some other goods).

But even if the allocation of resources is efficient, it still may not be satisfactory to society, primarily because of two reasons: public goods are not produced in response to market incentives, and markets tend to over- or under-produce social goods, that is, those resulting in externalities. It may then be said in regard to society's preferences that resources are misallocated, and that there is a justification for government to act to reallocate resources. Chapter 21 is devoted to the issue of governmental reallocation of resources.

ETHICS AND THE BUSINESS COMMUNITY

It is sometimes suggested that people in the business community are more likely to behave in an illegal or unethical manner than are people in other occupations. There is no evidence that people who become managers of business enterprises are by race, ethnicity, religion, education, training, cultural conditioning, or heredity significantly different from people who enter other walks of life. Unethical people may become teachers, ministers, plumbers, doctors, politicians, or managers of business enterprises; by the same token, ethical people may likewise enter any of these occupations.

People 'in business' have the same responsibilities of citizenship as do people in other fields. It may be true that businessmen and businesswomen, because they are trustees of corporate assets and exercise decision-making authority over other people, are subjected to temptations to engage in questionable behaviour which are commensurate with their positions of authority. Does this mean that they should be held to higher standards of honesty and integrity than people in other occupations?

These are certainly foundation blocks for a workable market economy. Market capitalism would cease to function efficiently, and might cease to function at all, in the absence of honour and trust in business dealings.

All people, irrespective of their occupations or positions, should be expected to behave according to the same high moral and ethical standards. To this point we have described the roles which business decision makers play in their societies, and implicitly the responsibilities which they incur to their societies to provide goods and services, employment, tax revenues, and good citizenship behaviour. But societies have a collateral responsibility to members of their business communities and indeed to all of their citizens, irrespective of occupation or position, to inculcate into them the virtues of honesty and integrity.

Business *per se* is neither ethical nor unethical, moral nor immoral. But positions of business leadership and authority may be filled with honest or dishonest people, just as can pulpits, classrooms, operating rooms, and legislatures. Society should expect no less (but also no more) of its business leaders than of its preachers, teachers, doctors, electricians, or legislators.

Summary of Important Points

1. The business firm is a creation of members of society to improve the efficiency of production by enabling specialization and division of labour and management.
2. In a centrally planned economy, the manager of the productive unit responds to the dictates of the planning authority, whereas in a market economy the manager responds to market incentives.
3. Alternatives to private enterprise include governmental efforts to modify or constrain management and operations, or to take over the enterprise and run it as an organ of the state.
4. Business firms in market capitalism make numerous contributions to their societies, including: the provision of goods and services demanded by society; productive employment; the payment of taxes; and citizenship.
5. Each of the roles played by the firm in its society is fraught with the potential for misbehaviour which may lead the society to become less tolerant of continued unfettered operation.
6. The business firm's societal contacts include: their customers, their owners, their employees, their suppliers, their competitors, third parties, and various other constituencies.
7. Although most firms are subject to consumer sovereignty, some firms aggressively attempt to establish producer sovereignty by creating or manipulating consumer demand; if producer sovereignty becomes troublesome, the government of the society may exercise state sovereignty to nationalize the firm.

Contd....

8. The firm's various constituencies continually pull at the management; the most vocal tend to get management's attention; if the management cannot or will not satisfactorily address the voiced concerns, it can expect intervention by governmental authority.
9. The economics of public choice is the study of how societies decide whether economic decisions are to be made in the private or the public sectors.
10. In a market economy, the perceptive, responsive, and efficient survive and prosper; the imperceptive, unresponsive, and inefficient suffer losses and fail.
11. Societies which favour dispersed and participatory decision making tend to leave economic decision making to members of society unless there emerges widespread belief that private decision making is detrimental to the general welfare of society.
12. When problems in the functioning of the private sector emerge, government has two fundamental alternatives: to try to make the private mechanism work satisfactorily, or to substitute public decision making in place of private discretion.
13. The principal means for improving the functioning of the private sector mechanisms are to reduce or eliminate market imperfections, and to curb the unbridled desires of decision makers to accumulate wealth or exercise control.
14. The relief of market imperfections often comes via technological advances which improve information flows or reduce the costs and time requirements of mobility.
15. It is often easier to substitute for private decision mechanisms than to make them work better; the obvious substitute is public or authoritarian decision making.
16. In authoritarian societies, the obvious substitute for faulty centralized decision making is individual discretion exercised through market mechanisms.
17. All real-world economies are mixed in the sense that they incorporate varying degrees of private discretion and authoritarian decision making.
18. The firm's situation within its host society provides innumerable opportunities which it may exploit, but also poses threats to private discretion.
19. Societies through their governments may intervene in their economies in a variety of ways including: determining weights and measures; providing a stable money supply; providing for law and order; establishing security of private property; maintaining competitive conditions; stabilizing the macro-economy; redistributing income and wealth; and reallocating resources.
20. Opportunities and threats to private business firms lie in how extensively government intervenes in the economy and how effectively it succeeds in achieving the goals of its interventions.
21. The private sector of an economy yields an allocation of resources which can be construed as efficient if there are few externalities and little exercise of monopoly power.

Contd.....

22. Even if a society's allocation of resources is efficient, it still may not be satisfactory because public goods are not produced, and because markets tend to over- or under-produce goods yielding externalities.
23. There is little evidence that people who become managers are more likely to behave in illegal or unethical manners; people 'in business' have the same responsibilities of citizenship as do people in other fields.
24. Market capitalism would cease to function efficiently in the absence of honour and trust in business dealings; societies have a responsibility to members of their business communities to indoctrinate them with the virtues of honesty and integrity.
25. Business *per se* is neither ethical nor unethical, but positions of business leadership may be filled with honest or dishonest people; society should expect no less or more of its business leaders than it does of other members of society.

Significant Terms

efficiency
specialization and division of labour
business related revenue sources
business citizenship
consumer, producer, state sovereignty
constituencies
dispersal of stock ownership
exploitation
monopolistic advantage
monopsony position
externalities, spill-overs
simultaneous pursuit of multiple goals
public choice
dispersed and participatory decision making
market imperfections
unethical, criminal behaviours
technological advances
authoritarian decision mechanisms
socialism
mixed economies
opportunities, threats
government intervention
efficient allocation of resources
public, social goods
under-, over-allocation of resources
socially responsible; social conscience
ethics

Questions for Discussion

1. Identify reasons that society is willing to create and tolerate the continued existence of business firms.
2. Distinguish between the circumstances of private business firms in market capitalism and state enterprises in authoritarian socialism.
3. Why might society cease to be tolerant of the existence or activities of privately owned and managed business firms?
4. Identify various contributions which business firms make to their host societies.
5. Discuss the citizenship presence of business firms in their communities.
6. Identify the various contacts which business firms have with their host communities; how are these contacts fraught with the potential for misbehaviour?
7. Distinguish producer from consumer sovereignty and discuss the managerial implications of each.
8. Explain why aggressive producer sovereignty might invoke an exercise of state sovereignty; what are the managerial implications?
9. Discuss the managerial implications of the progressive dispersion of ownership shares in the modern corporation.
10. Explain how exploitation of a resource can occur in a business firm in a market economy.
11. Discuss the managerial implications of the political influence over elected or appointed government officials which can be mustered by labour.
12. Discuss the managerial implications of the achievement of monopolistic advantage by a supplier in regard to a resource required by the firm.
13. Why may competitors of a firm be construed as one of the firm's constituencies?
14. Why might managers feel some sense of social responsibility with respect to 'third parties' in their host societies? How does social responsibility impact the profit position of the firm?
15. How can managers rationally approach the problem of multiple constituencies which continually make demands upon their firms?
16. Describe the working of the economic mechanism in a market economy; why does it require a 'visible hand' to order its relationships?
17. Discuss the consequences in a market economy for firms whose managements are imperceptive, unresponsive, or inefficient.

18. Identify the alternative approaches open to governments of democratic societies when faults are discovered in the functioning of their market economies.
19. Why does it seem easier to replace private discretion with authoritarian decision making than to repair the private decision making mechanism?
20. Explain how technological advance may relieve market imperfections in a capitalistic economy.
21. Describe the irony in the obvious substitutes for the preferred decision making modes in capitalism and socialism when those modes are found to be faulty.
22. Explain the sense in which all real-world economies are 'mixed.'
23. Identify ways in which societies through their governments may intervene in their economies; discuss the managerial implications of each.
24. Discuss the implications of a failure of a society to secure the ownership of private property.
25. Identify the conditions under which a society's allocation of resources may be judged to be efficient.
26. Explain why an efficient allocation of society's resources might not be satisfactory.

—oo(O)oo—

Chapter **21**

Reallocation of Resources by Government

Topics covered in this chapter

• Why an efficient allocation of resources may not be satisfactory • Roles for government in regard to private, public, and social goods. • Opportunities and threats to business firms in regard to public and social goods. • Resource misallocation due to social goods. • Governmental responses to social goods. • Resource misallocation due to spill-over costs. • Managerial implications of governmental responses to spill-over costs. • Opportunities associated with spill-over costs.

The private sector of any economy will yield a certain allocation of resources which can be construed as efficient if there are few externalities and little exercise of monopoly power. It is efficient in the sense that under competitive conditions, output of each good will be adjusted until its marginal cost (society's valuation of the resources used to produce the good instead of some other goods) is just equal to its marginal revenue (or price, society's valuation of having one more unit of the good rather than some other goods).

But even if the allocation of resources is efficient, it still may not be satisfactory to the society, primarily because of two reasons: public goods are not produced in response to market incentives, and markets tend to over- or under-produce social goods, that is, those resulting in externalities. It may then be said in regard to society's preferences that resources are misallocated, and that there is a justification for government to act to reallocate resources. The remainder of this chapter is devoted to the issue of governmental reallocation of resources.

PUBLIC VS. PRIVATE GOODS

In the ensuing discussion we use the term 'goods' to refer to both goods and services. Private goods are those which are provided by firms in the private sector in response to profit incentives. Private goods involve expense outlays which can be handled by individual members of society. Because there are clear correspondences between the benefits which the purchaser might receive and the costs which must be paid, it is possible for the purchaser to reach a rational decision to buy the private good. Private goods are subject to the so-called 'exclusion principle,' that is, the private purchaser can exclude other members of society from enjoying the benefits of the good.

A competitive market economy can be expected to yield an efficient allocation of resources to the production of private goods which involve no externalities. Except for providing an environment conducive to their production and maintaining competition, there is very little other role for government to play in regard to private goods. We note below that there may occur special cases of private goods where too little or too much of them is produced, and that this may warrant a role for government.

In contrast to private goods, public goods are not produced by the private sector in response to profit incentives. This is because they tend to be large and 'lumpy' in the sense that they involve larger outlays than can be undertaken by most single members of society, and they must be purchased '*in toto*' rather than in small pieces. Public goods may yield benefits to society at large, but it is often difficult for individual members of society to identify any particular benefit which accrues to them personally. With such a lack of clear correspondence between outlay and benefit, it is usually not possible for the individual to reach a rational decision to purchase a public good, or even his or her small share of one. Also, public goods typically are not subject to the exclusion effect, that is, it is not possible for the purchaser(s) to prevent other members of society from enjoying benefits flowing from the public good. A corollary of this feature of the public good is the so-called 'free-rider' effect, that is, that other members of society tend to 'ride free' because they can enjoy the benefits without paying the cost of acquisition.

Examples of public goods include national defence, local police services, fire departments, parks, and a variety of infrastructure facilities such as highways and streets, water, sewer, and refuse collection systems, and in some places electricity and gas generation and transmission systems. As soon as we have identified possible examples of public goods, readers may begin to think of possible exceptions; private amusement parks, toll roads, private security services, etc. But the principle still holds as a general phenomenon, even if we can think of possible exceptions.

The salient point for our purposes is that a market economy will not of its own volition allocate resources to the production of public goods. It usually takes a social decision reached by some governmental body in order for a public good to be produced, and for resources to be reallocated to the production of the public good. However, in Western democratic societies which organize their economies around markets, public goods are not produced in the public sector. Rather, they are provided by the public sector in the sense that a social decision is reached to commission their production and public funds are budgeted to pay for them. Their actual production occurs in the private sector as public agencies contract with private firms to build the public goods. The incentive for a private sector business firm to contract to produce such a public good is that the contracted price is expected to more than cover the estimated expenses in order to allow a 'profit.' However, this is not the basis for a conclusion that public goods are produced in the private sector in response to profit incentives.

Now we come to the important point: the social decision to commission and fund the construction of a public good provides opportunities for private sector firms. The usual procedure is for the commissioning authority to make public announcement that competitive bids will be entertained from private sector firms. The criteria for 'letting a contract' to one of the bidding firms include the bid price, the estimated completion date, and a variety of possible design or performance conditions. Often the 'low bidder' gets the contract, but this does not always occur.

Threats to private sector firms may be contingent upon the bidding process if firms conspire to 'rig bids' so that one of them gets the particular job while others anticipate getting other jobs in the future. Also, the firm which wins the contract to construct the public good may suffer a threat of a lawsuit if it fails to meet any of the contracted conditions, including the bid price, the completion date, or any of the design or performance conditions.

There are yet other threats to private sector firms in that the societal decision to commission the production of a public good has the effect of reallocating resources away from the production of private goods. The problem is less critical in an economy suffering significant unemployment, but in a nearly fully-employed economy, the prices of resources tend to rise as they are bid away from the production of private goods. This will have the effect of increasing production costs and narrowing profit margins for private goods producers which use the same resources. If this process results in rising market prices for the private goods, less of them will be sold (their demand curves slope upwards from right to left) at the same time that more of the public good is produced. Private goods producers who can no longer earn at least normal returns can be expected to exit their respective industries.

SOCIAL GOODS YIELDING POSITIVE SPILL-OVERS

Social goods are special cases of private goods. They are private goods because some quantities of them will be produced in the private sector in response to profit incentives. They are special cases in that while their private-intentions market demand curves recognize the explicit demands for them at going market prices, they fail to recognize any positive or negative spill-over effects (or externalities) resulting from either their production or their consumption.

Examples of positive spill-overs include the satisfactions enjoyed by passers-by because a firm has beautified its buildings or grounds, and the fact that health services tend to benefit many people other than those who directly receive them. Also, while education or training benefits the recipient by increasing the income-earning potential, other members of society also are made better off when the recipient becomes productive. The sense in which markets misallocate resources in the production of goods yielding spill-over benefits is that they are produced in inadequate quantities.

Figure 21.1 illustrates this point. A normal market supply is represented as S. The demand curve labelled D_p represents the private intentions market demand curve, that is, the quantities of the good which would be purchased at each possible price by those who benefit directly from the consumption of the good. Suppose that the good yields spill-over benefits to other members of

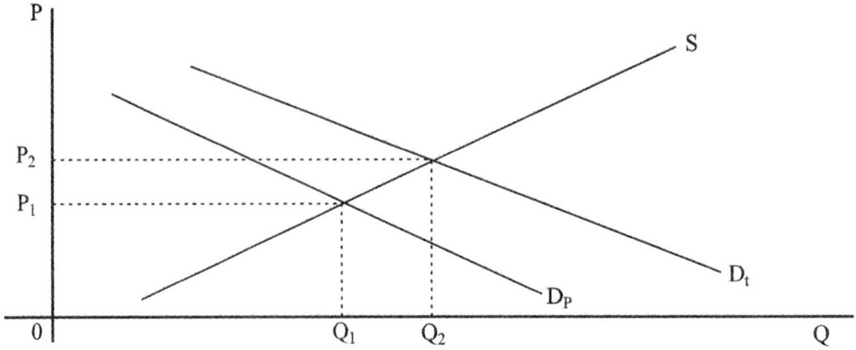

Figure 21.1. Demand & supley curve for social good.

society who did not directly demand the good. Their implicit demand for the good can be represented by an addition to the private intentions demand which shifts the demand curve outward to a new locus, D_t, representing the 'total' demand for the good.

The problem for society is that the locus of D_t is virtual rather than actual. The relevant market demand curve which interacts with the market supply curve is D_p. This market interaction will result in the production of only Q_1 which is sold at market price P_1. But if the market could in some way be made to recognize in an explicit sense the spill-over benefits included in the virtual demand curve D_t, a larger quantity, Q_2, would be transacted at a higher price, P_2. Because the market produces only the smaller quantity, Q_1, it may be said that resources are under-allocated to the production of the good. But it would be desirable from a social perspective for the larger quantity, Q_2, to be produced and consumed. Recognition of this desirability constitutes the basis for some action by society to try to reallocate resources towards the production of more of the good which yields spill-over benefits.

How can government attempt to correct this misallocation of resources? It could attempt to adjust the locus of the market demand curve, but this is a very difficult thing to do. The government could mount an advertising campaign which encourages people to consume more of the good ('Take flu shots....They are good for you and others as well!' 'Stay in school....You will benefit and the rest of society will as well!'), and this might have some effect in shifting the market demand curve to the right towards D_t in Figure 21.1. However, such admonitions are unlikely to have the desired social impact.

Governments have found it to be much more effective to manipulate the locus of the supply curve than the locus of the demand curve. The principal means of doing this is to provide a subsidy which shifts the market supply curve far enough to intersect the market demand curve at the desired quantity. In Figure 21.2, S' lies below (and to the right of) market supply curve S by enough to allow it to intersect the market demand curve, D_p, at the quantity Q_2. This is the quantity which would be transacted in the market if the market demand curve reflected the spill-over as well as the direct benefits. The vertical distance between S' and S is the per-unit amount of the subsidy.

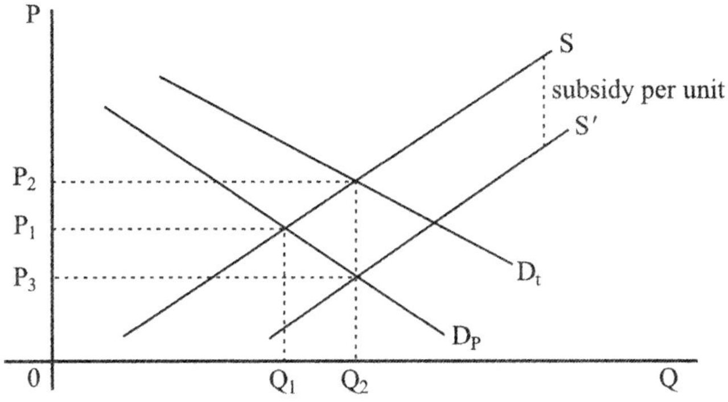

Figure 21.2. Demand & supply curve in case subsidy.

The subsidy, if provided to the consumer, has the effect of reducing the purchase price of the good so that a larger quantity, Q_2, is bought at the lower price, P_3. If the subsidy is paid to the producer, it serves as an off-set to the cost of production, thereby shifting the supply curve downwards. In a competitive market the reduced production costs can be expected to be passed through to consumers in the form of lower market prices. But in any imperfectly competitive market, the exercise of monopoly power may result in the subsidy being internalized to allow a wider profit margin.

A practical problem from the perspective of public policy is recognizing the effect that the spill-over benefit should have on the locus of the demand curve, that is, the true locus of the virtual demand curve, D_t. If the responsible government officials overestimate the effect of the spill-over benefit, the subsidy may be set at too large an amount with the effect of inducing an over-allocation of resources to the production of the good. On the other hand, if the government officials underestimate the effect of the spill-over benefit, the subsidy will be too small, which will leave resources under-allocated to production of the good. It is almost heroic to think that government officials (or anyone else) are perceptive and astute enough to estimate just the right magnitude of a required subsidy so as to achieve a correct allocation of resources to the production of the spill-over benefit good.

This problem aside, what are the opportunity and threat potentials for firms in the private sector? Producers of goods for which subsidies are provided may find market opportunities to expand both production and profit margins. These opportunities will be greater to the extent that government officials tend to overestimate spill-over benefits and thus set subsidies at levels which are too large, and *vice versa* if they underestimate the spill-over benefits. This is a persisting problem for officials at state universities which receive subsidies from state government treasuries. Since the subsidies have the effect of allowing the state universities to price their products below their per unit cost of production, the quantity demanded of higher education is typically larger than would be the case in the absence of such subsidies. The relevant question is how much additional higher education should be provided to society to recognize the spill-over benefits. Similar questions

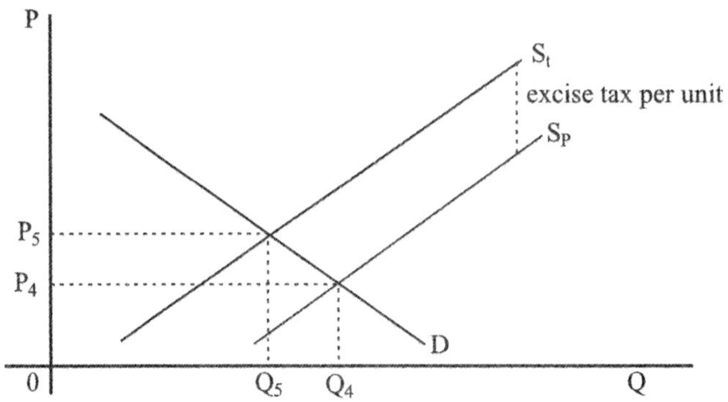

Figure 21.3. Demand & supply curve in case excise tax.

arise in regard to subsidy and pricing of health services. We shall not attempt to address questions in either area.

There are also threats consequent upon the provision of subsidies to the production of goods yielding spill-over benefits. If the subsidies have the effect of reallocating resources towards the production of the spill-over benefit good, they also have the effect of reallocating resources away from other private goods. This will be to the detriment of the other private goods producers, and the effect will be the greater if the responsible government officials tend to overestimate the spill-over benefits.

SPILL-OVER COSTS

Private goods may result in negative spill-overs, or spill-over costs, although such goods are not customarily referred to as 'social goods.' Spill-over costs are the negative effects that descend upon innocent bystanders to the activities of the firm. Examples of spill-over costs include the unsightliness of 'rust-belt' manufacturing plants, the noise and odours resulting from some manufacturing processes, the entire variety of industrial effluents ejected into the atmosphere and waterways, and congestion on the highways attributable to concentrated industrial or commercial activity.

The analysis of spill-over costs starts with a normal market demand curve, D, as illustrated in Figure 21.3. Superimposed over it is a private-intentions market supply curve, S_p, showing the quantities of the good which producers would offer on the market at possible alternative prices. The market can be expected to adjust to an equilibrium at quantity Q_4 which is sold at price P_4. The market supply curve is a summation of the individual supply curves of all of the firms producing the good. Each of their supply curves reflects all of the costs which are relevant to the production process, whether they are explicit or implicit costs. The relevant-cost supply curves include none of the costs which are irrelevant to current decision making. This means that the market supply curve excludes all spill-over costs because such costs descend upon members of society other than those who make production decisions within the producing firms.

If such spill-over costs could be incorporated into the market supply curve for the good in question, it might lie at locus S_t, above S_p by an amount which reflects the magnitude of the spill-over costs. Supply curve S_t represents the total of the costs of production, including relevant and spill-over costs. S_t is only a virtual supply curve, but if it were the actual market supply curve, a smaller quantity, Q_5, would be transacted in the market at a higher market price, P_5.

Because quantity Q_4 (which does not recognize the spill-over costs) is larger than quantity Q_5 (which would recognize the spill-overs), it may be said from a social perspective that too much of the good is being produced and sold, and thus that resources are over-allocated to the good which yields spill-over costs. This then constitutes a justification for society to act through its government to deal with the spill-overs.

There are a variety of ways in which government might attempt to address the spill-over cost problem. We shall examine the managerial implications of four possibilities:

1. Government enacts legislation which prohibits and forbids the continuance of the problem.
2. Government permits the process causing the social cost to continue but requires the offending firms to compensate those who are harmed.
3. Government auctions pollution rights to the highest-bidding firms.
4. Government imposes a punitive tax in the form of an excise on each unit of the good sold.

A governmental edict that a social cost must cease will be ineffective unless backed by a further provision in the law which makes the action a criminal offence with serious penalties, or makes the innocent third parties harmed by the social cost eligible to collect civil damages. In either case, the expense of legal defence, court costs, and penalties or damages will become explicit costs to the firm or to its managers personally, and will thus become costs which are relevant to operating conditions. The higher explicit costs will narrow profit margins and thereby discourage production and further entry into the market. Or if the costs can be passed along to consumers in the form of higher prices, consumers will purchase less of the good yielding the spill-over cost. In either case, the social objective of reallocating resources away from production of the good will be accomplished.

If government permits the socially offending activity to continue but requires compensation of all who are harmed, the compensation outlays will likewise become explicit costs of operation and hence relevant to decision making. The same resource reallocation effects will follow.

A popularly-discussed approach to dealing with spill-over costs is for government to auction rights to continue the process. The outlays paid by the highest bidders will also become explicit costs of production which are relevant to production decision making, and again the desired resource reallocation effects will follow. A further possibility is that if the prices bid for the pollution rights are higher than the costs of abating the spill-over costs (for example, by making capital expenditures to filter, scrub, dampen, or otherwise diminish the air, water, or noise pollution), some firms will incur the expense of abatement rather than bid on the pollution rights. Such expenses will also become explicit and hence relevant costs to the production processes.

Finally, a responsible government authority might opt for a punitive excise tax which would shift the market supply curve upward to the position of St in Figure 21.3. The per-unit amount of the excise tax is represented by the vertical distance between S_p and S_t. The market price would be expected to rise to P_5 and quantity transacted to fall to Q_5 (because consumers purchase less at higher prices). The declining production is accompanied by the desired reallocation of resources away from production of the offending good. Just as in the case of spill-over benefits, there is also the practical problem of whether the responsible government official can accurately estimate the magnitude of the spill-over cost so as to determine just the right level of excise tax. If the spill-over cost is overestimated, the excise tax will be too large, and a further misallocation of resources will occur as output of the good decreases below Q5. If the spill-over cost is underestimated, the amount of the excise tax will be too small, and the existing misallocation of resources will persist.

These four alternatives have all assumed deliberate action on the part of government to bring about the socially desired resource reallocation. The same end might be accomplished with no government action at all if managers of firms causing spill-over costs become aware of the problem (possibly because of complaints by one or more of their constituencies), and with a twinge of conscience become more 'socially responsible.' Irrespective of whether the adjustment ensues as a matter of social conscience or in response to governmental action, the spill-over costs which formerly were not relevant to managerial decision making have become explicit costs of production which are relevant. One moral of the story, as first noted in Chapter 8, is that costs which are presently irrelevant to managerial decision making always have the potential to become relevant, and thus should never be completely ignored.

Thus far our discussion has focused upon threats to society and to firms which are producing goods involving spill-over costs. Are there any opportunities to be exploited in regard to spill-over costs? Resources which are reallocated away from production of goods involving spill-overs are released for use in producing other goods. Firms using such resources may enjoy falling input prices which expand profit margins and encourage increased production. There are also opportunities in industries which produce the equipment which accomplishes abatement or clean-up of the effects of the cost spill-overs.

Summary of Important Points

1. The private sector of an economy yields an allocation of resources which can be construed as efficient if there are few externalities and little exercise of monopoly power.
2. Even if a society's allocation of resources is efficient, it still may not be satisfactory because public goods are not produced, and because markets tend to over- or under-produce goods yielding externalities.
3. Private goods are those which are provided by firms in the private sector in response to profit incentives; except for providing an environment conducive to their production and maintaining competition; there is very little other role for government to play in regard to private goods.

Contd....

4. Public goods are not produced by the private sector in response to profit incentives; it usually takes a social decision reached through the offices of a governmental body for a public good to be produced.
5. The social decision to commission and fund the construction of a public good provides opportunities for private sector firms; threats may be contingent upon the bidding process if firms conspire to 'rig bids.'
6. A societal decision to commission the production of a public good has the effect of reallocating resources away from the production of private goods; private goods producers who can no longer earn at least normal returns can be expected to exit their industries.
7. Social goods are special cases of private goods because while they are produced in the private sector, their demands fail to recognize externalities and result in misallocation of resources.
8. Because it is very difficult for government to adjust the locus of the market demand curve, the usual procedure is to attempt to shift the locus of the supply curve of a product involving an externality.
9. When a social good involves a positive externality, a subsidy has the effect of shifting the supply curve downwards (or to the right) so that at a lower market price more of the good will be produced and sold, thereby relieving the under-allocation of resources.
10. When a social good involves a spill-over cost, a tax has the effect of shifting the supply curve upward (or to the left) so that at a higher price less of the goodwill be purchased, thereby relieving the over-allocation of resources.
11. If the responsible government agency over-estimates a spill-over benefit, the subsidy may be set at too large an amount, thereby inducing an over-allocation of resources; a similar conclusion follows for overestimation of a spill-over cost.
12. Producers of goods for which subsidies are provided may find market opportunities to expand both production and profit margins; subsidies to some goods also have the effect of reallocating resources away from other goods.
13. Producers of goods upon which taxes are imposed must either absorb the taxes or raise prices, and will thus suffer declining sales and decreased resource usage.
14. Means by which government might attempt to address the spill-over cost problem include: legislation which forbids the continuance of the problem; requirement that the causer of the spill-over cost compensate those who are harmed; auctions of pollution rights; and punitive taxes.
15. Appropriate governmental response to a spill-over cost has the effect of converting the spill-over cost from an irrelevant to a relevant cost.
16. A socially responsible twinge of conscience might have the same effect as a governmental action to redress a spill-over cost.
17. Resources which are reallocated away from the production of goods involving spill-over costs are released for use in producing other goods; firms using those resources may enjoy falling input prices which expand profit margins and encourage expanded production.

Significant Terms

private, social, public goods

competitive market economy

efficient allocation of resources

free-rider effect

market opportunities

bid rigging

unemployment

externalities, spill-overs

private-intentions demand curve

over-, under-allocation of resources

subsidy

relevant-cost supply curve

explicit, relevant costs

auction rights

abatement, clean-up, compensation, punishment

punitive excise tax

over-, under-estimation of effect

social responsibility conscience

Questions for Discussion

1. What constitutes an efficient allocation of resources?
2. Why might an efficient allocation of resources not be desirable?
3. Identify the characteristics of private goods.
4. What is the legitimate role of government in regard to private goods?
5. Distinguish public goods from private goods and identify the characteristics of public goods.
6. What is the legitimate role of government in regard to public goods?
7. Distinguish social goods from purely private goods and from public goods.
8. What is the legitimate role of government in regard to social goods?
9. How does the exclusion principle distinguish between private and public goods?
10. Explain the role of the private sector in the provision of public goods in a democratic society.

11. Identify possible opportunities to the private sector resulting from a social decision to commission the acquisition of a public good.

12. Identify possible threats to private sector firms resulting from a social decision to commission the acquisition of a public good.

13. In what sense are social goods special cases of private goods? Or, are private goods special cases of social goods?

14. Explain why there is a problem with the market demand curve in the case of a social good.

15. How can a market demand curve be made to account for all of the benefits accruing to society from the consumption of a social good?

16. Explain how the incidence of a social good results in a misallocation of resources.

17. Why is the social approach to dealing with a social good usually in terms of the good's supply curve? What is done in regard to the supply curve?

18. Distinguish a subsidy from a tax and explain how they can be used in addressing the problems of externalities.

19. Explain why it might be more appropriate to provide a subsidy to consumers rather than producers of a social good. What are the managerial implications?

20. Discuss the implications of providing a subsidy to the producer rather than consumers of a social good. What are the managerial implications?

21. Discuss the implications of the government's over- (under-) estimating the magnitude of a spill-over benefit resulting from a social good.

22. Identify possible opportunities to private sector producers consequent upon public determination to do something about the misallocation of resources attributable to a social good.

23. Identify possible threats to private sector firms consequent upon a governmental resolve to address a social good misallocation of resources.

24. Explain why the incidence of spill-over costs results in a misallocation of resources.

25. What is the problem with the market supply curve in the case of a spill-over cost?

26. Why might the relevant-cost supply curve result in a misallocation of resources?

27. What is the justification for society to act through its government in regard to spill-over costs?

28. Identify various approaches which governments might implement in addressing a spill-over cost problem. How does each affect the relevant costs of private sector business firms?

29. How can the auction of pollution rights have the effect of diminishing the pollution?
30. Discuss the implications of over- (under-) estimation of the magnitude of a spill-over cost by government authority.
31. Explain how a twinge of social conscience might accomplish the same end as an explicit governmental response to a spill-over cost.
32. Identify possible opportunities to be exploited in regard to spill-over costs.
33. Explain the sense in which business *per se* is neither moral nor immoral.
34. Discuss the citizenship responsibilities of people who are 'in business.'
35. Discuss the social implications of a breakdown of honesty and integrity in business dealings.
36. Discuss the responsibilities of society in regard to the indoctrination of its business leaders.
37. Critically evaluate the statement that society should expect no less or more of its business leaders than of its preachers, teachers, doctors, electricians, or legislators.

—oo(O)oo—

Chapter 22

International Commerce

Topics covered in this chapter

• The distinction between international and domestic business operations. • Differences between international and interregional commerce. • Possible bases for interregional trade. • The changeability of regional advantages. • The impact of nationalism on international commerce. • The effects of using different currencies. • The significance of cultural differences. • Means of acquaintance with target markets.

We open this chapter with a half-serious apology for including a chapter which focuses upon the international dimension of business. The reason for the apology is that in much of the rest of the world outside of the United States of America, there is little significant distinction between international and domestic business operations. If one is in business at all, he or she automatically engages in international business operations. Managers of such firms hardly give second thoughts to the requisites for sourcing supplies, selling products, or locating production in countries other than that within which the firm's home office is located.

The apology is only half serious because many people in various countries, and notably the United States of America, are somewhat intimidated by the international dimension. It is a mixed blessing to the U.S.A. that it has a rich endowment of natural resources and a huge internal economy. Domestic firms have been able to rely upon the internal economy for both sources of supply and markets for their domestically-produced products. Because they have been able to look inwards for over two centuries, managers of American firms have tended to regard the outside world as marginal or peripheral to their activities. Many view the international sector as possessing some mystique which requires special capabilities to penetrate. This perception is enhanced by the fact that Americans are for the most part monolingual. Although English is the only language spoken and understood by the majority of Americans, Spanish may yet overtake English as the American *lingua franca*.

If much of American business has seemed intimidated by international involvements, post-war American consumers have carried on a love affair with foreign-made goods and services. During much of the post World War II era, U.S. balance of payments deficits have been the rule rather than the exception. Concerns about on-going trade deficits and mounting international debt to foreigners have led various U.S. governmental agencies to devise programmes to promote exports and discourage imports. American experience with protecting domestic industries from foreign commercial incursions spans more than two centuries.

On-going trade and payments deficits and official concern about them have aroused the interest of the American academic community in international commercial relations. Some graduate programmes have specialized in international commerce; examples include the American Graduate School of International Management (the "Thunderbird School") in Phoenix, Arizona, and the Masters of International Business Studies (MIBS) offered by the Business School of the University of South Carolina. Beginning in the 1970s, a deliberate effort was mounted by business studies programmes to internationalize their curricula.

By the early 1980s the principal business studies accrediting organization, the American Assembly of Collegiate Schools of Business (AACSB), had established a standard requiring any programme seeking accreditation or re-accreditation to achieve a satisfactory internationalization of its curriculum. The most commonly used models for such internationalization have been to employ foreign faculty and recruit foreign students, to introduce new courses focusing upon international business problems and procedures (for example, international marketing, international finance, international management), and to infuse international concepts into existing courses as appropriate. The latter two models have spawned a flock of new textbook titles as well as revisions of existing texts to incorporate references to the international arena.

In a sense, the recent obsession of American commerce and academia with anything international is only a transitional phase. With the passage of time, international commercial activity will become more commonplace; eventually business studies curricula will become sufficiently internationalized that special commentary about the international sector will no longer be warranted. Three phenomena militate in favour of this transition.

1. Technological advances in communications and transportation shorten the time and costs of distance, thereby diminishing market imperfections and facilitating international exchange.
2. English, the language spoken by the majority of Americans, seems to have emerged as the global language of commerce as well.
3. Efforts underway in various regions of the world to achieve both economic and political integration (the European Union, a 'single market' by 1993, currency union by 1999, and a 'United States of Europe' by some point in the twenty-first century) tend to render concepts of the international ever less significant.

But until such transformation is completed (if ever), we shall be compelled to include chapters such as this in our texts.

BASES FOR INTERREGIONAL COMMERCE

John Donne has said that 'No man is an island, entire of itself...' (Devotions upon Emergent Occasions, Meditation 17). It is surely true that no nation can be an island completely unto itself either. Some have tried. After both its Revolutionary War and World War I, the U.S.A. seemed to withdraw into isolationism in order to avoid further international entanglements, both political and commercial. After its establishment in 1918, the Union of Soviet Socialist Republics (U.S.S.R.) pursued a *de facto* strategy of autarky, that is, internal self-sufficiency. Of all of the nations in the world, these two might have come closest to functional autarky because of the immense richness of their natural resource endowments. But neither of these nor any other nation in the world has been able to achieve absolute autarky. There are several fundamental reasons why they have found it either necessary or beneficial to engage in international commercial relations. There is a very significant difference between international and interregional commerce, but we shall defer consideration of it until a later section. For the moment we shall focus attention upon bases for interregional commerce.

It is a fact of physical nature that resources are unequally distributed across the earth's geographic space. Some resources approach ubiquity (found everywhere); others are concentrated by regions. Resources which are found in only one or two places on earth may be referred to as geographic uniquities. Examples include rare elements or precious gems or metals, agricultural commodities which grow only under very special conditions, and natural tourist attractions. Populations of regions possessing such uniquities are fortunate in having access to such resources which they are able to exploit; populations elsewhere are correspondingly unfortunate. Populations of regions devoid of such uniquities may acquire them (or things produced using them) by engaging in interregional trade or military aggression to capture them.

There are few perfect ubiquities or uniquities among productive resources. Most resources are found in many places across the globe, although in greater or lesser geographic concentrations. Goods and services requiring those resources as inputs may be produced more cheaply in regions where they are found in abundance than in other regions where they are scarce.

THE PRINCIPLE OF COMPARATIVE ADVANTAGE

Economists have enunciated the so-called **principle of comparative advantage** to explain regional specialization in the production of goods and services. According to this principle, people in each region should specialize in producing those goods and services which can be produced most efficiently in their region compared to other regions. 'Most efficiently' means at least opportunity cost (in terms of other goods and services forgone) compared to the other regions. Since the production of goods becomes geographically specialized, people in different regions must trade their specialties for the specialities of people in other regions.

Generalization in consumption is enabled everywhere through trade even though there is regional specialization in production. It can be shown with theoretical exercises as well as empirical information that those who specialize their production according to the principle of comparative advantage and trade with one another enjoy higher welfare than they would under conditions of autarky.

It is sometimes suggested that there are regions of the world which are essentially devoid of productive advantages, whereas other regions seem to possess all of the advantages (veritable 'Gardens of Eden'). We can resolve this problem by further refining the definition of comparative advantage. A region's absolute advantages include all of those things which it can produce at lower opportunity costs than can be achieved in other regions. A region's absolute disadvantage is anything which can be produced elsewhere at lower costs in terms of other goods and services which must be forgone.

It may well be that opportunity costs of most things are lower in one region relative to all others, but this does not mean that the region should generalize in production. Its comparative advantages lie in those things for which it has **greatest absolute** advantage(s), while the comparative advantages of other regions lie in the things for which they have **least absolute** disadvantages. They should still specialize in production, but the one in its greatest absolute advantage and all the rest in their least absolute disadvantages. It follows logically from this definition of comparative advantage that it is not possible for a region to have no comparative advantage(s). Furthermore, it can be shown that all of the regions of the world, the sparsely-endowed as well as the abundantly endowed, will enjoy higher welfare with specialization according to the principle of comparative advantage and trade with one another unencumbered by politically imposed constraints.

Modern elaborations of the theory of comparative advantage recognize at least five bases for regional comparative advantages: resource endowments, cultural preferences, known technologies, scale economies, and company-specific knowledge. The first three are endogenous to locale; the last two technically are independent of geography, but may become location specific at the discretion of production decision makers. For purpose of illustration, it is usual in trade theory to hypothesize a two-resource, two-commodity, two-region world. Suppose one of the regions, A, is abundantly endowed with capital resources but has only enough labour to operate its capital stock, and that the other region, B, is abundantly endowed with labour but has a small amount of capital which serves as minimal tools for the labour. The two regions produce two commodities, X which under technologies known in both regions requires a great deal of labour but not much capital, and Y which uses substantial amounts of capital but only a little labour. If the two regions employ identical technologies for producing the two goods and further have identical preference functions, region A should specialize in producing good Y, whereas region B should produce more of good X. Each should trade some of its specialty to the other in exchange for some of the other's specialty.

Suppose that the two regions have identical resource endowments and know the same productive technologies. While people in both regions consume both goods, suppose that people in region A have a stronger preference for X, the labour intensive good, while people in region B like Y, the capital intensive good. In this case, it would be appropriate for region A to specialize in producing X and region B in producing Y. Each should trade some of its output to the other in order to achieve consumption generalization in both regions. In this case, the basis for comparative advantage is differential preferences rather than resource endowments.

As a third possibility, suppose that the two regions possess identical resource endowments and share a common preference system, but that scientists and engineers in region A have advanced technology with respect to the production of X so as to economize on labour, whereas common technology continues to be used in the production of Y, the capital intensive good, in both countries. Again, intuition suggests that region A should specialize in the production of X leaving region B to specialize in production of Y. They should trade some of their respective specialties to each other. The basis of comparative advantage here is differential technologies rather than resource endowments or preferences. Scale economies and company-specific knowledge may also serve as bases for regional comparative advantage.

It would be highly unlikely in any of these cases that perfect specialization (that is, only X is produced in A and only Y is produced in B) would result. Both goods would continue to be produced in both regions, but in each region more of the comparative advantage good would be produced, and less of the comparative disadvantaged good(s). Also, the real world is composed of many regions, some of which are similar to others in respect to resource endowments, preferences, or technologies, and different from the other regions in various respects. The basis for comparative advantage of each may lie in one of these areas or a combination of them. Empirical evidence suggests that a larger volume of the world's trade is conducted among regions which are similar in income levels and preferences, than among regions which are widely divergent in any of these areas.

QUALIFICATIONS TO THE PRINCIPLE OF COMPARATIVE ADVANTAGE

As noted in previous chapters, managerial opportunities and threats are to be found in almost any circumstances, including those of interregional trade. Certain qualifications to the argument presented to this point should be noted. One is that comparative advantages, whether attributable to resource endowments, preferences, or technologies, are not 'struck in stone,' that is, they are changeable. Circumstances of resource depletion can terminate a former comparative advantage based on the richness of a resource endowment. The discovery of a new deposit or pool of a natural resource can confer a comparative advantage. Population growth or immigration may confer a comparative advantage in producing labour intensive goods where one formerly did not exist. By the same token, emigration may result in depletion of a former comparative advantage based on labour abundance. Natural disasters such as a volcanic eruption, a hurricane, or a freeze which destroys a crop stock may bring to an end some historic comparative advantage. Changing preferences away from 'old' goods and towards newly developed ones may shift comparative advantage from regions specializing in the 'old' and towards regions specializing in the 'new.'

The forms of comparative advantage transition noted above follow from natural or market phenomena which are not under the control of the firm. One of the most significant forms of change in comparative advantages comes about through technological advances which develop new items or new processes which economize on scarce resources. Another significant phenomenon which may change comparative advantage is capital investment. Regions which formerly were capital scarce may become capital abundant, as for example the newly industrialized countries ('NICs') of South Asia. The reason that these two forms of comparative advantage transition are significant to managerial decision making is that they are implemented at the discretion of managers of firms. It is by mounting an effort at research and development (R&D) or by capital investment that managerial decision makers may seize entrepreneurial opportunities and deliberately change the competitiveness of their firms and the comparative advantages of their regions.

THE INTERNATIONAL DIMENSION

To this point we have been discussing **interregional** trade; in the so-called 'pure theory of trade' there is no distinction between interregional and international trade. The emergence of national identity and the nation state over the past four centuries have enabled two additional factors which provide for regional differentiation: nationalism and the operations of government.

The interests of governments in international commerce have necessitated another qualification to the comparative advantage theory. The government may attempt to protect an old domestic industry in order to preserve a comparative advantage which is fleeing to foreign regions. An example is the cotton textile industry as it moves from the South of the U.S.A. to East and South Asia. Such protection may take the forms of subsidies to the domestic industry or quotas or tariffs imposed on imported merchandise. Or the government may promote the development of what is believed to be a latent comparative advantage of the region by subsidizing a so-called 'infant industry.' A recent example of this may be the developing electronics industries in India and Singapore.

Government may attempt to neutralize another region's comparative advantage by imposing an import tariff which is intended to eliminate a foreign cost advantage ('levelling the playing field'). The government may impose an import quota as a means of limiting the damage resulting from importation of an item which can be produced at lower cost elsewhere. Or the government may take 'compensatory' action in any of these areas to offset some policy being implemented by the government of another region. In any of these cases of protection, the effect will be to diminish any potential for gain by comparative advantage specialization.

National identity leads to **nationalism**, a sort of emotional cement which binds together people of the same cultural background. They may share a common history and heritage; they may be more-or-less homogeneous with respect to race and ethnicity; typically they subscribe to the same religion or various sects or denominations of a common religion; the vast majority of them speak the same language; and, most importantly, they share a common vision about what it means to be a citizen of the nation. The term is often used to describe a 'nation of people' or simply 'a people' in the biblical sense (the 'Children of Israel' in the Bible are an example of a nation in this sense). The emotional cement of nationalism may reveal itself in the form of patriotism, that is, love of homeland, its cultural and political heritage, its flag.

Other terms such as provincialism or regionalism may attain almost the same sense of nationalism, but with respect to the attitudes of people in more restricted geographic locales. Belgians typically are much more nationalistic with respect to being Flemish or Walonian than they are about being Belgian. It is more important to some in the U.S.A. to be Texans or Southerners than it is to be American. The European Union is attempting to establish a sort of super-national regionalism so that citizens of the 15 member states will begin to feel a sense of European nationalism which eventually may displace nation-state nationalism. Although there is no good term to describe it, a similar emotional cement often exists among the students and alumni of an American state university, especially when in athletic competition with a rival state university.

Nation states are political entities defined by boundaries encompassing areas which may coincide closely with that populated by a 'nation of people' in the biblical sense. Sometimes a nation state encompasses two or more nations of peoples. American Indian tribes have often been referred to as 'nations;' there were many nationalities in the former Soviet Union; modern India encompasses numerous tribal peoples. In the early 1990s, the various nationalities contained by both the Soviet Union and Yugoslavia began to pull apart.

Occasionally political boundaries separating nation states divide peoples of the same nationality. The post-war political division of Europe left the German people separated by 'walls' as well as borders. In South Asia, the Bengali tribal people are split by the India-Bangladesh border. The Pakistan-Afghanistan border divides the Baluchi people, while the Pakistan-India border separates Punjabi tribal people. Separatist movements in these and other areas may have as their goal the reunification of peoples of the same nationality which have been separated by political boundaries.

Nation states also may not coincide with economic regions which are characterized by the possession of natural resources. Both the United States of America and the Russian Republic include numerous uniquely definable economic regions. Sometimes national boundaries split a common resource endowment region. Europeans have often redrawn national boundaries across the rich coal and iron deposits of the Alsace-Lorraine region.

The essential characteristic of the nation state is its possession and exercise of national sovereignty by the government of the nation state. 'National sovereignty' means that the government of the state has the authority and the power to do anything it wishes with respect to the peoples and resources contained within its political boundaries. This power includes the ability to determine the form of economic organization of the economy of the state (until recently, the government of the former U.S.S.R. mandated socialism), and to impose protectionist measures with respect to the industries within the economy (the government of the U.S.A. has a long history of protectionism). It includes the right to insist upon the use of a national currency within the realm and to exclude the use of currencies preferred by others. Sometimes this authority and power leads to human rights abuses to which people and authorities in other nation states raise objections. Such exercise of discretion by the state is constrained only by the tolerance of its citizens and by attitudes and military prowess of other nation states.

CURRENCY DIVERSITY

One of the most critical factors which sets international trade apart from interregional trade is a consequence of the exercise of national sovereignty: the use of different currencies in different nation states. Because the dollar in used in the U.S. economy while the pound sterling is accepted exclusively in the United Kingdom, the balance of payments between the U.S. and the U.K. is important to economic and political considerations in both countries. The dollar-sterling exchange rate is critical to the volume of goods and services entering into international commerce between the two countries at any point in time.

Where the same currency is used throughout a region, these matters should become irrelevant. In the United States, who is concerned about the balance of payments between South Carolina and New York? And what about the exchange rate between the currency used in South Carolina and that accepted in New York (both use the U.S. dollar)? In the European Union the British still insist upon the pound sterling while the French and the Germans use euros as do the majority of EU countries. The U.K.-euro balance of payments continues as a hot issue, just like the pound-dollar and dollat-yuan exchange rates. This is true especially since the European Central Bank insists upon stabilizing the exchange rates while the UK governments is inclined to use currency devaluation or exchange rate fluctuation as means of correcting balance of payments disequilibria.

Currency matters spill over upon the commercial sectors of the international trading partners. That these issues are still not entirely irrelevant in Europe where the Central Bank sets economic conditions (such as interest rates) which adversely affect the economies of some countries in the eurozone but have an overall neutral or beneficial effect for others. And there is still the problem in the balance of payments between the U.S.A. and Europe and with the dollar-Euro exchange rate until such time as Americans and Europeans can agree to use a common currency!

THE CULTURAL DIMENSION

The analysis of nationalism would be much simpler if every nation state were associated exclusively with a certain nation of people. But as we have already noted, this is not the case. Whether we are speaking of the nation state or a particular nation of people who share a common heritage, the principal implication of nationalism is that there are significant differences among populations which yield important consequences for trade and the location of economic activity. These differences may spring from natural phenomena such as heritage, customs, language, etc., or they may be artificially imposed by the behaviour of the governments of the nation states.

Even if political relationships are not involved, differences of national heritages and languages lead to suspicions about the customs and intentions of 'foreigners,' and in extreme cases to xenophobia, that is, fear and hatred of foreigners. An extreme economic consequence of xenophobia is the attempt to achieve autarky. The important point is that nationalism, whether emanating from cultural differences or state sovereignty, tends to diminish the potential for gains from interregional and international specialization and trade. In the extreme, nationalism can completely eliminate such potential gains if sovereign national governments pursue strategies of extreme political isolation and economic autarky.

Because of nationalism, it is necessary to recognize that comparative advantage may be based upon preferences which differ by regions which are defined by national boundaries as well as by cultural heritage. It is also necessary to note that natural comparative advantages may be enhanced or neutralized by the discretionary actions of government officials.

The managerial implications of nationalism, whether based in cultural differences or the exercise of state sovereignty, is that business decision makers wishing to buy, sell, or produce in other countries must come to an understanding of the cultural characteristics and governmental practices of the other countries. It is these differences which make foreign dealings appear to be mysterious, difficult, and risky. The antidotes are acquaintance and familiarity with the foreign environments within which the firm expects to operate. Acquaintance and familiarity can be achieved through study, travel, and interaction with nationals from the target markets. The study should include examination of cross-cultural differences which lead to appreciation of customs and practices different from one's own.

One of the best ways to achieve such appreciation is to learn the languages of the peoples who live in the regions where the firm wishes to operate. Competence in the languages of the target markets may also be crucial to successful business dealings. Peoples in most countries of the world are multilingual; in some countries (notably the U.S.A.) the norm seems to be mono-linguality. A business negotiator who is knowledgeable of the trading partner's language as well as his or her own will likely have the upper hand over a negotiator who speaks only one language. Also, if one is not familiar with the trading partner's language, the partner will be able to lapse into his or her own language when speaking with associates. Finally, we may note that most people in other lands have greater appreciation of their trading partners if they can at least attempt to speak the local language.

WHAT'S AHEAD

In this chapter we have explored the possibilities of engaging in international commerce, that is, exporting to or importing from other regions of the world. But it is also feasible and potentially profitable to engage in direct foreign investment, that is, to locate production in other regions of the world than the home country, and to engage in direct foreign investment to establish the foreign domiciled production facilities. The next chapter is devoted to the multi-nationalization of enterprise.

Summary of Important Points

1. In much of the world outside of the U.S.A. little significant distinction is made between international and domestic business operations; Americans often seem intimidated by the international dimension.
2. On-going trade and payments deficits and official concern about them have heightened the interest of the American academic community in international commercial relations.
3. With the passage of time, international commercial activity will become more commonplace so that special commentary in the academic curriculum will no longer be warranted.
4. Some nations have pursued strategies of autarky, but none has been able to achieve such a state.
5. In the end there is very little difference between interregional and international commerce.

Contd.....

6. The fundamental explanation of interregional commerce is that resources are unequally distributed across the earth's geographic space, but other explanations lie in different preferences and technologies.
7. According to the theory of comparative advantage, people in each region should specialize in producing those goods and services which can be produced most efficiently in their region in comparison to other regions.
8. Interregional trade enables consumption generalization even though there is regional production specialization; such specialization and trade enables the achievement of higher welfare.
9. Because comparative advantage consists in a region's greatest absolute advantage or least absolute disadvantage, it is logically impossible for a region to have no comparative advantage.
10. Regions with identical resource endowments but different tastes or technologies may have comparative advantages based in these differences.
11. Comparative advantages are subject to change over time and may be changed by technological change and capital investment.
12. The government of a region may act to change or subvert the natural comparative advantages of its region or others.
13. Nationalism and national differences may constitute a basis for exchange where none otherwise exist in resource endowments, preferences, or technologies; nationalism may also serve to nullify natural comparative advantages.
14. The use of different currencies in different nations distinguishes international commerce and may constitute an impediment to trade unless currencies may be freely converted into one another.
15. Nationalism tends to diminish the potential for gains from interregional and international specialization and trade.
16. Business decision makers wishing to buy, sell, or produce in other countries must come to an understanding of the cultural differences and governmental practices of the other countries.
17. Acquaintance and familiarity may be achieved through study, travel, and interaction with nationals from the target market; one of the best means is to learn the languages of the peoples who live in the regions where the firm wishes to do business.

Significant Terms

international business	international market imperfections
resource endowments	isolationism
trade deficits, international debt	autarky
internationalization of the curriculum	interregional commerce

unequal resource distribution
ubiquities, uniquities
comparative advantage
opportunity cost
generalization in consumption
specialization in production
trade
absolute advantages, disadvantages
non-endowment explanations
opportunities, threats
immigration, emigration
comparative advantage transition
protection
nationalism
peoples
borders, walls
economic regions
national sovereignty
national currencies
exchange rates
devaluation
payments
cultural heritage
xenophobia

Questions for Discussion

1. Explain why in most of the world there is little distinction made between international and domestic business. Why in the United States is there a significant distinction made between them?
2. Why might the American emphasis on international business diminish with the passage of time?
3. Why do nations like the U.S.A. and the Soviet Union sometimes retreat into isolationism and autarky? What are the economic implications?
4. Identify possible bases for interregional specialization and trade.
5. Distinguish comparative from absolute advantage and discuss the relationship between the two.
6. Explain how generalization in consumption can be achieved even though regions specialize in production.
7. Explain why it is logically impossible for a region to have no comparative advantage.
8. Beyond generalization in consumption, explain why the people of a region should go to the trouble to specialize in production.
9. Identify the economic criterion for specialization in production; what are the implications of specialization on some other (non-economic) ground?

10. Explain how preference diversity between regions can serve as a basis for trade.
11. Explain how the use of different technologies in different regions can serve as the basis for specializing their production in different goods.
12. Why do trading partners rarely achieve perfect specialization in producing different commodities?
13. Explain how regional comparative advantages may change or be changed over time.
14. Discuss the consequences for the industries and the workers of a region when one of its historic comparative advantages moves elsewhere.
15. Why do governments often try to protect a domestic industry from which the comparative advantage has shifted to other regions? What are the economic implications of such protection?
16. How can government promote the development of what is believed to be a latent comparative advantage of its region?
17. Explain how nationalism in different countries may serve to enhance their potentials for trade with one another.
18. Explain how nationalism in different countries may become an impediment to capturing the potential gains from specialization and trade.
19. How do the behaviours and relationships among alumni of the same college or university resemble nationalism? What are the economic implications?
20. Discuss the economic consequences of a division of a nation of people by artificial boundaries or walls.
21. Discuss the economic implications of the exercise of national sovereignty by the government of potential trading partners.
22. Why might the use of different national currencies in different countries constitute a problem for international trade? How can this problem be averted?
23. Identify possible ways in which international cultural diversity might pose problems for international trade. What are the managerial implications?
24. Why does nationalism, whether based on cultural diversity or the exercise of state sovereignty, diminish the potential for gains from interregional and international trade?
25. Identify means by which business decision makers wishing to buy, sell, or produce in other countries can become acquainted with the cultures of their target markets?
26. Discuss the implications of a lack of understanding of a prospective trading partner's language.

—oo(O)oo—

Chapter 23

The Multinationalization of Enterprise

Topics covered in this chapter

• Principles of industry location. • The significance of comparative advantage in industry location. • Opportunities and threats in an open economy. • The entrepreneurial nature of international decision making. • The nature of multi-nationalization. • Why multinational enterprises engage in foreign direct investment. • The monopolistic advantages of oligopolistic multinational firms. • The sunk-cost nature of product development expenses. • Development of knowledge assets as a source of comparative advantage. • Definitions of dumping. • The relationship between protection and comparative advantage. • Consequences of shifts of comparative advantage.

We finished Chapter 22 with a notation that while regions of the world may have macro level comparative advantages, the operatives who have to discover and exploit those comparative advantages are micro level people who function as decision making agents of business firms. We should also note that business decision makers can attempt to change a region's comparative advantages through implementing technological change and capital investment. The acts of discovering, exploiting, and changing comparative advantages are essentially entrepreneurial in nature.

Macro level **comparative** advantages are region (or country) specific. The micro-economic vehicles for discovering, exploiting, and changing comparative advantages are **competitive** advantages which are company specific. Another way to say this is that no latent comparative advantages can be discovered or developed unless managers of business enterprises can establish and exploit competitive advantages over actual or potential rivals. The entrepreneurial motivations to do so are profitability, growth potential, and control over markets and production processes. How are these decision making goals pursued?

THE LOCATION OF ECONOMIC ACTIVITY

Some economic activity, by its very nature, must take place in close proximity to the markets which it serves. The restaurant and real estate businesses come readily to mind. In fact, most services must be rendered at the site of consumption (financial and insurance services may constitute exceptions). Other economic activity is more appropriately located nearer to sources of supply of the raw materials which are required as inputs in the final products.

The over-riding principle is that under sufficiently competitive market conditions, commercial activity tends to locate relative to markets and input supplies where it can operate most profitably. Inappropriately located productive sites will yield lower returns or losses, and ultimately may result in failure and exit from the market.

Two further locational principles can be identified. In order to minimize the combination of production and shipping costs, products which lose weight in the manufacturing process tend to be produced closer to sources of supplies of the inputs of greatest weight per unit cost. Products which gain weight in the production process tend to be produced nearer to their final markets. Examples of weight-losing manufacturing processes are found in the refinement of ores to produce metals of high purity. Any product which is assembled in stages from materials or components may serve as an example of a weight-gaining process.

Economic activity may relocate for a variety of reasons. One is simply that producers realize that their former sites are uneconomic relative to other sites. This realization may be brought upon them by the subnormal returns or outright losses which they suffer compared to those realized by producers in other locales. One of the most potent forms of industry relocation is the failure of productive ventures in one region at the same time that new ventures producing the same goods or services are started in another region. Capital is withdrawn and labour displaced at the former site, and new capital is invested and employees are recruited at the new site, but rarely by the same people.

One of the principal vehicles for industry relocation is changing comparative advantage. As we have already noted, comparative advantages are not 'struck in stone.' When comparative advantages change, either for natural reasons or because of human intervention, industry tends to relocate away from the former locus of the comparative advantage, and towards its new locus. Whether the comparative advantage has shifted regionally or from one country to others, locales where the advantage is departing may resist as strongly as possible their loss of advantage, and may solicit the offices of the governments of their countries to prevent the flight.

When a region's comparative advantages change, what business decision makers see are changing **competitive** advantages, not macro level comparative advantages. The entrepreneurially perceptive firm managers will see competitive opportunities in other industries or other locales sooner; the less perceptive and more risk averse will remain too long in their current industries or locales and ride their firms into decline and failure.

Economists can with confidence argue that specialization according to comparative advantage will maximize world welfare. One of the great ironies of the principle of comparative advantage is that the adjustment to a shift of comparative advantage can be extremely painful in regions which lose it, even while the gainers enjoy the ebullience associated with expanding output, employment, and profits. Usually all of the pains are suffered in one region, while all of the benefits are enjoyed in another. A loss of comparative advantage will be manifested to business firms by operating losses, business failures, distress sales of plant and equipment, a declining tax base, and dis-employment. It is these conditions, especially when they result in threats of political instability, which command the attention of government officials. But if international economic realities truly have changed, any governmental action to 'stem the tide' of a fleeing comparative advantage can only distort the international allocation of resources and lower efficiency and welfare, both at home and abroad.

Some productive resources tend to be more mobile than do others. It is often thought that labour is the most mobile resource while capital and natural resources are less mobile. There have been historical instances of human migrations for economic reasons. From the sixteenth century forward, people have left Western Europe for North and South America, South Africa, and Australia in search of greater opportunity, that is, richer endowments of natural resources. The nineteenth century in the U.S.A. saw a great westward migration for similar reasons. Today, people are fleeing certain Eastern European countries for both political and economic reasons.

It is also possible to extract and ship natural resources to remote locations for processing, as it is possible to take the processing to the site of the extraction. A footloose industry is one in which both materials and capital are more mobile than the labour necessary to produce the output. A footloose industry need not locate either near sources of raw materials or to markets for the product. The cotton textile industry may be an example of a footloose industry because it seems to move continually across the earth's geographic space in search of the lowest cost labour. This seems to be a case of 'the mountain going to Mahomet,' that is, the industry going to the labour. Cultural heritage tends to militate against the mobility of labour across national boundaries. Technological advances in communications and transportation tend to render all industries ever more footloose because the declining costs of shipping materials and capital resources make them ever more mobile relative to labour.

OPPORTUNITIES IN AN OPEN ECONOMY WORLD

Our discussion is intended to be suggestive of the many opportunities as well as threats to business enterprises in a world characterized by open economies. The term 'open economy' refers to a situation where neither cultural nor governmental hindrances to enterprise prevent international trade, requirements sourcing, the location of production, or immigration. In a closed economy, the business decision maker has only to decide where within the economy to locate the enterprise, from whom to source materials requirements, and in which domestic markets to offer the produced goods and services. An economy becomes closed either because its people are so xenophobic and isolationist that they will not interact with foreigners, or because the government acts to diminish or prohibit foreign commerce. Even if an economy is not entirely closed by xenophobic attitudes or governmental hindrances to trade, the presence of such forces tend to constrain international commerce and diminish the potential benefits.

When an economy is more-or-less open to international commerce, the range of decision options available to the business decision maker extend to considerations of

(a) whether to sell the firm's output in foreign markets;

(b) whether to source materials requirements abroad;

(c) whether to locate production in other countries;

(d) whether to raise financial capital abroad; and

(e) whether to recruit employees and managerial personnel internationally.

All of these are essentially entrepreneurial (to be distinguished from routine managerial) decisions. The motivations to such entrepreneurial decisions are profitability, growth, and control.

As we noted, business decision makers in many countries do not make serious distinctions between domestic and international commerce. But for business decision makers in a large, inward looking country such as the U.S.A., it may take a special orientation for a decision maker even to perceive the 'foreign' opportunities, and an even more special attitude towards risk to be willing to delve into the unknown or mysterious facets of foreign commerce. This is what renders international operating decisions essentially entrepreneurial in nature.

The same decision criteria may be employed by the entrepreneurial decision maker irrespective of whether domestic or international operations are at issue. If the anticipated benefits of undertaking a new international operation exceed the estimated costs, the operation is economically justifiable. In case of an anticipated expansion of an on-going activity in the international arena, an excess of marginal benefits over marginal costs warrants the expansion. Similar criteria can be specified for contracting or terminating any international operation. The additional difficulty for international considerations is identifying all of the relevant benefits and costs. Because of the uncertainty and variability associated with the international arena, risk factors may be more significant than in known domestic markets.

It is a classification of convenience to identify four types of enterprises on the basis of their engagement in international commerce:

1. A domestic firm is one which, with respect to a particular nation state, conducts all of its business relationships exclusively in the domestic economy of that nation state; it may find itself serving an occasional foreign customer travelling in its nation state even though it does not solicit foreign business.

2. A foreign firm is one which, with respect to a particular nation state, is organized or incorporated in a second nation state, but which is doing business by way of buying or selling in the domestic economy of the first nation state.

3. An international firm is one which maintains a principal office and productive facilities in one nation state and conducts buying and selling activity in that and other nation states.

4. A multinational firm is one which maintains offices and productive facilities in multiple nation states and determines executive policy without preference or prejudice with respect to national origin or location.

A true multinational firm may both sell output and source materials and financing requirements internationally; it may locate production anywhere in the world that its management sees fit; it may seek financing and technologies anywhere in the world, and it may recruit employees and managerial personnel anywhere in the world. A firm has risen to the height of multi-nationality if in its management recruiting it can be blind with respect to nationality, race, ethnicity, language, and cultural heritage.

The more risk averse the management of a firm is, the more likely it is to remain a purely domestic firm. Venturing into the realms of international and multinational operations requires willingness to assume risk. Needless to say, the vast majority of business firms in the world are either domestic or international firms; some of the latter are in the process of becoming true multinationals; there are indeed only a few firms in the world which have achieved true multi-nationality.

All firms engaged in international operations facilitate the mobility of resources and goods, and thereby contribute to allocative efficiency across national boundaries. International importers and exporters do so in response to international market incentives. Franklin R. Root (*International Trace and Investment*, South-Western Publishing Company, Sixth Edition, 1991) characterizes the multinational enterprise as an international transfer agent. Although it responds to external market forces, the multinational enterprise employs managerial discretion rather than market incentives to direct the flows of resources, capital, product, technology, and managerial expertise within itself and among its affiliates in other countries. In doing so it surmounts both market imperfections and political hindrances to market-initiated flows. The multinational enterprise thereby achieves greater allocative efficiency through the exercise of managerial discretion than can be achieved purely through international market transactions, especially if market transactions involve externalities.

The international opportunities open to a purely domestic firm are limited exclusively to the unsolicited interaction with foreign nationals who happen into the firm's place of business. The broader horizons of the international firm include possibilities of both importing and exporting as well as licensing and participating in joint ventures. The international firm may import final products to be marketed to customers within its economy, or to be re-exported to customers in other countries. It may also import raw materials, partially processed goods, or components to which it adds value in further processing, assembly, and packaging. These goods may then be marketed domestically or re-exported for sale or further processing in other countries. Even if the international firm has not imported materials or finished goods, it may export its domestically produced goods and services.

The impetus to export domestically produced goods is the perception of market opportunities in other countries which appear more profitable (or no less so) than domestic distribution. The impetus to import materials or components is the discovery of cost advantages in international sourcing compared to domestic sourcing.

The impetus to import finished goods for domestic distribution may be either foreign cost advantage, the perception of domestic markets for uniquely foreign merchandise, or both. In fact, the strength of domestic demand for a foreign-made item may be great enough to outweigh its cost disadvantage; many American consumers appear willing to pay higher prices for certain foreign-made automobiles (for example, Mercedes Benz, BMW, Jaguar) than for comparable domestically assembled vehicles (Cadillac, Lincoln).

DRIVES TO MULTI-NATIONALIZATION

The multinational enterprise is subject to all of these drives plus others which lead it to establish or acquire productive facilities in countries other than that where its principal office is located. The establishment of such productive subsidiaries or affiliates requires foreign direct investment which is distinguished from portfolio investment. The former involves the construction or acquisition of facilities over which the firm exercises exclusive control while the latter involves only the acquisition of a small-enough share of outstanding stock that control is not intended or possible. The motivation to foreign portfolio investment is usually found in the anticipation that foreign rates of return are higher than domestic rates of return after allowing for risk differentials. However, there is little evidence to the effect that differences in expected rates of return alone can account for foreign direct investment by multinational enterprises.

There is an extensive literature focusing upon the motives to undertake direct foreign investment. We shall here attempt only to examine the prominent theories and summarize the conclusions. Virtually all multinational enterprises are large concerns (in terms of invested capital, sales volumes, number of employees, etc.) which operate in oligopolistic markets. They therefore possess varying amounts of monopoly power in the sense of being able to exercise pricing discretion. Their monopoly power is based upon either scale economies or superior knowledge which confer firm-specific competitive advantages. Such competitive advantage may be applied anywhere in the world, and thus can serve as the basis of a region-specific comparative advantage only at those sites where management chooses to establish operations.

If the benefits of scale economies or knowledge assets are sufficient to outweigh the costs of distance, cultural differences, and dealings with foreign governments, the management of the multinational enterprise may expect greater income from operating in the foreign market than local firms can expect. To realize the larger incomes, the local firms would have to achieve comparable size (to exploit the economies of scale) or in some way acquire similar knowledge assets (which are costly to acquire). The reason that the multinational enterprise may be able to operate more economically in the foreign market than can local firms is that their knowledge assets were developed for the 'home market,' and thus are sunk costs; the marginal cost of development of the knowledge assets for the foreign market is therefore zero. But the marginal cost of acquiring such knowledge assets by local firms would be significantly non-zero. The exercise of superior knowledge by the multinational enterprise allows it to produce and sell differentiated products in the foreign market. This enables it to exercise monopoly pricing and capture economic rent for the knowledge assets.

A typical life cycle can be described for a product developed by a multinational enterprise. When the new product is introduced, production is initially retained in the home country (or where an affiliate first developed the new product) to allow close contact with design and production technical expertise. The product is sold in the domestic market and may be exported to foreign markets. However, as the product becomes standardized, the enterprise is able to shift production to affiliates in lower-cost foreign locales, most likely in other industrialized countries with large domestic and export markets so that scale economies can be exploited. A collateral phenomenon is that with standardization of the product, local firms can imitate the product (the competitive advantage of the superior knowledge assets begins to erode) to capture some of the multinational enterprise's export market. Foreign production at lower costs may then be a defensive measure undertaken by the multinational enterprise in order to preserve market share.

In the latter stages of the product's life cycle, production in the multinational enterprise's home market may cease as the product continues to be available only as an import from its foreign affiliates. Continuing developments of new knowledge assets by the multinational enterprise are needed to sustain its home-country operations. It is in the continuing development of knowledge assets that the home country of the multinational enterprise may have its real comparative advantage.

Because the multinational enterprise is likely to be an oligopoly with wide dispersion of ownership shares, its management may be more attuned to growth and share-of-market objectives than to profit *per se*. The Baumol sales optimization model may be an appropriate vehicle for analysis of the typical multinational enterprise. The development of differentiated products and their sale in world markets is one means by which the multinational may be able to achieve an increased market share or a continually growing volume of sales. Competitor oligopolists are likely to feel compelled to follow a leader into international production and marketing as defensive measures in order to preserve their market shares. Such oligopolistic bunching of entry into foreign markets by competing multinational enterprises tends to be a common phenomenon.

Multinational enterprises may be more inclined to enter into foreign production of their products rather than exporting from the home country or licensing foreign producers. The reason is that by doing so they can internalize control of their superior knowledge assets and thereby protect them from erosion for a longer time. Because a newly developed superior knowledge tends to become a public good very quickly as others master or imitate it, the developer can capture an economic rent for it only as long as the knowledge is secret or can be held proprietary. Exporting the good from the domestic productive facilities, or licensing the production technology to foreign producers, tends to accelerate the deterioration of the proprietary nature of the knowledge assets. This may be regarded as an externality of market-organized transactions, that is, the market price after the newly developed knowledge becomes a public good fails to reward the developer for the costs of developing the new knowledge. This market imperfection can be averted by the multinational enterprise by retaining sole proprietary exploitation of its superior knowledge assets within the firm and its foreign affiliates rather than letting the knowledge assets leak to the rest of the world through market transactions.

THREATS IN AN OPEN ECONOMY

While the open economy provides a whole range of opportunities for the enterprise, it also holds some threats. The principal threat to domestic producers comes from foreign producers, especially if they can achieve lower production costs or produce products which are differentiated by virtue of their foreign manufacture. Foreign producers are often perceived to 'dump' their products in domestic markets as a means of driving domestic producers from the market, thereby conferring monopoly power upon the foreign producers.

Although lower prices of foreign products may reflect lower direct (variable) production costs, another rationale for such apparent dumping is that overhead costs typically have been fully allocated by the foreign producer to the output produced for its domestic market. In this case the price of output destined for foreign markets needs to cover only the direct (or variable) costs. Hence the price of the output produced for the foreign market (excluding any allowance for overhead costs) can be lower than the domestic price (including full allocation of overhead costs).

Technically, 'dumping' means that a foreign producer is selling in a domestic market at a price below the foreign producer's full cost of production (including overhead cost allocation). However, it is virtually never possible for one who charges another with dumping to gain adequate information about the other's costs (direct or overhead) of production. For this reason, the 'political' definition of dumping is sale by the foreign producer in the domestic market at a price below the domestic producer's full cost of production (including overhead cost allocation). Sometimes domestic producers claim that the foreign producer is dumping when the price is simply below domestic prices. This is a 'political' definition because it usually serves as the basis for an appeal by domestic producers to their governments for protection from the foreign producers who are reputed to be engaged in dumping.

The problem with the political definition of dumping is that it really cannot be distinguished from the phenomenon of competitive pricing. For example, if another domestic producer were selling at a price below our own preferred price, or even at a price below our own per-unit cost of production including overhead cost allocation (ATC), we could hardly charge our domestic competitor with dumping. The most that we could do is complain about competitive pricing which may be predatory in nature. But if a foreign firm engages in exactly the same behaviour, domestic producers are quick to charge dumping and appeal to their governments for relief.

Actions by governments are also potential sources of threats as well as opportunities. If domestic producers can enlist the authority of government to protect them by imposing tariffs or quotas, this constitutes an opportunity for domestic producers to sustain or expand production and employment (in spite of a lack of comparative advantage), but it is a threat both to foreign exporters and to domestic importers. By the same token, actions by foreign governments to protect their industries will constitute threats to domestic firms which may have real competitive advantages. As we have already noted, protection also tends to distort the world-wide allocation of resources and diminish the potential for gains from trade.

Governmentally imposed quotas implemented by import or export licensing also constitutes a source of threat for domestic firms. Import licensing is more commonly used as a means of protecting domestic producers, but governments of resource-rich regions (particularly petroleum exporting countries) may use export licensing as a means of capturing income from the foreign sale of the resource. The source of the threat is that uncertainty arises as to which firms can acquire licences to import or export what quantities of goods. Production and shipping schedules may be significantly disrupted, and earnings from sales of imported materials or goods for export may be jeopardized.

But the greatest threat to domestic producers in any country is an adverse shift of comparative advantage. Such may come about because of a natural disaster which destroys a productive advantage, or it may result simply from depletion of an historic natural resource endowment. In the modern world, an adverse shift of comparative advantage is more likely to have been engineered by foreign competitors who develop superior knowledge assets or engage in such massive capital investment as to create a capital-abundant productive environment. Also, technical advances in communications and transportation may render capital and resources so much more mobile than labour that footloose industries move very easily from one part of the world to another in search of ever lower-cost labour. Such a fleeting comparative advantage will severely threaten the viability of firms where the industry historically has been located.

Finally, we note that in oligopolistic markets (which may characterize most of the markets in the modern world) the competitive actions by any single firm can be expected to threaten the market share and profitability of any other firm in the market. If the others do not rise to the occasion they will certainly suffer declining market shares and operating losses which may culminate in failure. This phenomenon is surely so much more intense in an open-economy world than in protected domestic economies.

Even though the threats in an open economy may appear substantial, the opportunities found in international commerce almost surely outweigh them. The evidence to support this contention lies in the expanding volume of both trade and direct foreign investment throughout the world. But as a re-visitation to the opening passages of the next chapter, we note that these concepts and problems of internationalism will tend to diminish in importance as economies become more open, as their peoples become more comfortable with international commerce, as economic and political integration ensues, and as market imperfections diminish with technological advances in communications and transportation.

As we end this chapter, perhaps it would be helpful to list some of the operational objectives which firms pursue in their quest for global competitive advantage. Firms attempt to establish market presences in other regions of the world in order to:

1. increase sales revenue and hence profitability;
2. achieve unit sales or revenue growth targets;
3. increase share of the market,
4. achieve enhanced oligopolistic position by pre-empting competitors;
5. preserve oligopolistic position by meeting or neutralizing competitors who have already arrived;
6. diminish dependence upon mature or stagnant markets;
7. increase demand to allow spreading overhead in existing plants; and
8. increase demand to exploit economies of scale from increasing plant size.

Firms engage in direct investment in other regions in order to:

1. surmount nationalistic preferences for domestically made goods;
2. seek higher rates of return than can be achieved elsewhere or by local competitors;
3. internalize control of knowledge assets while exploiting them;
4. acquire new knowledge resources; and
5. circumvent trade barriers.

WHAT'S AHEAD

The next chapter extends the international scope into the realm of developing economies. Because trade and development are inextricably intertwined, we shall use the international dimension as the platform for launching our survey of entrepreneurial opportunities in developing economies.

Summary of Important Points

1. The overriding principle of industry location is that under sufficiently competitive market conditions, industry tends to locate relative to markets and input supplies where it can operate most profitably.
2. The production of weight-losing products tends to be located closer to sources of supplies; weight-gaining product production tends to be located closer to final markets.
3. One of the most potent forms of industry relocation is the failure of productive ventures in one region at the same time that new ventures producing the same goods or services are started in another region.
4. One of the principal vehicles for industry relocation is shifting comparative advantage.
5. Usually all of the pains of a comparative advantage shift are suffered in one nation while all of the benefits are enjoyed in another.
6. Any governmental action to 'stem the tide' of a fleeing comparative advantage can only distort the international allocation of resources.
7. Technological advances in communications and transportation tend to render both materials and capital resources ever more mobile relative to labour.
8. Business firms may find both opportunities and threats in an open economy, one where neither cultural nor governmental hindrances to enterprise prevent international trade, requirements sourcing, production, or immigration.
9. In an open economy the range of decision options available to the entrepreneur include: selling in foreign markets; sourcing requirements (materials and financial) abroad; producing in other countries; and recruiting managerial personnel internationally.
10. For decision makers in a country such as the U.S.A., it may take a special orientation to perceive foreign opportunities and assume risk in exploiting them; international operating decisions are essentially entrepreneurial in nature.
11. Because of the uncertainty and variability associated with the international arena, risk factors may be more significant than in known domestic markets.
12. Enterprises may be classified into four categories: domestic firms, foreign firms, international firms, and multinational firms.

Contd.....

13. A firm has risen to the height of multi-nationality if in its management recruiting it can be blind with respect to nationality, race, ethnicity, language, and cultural heritage.
14. The multinational enterprise is characterized as an international transfer agent which contributes to allocative efficiency across national boundaries.
15. The establishment of foreign productive subsidiaries by a multinational firm requires foreign direct investment (rather than portfolio investment); there is no evidence that differences in expected rates of return can account for foreign direct investment.
16. Virtually all multinational firms are large concerns which operate in oligopolistic markets; their monopoly power is based upon scale economies or superior knowledge.
17. If the benefits of scale economies or knowledge assets are sufficient to outweigh the costs of distance, cultural differences, and dealings with foreign governments, the multinational firm may expect greater operating income in the foreign market than can local firms.
18. The multinational's knowledge assets were developed for the home market and are thus sunk costs; the marginal cost of acquiring such knowledge assets by local firms is significantly non-zero.
19. A newly-introduced product follows a typical life cycle: home country production, export, foreign subsidiary production, foreign imitation, import.
20. Continuing developments of new knowledge assets by the multinational may confer true comparative advantage on the multinational's home country.
21. The management of an oligopolistic multinational enterprise may be more attuned to growth and share-of-market than to profits.
22. Oligopolistic bunching of entry into foreign markets results from feelings of compulsion to follow the leader as a defensive measure.
23. Multinational enterprises are more inclined to establish subsidiaries to produce their products in foreign locales than to export the products in order to internalize control of their superior knowledge assets.
24. A principal threat to local producers comes from foreign or multinational producers who can achieve lower production costs or who have already allocated the product development costs to the quantities produced for their home markets.
25. The political definition of dumping is sale by the foreign producer in the domestic market at a price below the domestic producer's cost of production.
26. The problem with the political definition of dumping is that it cannot be distinguished from the phenomenon of competitive pricing.
27. The enlistment by domestic producers of governmental protection constitutes an opportunity for domestic producers to expand production and employment in

Contd.....

spite of a lack of true comparative advantage; if foreign producers do this, it constitutes a threat to domestic firms which might want to export.

28. Threats are consequent upon government-imposed quotas because uncertainty arises as to which firms can acquire licences to import or export what quantities.
29. The greatest international threat to domestic producers is adverse shift of comparative advantage which may have natural causes, or which may have been engineered by foreign competitors who develop superior knowledge assets or engage in massive capital investments.
30. In oligopolistic international markets, the competitive actions by any single firm can threaten the market shares and profitability of other firms.
31. The evidence is that opportunities found in international commerce almost surely outweigh the threats.

Significant Terms

industry location, relocation

weight-losing, -gaining products

business failure

comparative advantage shifts

protection

resource mobility

footloose industry

cultural heritage

open, closed economy

sourcing

foreign opportunities, risks

entrepreneurial decision

domestic, foreign, international, multinational

allocative efficiency

international transfer market imperfections

managerial discretion

externalities

export, import

direct, portfolio investment

expected rates of return

oligopolistic markets

pricing discretion

scale economies

superior knowledge assets

sunk costs

product life cycle

competitive, comparative advantage

growth, share-of-market

oligopolistic bunching of entry

internalize control

economic rent

Questions for Discussion

1. Why are all industries not located everywhere on the face of the earth?
2. Identify the overriding principle of industry location.
3. Why do some industries locate closer to material sources, while others locate closer to markets?
4. Why do industries tend to relocate?
5. Discuss the political and social consequences of shifting comparative advantage.
6. Explain how shifting comparative advantage can cause industry relocation.
7. Discuss the comparative mobilities of materials, labour, and capital.
8. Distinguish an open economy from a closed economy and discuss the entrepreneurial opportunities associated with each.
9. Explain the sense in which international business decisions are essentially entrepreneurial in nature.
10. Why do international business operations tend to be more risky than domestic operations?
11. Classify business firms as to their international orientation and discuss the managerial/ entrepreneurial decision options of each.
12. How may the degree of multi-nationalization of orientation of a business firm be discerned?
13. Explain the sense in which a multinational enterprise functions as an international transfer agent.
14. Explain why the operating horizons of an international firm are broader than those of a purely domestic firm.
15. Distinguish direct from portfolio foreign investment and discuss them in the context of multinational enterprise.
16. Why do multinational enterprises engage in foreign direct investments?
17. Explain the sense in which knowledge asset development expenses are sunk costs. What are the multinational decision implications?
18. Describe the product life cycle in its multinational dimension. What are the managerial/ entrepreneurial implications?
19. How can oligopolistic bunching of entry into foreign markets be explained?
20. Explain the likely relationship between knowledge asset development and comparative advantage.

21. Distinguish competitive advantage from comparative advantage and explain how they may be related.

22. Why are multinational enterprises more inclined to enter into foreign production of their products than to export them or licence their production by foreign firms?

23. Why might the exporting of a product or the licensing of its foreign production result in an externality of the market-organized transaction?

24. How can externalities of market-organized transactions be averted by multinational enterprises?

25. Survey the threats to the operations of multinational enterprises; given the threats, why do enterprises engage in multinational operations?

26. How might the firm's allocation of overhead costs lead to a charge that it is dumping in foreign markets?

27. Distinguish the political definition of dumping from the technical definition and discuss the economic implications of the distinction.

28. Distinguish dumping from competitive pricing and discuss the political and economic implications.

29. Discuss the likely implications of governmental protection of domestic industry for the world-wide allocation of resources and welfare.

30. Explain why comparative advantages might shift from one region of the world to another and discuss the managerial/entrepreneurial implications.

31. Why will the problems of international commerce diminish over time?

—oo(O)oo—

Chapter 24

Opportunities in Developing Economies

Topics covered in this chapter

• The nature of lesser developed countries. • Managerial and entrepreneurial decision making in lesser developed economies. • Entrepreneurial capacity as comparative advantage. • Cultural environments of lesser developed countries. • The underdevelopment of infrastructure. • The scarcity of capital. • Labour in the lesser developed economy. • The appropriateness of technology. • The potential of trade for development. • The role of the government in the developing economy. • Entrepreneurial opportunities in the developing economy.

DEVELOPING ECONOMY TERMINOLOGY

We choose the term 'lesser developed country' (LDC) as perhaps the least problematic of the terms which have been employed in the literature to refer to low-income countries in the 'third world' which are characterized by primary product production and the use of primitive productive techniques. (The 'first world' consists of the industrialized market economies of Europe and North America; the 'second world' encompasses the socialistic economies of the former Sino-Soviet bloc; the 'third world' consists of the low-income and underdeveloped countries of the South and East.) The distinction between the 'first' and 'second' worlds is being made obscure by the transitions from socialism to market economy in the latter, and by experimentations with statism in the former.

The concept of 'lesser developed' is of course relative. All economies except some in the very most remote and primitive parts of the world have experienced some development, some income growth, some adoption of advanced technologies, and some industrialization. And many technologically advanced, financially mature economies surely still are underdeveloped relative to their resource endowments and potentials for continued development.

We shall take the term 'LDC' to refer to countries which lag behind the technological conditions and income levels of the typical higher income, more industrialized, more technologically advanced economies of North America, Europe, and the Pacific rim. The term 'newly industrialized country' (NIC) signifies countries in an intermediate state which are making progress from conditions of underdevelopment towards development.

RISK FACTORS

Managerial and entrepreneurial decision making in LDC economies should employ the same benefit-cost criteria as employed in advanced economies when considering either domestic or international operations. The problems of LDC decision making centre about even greater market imperfections, even less market information, and ever greater market externalities than are found in more advanced economies. This means that risks may be greater in any or all decision settings in the LDC economy. It also means that decision making in regard to business operations in LDC economies should be characterized more as entrepreneurial than managerial. As we noted, the decision maker must compile a storehouse of experience upon which to base assessments of risk. And as noted above in discussing prospects for international operations, the best way to do this is to become as familiar as possible with the LDC decision setting. This may prove difficult without direct involvement within the LDC environment.

THE ROLE OF ENTREPRENEURSHIP

Development economists have come to the conclusion that one of the most significant reasons for underdevelopment in the third world is lack of entrepreneurship. A region may have a rich endowment of various natural resources, but it will not be exploited without entrepreneurs to assume risk in innovation. Another region may be essentially devoid of natural resource endowments, but an entrepreneur may still perceive a productive opportunity and 'make it happen.'

A prerequisite to initiating an on-going development process is to provide conditions conducive to entrepreneurship and tolerant of entrepreneurship. Where enterprise is essentially lacking in a third world country, the avenues of international trade and investment may provide just the 'jump start' necessary to promote on-going development.

We may hypothesize that one of the important comparative advantages of the developed part of the world lies in its endowment of entrepreneurial capacity. The exercise of entrepreneurship may be one of the most valuable contributions of the multinational enterprise to the LDC economies within which they operate. The problem for the LDC then is to indigenize the entrepreneurial process so that it will be taken over by local business interests.

THE CULTURAL ENVIRONMENT

Foreign involvement in the LDC environment begs even greater questions about cross-cultural differences than occur when firms become involved in other economies which are similar to their own. Customs and dress are even more exotic. Business practices are likely to be even more closely tied to cultural heritage than the standards of business dealings which have emerged among European and North American countries. In many third world countries, women do not enjoy the same acceptance in business dealings as do male managers.

A wide variety of national and tribal languages and dialects are spoken in the third world, although nineteenth and early-twentieth century colonialism has left a legacy of European language blocs in the third world. But the managers of a multinational enterprise attempting to do business in a third-world country should not expect to rely upon his or her native language or that studied in high school or college even though many people in the LDC may understand it as a second or third language. The foreign manager will find greater acceptance and business dealings will be facilitated if he or she can speak (even meagrely) the language of the realm and avoid *faux pas* related to cultural differences.

INFRASTRUCTURE

One of the crucial problems of the LDC decision setting is the underdeveloped nature of infrastructure facilities which can be taken for granted in a more advanced economy. Transportation and communications facilities may be primitive; electricity and gas generation and transmission facilities may be lacking; sanitation and health care may be at an entirely different level than in the more advanced economy. The firm may find itself having to provide several of these services or facilities simply to be able to conduct its intended lines of business. Indeed, the scarcity of such infrastructure facilities may constitute rich entrepreneurial opportunities for both domestic and foreign firms.

One of the consequences of infrastructure underdevelopment is that it may not be possible to rely upon the commercial environment of the LDC to provide input supplies, complementary services, maintenance and repair support, or even marketing channels for distribution of outputs. A productive facility in an LDC is much more likely to have to be more vertically integrated, self-contained, and stand-alone than needs to be planned for and achieved in a more advanced economy.

CAPITAL SCARCITY

A common problem of most of the LDC economies is that directly productive capital is scarce and technologies are primitive. The so-called 'vicious circle of poverty' turns upon the capital scarcity which ensures low labour productivity. The low productivity enables only meagre wages. Incomes which are near (or below) the threshold of subsistence needs limit the capacity of the society to save. Little indigenous saving limits the investment potential of society. Finally, inadequate investment ensures that capital will remain scarce.

But the circle of poverty may be broken at numerous points, any of which may provide entrepreneurial opportunities for interests within or from outside the LDC economy. The capital scarcity itself may pose investment opportunities since interest rates should provide higher returns than available in capital abundant parts of the world. Higher interest rates should attract foreign savings either through portfolio or direct foreign investment, or through international bank lending. Foreign lenders will also insist upon even higher interest rates than warranted by capital scarcity so as to include risk premiums against the unknown and uncertain conditions in the LDC environment. Low wages should attract footloose industries from other parts of the world, but they may be perceived to be attempting to exploit an impoverished population.

LABOUR AND TECHNOLOGY

In an LDC the manager should expect to employ labour of pre- or early-industrial attitudes and conditioning. Such a labour force may be attuned to the agricultural sector during peak planting and harvesting seasons, and may thus be absent from the commercial or industrial work place at those times. Labour in an LDC is typically not (yet) attuned to the discipline of the clock or to required manufacturing tolerances.

A critical problem of decision making in the LDC setting is choice of 'appropriate technologies.' The newest and most advanced technology employed in 'the West' is not likely to be appropriate to the LDC, but numerous mistakes have been made in adopting Western technologies in LDC economies. The 'appropriateness' of a technology should be judged with respect to the resource endowments of the region.

A region which enjoys an abundance of labour but a scarcity of capital should employ labour-using and capital-saving technologies. Unfortunately for many LDC economies, the technologies employed in the West have been developed in capital abundant settings to conserve upon scarce labour, and thus are not appropriate to the LDC setting without extensive adaptation.

TRADE AND DEVELOPMENT

International trade and foreign direct investment are recognized by development economists to be two of the potentially most effective routes to the further development of an LDC economy. Specialization according to comparative advantage and trade can allow the LDC to develop its latent potentials. Foreign direct investment may help to change comparative advantages by relieving capital scarcity and technological backwardness. It may also help to diversify the LDC economy so that it is not so reliant upon one or a few crops or industries.

The operations of international and multinational firms can bring labour skills, managerial expertise, and new technologies to the LDC when the firms function as international transfer agents. Multinational enterprises prefer to establish subsidiaries or affiliates in the foreign environment in order to earn rents from their superior knowledge assets while maintaining control over them. The LDC economy will be the beneficiary of the employment and training provided by the multinational firm, and inevitably knowledge asset transfers to people in the LDC will occur deliberately or by leakage.

THE ROLE OF THE GOVERNMENT

The government of the LDC may pose additional dimensions in the managerial decision setting which are not significant factors in the Western economy. An enlightened government will welcome both international trade and foreign direct investment by multinational enterprises; some have been willing to provide 'tax holidays' as inducements to new foreign investment. However, governments of some LDC economies are suspicious of foreign involvements in their economies to the point of regulating and constraining the operations of foreign firms in their economies. One reason is that a multinational enterprise may generate larger gross revenues from its worldwide operations than the annual gross domestic product of the LDC.

It is not unusual for LDC governments to subsidize domestic 'infant industries' in their economies, and to protect them from foreign competition with restrictive import quotas or tariffs. The government of the LDC may limit foreign investors to only minority (less than 50 per cent) positions in domestic ventures, and may also impose a 'sunset law' requiring the foreign investor to withdraw within a specified time period. Laws may also require the progressive indigenization of the labour force and the management. Affiliates of multinational enterprises may find difficulties in importing materials requirements or needed machinery.

The multinational firm is likely to face high taxes on inventories, sales, and plant and equipment, and tax rates may be unexpectedly increased after local operations are started. The multinational may also encounter difficulties in repatriating profits earned by its affiliate in the LDC. Finally, we should note that in some LDCs there are distinct risks of nationalization of foreign-owned facilities, and there is no guarantee that the government will provide adequate (or any) compensation for the assets nationalized.

ENTREPRENEURIAL OPPORTUNITIES

Our discussion of the LDC setting has of course not been exhaustive; it is intended only to give the reader an overview of some of the problems to be encountered in decision settings in lesser developed countries. But we do not intend with this overview to discourage the manager from considering operations within the LDC. There are great opportunities to be considered in the LDC decision setting. A rational approach to such involvement is to identify all of the relevant benefits and costs emanating from such involvement, carefully assess the attendant risks, make adjustments to estimates of benefits and costs to account for the risks, and proceed if the involvement appears viable after allowing for the risks.

Summary of Important Points

1. Lesser developed countries are those which lag behind the technological conditions and income levels of the typical higher income economies of North America, Europe, and the Pacific Rim.
2. Managerial and entrepreneurial decision making in LDC economies should employ the same benefit-cost criteria as employed in advanced economies, but decision making in LDCs involve greater market imperfections, less information, and more externalities.
3. The decision maker should compile a storehouse of experience with the LDC environment upon which to base assessments of risk.

Contd....

4. One of the most significant reasons for under-development is lack of entrepreneurship; on-going development requires conditions conducive to entrepreneurship.
5. Comparative advantage of advanced countries may lie in their endowments of entrepreneurial capacity, the exercise of which may benefit the economies of LDCs.
6. Cross-cultural differences with LDC economies are greater than with foreign markets in economies which are similar to the multinational enterprise.
7. The foreign manager will find greater acceptance and business dealings will be facilitated if he or she can speak the language of the LDC realm.
8. The underdevelopment of infrastructure facilities severely limits conducting business in the LDC, but may also constitute rich entrepreneurial opportunities.
9. Because of the underdevelopment of infrastructure facilities, a productive facility in the LDC is likely to have to be more vertically integrated, self-contained, and stand alone than in an advanced economy.
10. Capital scarcity is at the heart of a vicious circle of poverty in the LDC, but the circle can be broken by entrepreneurship from within or outside the LDC economy.
11. In an LDC the manager should expect to employ labour of pre- or early-industrial attitudes and conditioning.
12. The appropriateness of the technology for implementation in an LDC economy should be judged with respect to the resource endowments of the region.
13. International trade and foreign direct investment are potentially the most effective routes to further development of the LDC economy.
14. The operations of international and multinational firms can bring labour skills, managerial expertise, and new technologies to the LDC when the firms function as international transfer agents.
15. An enlightened host government will welcome both international trade and foreign direct investment by multinational enterprises, but the government may also be suspicious of the motives of the multinational.
16. Governments of LDCs are prone to protect and subsidize their domestic industries, and to limit the involvement of multinational enterprises in their economies.
17. Multinational enterprises often face high taxes in LDCs, and may be subject to risks of nationalization.
18. A rational approach to involvement in an LDC economy is to identify all of the relevant benefits and costs emanating from such involvement, assess the attendant risks, make risk adjustments to benefits and costs, and proceed if involvement still appears viable.

Significant Terms

- lesser developed country
- first, second, third world
- advanced technologies
- advanced economy
- benefit-cost criteria
- market imperfections
- externalities
- entrepreneurial, managerial decision making
- comparative advantage
- cross-cultural differences
- language of the realm
- infrastructure
- vertically integrated
- capital scarcity
- circle of poverty
- interest rates
- risk premiums
- foot-loose industries
- appropriate technologies
- international trade
- foreign direct investment
- multinational enterprise
- infant industries
- protection
- sunset law
- repatriating profits
- nationalization
- opportunities, threats

Questions for Discussion

1. Why is the concept of 'lesser developed' a relative term?
2. Explain why the terms 'first world,' 'second world,' and 'third world' may have begun to lose meaning.
3. Why are risks typically greater in lesser developed countries? What are the entrepreneurial risks that one should expect to confront?
4. How can the risks encountered in dealings in lesser developed countries be handled?
5. Why is entrepreneurship critical to development?
6. Discuss the relationship between entrepreneurial capacity and comparative advantage in advanced and developing countries.
7. How does the cultural environment of a lesser developed country bear upon managerial and entrepreneurial decision making there?

8. Discuss the implications of the inability of a manager of the subsidiary of a multinational enterprise to speak the language where the subsidiary is located.
9. Discuss the consequences and identify the opportunities of infrastructure underdevelopment in a lesser developed economy.
10. Discuss the managerial and entrepreneurial implications of capital scarcity in lesser developed countries.
11. Why might 'vicious circles of poverty' not be nearly as vicious as they are described?
12. Discuss entrepreneurial opportunities found in 'vicious circles of poverty.'
13. Identify the likely problem of employment of labour in a lesser developed country by the subsidiary of a multinational enterprise.
14. Why are Western technologies often not appropriate for implementation in lesser developed economies?
15. Identify the economic criterion for selection of an appropriate technology.
16. Discuss the potential for trade and foreign direct investment to contribute to the development experience of a lesser developed economy.
17. Explain how the operations of multinational enterprises may benefit the development processes in lesser developed economies; what are the risks to the lesser developed countries of accepting such operations?
18. What problems with government administration do multinational enterprises typically encounter in developing countries? What are the managerial and entrepreneurial implications?
19. Discuss the consequences of protectionism in lesser developed economies for development and for entrepreneurial decision making.
20. Discuss the implications for a multinational enterprise's local operations in a lesser developed country if it has a history of nationalizing foreign-owned facilities.
21. What is the evidence that the opportunities outweigh the threats of involvement by multinational firms in lesser developed countries?

—oo(O)oo—

Part - II

- **History of International Trade**
- **Absolute Advantage Theory of International Trade**
- **Comparative Advantage Theory of International Trade**
- **Heckscher-Ohlin Model**
- **Terms of Trade**
- **Gains from International Trade**
- **Balance of Payment**
- **The Foreign Exchange Market**
- **Financial Market**
- **Purchasing Power Parity**
- **Indian Foreign Exchange Market—Basic Information**
- **International Monetary Fund**
- **World Trade Organization**
- **Composition and Direction of Foreign Trade**

Chapter 25

History of International Trade

The history of international trade chronicles notable events that have affected the trade between various countries. In the era before the rise of the nation state, the term 'international' trade cannot be literally applied, but simply means trade over long distances; the sort of movement in goods which would represent international trade in the modern world.

Chronology of Events

- 1.1 1500 – 1776
- 1.2 1776 – 1841
- 1.3 1889 – 1945
- 1.4 1946 – 1995
- 1.5 1996 - Present day

CHRONOLOGY OF EVENTS

- **1157:** The Hanseatic League secures trading privileges and market rights in England for goods from the League's trading cities.
- **1498:** Vasco da Gama opens up the spice trade.

1500 – 1776

- **1500:** In the sixteenth century Antwerp was the centre of trade. After the siege of Antwerp (1584-1585) trade moved to Amsterdam.

- **1580:** Portugal's loss of independence to Spain creates a monopoly in spices from the Indies; without competition the Spanish were able to raise European prices, and shut the free-trading Dutch out of the market.
- **1592:** Japan introduced a system of foreign trade licences to prevent smuggling and piracy.
- **1602:** The Dutch East India Company is formed.
- **1604:** Hugo Grotius publishes *Mare liberum* (The Free Seas), advocating open use of the sea by maritime trade of all nations. In Britain, parliament moves in favour of free trade, but opposes the Dutchman's call for unlimited navigation rights; English and Dutch Republic traders are fierce rivals.
- **1651:** Act of Navigation permits only English or originating-country ships to carry goods into England.
- **1654:** After defeat in the First Anglo-Dutch War the Dutch agreed to respect the Act of Navigation in the Treaty of Westminster.
- **1685:** The first British outpost in the East Indies was established in Sumatra.
- **1713:** Important international trading rights are mostly assigned by monopoly contract. In the Treaty of Utrecht Britain receives the Asiento slave-trading contract, and secures the Canadian fur trade for the Hudson Bay Company.
- **1751:** Benjamin Franklin's *Observations Concerning the Increase of Mankind, Peopling of Countries, &c.* argues that competition from third-country suppliers would prevent British merchants selling manufactured goods above world prices to the American colonies, in the liberal tradition of free trade. However, the same document advocates mercantile laws as 'generative laws' which 'strengthen a Country doubly'. Mercantilism was a nationalist theory which dominated thought about the correct trade policy to adopt in eighteenth century Europe: Export as much as possible, but import the minimum to create a 'favourable' trade balance.
- **1756:** Richard Cantillon criticized the prevailing mercantile approach to trade which emphasised manufacturing; the Physiocrats emphasized the domestic agricultural sector.
- **1764:** The Sugar Act raises a 3 pence per gallon tariff on molasses imported from the French West Indies, to make British West Indies sugar more competitive in the American colonies. Since there is insufficient supply from the British West Indies, New England merchants are forced to buy the taxed sugar from the French West Indies anyway, with the tariff acting as an unpopular means of wealth transfer to the British exchequer from consumers in the colonies.

- **1770:** Turgot's *Lettres sur la liberté du commerce des grains* demands the end to restrictions on free trade in grain, with the claim that all parties would thereby benefit.

1776 - 1841

- **1776:** *An Inquiry into the Nature and Causes of the Wealth of Nations,* questioned the wisdom of Mercantilism. Adam Smith argued that economic specialization could benefit nations just as much as firms. Since the division of labour was restricted by the size of the market, he said that countries having access to the largest markets would be able to divide labour more efficiently and thereby become more productive. Smith was later to say that he considered all rationalizations of import and export controls 'dupery', which hurt the trading nation at the expense of specific industries.
- **1799:** The Dutch East India Company, formerly the world's largest company, goes bankrupt, partly due to the rise of competitive free trade.
- **1815:** The British Corn Laws are introduced, preventing grain imports.
- **1816:** In line with protectionist opinion, the U.S. Congress extended its 1789 tariff to manufactured goods. The intention of limiting free trade was to help local industries compete with the products of industrial England.
- **1817:** James Mill, Robert Torrens, and especially David Ricardo showed that free trade might benefit the industrially weak as well as the strong, in the famous theory of comparative advantage. In *Principles of Political Economy* Ricardo advanced the doctrine still considered the most counterintuitive in economics:

  Both countries benefit when a totally inefficient producer sends the merchandise it produces least badly to a country able to produce it more efficiently at home.
- **1828:** The 'Tariff of Abominations' is signed into U.S. law with the express intention of raising the domestic price of British manufactured goods. This was in the interests of Northern producers, but was unpopular in the South, especially because England reduced agricultural imports in response.
- **1832:** The U.S. starts to lower tariffs, but not enough to avoid the Nullification Crisis; South Carolina felt that the tariffs of 1828 and 1832 were against its vital economic interests and tried to pass the Ordinance of Nullification, declaring both federal tariffs null and void within state borders.

- **1833:** The U.S. tariff issue is defused by a protectionist, Henry Clay, who promotes a staged reduction of tariffs down to the levels of 1816.
- **1840:** Opium War—Britain invades China to overturn the Chinese bar on opium imports (Britain was shipping a ton of opium per day from India into Chinese ports). The British case was argued in Ricardian terms against the import barriers the Chinese wished to impose; parliament argued that the trade in opium should not be restrained.
- **1841:** Friedrich List's *Das Nationale System der Politischen Okonomie* disputed the equivalence between individuals and countries in the conduct of trade. Within a country the ideal economic system would be the free market, but the importance of developing national productive power made free trade between nations a danger for a country specializing in agriculture. He said that such a country would stagnate and never reach an industrial stage of development. He compared a period of protectionism for an industrially weak nation to a period of education for an individual; costly in the short term, but paying off in time. He acknowledged the immediate economic advantages of free trade, and advocated returning to this policy as soon as the 'industrial education' of Germany was complete.

1842 - 1889

- **1842:** first opium war ends.
- **1844:** The ascendancy of free trade was primarily based on national advantage. That is, the calculation made was whether it was in any particular country's self-interest to open its borders to imports. Ricardo and others had shown that it might well be, but John Stuart Mill proved that a country with monopoly pricing power on the international market could manipulate the terms of trade through maintaining tariffs, and that the response to this might be reciprocity in trade policy. This was taken as evidence against the universal doctrine of free trade, as it was believed that more of the economic surplus of trade would accrue to a country following *reciprocal*, rather than completely free, trade policies.
- **16 May 1846:** Repeal of the Corn Laws passed by the British House of Commons.
- **1848:** The infant industry scenario developed by J. S. Mill anticipated New Trade Theory by promoting the theory that government had the 'duty' to protect young industries, although only for such a time as would be necessary for them to develop full capacity. This theory became policy in many countries, these nations attempting to industrialize and out-compete English exporters.

- **1860:** Free trade agreement finalized between Britain and France under the presidency of Napoleon III, prepared by Michel Chevalier and Richard Cobden, sparking off successive agreements between other countries in Europe.
- **1868:** The Japanese Meiji Restoration lead the way to Japan opening its borders and quickly industrializing through free trade. Under bilateral treaties restraint of trade imports to Japan were forbidden.
- **1873:** The Wiener Börse slump signals the start of the continental Long Depression, during which support for protectionism grows.
- **1879:** Influenced by List's nationalist argument for industrial protection Bismarck abandons the German free trade policy, enacting tariffs over the objections of his National Liberal Party allies.
- **1888:** Benjamin Harrison wins the U.S. presidency on a protectionist ticket.

1889 - 1945

- **1890:** William McKinley argued that the revenues generated from the current tariff levels were too high; by raising import barriers it was said that imports would drop sufficiently to lower tariff income, reducing the dangerously high treasury surplus. President Harrison tried to make the tariff more acceptable by writing in reciprocity provisions, and through direct payments to domestic sugar producers rather than tariffs on sugar imports. The McKinley tariff sets U.S. rates to 50 per cent, and was widely blamed for substantial consumer price inflation.
- **1892:** France introduces the Méline Tariff, ushering in an era of protectionist measures.
- **1897:** In the Dingley Tariff, U.S. import duty is raised to a 46.5 per pent average.
- **1904:** George Reid, leader of the Australian Free Trade Party becomes Prime Minister, and with the support of parliament abolishes protective tariffs, against the opposition of the Protectionist Party.
- **1909:** Payne-Aldrich tariff
- **1930:** The most famous trade restriction in history was passed in the wake of the Stock Market Crash of 1929: the Smoot-Hawley Tariff Act roughly doubled the U.S. tariff levels from those set in 1913.
- **1933:** Bertil Ohlin publishes *Interregional and International Trade*, giving conditions under which a comparative advantage can exist despite identical technologies internationally (the Heckscher-Ohlin model).

- **1934:** The Reciprocal Trade Agreements Act (RTAA) is passed in the U.S.A., allowing for bilateral trade agreements to be made with other countries without a most favoured nation clause.
- **1945:** MITI is given powers to control imports to post war Japan, in the hope of helping reconstruction.

1946 - 1995

- **1946:** The Bretton Woods system goes into effect; it had been planned since 1944 as an international economic structure to prevent further depressions and wars. It included institutions and rules intended to prevent national trade barriers being erected, as the lack of free trade was considered by many to have been a principal cause of the war.
- **1947:** 23 countries agree to the General Agreement on Tariffs and Trade to rationalize trade among the nations. Low tariffs are beneficial to the economies of the nations in that it encourages imports, increases government revenues and gives local industries some motivation to improve their efficiency. High tariffs discourage trade between the nations, reduce or eliminate government revenues from this sector of taxation, and give more monopoly power to local industry. So low tariffs are beneficial to the world economy but not free trade. Free trade does not necessarily mean increased trade among the nations. Nations who cannot compete in the world market will have their standard of living reduced and this reduction in their standard of living will reduce world trade. Free trade does not enable governments to earn taxes from this sector. Free trade transfers monopoly power from local industry to foreign companies and the job of government regulating the economy for the common benefit of everybody will be lost. Foreign companies cannot be regulated by government because they are aliens to a local economy.
- **1948:** Ludwig Erhard's trade liberalization is credited by some with making Germany quickly competitive in industrial production after the damage of the Second World War.
- **1948:** The International Trade Organization's charter is agreed at the U.N. Havana Conference on Trade and Employment, but blocked in the U.S. Senate.
- **1951:** The European Coal and Steel Community, forerunner of the European Union, creates a free trade area for certain raw materials inside Europe.
- **1959:** Oxfam opens the first Worldshop, retailing foreign goods under fair trade principles.

- **1960:** European Free Trade Association established.
- **1971:** Zangger Committee formed to advise on the interpretation of nuclear goods in relation to international trade and the Nuclear Non-Proliferation Treaty (NPT).
- **1971:** Without accepting the doctrines of free trade the, 'Comprehensive Program for Socialist Economic Integration' moved the Comecon countries to world prices in calculating the value of intra-Comecon trade. The free market price was observed for five years and the mean of these prices used to give the relative value of the imports and exports between communist countries in the trading group over the following five years.
- **October 16, 1973:** OPEC raises the Saudi light crude export price, and mandates an export cut the next day, plus an embargo on oil exports to nations allied with Israel in the course of the Yom Kippur War. The cartel's apparent ability to manipulate prices by restricting supply was taken by many oil importers as an example of the 'reciprocity' violation of free trade advanced by John Stuart Mill in 1848. See: A detailed chronology of the embargo, and Fuel price chronology from NPR.
- **1974:** The oil price shock was felt around the world, because production reductions increased the international price even on the open market (to countries outside the OPEC embargo). Some oil importing countries respond with the reduction of oil consumption.
- **1974:** The Nuclear Suppliers Group (NSG) was created to moderate international trade in nuclear related goods, after the explosion of a nuclear device by a non-nuclear weapon state.
- **1975:** Inter-Comecon trade tied even more closely to the 'world price' dictated by free trade.
- **1985:** The Australia Group was formed to moderate international trade in chemical and biological weapons and associated goods.
- **1987:** The Missile Technology Control Regime came into being with the aim of limiting the proliferation of the means of delivery of weapons of mass destruction, using international trade controls.
- **1988:** Solidaridad launches 'Fair trade' labelling with the sale of Mexican coffee which was certified to meet ethical standards of sustainable development. This and other initiatives promoted the idea that some trade between regions could be socially beneficial (outside of the economic elites). The movement is especially active in campaigning to remove agricultural subsidies in the developed world (which some see as campaigning for free trade).

- **1992:** European Union lifts barriers to internal trade in goods and labour.
- **January 1, 1994:** NAFTA takes effect.
- **1994:** The GATT Marrakech Agreement specifies formation of the WTO.
- **January 1, 1995:** The World Trade Organization is created to facilitate free trade, by mandating mutual most favoured nation trading status between all signatories.

1996 - PRESENT DAY

- **1996:** The Wassenaar Arrangement moderates international trade in conventional arms and associated goods.
- **March, 1996:** IMF approves major loan to Russia.
- **November, 1996:** US Stock Market rises 10 days in a row.
- **September, 1996:** Alan Greenspan, Chairman of the US Federal Reserve Board, suggests that "irrational exuberance" may have "unduly escalated asset values".
- **October, 1997:** Global stock markets fall. NYSE invokes "circuit breaker for first time to stop trading.
- **January, 1998:** Russia issues new rubles.
- **February, 1998:** Standard & Poor's 500 Index closes above 1,000 for first time.
- **August, 1998:** Russia defaults on state short-term bonds and devalues ruble.
- **November, 1998:** The first dotcom, Theglobe.com, goes public.
- **January 1, 1999:** The euro is established.
- **January 1, 2001:** European single currency (euro) comes into effect.
- **November, 2001:** China joins WTO.
- **December, 2001:** Bankruptcy of Enron.
- **September, 2002:** United Nations World Summint on Sustainable Development opens.

—oo(O)oo—

- **October, 2002:** Dotcom bubble ends on world stock markets.
- **December, 2005:** Sixth WTO Ministerial Conference, Hong Kong.
- **July, 2007:** The sub prime mortgage crisis in the United States starts what comes to be called the Credit Crunch.
- **September, 2008:** Bankruptcy of Lehman Brothers.

Chapter 26

Absolute Advantage Theory of International Trade

A country has an **absolute advantage** economically over another, in a particular good, when it can produce that good more cheaply. A country also has an absolute advantage if it can produce more of the good than another country can, with the same amount of resources.

The term is important in the theory of international trade because it is often mistakenly assumed that (to take an example) if France has an absolute advantage over England in some product, say cheese, then France will not normally import cheese from England.

A seminal analysis by the 19th-century English economist David Ricardo showed that despite France's absolute advantage, it may well benefit both countries for England to produce and export cheese to France.

Ricardo identified comparative advantage, rather than absolute advantage, as the correct concept for understanding efficient patterns of production and exchange across countries. His discussion is central to modern trade theory.

The two concepts have applications outside international trade, though this is where they are most commonly used. Suppose that two castaways on a desert island gather both fruit and grain, which they then share equally between them.

Suppose that Castaway A can gather more fruit per hour than Castaway B, and therefore has an absolute advantage in this good. Nonetheless, it may well make sense for A to leave some fruit-gathering to B.

One needs to look at comparative advantage rather than absolute advantage, to discover how A and B can each best allocate their effort. If A's initial advantage over B in grain-gathering is greater than his or her advantage in fruit-gathering, then fruit-effort should be transferred from A to B, to the point where A's comparative advantages in the two goods are equal. Thus it may be rational for fruit to flow from B to A, despite A's absolute advantage.

Examples

Country A can produce product z for $ 1.

Country B can produce product z for $ 2.

Country A has an absolute advantage over Country B in product z.

•

Kentucky has significant coal reserves.

Illinois does not use nuclear energy.

Energy production is cheaper with coal than with nuclear energy. <— Assumption

Kentucky has an absolute advantage in energy production.

—oo(O)oo—

Chapter 27

Comparative Advantage Theory of International Trade

In economics, the theory of **comparative advantage** explains why it can be beneficial for two parties (countries, regions, individuals and so on) to trade if one has a lower relative cost of producing some good. What matters is not the absolute cost of production but the opportunity cost, which measures how much is given up of one good to produce a unit of the other good. Comparative advantage is critical to understanding modern international trade theory.

Under absolute advantage, one country can produce more output per unit of productive input than another. With comparative advantage, even if one country has an absolute (dis)advantage in every type of output, it can benefit from specializing in and exporting those products in which it has a relative advantage (that is, a lower opportunity cost) and importing the good in which it has a relative disadvantage.

ORIGINS OF THE THEORY

Comparative advantage was first described by Robert Torrens in 1815 in an essay on the corn trade. He concluded that it was to England's advantage to trade various goods with Poland in return for corn, even though it might be possible to produce that corn more cheaply in England than Poland.

However, the theory is usually attributed to who created a systematic explanation in his 1817 book, *The Principles of Political Economy and Taxation,* using an example involving England and Portugal. In Portugal it is possible to produce both wine and cloth with less work than it takes in England. However, the **relative costs** of producing those two goods are different in the two countries. In England it is very hard to produce wine, and only moderately difficult to produce cloth. In Portugal both are easy to produce. Therefore, while it is cheaper to produce cloth in Portugal than England, it is cheaper still for Portugal to produce excess wine, and trade that for

English cloth. Conversely, England benefits from this trade because its cost for producing cloth has not changed but it can now get the cheaper Portuguese wine.

Stanislaw Ulam once challenged Nobel laureate Paul Samuelson to name one theory in all of the social sciences which is both true and nontrivial. Several years later, Samuelson responded with David Ricardo's theory of comparative advantage:

> That it is logically true need not be argued before a mathematician; that it is not trivial is attested by the thousands of important and intelligent men who have never been able to grasp the doctrine for themselves or to believe it after it was explained to them.

EXAMPLES

The following worked examples explain the reasoning behind the theory. In Example 3 all assumptions are italicized for easy reference, and some are explained at the end of the example.

EXAMPLE 1

Two men land alone in an isolated island. To survive they must undertake a few basic economic activities like water carrying, fishing, cooking and shelter construction and maintenance. The first man is young, strong, and educated and is faster, better, more productive at everything. He has an absolute advantage in all activities. The second man is old, weak, and uneducated. He has an absolute disadvantage in all economic activities. In some activities the difference between the two is great; in others it is small.

Is it in the interest of either of them to work in isolation? No, specialization and exchange (trade) can benefit both of them.

How should they divide the work? According to comparative, not absolute advantage: the young man must spend more time on the tasks in which he is much better and the old man must concentrate on the tasks in which he is only a little worse. Such an arrangement will increase total production and/or reduce total labour. It will make both of them richer.

EXAMPLE 2

A needs 100 P1 and 100 P2

B needs 100 P1 and 100 P2

So A saved 120 cost units or 4 per cent and B saved 100 cost units or 2.5 per cent. Clearly A gained more from the trade, but both parties experienced growth. Now if B adds some taxes to protect the producers of P1 he can try to get a larger percentage of the trade but his savings goes down as do the overall savings.

EXAMPLE 3

Suppose, for example, we have two countries *of equal size*, **Northland** and **Southland**, that both produce and consume two goods, **Food** and **Clothes**. The productive capacities and

A: No trade

Product	Cost	Produced	Cost
P1	10	100	1000
P2	20	100	2000
Net	–	200	3000

B: No trade

Product	Cost	Produced	Cost
P1	15	100	1500
P2	25	100	2500
Net	–	200	4000

A with trade: 100 P1 for 56 P2

Product	Cost	Produced	Cost
P1	10	200	2000
P2	20	44	880
Net	–	244	2880

B with trade: 56 P2 for 100 P1

Product	Cost	Produced	Cost
P1	15	0	0
P2	25	156	3900
Net	–	156	3900

efficiencies of the countries are such that if both countries devoted all their resources to food production, output would be as follows:

- Northland: 100 tonnes
- Southland: 200 tonnes

Conversely if all of the resources of the countries were allocated to the production of clothes, output would be:

- Northland: 100 tonnes
- Southland: 100 tonnes

We need to assume that each of the countries has *constant opportunity costs of production* between the two products, and that both economies have *full employment at all times*. Also all *factors of production are perfectly mobile within the countries* between clothing and food industries, but are *immobile between the countries*. Finally *the price mechanism must be working to provide perfect competition.*

So Southland has an absolute advantage over Northland in the production of food, and both countries are equally efficient in the production of clothes. Intuitively it would seem that there is no mutual benefit in trade between the economies. But an examination of the **opportunity costs** shows something different. For Northland, the opportunity cost of producing one tonne of food is one tonne of clothes and vice versa.

But for Southland, the opportunity cost of one tonne of food is 0.5 tonne of Clothes; and the opportunity cost of one tonne of Clothes is 2 tonnes of Food. Looked at this way, Southland has a comparative advantage in Food production because of its lower opportunity cost of production with respect to Northland. And Northland also has a comparative advantage over Southland in the production of Clothes, the opportunity cost of which is lower in Southland with respect to Food than in Northland.

To show that these different opportunity costs can lead to mutual benefit if the countries specialise production and trade, consider the following starting position. Both countries produce and consume only domestically. The volumes are:

Production and Consumption before Trade

	Food	Clothes
Northland	50	50
Southland	100	50
World total	150	100

We now examine the consequences of trade between the two countries. This example includes no formulation of the preferences of consumers in the two economies which would allow the determination of the international exchange rate of Clothes and Food. But given the production capabilities of each country, in order for trade to be worthwhile Northland requires a price of at least one tonne of Food in exchange for one tonne of Clothes; and Southland requires at least one tonne of Clothes for two tonnes of Food.

It follows that the actual exchange price will be somewhere between the two. The remainder of the example works with an international trading price of one tonne of Food for 2/3 tonne of Clothes.

If both countries specialise completely in the goods in which they have comparative advantage, their outputs will be:

Production after Trade

	Food	Clothes
Northland	0	100
Southland	200	0
World total	200	100

Note that world production of Food had increased and Clothing production has remained the same. Using the exchange rate of one tonne of Food for 2/3 tonne of Clothes, Northland and Southland are able to trade to yield the following level of consumption:

Consumption after Trade

	Food	Clothes
Northland	75	50
Southland	125	50
World total	200	100

Northland has traded 50 tonnes of Clothing for 75 tonnes of Food. Both countries have benefited. In fact, both countries are now consuming at points outside their production possibility frontiers.

Assumptions in Example 3

- **Two countries, two goods**—the theory is no different for larger numbers of countries and goods, but the principles are clearer and the argument easier to follow in this simpler case.
- **Equal size economies**—again, this is a simplification to produce a clearer example.
- **Full employment**—if one or other of the economies has less than full

employment of factors of production, then this excess capacity must usually be used up before the comparative advantage reasoning can be applied.

- **Constant opportunity costs**—a more realistic treatment of opportunity costs the reasoning is broadly the same, but specialization of production can only be taken to the point at which the opportunity costs in the two countries become equal. This does not invalidate the principles of comparative advantage, but it does limit the magnitude of the benefit.
- **Perfect mobility of factors of production within countries**—this is necessary to allow production to be switched *without cost*. In real economies this cost will be incurred: capital will be tied up in plant (sewing machines are not sowing machines) and labour will need to be retrained and relocated. This is why it is sometimes argued that 'nascent industries' should be protected from fully liberalised international trade during the period in which a high cost of entry into the market (capital equipment, training) is being paid for.
- **Immobility of factors of production between countries**—why are there different rates of productivity? Capital includes production technology and know-how. If it can be moved between countries then the production capabilities of the countries will change. Similarly the movement of labour will change that factor cost and productivity. *Perfect* transnational mobility of factors of production would invalidate comparative advantage. *Imperfect* transnational mobility reduces the mutual benefit of trade.
- **Perfect competition**—this is a standard assumption that allows perfectly efficient allocation of productive resources in an idealized free market.

MORE COMPLEXITIES

While the Ricardian model has only one input, we could extend the model both increasing the number of goods from two goods to **n** goods and by allowing the productivity coefficient to vary.

CRITICISMS

Few criticisms exist of the basic insight that rational division of labour depends on comparative and not absolute advantage. However, there are many who question that this requires support for free trade.

—oo(O)oo—

Chapter 28

Heckscher-Ohlin Model

The **Heckscher-Ohlin model** (H-O model) is a general equilibrium mathematical model of international trade, developed by Eli Heckscher and Bertil Ohlin at the Stockholm School of Economics. It builds on David Ricardo's theory of comparative advantage by predicting patterns of trade and production based on the factor endowments of a trading region. The model essentially says that countries will export products that utilize their abundant factor(s) of production and import products that utilize the countries' scarce factor(s).

FEATURES OF THE MODEL

Relative endowments of the factors of production (land, labour, and capital) determine a country's comparative advantage. Countries have comparative advantages in those goods for which the required factors of production are relatively abundant locally. This is because the prices of goods are ultimately determined by the prices of their inputs. Goods that require inputs that are locally abundant will be cheaper to produce than those goods that require inputs that are locally scarce.

For example, a country where capital and land are abundant but labour is scarce will have comparative advantage in goods that require lots of capital and land, but little labour—grains, for example. If capital and land are abundant, their prices will be low. As they are the main factors used in the production of grain, the price of grain will also be low—and thus attractive for both local consumption and export. Labour intensive goods on the other hand will be very expensive to produce since labour is scarce and its price is high. Therefore, the country is better off importing those goods.

THEORETICAL DEVELOPMENT OF THE MODEL

The Ricardian model of comparative advantage has trade ultimately motivated by differences in labour productivity using different *technologies*. Heckscher and Ohlin did not require production technology to vary between countries, so (in the interests of simplicity) the *H-O model has identical production technology everywhere*. Ricardo considered a single factor of production (labour) and would not have been able to produce comparative advantage without technological differences between countries (all nations would become autarkies at various stages of development, with no reason to trade with each other). The H-O model removed technology variations but introduced variable capital endowments, recreating endogenously the inter-country variation of labour productivity that Ricardo had imposed exogenously. With international variations in the capital endowment (that is, infrastructure) and goods requiring different factor *proportions*, Ricardo's comparative advantage emerges as a profit-maximizing solution of capitalist's choices from *within* the model's equations. (The decision capital owners are faced with is between investments in differing production technologies: The H-O model assumes capital is privately held.)

ORIGINAL PUBLICATION

Bertil Ohlin published the book which first explained the theory in 1933. Although he wrote the book alone, Heckscher was credited as co-developer of the model, because of his earlier work on the problem, and because many of the ideas in the final model came from Ohlin's doctoral thesis, supervised by Heckscher.

Interregional and International Trade itself was verbose, rather than being pared down to the mathematical, and appealed because of its new insights.

THE 2 × 2 × 2 MODEL

The original H-O model assumed that the only difference between countries was the relative abundances of labour and capital. The original Heckscher-Ohlin model contained two countries, and had two commodities that could be produced. Since there are two (homogeneous) factors of production this model is sometimes called the '2 × 2 × 2 model'.

The model has *variable factor proportions* between countries: Highly developed countries have a comparatively high ratio of capital to labour in relation to developing countries. This makes the developed country capital-abundant relative to the developing nation, and the developing nation labour-abundant in relation to the developed country.

With this single difference, Ohlin was able to discuss the new mechanism of comparative advantage, using just two goods and two technologies to produce them. (One technology would be a capital intensive industry, the other a labour intensive business—see 'assumptions' below).

EXTENSIONS

The model has been extended since the 1930s by many economists. These developments did not change the fundamental role of variable factor proportions in driving international trade, but added to the model various real-world considerations (such as tariffs) in the hopes of increasing the model's predictive power, or as a mathematical way of discussing macroeconomic policy options.

Notable contributions came from Paul Samuelson, Ronald Jones, and Jaroslav Vanek, so that variations of the model are sometimes called the Heckscher-Ohlin-Samuelson model or the Heckscher-Ohlin-Vanek model in the modern synthesis.

Assumptions of the Model

The original, $2 \times 2 \times 2$ model was derived with restrictive assumptions, partly for the sake of mathematical simplicity. Some of these have been relaxed for the sake of development. These assumptions and developments are listed here.

BOTH COUNTRIES HAVE IDENTICAL PRODUCTION TECHNOLOGY

As mentioned above, the HO model differs from Ricardo's most drastically by assuming that the production functions available in each country are identical. The production functions simply convert labour and capital input to output. This assumption means that producing the same output of either commodity *could* be done with the same level of capital and labour in either country. Actually, it would be inefficient to actually use the same balance in either country (because of the relative availability of either input factor) but, in principle this would be possible. Another way of saying this is that the per-capita productivity is the same in both countries in the same technology with identical amounts of capital.

Countries have natural advantages in the production of various commodities in relation to one another, so this is an 'unrealistic' simplification designed to highlight the effect of variable factors. (This meant that the original HO-model produced an alternative explanation for free trade to Ricardo's, rather than a complementary one). In reality, both effects may occur (differences in technology and factor abundances). In addition to natural advantages in the production of one sort of output over another (wine versus rice, say) the infrastructure, education, culture, and 'know-how' of countries differ so dramatically that the idea of identical technologies is a theoretical notion. Ohlin said that the HO model was a long run model, and that the conditions of industrial production are 'everywhere the same' in the long run.

PRODUCTION OUTPUT MUST HAVE CONSTANT RETURN TO SCALE

Both of the countries in the simple HO model produced both commodities, and both technologies have constant returns to scale (CRS). (CRS production has twice the output if both capital and labour inputs are doubled, so the two production functions must be 'homogeneous of degree 1').

These conditions are required to produce a mathematical equilibrium. With increasing returns to scale it would likely be more efficient for countries to specialize, but specialization is not possible with the Heckscher-Ohlin assumptions.

THE TECHNOLOGIES USED TO PRODUCE THE TWO COMMODITIES DIFFER

The CRS production functions must differ to make trade worthwhile in this model. For instance, if the functions are Cobb-Douglas technologies the parameters applied to the inputs must vary. An example would be:

Arable industry: $A = K^{1/3}L^{2/3}$

Fishing industry: $F = K^{1/2}L^{1/2}$

where A is the output in arable production, F is the output in fish production, and K, L are capital and labour in both cases.

In this example, the marginal return to an extra unit of capital is higher in the fishing industry, assuming units of F(ish) and A(rable) output have equal value. The more capital-abundant country may gain by developing its fishing fleet at the expense of its arable farms. Conversely, the workers available in the relatively labour-abundant country can be employed relatively more efficiently in arable farming.

LABOUR MOBILITY WITHIN COUNTRIES

Within countries, capital and labour can be reinvested and re-employed to produce different outputs. Like the comparative advantage argument of Ricardo, this is assumed to happen without cost.

If the two production technologies are the arable industry and the fishing industry it is assumed that farmers can shift to work as fishermen with no cost, and vice versa.

CAPITAL MOBILITY WITHIN COUNTRIES

It is further assumed that capital can shift easily into either technology, so that the industrial mix can change without adjustment costs between the two types of production.

For instance, if the two industries are farming and fishing it is assumed that farms can be sold to pay for the construction of fishing boats with no transaction costs.

CAPITAL IMMOBILITY BETWEEN COUNTRIES

The basic Heckscher-Ohlin model depends upon the relative availability of capital and labour differing internationally, but if capital can be freely invested anywhere, competition (for investment) will make relative abundances identical throughout the world. (Essentially, Free Trade in capital would provide a single worldwide investment pool.)

Differences in labour abundance would not produce a difference in *relative* factor abundance (in relation to mobile capital) because the labour/capital ratio would be identical everywhere. (A large country would receive twice as much investment as a small one, for instance, maximizing capitalist's return on investment).

As capital controls are reduced, the modern world has begun to look a lot less like the world modelled by Heckscher and Ohlin. It has been argued that capital mobility undermines the case for Free Trade itself, see: Capital mobility and comparative advantage Free trade critique. Capital is mobile when:

- There are limited exchange controls
- Foreign Direct Investment (FDI) is permitted between countries, or foreigners are permitted to invest in the commercial operations of a country through a stock or corporate bond market

LABOUR IMMOBILITY BETWEEN COUNTRIES

Like capital, labour movements are not permitted in the Heckscher-Ohlin world, since this would drive an equalization of relative abundances of the two production factors, just as in the case of capital immobility above. This condition is more defensible as a description of the modern world than the assumption that capital is confined to a single country.

COMMODITIES HAVE THE SAME PRICE EVERYWHERE

The $2 \times 2 \times 2$ model originally placed no barriers to trade, had no tariffs, and no exchange controls (capital was immobile, but repatriation of foreign sales was costless). It was also free of transportation costs between the countries, or any other savings that would favour procuring a local supply.

If the two countries have separate currencies, this does not affect the model in any way (Purchasing Power Parity applies). Since there are no transaction costs or currency issues the law of one price applies to both commodities, and consumers in either country pay exactly the same price for either good.

In Ohlin's day this assumption was a fairly neutral simplification, but economic changes and econometric research since the 1950s have shown that the local prices of goods tend to be correlated with incomes when both are converted at money prices (although this is less true with traded commodities).

PERFECT INTERNAL COMPETITION

Neither labour nor capital has the power to affect prices or factor rates by constraining supply; a state of perfect competition exists.

—oo(O)oo—

Chapter 29

Terms of Trade

In international economics and international trade, **terms of trade** or TOT are the ratio of the price of an export commodity/-ies to the price of an import commodity/-ies. 'Terms of trade' are sometimes used as a proxy for the relative social welfare of a country, but this heuristic is technically questionable and should be used with extreme caution. An improvement in a nation's terms of trade is good for that country in the sense that it has to pay less for the products it imports, that is, it has to give up fewer exports for the imports it receives.

TWO COUNTRY MODEL CIE ECONOMICS

In the simplified case of two countries and two commodities, terms of trade is defined as the ratio of the price a country receives for its export commodity to the price it pays for its import commodity. In this simple case the imports of one country are the exports of the other country. For example, if a country exports 50 dollars worth of product in exchange for 100 dollars worth of imported product, that country's terms of trade are 50/100 = 0.5. The terms of trade for the other country must be the reciprocal (100/50 = 2). When this number is falling, the country is said to have 'deteriorating terms of trade'. If multiplied by 100, these calculations can be expressed as a per cent (50 per cent and 200 per cent, respectively). If a country's terms of trade fall from say 100 per cent to 70 per cent (from 1.0 to 0.7), it has experienced a 30 per cent deterioration in its terms of trade. When doing longitudinal (time series) calculations, it is common to set the base year to 100 per cent to make interpretation of the results easier.

In basic microeconomics, the terms of trade are usually set in the interval between the opportunity costs for the production of a given good of two countries.

MULTI-COMMODITY MULTI-COUNTRY MODEL

In the more realistic case of many products exchanged between many countries, terms of trade can be calculated using a Laspeyres index. In this case, a nation's terms of trade is the ratio of the Laspeyre price index of exports to the Laspeyre price index of imports. The Laspeyre export index is the current value of the base period exports divided by the base period value of the base period exports. Similarly, the Laspeyre import index is the current value of the base period imports divided by the base period value of the base period imports.

$$\frac{p^c q^0}{p^0 q^0} \Big/ \frac{p^c q^0}{p^0 q^0}$$

where

p_x^c = price of exports in the current period

q_x^0 = quantity of exports in the base period

p_x^0 = price of exports in the base period

p_m^c = price of imports in the current period

q_m^0 = quantity of imports in the base period

p_m^0 = price of imports in the base period

OTHER TERMS-OF-TRADE CALCULATIONS

1. **The net barter terms of trade** is the ratio (expressed as a percentage) of relative export and import prices when volume is held constant.
2. **The gross barter terms of trade** is the ratio (expressed as a per cent) of a quantity index of exports to a quantity index of inputs.
3. **The income terms of trade** is the ratio (expressed as a per cent) of the value of exports to the price of imports.
4. **The single factorial terms of trade** is the net barter terms of trade adjusted for changes in the productivity of exports.
5. **The double factorial terms of trade** adjusts for both the productivity of exports and the productivity of imports.

LIMITATIONS

Terms of trade should not be used as synonymous with social welfare, or even Pareto economic welfare. Terms of trade calculations do not tell us about the volume of the countries' exports, only relative changes between countries. To understand how a country's social utility changes, it is necessary to consider changes in the volume of trade, changes in productivity and resource allocation, and changes in capital flows.

In the real world of over 200 nations trading hundreds of thousands of products, terms of trade calculations can get very complex. Thus, the possibility of errors is significant.

—oo(O)oo—

Chapter 30

Gains from International Trade

The main reason why the presence of economies of scale can generate trade gains is because the reallocation of resources can raise world productive efficiency. To see how, we present a simple example using a model similar to the Ricardian model.

BASIC ASSUMPTIONS

Suppose there are two countries, the U.S.A. and France, producing two goods, clothing and steel, using one factor of production, labour. Assume the production technology is identical in both countries and can be described with the following production functions.

Production of Clothing

USA	France
$Q_C = \dfrac{L_C\ [\text{hrs}]}{a_{LC}\ [\frac{\text{hrs}}{\text{rack}}]}$	$Q_C^* = \dfrac{L_C^*}{a_{LC}}$

where

Q_C = quantity of clothing produced in the U.S.A.

L_C = amount of labour applied to clothing production in the U.S.A.

a_{LC} = unit-labour requirement in clothing production in the U.S.A. and France (hours of labour necessary to produce one rack of clothing) and where all starred variables are defined in the same way but refer to the process in France. Note that since production technology is assumed the same in both countries, we use the same unit-labour requirement in the U.S.A. and the French production function.

Production of Steel: The production of steel is assumed to exhibit economies of scale in production.

USA	France
$Q_S = \dfrac{L_S\ [\text{hrs}]}{a_{LS}(Q_S)[\frac{\text{hrs}}{\text{tons}}]}$	$Q_S^* = \dfrac{L_S^*}{a_{LS}(Q_S^*)}$

where

Q_S = quantity of steel produced in the U.S.A.

L_S = amount of labour applied to steel production in the U.S.A.

$a_{LS}(Q_S)$ = unit-labour requirement in steel production in the U.S.A. (hours of labour necessary to produce one ton of steel). Note, it is assumed that the unit labour requirement is a function of the level of steel output in the domestic industry. More specifically we will assume that the unit-labour requirement falls as industry output rises.

Resource Constraint: The production decision is how to allocate labour between the two industries. We assume that labour is homogeneous and freely mobile between industries. The labour constraints are given below.

USA	France
$L_C + L_W = L$	$L_C^* + L_C^* = L^*$

where L is the labour endowment in the U.S.A. and L* is the endowment in France. When the resource constraint holds with equality it implies that the resource is fully employed.

Demand: We will assume that the U.S.A. and France have identical demands for the two products.

A Numerical Example

We proceed much as Ricardo did in presenting the argument of the gains from specialization in one's comparative advantage good. First, we will construct an autarky equilibrium in this model assuming that the two countries are identical in every respect. Then we will show how an improvement in world productive efficiency can arise if one of the two countries produces all of the steel that is demanded in the world.

Suppose the exogenous variables in the two countries take the values in the following table.

USA	$a_{LC} = 1$	$L = 100$
France	$a_{LC} = 1$	$L^* = 100$

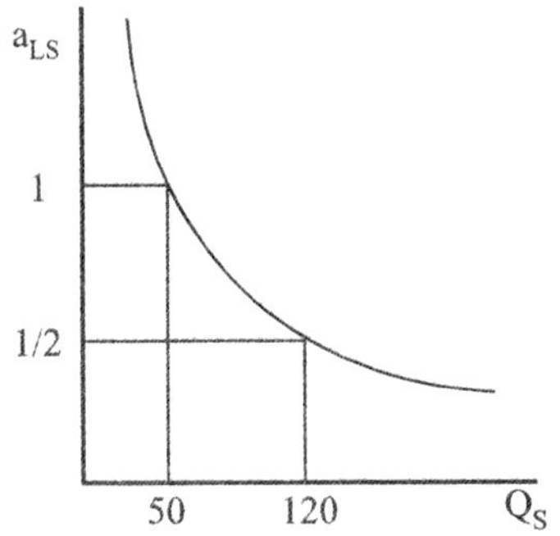

Let the unit-labour requirement for steel be read off the adjoining graph. The graph shows that when 50 tons of steel are produced by the economy, the unit-labour requirement is 1 hour of labour per ton of steel. However, when 120 tons of steel are produced, the unit-labour requirement falls to half an hour of labour per ton of steel.

An Autarky Equilibrium

The U.S.A. and France, assumed to be identical in all respects, will share identical autarky equilibriums. Suppose the equilibriums are such that production of steel in each country is 50 tons. Since at 50 tons of output, the unit-labour requirement is 1, it means that the total amount of labour used in steel production is 50 hours. That leaves 50 hours of labour to be allocated to the production of clothing, which with a unit-labour requirement of 1 also, means that total output of clothing is 50 racks. The autarky production and consumption levels are summarized below.

Autarky Production/Consumption		
	Clothing (racks)	Steel (tons)
USA	50	50
France	50	50
World Total	100	100

The problem with these initial autarky equilibriums is that because demands and supplies are identical in the two countries, the prices of the goods would also be identical. With identical prices, there would be no incentive to trade if trade suddenly became free between the two countries.

GAINS FROM SPECIALIZATION

Despite the lack of incentive to trade in the original autarky equilibriums, we can show, nevertheless, that trade could be advantageous for both countries. All that is necessary is for one of the two countries to produce all of the good with economies of scale and let the other country specialize in the other good.

For example, suppose we let France produce 120 tons of steel. This is greater than the 100 tons of world output of steel in the autarky equilibriums. Since the unit-labour requirement of steel is ½ when 120 tons of steel are produced by one country, the total labour can be found by plugging these numbers into the production function. That is, since $Q_S^* = L_S^*/a_{LS}$, $Q_S^* = 120$ and $a_{LS} = ½$, it must be that $L_S^* = 60$. In autarky it took 100 hours of labour for two countries to produce 100 tons of steel. Now it would take France 60 hours to produce 120 tons. That means more output with less labour.

If France allocates its remaining 40 hours of labour to clothing production and if the U.S.A. specializes in clothing production, then production levels in each country and world totals after the reallocation of labour would be as shown in the following table.

Reallocated Production		
	Clothing (racks)	Steel (tons)
USA	100	0
France	40	120
World Total	140	120

The important result here is that it is possible to find a reallocation of labour across industries such that **world output of both goods rises**. Or in other words, there is **an increase in world productive efficiency**. If output of both goods rises then surely it must be possible to find a terms of trade such that both countries would gain from trade. For example, if France were to export 60 tons of steel and import 30 racks of clothing then each country would consume 70 units of clothing (20 more than in autarky) and 60 tons of steel (10 more than in autarky).

The final conclusion of this numerical example is that when there are economies of scale in production then free trade, after an appropriate reallocation of labour, can improve national welfare for both countries relative to autarky. The welfare improvement arises because by concentrating production in the economies of scale industry in one country, advantage can be taken of the productive efficiency improvements.

—oo(O)oo—

Chapter 31

Balance of Payment

The Balance of Payment (BOP) Accounts are an important aspect of the study of macro economy. In our four sector circular flow diagram given in Chapter 2, it has been shown that the external sector influences the working of an open economy. Macroeconomic phenomena cannot be confined within a particular economy. On the other hand, open economies react sharply to events that are occurring in the rest of the world sector. In order to record the overseas transactions of a country, the BOP accounts are maintained and they constitute an important part of the national income accounts. The BOP accounts are a summary of international transaction of a country for a given period, that is a financial year. 'The balance of payments of a country is a systematic record of all economic transactions between the residents of the reporting country and the residents of foreign countries during a given period of time'.[1] Here, are two questions that need to be answered. They are: who is a resident? What is an economic transaction? Resident of a country ordinarily includes individuals, business units, government and their agencies. An economic transaction is an exchange of value: a process in which 'there is transfer of title to an economic good, the rendering of an economic service from residents of one country to residents of other countries'.[2]

RELATION BETWEEN NATIONAL INCOME AND BALANCE OF PAYMENTS

Economic activity usually generates two types of transactions that give rise to international payments and receipts. Firstly, activities arising from production and sale of current output and secondly, those arising from the purchase and sale of existing assets, both real and financial. Let us consider the first, which is production and sale of current output. In an open economy, the expenditure

1. *International Economics,* Charles P. Kindleberger Homeward, Illinois, U.S.A.: Irwin, p. 457.
2. *Ibid.*

of consumers, investors and government in addition to the expenditure of foreigners on the country's exports generates the nation's production of goods and services. The income generated by this can be shown in the following expression:

$$Y = C + I + G + X$$

This income is disposed off in the purchase of consumer goods and services (C), savings (S) and taxes (T). Add the goods and services purchased from abroad by the domestic sectors, that is imports (M). The following expression gives the way income is disposed off:

$$Y = C + S + T + M$$

According to national income accounting, income generated must be equal to income disposed off. Therefore,

$$C + I + G + X = C + S + T + M$$

Simplifying this we obtain

$$I + X + G = S + T + M$$

Here I, G and X are *injections* into the income stream and S, T and M are *leakages* therefrom. So, in equilibrium planned injections must be equal to total planned leakages.

BALANCE OF TRADE AND BALANCE OF PAYMENTS

Balance of Trade takes into account only those transactions arising out of the exports and imports of goods (the visible items). It does not consider the exchange of services rendered such as shipping, insurance and banking, payment of interest and dividend or expenditure by tourists which are also known as invisible items.

Balance of Payments takes into account the exchange of both visible and invisible items. Hence, the balance of payments represents a better picture of a country's economic transactions with the rest of the world than the Balance of Trade.

STRUCTURE OF BALANCE OF PAYMENT ACCOUNTING

The transactions are recorded in the balance of payments accounts in double-entry bookkeeping. Each international transaction undertaken by the country will result in a credit entry and debit entry of equal size.

As international transactions are recorded in double-entry accounting, the BOP accounting must always balance: that is, total amount of debits must equal total amount of credits. Of course, the balancing item Errors and Omissions must be included to 'balance' the BOP accounts. By convention, debit items and credit items are entered with a minus sign and plus sign respectively.

Transactions in BOP are classified into five major categories as given below:

1. Goods and services account
2. Unilateral transfer account
3. Long-term capital account
4. Short-term private capital account
5. Short-term official capital account

For each of these given categories, specific types of transactions are shown as debits or credits. This is shown in Table 31.1.

Since there are two major categories of accounts in the BOP accounts statement, that is, current and capital accounts, an explanation of current and capital account is in order at this stage to understand their components.

Table 31.1: Classification on System of Debits and Credits in the Balance of Payments Accounts

Debits (–)	Credits (+)
A. Imports of goods	A. Exports of goods
B Imports of services Unilateral transfers (gifts) made	B. Exports of Services Unilateral transfers (gifts) received
A. Increase in long-term foreign assets owned by home country private citizens and government	A. Decrease in long-term foreign assets owned by home country citizens and government
B. Decrease in long-term home country assets owned by foreign private citizens and governments	B. Increase in long-term home country assets owned by foreign private citizens and governments
A. Increase in short-term foreign assets owned by home country private citizens	A. Decrease in short-term foreign assets owned by home country private citizens
B. Decrease in short-term home country assets owned by foreign private citizens	B. Increase in short-term home country assets owned by foreign private citizens
A. Increase in short-term foreign assets owned by home country government (official monetary authorities)	A. Decrease in short-term foreign assets owned by home country government (official monetary authorities)
B. Decrease in short-term home country assets owned by foreign governments (official monetary authorities)	B. Increase in short-term home country assets owned by foreign governments (official monetary authorities)

Current Account

The Current Account records imports and exports of goods and services and unilateral transfers. Exports, whether of goods (steel, machinery, rice, etc.) or services (banking services, insurance services, tourism services to foreign tourists, etc.) are entered as positive items in the account. This is because exports cause an inflow of foreign exchange into the country. Imports are recorded as negative items in the account because imports cause an outflow of foreign exchange from the country.

1. BOP accounts differentiate between trade in goods and trade in services. The balance of exports and imports of goods is called the *balance of visible trade*, and the balance of exports and imports of services is called the *balance of invisible trade*. The terms are used because goods are visible to the eye but services are invisible to the eye.
2. Unilateral transfers or unrequited transfers are receipts which residents of a country receive, or payments that the residents of a country make without getting anything in return, that is, receipts or payments for which there is *no quidpro quo*. Receipts from abroad are entered as positive items and payments abroad are entered as negative items. Private unrequited transfers are gifts that domestic residents receive from or make to foreign residents. An example of this would be Indians in the Gulf countries sending back money to their relatives in India. Official unrequited transfers is the receipt of or giving of foreign aid, from developed countries or to developing countries. The net value of balances of visible trade and of invisible trade and of unilateral transfers is the *balance on current account.*

Capital Account

The Capital Account records all international transactions that involve a resident of the domestic country changing his assets with a foreign resident or his liabilities to a foreign resident. The various forms of capital account transactions are given below.

1. *Private transactions*: These are transactions that are affecting assets or liabilities by individuals, businesses, etc. and other non-government entities. The bulk of foreign investment is private.
2. *Official transactions*: Transactions affecting assets and liabilities by the government and its agencies.
3. *Direct investment*: It is the act of purchasing an asset and at the same time acquiring control of it (other than the ability to re-sell it). An example of such an investment is the acquisition of a firm in one country by a firm in another country. The transfer of funds from the parent company abroad to the subsidiary company in the domestic country so that the subsidiary can acquire assets in the domestic country is another type of direct investment. Such business transactions form the major part of private direct investment overseas. Similar transactions by individuals could be the purchase of a house abroad, etc.

4. *Portfolio investment*: It is the acquisition of an asset that does not give the purchaser control over the asset. An example of such investment is the purchase of shares in a foreign company or of bonds issued by a foreign government, or loans made to foreign firms or governments. By convention, the purchase of an asset from another country appears as a negative item on the capital account for the purchasing country (there is an outflow of foreign exchange). Thus, capital outflows are awarded a negative sign and capital inflows are awarded a positive sign. The net value of the balances of direct and portfolio investment is called the *balance on capital account.*

OTHER ITEMS IN THE BALANCE OF PAYMENTS

The remaining items that cannot be categorised into the two preceding categories constitute the other items in the balance of payments. They are included since the full balance of payments account must balance. These items are as follows:

1. *Errors and Omissions*: These are to take into account the difficulty of accurately recording all the wide variety of transactions that take place in the accounting period. They may arise due to the presence of sampling of transactions rather than recording each individual transaction (for example, instead of recording each of a thousand exports of lemons, they may multiply an average lemon export figure by thousand), due to dishonesty, that is, businessmen under-reporting sales abroad to avoid taxes, or when smuggling occurs, etc.
2. *Official Reserve Transactions*: All transactions except those in this category may be termed as *autonomous transactions*. They are so called because they are entered into with some independent motive, that is, not with a view to bring their consequences on the balance of payments or on the exchange rate. In contrast to this, official reserve transactions are carried out by the government and the central banks in pursuit of some international economic policy objective; while keeping an eye on the effect of such transactions on the BOP and the exchange rate. As a result such transactions are not autonomous. The first of these items is the change in the domestic country's official reserve assets. These reserves of a country are held in the form of foreign currency or foreign currency securities, gold and Special Drawing Rights (SDR) with the IMF. SDR allows a country to avail of foreign exchange in proportion to the quantum of the country's deposit of its currency with the IMF under the SDR scheme. The changes in the country's reserves must reflect the net value of all other items in the BOP. Reduction in these assets will be used to finance expenditures abroad. Reductions appear as a credit item in the BOP (because their sale causes foreign exchange inflow into the country). An increase in these reserves will appear as a debit because purchasing assets. The second of these transactions is the change in foreign official assets in India. Foreign central banks will hold part of

their reserve assets in the form of rupees. If foreign central banks increase the amount of official reserve assets held in India it will appear as a positive item because their purchase of our rupee securities or rupees will cause inflow of foreign exchange into India. Table 10.1 gives the components of India's Balance of Payments and changes over the last decade.

AUTONOMOUS AND ACCOMMODATING ITEMS

In the discussion of these various balances in BOP account, economists use the terms such as *autonomous items*, *accommodating items*, *above the line items* and *below the line items* in the balance of payments. Let us explain their meaning. *Autonomous items* in the BOP refer to international economic transactions that take place due to some economic motive such as profit maximization. These transactions are independent of the state of the country's balance of payments. These items are often called *above the line items* in the BOP. The balance of payments is in deficit if the autonomous receipts are less than autonomous payments. This means that the foreign country has some net claims against the domestic country. The BOP is in surplus if the autonomous receipts are greater than autonomous payments. This means that the domestic country has some net claims against the foreign country.

The monetary authorities may finance a deficit by depleting their reserves of foreign currencies, or by borrowing from the IMF, or by borrowing from foreign monetary authorities. This will be shown as decrease in reserves. The monetary authority may deploy a surplus by purchasing foreign securities, foreign currency or gold. This appears as an increase in reserves. *Accommodating items* in the BOP refer to transactions that occur because of other activity in the BOP, such as government financing. Accommodating items are also referred to as *below the line items*. The official settlements are seen as an accommodating item in order to keep the BOP identity. The official settlements approach to the balance of payments looks at the net monetary transfer that has been made by the monetary authorities in settlement. The assumption made in this approach is that the monetary authority is the ultimate financier of any deficit in the balance of payments or the ultimate recipient of any surplus. Note that the official settlements approach assumes importance in a fixed exchange rate set-up. In a flexible rate set-up, much of the deficit and surplus will be automatically wiped out by an adjustment in the exchange rates, leaving less settlement work for the monetary authorities.

DISEQUILIBRIUM IN BALANCE OF PAYMENTS

There are a number of factors that cause disequilibrium in the balance of payments showing either a surplus or deficit. These causes are broadly categorized into

(a) Economic factors;

(b) Political factors; and

(c) Social factors.

Table 31.2: Example of a Country's Balance of Payments

No.	Item	1990–91	2001–02
1.	Exports	18,477	44,915
2.	Imports	27,915	57,618
3.	Trade balance	–9,438	–12,703
4.	Invisibles (net)	–242	14,054
4(i)	Non-factor services	980	4,199
4(ii)	Investment income	–3,752	–2,654
4(iii)	Private transfers	2,069	12,125
4(iv)	Official transfers	461	384
5.	Current account balance	–9,680	1,351
6.	External assistance (net)	2,210	1,204
7.	Commercial borrowing (net)	2,248	–1,147
8.	IMF (net)	1,214	0
9.	NR deposits (net)	1,536	2,754
10.	Currency debt service	–1,193	–519
11.	Foreign Investment (net) of which	103	5,286
11(i)	FDI (net)	97	3,266
11(ii)	FIIs	0	1,505
11(iii)	Euro equities and others	6	515
12.	Other flows (net)	2,284	2,828
13.	Capital account total (net)	8,402	10,406
14.	Reserve use (–increase)	1,278	–11,757

Economic Factors

- Large-scale development expenditure that may cause large imports.
- Cyclical fluctuations in general business activity such as recession or depression.
- High domestic prices may result in imports.
- New sources of supply, new and better substitutes to existing products and changes in costs will bring about a change in trade flows and hence BOP over a period of time.

Political Factors

Political instability may cause large capital outflows and dampen the inflows of foreign capital.

Social Factors

Changes in tastes, preference and fashions may affect imports and exports. Balance of payments disequilibrium is a serious issue for policy makers. A chronic BOP deficit leads to downgrading the economy in the world community. Domestic sectors also receive the impact of BOP deficit. Hence, the monetary authority of the country concerned and the IMF undertake certain corrective measures to deal with the disequilibrium in the BOP. So, every country in its economic agenda strives hard to perform well in its international trade in order that it will not enter into problems of BOP disequilibrium.

—oo(O)oo—

Chapter 32

The Foreign Exchange Market

EXCHANGE RATE

The exchange rate represents the number of units of one currency that exchanges for a unit of another. There are two ways to express an exchange rate between two currencies (for example, the \$ and £ [pound]). One can either write \$/£ or £/\$. These are reciprocals of each other. Thus if E is the \$/£ exchange rate and V is the £/\$ exchange rate then $E = 1/V$.

For example, on January 8, 1997, the following exchange rates prevailed,

$$E_{\$/£} = 1.69 \text{ which implies } V_{£/\$} = 0.59$$

$$V_{¥/\$} = 116. \text{ which implies } E_{\$/¥} = 0.0086$$

CURRENCY VALUE

It is important to note that the value of a currency is always given in terms of another currency. Thus the value of a US dollar in terms of British pounds is the £/\$ exchange rate. The value of the Japanese yen in terms of the dollar is the \$/¥ exchange rate.

[Note: We always express the value of all items in terms of something else. Thus, the value of a quart of milk is given in dollars, not in milk units. The value of a car is also given in dollar terms, not in terms of cars. Similarly, the value of a dollar is given in terms of something else, usually another currency. Hence the rupee/\$ exchange rate gives us the value of the dollar in terms of rupees.]

This definition is especially useful to remember when one is dealing with unfamiliar currencies. Thus the value of the euro (€) in terms of British pounds is given as the £/€ exchange rate.

The peso/€ exchange rate refers to the value of the euro in terms of pesos.

CURRENCY APPRECIATION

A currency *appreciates* with respect to another when *its value rises* in terms of the other. The dollar appreciates with respect to the yen if the ¥/$ exchange rate rises.

CURRENCY DEPRECIATION

A currency *depreciates* with respect to another when *its value falls* in terms of the other. The dollar depreciates with respect to the yen if the ¥/$ exchange rate falls.

Note that if the ¥/$ rate rises, then its reciprocal, the $/¥ rate falls. Since the $/¥ rate represents the value of the yen in terms of dollars, this means that when the dollar appreciates with respect to the yen, the yen must depreciate with respect to the dollar.

The ***rate of appreciation*** (or depreciation) is the percentage change in the value of a currency over some period of time.

EXAMPLE 1

On Jan. 8 1997, $E_{¥/\$} = 116$

On Jan. 8 1996, $E_{¥/\$} = 105$

Use percentage change formula: (New value – Old value)/Old Value

$$\frac{(116-105)}{105} = \frac{11}{105} = 0.105$$

Multiply by 100 to write as a percentage to get,

$$0.105 \times 100 = +\ 10.5\%$$

Since we have calculated the change in the value of the $, in terms of the yen, and since the percentage change is positive, this means that the dollar has appreciated by 10.5 per cent with respect to the yen during the past year.

EXAMPLE 2

On Jan. 8 1997, $E_{£/\$} = 0.59$

On Jan. 8 1996, $E_{£/\$} = 0.65$

Use percentage change formula: (New value – Old value)/Old Value

$$\frac{(0.59-0.65)}{0.65} = -\frac{0.06}{0.65} = -\ 0.092$$

Multiply by 100 to write as a percentage to get,

$$-0.092 \times 100 = -9.2\%$$

Since we have calculated the change in the value of the \$, in terms of pounds, and since the percentage change is negative, this means that the dollar has depreciated by 9.2 per cent with respect to the pound during the past year.

ARBITRAGE

Arbitrage, generally means buying a product when its price is low and then reselling it after its price rises in order to make a profit. Currency arbitrage means buying a currency in one market (say New York) at a low price and reselling, moments later, in another market at a higher price.

SPOT EXCHANGE RATE

The spot exchange rate refers to the exchange rate that prevails *on the spot*, that is, for trade to take place immediately.

FORWARD EXCHANGE RATE

The forward exchange rate refers to the rate which appears on a contract to exchange currencies either 30, 60, 90 or 180 days in the future.

For example a corporation might sign a contract with a bank to buy DMs for dollars 60 days from now at a predetermined ER. The predetermined rate is called the 60-day forward rate. Forward contracts can be used to reduce exchange rate risk.

For example, suppose an importer of BMWs is expecting a shipment in 60 days. Suppose that upon arrival the importer must pay € 1,000,000. The current spot ER is 1.20 \$/€ thus if the payment were made today it would cost \$ 1,200,000. Suppose further that the importer is fearful of a \$ depreciation. He does not currently have the \$ 1,200,000 but expects to earn more than enough in sales over the next two months. If the \$ falls in value to, say, 1.3 \$/€ in 60 days time, how much would it cost the importer in dollars to purchase the BMW shipment?

A. The shipment would still cost € 1,000,000. To find out how much this is in dollars multiply € 1,000,000 by 1.3 \$/€ = \$ 1,300,000.

Note this is \$ 100.000 more for the cars simply because the \$ value changed.

One way the importer could protect himself against this potential loss is to purchase a forward contract to buy € for \$ in 60 days. The ER on the forward contract will likely be different from the current spot ER. In part its value will reflect market expectations about the degree to which currency values will change in the next two months. Suppose the current 60-day forward ER is 1.25 \$/€ reflecting the expectation that the \$ value will fall. If the importer purchases a 60-day contract to buy € 1,000,000 it will cost him (1,000,000 × 1.25) = \$ 1,250,000. Although this is higher than what it would cost if the exchange were made today, the importer does not have the cash available to make the trade today, and the forward contract would protect the importer from even an even greater \$-depreciation.

When the forward ER is such that a forward trade costs more than a spot trade today costs, there is said to be a *forward premium*. If the reverse were true, such that the forward trade were cheaper than a spot trade then there is a *forward discount*.

HEDGING

A currency trader is hedging if he or she enters into a forward contract to protect oneself from a downside loss. However by hedging the trader also forfeits the potential for an upside gain. Suppose in the story above that the spot ER falls. Suppose the ER fell to 1.10 \$/€. In this case, had the importer waited the € 1,000,000 would only have cost (1,000,000 × 1.10) = \$ 1,100,000. Thus, hedging protects against loss but at the same time eliminates potential unexpected gain.

PARTICIPANTS IN THE FOREX

The foreign exchange market (FOREX) is not a market like the New York stock exchange, where daily trades of stock are conducted in a central location. Instead, a FOREX market refers to the activities of major international banks that engage in currency trading. These banks act as intermediaries between the true buyers and sellers of currencies, that is, governments, businesses, and individuals. These banks will hold foreign currency deposits and stand ready to exchange these for domestic currency upon demand. The exchange rate will be determined independently by each bank but will essentially be determined by supply and demand in the market. In other words, the banks set the exchange rate at each moment to equalize its supply of foreign currency with the market demand. Each bank makes money by collecting a transactions fee for its 'exchange services.'

It is useful to categorize two distinct groups of participants in the FOREX, those whose transactions are recorded on the current account (importers and exporters) and those whose transactions are recorded on the financial account (investors).

1. Importers and Exporters

Anyone who either imports or exports goods and services will need to exchange currencies to make the transactions. This includes tourists who travel abroad since their transactions would appear as services in the current account. These businesses and individuals will engage in currency trades daily; however, these transactions are small in comparison to those made by investors.

2. International Investors, Banks, Arbitrageurs, etc.

Most of the daily currency transactions are made by investors. These investors, be they investment companies, insurance companies, banks or others, are making currency transactions to realize a greater return on their investments or holdings. Many of these companies are responsible to manage the savings of others. Pension plans and mutual funds buy and sell billions of dollars worth of assets daily. Banks, in the temporary possession of the deposits of others do the same. Insurance companies manage large portfolios which act as their capital to be used to pay off claims on accidents, casualties and deaths. More and more these companies look internationally to make the most of their investments.

It is estimated that over \$ 1 trillion (or \$ 1,000 billion) worth of currency is traded every day. Only about \$ 70-\$ 100 billion of trade in goods and services takes place daily worldwide. This suggests that much of the currency exchanges are done by international investors rather than importers and exporters.

INVESTMENT CONCERNS—INTERNATIONAL OR DOMESTIC

Investors generally have three broad concerns when an investment is made. They care about how much money the investment will earn over time, they care about how risky the investment is, and they care about how liquid, or convertible, the asset is.

1. Rate of Return

The percentage change in the value of an asset over some period of time.

Investors purchase assets as a way of saving for the future. Any time an asset is purchased the purchaser is forgoing current consumption for future consumption. In order to make such a transaction worthwhile the investor hopes (sometimes expects) to have more money for future consumption than the amount they give up in the present. Thus investors would like to have as high a rate of return on their investments as possible.

Example 1

Suppose a Picasso painting is purchased in 1996 for \$ 500,000. One year later the painting is resold for \$ 600,000. The rate of return is calculated as,

$$\frac{(600{,}000 - 500{,}000)}{500{,}000} \times 100 = \frac{100{,}000}{500{,}000} \times 100 = 0.20 \times 100 = 20\%$$

Example 2

\$ 1,000 is placed is a savings account for one year at an annual interest rate of 10 per cent. The interest earned after one year is \$ 1,000 × 0.10 = \$100. Thus the value of the account after one year is \$ 1,100. The rate of return is,

$$\frac{1100 - 1000}{1000} \times 100 = \frac{100}{1000} \times 100 = 0.10 \times 100 = 10\%$$

This means that the rate of return on a domestic interest bearing account is merely the interest rate.

2. Risk

The second primary concern of an investor is the risk of the assets. Generally, the greater the expected rate of return, the greater the risk. Invest in an oil wildcat endeavour and you might get a 1,000 per cent return on your investment...if you strike oil. The chances of doing so are likely to be very low however. Thus, a key concern of investors is how to manage the trade-off between risk and return.

3. Liquidity

Liquidity essentially means the speed with which assets can be converted to cash. Insurance companies need to have assets which are fairly liquid in the event that they need to pay out a large number of claims. Banks have to stand ready to make payouts to depositors, etc.

FOREIGN EXCHANGE MARKET

The **foreign exchange** (**currency** or **forex** or **FX**) **market** exists wherever one currency is traded for another. It is by far the largest market in the world, in terms of cash value traded, and includes trading between large banks, central banks, currency speculators, multinational corporations, governments, and other financial markets and institutions. The trade in the forex markets across the globe currently exceeds $ 1.9 trillion/day (on average). Retail traders (individuals) are currently a very small part of this market and may only participate indirectly through brokers or banks and may be targets of forex scams.

MARKET SIZE AND LIQUIDITY

The foreign exchange market is unique because of:

- its trading volume,
- the extreme liquidity of the market,
- the large number of, and variety of, traders in the market,
- its geographical dispersion,
- its long trading hours—24 hours a day (except on weekends), and
- the variety of factors that affect exchange rates.

Average daily global turnover in traditional foreign exchange market transactions totalled $ 2.7 trillion in April 2006 according to IFSL estimates based on semi-annual London, New York, Tokyo and Singapore Foreign Exchange Committee data. Overall turnover, including non-traditional foreign exchange derivatives and products traded on exchanges, averaged around $ 2.9 trillion a day. This was more than 10 times the size of the combined daily turnover on all the world's equity markets. Foreign exchange trading increased by 38 per cent between April 2005 and April 2006 and has more than doubled since 2001. This is largely due to the growing importance of foreign exchange as an asset class and an increase in fund management assets, particularly of hedge funds and pension funds. The diverse selection of execution venues such as internet trading platforms has also made it easier for retail traders to trade in the foreign exchange market.

Unlike a stock market, where all participants have access to the same prices, the forex market is divided into levels of access. At the top is the inter-bank market, which is made up of the largest investment banking firms. Within the inter-bank market, spreads, which are the difference between the bid and ask prices, are razor sharp and usually unavailable, and not known to players outside the inner circle. As you descend the levels of access, the difference between the bid and ask prices widens. This is due to volume. If a trader can guarantee large numbers of transactions for large amounts, they can demand a smaller difference between the bid and ask price, which is referred to as a better spread. The levels of access that make up the forex market are determined by the size of the 'line' (the amount of money with which they are trading). The top-tier inter-bank market accounts for 53 per cent of all transactions. After that there are usually smaller investment banks, followed by large multi-national corporations (which need to hedge risk and pay employees in different countries), large hedge funds, and even some of the retail forex market makers. According to Galati and Melvin, "Pension funds, insurance companies, mutual funds, and other institutional investors have played an increasingly important role in financial markets in general, and in FX markets in particular, since the early 2000s" (2004). In addition, they note, "Hedge funds have grown markedly over the 2001–2004 period in terms of both number and overall size." Central banks also participate in the forex market to align currencies to their economic needs.

BANKS

The inter-bank market caters for both the majority of commercial turnover and large amounts of speculative trading every day. A large bank may trade billions of dollars daily. Some of this trading is undertaken on behalf of customers, but much is conducted by proprietary desks, trading for the bank's own account.

Until recently, foreign exchange brokers did large amounts of business, facilitating inter-bank trading and matching anonymous counterparts for small fees. Today, however, much of this business has moved on to more efficient electronic systems, such as EBS, Reuters Dealing 3000 Matching (D2), the Chicago Mercantile Exchange, Bloomberg and TradeBook(R). The broker squawk box lets traders listen in on ongoing inter-bank trading and is heard in most trading rooms, but turnover is noticeably smaller than just a few years ago.

COMMERCIAL COMPANIES

An important part of this market comes from the financial activities of companies seeking foreign exchange to pay for goods or services. Commercial companies often trade fairly small amounts compared to those of banks or speculators, and their trades often have little short term impact on market rates. Nevertheless, trade flows are an important factor in the long-term direction of a currency's exchange rate. Some multinational companies can have an unpredictable impact when very large positions are covered due to exposures that are not widely known by other market participants.

CENTRAL BANKS

National central banks play an important role in the foreign exchange markets. They try to control the money supply, inflation, and/or interest rates and often have official or unofficial target rates for their currencies. They can use their often substantial foreign exchange reserves to stabilize the market. Milton Friedman argued that the best stabilization strategy would be for central banks to buy when the exchange rate is too low, and to sell when the rate is too high—that is, to trade for a profit based on their more precise information. Nevertheless, the effectiveness of central bank 'stabilizing speculation' is doubtful because central banks do not go bankrupt if they make large losses, like other traders would, and there is no convincing evidence that they do make a profit in trading.

The mere expectation or rumour of central bank intervention might be enough to stabilize a currency, but aggressive intervention might be used several times each year in countries with a dirty float currency regime. Central banks do not always achieve their objectives, however. The combined resources of the market can easily overwhelm any central bank. Several scenarios of this nature were seen in the 1992-93 ERM collapse, and in more recent times in Southeast Asia.

INVESTMENT MANAGEMENT FIRMS

Investment management firms (who typically manage large accounts on behalf of customers such as pension funds and endowments) use the foreign exchange market to facilitate transactions in foreign securities. For example, an investment manager with an international equity portfolio will need to buy and sell foreign currencies in the spot market in order to pay for purchases of foreign equities. Since the forex transactions are secondary to the actual investment decision, they are not seen as speculative or aimed at profit-maximization.

Some investment management firms also have more speculative specialist currency overlay operations, which manage clients' currency exposures with the aim of generating profits as well as limiting risk. Whilst the number of this type of specialist firms is quite small, many have a large value of assets under management (AUM), and hence can generate large trades.

HEDGE FUNDS

Hedge funds, such as George Soros's Quantum fund have gained a reputation for aggressive currency speculation since 1990. They control billions of dollars of equity and may borrow billions more, and thus may overwhelm intervention by central banks to support almost any currency, if the economic fundamentals are in the hedge funds' favour.

RETAIL FOREX BROKERS

Retail forex brokers or market makers handle a minute fraction of the total volume of the foreign exchange market. According to CNN, one retail broker estimates retail volume at $ 25-50 billion daily, which is about 2 per cent of the whole market.

TRADING CHARACTERISTICS

There is no single unified foreign exchange market. Due to the over-the-counter (OTC) nature of currency markets, there are rather a number of interconnected marketplaces, where different currency instruments are traded. This implies that there is no such thing as *a single* dollar rate - but rather a number of different rates (prices), depending on what bank or market maker is trading. In practice, the rates are often very close, otherwise they could be exploited by arbitrageurs.

The main trading centres are in London, New York, Tokyo, and Singapore, but banks throughout the world participate. As the Asian trading session ends, the European session begins, then the U.S. session, and then the Asian begin in their turns. Traders can react to news when it breaks, rather than waiting for the market to open.

There is little or no 'inside information' in the foreign exchange markets. Exchange rate fluctuations are usually caused by actual monetary flows as well as by expectations of changes in monetary flows caused by changes in GDP growth, inflation, interest rates, budget and trade deficits or surpluses, large cross-border M&A deals and other macroeconomic conditions. Major news is released publicly, often on scheduled dates, so many people have access to the same news at the same time. However, the large banks have an important advantage; they can see their customers' order flow.

Currencies are traded against one another. Each pair of currencies thus constitutes an individual product and is traditionally noted XXX/YYY, where YYY is the ISO 4217 international three-letter code of the currency into which the price of one unit of XXX is expressed. For instance, EUR/USD is the price of the euro expressed in US dollars, as in 1 euro = 1.3045 dollar. Out of convention, the first currency in the pair, the base currency, was the stronger currency at the creation of the pair. The second currency, counter currency, was the weaker currency at the creation of the pair.

The factors affecting XXX will affect both XXX/YYY and XXX/ZZZ. This causes positive currency correlation between XXX/YYY and XXX/ZZZ.

On the spot market, according to the BIS study, the most heavily traded products were:

- EUR/USD - 28 %
- USD/JPY - 18 %
- GBP/USD (also called *sterling* or *cable*) – 14 %

and the US currency was involved in 89 per cent of transactions, followed by the euro (37 per cent), the yen (20 per cent) and sterling (17 per cent). (Note that volume percentages should add up to 200% – 100% for all the sellers, and 100 per cent for all the buyers).

Although trading in the euro has grown considerably since the currency's creation in January 1999, the foreign exchange market is thus far still largely dollar-centered. For instance, trading the euro versus a non-European currency ZZZ will usually involve two trades: EUR/USD and USD/ZZZ. The only exception to this is EUR/JPY, which is an established traded currency pair in the inter-bank spot market.

FACTORS AFFECTING CURRENCY TRADING

Although exchange rates are affected by many factors, in the end, currency prices are a result of supply and demand forces. The world's currency markets can be viewed as a huge melting pot: in a large and ever-changing mix of current events, supply and demand factors are constantly shifting, and the price of one currency in relation to another shifts accordingly. No other market encompasses (and distils) as much of what is going on in the world at any given time as foreign exchange.

Supply and demand for any given currency, and thus its value, are not influenced by any single element, but rather by several. These elements generally fall into three categories: economic factors, political conditions and market psychology.

ECONOMIC FACTORS

These include economic policy, disseminated by government agencies and central banks, economic conditions, generally revealed through economic reports, and other economic indicators.

Economic policy comprises government fiscal policy (budget/spending practices) and monetary policy (the means by which a government's central bank influences the supply and 'cost' of money, which is reflected by the level of interest rates).

Economic conditions include:

Government budget deficits or surpluses: The market usually reacts negatively to widening government budget deficits, and positively to narrowing budget deficits. The impact is reflected in the value of a country's currency.

Balance of trade levels and trends: The trade flow between countries illustrates the demand for goods and services, which in turn indicates demand for a country's currency to conduct trade. Surpluses and deficits in trade of goods and services reflect the competitiveness of a nation's economy. For example, trade deficits may have a negative impact on a nation's currency.

Inflation levels and trends: Typically, a currency will lose value if there is a high level of inflation in the country or if inflation levels are perceived to be rising. This is because inflation erodes purchasing power, thus demand, for that particular currency.

Economic growth and health: Reports such as gross domestic product (GDP), employment levels, retail sales, capacity utilization and others, detail the levels of a country's economic growth and health. Generally, the more healthy and robust a country's economy, the better its currency will perform, and the more demand for it there will be.

POLITICAL CONDITIONS

Internal, regional, and international political conditions and events can have a profound effect on currency markets. For instance, political upheaval and instability can have a negative impact on a nation's economy. The rise of a political faction that is perceived to be fiscally responsible can have the opposite effect. Also, events in one country in a region may spur positive or negative interest in a neighbouring country and, in the process, affect its currency.

MARKET PSYCHOLOGY

Perhaps the most difficult to define (there are no balance sheets or income statements), market psychology influences the foreign exchange market in a variety of ways:

Flights to quality: Unsettling international events can lead to a 'flight to quality'—with investors seeking a 'safe haven'. There will be a greater demand, thus a higher price, for currencies perceived as stronger over their relatively weaker counterparts.

Long-term trends: Very often, currency markets move in long, pronounced trends. Although currencies do not have an annual growing season like physical commodities, business cycles do make themselves felt. Cycle analysis looks at longer-term price trends that may rise from economic or political trends.

'Buy the rumour, sell the fact:' This market truism can apply to many currency situations. It is the tendency for the price of a currency to reflect the impact of a particular action before it occurs and, when the anticipated event comes to pass, react in exactly the opposite direction. This may also be referred to as a market being 'oversold' or 'overbought'.

Economic numbers: While economic numbers can certainly reflect economic policy, some reports and numbers take on a talisman-like effect—the number itself becomes important to market psychology and may have an immediate impact on short-term market moves. 'What to watch' can change over time. In recent years, for example, money supply, employment, trade balance figures and inflation numbers have all taken turns in the spotlight.

ALGORITHMIC TRADING IN FOREX

With steady growth of the FX markets and the increasing adoption of E-FX among the market participants, algorithmic trading is emerging as the next level of trading technology for market participants to contend with. Although there is much confusion about the technique, most market participants seem to agree that it will be used increasingly frequently. According to financial consultancy Celent estimates, by 2008 up to 25 per cent of all trades by volume will be executed using algorithm, up from about 18 per cent in 2005.

FINANCIAL INSTRUMENTS

There are several types of financial instruments commonly used.

Spot

A spot transaction is a two-day delivery transaction, as opposed to the futures contracts, which are usually three months. This trade represents a 'direct exchange' between two currencies, has the shortest time frame, involves cash rather than a contract; and interest is not included in the agreed-upon transaction. The data for this study come from the spot market. Spot has the largest share by volume in FX transactions among all instruments.

Forward Transaction

One way to deal with the Forex risk is to engage in a forward transaction. In this transaction, money does not actually change hands until some agreed upon future date. A buyer and seller agree on an exchange rate for any date in the future, and the transaction occurs on that date, regardless of what the market rates are then. The duration of the trade can be a few days, months or years.

Futures

Foreign currency futures are forward transactions with standard contract sizes and maturity dates—for example, 500,000 British pounds for next November at an agreed rate. Futures are standardized and are usually traded on an exchange created for this purpose. The average contract length is roughly three months. Futures contracts are usually inclusive of any interest amounts.

Swap

The most common type of forward transaction is the currency swap. In a swap, two parties exchange currencies for a certain length of time and agree to reverse the transaction at a later date. These are not contracts and are not traded through an exchange.

Options

A foreign exchange option (commonly shortened to just FX option) is a derivative where the owner has the right but not the obligation to exchange money denominated in one currency into another currency at a pre-agreed exchange rate on a specified date. The FX options market is the deepest, largest and most liquid market for options of any kind in the world.

THE DIFFERENCE BETWEEN SPOT AND FUTURES IN FOREX

Before a description of retail trading, it is important to understand the difference between the spot and futures markets. Futures are generally based on contracts, with typical durations of three months. Spot, on the other hand, is a two-day cash delivery. While the futures markets were created to hedge out risks and speculate on future market conditions, spot was created to allow actual cash deliveries. Spot developed a two-day delivery date to give those transporting the actual cash a window of time to receive it. While in theory there still is a two-day delivery date imposed after a forex transaction, this is no longer used effectively. Every day, at 5 pm EST (the predetermined end of the trading day) spot positions are closed and then reopened. This is done to guarantee an unlimited timeline for delivery. For example, if a spot transaction occurs on a Monday, the delivery date is Wednesday. At 5 pm on Monday, the position is closed and then immediately re-opened; now this is a new position with the close date of Thursday. This daily process allows an investor to hold open a position indefinitely.

Another important difference between futures and spot is how interest is credited. Each currency in a forex transaction has an inherent interest rate attached to it. In the case of the U.S. dollar, this is the Federal Funds Rate. This interest is added every day whether the market is trading or not. Interest cannot take a vacation; money and its loaning value are still important even if the financial world has stopped dealing. In futures, the interest is built into the price of the contract. In spot, however, interest is not taken into account in the offering price because the spot market is a cash market, not a contract market. There must be some mechanism for crediting interest, and various institutions have developed ways to do it. The most common method is to credit that day's worth of interest at the same time they 'flip' the position, or carry it over to the next day. This is important for later discussions and analysis because the transactions examined in this study had interest credited at the end of the business day at exactly 5 pm EST. If a position was held from

5:01 pm on Tuesday and closed at 4:59 pm on Wednesday, no interest would be credited for that day. If, on the other hand, a position was opened on Tuesday at 4:59 pm and closed on the same day 5:01 pm, a full day's interest would be credited. This has interesting ramifications; traders who work intra-day, or 'day traders,' often do not use interest for either gain or loss.

SPECULATION

Controversy about currency speculators and their effect on currency devaluations and national economies recurs regularly . Nevertheless, many economists (for example, Milton Friedman) argue that speculators perform the important function of providing a market for hedgers and transferring risk from those people who do not wish to bear it, to those who do. Other economists (for example, Joseph Stiglitz) however, may consider this argument to be based more on politics and a free market philosophy than on economics.

Large hedge funds and other well capitalized 'position traders' are the main professional speculators.

—oo(O)oo—

Chapter 33

Financial Market

In economics, a **financial market** is a mechanism that allows people to easily buy and sell (trade) financial securities (such as stocks and bonds), commodities (such as precious metals or agricultural goods), and other fungible items of value at low transaction costs and at prices that reflect efficient markets.

Financial markets have evolved significantly over several hundred years and are undergoing constant innovation to improve liquidity.

Both general markets, where many commodities are traded and specialised markets (where only one commodity is traded) exist. Markets work by placing many interested sellers in one 'place', thus making them easier to find for prospective buyers. An economy which relies primarily on interactions between buyers and sellers to allocate resources is known as a market economy in contrast either to a command economy or to a non-market economy that is based, such as a gift economy.

In finance, financial markets facilitate:

- The raising of capital (in the capital markets);
- The transfer of risk (in the derivatives markets); and
- International trade (in the currency markets).

They are used to match those who *want* capital to those who *have* it.

Typically a borrower issues a receipt to the lender promising to pay back the capital. These receipts are *securities* which may be freely bought or sold. In return for lending money to the borrower, the lender will expect some compensation in the form of interest or dividends.

DEFINITION

The term **'Financial markets'** can be a cause of much confusion.

Financial markets could mean:

1. organisations that facilitate the trade in financial products, that is, *stock exchanges facilitate the trade in stocks, bonds and warrants.*
2. the coming together of buyers and sellers to trade financial products, that is, *stocks and shares are traded between buyers and sellers in a number of ways including: the use of stock exchanges; directly between buyers and sellers, etc.*

In academia, students of finance will use both meanings but students of economics will use only the second meaning.

Financial markets can be domestic or they can be international.

TYPES OF FINANCIAL MARKETS

The financial markets can be divided into different subtypes:

- Capital markets which consist of:
    - Stock markets, which provide financing through the issuance of shares or common stock, and enable the subsequent trading thereof.
    - Bond markets, which provide financing through the issuance of b, and enable the subsequent trading thereof.
- Commodity markets, which facilitate the trading of commodities.
- Money markets, which provide short term debt financing and investment.
- Derivatives markets, which provide instruments for the management of financial risk.
    - Futures markets, which provide standardised forward contracts for trading products at some future date; see also forward market.
- Insurance markets, which facilitate the redistribution of various risks.
- Foreign exchange markets, which facilitate the trading of foreign exchange.

The capital markets consist of primary markets and secondary markets. Newly formed (issued) securities are bought or sold in primary markets. Secondary markets allow investors to sell securities that they hold or buy existing securities.

RAISING CAPITAL

To understand financial markets, let us look at what they are used for, that is, what is their purpose?

Without financial markets, borrowers would have difficulty finding lenders themselves. Intermediaries such as banks help in this process. Banks take deposits from those who have money to save. They can then lend money from this pool of deposited money to those who seek to borrow. Banks popularly lend money in the form of loans and mortgages.

More complex transactions than a simple bank deposit require markets where lenders and their agents can meet borrowers and their agents, and where existing borrowing or lending commitments can be sold on to other parties. A good example of a financial market is a stock exchange. A company can raise money by selling shares to investors and its existing shares can be bought or sold.

The following table illustrates where financial markets fit in the relationship between lenders and borrowers:

Relationship between Lenders and Borrowers

Lender	Financial Intermediaries	Financial Markets	Borrowers
Individuals	Banks	Interbank	Individuals
Companies	Insurance companies	Stock Exchange	Companies
	Pension funds	Money Market	Central Government
	Mutual funds	Bond Market	Municipalities
		Foreign Exchange	Public Cooperatives

LENDERS

Individuals do not think of themselves as lenders but they lend to other parties in many ways. Lending activities may be:

- putting money in a savings account at a bank;
- contributing to a pension plan;
- paying premiums to an insurance company;
- investing in government bonds; or
- investing in company shares.

Companies tend to be borrowers of capital. When companies have surplus cash that is not needed for a short period of time, they may seek to make money from their cash surplus by lending it via short term markets called money markets.

There are a few companies that have very strong cash flows. These companies tend to be lenders rather than borrowers. Such companies may decide to return cash to lenders (for example, via a share buyback). Alternatively, they may seek to make more money on their cash by lending it (for example, investing in bonds and stocks).

BORROWERS

Individuals borrow money via bankers loans for short term needs or longer term mortgages to help finance a house purchase.

Companies borrow money to aid short term or long term cash flows. They also borrow for fund modernisation or future business expansion.

Governments often find that their spending requirements exceed their tax revenues. To make up this difference, they need to borrow. Governments also borrow on behalf of nationalised industries, municipalities, local authorities and other public sector bodies. In the U.K., the total borrowing requirement is often referred to as the public sector borrowing requirement (PSBR).

Governments borrow by issuing bonds. In the U.K., the government also borrows from individuals by offering bank accounts and premium bonds. Government debt seems to be permanent. Indeed the debt seemingly expands rather than being paid off. One strategy used by governments to reduce the *value* of the debt is to influence *inflation*.

Municipalities and local authorities may borrow in their own name as well as receive funding from national governments. In the U.K., this would cover an authority like Hampshire County Council.

Public Corporations typically include nationalised industries. These may include the postal services, railway companies and utility companies.

Many borrowers have difficulty raising money locally. They need to borrow internationally with the aid of foreign exchange markets.

DERIVATIVE PRODUCTS

During the 1980s and 1990s, a major growth sector in financial markets is the trade in so-called **derivative products**, or **derivatives,** for short.

In the financial markets, stock prices, bond prices, currency rates, interest rates and dividends go up and down, creating *risk*. Derivative products are financial products which are used to *control* risk or paradoxically *exploit* risk.

CURRENCY MARKETS

Seemingly, the most obvious buyers and sellers of foreign exchange are importers/exporters. While this may have been true in the distant past, whereby importers/exporters created the initial demand for currency markets, importers and exporters now represent only 1/32 of foreign exchange dealing, according to BIS.

The picture of foreign currency transactions today shows:

- Banks and institutions
- Speculators

- Government spending (for example, military bases abroad)
- Importers/Exporters
- Tourists

ANALYSIS OF FINANCIAL MARKETS

Much effort has gone into the study of financial markets and how prices vary with time. Charles Dow, one of the founders of Dow Jones & Company and *The Wall Street Journal*, enunciated a set of ideas on the subject which are now called the Dow Theory. This is the basis of the so-called technical analysis method of attempting to predict future changes. One of the tenets of 'technical analysis' is that market trends give an indication of the future, at least in the short term. The claims of the technical analysts are disputed by many academics, who claim that the evidence points rather to the random walk hypothesis, which states that the next change is not correlated to the last change.

The scale of changes in price over some unit of time is called volatility. It was discovered by Benoît Mandelbrot that changes in prices do not follow a Gaussian distribution, but are rather modelled better by Lévy stable distributions. The scale of change, or volatility, depends on the length of the time unit to a power a bit more than half. Large changes up or down are more likely than what one would calculate using a Gaussian distribution with an estimated standard deviation.

FINANCIAL MARKETS IN POPULAR CULTURE

Gordon Gekko is a famous caricature of a rogue financial markets operator, famous for saying 'greed ... is good'.

Only negative stories about financial markets tend to make the news. The general perception, for those not involved in the world of financial markets is of a place full of crooks and con artists. Big stories like the Enron scandal serve to enhance this view.

Stories that make the headlines involve the incompetent, the lucky and the downright skilful. The Barings scandal is a classic story of incompetence mixed with greed leading to dire consequences. Another story of note is that of Black Wednesday, when sterling came under attack from hedge fund speculators. This led to major problems for the United Kingdom and had a serious impact on its course in Europe. A commonly recurring event is the stock market bubble, whereby market prices rise to dizzying heights in a so-called exaggerated bull market. This is not a new phenomenon; indeed the story of Tulip mania in the Netherlands in the seventeenth century illustrates an early recorded example.

Financial markets are merely tools. Like all tools they have both *beneficial* and *harmful* uses. Overall, financial markets are used by honest people. Otherwise, people would turn away from them *en masse*. As in other walks of life, the financial markets have their fair share of rogue elements.

—oo(O)oo—

Chapter 34

Purchasing Power Parity

The **Purchasing Power Parity (PPP)** theory was developed by **Gustav Cassel** in 1920. It is the method of using the long-run equilibrium exchange rate of two currencies to equalize the currencies' purchasing power. It is based on the law of one price, the idea that, in an efficient market, identical goods must have only one price.

Purchasing power parity is often called ***absolute* purchasing power parity** to distinguish it from a related theory ***relative* purchasing power parity**, which predicts the relationship between the two countries' relative inflation rates and the change in the exchange rate of their currencies.

A purchasing power parity exchange rate equalizes the purchasing power of different currencies in their home countries for a given basket of goods. These special exchange rates are often used to compare the standards of living of two or more countries. The adjustments are meant to give a better picture than comparing gross domestic products (GDP) using market exchange rates. This type of adjustment to an exchange rate is controversial because of the difficulties of finding comparable baskets of goods to compare purchasing power across countries.

Market exchange rates fluctuate widely, but many believe that PPP exchange rates reflect the long run equilibrium value. The distortions caused by using market rates are accentuated because prices of non-traded goods and services are usually lower in poorer economies. For example, a U.S. dollar exchanged and spent in the People's Republic of China will buy much more than a dollar spent in the U.S.A.

The differences between PPP and market exchange rates can be significant. For example, the World Bank's *World Development Indicators 2005* estimates that one United States dollar is equivalent to approximately 1.8 Chinese yuan by purchasing power parity in 2003. However, based on nominal exchange rates, one U.S. dollar is currently equal to 7.9 yuan. This discrepancy has large implications; for instance, GDP per capita in the People's Republic of China is about

US$ 1,800, while on a PPP basis it is about US$ 7,204. This is frequently misused to assert that China is the world's second largest economy, but such a calculation would be invalid under the PPP theory. At the other extreme, Japan's nominal GDP per capita is around US$ 37,600, but its PPP figure is only US$ 30,615.

Estimation of purchasing power parity is complicated by the fact that countries do not simply differ in a uniform price level; rather, the difference in food prices may be greater than the difference in housing prices, while also less than the difference in entertainment prices. People in different countries typically consume different baskets of goods. It is necessary to compare the cost of baskets of goods and services using a price index. This is a difficult task because purchasing patterns and even the goods available to purchase differ across countries. Thus, it is necessary to make adjustments for differences in the quality of goods and services. Additional statistical difficulties arise with multilateral comparisons when (as is usually the case) more than two countries are to be compared.

When PPP comparisons are to be made over some interval of time, proper account needs to be made of inflationary effects.

EXPLANATION

For a U.S. dollar to buy as much in the U.K. as in the U.S.A., as is assumed under the *law of one price*, the price of a basket of goods in pounds in the U.K. (denoted as: £P) times the spot exchange rate (denoted as: \$/£) should equal the price of the same basket in the U.S.A. priced in dollars (denoted as: \$P).

$$£P\ (\$/£) = \$P$$

This implies that the exchange rate that equalizes the value of a dollar of purchasing power (the PPP exchange rate) is:

$$(\$/£) = \$P/£P$$

If the actual spot rate is greater, it suggests that the £ is over-valued against the \$. If the actual spot rate is less, it suggest that the \$ is over-valued against the £.

For example if a 'representative' consumption basket costs \$ 1,500 in the U.S.A. and £ 1,000 in the U.K. the PPP exchange rate would be \$ 1.50/£.

If the actual spot rate was \$ 1.80/£ this would indicate that the pound is overvalued by 20 per cent, or equivalently the dollar is undervalued by 16.7 per cent.

RELATIVE PPP

Relative PPP relates the inflation rate (the change of price levels) in each country to the change in the market exchange rate.

$$\frac{S_t}{S_{t-1}} = \frac{P_t^* / P_{t-1}^*}{P_t / P_{t-1}}$$

where S_t is the spot rate in Foreign Currency/Domestic Currency and P_t is the price level in period t (foreign values are marked by an asterisk). This relation is necessary but not sufficient for absolute purchasing power parity.

According to this theory, the change in the exchange rate is determined by price level changes in both countries. For example, if prices in the U.S.A. rise by 3 per cent and prices in the European Union rise by 1 per cent the purchasing power of the USD should depreciate by 2 per cent compared to the purchasing power of the EUR (equivalently the EUR will appreciate by about 2 per cent)

PPP EQUALIZATION AND THE LAW OF ONE PRICE

The law of one price states that differing prices of a traded good will tend to equalize in the absence of tariffs, other barriers to trade and prohibitively high shipping rates. The law of one price can also be stated as: "In an efficient market all identical goods must have only one price."

The naïve PPP hypothesis is that free trade of goods should revert exchange rates to their PPP values. However, econometric analysis rejects this hypothesis, and gives a better prediction of the PPP/exchange rate relationship (the CPI) based on relative GDPs. Neo-classical economics includes the Balassa-Samuelson effect theory, which explains the PPP model adjustment giving the equilibrium CPIs.

BIG MAC INDEX

An entertaining example of one measure of PPP is the Big Mac index popularised by *The Economist*, which looks at the prices of a Big Mac burger in McDonald's restaurants in different countries. If a Big Mac costs US$ 4 in the U.S.A. and GBP£ 3 in Britain, the PPP exchange rate would be £ 3 for $ 4. The Big Mac Index is presumably useful because it is based on a well-known good whose final price, easily tracked in many countries, includes input costs from a wide range of sectors in the local economy, such as agricultural commodities (beef, bread, lettuce, tomatoes), labour (blue and white collar), advertising, rent and real estate costs, transportation, etc.

WEST AND CENTRAL AFRICAN FRANC

In 2003, the U.S. dollar bought on average about 550 CFA francs. Because of a difference in purchasing power within some of the regions using the CFA franc, their purchasing power parity exchange rate differed greatly (lower implies a stronger currency): Cameroon 240, Central African Republic 166, Chad 172, Republic of the Congo 677, Equatorial Guinea 114, Gabon 413, Benin 273, Burkina Faso 167.

NEED FOR PPP ADJUSTMENTS TO GDP

Using market exchange rates to compare the standard of living in countries or per capita Gross Domestic Product can give a very misleading picture. The exchange rate only reflects traded goods in contrast to non-traded ones. Also, currencies are traded for purposes other than trade in goods and services, for example, to buy capital assets whose prices vary more than those of physical goods. Also, different interest rates, speculation, hedging or interventions by central banks can influence the foreign-exchange market.

The PPP method is used as an alternative.

For example, if the value of the Mexican peso falls by half compared to the U.S. dollar, the Mexican Gross Domestic Product measured in dollars will also halve. However, this exchange rate results from international trade and financial markets. It does not necessarily mean that Mexicans are any poorer; if incomes and prices measured in pesos stay the same, they will be no worse off assuming that imported goods are not essential to the quality of life of individuals. Measuring income in different countries using PPP exchange rates helps to avoid this problem.

PPP exchange rates are especially useful when official exchange rates are artificially manipulated by governments. Countries with strong government control of the economy sometimes enforce official exchange rates that make their own currency artificially strong. By contrast, the currency's black market exchange rate is artificially weak. In such cases a PPP exchange rate is likely the most realistic basis for economic comparison.

DIFFICULTIES

The main reasons why PPP does not perfectly reflect standards of living are

- PPP numbers can vary with the specific basket of goods used, making it a rough estimate.
- Preferences and choices can vary from country to country. Goods then differ in their contribution to welfare.
- International competitiveness is mainly affected by the exchange rate and not by PPP.
- Differences in quality of goods are not sufficiently reflected in PPP.
- The price of a product within one currency-zone may vary drastically (for example, the average price of a can of soda is drastically lower in Lexington, Kentucky than in New York, New York. This is even more noticeable within the Euro zone.
- Imported goods are purchased at market exchange rates, and thus a country that has to import all of its food would appear better off than it actually is if the PPP is used as the measurement of well-being.

PPP calculations are often used to measure poverty rates.

RANGE AND QUALITY OF GOODS

The goods that the currency has the 'power' to purchase are a basket of goods of different types:

1. Local, non-tradable goods and services (like electric power) that are produced and sold domestically.
2. Tradable goods such as non-perishable commodities that can be sold on the international market (for example, diamonds).

The more a product falls into category 1 the further its price will be from the currency exchange rate (Moving towards the PPP exchange rate). Conversely, category 2 products tend to trade close to the currency exchange rate.

More processed and expensive products are likely to be tradable, falling into the second category, and drifting from the PPP exchange rate to the currency exchange rate. Even if the PPP 'value' of the Chinese currency is five times stronger than the currency exchange rate, it will not buy five times as much of internationally traded goods like steel, cars and microchips, but non-traded goods like housing, services ('haircuts'), and domestically produced rice. The relative price differential between tradables and non-tradables from high-income to low-income countries is a consequence of the Balassa-Samuelson effect, and gives a big cost advantage to labour intensive production of tradable goods in low income countries (like China), as against high income countries (like Switzerland). The corporate cost advantage is nothing more sophisticated than access to cheaper workers, but because the pay of those workers goes further in low-income countries than high, the relative pay differentials (inter-country) can be sustained for longer than would be the case otherwise. (This is another way of saying that the wage rate is based on average local productivity, and that this is below the per capita productivity that factories selling tradable goods to international markets can achieve. This is sometimes called exploitation.) An equivalent cost benefit comes from non-traded goods that can be sourced locally (nearer the PPP-exchange rate than the nominal exchange rate in which receipts are paid). These act as a relatively cheaper factor of production than is available to factories in richer countries.

DIFFICULTIES WITH PPP COMPARISONS IN WELFARE ECONOMICS

While using PPP exchange rates for income comparison is an improvement over using market exchange rates, it is still imperfect, and comparisons using the PPP method can still be misleading. Comparing standards of living using the PPP method implicitly assumes that the real value placed on goods is the same in different countries. In reality, what is considered a luxury in one culture could be considered a necessity in another. The PPP method does not account for this. (This is not primarily a flaw in the exchange rate methodology, as cultural and interpersonal differences in utility functions are a more fundamental microeconomic problem.)

A PPP exchange rate varies depending on the choice of goods used for the index (CPI). Hence, it is possible to deliberately or accidentally bias a PPP exchange rate by the choice of a bundle. Indeed, it may be hard to construct equivalent representative bundles for the consumption habits of very different societies. PPP could also have difficulty accounting for differences in quality between goods in one country and equivalent goods in another.

Even if a good PPP is used, GDP per capita is still a measure of the economic output of the whole economy, not a direct measure of the mean or median person's *quality of life*. Other factors such as the standards of homes and schools, access to public services, the extent of pollution, and strength of consumer protection laws are hard to quantify and generally not fully reflected in the GDP. Even a PPP-adjusted measure of GDP per capita must be used with caution, for all the usual reasons that the GDP figure itself is limited (for instance, its inability to capture the surplus between subjective value and payment price).

For example, in 2002, the nominal GDP per capita in Japan was about US$ 40,000, while the equivalent PPP into a U.S. goods basket was estimated at $ 27,000. In the U.S.A., GDP per capita was about $ 36,400 (nominal and real if based on 2002 dollars). This means that the average U.S. citizen could enjoy slightly more consumption than the average Japanese (vastly more if private saving is removed from consumption income). However, it does not necessarily follow that this implies a 'higher standard of living' in the sense of 'enjoying life' more; the U.S.A. has higher crime rates and less social cohesion than Japan, while Japan has much less physical space per person and arguably less individual freedom. Ultimately, the quality of life will depend on subjective judgement and individual preferences.

While per-capita income does not take into account inequalities in wealth distribution, neither does the PPP-scaled income.

—oo(O)oo—

Chapter 35

International Monetary Fund

The International Monetary Fund—also known as the 'IMF' or the 'Fund—was conceived at a United Nations conference convened in Bretton Woods, New Hampshire, U.S.A. in July 1944. The 45 governments represented at that conference sought to build a framework for economic cooperation that would avoid a repetition of the disastrous economic policies that had contributed to the Great Depression of the 1930s.

FAST FACTS ON THE IMF

- Current membership: 185 countries
- Staff: approximately 2,716 from 165 countries
- Total quotas: $ 317 billion (as of 31.7.2006)
- Loans outstanding: $ 28 billion to 74 countries, of which $ 6 billion to 56 on concessional terms (as of 31.7.2006)
- Technical assistance provided: 429.2 person years during FY2006
- Surveillance consultations concluded: 128 countries during FY2006, of which 122 voluntarily published information on their consultation.

Article I of the Articles of Agreement sets out the IMF's main responsibilities:

- promoting international monetary cooperation;
- facilitating the expansion and balanced growth of international trade;
- promoting exchange stability;
- assisting in the establishment of a multilateral system of payments; and
- making its resources available (under adequate safeguards) to members experiencing balance of payments difficulties.

IMF ACTIVITIES

More generally, the IMF is responsible for ensuring the stability of the international monetary and financial system—the system of international payments and exchange rates among national currencies that enable trade to take place between countries. The Fund seeks to promote economic stability and prevent crises; to help resolve crises when they do occur; and to promote growth and alleviate poverty. It employs three main functions—surveillance, technical assistance, and lending—to meet these objectives.

- The IMF works to **promote global growth and economic stability**—and thereby prevent economic crisis—by encouraging countries to adopt sound economic policies.

  Surveillance is the regular dialogue and policy advice that the IMF offers to each of its members. On a regular basis—usually once each year—the Fund conducts in-depth appraisals of each member country's economic situation. It discusses with the country's authorities the policies that are most conducive to stable exchange rates and a growing and prosperous economy. Members have the option to publish the Fund's assessment, and the overwhelming majority of countries opt for transparency, making extensive information on bilateral surveillance available to the public. The IMF also combines information from individual consultations to form assessments of global and regional developments and prospects. These views on the IMF's multilateral surveillance are published twice each year in the *World Economic Outlook* and the *Global Financial Stability Report.*

  Technical assistance and training are offered—mostly free of charge—to help member countries strengthen their capacity to design and implement effective policies. Technical assistance is offered in several areas, including fiscal policy, monetary and exchange rate policies, banking and financial system supervision and regulation, and statistics.

- In the event that member countries do experience difficulties financing their balance of payments, the IMF is also a fund that can be tapped to **help in recovery**.

  Financial assistance is available to give member countries the breathing room they need to correct balance of payments problems. A policy programme supported by IMF financing is designed by the national authorities in close cooperation with the IMF, and continued financial support is conditional on effective implementation of this programme.

- The IMF is also actively working to **reduce poverty** in countries around the globe, independently and in collaboration with the World Bank and other organizations.

  The IMF provides financial support through its concessional lending facility—the Poverty Reduction and Growth Facility (PRGF) and the Exogenous Shocks Facility (ESF)—and through debt relief under the Heavily Indebted Poor Countries (HIPC) Initiative and the Multilateral Debt Relief Initiative (MDRI).

In most low-income countries, this support is underpinned by Poverty Reduction Strategy Papers (PRSP). These papers are prepared by country authorities—in consultation with civil society and external development partners—to describe a comprehensive economic, structural and social policy framework that is being implemented to promote growth and reduce poverty in the country.

IMF GOVERNANCE AND ORGANIZATION

The IMF is accountable to the governments of its member countries. At the apex of its organizational structure is its Board of Governors, which consists of one governor from each of the IMF's 185 member countries. All governors meet once each year at the IMF-World Bank Annual Meetings; 24 of the governors sit on the International Monetary and Finance Committee (IMFC) and meet twice each year. The day-to-day work of the IMF is conducted at its Washington DC headquarters by its 24-member executive board; this work is guided by the IMFC and supported by the IMF's professional staff. The managing director is head of IMF staff and chairman of the executive board, and is assisted by three deputy managing directors.

The IMF's **resources** are provided by its member countries, primarily through payment of quotas, which broadly reflect each country's economic size. The total amount of quotas is the most important factor determining the IMF's lending capacity. The annual expenses of running the Fund are met mainly by the difference between interest receipts (on outstanding loans) and interest payments (on quota 'deposits').

HOW THE IMF PROMOTES GLOBAL ECONOMIC STABILITY

The IMF advises and assists member countries in implementing economic and financial policies that promote stability, reduce vulnerability to crisis, and encourage sustained growth and high living standards. It also promotes dialogue among member countries on the regional and international consequences of their economic and financial policies, and reviews global economic trends and developments that affect the health of the international monetary and financial system. Since greater transparency, both in economic policy and in data on economic and financial developments, is critical for smoothly functioning economies and a stronger international monetary system, the IMF has taken steps to provide more information about its operations and analyses and to encourage greater openness on the part of member countries.

WHY IS ECONOMIC STABILITY IMPORTANT?

Promoting economic stability is partly a matter of avoiding economic and financial crisis. As recent experiences in Argentina, Turkey, and other countries have shown, crises can destroy jobs, slash incomes, and cause great human suffering—both nationally and beyond a country's borders if the crisis spreads. But economic stability also means avoiding large swings in economic activity, high inflation, and excessive volatility in exchange rates and financial markets. Any of these types of instability can increase uncertainty and discourage investment, impede economic growth, and hurt living standards.

A dynamic market economy necessarily involves some degree of instability, as well as gradual structural change. The challenge for policymakers is to minimize this instability without reducing the ability of the economic system to raise living standards through the increasing productivity, efficiency, and employment that it generates. Experience has shown that countries with the strongest growth and employment rates, and the least economic instability, follow sound macroeconomic (fiscal, monetary, and exchange rate) policies.

Economic stability is also fostered by robust economic and financial institutions and regulatory frameworks. They support, among other things, transparency of financial transactions in the government budget, central bank, and the public sector, along with strong standards and systems for accounting, auditing, and data provision.

HOW THE IMF HELPS

The IMF helps countries to implement these good practices through its key functions of surveillance, technical assistance, and lending, including initiatives to improve governance and the quality and availability of data and economic information.

SURVEILLANCE

Every country that joins the IMF accepts the obligation to subject its economic and financial policies to the scrutiny of the international community. Accordingly, the IMF conducts surveillance (or oversight) of economic policies at the country, regional, and global levels. The core of bilateral surveillance is the regular—usually annual—consultations that the IMF holds with each member country. During these consultations, Fund staff discuss economic developments and policies with national policymakers, and often with representatives of business and civil society. The IMF provides advice on macroeconomic policies and ways to strengthen financial sectors and trade competitiveness. The consultations also consider potential national and international consequences of domestic policies, and possible domestic repercussions of developments in other countries or regions.

The IMF also closely monitors economic and financial developments at the regional and global levels. Among the initiatives used to inform bilateral surveillance and aimed at promoting global economic stability:

- The IMF works to improve its ability to **assess countries' vulnerabilities to crisis**, identifying and promoting effective responses to risks to economic stability, including from payments imbalances, currency misalignments, and financial market disturbances.
- In collaboration with the World Bank, the IMF conducts in-depth assessments of countries' financial sectors under the **Financial Sector Assessment Programme (FSAP)**. The purpose is to identify the strengths, risks, and vulnerabilities of countries' financial systems and help formulate appropriate policy responses. The Fund is further deepening financial and capital market surveillance, particularly in its analysis of emerging market members.

- The IMF has developed and actively promotes **standards and codes** of good practice in economic policymaking. It is also involved in international efforts to combat money laundering and the financing of terrorism.

Recently, the IMF began implementing a **Medium-Term Strategy**, which will guide the institution's evolution to help members face the challenges of 21st century globalization. Specific proposals include the introduction of *multilateral consultations* aimed at addressing issues of global or regional significance, the first of which is underway; broadening exchange rate analysis to include major emerging market currencies; and strengthening the analysis in the *World Economic Outlook* and the *Global Financial Stability Report* of macroeconomic and financial risks and their interactions.

Technical Assistance

The IMF helps countries strengthen their capacity to design and implement sound economic policies. The Fund provides advice and training on a range of institutional and policy issues within its areas of responsibility, including fiscal, monetary, and exchange rate policies; the regulation and supervision of banking and financial systems; the development of statistical systems; and of associated legal frameworks.

Lending

Even the best economic policies cannot completely eradicate instability or avert crises. In the event that a member country does experience financing difficulties, the IMF can provide financial assistance to support policy programmes that will correct underlying macroeconomic problems, limit disruption to the domestic and global economies, and help restore confidence, stability, and growth. IMF financing instruments can also support **crisis prevention**.

HOW THE IMF HELPS TO RESOLVE ECONOMIC CRISES

Balance of payments difficulties can arise—and, in the worst case, build into crises—even in the face of strong prevention efforts. The IMF assists countries in restoring economic stability by helping to devise programmes of corrective policies and providing loans to support them. Since unsustainable debt burdens are sometimes part of the problem, the IMF has also been encouraging actions by debtor countries and their creditors to facilitate a more orderly process for debt restructuring.

WHY DO ECONOMIC CRISES OCCUR?

Bad luck, inappropriate policies, or a combination of the two may create balance of payments difficulties in a country—that is, a situation where sufficient financing on affordable terms cannot be obtained to meet international payment obligations. In the worst case, the difficulties can build into a crisis. The country's currency may be forced to depreciate rapidly, making international goods and capital more expensive, and the domestic economy may experience a painful disruption. These problems may also spread to other countries.

The causes of such difficulties are often varied and complex. Key factors have included weak domestic financial systems; large and persistent fiscal deficits; high levels of external and/or public debt; exchange rates fixed at inappropriate levels; natural disasters; or armed conflicts. Some of these factors can directly affect a country's trade account, reducing exports or increasing imports. Others may reduce the financing available for international transactions; for example, investors may lose confidence in a country's prospects leading to massive asset sales, or 'capital flight.' In case, diagnoses of, and responses to, crises are complicated by linkages between various sectors of the economy. Imbalances in one sector can quickly spread to other sectors, leading to economic disruption.

HOW IMF LENDING HELPS

IMF lending aims to give countries breathing room to implement adjustment policies and reforms that will restore conditions for strong and sustainable growth, employment, and social investment. These policies will vary depending upon the country's circumstances, including the causes of the problems. For instance, a country facing a sudden drop in the price of a key export may simply need financial assistance to tide it over until prices recover and to help ease the pain of an otherwise sudden and sharp adjustment.

A country suffering from capital flight needs to address whatever problems led to the loss of investor confidence: perhaps interest rates that are too low, a large government budget deficit and debt stock that is growing too fast, or an inefficient, poorly regulated domestic banking system.

Before a member country can receive a loan, the country's authorities and the IMF must agree on a programme of economic policies. A country's commitments to undertake certain policy actions are an integral part of IMF lending. They are designed to ensure that the funds will be used to resolve balance of payments problems. They would also help to restore or create access to support from other creditors and donors. A country's return to economic and financial health allows the IMF to be repaid, making the funds available to other members.

IMF loan programmes are tailored to the specific circumstances of individual countries. In recent years, the largest number of loans has been made through the Poverty Reduction and Growth Facility (PRGF), which provides funds at a concessional interest rate to low-income countries to address protracted balance of payments problems. However, the largest amount of funds is provided through Stand-By Arrangements (SBA), which charge market-based interest rates on loans to assist with short-term balance of payments problems.

The IMF also provides concessional loans under the Exogenous Shocks Facility (ESF) to meet low-income countries' temporary needs arising from exogenous shocks, and emergency assistance to countries that have experienced a natural disaster or are emerging from armed conflict.

Globalization has vastly increased the size of private capital flows relative to official flows and IMF quotas, albeit unevenly so. Many emerging-market countries currently see an unmet need for insurance against large and volatile capital flows. Under its Medium-Term Strategy, the IMF will re-examine its instruments that help prevent and respond to crises to ensure they continue to meet emerging-market members' needs. Low-income countries have differing needs. Some require debt relief, and others concessional financing. Meanwhile, some no longer need financing, but seek the reassurance of policy support and signalling.

RESOLVING EXTERNAL DEBT CRISES

Some balance of payments difficulties arise because countries amass debt burdens that are not sustainable; they cannot be repaid under any feasible set of policies. In these circumstances, a country and its creditors must restructure the debt. This may involve some easing of the repayment terms, like an increase in maturities, or, in the most severe cases, a reduction in the face value of the debt.

As the multilateral institution at the centre of the global financial system, the IMF works to help improve the debt restructuring process between countries and their private creditors. For example, the IMF actively encourages member countries to include Collective Action Clauses in new international sovereign bonds, to facilitate restructuring of individual issues, when needed. The IMF is also following efforts by sovereign debtors and private sector creditors to implement a broad set of voluntary principles formulated in the context of a private sector-led initiative—the 'Principles for Stable Capital Flows and Fair Debt Restructuring in Emerging Markets'—for emerging market crisis management and debt restructuring. The IMF's Lending into Arrears (LIA) policy is aimed at ensuring that debtor countries with arrears to private creditors have access to the funds necessary to implement their economic programmes, while seeking to eliminate those arrears by engaging in a constructive dialogue with their creditors.

Together with the World Bank, the IMF has also been working to reduce to sustainable levels the debt burdens of heavily indebted poor countries under the enhanced Heavily Indebted Poor Countries (HIPC) Initiative and the Multilateral Debt Relief Initiative (MDRI).

HOW THE IMF HELPS POOR COUNTRIES

The IMF provides low-income countries with policy advice, technical assistance, and financial support. Low-income countries receive more than half of the technical assistance provided by the Fund, and financial support is extended at low interest rates and over relatively long time horizons. Low-income countries with high external debt burdens are also eligible for debt relief.

WHAT CAN BE DONE TO REDUCE POVERTY?

Despite progress in recent decades, the extreme poverty prevalent in low-income countries is a critical problem facing the global community. At present, more than a billion people are living on less than $ 1 a day. More than three-quarters of a billion people are malnourished—about a fifth of them children. One-hundred and sixteen of every 1,000 children born in low-income countries die before reaching the age of five, the majority from malnutrition or disease that is readily preventable in high-income countries.

The Millennium Development Goals (MDGs) set by the United Nations are centered on halving poverty between 1990 and 2015. How can they be achieved, when the causes of poverty and the reasons it persists are complex, varied, and not fully understood? There is little dispute that a sustained, rapid rate of growth in average per capita incomes is essential for meaningful poverty reduction. In turn, the factors that have been shown to promote such growth include openness to international trade, sound economic policies, strong institutions and legal frameworks, and good governance.

Accordingly, in the March 2002 Monterrey Consensus, the international community adopted a two-pillar strategy for achieving the MDGs. The first is the pursuit of sound policies and good governance by the low-income countries themselves. The second is larger and more effective international support, including official development assistance and trade liberalization to open markets to developing country exports.

THE ROLE OF THE IMF

The IMF is helping low-income countries make progress towards the MDGs and contributing to the approach embodied in the Monterrey Consensus through each of the Fund's three key functions—lending, technical assistance, and surveillance.

LENDING

The IMF provides financial assistance to low-income countries experiencing balance of payments problems through its Poverty Reduction and Growth Facility (PRGF) and for temporary needs arising from exogenous shocks through the Exogenous Shocks Facility (ESF). The interest rate on PRGF and ESF loans is concessional (only 0.5 per cent), and loans are repaid over a period of 10 years (with 5½ years' grace).

PRGF and ESF lending programmes are based on Poverty Reduction Strategy Papers (PRSP). A PRSP is prepared by the government of a low-income country, in concert with civil society and development partners such as the IMF and the World Bank, to describe the policies that will be employed to promote growth and reduce poverty in the country.

In addition to economic policies, PRSPs typically cover structural and social policies that are needed to improve health and education, safeguard the environment, and combat HIV/AIDS, malaria, and other diseases. The IMF sees the PRSP approach as a key framework for implementing the Monterrey Consensus, and is working to ensure better alignment of PRGF lending programmes with PRSPs.

Some low-income countries are eligible for the Heavily Indebted Poor Countries (HIPC) Initiative and the Multilateral Debt Relief Initiative (MDRI). The joint IMF-World Bank HIPC Initiative entails coordinated action by the international financial community, including multilateral organizations and governments, to reduce to sustainable levels the external debt burdens of heavily indebted poor countries.

The MDRI aids full debt relief by three multilateral institutions—the IMF, the International Development Association (IDA) of the World Bank, and the African Development Fund (AfDF). The HIPCs that have already obtained debt service relief are spending much more on social services than on debt service—on average four times as much—and have shown a marked increase in the share of health and education in the budgets under their PRGF programmes.

The Policy Support Instrument offers support for low-income countries that do not want or do not need financial assistance from the IMF but want its advice, monitoring, and endorsement of their economic policies. It is a vehicle intended to help them design effective economic programmes and provide signalling to donors, the multilateral development banks, and markets.

Technical Assistance

Adequate policy-making capacity is critical for sustainable development and growth. The IMF provides assistance and training—generally free of charge—to help member countries strengthen the capacity of their institutions and officials to manage economic and financial policies. In recent years, the Fund has reinforced its efforts in low-income countries by establishing regional technical assistance centres in the Pacific, the Caribbean, East, West, and Central Africa, and in the Middle East.

Surveillance

Low-income countries benefit from the full range of policy advice that is provided regularly to all 184 members through IMF surveillance. The objectives of this advice are to help countries:

(i) establish economic frameworks that can support sustained high growth and poverty reduction;

(ii) identify and manage sources of macroeconomic risks and vulnerabilities; and

(iii) strengthen institutions and policies that underpin sound macroeconomic management.

Low-income countries also benefit from the Fund's surveillance over the policies of other countries and the international monetary system, which promotes global growth and economic stability. The IMF also uses the surveillance process to encourage developed countries to live up to their pledges towards the MDGs—especially, the long-standing target of 0.7 per cent of GNP of official development assistance, and the need to reduce subsidies and other barriers to trade in order to improve access to their markets for low-income country exports.

Progress in implementing the policies and actions needed to achieve the MDGs and related outcomes is assessed annually in the *Global Monitoring Report*, a publication produced jointly by the IMF and the World Bank, in collaboration with other international partners.

—oo(O)oo—

Chapter 36

World Trade Organization

The World Trade Organization (WTO) is an international organization designed to supervise and liberalize international trade. The WTO came into being on January 1, 1995, and is the successor to the General Agreement on Tariffs and Trade (GATT), which was created in 1947, and continued to operate for almost five decades as a *de facto* international organization.

The WTO deals with the rules of trade between nations at a global or near-global level; it is responsible for negotiating and implementing new trade agreements, and is in charge of policing member countries' adherence to all the WTO agreements, signed by the bulk of the world's trading nations and ratified in their parliaments. Most of the WTO's current work comes from the 1986-94 negotiations called the Uruguay Round, and earlier negotiations under the GATT. The organization is currently the host to new negotiations, under the Doha Development Agenda (DDA) launched in 2001

The WTO is governed by a ministerial conference, which meets every two years; a general council, which implements the conference's policy decisions and is responsible for day-to-day administration; and a director-general, who is appointed by the ministerial conference. The WTO's headquarters are in Geneva, Switzerland.

John Maynard Keynes and Harry Dexter White at the Bretton Woods Conference—both economists had been strong advocates of a liberal international trade environment, and recommended the establishment of three institutions: the IMF (fiscal and monetary issues), the World Bank (financial and structural issues), and the ITO (international economic cooperation).

The WTO's predecessor, the General Agreement on Tariffs and Trade (GATT), was established after World War II in the wake of other new multilateral institutions dedicated to international economic cooperation—notably the Bretton Woods institutions now known as the World Bank and the International Monetary Fund. Although an agreement covering trade was not negotiated at Bretton Woods, the Conference did recognize the need for a comparable international institution. In December 1945, the U.S.A. invited its wartime allies to enter into negotiations to conclude a multilateral agreement for the reciprocal reduction of tariffs on trade in goods. At the proposal of the U.S.A., the United Nations Economic and Social Committee adopted a resolution, in February 1946, calling for a conference to draft a charter for an International Trade Organization (ITO). A Preparatory Committee was established in February 1946, and worked until November 1947 on the charter of an international organization for trade. By October 1947 an agreement on the GATT was reached in Geneva, and on October 30, 1947, twenty three countries signed the 'Protocol of Provisional Application of the General Agreement on Tariffs and Trade'. In March 1948, the negotiations on the ITO Charter were successfully completed in Havana. The Charter provided for the establishment of the ITO, and set out the basic rules for international trade and other international economic matters. The ITO Charter, however, never entered into force; while repeatedly submitted to the U.S. Congress, it was never approved. The most usual argument against the new organization was that it would be involved in internal economic issues. On December 6, 1950, President Truman announced that he would no longer seek Congressional approval of the ITO Charter. In the absence of an international organization for trade, the GATT would over the years 'transform itself' into a *de facto* international organization.

GATT ROUNDS OF NEGOTIATIONS

The GATT was the only multilateral instrument governing international trade from 1948 until the WTO was established in 1995. Despite attempts in the mid 1950s and 1960s to create some form of institutional mechanism for international trade, the GATT continued to operate for almost half a century as a semi-institutionalized multilateral treaty regime on a provisional basis.

From Geneva to Tokyo

Seven rounds of negotiations occurred under the GATT before the first GATT trade rounds concentrated on further reducing tariffs. Then, the Kennedy Round in the mid-Sixties brought about a GATT anti-dumping Agreement and a section on development. The Tokyo Round during the Seventies was the first major attempt to tackle trade barriers that do not take the form of tariffs, and to improve the system, adopting a series of agreements on non-tariff barriers, which in some cases interpreted existing GATT rules, and in others broke entirely new ground. Because these plurilateral agreements were not accepted by the full GATT membership, they were often informally called 'codes'. Several of these codes were amended in the Uruguay Round, and turned into multilateral commitments accepted by all WTO members. Only four remained plurilateral (those on government procurement, bovine meat, civil aircraft and dairy products), but in 1997 WTO members agreed to terminate the bovine meat and dairy agreements, leaving only two.

Uruguay Round

Well before GATT's 40th anniversary, its members concluded that the GATT system was straining to adapt to a new globalizing world economy. In response to the problems identified in the 1982 Ministerial Declaration (structural deficiencies, spill-over impacts of certain countries' policies on world trade GATT could not manage, etc.), the eighth GATT round—known as the Uruguay

Round—was launched in September 1986, in Punta del Este, Uruguay. It was the biggest negotiating mandate on trade ever agreed: the talks were going to extend the trading system into several new areas, notably trade in services and intellectual property, and to reform trade in the sensitive sectors of agriculture and textiles; all the original GATT articles were up for review.

The round was supposed to end in December 1990, but the U.S.A. and the EU disagreed on how to reform agricultural trade and decided to extend the talks. Finally, in November 1992, the U.S.A. and the EU settled most of their differences in a deal known informally as 'the Blair House Accord', and on April 15, 1994, the deal was signed by ministers from most of the 123 participating governments at a meeting in Marrakech, Morocco. The agreement established the World Trade Organization, which came into being upon its entry into force on January 1, 1995, and replaced GATT as an international organization. It is widely regarded as the most profound institutional reform of the world trading system since GATT's establishment.

During the Doha Round, the U.S. government blamed Brazil and India for being inflexible, and the EU for impeding agricultural imports. Brazil President Luiz Inácio Lula da Silva, responded to the criticism arguing that progress will be only achieved if the richest countries (especially the U.S.A. and the EU) make deeper cuts in their agricultural subsidies, and open their markets further for agricultural goods.

The GATT still exists as the WTO's umbrella treaty for trade in goods, updated as a result of the Uruguay Round negotiations (a distinction is made between GATT 1994, the updated parts of GATT, and GATT 1947, the original agreement which is still the heart of GATT 1994). GATT 1994 is not however the only legal binding agreement included in the Final Act; a long list of about 60 agreements, annexes, decisions and understandings was adopted. In fact, the agreements fall into a simple structure with six main parts: an umbrella agreement (the Agreement establishing the WTO); agreements for each of the three broad areas of trade that the WTO covers (goods and investment (the Multilateral Agreements on Trade in Goods including GATT 1994 and TRIMS), services (GATS) and intellectual property (TRIPS); dispute settlement (DSU); and reviews of governments' trade policies (TPRM).

Doha Round

The WTO launched the current round of negotiations, the Doha Development Agenda (DDA) or Doha Round, at the Fourth Ministerial Conference in Doha, Qatar, in November 2001. The Doha Round was to be an ambitious effort to make globalisation more inclusive and help the world's poor, particularly by slashing barriers and subsidies in farming. The initial agenda comprised both further trade liberalization and new rule-making, underpinned by commitments to strengthen substantially assistance to developing countries.

The talks have been highly contentious and agreement has not been reached, despite the intense negotiations at the Fifth Ministerial Conference in Cancún in 2003 and at the Sixth Ministerial Conference in Hong Kong on December 13–18, 2005 and the Seventh Ministerial Conference in Geneva (July, 2006). On July 24, 2006, at the end of yet another futile gathering of trade ministers in Geneva, Pascal Lamy, the WTO's Director-General, formally suspended the negotiations. Nevertheless, in his report to the WTO General Council on February 7, 2007, Lamy said that "political conditions are now more favourable for the conclusion of the Round than they have been for a long time'. He then added that "political leaders around the world clearly want us to get fully back to business, although we in turn need their continuing commitment".

MISSION, FUNCTIONS AND PRINCIPLES

The WTO's stated goal is to improve the welfare of the peoples of its member countries, specifically by lowering trade barriers and providing a platform for negotiation of trade. Its main mission is "to ensure that trade flows as smoothly, predictably and freely as possible". This main mission is further specified in certain core functions serving and safeguarding five fundamental principles, which are the foundation of the multilateral trading system.

FUNCTIONS

Among the various functions of the WTO, these are regarded by analysts as the most important:

- It oversees the implementation, administration and operation of the covered agreements.
- It provides a forum for negotiations and for settling disputes.

Additionally, it is WTO's duty to review the national trade policies, and to ensure the coherence and transparency of trade policies through surveillance in global economic policy-making. Another priority of the WTO is the assistance of developing, least-developed and low-income countries in transition to adjust to WTO rules and disciplines through technical cooperation and training. The WTO is also a centre of economic research and analysis: regular assessments of the global trade picture in its annual publications and research reports on specific topics are produced by the organization. Finally, the WTO cooperates closely with the two other components of the Bretton Woods system, the IMF and the World Bank.

PRINCIPLES OF THE TRADING SYSTEM

The WTO establishes a framework for trade policies; it does not define or specify outcomes. That is, it is concerned with setting the rules of the trade policy games. Five principles are of particular importance in understanding both the pre-1994 GATT and the WTO:

1. **Non-discrimination.** It has two major components: the most favoured nation (MFN) rule, and the national treatment policy. Both are embedded in the main WTO rules on goods, services, and intellectual property, but their precise scope and nature differ across these areas. The MFN rule requires that a product made in one member country be treated no less favourably than a very similar good that originated in any other country. "Grant someone a special favour and you have to do the same for all other WTO members." According to national treatment, imported and locally-produced goods should be treated equally (at least after the foreign goods have entered the market).

National treatment ensures that liberalization commitments are not offset through the imposition of domestic taxes and similar measures

2. **Reciprocity.** It reflects both a desire to limit the scope of free-riding that may arise because of the MFN rule, and a desire to obtain better access to foreign markets. A related point is that for a nation to negotiate, it is necessary that the gain from doing so be greater than the gain available from unilateral liberalization; reciprocal concessions intend to ensure that such gains will materialize.

3. **Binding and enforceable commitments.** The tariff commitments made by WTO members in a multilateral trade negotiation and on accession are enumerated in a schedule (list) of concessions. These schedules establish 'ceiling bindings': a country can change its binding, but only after negotiating with its trading partners, which could mean compensating them for loss of trade. If satisfaction is not obtained, the complaining country may invoke the WTO dispute settlement procedures.

4. **Transparency.** The WTO members are required to publish their trade regulations, to maintain institutions allowing for the review of administrative decisions affecting trade, to respond to requests for information by other members, and to notify changes in trade policies to the WTO. These internal transparency requirements are supplemented and facilitated by periodic country-specific reports (trade policy reviews) through the Trade Policy Review Mechanism (TPRM). The WTO system tries also to improve predictability and stability, discouraging the use of quotas and other measures used to set limits on quantities of imports.

5. **Safety valves.** In specific circumstances, governments are able to restrict trade. There are three types of provisions in this direction: articles allowing for the use of trade measures to attain non-economical objectives; articles aimed at ensuring 'fair competition'; and provisions permitting intervention in trade for economic reasons.

FORMAL STRUCTURE

According to WTO rules, all members may participate in all councils, committees, etc., except Appellate Body, Dispute Settlement panels, and plurilateral committees.

Highest Level: Ministerial Conference

The topmost decision-making body of the WTO is the ministerial conference, which has to meet at least every two years. It brings together all members of the WTO, all of which are countries or separate customs territories. The ministerial conference can make decisions on all matters under any of the multilateral trade agreements.

Second Level: General Council

The daily work of the ministerial conference is handled by three groups: the general council, the dispute settlement body, and the trade policy review body. All three consist of the same membership—representatives of all WTO members—but each meets under different rules.

1. The general council is the WTO's highest-level decision-making body in Geneva, meeting regularly to carry out the functions of the WTO. It has representatives (usually ambassadors or equivalent) from all member-governments and has the authority to act on behalf of the ministerial conference which meets about every two years. The council acts on behalf of the ministerial council on all WTO affairs. The current chairman is Amb. Eirik Glenne (Norway).
2. The Dispute Settlement Body - Made up of all member governments, usually represented by ambassadors or equivalent. The current chairperson is H. E. Muhamad Noor Yacob (Malaysia).
3. The Trade Policy Review Body (TPRB) - the WTO general council meets as the trade policy review body to undertake trade policy reviews of members under the TRPM. The TPRB is thus open to all WTO members. The current chairperson is H. E. Claudia Uribe (Colombia).

Third Level: Councils for Trade

The councils for trade work under the general council. There are three councils—Council for trade in goods, Council for trade-related aspects of intellectual property rights, and Council for trade in services—each council works in different fields. Apart from these three councils, six other bodies report to the general council reporting on issues such as trade and development, the environment, regional trading arrangements and administrative issues.

1. Council for Trade in Goods—The working of the General Agreement on Tariffs and Trade (GATT) which covers international trade in goods, is the responsibility of the council for trade in goods. It is made up of representatives from all WTO member countries. The current chairperson is Amb. Yonov Frederick Agah (Nigeria).
2. Council for Trade-Related Aspects of Intellectual Property Rights—Information on intellectual property in the WTO, news and official records of the activities of the TRIPS council, and details of the WTO's work with other international organizations in the field.
3. Council for Trade in Services—The council for trade in services operates under the guidance of the general council and is responsible for overseeing the functioning of the General Agreement on Trade in Services (GATS). It is open to all WTO members, and can create subsidiary bodies as required.

Fourth Level: Subsidiary Bodies

There are subsidiary bodies under each of the three councils.

1. The Goods Council—subsidiary under the council for trade in goods. It has 11 committees consisting of all member countries, dealing with specific subjects

such as agriculture, market access, subsidies, anti-dumping measures and so on. The committees include the following:

- Information Technology Agreement (ITA) Committee
- State Trading Enterprises
- Textiles Monitoring Body—Consists of a chairman and 10 members acting under it.
- Groups dealing with notifications—process by which governments inform the WTO about new policies and measures in their countries.

2. The Services Council—subsidiary under the council for trade in services which deals with financial services, domestic regulations and other specific commitments.
3. Dispute settlement panels and appellate body—subsidiary under the dispute settlement body to resolve disputes and the appellate body to deal with appeals.

Other Committees

Committees on

- Trade and Environment
- Trade and Development (Subcommittee on Least-Developed Countries)
- Regional Trade Agreements
- Balance of Payments Restrictions
- Budget, Finance__ and Administration

Working parties on

- Accession

Working groups on

- Trade, debt and finance
- Trade and technology transfer

TRADE NEGOTIATIONS

While most international organizations operate on a *one country, one vote* or even a *weighted voting* basis, many WTO decisions, such as adopting agreements (and revisions to them) are officially determined by consensus of all members. The advantage of consensus decision-making is that it encourages efforts to find the most widely acceptable decision. Main disadvantages include large time requirements and many rounds of negotiation to develop a consensus decision, and the tendency for final agreements to use ambiguous language on contentious points that makes future interpretation of treaties difficult.

In reality, WTO negotiations proceed not by consensus of all members, but by a process of informal negotiations between small groups of countries. Such negotiations are often called 'Green Room' negotiations (after the colour of the WTO Director-General's Office in Geneva), or 'Mini-Ministerials', when they occur in other countries. These processes have been regularly criticized by many of the WTO's developing country members which are often totally excluded from the negotiations.

Richard Steinberg (2002) argues that although the WTO's consensus governance model provides law-based initial bargaining, trading rounds close through power-based bargaining favouring Europe and the U.S.A., and may not lead to Pareto improvement.

DISPUTE SETTLEMENT

> " Prompt compliance with recommendations or rulings of the DSB is essential in order to ensure effective resolution of disputes to the benefit of all members.
> — *World Trade Organization, Article 21.1 of the DSU*

In 1994, the WTO members agreed on the Understanding on Rules and Procedures Governing the Settlement of Disputes (DSU) annexed to the 'Final Act' signed in Marrakech in 1994. Dispute settlement is regarded by the WTO as the central pillar of the multilateral trading system, and as a 'unique contribution to the stability of the global economy' WTO members have agreed that if they believe fellow-members are violating trade rules, they will use the multilateral system of settling disputes instead of taking action unilaterally.

The operation of the WTO dispute settlement process involves the DSB panels, the appellate body, the WTO secretariat, arbitrators, independent experts and several specialized institutions. The general council discharges its responsibilities under the DSU through the Dispute Settlement Body (DSB). Like the general council, the DSB is composed of representatives of all WTO members. The DSB is responsible for administering the DSU, that is, for overseeing the entire dispute settlement process... If a member state considers that a measure adopted by another member state has deprived it of a benefit accruing to it under one of the covered agreements, it may call for consultations with the other member state.

If consultations fail to resolve the dispute within 60 days after receipt of the request for consultations, the complainant state may request the establishment of a panel. It is not possible for the respondent state to prevent or delay the establishment of a panel, unless the DSB by consensus decides otherwise. The panel, normally consisting of three members appointed *ad hoc* by the secretariat, sits to receive written and oral submissions of the parties, on the basis of which it is expected to make findings and conclusions for presentation to the DSB. The proceedings are confidential, and even when private parties are directly concerned, they are not permitted to attend or make submissions separate from those of the state in question.

The final version of the panel's report is distributed first to the parties, and two weeks later it is circulated to all the members of the WTO. The report must be adopted at a meeting of the DSB within 60 days of its circulation, unless the DSB by consensus decides not to adopt the report or a party to the dispute gives notice of its intention to appeal. A party may appeal a panel report to a standing appellate body, but only on issues of law, and legal interpretations developed by the panel. Members may express their views on the report of the appellate body, but they cannot derail it: an appellate body report shall be adopted by the DSB and unconditionally accepted by the parties, unless the DSB decides by consensus within 30 days of its circulation not to adopt the report.

Within 30 days of the adoption of the report, the member concerned is to inform the DSB of its intentions; if the member explains that it is impracticable to comply immediately with the recommendations and rulings, it is to have a 'reasonable period of time' in which to comply. If no agreement is reached about the reasonable period for compliance, that issue is to be the subject of binding arbitration. If there is a disagreement as to the satisfactory nature of the measures adopted by the respondent state to comply with the report that disagreement is to be decided by a panel, if possible the same panel that heard the original dispute, but apparently without the possibility of appeal from its decision.

If all else fails, two more possibilities are set out in the DSU:

- If a member fails within the 'reasonable period' to carry out the recommendations and rulings, it may negotiate with the complaining state for a mutually acceptable compensation.
- If no agreement on compensation is reached within 20 days of the expiry of the 'reasonable period', the prevailing state may request authorization from the DSB to suspend application to the member concerned of concessions or other obligations under the covered agreements. In contrast to prior GATT practice, authorization to suspend concessions in this context is semi-automatic, in that the DSB "shall grant the authorization within thirty days of the expiry of the reasonable period", unless it decides by consensus to reject the request.

The DSU states that fellow members should give 'special attention' to the problems and interests of the developing countries. If one party to a dispute is a developing country, that party is entitled to have at least one panellist who comes from a developing country. Further, if a complaint is brought against a developing country, the time for consultations (before a panel is convened) may be expended, and if the dispute goes to a panel, the deadlines for the developing country to make its submissions may be relaxed. Formal complaints against least developed countries are discouraged, and if consultations fail, the Director-General and the Chairman of the DSB stand ready to offer their good offices before a formal request for a panel is made. As to substance, the DSU provides that 'particular attention' is to be paid to the interests of the developing countries, and that the report of panels shall 'explicitly indicate' how account has been taken of the 'differential and more favourable treatment' provisions of the agreement under which the complaint is brought. In order to assist developing countries overcome their limited expertise in WTO law and assist them in the management of complex trade disputes, an advisory centre on WTO law was established in 2001.

ACCESSION AND MEMBERSHIP

The process of becoming a WTO member is unique to each applicant country, and the terms of accession are dependent upon the country's stage of economic development and current trade regime. The process takes about five years, on average, but it can last more if the country is less than fully committed to the process or if political issues interfere. As is typical of WTO procedures, an offer of accession is only given once consensus is reached among interested parties.

A country wishing to accede to the WTO submits an application to the general council, and has to describe all aspects of its trade and economic policies that have a bearing on WTO agreements. The application is submitted to the WTO in a memorandum which is examined by a working party open to all interested WTO members. After all necessary background information has been acquired, the working party focuses on issues of discrepancy between the WTO rules and the applicant's international and domestic trade policies and laws.

The working party determines the terms and conditions of entry into the WTO for the applicant nation, and may consider transitional periods to allow countries some leeway in complying with the WTO rules. The final phase of accession involves bilateral negotiations between the applicant nation and other working party members regarding the concessions and commitments on tariff levels and market access for goods and services. The new member's commitments are to apply equally to all WTO members under normal non-discrimination rules, even though they are negotiated bilaterally

When the bilateral talks conclude, the working party sends to the general council or ministerial conference an accession package, which includes a summary of all the working party meetings, the protocol of accession (a draft membership treaty), and lists ('schedules') of the member-to-be's commitments. Once the general council or ministerial conference approves of the terms of accession, the applicant's parliament must ratify the protocol of accession before it can become a member.

MEMBERS AND OBSERVERS

The WTO has 150 members (almost all of the 123 nations participating in the Uruguay Round signed on at its foundation, and the rest had to get membership). The 27 states of the European Union are represented also as the European communities. WTO members do not have to be full sovereign nation-members. Instead, they must be a customs territory with full autonomy in the conduct of their external commercial relations. Thus Hong Kong became a GATT contracting party, and Chinese Taipei (Taiwan) acceded to the WTO in 2002. A number of non-members have been observers (31) at the WTO and are currently negotiating their membership. With the exception of the Holy See, observers must start accession negotiations within five years of becoming observers. Some international intergovernmental organizations are also granted observer status to WTO bodies; 15 states and 2 territories so far have no official interaction with the WTO.

AGREEMENTS

The WTO oversees about 60 different agreements which have the status of international legal texts. Member countries must sign and ratify all WTO agreements on accession.

AGREEMENT ON AGRICULTURE (AOA)

The AoA came into effect with the establishment of the WTO at the beginning of 1995. The AoA has three central concepts, or 'pillars': domestic support, market access and export subsidies.

Domestic Support

The first pillar of the AoA is 'domestic support'. The AoA structures domestic support (subsidies) into three categories or 'boxes': a green box, an amber box and a blue box. The green box contains fixed payments to producers for environmental programmes, so long as the payments are 'decoupled' from current production levels. The amber box contains domestic subsidies that governments have agreed to reduce but not eliminate. The blue box contains subsidies which can be increased without limit, so long as payments are linked to production-limiting programmes.

The AoA's domestic support system currently allows Europe and the U.S.A. to spend $ 380 billion annually on agricultural subsidies alone. "It is often still argued that subsidies are needed to protect small farmers but, according to the World Bank, more than half of EU support goes to 1 per cent of producers while in the U.S.A. 70 per cent of subsidies go to 10 per cent of producers, mainly agri-businesses". The effect of these subsidies is to flood global markets with below-cost commodities, depressing prices and undercutting producers in poor countries—a practice known as dumping.

Market Access

'Market access' is the second pillar of the AoA, and refers to the reduction of tariff (or non-tariff) barriers to trade by WTO members. The 1995 AoA required tariff reductions of:

- 36 per cent average reduction by developed countries, with a minimum per tariff line reduction of 15 per cent over five years.
- 24 per cent average reduction by developing countries with a minimum per tariff line reduction of 10 per cent over nine years.

Least Developed Countries (LDCs) were exempted from tariff reductions, but either had to convert non–tariff barriers to tariffs—a process called tariffication—or 'bind' their tariffs, creating a 'ceiling' which could not be increased in future.

Export Subsidies

'Export subsidies' is the third pillar of the AoA. The 1995 AoA required developed countries to reduce export subsidies by at least 35 per cent (by value) or by at least 21 per cent (by volume) over the five years to 2000.

Criticism

The AoA is criticized for reducing tariff protections for small farmers—a key source of income for developing countries—while allowing rich countries to continue to pay their farmers massive subsidies which developing countries cannot afford.

SPS AND GENETICALLY MODIFIED ORGANISMS (GMOS)

In 2003, the U.S.A. challenged a number of EU laws restricting the importation of Genetically Modified Organisms (GMOs), arguing they are 'unjustifiable' and illegal under SPS agreement. In

May 2006, the WTO's dispute resolution panel issued a complex ruling which took issue with some aspects of the EU's regulation of GMOs, but dismissed many of the claims made by the U.S.A.

CRITICISM

Quarantine policies play an important role in ensuring the protection of human, animal and plant health. Yet under the SPS agreement, quarantine barriers can be a 'technical trade barrier' used to keep out foreign competitors.

The SPS agreement gives the WTO the power to override a country's use of the precautionary principle—a principle which allows them to act on the side of caution if there is no scientific certainty about potential threats to human health and the environment. Under SPS rules, the burden of proof is on countries to demonstrate scientifically that something is dangerous before it can be regulated, even though scientists agree that it is impossible to predict all forms of damage posed by insects or pest plants.

AGREEMENT ON TECHNICAL BARRIERS TO TRADE (TBT)

The **Agreement on Technical Barriers to Trade**—also known as the TBT Agreement is an international treaty of the World Trade Organization. It was negotiated during the Uruguay Round of the General Agreement on Tariffs and Trade, and entered into force with the establishment of the WTO at the end of 1994.

The object of the TBT Agreement is to "to ensure that technical negotiations and standards, as well as testing and certification procedures, do not create unnecessary obstacles to trade".

Although the stated aim of the WTO is to promote free trade and stimulate economic growth, much of public discourse and a considerable body of expert literature believe that globally free trade results in the rich (both people and countries) becoming richer, while the poor are getting poorer. Martin Khor, Director of the Third World Network, argues that the WTO does not manage the global economy impartially, but in its operation has a systematic bias towards rich countries and multinational corporations, harming smaller countries which have less negotiation power. He argues that developing countries have not benefited from the WTO agreements of the Uruguay Round, because (among other reasons): market access in industry has not improved; these countries have had no gains yet from the phasing out of textiles quotas; non-tariff barriers such as anti-dumping measures have increased; domestic support and export subsidies for agricultural products in the rich countries remain high. Jagdish Bhagwati asserts however that there is greater tariff protection on manufacturers in the poor countries, which are also overtaking the rich nations in the number of anti-dumping filings.

Other critics claim that the issues of labour and environment are steadfastly ignored. Steve Charnovitz, former Director of the Global Environment and Trade Study (GETS), believes that the WTO "should begin to address the link between trade and labour and environmental concerns." Further, labour unions condemn the labour rights record of developing countries, arguing that to the extent the WTO succeeds at promoting globalization, then in equal measure do the environment and labour rights suffer. On the other side, Khor responds that "if environment and labour were to enter the WTO system it would be conceptually difficult to argue why other social and cultural issues should also not enter." Bhagwati is also critical towards "rich-country lobbies seeking on imposing their unrelated agendas on trade agreements". Therefore, both Bhagwati and Arvind Panagariya have criticized the introduction of TRIPs into the WTO framework, fearing that such non-trade agendas might overwhelm the organization's function.

Other critics have characterized the decision making in the WTO as complicated, ineffective, unrepresentative and non-inclusive, and they have proposed the establishment of a small, informal steering committee (a 'consultative board') that can be delegated responsibility for developing consensus on trade issues among the member countries. The Third World Network has called the WTO 'the most non-transparent of international organisations', because 'the vast majority of developing countries have very little real say in the WTO system'; the Network stresses that 'civil society groups and institutions must be given genuine opportunities to express their views and to influence the outcome of policies and decisions'. Certain non-governmental organizations, such as the World Federalist Movement, argue that democratic participation in the WTO could be enhanced through the creation of a parliamentary assembly, although other analysts have characterized this proposal as ineffective.

—oo(O)oo—